D0856876

THE
POPES
AND THE
PAPACY
IN THE EARLY MIDDLE AGES
476–752

THE
POPES
AND THE
PAPACY
IN THE EARLY MIDDLE
AGES
476–752

Jeffrey Richards

Department of History
Lancaster University

ROUTLEDGE & KEGAN PAUL
LONDON, BOSTON AND HENLEY

First published in 1979
by Routledge & Kegan Paul Ltd
39 Store Street, London WC1E 7DD,
Broadway House, Newtown Road,
Henley-on-Thames,
Oxon RG9 1EN and
9 Park Street,
Boston, Mass. 02108, USA
Phototypeset in V.I.P. Bembo by
Western Printing Services Ltd, Bristol
and printed in Great Britain by
Redwood Burn Ltd Trowbridge and Esher

British Library Cataloguing in Publication Data

Richards, Jeffrey
    The Popes and the Papacy in the early Middle
    Ages, 476–752
    1. Papacy – History – To 1309
    I. Title
    262'.13'09021   BX965   78–41023

ISBN 0 7100 0098 7

This book is dedicated with gratitude and respect to those gallant gentlemen whose example of courage, dedication and determination both in victory and in defeat has proved a constant inspiration:

John Gidman   Brian Little   Andy Gray
John Deehan   Alex Cropley   Dennis Mortimer
Leighton Phillips   Chris Nicholl   Jimmy Rimmer
Frank Carrodus   Gordon Cowans   John Robson
Ian Ross   Charlie Aitken   Ron Saunders
Ken McNaught   John Gregory   Gordon Smith
Keith Leonard   Allan Evans   Tommy Craig

I humbly ask that the ears of the learned tolerate some rustic expressions without complaining so that the Lord's flock receive celestial nourishment in simple and down to earth language.

St Caesarius of Arelate

Contents

Acknowledgments

I am indebted to the following friends and colleagues for advice, assistance and suggestions: the late Professor A. H. M. Jones, Professor M. I. Finley, Professor R. A. Markus, Professor A. L. F. Rivet, Dr P. D. King, Mr S. A. C. Lamley, Mr J. Stevenson, Mr J. Martindale, Mrs E. Scott, Miss L. Parkinson, Mrs M. Jackson and Miss S. Hall. I would like to thank the staffs of the Cambridge University Library, the Lancaster University Library, the British Museum Reading Room and the Birmingham Reference Library for their unfailing courtesy and helpfulness. I owe a special debt to Professor H. J. Perkin, Dr E. J. Evans and Dr J. A Tuck, who read the entire book in manuscript and made many helpful comments. All opinions and errors are of course my own.

Introduction

There has been a tendency in recent years to view the history of the early medieval papacy in predominantly, if not exclusively, ideological terms. This has resulted in a one-sided view of papal history in which certain periods, indeed whole centuries, have been downgraded because they are not eras of 'significant ideological advance'. One such period is that beginning with the re-establishment of imperial rule in Italy in 554 and ending with the fall of the exarchate of Ravenna in 751. It has been described, indeed dismissed, as 'the Byzantine captivity' of the papacy, implying its unwilling subjection to the Eastern Empire and the stifling of its mission and character. It is the purpose of this study to try to correct that imbalance and emphasize other positive aspects of papal history, political, administrative and social, which just as much as theory were to change the shape and direction of papal development.

The papacy, of course, had an ideology, but it was an ideology that had been arrived at by the opening date of this study, was not departed from during the period covered and in particular not in the direction of papal monarchy. It is anachronistic and without foundation to view this period in terms of the progressive and systematic elaboration of an idea of papal monarchy or of the superseding of the emperor by the pope at the head of the Christian hierarchy. To take this view is to reformulate early medieval history in terms of the late medieval papal masterplan, which undoubtedly did exist, and to give papal history an illusion of inevitability that the facts themselves belie. What eleventh-century canonists may or may not have made of the writings of Pope Gelasius I is utterly irrelevant to any realistic appreciation of how the papacy changed in the sixth and seventh centuries. The papacy's power and responsibility unquestionably grew during this period, but by a series of historical accidents rather than by a coherent radical design, by its response to the immediate rather than concentration on the theoretical, by being the right

1

institution in the right place at the right time. It is hoped that by giving prominence to social, economic and political factors it will be possible to view early-medieval papal history in terms other than those of a rigid, foreordained theoretical structure in which the people involved were simply pawns in a gigantic, centuries-long, hierocratic chess game, in which the papal queen moved gradually and inexorably to checkmate the imperial king, a view which in the light of the facts is not only fanciful but wayward.

The period under review is that from 476 to 752, that fascinating, darkling, interstitial period, marked at one end by the fall of the Western Roman Empire and at the other by the rise of the Frankish Empire. Beneath the protective umbrella provided by these two very different imperial entities, the prestige, power and influence of the papacy grew and prospered. But in the intervening centuries there was no such towering presence in the West on whom papal Rome could safely rely. The papacy was thrown back on its own resources and came to rely more and more on the character and qualities of the individual popes. This study will therefore lay much more stress on the individual figures of the popes and their shifts of policy and principle than it has been customary to do in recent years.

For the popes were not merely the depersonalized executors of some grand monarchical strategy, they were flesh-and-blood figures, subject to temper and caprice, bodily infirmity and human error. The system of election ensured that all sorts of men would jostle for power – saints and sinners, knaves and nonentities, states-men and scoundrels. Once in office, they would be subject to changes of policy and direction, shifts in the balance of Mediter-ranean world power, changes in the nature of society, which made for a situation of considerably more variety and fluidity than is allowed for in that monolithic view which looks at papal history as the working out of a monarchical blueprint.

The social context is one of increasing separatism in Italy. The province, peripheral to mainstream developments in the Eastern Roman Empire, was frequently left to cope with its problems alone. These problems were very real and far-reaching ones, involving as they did the onset both of barbarian invaders and the plague. The financial burdens imposed on the province, the oppressive presence of a largely Greek administration, the often feeble response of the imperial government to the threats to Italy's survival and the involvement of the East in a succession of heresies, all combined in the space of two centuries to induce the growth of a specifically Italian interest, at odds on many fundamental matters with the imperial government in Constantinople. Against this background, the three continuing strands of religious, social and political circumstances in papal history all contrived to make the papacy seem, in the absence of any comparable Italian institution, to be a figurehead for those interests. It was never the wish of the papacy that this should be so, but it came to be so nevertheless.

First, there was a succession of doctrinal conflicts with Constantinople. But this led to no substantial ideological change. Each time papal Rome, in what can almost be seen as a Pavlovian response, took up exactly the same position, one of affirming the pre-existing ideas and the basic, already defined and agreed tenets of the faith. The consequence of this was a practical one. In an age when the articles of faith were for the man in the street a matter of life and death, the pope came to be seen as the champion of orthodoxy, the spiritual leader of Italy and ultimately the successful resister of the imperial government, which invariably backed these Eastern bids to tamper with the faith.

It is in this context that we must place the constant assertion of Rome's primacy. It was an affirmation of papal seniority in the ecclesiastical hierarchy as the best guarantee of the maintenance of orthodoxy rather than a first step in a bid to establish monarchical supremacy over all other authorities, lay and ecclesiastical. The arguments to justify the primacy – the Petrine Commission, apostolic foundation, etc. – had been largely developed before the period of this study begins. During it, they were emphasized rather than added to.

Second, at a time of considerable social and economic dislocation, due to the effects of plague and war, new emphasis was placed on the traditional role of the papacy both as intercessor with God and as dispenser of help to the hungry, the homeless and the sick. More and more, people turned to Rome as the one stable and settled force, and sure and certain source of spiritual and material help. So, as the volume of work increased and the range of responsibilities widened, the papal administration expanded and diversified until it came to rival that of the provincial government.

Third, the role of the pope as intercessor with barbarian invaders – on the hallowed model of Pope Leo the Great's famous interview with Attila which turned the Huns back from the gates of Rome – and the papacy's activity in the field of ransoming prisoners broadened to include the actual negotiation of truces and treaties. When the Lombards were converted to Catholicism, this became even more common, because the Lombards would defer to papal arguments far more readily than they would to Exarchal persuasion. Ultimately, indeed, the exarch of Ravenna was reduced to asking the pope for help in warding off the Lombard threat from his capital. By the seventh century, with the Roman senate gone and the Roman aristocracy dispersed, with the government of the exarch unpopular, starved of resources and stretched to its limits, the Italian people came to look to the pope for political as well as spiritual leadership.

It was, therefore, the combination of these three continuing trends – the successful resistance to a succession of Eastern heresies; the increasing involvement in the social services; the increasing involvement in politics, diplomacy and war – that made the papacy a power in the land. None of these developments took place because of any new-fangled monarchical ideology. All were extensions of the traditional and time-honoured role of the pope, in defending orthodoxy, ransoming prisoners and feeding the poor. The papal administration expanded because the work increased. The popes took on secular functions not at the dictates of theory but out of sheer desperate necessity. The combined result was a papacy whose power was enhanced beyond its wildest dreams. But this was a cause for concern rather than rejoicing on the part of the papacy. The extent to which the pope came to be idolized by the people and the worry to which this gave rise is reflected in the synodical decree introduced by Gregory the Great in 595. The custom of covering the pope's bodies with *dalmatics* for their funeral processions had grown up. But these *dalmatics* were being torn to pieces and carried off by the people, who preserved them as holy relics and held them in greater esteem than the relics of the apostles and martyrs. Gregory therefore had to order that this should stop. But it reflects the position in popular esteem already held by the papacy at the end of the sixth century.

Nowhere is the blend of political, religious and social elements more apparent than in the papal elections. In their intensity and passion, they matched, in some cases even surpassed, the turbulence surrounding imperial elections. Many papal elections involved violence, chicanery and corruption on a grand scale. Blood ran in the streets of Rome, gold changed hands in the corridors of power, rival factions pumped out propaganda and ambitious men caballed around the deathbeds of the popes. The high passions and low intrigues that this involved have a familiar, almost contemporary ring. The fire and spice of those times comes through to us in the surviving documents of the period. This is the raw, red meat of papal history, this and not the desiccated, pre-packed portions often served up in the guise of papal history. This day-to-day reality will be highlighted as a counterbalance to the dominance of monarchical theory in some versions of papal history.

In pursuit of the facts and in humble emulation of my revered mentor A. H. M. Jones, I have concentrated my researches on the primary sources, preferring to allow the authentic voices of the period to speak for themselves and their time rather than to synthesize the views of the sometimes tendentious later commentators. Nevertheless, students of the period will recognize the debt I owe, and which I freely acknowledge, to those modern scholars whose pioneering work has made the trip through the minefield of early medieval history that bit less precarious, men such as Dvornik, Duchesne, Hefele, Jones, Frend, Caspar and Llewellyn.

The book falls into five sections. The first section will set the context of the study, along the lines suggested above. The second and third sections present an interpretive narrative of the period. The fourth section analyses the background and qualifications for office of the popes. The fifth section traces the growth of the papal administration and examines the neglected subject of papal personnel management. The whole adds up, I hope, to an examination of papal history from a new perspective.

Part I

The Context

Chapter 1

The Ideological Context

The papacy based its ideology on two fundamental beliefs, which it clung to with a fanatical tenacity. The first was Rome's primacy, and the papacy was extraordinarily sensitive on that subject. Roman primacy in the church derived initially from the fact that the papal see was sited in the capital of the Roman Empire. It was a considerable blow to papal prestige when the Western capital was shifted first to Milan, then to Ravenna, and finally, when the Western Empire fell, vanished altogether. That melancholy event meant that the sole and undisputed imperial capital was now Constantinople, the so-called New Rome beside the Bosphorus, which was the heart and power-house of the Eastern Roman Empire.

It was in response to this undermining of a political reason for the primatial claim that Rome developed the theory of a primacy based on apostolic and Petrine foundation. The enthusiasm with which these claims were elaborated testifies to Rome's sensitivity on the subject. In the East, on the other hand, political status still determined ecclesiastical status and it was only natural that Constantinople should seek in the ecclesiastical hierarchy a ranking order commensurate with her status as imperial capital. It is no surprise, then, that the General Council of the church meeting at Constantinople in 381 decreed that Constantinople should rank second after Rome in status.[1]

The pope made no objection to this. But in 451, when the Council of Chalcedon met, it was decreed that Constantinople should equal Rome in status.[2] Pope Leo I, architect of the Chalcedonian settlement, interpreted this as an attack on Rome's primacy and refused to accept that particular canon. While there is reason to believe that the idea behind this canon was to humble not Rome but Alexandria, Constantinople's main rival to supremacy in the Eastern church, Leo's reaction was predictable. For to him it must have looked like the prelude to a proclamation of Constantinopolitan supremacy over Rome.

9

In fact Constantinople never sought a position superior to Rome's. Rome's Petrinity and apostolicity were never challenged either by the emperor, the patriarch or the Eastern church. Even though Rome had ceased to be the capital, she had given the empire its name, its laws, its governmental system, its ethos. Accordingly she was revered by the inhabitants of the Eastern Empire who, though Greek in language, culture and outlook, continued to call themselves 'Romans'. This did not stop papal-imperial relations being marred by periodic papal outbursts on the subject of the primacy, outbursts sufficiently intemperate as to suggest that Rome never really recovered from the shock of ceasing to be the imperial capital. For all its battery of claims – the 'keys of the kingdom', the Petrine commission, double apostolic foundation and the rest – there remains the suspicion that for an institution as rooted in the psyche and traditions of the Roman world as the papacy was there could be no real peace of mind until Rome was once again the capital of the Roman Empire.

The claim to equal status by Constantinople remained a permanent worry to the papacy and exacerbated the difficulties which arose between Rome and Constantinople during the Acacian schism. Already divided by doctrinal differences, relations between the two churches were hardly improved when Pope Gelasius I – with characteristic lack of tact – dragged in the status question. He firmly rejected the Chalcedonian pronouncement on equal status[3] and went so far as to deny Constantinople even metropolitan status.[4] Even as the doctrinal differences underlying the schism were being resolved under Pope Hormisdas, the status question still nagged. At the same time as he signed the pope's *libellus* of orthodoxy and renounced the heresy of his predecessors, the Constantinopolitan patriarch John II reaffirmed the equality of status between the two sees.[5]

The problem was finally resolved by Emperor Justinian I, the supreme autocrat but also the supreme Roman, who issued a law which stated:[6]

> We decree in accord with the decisions of the Councils that the most holy pope of Ancient Rome is the first of all the priests and the holy bishop of Constantinople occupies the second see after the holy and apostolic see of Rome.

In effect Justinian was repealing the Chalcedonian canon and reinstating the Constantinople canon of 381. Justinian was one of the most active defenders of the theory of papal primacy, acknowledging it in a letter to Pope John II, 'the head of all the holy churches'[7], and in several laws.[8] It was also widely accepted in the Eastern church, being confirmed, for instance, in a letter of the Syrian monks to Pope Hormisdas[9] and in a letter from the bishops of Epirus to the same pope, grandly addressed as *Princeps Episcoporum*.[10]

Yet there was another quarrel between Rome and Constantinople under Popes Pelagius II and Gregory I when the assumption by Patriarch John IV of the title 'Oecumenical Patriarch' was assumed to be another attack on the Roman primacy. In fact it was not, because 'Oecumenical Patriarch' simply meant supreme within his own patriarchate. It was a title that had been accorded to Popes Leo I, Hormisdas and Agapitus, just as it was accorded to Patriarchs John II, Epiphanius, Anthimus and Menas. The emperor Constantine IV, when inviting Pope Donus and Patriarch George to attend the sixth General Council of the church, calls them both 'Oecumenical', confirming its non-exclusivity.[11] The Gregorian quarrel was resolved in 607 by the issue of an edict by the emperor Phocas to Pope Boniface III confirming Rome's primacy.[12] It was reconfirmed during the seventh century by Emperor Constans II to Pope Vitalian, by Emperor Justinian II to Pope Constantine and by the sixth General Council of the church at Constantinople in 680–1.[13]

Despite Rome's hypersensitivity about her status, there is no sign anywhere in the period of a bid by Constantinople to topple Rome or usurp the primacy. Even the attempt to secure equality was abandoned. The ready use by Easterners of the apostolic and Petrine terminology when addressing or referring to Rome shows a perfect willingness to accept Rome on her own stated terms. So, for instance, at the Council of Chalcedon, the entire assembly rose to its feet, crying: 'St Peter has spoken through Leo.' So wrote the bishops of Cyprus to Pope Theodore in 643:[14]

> Christ our God has instituted your apostolic see, o holy head, as a God-fixed and immovable foundation. For you, as truly spoke the Divine Word, are Peter, and upon your foundation the pillars of the church have been fixed and to you he committed the keys of the kingdom. He ordered you to bind and to loose with authority on earth and in heaven. You are set as the destroyer of profane heresies, as teacher and leader of the orthodox and unsullied faith.

In similar terms, the Palestinian bishop Stephen of Dor announced to the 649 Lateran synod that Palestine looked to Rome, 'to the chair which rules and presides over all, the head and the highest'.[15] These examples could be multiplied many times over, and under the circumstances Rome's concern seems thoroughly unjustified.[16]

The concrete expression of Rome's primacy is to be found in the claim to appellate jurisdiction over the whole church, first enunciated at the Council of Sardica in 343. It gained acceptance in the West, helped by the endorsement of Western emperors. It was a principle frequently stressed by the popes in their dealings with the East, notably by Gelasius I, who typically and bluntly claimed: 'that the voice of Christ, the traditions of the elders and the authority of the canons confirms that (Rome) may always judge the whole church'.[17] But it seems to have been resented by the Eastern church, which was perfectly prepared to concede a primacy of respect but rarely of jurisdiction to Rome. Such cases as did go to Rome on appeal seem to have been mainly those of condemned clerics turning to the pope as a desperate last resort. Typical perhaps is the case recounted in the *Vitae Patrum* of two Egyptian monks, who having castrated themselves to avoid the temptations of the flesh, were excommunicated by the patriarch of Alexandria. They appealed against the sentence both to the patriarch of Jerusalem and to the patriarch of Antioch and when these appeals failed, they tried the pope, who also confirmed the excommunication.[18] Whether or not the principle was put into practice seems to have depended entirely on personality and circumstance.

The other basic belief and one which is closely related to the primacy is Rome's belief in itself as the bastion of orthodoxy, or as Pope Felix III put it, 'executrix of the Chalcedon council on behalf of the Catholic faith'.[19] It was this which caused Rome to seek to implement her primacy. Rome's experience since the legalization of Christianity by Constantine the Great in 313 had been that the Eastern churches were fundamentally unsound on the definition of the faith. Pope Gelasius put it into words when he talked slightingly of 'the Greeks, among whom there is no doubt that many heresies abound'. Gregory I echoed him a century later saying: 'We know of a truth that many bishops of Constantinople have fallen into the whirlpool of heresy and have become not only heretics but heresiarchs'.[20] First Arianism and then Monophysitism had arisen, heretical interpretations of Christianity which had gained not only wide currency in the East but also patrons at the imperial court. It was this experience which confirmed Rome in its belief that the primacy must be asserted in order to ensure that the true faith remained inviolable. For Rome the true faith was enshrined in the Chalcedonian Creed, the definition of orthodoxy based on Pope Leo's *Tome*, presented to the Council of the Church called by the emperor Marcian in 451 to solve the christological controversy and accepted by it. Rome's position in the controversy had been vindicated and the papacy, buttressed by this considerable theological triumph, became entrenched in the idea that it was the guardian and protector of the true orthodoxy. For Rome there could be no departure whatever from the Chalcedonian principles laid down by Pope

Leo. Pope Hormisdas summarized this view perfectly when he wrote in his *libellus*:[21] 'It is in the apostolic see that the Catholic religion has always been preserved without stain.' Justinian too acknowledged this when he wrote: 'each time heretics have arisen in our midst, it is by a sentence and a true judgment of this venerable see [i.e. Rome] that they have been condemned'.[22]

Papal Rome's actions throughout this period were dictated not by an ideological blueprint for the establishment of a governmental scheme in which the Pope outranked everyone but by two very precisely defined ideas – that the papacy had primacy within the church and that it was the defender of an already defined, perfect and unalterable orthodoxy. Against the first, there was little argument from the rest of the church. Against the second, there was much, for when orthodoxy came into question, complex theological issues were raised.

What the papacy did not do in this period was to seek a position of permanent superiority to the emperor, and herein lies the kernel of the dominant theme – if one is required – for papal history between 476 and 752. It was not a conflict between cultures (East versus West) or between institutions (*imperium* versus *sacerdotium*) or between jurisdictions (Rome versus Constantinople) so much as the essential schizophrenia of the papal position which accurately reflects the uneasy dualism of the world in which it found itself, an inner tension that could never be resolved without some drastic step that in this period was never contemplated or even articulated.

The prevailing view of society was of two coterminous bodies, the Roman Empire and the Christian church, both divinely ordained but with essentially different if complementary spheres of influence. The Christian Roman Empire – the *Sancta Respublica* – represented a fusion of two elements which when in harmony strengthened and unified, but when in disharmony provoked in the papacy a crisis of identity. It was under Constantine I that the Roman imperial tradi-tion, reinforced by Hellenistic divine kingship theory, was fused with Greek Christian thought. The result was a concept of a world state ruled by the emperor, God's chosen vicegerent, which in its order and harmony and devotion to the ruler reflected the order and harmony and devotion to God in the kingdom of heaven.

It was not just a fusion of ideas that the Christian Roman Empire involved, it was also a fusion of structures. In every aspect of the Christian church can be seen reflections of the empire. The provin-cial structure of the church and its hierarchical chain of command were clearly based on that of the empire. Indeed the Council of Chalcedon decreed that the church should adapt its organization to conform with changes in the civil organization. Thus when the civil diocese of Italy was divided in two during the Diocletianic reforms, the ecclesiastical diocese was divided also. *Italia Annonaria* in the north formed a diocese headed by the archbishop of Milan; *Italia Suburbicaria* in the centre and the south formed a diocese headed by the pope in Rome. But when the pope's practical everyday jurisdiction was thus reduced, his patriarchal authority over Italy remained undiminished, since he was and remained the only Western patriarch. Rome accepted the change without protest, and it continued to be a cardinal principle. So much so that when Gregory I was planning a provincial structure for the English church, he drew on the details of the old imperial civil organization in a version of the *Notitia Dignitatum*.[23]

Similarly, the papal chancery was modelled on its imperial counterpart, its methods, documents, forms of address closely copied. In the late seventh and early eighth centuries, the introduction of elaborate court ceremonial into the Lateran Palace, complete with tiara, *proskynesis*, Greek hymns and sumptuous liturgical ritual, indicated not so much a desire to turn the papacy into a monarchy as a further example of a long tradition of adoption of the externals of *Romanitas*, demonstrating by imitation the most sincere form of flattery.

Nothing better indicates the creative fusion of *Romanitas* and *Christianitas* in the papacy than the character and achievements of Pope Gregory the Great. On the one hand in his loyalty to the Empire, his meticulous attention to estate management and the *clientela* principles underlying his personnel policy, Gregory, like so many sixth-century popes, was every inch a Roman gentleman. On the other hand, in his monastic avocation, the austere communal lifestyle described by his biographer as 'apostolic' and the enthusiastic devotion to teaching, preaching, conversion and exegesis, he was every inch a Christian. This dualism was recognized and acknowledged in the absolutely accurate description of him on his tombstone as 'the consul of God'.

The role of the emperor in the church had been defined and established under Constantine. According to the Christian Roman kingship theory, the emperor was responsible to God for the well-being of his subjects and this included their spiritual well-being. For it was his duty to maintain the unity and purity of the true faith. It was not the emperor's duty to define doctrine, as Constantine himself admitted when he said to the council of Nicaea in 313: 'You are bishops for all which is internal to the church; I am bishop for all external affairs of the church.' The church, whose ministers also received their power from God, decided doctrine, therefore, and the emperor enforced it. The concrete expression of this arrangement was the great church councils, convoked and sometimes presided over by the emperor but deciding doctrine by themselves. The emperor's role was to enforce doctrinal decisions, root out heresy, maintain ecclesiastical discipline and unity.

Constantine took this duty very seriously, as he reveals in a letter to Celsus, Vicar of Africa:[24]

> With favour of the divine piety I shall come to Africa and shall most fully demonstrate, by pronouncing a clear judgment, to all what kind of veneration is to be rendered to the Highest Divinity and what sort of worship appears to please him. And since it is obvious enough that no one can gain the blessings of a martyr from that crew who seem to be alienated and divorced from the truth of religion, I shall without any hesitation cause those whom I shall judge hostile to the divine law and to religion itself and shall find guilty of violence against the proper worship, to pay the penalty which that mad and reckless obstinacy deserves. . . . I am going to make plain to them what kind of worship is to be offered to the Divinity. For in no other way do I believe that I can escape the greatest guilt than by refusing to connive at their wickedness. What higher duty have I in virtue of my Imperial office and policy than to dissipate errors and repress rash indiscretions, and so to cause all to offer to Almighty God true religion, honest concord and due worship.

This makes clear Constantine's view that God had appointed him emperor and that it was his duty to see God properly worshipped. The emperor therefore accepted the role of the church – and the pope as its primate – within the divinely ordained scheme of things. The normal and natural relationship of emperor and churchman was summed up by Justinian in one of his novels:[25]

> The greatest of the gifts of God to men granted by divine generosity are the priesthood and the imperial authority: the one serves divine ends, the other rules over and cares for human affairs: and each of these springs from one and the same source, and each adorns the life of Man. For if the priest is blameless in every respect and enjoys free access to God and if the emperor duly and rightly adorns the state which is entrusted to him, then there will result a certain fair harmony, which will furnish every good thing for the human race. So we take the greatest care of the true doctrine of God and the good character of priests. If they have this quality we believe that through it the greatest benefits will be given us by God.

This harmony and working together are the keynotes of the ideal relationship envisaged between the Christian emperor and the Christian church.

It is a relationship which papal Rome showed no reluctance in accepting. Pope Celestine wrote to the Emperor Theodosius II:[26] 'You who reign by the authority of Christ our God have by the virtue of your faith conquered its impious foes winning a celestial triumph, whereby you religiously furnish a bulwark for your empire for all time.' Leo the Great also wrote to Theodosius II:[27] 'so we rejoice that there is in you not only a royal but also a priestly mind.' Pope Vigilius wrote in similar terms to the Emperor Justinian:[28] 'It is meet that we should glory in the Lord because he has deigned in his mercy to give you not only an imperial but a priestly soul.' So the emperor, like the church, represented a fusion of Christian and Roman elements, agreed, as Constantine had suggested, to have a priestly function as well as an imperial one.[29]

As long as pope and emperor were content to maintain this division of labour, then the relationship worked. But during the fifth and sixth centuries successive emperors sought to make permanent a radical departure from it – the alteration of doctrine by imperial edict without recourse to church councils. It was this policy which was to provoke the crisis of identity in the papacy. Pope Gelasius summed up the papal dilemma perfectly when he wrote: 'As a Roman-born, I love, honour and revere the Roman emperor, and as a Christian, I desire that he who has a zeal for God shall have with it an accompanying knowledge of the truth.'[30] There were times when the papacy found it impossible to reconcile the two elements, but this was never of its own choosing. It was never the pope, always the emperor, who rocked the boat when he got himself enmeshed in some new theological speculation and started tampering with the Chalcedonian settlement. Rome's answer each time was not to attempt to redefine the relationship between them but to urge a return to the previously agreed position, to stress the fundamentals of the Constantinean settlement. There is then no ideological advance, no questioning of traditional roles on the part of the papacy. What there is from time to time is an uncomfortable awareness of the irreconcilable tension between their *Romanitas* and their *Christianitas*.

Most of the time, however, the papacy was quite content 'to render unto God that which was God's and unto Caesar that which was Caesar's'. Gregory the Great in his handbook for bishops, the *Regula Pastoralis*, made it quite plain that a lay ruler, however wicked, had to be obeyed. For failure to obey would upset the earthly structure, ordained by God: 'When we offend against those who are set over us, we go against the ordinance of Him who set them over us.'[31]

Whatever the dispute between the pope and the emperor on points of faith, the pope remained loyal to the emperor. When the Emperor Anastasius I accused Pope Symmachus, perhaps the fiercest of all his papal opponents, of conspiring with the senate to excommunicate him, Symmachus indignantly denied it.[32] Indeed, no Pope demanded the condemnation of either the emperor Zeno or Anastasius throughout the whole Acacian schism. When it came, as part of the reconciliation, it was at the instigation of the East. Even while attacking the Monothelete religious policy of the imperial goverment, Pope Martin protested his loyalty to the crown in fulsome terms.[33] Gregory II, when writing to the emperor Leo III to attack Iconoclasm, not only accorded him his traditional role of 'emperor and priest' but also stressed that he had taken care to see that his orders had been transmitted to the nations of the West whose kings had been besought by the pope to remain faithful to the emperor.[34] In much more practical terms, successive popes expended untold amounts of money from the papal coffers in buying back conquered towns and territories from the Lombards not for themselves but for the empire.

Throughout the period of imperial rule from Constantinople, the images of the emperor and the empress were placed in positions of honour in the church. Gregory the Great, for instance, attended by both clergy and senate, presided over the installation of the images of Phocas and Leontia in the oratory of St Caesarius in the imperial palace on the Palatine, powerfully betokening the presence of the rulers in the midst of the ancient capital.[35] The refusal of the people to venerate images of the short-lived Monothelete emperor Philippicus at the time of Pope Constantine was so unusual that it merited inclusion in the pope's 'official' biography.[36]

One thing remains constant in this period. The people may revolt; the army may revolt; but the loyalty of the papacy to the empire endures and indeed becomes its principal bulwark in the fraught last years of the exarchate. One of the byproducts of calling this period 'the Byzantine captivity of the papacy' is the idea that the papacy was – or should have been – seeking emancipation from the empire. Nothing could be further from the truth. The popes accepted the emperor's traditional role with regard to the church, felt themselves to be an integral part of the Christian Roman Empire. It was unthinkable that they should seek or even contemplate withdrawal.

The proponents of the monarchical ideology theory point to several developments in this period to support their case. Let us examine them. Great play is always made with papal pronouncements during the Acacian schism and it is necessary to put them firmly in context. It was the Monophysite crisis which provoked the first quarrel between the pope and the Eastern Roman Empire in this period. Essentially the Monophysite controversy was a debate about the nature of Christ. The Monophysites maintained that Christ had a single nature, blending human and divine elements; the Dyophysites maintained that he had a single person but two unconfused natures, one human and one divine. What made the matter doubly serious was that it divided the empire along geographical lines, with the Oriental provinces, Egypt, Palestine and Syria, drawn towards Monophysitism, and Asia Minor and the Balkans pulled in the opposite direction. There was a further dimension too, that of ecclesiastical politics, with the Monophysite patriarch of Alexandria and the Dyophysite patriarch of Constantinople struggling for hierarchical pre-eminence in the Eastern church.[37]

The danger to the empire of such internal divisions was not lost on the imperial government, and successive church councils were held to resolve the matter. The struggle between Alexandria and Constantinople led inevitably to both sides appealing for support to the third major patriarchate – Rome. It was from Rome that the definition of the faith – essentially an endorsement of the Dyophysite position – came, established at the Council of Chalcedon and based on Pope Leo's *Tome*. Its importance cannot be overestimated. For while it was to prove acceptable to the West, the Balkans and much of Asia Minor, it was rejected by the Monophysite provinces and its overthrow became thereafter one of the Monophysites' principal aims.

The papacy came into collision with the empire during the reign of Zeno (474–91). The gulf between the Orthodox and Monophysite provinces of the empire had remained as wide as ever and to bridge it he sought a compromise formula. Aided by the patriarch Acacius of Constantinople therefore, he drew up an imperial edict known as the *Henotikon* or Act of Union, promulgated on 28 July 482. The basic idea of the *Henotikon* was to ignore Chalcedon and take its stand on the three previous general councils of the church: Nicaea, Ephesus and Constantinople. But it did not say anything contrary to the Chalcedonian agreement, and the government seems to have hoped that the two sides would simply agree to differ on the particular matter of the nature of Christ.

Many moderates of both sides, worn out by the bloody strife which had followed Chalcedon, accepted the *Henotikon*. But Rome did not. Its reasons were the predictable and fundamentalist ones that the *Henotikon* was a violent subversion of Chalcedon, of which Rome was the guardian, and a breach with the tradition that doctrinal changes were decided by church council and not by imperial edict.

Rome acts, then, in defence of the *status quo* both in religion and with regard to the role of the emperor. The controversy produced correspondence between pope and emperor which, it has been argued, fundamentally altered the theoretical balance of power in Christendom by exalting the spiritual above the temporal and asserting the papacy's superiority to the empire. But to argue this is to divorce the letters from the background which produced them and to select phrases and paragraphs with scant regard for context, circumstance or contemporary psyche.

The key figure in this development is said to be Pope Gelasius I, several of whose letters are quoted in support of the theory of redefinition of the balance of power. His importance is enhanced by the fact that close textual exegesis has demonstrated that, in his capacity as 'secretary of state', he also wrote the letters of his predecessor Pope Felix III to the East.[38] But it is necessary to get Gelasius and his letters clearly in perspective.

Taking the run of letters between pope and emperor as a whole, several factors strike the objective observer. First, there is the inconsistency of tone. Towards Zeno the papal letters begin cordially enough, but exasperation creeps in as the pope is unable to convince the emperor of his point of view. But when Zeno is replaced as emperor by Anastasius I, the tone once again becomes cordial until he too proves impervious to papal eloquence and the papal letters come to be characterized by terseness and impatience.

For instance, Felix III's first letter to Zeno, written in March 483, begins:[39]

> It was surely proper, venerable emperor, after the death of
> Pope Simplicius my predecessor of holy memory, and my
> own election to his place, that I should write to your clemency
> to announce the events as the course of things required and to
> show my first courtesies. . . . Let not your piety conceive that
> anyone loves you more sincerely than he who wishes you to
> have perpetual peace with God.

Again in May 590, Felix writes:[40]

> I confess that the human mind cannot thank God enough that
> the divine mercy should have planted in the mind of your
> piety such a love of religion as to make you esteem it above
> everything and see in it an element of solidity for your
> empire. . . . I know that it is the wonderful devotion of your
> clemency that has inspired all the admirable words of your
> gentleness in favour of a reverent exercise of divine worship. It
> has made you wish to intensify the unity of the catholic faith,

strenuously to promote the peace of the churches and to try to appoint as the bishop of the people of Constantinople, one who, under the influence of supernatural grace, would excel by the soundness of his character and above all be devoted to the orthodox faith.

This is the same man as had in August 484 written sternly:[41]

> I am certain that it would serve your interests best whenever the affairs of God are at stake both to try and subject your royal will to the priests of God according to his ordinance and to learn about sacred matters from the bishops rather than to teach them.

What is the cause of the change of tone? In 484 the pope has just excommunicated the patriarch Acacius after a crude attempt to corrupt the papal legates, undertaken with the apparent backing of the emperor. By 490, the wicked Acacius is dead, Fravitta is patriarch and there is hope of reconciliation. The changes of tone in the papal letters throughout this period are not dictated by the emergence of a programmatic dogma about temporal and spiritual relations but by the everyday ebb and flow of diplomacy and negotiation. There is no reason to assume that the language of the pope is dictated by anything other than an immediate response to events and situations.

Pope Gelasius did not announce his election to the emperor and much play is made of this. But in fact when Emperor Anastasius reproached him for this omission, Gelasius wrote with an immediate explanation.[42] Royal envoys returning from the East in 492 had refused to see the pope, claiming that the emperor had forbidden it. So Gelasius had feared to write lest he offend. But now he freely confessed 'as a Roman-born, I love, honour and revere the Roman Emperor'. This love and reverence, however, did not prevent Gelasius laying down the law sometimes acrimoniously both to the emperor and to the Eastern church.

The fierceness of Gelasian pronouncements upon the Acacian schism were a matter of character and temperament. For he was a fierce opponent of heresy and schism wherever it appeared. The counterpart of his attitude towards the East is to be found in his unrelenting opposition to variations in the faith, against which he proceeded without fear or favour wherever they appeared. He wrote a denunciation of the pagan festival of *Lupercalia*, which was still being practised in Rome with the backing of prominent senators.[43] He uncovered a nest of Manichaeans in Rome and drove them into exile, publicly burning their books in a grand *auto da fé* before the doors of the basilica of Santa Maria.[44] He campaigned against the

Pelagian heresy, writing to urge its suppression by the bishops of Picenum[45] and the metropolitan of Dalmatia.[46] His extensive polemical writings include a tractate attacking Pelagianism,[47] two books attacking Arianism,[48] a historical account of the growth of Monophysitism,[49] an attack on its theological basis[50] and a defence of the anathematization of Acacius.[51] All of this shows the pope to have been a man concerned to preserve Chalcedonian orthodoxy and not a seeker after innovation.

Much has hinged on the famous letter of Gelasius I to the emperor Anastasius, in which he wrote:[52]

> There are two powers by which the world is chiefly governed, the sacred authority of the priesthood and the royal power. Of these the responsibility of the priests is more weighty in so far as they will answer for the kings of men themselves at the divine judgment. You know, most clement son, that, although you take precedence over all mankind in dignity, nevertheless you piously bow the neck to those who have charge of divine affairs and seek from them the means of your salvation and hence you realize that, in the order of religion, in matters concerning the reception and right administration of the heavenly sacraments, you ought to submit yourself rather than rule, and that in these matters you should depend on their judgment rather than seek to bend them to your will.

In this letter Gelasius appears to contrast *auctoritas* and *potestas*. Much ink and fury has been expended over the years in trying to define just what he meant. There have been four main interpretations. Erich Caspar argued that *potestas* meant power and *auctoritas* moral authority and that Gelasius was restating the strictly dualist view of the world.[53] Walter Ullmann has argued that in Roman legal terms, *auctoritas* meant the God-given right to rule and *potestas* merely delegated executive power and that this is a statement of papal supremacy.[54] Francis Dvornik has argued that in Roman legal terms, *potestas* meant sovereignty and *auctoritas* merely traditional authority and that it is a statement of imperial supremacy.[55] A. K. Ziegler has suggested that it is merely a rhetorical device to avoid using the same word twice, and he quotes a letter written by Gelasius for Felix III in which he is clearly using *auctoritas* and *potestas* as synonyms.[56] The whole situation is further complicated by the fact that in the High Middle Ages Gelasius's letters were plundered by propagandists seeking to buttress new papal pretensions with time-honoured quotations from past popes.

In fact the whole argument is a dangerous red-herring, distracting attention from the more important considerations of context and character already mentioned. The letter is haughty and high-handed, but that was the nature of this particular pope. His successor, Pope Anastasius II, was quite the reverse, a mild, conciliatory man who rejected the Gelasian manner when he wrote to the emperor:[57]

> The heart of your pious majesty is the holy shrine of public welfare so that through the intervention of yours whom God has ordered to govern the world as his vicar, the evangelical and apostolic precepts are not resisted in false pride, but, in obedience to what is salutary are carried out.

Tone and temperament then should not mislead us.

The letter itself must be placed in the context both of the whole sequence of papal letters and of Gelasius's own *Zeitgeist*. Gelasius himself supplied the key to his 494 letter when two years later he made it quite clear that he was not advocating supremacy:[58]

> For Christ, mindful of human frailty, regulated with an excellent disposition what pertained to the salvation of his people. Thus he distinguished between the offices of both powers according to their own proper activities and separate dignities, wanting his people to be saved by healthful humility and not carried away again by human pride, so that Christian emperors would need priests for attaining eternal life, and priests would avail themselves of imperial regulation in the conduct of temporal affairs. In this fashion spiritual activity would be set apart from worldly encroachments and the 'soldier of God' would not be involved in secular affairs, while on the other hand he who was involved in secular affairs would not seem to preside over divine matters. Thus the humility of each order would be preserved, neither being exalted by the subservience of the other and each profession would be especially fitted for its appropriate functions.

It is an unambiguous statement of the dualist position originally taken by Constantine and later reiterated by Justinian.

The difference between Gelasius and his predecessors is not that he wanted to change the traditional relationship of the temporal and spiritual authorities but that he wanted it more clearly defined. The two spheres were agreed to exist with some degree of overlap. The Acacian schism had brought into question the degree of overlap, forcing Gelasius to seek clarification.

In essence there is nothing radical or revolutionary in the papal letters. They are not written as abstract statements of principle but as arguments to convince. They seek no great leap-forward, rather a return to the *status quo*. That is why the letters are filled with references to tradition. That is why Felix III constantly reminds the emperor of the examples of his predecessors Marcian and Leo. For they upheld the *status quo* which Zeno and Anastasius have departed from. When Felix writes that it is 'for the emperor to learn rather than teach', he is saying nothing new. He is simply reminding the emperor that traditionally doctrine was decided by the bishops in council and not by the emperor by edict. Exactly the same intention underpins the Gelasian letters. Throughout the schism the papal position remains consistent. Chalcedonian orthodoxy must not be impaired and doctrine should not be decided by imperial edict. Different popes express themselves in different ways. Anastasius II is extremely courteous, Symmachus extremely surly. But the message remains the same.

An attempt to redefine the relationship with the temporal sphere, then, is not only outside papal policy as perceived throughout this period, it would also be extremely uncharacteristic of Gelasius himself. His activities in other fields show him to be an intense traditionalist. In 494 he was prompted by the dislocation and confusion caused by the Ostrogothic invasion to issue a major *Constitutum*,[59] in which he specifically pledged the papacy to avoid innovation (precept 9). Throughout the *Constitutum* there is evidence of papal concern to maintain existing and time-honoured practices. Priests must not usurp episcopal functions (precept 6) nor deacons, the functions of priests (precept 7). Ordinations and baptisms must be carried out on the traditionally appointed days (precept 11). No new basilicas may be dedicated without papal permission (precept 4).

Gelasius's letters and decretals on non-doctrinal matters resound with a deep and pervasive conservatism. Promotion must be by seniority.[60] Younger bishops must get papal permission to visit the royal court.[61] Bishops must as a general rule preserve as just and legitimate the decisions of their predecessors.[62] When judging a boundary dispute, Gelasius wrote: 'The parishes of each church fixed by ancient disposition cannot for any reason be changed lest by the bad example of one change, instability increases and universal confusion is created everywhere.'[63] These are the words of a man to whom tradition is everything and the *status quo* an axiom.

Gelasius sought everywhere to stress the traditional rights not only of the church but also of the laity. But he did so not to try to elevate the church in any way but to ensure that both sides retained their proper authority. There was here as elsewhere a desire not to innovate but to preserve. Thus when in precept 14 of his *Constitutum*, Gelasius says that 'no cleric may take as tenant, slave or cleric anyone who belongs to someone else without written permission of the lord on pain of excommunication and deposition,' he is demonstrating both a desire to protect the rights of masters over their slaves and tenants in order to preserve the social order and a wish to prevent the lowering of standards in the priesthood. His consistent aim was to retain papal control over matters involving church personnel and church property and also carefully to define church rights in this field.

Above all his policy towards the Ostrogothic regime in Italy parallels exactly his attitude to the emperor's role in the church. For it too is prompted not by a desire to redefine but rather to define and delimit because of the arrival in Italy of an alien presence which might seek to interfere in church affairs. There is no doubt that King Theodoric subscribed to this distinction of spheres and we know of at least one case in which clerical personnel, having appealed to the royal court in a case of dispute, were remitted back to the Pope's jurisdiction. But other laymen were less scrupulous and Gelasius made plain his position when writing to Count Teias:[64]

> We urge your nobility more and more that you should refrain from interfering in ecclesiastical cases and affairs and that ceasing all disturbance, you should allow the rule of religion to be preserved, especially since there can be no doubt that you are of another communion and you ought not to involve yourself in things which do not concern you, whatever your intentions, lest you compel us to refer all these things to my lord and son the King. Because as he in his wisdom wishes to act in no way contrary to ecclesiastical rights, it is proper that whoever lives under his dominion should imitate the deeds of the magnificent king, so that he does not seem to act against the will of the King.

The simple fact of the matter is that the popes can speak with asperity to the emperors during these years, because the emperors cannot get at them. Italy is ruled by barbarian kings and the emperor is far away. They change their tune quickly enough when the province comes back under imperial rule and popes who do not behave find themselves being hauled off to Constantinople under guard. The attitude adopted by popes like Gelasius and Symmachus to the East then can be explained in political rather than ideological terms. Given all this evidence of context and character, the question of what Gelasius actually meant by *auctoritas* and *potestas* pales into insignificance.

The problem presenting itself to the papacy in the eighties of the fifth century was not, as has been claimed, concerned with the qualification for governing the church as the congregation of all Christians. To say that is to see the fifth century in terms of the eleventh and twelfth centuries. The problem presenting itself to the papacy was quite simply how to get back the *status quo ante Henotikon*. That was its object in 519 just as it had been its object in 484.

However, those who argue that a papal monarchical theory emerged in the last years of the fifth century are faced with a succession of facts which requires remarkable mental gymnastics to surmount. The so-called 'charter of liberty' of the papacy had no sooner been promulgated than there was a schism between two factions in the Roman church, one favouring *détente* with the East and the other the maintenance of a Gelasian hard-line. The hard-liners triumphed but only by abasing themselves before King Theodoric, negating any concept of papal supremacy over lay authorities. When Theodoric, repeatedly asked to decide who was the rightful pope, refused to intervene in church affairs and appointed a synod of bishops to decide, the bishops sent a petition to the king in which they made a grovelling statement of their utter incapability:[65]

> It is therefore the concern of your *imperium* by God's will to see to the conciliation of the church and the peace of the city of Rome and the provinces. So we beg you as a pious ruler to come to the aid of our weakness and powerlessness since the simplicity of priests is not equal to the cunning of the laity and we can no longer bear the deaths of our servants and the dangers to ourselves here in Rome.

In somewhat less lachrymose but none the less humble terms Pope Symmachus himself, at the same time as he was writing intemperate and offensive letters to the Christian Eastern emperor, threw himself on the mercy of the Arian and barbarian king of Italy. As one historian admits wryly, 'there was a considerable gulf between the highly developed governmental doctrine of the papacy and actual reality – concrete papal actions in the early sixth century can hardly be detected.'[66] If the idea of a highly developed governmental doctrine is abandoned, then this absence of concrete papal actions in pursuit of it becomes entirely explicable.

Eventually the Acacian schism ended and good relations between Rome and Constantinople were restored on Rome's terms – the restoration of the *status quo ante Henotikon*. But this did not occur because Rome was strong or had made her point, it occurred because a new dynasty came to power in the East with a very different set of policies from the old. Justin I and Justinian I were both by personal conviction Chalcedonians. But more than this, their foreign policy priorities included the re-establishment of concrete imperial authority in the West, which needed the goodwill of the pope. Zeno and Anastasius, whose priority had been religious and political union in the East, had ignored Italy and consequently the pleas and protests of the pope had fallen on deaf ears.

Gregory the Great is perhaps the most celebrated pope in the sixth and seventh centuries, and supporters of the monarchical ideology theory have sought to fit him into the development pattern as they see it. According to this view, Gregory's sojourn in Constantinople led to his 'clear realization that the claim to primatial authority in matters of jurisdiction had no hope whatsoever of being acknowledged in Constantinople'.[67] If so, the evidence is hard to find. Gregory played the same game as all the popes, asserting the right to withdraw certain cases involving the Eastern church to Rome. Indeed he had rather more success in this field than many popes. He also pressed the emperor vigorously about the assumption of the title 'Oecumenical Patriarch' by John IV of Constantinople, fearing an infringement of Roman primacy.

In the light of this 'clear realization', according to the same view, Gregory conceived a new strategy:[68]

> He decided that if the papacy was to fulfil its true vocation without interference by the imperial government and without being constantly exposed to serious accusations, it could only do so if it extended its concrete influence to regions and districts which were of no concern to the imperial government. In practical terms, this meant the beginning or intensification of papal operations in Spain, Gaul and Britain.

Again, this is not supported by the evidence. First, there was virtually no contact with Spain at all. Second, Gregory's contacts with Gaul consisted largely of his attempts to persuade the Merovingian rulers to initiate a reform synod to clear up the abuses in the church, attempts which failed miserably. Third, Gregory undertook the English mission not in order to extend papal influence but because the English were heathen and needed converting. Like Gelasius, Gregory was a fervent opponent of heresy, paganism and schism. His efforts to convert the English must be seen alongside his equally determined bids to suppress the Donatists of Africa, the 'Three Chapters' schismatics of Istria, the worshippers of stone idols in Sardinia and of trees in Campania, all of them areas within the confines of the empire.

The 'policy of bifurcation', with Gregory writing high-handedly to Western rulers while speaking humbly to the empire, is not borne out by the facts. He was almost as deferential to the bloodthirsty and ruthless queen Brunhilda of the Franks as he was to the emperor

Maurice – although his attitude to neither compares with the sicken-
ing servility he displayed towards Phocas, largely because Phocas
had disposed of Maurice, with whom Gregory had had his differences. The acts Gregory took which in the long run did enhance
papal power – paying imperial troops, negotiating treaties, appointing military commanders – were undertaken not in accordance with
any ideological plan but out of sheer desperate necessity. If he had
not done these things, Rome would have fallen to the Lombards.
One historian has written: 'it is nevertheless true that Gregory I did
not materially contribute to the development of the hierocratic
theme.'[69] This is perhaps not surprising. For Gregory's mind did not
work in that way. His actions were dictated by the fact that he was a
Roman and a Christian and not a would-be papal monarch eman-
cipating himself from imperial control. People simply did not think
in that way at the end of the sixth century.

In the seventh and early eighth centuries, too, there was a marked
absence of ideological developments. There were doctrinal struggles
certainly, but they followed the same pattern as the Monophysite
crisis. The emperor imposed a new religious policy by edict. Rome
objected on the familiar grounds. The emperor tried to enforce his
policy. Rome resisted. Ultimately the crisis was settled on Rome's
terms, but only because circumstances in the East had changed: there
was a new emperor and a reversal of government policy.

Rome certainly stressed her primatial role in the West. Since the
pope was the only Western patriarch, this was both proper and
inevitable. The barbarian states, as they gradually acquired catholicism and civilization, accorded Rome due respect. But there is no
evidence of substantial contact between Gaul and Rome during the
century following the death of Gregory the Great. There seems to
have been little contact with Spain either and when it did occur it was
usually acrimonious.[70] But whatever the nature of the relations
between Rome and the barbarian states, the papacy sees itself consistently and unshakably as subject to the Roman Empire. Only when
the imperial presence vanishes does it consciously look for another
secular protector and settle on the Franks.

This, then, was not a period of ideological growth. There was no
monarchical masterplan to which some popes adhered and from
which others deviated. Rome's position, based on the trinity of
harmony, orthodoxy and primacy, was profoundly conservative,
traditional and rooted in the past. Contemporaries saw the period in
terms of the coexistence of *Romanitas* and *Christianitas*. The period
between 476 and 554, during which the barbarians ruled Italy, briefly
distorted the relationship. Thereafter it was restored. The popes saw
themselves as both Christians and Romans. When it came to a

doctrinal crunch, they were Christians first. But they clung to their *Romanitas* even when at odds with the East and they were still clinging to it when Imperial rule in Italy crumbled into dust.

Chapter 2

The Political and Religious Context

Despite the importance to papal thinking of primacy and apostolicity, it is quite evident that the papacy's development in this period was not primarily determined by theory but by personalities and events. The subordination of theory to circumstance can be simply demonstrated. No one made more frequent or regular declarations of papal primacy than Justinian I. Yet it was Justinian who took imperial interference in papal affairs to its highest level. He successfully deposed one pope, kidnapped a second and forcibly installed a third. He imposed his doctrinal changes with ruthless single-mindedness. A perfect example of this is his success with Theopaschism.

Theopaschism was based on the idea that the Trinity remained the Trinity even after the Incarnation. Strict Chalcedonian orthodox opinion rejected this idea on the grounds that it implied that God could die. When it was advanced in Rome by Scythian monks in 521, it was decisively rejected by Pope Hormisdas who regarded it as crypto-Monophysite. Yet Justinian, who saw it as a possible formula to reunite the rival religious factions in his empire, took it up enthusiastically and promulgated without consulting either the pope or the patriarch of Constantinople two successive edicts introducing Theopaschism into the canons of the faith.[1] After the proclamation of the second of these in 533, Justinian wrote to Pope John II confirming papal primacy but also inviting him to endorse the Theopaschite edict.[2] Despite his predecessor's clear condemnation of the doctrine, John II not only dutifully endorsed it but also said that it conformed to the long-established beliefs of the Roman church. He went so far as to condemn the *Akoimetae*, the Constantinople monks who were Rome's staunchest allies in the Eastern capital, for their opposition to Theopaschism.[3] Three years later Pope Agapitus, one-time colleague of Hormisdas, confirmed John's declaration.[4]

The ideas had not changed during these years, and therefore the variations in the papal response to Theopaschism can only be attri-

29

buted to the interplay of personality and circumstance, factors which, though often underrated by historians, played crucial roles in the development of the papacy. In particular, the influence of personality was pivotal. The course and destiny of the papacy was decisively shaped by the succession of very different personalities who occupied the throne of St Peter: pontiffs like the austere, prickly and rigidly unbending legalist Gelasius I; the fiery, passionate and uncouth 'Young Turk' Symmachus; the ambitious, guileful and manoeuvring politico Vigilius; the tireless monastic missionary-administrator Gregory the Great; the suave, witty and dynamic statesman Zacharias; the cautious, prudent, fussily meticulous Hormisdas; the forceful, direct and practical man of affairs Honorius I; each played his part in his own way and each left his legacy to the institution.

Almost as important as the character of the pope were the character and interests of the emperor. The Roman Empire was, after all, an autocracy, and imperial government policy took its direction from the personality and preoccupations of the autocrat. For instance, where Justinian I was vitally interested both in theology and in Italy, the Emperor Maurice was interested in neither, facts which were to have profound importance for Rome and the papacy.

As the years passed, the attitudes and attributes of the popes became more rather than less important, as imperial influence in Italy weakened and the papacy, for so long used to a secular protector, was thrown back more and more on its own resources. The first great shock it had to weather was the end of the Western Roman Empire in 476. Despite the fact that it must have seemed to many the logical culmination of centuries of decay, as Italy embarked on a new and uncharted course there must have been considerable uncertainty about how the papacy would fare in a country ruled by heretic barbarians.

The combination of continuous barbarian pressure on long, exposed frontiers and a stagnating economic system, increasingly unable to sustain the burdens placed upon it, rotted the fabric of the Western Roman Empire. One after another its provinces fell, until finally only Italy remained, ruled by powerful Germanic generalissimos, who exercised power through a succession of puppet emperors in Ravenna.

When Odoacer, the Herulian mercenary leader, finally pensioned off the last of the puppets, the aptly named Romulus Augustulus, and sent him into comfortable retirement in Campania, the sovereignty technically reverted to the Eastern Roman emperor in Constantinople. It is a measure of the respect that Odoacer, and Theodoric after him, held for imperial traditions and constitutional theory that one of their continuing policies was the quest for legitimacy. Neither ruled as Emperor but both exercised a dual role, ruling their own people as king and governing the Romans as viceroy in the name of the distant Eastern emperor. But the emperor was so distant and so ineffective that despite its technical status within the imperial orbit, Italy was effectively an independent barbarian kingdom.[5]

Odoacer ruled for nearly fifteen years before falling victim to the superior strength of another barbarian ruler, Theodoric the Amal, who swept into Italy at the head of his Ostrogoths. It took three years of war but by 493 Theodoric had established himself as king of Italy. Few can have foreseen that the rule of this enlightened heretic would provide Italy with its last period of stable and peaceful government for centuries. Theodoric, brought up at the imperial court in Constantinople, had like Odoacer, an intense admiration for the Roman system. Indeed his dying advice to his court was to love the senate and people of Rome and make sure of the peace and goodwill of the Eastern emperor.[6] He settled his Ostrogoths in Northern Italy, endowing them with land but largely without expropriating the Roman ruling classes. Like Odoacer before him he preserved the administrative system intact, though there were inevitably some adjustments to accommodate the reality of the barbarian presence.[7] Although of a different religious persuasion, he maintained good relations with the Roman church. He enforced law and order, encouraged peace and prosperity and worked for harmony between Goths and Romans. In this he was aided by a powerful faction of the Roman aristocracy, notably two outstanding chief ministers, the cool and judicious Liberius and the wise and learned Cassiodorus. In retrospect, his reign can be seen as the Indian summer of the Western Roman Empire.

A contemporary chronicler, the *Anonymus Valesianus*, paid eloquent tribute to him:[8]

Theodoric was a man of great distinction and of goodwill towards all men. He reigned thirty-three years. For thirty of these years Italy enjoyed such good fortune that even travellers journeyed in peace. For he did nothing wrong. He governed the two nations of Goths and Romans as if they were one people. Although he himself was an Arian, he attempted nothing against the catholic religion. He ordered the Roman administration to continue as it had under the emperors. He was generous with gifts and grain doles. Although he found nothing in the treasury but hay, by his efforts he restored it and filled it up.

Even more impressive, coming as it does from the East, is the verdict of the historian Procopius:[9]

> Theodoric was an extraordinary lover of justice and adhered rigorously to the laws. He guarded the country from barbarian invasion and displayed both intelligence and prudence in the highest degree. Of injustice towards his subjects there was hardly a trace in his government nor would he allow any of his subordinates to attempt anything of the kind, save only that the Goths divided among themselves the same proportion of the land of Italy which Odoacer had given to his partisans. So then Theodoric was in name a tyrant but died a true king, not inferior to the best of his predecessors and his popularity grew greatly, contrary to the ordinary fashion of human affairs, both among Goths and Italians.

His success was due to a policy of communal segregation. He ruled the Goths through his counts, but the Romans through the traditional administrative structure. Although an Arian himself, he insisted on strict religious toleration and this extended even to the Jews.[10] 'We cannot give orders about religious belief because no one can be forced to believe against his will,'[11] was the enlightened summary of his religious policy. Thus the Arian church, with its own buildings, hierarchy, services and estates, existed side by side with the Catholic church,[12] though neither church had anything to do with the other. But Theodoric scrupulously maintained the jurisdictional rights of the Catholic church intact, refusing to judge cases involving clerical personnel and remitting them to the appropriate ecclesiastical authority.[13]

During his reign there was a flowering of culture, much of it religion-based but fostered by the general atmosphere of peace and toleration. Cassiodorus, Boethius, Symmachus, Ennodius, Eugippius and Dionysius Exiguus in particular stand out, constituting a talented, prolific and erudite generation whose like was not to be seen again for centuries. Theodoric extended his rule outside Italy over Provence, northern Illyricum, Dalmatia, Rhaetia, part of Pannonia, and he established marriage alliances with most of the other barbarian rulers of the West.

It might seem as if Theodoric's rule was Roman imperialism without the empire. But this is not so. For the Ostrogothic achievement, however impressive, rested on very insecure foundations. For all his brilliant record, for all the fact that many of the aristocracy served their barbarian masters loyally and well in government positions, something had gone out of Italy and that something was the imperial spirit. There was a widespread feeling that these barbarian kings were just not *pukka*. There was still an overwhelming affinity with the empire of the East, which now alone embodied their Roman heritage, their imperial traditions, in many cases even their kith and kin. Strong religious, intellectual, cultural and family ties still bound the Roman aristocracy to the East. The spirit of empire, unique and irreplaceable, now dwelt in that New Rome beside the Bosphorus. Typical of this feeling is the wistful statement of Pope Felix III, himself a scion of the Roman aristocracy, to the emperor Zeno:[14] 'In you alone now survives the ancient name of Empire.' It was for this reason that Theodoric laid such store by the gaining of Eastern recognition. But, for all that, many regarded Theodoric as at best a tolerable stopgap until the Roman unity could be restored.

What created an illusory sense of unity between Theodoric and the Romans for the first half of his reign was the religious situation. While papal Rome was in schism from the Greek East, cordial relations between Romans of East and West were suspended and this strengthened Theodoric's position. But once the schism was ended, then the Romans were free to see Theodoric as an alien and a heretic, particularly since the ending of the schism was largely the work of Justin I and his nephew Justinian, whose policies also included the reconquest of Italy. The days of the Ostrogothic kingdom were clearly numbered.

Barely ten years after Theodoric's death, the imperial reconquest of Italy was launched. But it took twenty years to accomplish and left Italy impoverished, depopulated and broken in spirit. In 554 Justinian issued the *Pragmatic Sanction* officially to re-establish Roman rule. But it was a hollow triumph. The senatorial aristocracy had collapsed, undermined by massacre, bankruptcy and migration to the East. The old administration was dismantled and a new provincial government created, staffed by Greek civil servants and headed by an Eastern military governor, eventually to be called the exarch of Ravenna. The Arian church was suppressed and its property handed over to the Catholic church. But the Roman church lost the freedom of action it had enjoyed under Theodoric.

Two aspects in particular of the new set-up had serious implications for the papacy. The emperors expected the popes to toe the imperial line even on matters of doctrine; as, for instance, when Justinian compelled the unwilling papacy to endorse the condemnation of the so-called 'Three Chapters', an action which many believed to compromise the Chalcedonian settlement. This led directly to the Istrian schism, with the churches of Northern Italy withdrawing from communion with the pope. The schism persisted for nearly 150 years, seriously damaging Italian unity both spiritual and political. Similarly the choice of Ravenna as capital of the exarchate led to the rapid rise of the archbishopric of Ravenna, which was to come increasingly to resent its subordinate position in the Italian hierarchy. From time to time it pursued a policy of seeking autonomy from Rome, often backed by the Imperial authorities who saw it as useful in terms of ecclesiastical politics to have a counterweight to the papacy, just in case the Pope stepped out of line.

But worse than this was to come. For in 568 while Italy was still assessing the cost of the war of liberation, she was faced with another, even more serious, threat, in the Lombards. They struck like a thunderbolt from a clear sky, this savage, ferocious warrior race who, under their shrewd, ruthless king Alboin, came in search of plunder and conquest. There was no one to oppose them as they swept into Northern Italy, carrying all before them. In September 569 the old imperial capital of Milan opened its gates to them and Alboin assumed the title 'Lord of Italy'. Only the coastal plains of Venetia and Liguria held out, largely ignored by the Lombards who pressed on down the central core of Italy. By 571 they had completed the conquest of the Po Valley, and were swarming southwards into Umbria and Tuscia. Then suddenly in 572, at the height of his triumphal career, Alboin was murdered. His successor, King Cleph, was also murdered two years later and the Lombard chieftains gathering at Ticinum decided against electing a new king. Instead the horde divided up into thirty-six separate duchies, based on the already conquered cities. The principal interests of the Lombards were hunting and warfare, and they retained their clan organization, geared for war and supplied with food and labour by the native population. There is comparatively little evidence about the condition of the Roman population in Lombard Italy but the most likely conclusion is that the great landowners either fled or were killed, their estates being expropriated by the warrior class; and the peasants carried on much as they had done before, tilling the soil and serving new masters.[15]

By the time the kingship was suspended in 574, the initial impetus of the Lombards had spent itself. But they had effectively gained control of half of Italy. They ruled most of the old province of *Italia Annonaria*, with the exception of the coastal areas of Liguria centred on Genoa, Istria-Venetia centred on Grado and Aemilia centred on Ravenna and the Pentapolis. In *Suburbicaria* they established control of the central spine via two powerful and important duchies based on Spoletium and Beneventum from which they effectively dominated the Italian interior. Imperial rule was maintained in the Duchy of Rome and in the coastal areas around Naples, Rhegium, Hortona, Sipontum and Tarentum. In effect the imperial province of Italy had been reduced to a series of coastal enclaves. The islands of Sicily,

Sardinia and Corsica remained untouched but they were organized separately and not part of the exarchate of Ravenna.

How could this happen? First and perhaps most important the imperial government was wholly unprepared for the invasion. Italy seems to have been very weakly garrisoned and decisive counter-measures were not immediately forthcoming, in part because the throne was occupied by the eccentric and unstable Justin II, who spent much of his time reversing the policies of his predecessor Justinian and finally went mad in 574. This led to the emergence of the able and farsighted Tiberius Constantine as regent, and under his direction the government acted. A mercenary army under Justin's son-in-law Count Baduarius was despatched to Italy in 575. It was annihilated by the Lombards. This disaster effectively precluded the government from taking any further direct military action in the West.

Justin II's successors, Tiberius Constantine (578–82) and Maurice (582–602), preoccupied with crises in the East and the Balkans and unable to spare any additional troops for the Italian front, took steps which in effect recognized the fact of the Lombard conquest. Maurice organized the provincial government into the exarchate, a militarized frontier province, consolidating what remained of imperial Italy into a defensive unit. Both he and Tiberius used the expedient of paying other barbarians like the Franks the harass the Lombards. The Franks invaded Lombard Italy in 584 but the only practical consequence of this was to convince the Lombards that they needed undivided command again and they elected the son of the late King Cleph, Autharis, as king in the same year.

From this time on until the end of the period, the story is a repetitive one of successive advances and retreats, sieges and reliefs, truces and treaties, which constitute a gradual process of erosion of imperial territory. The empire was not without its spectacular counterstrikes from time to time and the eighteen-year exarchate of Isaac, ending with his death in 643 at the battle of Panaro, marked a notable period of imperial consolidation and military success. But during the seventh century the Ligurian and Istrian enclaves were mopped up and during the first half of the eighth century the frontiers of the exarchate were pushed further and further back until in 751 Ravenna itself fell and the exarchate was finally extinguished. The southernmost parts of Italy were reorganized into a Byzantine province, their long traditions of Greek speech and culture binding them much more closely to the main body of the Eastern Empire than the only recently Hellenized centre and the Latinate north. Throughout this period, too, the Lombards were digging in and settling down. They organized an administration, acquired a law

35

code and established diplomatic relations with other states. In other words the Lombard horde was transmuted into a meaningful and stable political entity.

Throughout the late sixth century and the whole of the seventh the papacy fought its own battle for survival and recovery. For Rome needed to survive both physical attack by the Lombards and the spiritual assault constituted by the revival of Arianism. Initially the papacy's position was extremely precarious, since it seemed to be caught literally between the devil and the deep blue sea. The papacy was situated within the Duchy of Rome, technically under an imperial military commander but one who was kept so short of troops and supplies that the popes found themselves having to step constantly into the breach. They had not only to provide material help in the form of money and grain but also to use their moral authority by appealing to all and sundry for aid and support. Pelagius II, for instance, elected in the midst of a Lombard siege, took it upon himself to appeal for Frankish intervention against the enemy, as well as making urgent representations to the emperor in Constantinople. Gregory I acted independently of the imperial authorities to secure a treaty with King Agilulf at a cost to the papal treasury of 500 pounds of gold. Apart from the external threat from the Lombards, the imperial province of Italy was far from stable internally as a whole succession of revolts (616, 619, 643, 652) testifies. There was indeed sufficient evidence of disaffection by the 660s for the emperor Constans II temporarily to transfer his headquarters to his Western dominions, partly in order to shore up their crumbling structure.

The course of Lombard history during this period is distinguished by three central continuing characteristics, all of which profoundly affected the papacy in one way or another. The first is the tensions between the Lombard kingdom, centred on Ticinum and controlling the north, and the largely autonomous southern duchies of Spoletium and Beneventum. The disaffection between these rival Lombard power centres was a two-edged sword for the beleaguered papal and imperial authorities. Sometimes it was a valuable weapon in the policy of 'divide and rule' and at others a potentially destructive one, especially if the pope chose to ally with the wrong side. The second is the permanent state of intermittent warfare between the imperial and Lombard forces, with frontiers eroded and Rome itself at least three times besieged. The third is the progressive civilization and conversion of the Lombards, which was ultimately to benefit the papacy most of all.

Rome's relations with the Lombards were dictated by the traditional desire to eradicate heresy and by the pressing practical need to keep them sweet to avoid its own extinction. There were in particular two continuing religious problems during the seventh century. The first was to convert the predominantly Arian Lombards to catholicism and the second was to reconcile the 'Three Chapters' schismatics of the north. The resolution of the two problems certainly enhanced Rome's power, but that was a byproduct of the main aim.

The swift and total success of the Lombards in northern Italy can be explained in part by the alienation of *Italia Annonaria* from Rome on account of the 'Three Chapters'. The archbishops of Milan and of Aquileia, the two senior churchmen of the north, had rejected the condemnation of the 'Three Chapters' by Popes Vigilius and Pelagius I and gone into schism. Whereas with the help of stalwart allies like the imperial governor Narses and Archbishop Agnellus of Ravenna Pope Pelagius had kept the centre and south of Italy loyal, the north had remained unreconciled. But this purely theological controversy had been overtaken by the political catastrophe of the Lombard invasion. For many Catholics in the north the rule of an Arian race must have seemed preferable to the rule of a heretical emperor and pope, and so there was almost no resistance.

Archbishop Honoratus of Milan and Archbishop Paulinus of Aquileia, however, fled from their sees and placed themselves under imperial protection, Paulinus transferring his see to the island of Grado off the Istrian coast and Honoratus taking refuge in Genoa in the imperial enclave of Liguria. It may be that they felt they had more to lose than most churchmen, for both are recorded as taking their treasures with them.[16] But not all churchmen followed their lead. Many must have imitated Bishop Felix of Tarvisium, who went out of his city to meet Alboin and asked for the property of his church to be spared. Alboin agreed and ordered a charter prepared to safeguard the rights and privileges of the church of Tarvisium.[17] Others were prepared to work with the Lombards, men like Bishop Agnellus of Tridentum, employed on a diplomatic mission.[18] This lack of resistance and willingness to oblige seems to have resulted in an uninterrupted episcopal succession being maintained in many cities of occupied northern Italy. It is only in the frontier areas of the north and the disputed areas of the centre and the south where populations dispersed, cities constantly changed hands and there was danger and instability that we find disruption in the episcopal succession and in the lives of sees. To all intents and purposes a catholic hierarchy was maintained in the north, though it was one which had no contact with Rome and remained faithful to the 'Three Chapters'. Regular episcopal succession is known to have been maintained in such key cities as Comum, Brixia, Novara, Verona and Bononia.[19] Also a

synod of schismatic prelates held at Marianum in 589 mustered the
bishops of Altinum, Sabiona, Tridentum, Tarvisium, Vicentia,
Verona, Concordia, Feltria, Acilum, Bellunum, Julium and Pola,
most of whom came from inside occupied territory, a clear indication of the general continuation of the hierarchy.[20] It was, however, a
headless hierarchy, since the two northern archbishops chose to
remain in the imperial refuges.

Both Honoratus of Milan and Paulinus of Aquileia died soon after
their flight. In 573 Laurentius II was elected in Genoa to succeed
Honoratus and he prudently abandoned support for the 'Three
Chapters' and signed a document to that effect, countersigned by
Gregory the Great, then prefect of Rome.[21] There were probably
two reasons for this. Laurentius depended for protection on the
goodwill of the imperial government, committed to a policy of
condemning the 'Three Chapters'. He also depended on the goodwill of Rome for the protection of the Milanese patrimony in Sicily,
one of his few remaining sources of revenue. Milan in fact fell under
the influence of Rome to a far greater extent than ever before. The
practice by which the archbishops of Milan and Aquileia consecrated each other was abandoned in view of the continued attachment of Aquileia to the 'Three Chapters' and suffragan bishops now
performed the consecration of the archbishop of Milan.[22] For the
first time, however, Rome began to oversee Milanese elections and
the pope began to refer to the archbishop as *filius noster* rather than
the usual *frater*.[23] Aware of the creeping influence of Rome, Milan
endeavoured to form an alliance with Ravenna and began making
special mention of the archbishop of Ravenna in the mass, something
of which the pope strenuously disapproved.[24]

It was the Lombard invasions rather than the exercise of ideological ambition that led to a real increase in papal influence. For just as
the exiled Milanese archbishop looked to the Western patriarch for
guidance and protection in his hour of need, and so was sucked into
his orbit, Ravenna too felt the effect of the long arm of Rome.
Uniquely two Romans were successively elected archbishops of
Ravenna. Even Grado eventually succumbed to pressure from
Rome, though at first Grado stubbornly persisted in support for the
'Three Chapters'. Archbishop Elias, elected in 571 to succeed
Paulinus, rallied the schismatic forces and rededicated Grado
cathedral to St Euphemia, the patron saint of Chalcedon, an important symbolic act since the condemnation of the 'Three Chapters'
was believed to have compromised the Chalcedonian settlement.
Pope Pelagius II attempted to win Elias over by argument and
remonstrance. But when this failed, the exarch Smaragdus took
sterner measures. Severus, who in 586 had succeeded Elias as arch-

bishop, was kidnapped with three of his bishops and an elderly *defensor* and carried off by the exarch to Ravenna. There he was held for a year until he agreed to condemn the 'Three Chapters'. The Venetian and Istrian bishops, meeting in synod, condemned the archbishop, but when he returned from Ravenna, he recanted his acceptance of the condemnation and was received back with rejoicing.[25]

The influence of both the empire and the papacy over Grado and the Istrian enclave still within imperial control eventually began to pay off, however. Three bishops from inside the imperially controlled area came over to orthodoxy under Gregory the Great[26] and on the death of Severus in 606 came the inevitable split. Abbot John was elected Archbishop in Aquileia with the support of the Lombards and the backing of the 'Three Chapters' hierarchy.[27] But in Grado, the orthodox Candidianus became archbishop with the backing of the empire, the papacy, the orthodox bishops, and, if Abbot John is to be believed, the use of force in the form of imperial troops.[28] Thereafter there were two rival archbishoprics in Istria and two rival hierarchies, one orthodox and one schismatic. In effect the split was between imperial and Lombard territory. The extent to which Grado depended on empire and papacy can be seen from the events of 628. There was a brief crisis when archbishop Fortunatus of Grado suddenly went schismatic and fled to the Lombards, taking the church treasures with him.[29] The clergy of Grado petitioned Pope Honorius I for a new archbishop and he sent them the Roman subdeacon Primogenius, who was duly installed.[30] Emperor Heraclius made good the loss of the treasure.[31]

The dreary 'Three Chapters' saga becomes intertwined with the more centrally important question of the conversion of the Lombards. The gradual process by which the Lombards ceased to be a mere warring horde and during the seventh century became a settled and organized state has already been mentioned. One of the major influences in this process was their conversion to Catholicism and the central figure in this was almost certainly Queen Theodelinda. A Catholic princess from Bavaria, she married King Autharis and rapidly established herself as a significant figure at the royal court. When Autharis died suddenly in 590, she was invited to choose and marry his successor, an indication of the appearance of dynastic sentiment. She chose, elevated and married Duke Agilulf of Turin.

Devoted to her faith, Theodelinda now sought to use her influence to advance it. Autharis had been intensely suspicious of Catholicism and had forbidden the sons of Lombards to be baptized as Catholics, for fear of sapping the warrior virility of the race.[32] But Agilulf was more accommodating to his wife's wishes. Although he himself remained an Arian, at Theodelinda's request 'he bestowed many possessions upon the church of Christ and restored to their wonted dignity bishops who were in a reduced and abject condition'.[33] Later, when their son Adaloald was born, Agilulf permitted him to be baptized as a Catholic. This new mood at the Lombard court paid off, for Gregory the Great inaugurated a correspondence with Theodelinda and she was influential in bringing about the *Generalis Pax* in 598, which provided a valuable breathing space during which Gregory was able to take steps to reconstitute the shattered ecclesiastical hierarchy in the duchy of Spoletium.[34] That he was permitted to do so and that the peace was signed and kept by the Lombards is an indication of a new reasonableness on their part.[35]

But all was not yet sweetness and light. There was a complicating factor. Theodelinda may have been a Catholic, but she was also a supporter of the 'Three Chapters', as was her principal religious adviser, Abbot Secundus of Tridentum. She intervened, for instance, in a dispute with the archbishop of Milan, some of whose suffragans, with her support, rejected his metropolitan authority on the grounds of his condemnation of the 'Three Chapters'.[36] The papacy had then to walk a very precarious diplomatic tightrope, given its own desire to win over the Arian Lombards to Catholicism and its simultaneous commitment to the condemnation of the 'Three Chapters'.

There were not just religious but also political complications about the increased interest shown in the Catholic hierarchy by the Lombard monarchy. For reasons both of doctrine and prestige, they wanted the archiepiscopal sees of Milan and Aquileia back under their control. When the see of Milan fell vacant in 600, Agilulf made strenuous efforts to persuade the handful of clergy still in Milan to elect their own archbishop. This bid failed. But in 606 the same ploy was tried with regard to the election of a new archbishop of Aquileia and resulted in the emergence of the two rival archbishops, one under Lombard protection and the other under imperial.

Strengthened by royal patronage, the Catholic hierarchy was able to hold its own against the Arian hierarchy established in the wake of the Lombard conquest. In fact important Lombard cities, such as Ticinum and Spoletium had two bishops, one Catholic and one Arian, recreating the situation that had existed under the Ostrogoths.[37] But the balance was tilting against the Arians. After the death of Abbot Secundus in 612, his place in the queen's confidence was taken by Abbot Columban of Bobbio whose arrival in Northern Italy from Gaul presaged an intellectual assault which left the Arians reeling. He successfully debated and disputed with them and spearheaded an internal missionary offensive. But at the same time he buttressed Queen Theodelinda in her support for the 'Three Chapters'. The 'Three Chapters' was increasingly seen to be the major obstacle standing between the full establishment of cordiality between Catholics inside and outside the Lombard kingdom. Columban indeed wrote to Pope Boniface IV urging him to with-draw the condemnation.[38] This was of course impossible, but Rome gave its backing to the work of converting the Arians and King Sisebut of Spain wrote to Theodelinda and Adaloald congratulating them on what they had managed to achieve in the field of conversion.[39]

Columban died at Bobbio in 615 and shortly afterwards King Agilulf died. He was succeeded as king by his son Adaloald (616–24) though the real power rested with the Queen Mother Theodelinda. Together they pressed on with advancing the Catholic cause. 'Under them', wrote Paul the deacon, 'many churches were restored and many gifts bestowed upon the holy places'.[40] The names of Theodelinda's advisers, Eusebius and Peter the son of Paul, how-ever, suggest along with the Catholic complexion, a creeping im-perial influence at court.[41] The feeling spread that the kingdom was being drawn into the orbit of the empire and when Adaloald became deranged, it was the signal for action. The Lombard aristocracy chose the King's Arian brother-in-law Arioald to be king and a period of civil war ensued, during which Pope Honorius I threw his support behind Adaloald. Certain Transpadane bishops had come out in support of the Arian usurper, perhaps because of fears that increased imperial influence on the royal regime presaged the end of the 'Three Chapters' in Lombardy. Honorius wrote to the exarch Isaac urging their arrest and transportation to Rome because of their disloyalty to Adaloald.[42]

Despite the stumbling block of the 'Three Chapters', it is obvious that the papacy set great store by the activities of Theodelinda and Adaloald, to the extent of punishing those bishops who failed to support the throne. There is similar evidence of cordiality between Rome and the Lombard authorities in the south. Pope Honorius wrote to Duke Arichis of Beneventum asking him to repatriate a runaway monk who had fled from the Roman *castrum* at Alatrium and taken refuge at Alifae inside the Lombard duchy, adding: 'We know from accounts given by many people that your glory has given justice in many different cases and particularly in those cases which appertain to the worship of God.'[43]

Already then there was evidence of the respect in which Rome was held by the Lombard powers. This respect survived the apparent catastrophe of the victory of Arioald and his assumption of the crown in 626, events accompanied by the deaths from poison of Adaloald and from natural causes of Theodelinda. Arioald showed

41

no desire to alienate the papacy and when for instance a jurisdictional dispute arose between the abbot of Bobbio and the bishop of Dertona, Arioald refused to judge it and instead referred it to Rome, paying the expenses of the abbot's journey there.[44] Theodelinda had died without seeing her plans fully realized but she had sown seeds that were very shortly to bear fruit.

Arioald was succeeded as king by Rothari (636–52) who played a major part in the consolidation of the Lombard kingdom. He promulgated the Lombard Law Code and inaugurated the first great advance since the invasion by overrunning Liguria to eliminate the imperial enclave around Genoa and advancing into the Istrian enclave by taking Opitergium. Although he was an Arian, he protected and tolerated the Catholic faith. This is reflected in the story that after his death and burial near the church of St John the Baptist, a thief robbed his tomb but St John appeared to the robber and rebuked him, saying: 'Why did you dare to touch the body of that man? Although he may not have been of the true faith, yet he has commended himself to me.'[45]

Rothari permitted ten Catholic bishops from Tuscia to attend the 649 Lateran Synod and four (Reate, Marsi, Asisium and Camerinum) went from the duchy of Spoletium. It was after all in the interests of the Lombards to encourage the papacy in its resistance to the empire. But it also reveals the continued or renewed existence of Catholic sees in Tuscia and Spoletium. There were in 649 bishops at Lucca, Luna, Pisa, Volaterra, Siena, Populonia, Rosellae, Tuscania, Tifernum Tiberinum and Clusium.[46] Some of these sees had maintained a continuous episcopal succession. But others had been revived as a result of the new favourable conditions. For instance, when the Lombards first invaded, the bishop of Populonia fled to Elba and died there.[47] But by 649 there was once again a bishop resident in that city. Siena, derelict between 570 and 640, and under the control of nearby Arretium, where a continuous episcopal succession was maintained, elected its own bishop, Maurus, in the early 640s, a clear indication of the rising tide of the Catholic revival.[48] But while there were encouraging signs for Rome in the kingdom and in the duchy of Spoletium, there was at least one black spot. In the duchy of Beneventum not a single Catholic see had survived, perhaps due to the large measure of paganism among the Lombard settlers of this part of Italy.

The revival of Catholic sees in Tuscia and Spoletium was symptomatic of the general Catholic advance, which reached its culmination after the death of Rothari. Rothari's son Rodoald was murdered after a five-month reign and in a political and religious revolution, Aripert, Catholic nephew of Queen Theodelinda, was elected king.

It was almost certainly during Aripert's reign (653–61) that the decisive step of decreeing Catholicism as the state religion was taken. It was a momentous occasion and one which was celebrated in the *Carmen de Synodo Ticinensi*, where Aripert was said to have 'abolished the heresy of the Arians and caused the Christian faith to flourish'.[49] The failing strength of Arianism is evidenced by the conversion to Catholicism of Anastasius, Arian bishop of the Lombard capital, Ticinum.[50]

There is evidence too that the change of official faith under Aripert heralded the arrival in the north of Catholic missionary clergy, some of them Greek, whose aim was now to confirm the Catholic preeminence and extinguish the still lingering adherence to the 'Three Chapters'. This missionary effort was probably signalled by the return to Milan after fifty years in Genoa of the metropolitan of northern Italy, an event which followed on from the fall of Genoa to the Lombards under Rothari. The presence of Archbishop John Bonus of Milan and the bishop of Dertona alone of all the north Italian bishops at the Lateran synod of 649 indicates that at that time there was still a widespread feeling of alienation from Rome in the north Italian hierarchy. But between 649 and 698 there was a major rethink of the position and this was probably in large measure attributable to the missionaries. There are recognizable traces of contemporary Greek and Oriental influence in seventh-century Milanese liturgical hymns and eucharistic prayers. More important, the missionary presence is attested by the appearance of a division of the clergy in the north called the *decumani*, who were still known several centuries later as *peregrini* – 'the foreigners'. *Decumani* clergy are known to have existed at Milan, Bergomum, Comum, Parma, Ticinum, Vercellae and Modicia.[51]

One of the most important missionary priests was Damian, who as a priest working under Archbishop Mansuetus of Milan helped to rally the northern church against Monotheletism and composed the official Milanese letter denouncing the heresy which was forwarded to the 6th General Council of the church in Constantinople in 681.[52] In recognition of his efforts he was ordained bishop of Ticinum by the pope. During his episcopate (c. 685–c. 715) Ticinum became an important centre for missionary clergy, among them the deacons Barionas and Thomas.[53] Damian then played a key role in the synod of Ticinum in 698 which finally extinguished the 'Three Chapters' schism and reunited the Catholic hierarchy of Italy.[54] It was perhaps in recognition of this that Pope Constantine restored the see of Ticinum to the jurisdiction of Milan.[55]

Kings Perctarit (672–88) and Cunincpert (688–700) consolidated the work begun by Aripert, encouraging and endowing the Catholic

43

church.[56] There was a brief Arian reaction c. 688–90 when Duke Alahis drove Cunincpert temporarily from the throne. Bishop Damian of Ticinum, trying to establish some kind of *rapport* with the usurper, was decisively snubbed and it was with relief that the Catholic priesthood welcomed the restoration of Cunincpert.[57] The ups and downs of the faith in Lombardy are effectively encapsulated in the story of one church, whose fortunes are recounted in a diploma of King Charles the Fat, dated 883, in which he confirms the right of the church of Bergomum to possession of the *Basilica Autareni*.[58] This edifice, as its name suggests, had been founded as an Arian church by King Autharis (584–90). It had been converted to Catholic use by Bishop John of Bergomum in the reign of King Grimoald (662–72). It was taken back by the Arian usurper Alahis but restored again to the Catholic bishop Antoninus by King Cunincpert between 690 and 700.

Despite the brief Arian reaction, the Catholic hierarchy went from strength to strength. By 680 ten bishops from the duchy of Spoletium were attending the Roman Synod.[59] The bishops of Tuscia Longobardorum were permitted upon election to go to Rome for ordination and there to take a special oath (*indiculum episcopi de Longobardie*)[60] in which they acknowledged Roman primacy, swore to maintain the unity and purity of the faith and, significantly, promised to work for peace between the empire and the Lombards. It is a measure of the extent to which the Lombard authorities respected the papacy. So too is the fact testified to by surviving eighth-century charters that boundary disputes between the Tuscian bishops were at the start of the century settled by representatives of the king but by 750 were being decided by representatives of the pope.[61]

There was even a Catholic revival in the duchy of Beneventum. The Catholic episcopate was revived in that city in 663, after the missionary priest Barbatus won the confidence of Duke Romuald by remaining in the city with him during a Byzantine siege. Permission was given to re-establish the long-derelict see and it provided a ready focus for the work of conversion and reconstruction.[62]

The climax of all this activity unquestionably came in 698 with the Synod of Ticinum, summoned by Cunincpert to set the seal on the extinction of the 'Three Chapters' schism. Legates from the synod took the joyful news to Pope Sergius I in Rome, who ordered the books of the Istrian schismatics to be ceremonially burned to prevent a revival of the heresy.[63] So by the end of the seventh century the twin purposes of the Roman church had been accomplished. The Lombards had been converted from Arianism to Catholicism, thanks to the patronage of devout Catholic monarchs like

Theodelinda, Aripert and Cunincpert; and the North Italians had been converted from the Istrian schism to the true faith, thanks to the arrival of the missionary clergy and the return of the metropolitan to Milan. The Catholic church now became part of the accepted establishment of Lombardy and Catholic Lombards were duly elected to bishoprics. In the first half of the eighth century, for instance, the wealthy Lombard landowner Talesperianus became bishop of Lucca and his brother Sichelm was archdeacon. One of the successors of Talesperianus was Walprand, son of Duke Walpert of Lucca. Increasingly Lombard names came to dominate the episcopal lists of Lombardic Italy: Teudald in Faesulae, Cunimund in Arretium, Gisulf in Clusium, Ausfred in Siena, etc.

Thereafter the Lombard kings accorded Rome particular respect. King Liutprand even confirmed by incorporating it into the Lombard Law Code the canon of the 721 Roman synod in which Gregory II, like so many of his predecessors, reaffirmed that Rome was 'the head of the church of God and the priests throughout the world'.[64] But while the religious problems had been resolved, there remained very real political dangers. The ambiguity of the situation is well expressed by the fact that in 723 Gregory II conceded the *pallium* of a metropolitan to Archbishop Serenus of Aquileia at the request of King Liutprand, but at the same time he wrote to Archbishop Donatus of Grado warning him of the danger from the wicked Lombards.[65] In 739 Liutprand ravaged the Roman church estates in Ravenna, and captured and held on to four frontier towns of the duchy of Rome. This prompted Pope Gregory III to write to the bishops of Tuscia Longobardorum urging them to intercede with the king for their return and reminding them of their oath of obedience to the papacy.[66]

In fact during the seventh and eighth centuries the four major powers on the Italian scene were engaged in a perpetual *danse macabre* with each other in which they generally adopted consistent positions. The Lombard kings, once they had become civilized and Catholic, accorded great respect to the pope as the patriarch of the Western church, but had no time for the emperor or the exarch whom they regarded as natural enemies. The pope, on the other hand, was devotedly loyal to the empire. At the same time he distrusted the Lombard king, referred to in the *Liber Pontificalis* as 'unspeakable', though being prepared to use him whenever possible in the interests of the church. The emperor accorded the pope respect as patriarch of the Western church while expecting him to obey imperial directives on doctrine, but he regarded the Lombard king as a natural enemy to be fought and disposed of. The exarch similarly regarded the Lombard king but also had his suspicions of the pope, whom he regarded as a potentially subversive force, in view of the extent to which the Italians were coming to look on him as 'a natural' leader. When it is all balanced out, it seems that the chief beneficiary of this *quadrille* was the papacy, its separate facets of *Christianitas* and *Romanitas* for once a strength rather than an embarrassment. By defending Catholic interests against the emperor and imperial interests against the Lombards, the papacy was in effect defending its own interests against all-comers.

Chapter 3

The Social and Economic Context

The social and economic context is perhaps the hardest to quantify because of the fragmentary nature of the evidence. Although social and economic statistics are virtually non-existent, it is possible to piece together an impressionistic view of the situation which lends credence to the famous lament of Gregory the Great. Shortly after his accession in 590 he penned a vivid picture of life in sixth-century Italy:[1]

> What happiness is there left in the world? Everywhere we see war. Everywhere we hear groans. Our cities are destroyed; our fortresses are overthrown; our fields laid waste; the land is become a desert. No inhabitants remain in the countryside, scarcely any in the towns. The small remnant of humanity surviving is daily and without cease borne down. Yet the scourge of divine justice has no end. . . . Some we have seen led into captivity, others mutilated, others killed. So what happiness is there left in the world? See to what straits Rome, once mistress of the world, is reduced. Worn down by her great and ceaseless sorrows, by the loss of her citizens, by the assault of the enemy, by the frequency of ruin – thus we see brought to pass the sentence long ago pronounced on the city of Samaria by the prophet Ezekiel.

This is no mere flight of rhetoric. It reflects fairly accurately the agony of a country racked for half a century by plague, famine and war. It seems clear that the period from the Byzantine Reconquest to the end of the seventh century was one of decline, depopulation and general stagnation. There had been destruction and dislocation caused by the four-year civil war between Odoacer and Theodoric at the end of the fifth century, particularly in Picenum and Aemilia. But the long and peaceful reign of Theodoric had allowed the damage to be made good. The occurrence of famine due to harvest failure or natural catastrophe in that reign had been met by prompt government action in the form of tax remission and emergency food supplies.[2]

But the twenty years of war accompanying the imperial conquest, the almost immediately ensuing Lombard invasions and the semi-permanent state of war which existed thereafter took a heavy toll on the life of Italy, both urban and rural. The destruction and social dislocation which occurred during the Gothic wars alone was immense. Rome was besieged three times, and in 546 actually captured by King Totila, who restrained his men from indiscriminate slaughter but permitted plundering and then evacuated the entire Roman population, leaving the eternal city for a while solely the domain of rats and grass. Each siege was accompanied by famine and disease and the suffering of the people was very great. Other great cities suffered similarly. At the outset of the war Naples fell after a twenty-day siege to the imperial forces and was given over to pillage and massacre.[3] Milan in 539 was taken by the Goths, its walls razed, its male population of some 300,000 slaughtered and its female population enslaved and handed over to the Burgundians.[4] In 545 the town of Tibur was taken and destroyed and its population put to the sword.[5]

The country areas were no better off. The provinces of Picenum, Aemilia and Tuscia were ravaged, plundered and fought over from end to end and in the ensuing famine some 50,000 people in Picenum alone died.[6] The population was reduced to eating acorns and in some cases to cannibalism. Two women near Ariminum, the sole survivors of their community, allegedly ate seventeen people and there were reports of women eating their children in Liguria.[7]

The wretched inhabitants of Italy suffered as much at the hands of their Byzantine 'liberators' as they did at the hands of the Goths. The Logothete Alexander, a man with a fearsome reputation for raising revenue for the state, was sent to Italy to squeeze out of the Italians all debts owed to the Gothic treasury. While imperial army commanders like Bessas, Constantine and John plundered and profiteered to enhance their own private fortunes. This all prompted King Totila with a fine sense of irony to write to the Senate in 544:

> Surely you must in these evil days sometimes remember the benefactions which you received not so very long ago at the hands of Theodoric and Amalasuntha. My dear Romans, compare the memories of these rulers with what you now know of the kindness of the Greeks towards their subjects. You received these men with open arms and how have they repaid you? With the griping exactions of Alexander the

Logothete and with the insolent oppressions of the petty
military tyrants who swagger in your streets.[8]

Devastated and depleted, Rome badly needed a breathing-space to
recover. But only thirteen years after the imperial provincial government had been established, the Lombards were at Italy's throat
and their impact was much more serious. For after the initial attack
they remained a continuing problem, making it impossible to settle
and cultivate the many frontier areas between their power centres
and the surviving imperial enclaves. Their initial advent was marked
by atrocities. Gregory the Great's *Dialogi* records the destruction of
groups as well as individuals: two monks in Valeria hanged, an abbot
at Sora killed, a deacon of the Marsian church beheaded but also four
hundred captives slaughtered in one massacre, forty peasants in
another and a group of Valerian monks in a third.[9] Large sections of
the population took to their heels desperately seeking the safety of
areas beyond the war zone. Sicily was the furthest and safest haven in
Italy and the Gregorian Register records the presence in Sicily of
refugees from places as diverse as Tauriana and Myria in Bruttium,
Canusium in Apulia, Formiae in Campania, Grumentum in Lucania,
Larinum in Samnium and Valeria province.[10] Gregory also records
that many men and women from different areas fled to the island of
Eumorphiana to escape the ferocity of the barbarians.[11] Discipline
and order, morale and supply amongst these refugees became prime
concerns of the pope.

Inevitably the areas from which they fled suffered. Gregory's
Register records the practical result of this as he authorizes the
unification of various border bishoprics because the reduction of
their populations or indeed the total dereliction of the sees renders
independent episcopal establishments superfluous.[12] One large tract
of Samnium around Saepinum and Bovianum, once a flourishing
agricultural area, remained deserted for nearly a hundred years after
the Lombard invasion until it was granted to a regiment of
Bulgarians for settlement by King Grimoald (662–71).[13] The grouping of whole areas under a single bishop, for instance Buxentum,
Velia and Blanda Julia under the bishop of Acropolis and of several
Apulian sees under the bishop of Sipontum, bespeaks considerable
abandonment of land and diminution of population. At least forty-
two previously attested sees perished during the troubles of the sixth
and seventh centuries, never to be revived. Most of them were in the
war zones of Picenum, Umbria, Apulia and Samnium.[14] There were
several new sees created, most of them inside imperial strongholds
(e.g. Acropolis, Castrum Valentini, Castrum Manturianum,
Balneum Regis) but by no means enough to compensate for the lost

49

sees, which must have witnessed both population decline and land abandonment.

As if this continual war damage were not enough, the period coincides almost exactly with the onset of the first plague pandemic. As far as can be computed from the scattered references, it subsisted from the 540s to the 760s. It seems to have originated in Ethiopia, whence, carried down the Nile, it struck in Egypt in 541.[15] It spread through the East like wildfire, carrying off some 300,000 of the population of Constantinople in 542–4, according to the chronicler Evagrius.[16] It even struck down the emperor Justinian who, with the singular good luck which attended his career, was one of the few recorded victims actually to recover.

It reached Italy in 543[17] and thereafter ravaged Italy and France in some ten successive waves, generally with a respite of several years in between. The cumulative effect of this pandemic must have been frightening. Specific figures of mortalities are rarely given. But it has been estimated that it 'probably caused as large a mortality in the empire as the Black Death of the 14th century did in the same countries'.[18] The toll of the Black Death has been put at approximately one-third of the population, and the Justinianic plague probably accounted for something like the same proportion.

It seems to have been the same disease as the Black Death, involving fever, hallucinations and a swelling in the groin or the armpit. It was carried by rats and reached the West in the holds of merchant ships. Its ravages were crippling. Gregory the Great records of one such outbreak that its effects were so serious in Rome that there were scarcely enough men to guard the walls and scarcely anyone, lay or cleric, who was strong enough to carry out his ordinary duties.[19] Paul the deacon, who lived at the end of the pandemic, paints a powerful picture of the onset of the plague in Liguria under Narses:[20]

There began to appear in the groins of men and in other rather delicate places, a swelling of the glands, after the manner of a nut or a date, presently followed by an unbearable fever, so that upon the third day the man died. But if any one should pass over the third day he had a hope of living. Everywhere there was grief and everywhere tears. For as common report had it that those who fled would avoid the plague, the dwellings were left deserted by their inhabitants, and the dogs only kept house. The flocks remained alone in the pastures with no shepherd at hand. You might see villas or fortified places lately filled with crowds of men, and on the next day, all had departed and everything was in utter silence. Sons fled, leaving the corpses of their parents unburied; parents forgetful of their duty abandoned their children in raging fever. If by chance long-standing affection constrained anyone to bury his near relative, he remained himself unburied, and while he was performing the funeral rites he perished; while he offered obsequies to the dead, his own corpse remained without obsequies. You might see the world brought back to its ancient silence: no voice in the field; no whistling of shepherds; no lying in wait of wild beasts among the cattle; no harm to domestic fowls. The crops, outliving the time of the harvest, awaited the reaper untouched; the vineyard with its fallen leaves and its shining grapes remained undisturbed while winter came on; a trumpet as of warriors resounded through the hours of the night and day; something like the murmur of an army was heard by many; there were no footsteps of passers by, no murderer was seen, yet the corpses of the dead were more than the eyes could discern; pastoral places had been turned into a sepulchre for men, and human habitations had become places of refuge for wild beasts.

With the ghastly spectre of plague added to those of war, famine and death, it must have seemed that the very four horsemen of the apocalypse had been unleashed on unhappy Italy. There can be little doubt that the ravages of the plague constitute one reason why the Lombards found conquest so easy. Paul the deacon discerned this: 'The Romans then had no courage to resist because the pestilence which occurred at the time of Narses had destroyed very many in Liguria and Venetia.'[21] The initial onset of the plague would have fastened on a population weakened by years of war and it would have in its turn led to famine and depopulation, precursors of the next round of plague. It seemed an unending cycle of decay.

Few historians have perhaps laid sufficient emphasis on the plague and the atmosphere of melancholy, introspection and imminent doom it engendered. Gregory the Great and Paul the deacon draw graphic pictures which indicate as much the psychological impact as the physical reality. It is small wonder that it was not a period of cultural creativity and it is hardly surprising that papal ideology was the last thing in the minds of contemporary churchmen, most of whom believed that the end of the world was at hand.

The 543 outbreak, beginning probably in Genoa and Massilia, chiefly affected southern France.[22] There was, however, a much more serious attack on Italy in the mid-560s during the governorship of Narses, when Ravenna, Istria, Liguria[23] and Rome were stricken.[24] Coming immediately after the end of the Gothic war and on the eve of the Lombard invasion, it was doubly serious. It returned in the early 570s,[25] accompanied this time by a serious famine which so affected Italy that, according to the *Liber Pontificalis*, many cities surrendered to the invading Lombards to avoid the rigours of want.[26]

The plague was back again in the 590s, this time in the aftermath of unprecedented floods, which swept Italy in the period 589–91. Paul the deacon writes,

> At this time there was a deluge of water in the territories of Liguria and Venetia and in other regions of Italy such as is not believed to have occurred since the time of Noah. Ruins were made of estates and country seats and at the same time a great destruction of men and animals. The paths were obliterated, the highways demolished and the River Athesis then rose so high around the church of the blessed martyr Zeno which is situated outside the walls of the city of Verona that the water reached the upper windows. Likewise the walls of the city of Verona itself were partly demolished by the same inundation. This inundation occurred on October 17, yet there were so many flashes of lightning and peals of thunder as are hardly wont to occur even in the summer time.[27]

To add insult to injury, much of Verona was burned down only two months later.

The flood also engulfed Rome, with the Tiber rising and inundating the city, destroying many ancient buildings and – more immediately serious – the church granaries containing thousands of measures of much-needed wheat. Contemporary eye-witness reports spoke of sea-beasts being stranded on the coast near Rome.[28] The inevitable corollary of this was a revival of the plague at Rome and at Portus, its most distinguished victim Pope Pelagius II who succumbed in the midst of these horrors on 7 February 590.[29] By September 591 the plague had reached Narnia[30] and by 592–3 it had arrived on the east coast, devastating Ravenna and Istria in an outbreak as severe as that under Narses.[31] On top of all this came an exceptional drought, gripping Italy for much of 591.[32]

There was barely a respite before the plague returned again, sweeping through Ravenna and the east coast in 598[33] and assaulting Rome in August 599.[34] Describing the debilitated condition of the inhabitants of the city, Gregory the Great reported that accounts of great mortality from the disease were reaching him from as far away as Africa and the East. In 604, apparently unconnected with the plague, but none the less unwelcome, there was a serious famine. The vines failed due to an unusually cold winter and the crops failed, partly destroyed by mice and partly by the blight.[35] But there was still no respite. The reign of Boniface IV (608–15) was marked by famine, flood and the return of the plague.[36] While under Pope Deusdedit (617–18) in the place of the plague, there was an outbreak of a scab disease which caused such swelling that it was impossible to identify the dead.[37]

After this battering the fates left Italy a breathing space, just long enough to recover from the previous assaults before it all started again. In the last year of Pope Adeodatus (672–6) there were such rainstorms and thunder as no men remembered before and many men and animals were killed by lightning.[38] The plague struck again in its wake,[39] returning in 680 to cause even greater havoc.

> So great was the multitude of those dying that even parents with their children and brothers with their sisters were placed on the same biers and conducted to their tombs in the city of Rome. And in like manner too this pestilence also depopulated Ticinum so that all citizens fled to the mountain ranges and to other places and grass and bushes grew in the market place and throughout the streets of the city.[40]

Not to be outdone, Vesuvius erupted in 684.[41] The last two recorded outbreaks of the pandemic were in southern Italy. Sicily and Calabria were devastated in 746–7[42] and Naples and southern Italy in 767.[43]

In the face of the considerable social and economic disasters engulfing Italy during these centuries, it was to the Roman church that the starving and oppressed Italians turned. In Rome itself, the papacy took over the social services. It was after all among the self-appointed duties of the church to use its resources to charitable ends. Pope Gelasius had victualled Rome from the church granaries during a famine[44] and Pope Vigilius sent back grain ships from Sicily to supply Rome during the Gothic wars.[45] Both these events merited contemporary mention because they were emergencies, but what happens from the mid-sixth century onwards is that the feeding of the people and the relief of need by the papacy became systematic and regularized.

After the end of the Gothic war, Pope Pelagius I sought to combat the famine and hardship with the produce and revenues of the papal estates[46] and by using his authority to appeal to outside sources, like the praetorian prefect Boethius of Africa, to whom he wrote in 560 complaining about the magnitude of the refugee problem and the devastation he was seeking to remedy.[47] By the time of Gregory the Great the church had organized its welfare and charitable works on proper administrative lines. A register was kept in the archives of everyone in receipt of church aid, the amounts paid out and the dates on which they were paid. On the first day of every month Gregory

distributed all the revenues in kind the church received to the poor –
grain, wine, cheese, vegetables, bacon, meat, fish and oil. He maintained a mobile meals service for the sick, sending out cooked food
from the papal palace by courier. He entertained refugees at his own
table.[48] This came to be so much expected that when on account of
the famine, his successor Pope Sabinian sold grain instead of giving it
away, he was publicly execrated.[49] But Gregory's charities extended
far beyond the city of Rome. The Register shows him authorizing
payment of subsidies to all sorts and conditions of people: decayed
gentlewomen in Campania, a refugee Samnite governor, a Neapolitan lawyer, the blind son of a *colonus*, a debt-ridden Syrian whose sons
had been sold into slavery, the children of a Jewish convert,[50] not to
mention 3,000 nuns, maintained in Rome on an annual subsidy of 80
pounds of gold.[51]

The other aspect of papal charity which was to result in a vast
extension of papal power was the payment of ransoms. As with food
supplies, the payment of ransoms was traditional. Pope Symmachus
is recorded as using church funds to ransom captives in Liguria.[52]
But with war becoming a permanent fact of life, the papacy was
called upon more and more frequently to buy off the enemy.
Gregory I found 500 pounds of gold to buy off the Lombard siege of
Rome.[53] Gregory II paid out 70 pounds of gold to recover the
captured city of Cumae for the empire and later unspecified but
extensive sums to regain Sutrium.[54] Gregory III bought off a Lombard attack on Castrum Gallensium for 'not a little money'.[55] Alongside these major transactions, there was the continuing payment of
ransoms for individuals, often raised by the sale of church plate.[56] It
was a natural step from the payment of ransom to the negotiation of
conditions, truces and and treaties and the gradual involvement of
the pope in diplomacy and power politics. Under these circumstances, it is small wonder that the people of Rome in particular, and
Italy in general, looking to the church as the agency of welfare and
charity and a bulwark against the barbarians, came to see its head, the
pope, as a natural leader, responsive to their needs in a way that the
imperial government was not.

Part II

The Papacy under the Ostrogoths

Chapter 4

The Acacian Schism

If we avoid imposing on papal history a prefabricated ideological pattern and concentrate on the immediate political and religious circumstances of the time, we get a more historically accurate insight into the course of papal development. During the centuries covered by this book, there are two distinct periods, during each of which the papacy's relationships with various secular powers are crucial and therefore deserving of close examination. The first period (476–554) is the period of the barbarian kings, chiefly Ostrogothic. The attitude of these kings to the papacy needs close scrutiny. So also does that of the senatorial aristocracy, which unlike the kings was largely Catholic and Rome-based. Many members of the aristocracy were as devout Christians as they were proud Romans. They endowed churches, bequeathed property and increasingly members of aristocratic families sought careers in the church. But it was not just for religious reasons that the aristocracy was interested in the affairs of the papacy. Rome's attitude towards the religious policies of the Eastern emperors played a vital role in determining the nature of the relationship between Italy and the East. Both those who envisaged a revival of Roman imperial authority in Italy and those who wanted to stabilize the barbarian regime on the basis of recognition by the East looked to the attitude of papal Rome as a crucial factor. It was an attitude that would be decided by belief and by personality, by circumstance and by political events.

The first papal election after 476 was obviously going to be crucially important for all the influential sections of Italian society. The crunch came in 483 when Pope Simplicius fell ill and was not expected to recover.[1] His death would be peculiarly significant for the Roman church, for several reasons. He had witnessed the final overthrow of the Western Roman Empire and the emergence in its place of a barbarian kingdom. His successor would be chosen in the first election since the papacy had been deprived of its traditional secular protector, the Western emperor. Also Simplicius had watched with growing alarm the revival of Monophysitism in the East and what he regarded as the feeble response of the imperial government in the face of this challenge. In consequence relations between Old Rome and New Rome had started to deteriorate in his last years, a fact which was seen to have profound religious and political implications.

Simplicius's successor would need to be equipped to deal with the delicate question of the relations of the Roman Catholic church with a king of Italy who was neither Roman nor Catholic and with the perhaps even more delicate question of relations between the Roman Catholic church of the West and the Christian Roman Empire of the East, whose emperor appeared to be tampering with the basic tenets of the faith. Both of these questions concerned the aristocracy just as much as the church. It is against this background that we need to view the events of March 483.

When it became clear that Simplicius's days were numbered, the praetorian prefect, Caecina Decius Maximus Basilius, summoned a meeting at the Imperial Mausoleum.[2] It was attended by members of the senate, the Roman clergy and leading local bishops – in effect the Catholic Roman establishment. The pope was not present and moreover he died during the course of these deliberations. He was buried in St Peter's on 10 March 483.

The meeting was presided over by Basilius and its subject was an *admonitio* issued by Simplicius to him saying that no election to the papacy was to be made without consulting Basilius. In effect it gave him a right of veto on the election of the next pope. Why was the pope making the enormous concession of granting the right of veto to a layman? The answer is to look at the layman in question. Basilius was both the leader of the aristocracy and the chief minister of King Odoacer. Any candidate approved by him would be likely to receive a smooth passage in both these quarters. It seems likely, too, that Simplicius sought to avoid the possibility of a disputed election after his death. In any such dispute, the aristocracy's role would be decisive. There had been several disputed elections in papal history, the last as recently as 418. Simplicius will have wanted to avoid a schism at a time when Roman Catholic Italy needed to present a united front in the face of an alien and Arian king. All this points to the involvement of Basilius as leader of the aristocracy. The pope will also have wanted to avoid the possibility of the intrusion of some royal favourite or foreigner onto the throne of St Peter, hence the involvement of Basilius in his role as the king's chief minister. It is also likely that Simplicius wanted to ensure that he was succeeded by a man with the ability to handle the looming political and religious problems. The election therefore was much too important to be left to the clergy alone, who might take it into their heads to elect some unworldly saint.

The idea that there was in 483 a conflict between Senate and clergy over the choice of the pope is not supported by the evidence. Admittedly, in the debate on the events of 483 held at the Symmachan victory synod of 502, it was implied that Basilius's actions constituted a violation of the tradition whereby the clergy played a major role in papal elections by transferring this majority to the laity and in particular the aristocracy. But this simply reflected the events of 499–502 when the senate and the clergy were engaged in strife over an election rather than the events of 483 when there is every appearance of concord with senate, clergy and bishops arranging between them the election of the new pope.

The assembly at the Mausoleum also promulgated an ecclesiastical law. This law forbade the alienation of ecclesiastical property by the popes on pain of anathema. What interpretation are we to place on this? The sinister theory is that it was a move to restrict the papacy to the independently wealthy who could gain election by the use of their private fortunes, eliminating from the race the less well-off, previously tempted to promise away papal property in order to secure votes; also that it was a move to prevent the popes utilizing the wealth of the church to further their own schemes, by eliminating their economic viability. But far more plausible – and supported by analogous laws issued in later reigns – is that it was aimed at cleaning up papal elections. At election time, intrigue and bribery were rife and the papal patrimony suffered from the repayment of debts incurred by the pope while campaigning for election. This law prevented him from promising away papal estates and thereby impoverishing the church.

This concern for the proper conduct of the election confirms the evidence of accord between aristocracy and clergy during the 483 election. The deliberations over a successor appear to have been completed by the time Simplicius died, for, three days after the funeral of his predecessor, the new Pope Felix III was consecrated. Felix seems to have been a man who satisfied the criteria of both parties to the election. He is the first known aristocrat to have been elected to the papacy, coming from a wealthy and propertied family of the middle aristocratic rank,[3] and has been described as 'the first pope conversant with the thought processes of the upper class'.[4] Socially and intellectually, then, he appealed to the aristocracy, but his religious credentials were also impeccable. He was a deacon, one of the senior administrators of the Roman church, and had been since at least 472 and probably earlier. His father had been a priest, his sister a nun and another relative, probably a younger brother, was also a priest.

As it transpired, relations between Rome and Odoacer proved to be no problem. Odoacer admired the Roman way, maintained the old imperial traditions and scrupulously avoided tangling with the church. The *Liber Pontificalis* makes no derogatory reference to Odoacer[5] and Felix III observed in a letter to Patriarch Acacius of Constantinople that he was secure in Italy and not oppressed by any violence.[6] But this did not lessen the dislike or distrust of Odoacer that clearly existed in papal Rome. After Odoacer's death Pope Gelasius referred to him as 'the barbarian heretic Odoacer then holding the kingdom of Italy',[7] indicating that constitutionally speaking the pope did not recognize him as king, though Felix probably refrained from telling Odoacer this when he was alive and capable of doing something about it.

On the other hand, relations between Rome and Constantinople got markedly worse. Pope Felix III was faced on his accession with the arrival in Rome of the fugitive Alexandrian patriarch John Talaia, telling horror stories about Monophysite persecutions of the orthodox Christians in Egypt. In addition there were the full implications of Zeno's *Henotikon*, promulgated in 482 and clearly seen as an imperial attempt to alter the faith without recourse to church council. The failure of either Patriarch Acacius or Emperor Zeno to answer Pope Simplicius's anxious letters, and the seriousness of the situation outlined by John Talaia, called for immediate action. But Felix had no desire to cause a breach with the East and he wrote a cordial letter to Zeno announcing his accession and affirming his loyalty to the empire.[8] But there was an urgent need to penetrate the silence from the East and the pope appointed a special embassy to go to Constantinople, carrying letters to the emperor, urging him to remain faithful to Chalcedon, and to Acacius, urging him not to split the church and to respect the Chalcedonian settlement.[9] In a typical piece of Primatial bravado they also carried copies to the patriarch and emperor of an official summons for Acacius to appear before a synod in Rome to answer the charges of John Talaia.

The embassy consisted of Bishop Vitalis of Truentum and Bishop Misenus of Cumae. They were to have been accompanied by the *defensor* Felix but he was delayed in Rome by illness. On their arrival at Abydos, the bishops were immediately arrested and cajoled by promises of gifts and threats of force into taking communion with Acacius and the legates of the Monophysite Alexandrian patriarch Peter Mongus, thus in effect cancelling out the purpose of their mission.

The *Akoimetae*, the 'Sleepless Monks of Constantinople', the

ultra-orthodox hard-liners who – in the absence of a permanent
papal representative in the imperial capital – kept the pope in touch
with developments in the East straightaway communicated the
news of the envoys' treachery to Rome.[10] On their return, the
envoys were put on trial before a synod of bishops held on 28 July
484, and were excommunicated and deposed for their crime.

The synod also excommunicated Acacius,[11] and Felix wrote
angrily to the Emperor Zeno on 1 August 484, informing him of the
excommunication and saying that he must choose between the
apostle Peter and Peter Mongus.[12] The letters were despatched via
the *defensor* Tutus to Constantinople. He handed over the sentence of
excommunication to the 'Sleepless Monks', one of whom pinned it
to Acacius's back while he was celebrating mass in Santa Sophia.
Acacius responded by excommunicating the pope and to make
matters worse he corrupted Tutus in the same way as he had the
bishops. On information again supplied by the 'Sleepless Monks'
Tutus was disgraced, deposed and excommunicated by a synod held
in October 485 after his return to Rome.[13]

What is clear from the evidence is that the Misenus–Vitalis case
was a *cause célèbre*. It dominates the account of Pope Felix's life in the
Liber Pontificalis.[14] It was this then rather than the theological issues,
which could probably have gone on being debated by Rome and
Constantinople, which precipitated the Acacian schism. Felix was
particularly scandalized because, as he had stressed in his letter to the
emperor, the bishops were not just bearers of letters but in a very real
sense the deputies of the Roman see.[15] The corruption of these
deputies provoked an immediate crisis between *Christianitas* and
Romanitas, in which the papacy stood on the former.

The Acacian schism was to last for thirty-four years. But except in
the later years of Pope Symmachus, embittered by a deep personal
antagonism existing between pope and emperor, a lively correspondence was maintained in order to resolve it. Equally clearly it
was just as much the personalities as the issues which determined the
course and the circumstances of the schism.

There could be no accommodation with Acacius, the man who
had sought to humiliate the papacy. But when he died in 489 and
Fravitta was appointed to succeed him, Felix III seized the opportunity to make a peace initiative. Fravitta sent a synodical letter to the
pope announcing his election and indicating his orthodoxy and
Felix III wrote fulsome letters of praise both to Fravitta[16] and to
Zeno,[17] extolling their Christian virtues and declaring: 'All the difficulties which previously had arisen, I believed to have been
removed by this appointment.' He added that it needed only the
condemnation of the names and memories of Peter Mongus of

Alexandria and Acacius of Constantinople to make reunion between the two sees complete, saying:

> These things, most reverent Emperor, I do not wrest from you as vicar of the blessed Peter, by the authority of the apostolic power as it were, but I confidently implore you as an anxious father desiring that the welfare and prosperity of my most clement son endure long.

But these conditions were not acceptable to the emperor and so although he was dead, Acacius's memory remained a stumbling block to the re-establishment of religious unity. Felix ordered the orthodox monks of Constantinople[18] not to communicate with the church or bishop of Constantinople until they received orders to do so from Rome and stressed in letters to prominent orthodox bishops that the solution to the schism must lie in the official condemnation of the memories of Peter Mongus and Acacius.[19] No headway at all had been made by the time Zeno died in 491. The new emperor was the elderly civil servant Anastasius I, who at 61 was one year older than the man he was replacing. He was chosen, married and elevated to the throne by Zeno's widow Ariadne and remained committed to Zeno's religious policy. Although Felix wrote to Anastasius[20] rejoicing in his election to the throne and hoping thus to get off to a good start with the new ruler, he found Anastasius no more flexible than Zeno had been. There was still an impasse between Rome and Constantinople when Felix himself died in February 492.

There was an obvious successor to Felix in his 'secretary of state' and the actual author of his correspondence with the East, Gelasius, who was certainly a deacon and probably archdeacon. Not only had he written the correspondence but also he and not the pope had briefed Senator Andromachus who had been sent in 489 to Constantinople to discuss the religious situation.[21] Although by birth an African, Gelasius had spent his formative years in Rome and shared his predecessor's commitment to the Roman Empire. As he wrote to the emperor Anastasius, 'As one who is Roman born, I love, revere and respect the Roman Emperor.'[22] He was duly elected to succeed Felix III and ordained on 1 March 492, a few days after the old pope's death.

There is no record of aristocratic involvement in or aristocratic opposition to his election, a further indication that the events of 483 had not been part of a concerted bid to subject the papacy to aristocratic control. The aristocracy were of course likely to be distracted by the still unresolved war between Odoacer and the invading Ostrogoths under Theodoric. There was subsequently friction between Gelasius and members of the senate. The pope's condemnation of the pagan festival of Lupercalia, favoured by a senatorial party headed by the senator Andromachus, so recently the papal emissary in the East, led to retaliatory attacks on Gelasius by senators who accused him of neglecting his disciplinary duties over his own clergy.[23] But at the time of the election Gelasius's credentials both as his predecessor's principal adviser in the matter of the Acacian schism and as a senior administrator with the experience to carry the church through the period of readjustment to Ostrogothic rule carried the day.

Gelasius I is one of the most celebrated of early medieval popes, but his importance lies not in his so-called ideological innovations, which are in the main merely the manifestations of spleen, but in his administrative reforms, his campaigns against heresy, his many theological writings, his establishment of a *modus vivendi* with the Ostrogoths. There was no area of papal activity in which Gelasius did not busy himself and in this he resembles no one so much as Gregory I. Both were personally austere, learned and munificent; both delighted in the company of their disciples; both spent their private fortunes on the poor; both detested and waged unrelenting war on heresy and above all, both were fiercely conservative.

A description of the life and character of Gelasius has survived in the letter of Dionysius Exiguus to Gelasius's disciple, the priest Julian:[24]

How great the merit of Pope Gelasius is before God we who have not seen him in bodily form easily perceive through you, his disciples, who were formed by his instruction and adorn the priesthood with your holy life, so that his works appear in a way to shine in your manifest good conduct. . . . He enjoyed especially communion and association with the servants of God and fired by their spiritual conversation he rejoiced in the pursuit of divine love and in meditation on the word of God. . . . He passed through the evil days of this world under the Lord's kindly guidance and bore all the dangers of life with wonderful prudence and patience; he preferred fasting to indulgence and trod pride underfoot by humility; he shone with such mercy and generosity as to endow almost all the poor and die poor himself. He was indeed blessed in this poverty, through which he persevered in the divine praises. His spirit was full of light, his life exemplary, his authority revered. Adorned with so many eminent virtues, he advanced not unworthily to his high office. Looking upon this position of highest dignity as a very grave charge, he maintained that a little neglect on the part of the pontiff is a serious danger for souls. Accordingly he gave himself up to no vain idling and wasteful banquets that bring maladies of soul and body. This pastor was an imitator of the great good shepherd, an outstanding bishop of the apostolic see, who lived the divine precepts and taught them.

Line for line, this might also be a description of Gregory I.

Judging by his letters, Gelasius was an altogether sterner and much less compromising figure than Felix III. His high sense of mission, his first-hand experience of Greek trickery and treachery and his natural frustration that a schism which had already imperilled the faith for six years showed no sign of resolution combined to ensure that there would be no alteration in the papal position and that it would be outlined in letters to the East with increasing impatience.

The continuation of the religious schism throughout Gelasius's reign had serious political implications. The legitimization of the position of Odoacer was not secured from the Eastern emperor and the embittering of relations between East and West as a result of the Acacian schism did nothing to further the cause of recognition. That the resolution of the Acacian schism and the legitimization of barbarian rule were closely linked is demonstrated by the fact that successive senatorial embassies were charged with discussing both topics together. The pope, having taken the hint about the danger to clerical embassies after the events of 483–4, did not send another ecclesiastical mission until 497. When Faustus undertook the joint mission in 493, Pope Gelasius warned him sourly of the tendency of the Greeks to try to corrupt embassies from the West.[25]

When Odoacer had first overthrown Romulus Augustulus, he had sent an embassy to Zeno, returning the imperial insignia as a token that he would not be appointing a Western emperor and asking that he be appointed *patricius* and entrusted with the government of Italy. His object was to occupy the same viceregal position as Ricimer, the difference being that his superior would now be not the Western emperor in Ravenna but the Eastern emperor in Constantinople. Zeno, however, rejected the proposal and suggested instead that he restore to the Western throne the ex-emperor Julius Nepos, then living in Dalmatia. Odoacer did not do that and, in the absence of formal recognition, simply called himself 'king'.[26]

But the question of legitimization continued to worry both Odoacer and the Romans. That he was regarded as not having obtained Eastern recognition is indicated by the slighting reference to him after his death by Pope Gelasius, who refers to him not as 'king' but as 'the barbarian heretic Odoacer then holding the kingdom of Italy'. So when in 489 the *Magister Officiorum* Andromachus was sent to Constantinople to negotiate about the Acacian schism, he was also entrusted with reopening the legitimization question. Zeno gave Odoacer an answer he did not expect. The capture of Dalmatia by Odoacer in 481 had brought him dangerously close to the European provinces of the Eastern empire and what was more he was also suspected of negotiating with the rebel Illus, who had sought to topple Zeno from his throne. Zeno, his hands full with both religious and political problems, saw an ideal way of killing two birds with one stone. The able and warlike young chieftain Theodoric and his Ostrogoths were menacing the Balkans. Zeno, in order to get rid of him, gave Theodoric the title and status Odoacer had requested – *patricius* – and despatched him to Italy to dispose of the troublesome Herulian.[27]

The Ostrogoths swept into Italy like a tidal wave, engulfing Odoacer's fledgling kingdom. Theodoric defeated him in several pitched battles and then bottled him up in Ravenna for three years. Odoacer finally surrendered after negotiating an agreement under which sovereignty was to be shared between them and Theodoric personally stabbed him to death at the official reconciliation banquet in 493.

The bulk of the Roman aristocracy had come over to Theodoric, who after all had the blessing of the Roman empire, as soon as it was clear that Odoacer could not win. But the same problem of legitimization arose. In 490, having broken the back of Odoacer's resistance, Theodoric sent an envoy to Zeno in the person of Rufius Postumius Festus, the senior member of the senate.[28] He was no longer content to be just *patricius* and wanted to be king as Odoacer had been. But Zeno would not accept this. Theodoric however was not to be denied and in 493 with Odoacer dead, he sent another embassy, headed this time by the new *Magister Officiorum*, Flavius Anicius Probus Faustus. Faustus was also entrusted by Gelasius with conducting negotiations about the Acacian schism. But the letter written by Gelasius to brief Faustus on what to expect from and how to react to the Greeks shows that the pope was in no mind to accept a compromise.[29] He warns Faustus about the sly tricks and obstinate heresy of the Greeks, refuting their likely arguments one by one and reacting angrily to suggestions that he and his predecessors had condemned the emperor. It is a bitter, sarcastic letter full of righteous indignation, dismissing the arguments of the patriarch of Constantinople as 'extremely impudent' and saying 'That one made me laugh' and 'They have dared to mention the canons to us when they have shown themselves constantly in breach of them in pursuit of their illicit ambitions'. It is no wonder then that when Anastasius proposed a compromise settlement, Gelasius rejected it and wrote his famous '*potestas* and *auctoritas* letter' in reply.[30] The details of this compromise are not recorded but it was probably the same compromise solution which Anastasius suggested in 497 and which decisively demonstrates that in the mind of the emperor and the aristocracy the schism and the legitimization issues were closely linked. With the failure of Faustus's mission, Theodoric simply assumed the title of 'king'.[31] But in 497, after the death of Gelasius, Theodoric sent a new mission to the East, again headed by Festus and this time a deal was struck *de praesumptione regni* – concerning the unauthorized assumption of the kingship.[32] The imperial insignia forwarded to the East by Odoacer were returned to Italy and Theodoric's assumption of the kingship was recognized. He ruled Italy as king by right henceforth, acknowledging the vague suzerainty of the Eastern empire. But the *quid pro quo* for the recognition of Theodoric demanded by Anastasius was the recognition by the pope of the validity of the *Henotikon* and that was to loose a hornet's nest.

Pope Gelasius's stubborn refusal to compromise and his unwillingness to shift Rome's stand on the Acacian schism led the Eastern bishops to write to him saying that his obstinacy threatened the standing of the entire church. Gelasius's reaction was 'a more in sorrow than in anger' complaint against the charge in which he compared himself to a doctor healing the sick.[33]

Not everyone shared the pope's rigidity and elsewhere in the Roman church there was a decisive softening of attitude towards the East. Several times the Eastern bishops had appealed to the pope for the reinstatement of the deposed episcopal envoys. Bishop Vitalis had died, but in a full dress Roman synod, held on 13 March 495, Bishop Misenus of Cumae was restored to office and held his see until his death in 511.[34] Significantly the synod was attended by only fifty-eight of the seventy-six Roman priests. At a time when 100 per cent attendance was usual, this suggests a hard core of eighteen unwilling to see the errant bishop forgiven. Considering the scandal which the case had caused it is hardly surprising that there should have been a hard-line core in the priesthood. What is perhaps surprising is that it should have been so small. It is a dramatic indication that clerical opinion was changing. The hard line towards Constantinople, hardening steadily since the death of Felix III, had produced nothing but acrimony between pope and emperor. The schism had now been running for more than ten years and there was no indication of any move likely to restore the unity of the Roman Catholic world. Yet no one wanted the schism really. The policies and priorities of Zeno and Anastasius, however, conflicted with the principles and temperament of Gelasius and made its resolution seem further away than ever. For many, especially in the aristocracy, the conflict of *Romanitas* and *Christianitas* had gone on far too long. It was time for a change.

The opportunity arose when Gelasius died in November 496 and, in an even more dramatic indication of the shift in opinion, the deacon Anastasius, who had played a leading part in the synod restoring Misenus, was elected Pope Anastasius II. He made his intentions clear at once by writing a humble letter to the emperor,[35] announcing his election, and declaring the restoration of peace as his aim: 'We do not want the controversy in the churches to continue any longer'. He ended with the prayer: 'May Almighty God place your kingdom and your person under his perpetual protection, most glorious and most clement emperor.' His sole condition was the condemnation of Acacius's memory. Apart from that he urged the emperor to use his influence to persuade the Alexandrians to return to Catholicism. But he gave an assurance that all the sacraments conferred by Acacius and his clergy would be recognized as valid by Rome. To be fair to Anastasius, he was not proposing a sell-out. He maintained the demand for the condemnation of Acacius, though he added that he did not think censures of the dead should be entered into rashly, implying that everything was negotiable. The recognition of sacraments was in line with Augustinian teaching and had already been accepted by Gelasius. But demand for the condemnation of Peter Mongus had been dropped, and above all there was here a clear desire for peace, a willingness to talk and a spirit of moderation, all of which had been absent from the pontificate of Gelasius. This demonstrates that Anastasius's intention was to reverse the hard line of his predecessor and this must have had some bearing on his election.

After the letter, the next stage was an embassy and once again political and religious issues were linked. In 497 Theodoric sent Festus to discuss recognition of his kingship and Anastasius II sent Bishops Cresconius of Tuder and Germanus probably of Pisaurum to discuss the schism. That the two missions were linked is evidenced by the letter the Alexandrian legates sent to 'the most glorious and excellent patrician Festus and the venerable Bishops Cresconius and Germanus sent as a legation from Rome with joint power',[36] and by the fact that Festus persuaded the Constantinople church to celebrate the festival of SS Peter and Paul.[37] Emperor Anastasius revived his compromise proposal – recognition of Theodoric in return for acceptance of the *Henotikon* by the pope. It was almost certainly rejected by the bishops since it went far beyond what the pope had in mind. But Festus proved more amenable, agreeing to persuade the pope to accept this compromise. On the basis of this, the emperor recognized Theodoric as king. It is clear that Festus was acting on his own initiative. But he must have had reason to believe that he could do what he promised. This confirms the suggestion that Pope Anastasius had been backed by a pro-Eastern faction, at least among the aristocracy, since it was this same faction, headed by Festus, which was to oppose Anastasius II's hard-line successor, Pope Symmachus.

The Bishop of Thessalonica, a church which Gelasius had fervently denounced for communicating with Acacius, was so struck by the new evidence of reasonableness on the part of the pope that he ordered the Gelasian letter against Acacius to be read publicly in the churches and sent his deacon Photinus to renew his communion with the Roman church. The pope admitted Photinus to communion, an act that was to set in train the ugly events which disfigured the next nine years of papal history.

The hostile *Vita Anastasii* in the *Liber Pontificalis*[38] described what happened next:

> At that time many clerics and priests withdrew from communion with him, because without consulting the priests or bishops or clergy of the whole catholic church, he had shared communion with a deacon of Thessalonica called Photinus, who was in communion with Acacius, and because he wished secretly to restore Acacius and could not. Then he was struck dead by divine will.

It is clear from this grimly vindictive notice that the hard-line faction saw the communion with Photinus as the last straw after the absolution of Misenus, the election of a soft-line pope and a conciliatory mission to the East. It is not true that Anastasius II wished to absolve Acacius from blame, but to his opponents it must have seemed the logical culmination of his actions. A section of the clergy withdrew from communion with the pope and at the height of the crisis in November 498 he died, an event attributed by his enemies with evident satisfaction to the wrath of God.

The death of Pope Anastasius provided the flashpoint for a major crisis within the Roman church. Both clergy and senate were deeply involved since the policy of *détente* inaugurated by Anastasius now hung in the balance and the very authority of the pope was under threat from a sizeable group of clerical rebels. At this absolutely crucial juncture there was going to have to be an election.

Chapter 5

The Symmachan Schism
(i) the events

Just four days after the death of Pope Anastasius, on 22 November 498, there was a divided election for the papal throne. One faction amongst clergy and senate gathered at the Lateran basilica and elected the deacon Symmachus. Another faction among clergy and senate gathered at the basilica of Santa Maria and elected the Archpriest Laurentius.[1] Fortunately a wealth of original material survives enabling us to reconstruct the events of the schism. There are versions of what occurred written by both sides: the 'official' biography of the pope, the *Vita Symmachi*, in the *Liber Pontificalis* and an unofficial biography by the opposition, the so-called 'Laurentian Fragment'. There are accounts of the three Roman synods: the reconciliation synod of 499, the trial synod of 502 and the victory synod of 502. There are the letters of Ennodius of Ticinum, one of the most active of Symmachus's supporters, and there are the various addresses and injunctions issued by King Theodoric.

It is necessary first to establish what happened before examining the standpoints and support of the protagonists. With both clergy and senate split, violent clashes breaking out between rival groups of supporters[2] and neither candidate prepared to back down, some form of arbitration was required. The *Vita Symmachi* says that the two parties agreed to take their case to King Theodoric at Ravenna;[3] the 'Laurentian Fragment' says that the parties were forced to accept the judgment of the king.[4] Either way it is a remarkable state of affairs when an Arian king has for whatever reason to choose a Catholic pope.

However, once the facts were made known to him, the king made his judgment 'that he who had been ordained first or was supported by the largest party should occupy the apostolic see'.[5] It was Symmachus who fulfilled these criteria and he was therefore duly consecrated pope. The 'Laurentian Fragment' claims that he obtained the verdict by paying large bribes.[6] Certainly money changed hands, though probably to influence important figures at court rather than the king himself. The Milanese deacon Ennodius, a prominent Symmachan, talks later in the schism of 400 *solidi* being distributed among grand personages whom it would be indiscreet to name.[7] The Laurentians also had access to money and apparently made full use of it. This fact was known as far away as the Eastern empire, where Theodore the Lector could write of the events of 498: 'And having corrupted many men with money [Festus] called upon a certain Roman whose name was Laurentius to be elected bishop contrary to custom.'[8] In view of the large number of aristocrats supporting Laurentius, it is likely that the Laurentians had even greater financial resources than the Symmachans.

For the time being, however, Symmachus was secure. He had the backing of the king and he proceeded to call a synod in Rome, which was attended by seventy-two bishops and all the Roman clergy, priests and deacons. It was held at the basilica of St Peter on 1 March 499, and its aim, as stated by Symmachus in his opening address, was to clear up the confused situation which had existed and to ensure that in future there would be no popular tumult or illegal canvassing at election time. A statute to this effect was read out, acclaimed by all those present and then signed by the pope and assembled church-men. Among those who signed was the Archpriest Laurentius, who shortly afterwards was appointed Bishop of Nuceria by the pope as a consolation prize for the loss of the holy see.[9]

The synod of 499 seemed to settle the matter of the election once and for all. Symmachus had been recognized as pope both by the Italian bishops and the Roman clergy and his opponent Laurentius had retired to his new bishopric. In 500 King Theodoric paid a state visit to Rome setting the seal on the reconciliation. The *Anonymus Valesianus* described his visit:[10]

> Pope Symmachus and the entire Senate and people of Rome
> met him amid general rejoicing outside the city. Then entering
> the city, he visited the Senate and he addressed the people at
> the Palma, promising that with God's help he would keep
> inviolate whatever the former Roman emperors had decreed.
> In celebration of his tenth anniversary, he entered the Palace in
> a triumphal procession for the entertainment of the people and he
> staged games in the Circus for the Romans.

Theodoric's pledge was inscribed on a bronze tablet and set up for all to see.

But for the opponents of Symmachus it marked only the end of the first round in the battle. Once again Festus took the lead. Together with a group of clerics and senators, presumably the activists of the Laurentian party, he laid charges against Pope Symmachus in a bid to secure his deposition. The initial charge was that in 501 he had celebrated Easter on the wrong date. The significance of this is that he had calculated the date according to the old Roman calendar, making Easter 25 March. His opponents reckoned that he should have calculated Easter according to the Greek calendar, making Easter 22 April. The accusation was laid before the king, who summoned the pope to Ariminum to answer the charge. Symmachus arrived at Ariminum with a high-powered group of deacons, priests and clergy, but discovered that other charges were to be brought against him, including unchastity and the misuse of church property. Symmachus took fright, fled from Ariminum with only one companion in the middle of the night and returning to Rome, locked himself up in St Peter's.[11]

The pope's flight proved to be a major miscalculation. It was widely regarded as an admission of guilt. It was probably at this point that Laurentius was reintroduced into Rome by his supporters and rallied his old faction. A sizeable section of the clergy, including many of the most senior clerics, withdrew from communion with Symmachus and communicated with Laurentius. The Laurentians seized the initiative. They called on the king to send a visitor to Rome to celebrate Easter on the correct (i.e. Greek) date and to summon a synod to examine the charges against Symmachus. The king agreed to both these requests. He appointed the Istrian Bishop, Peter of Altinum, as visitor and Peter came to Rome in time to celebrate Easter in 502.[12] He also took over the administration of the Roman see pending a decision about Symmachus. Immediately after Easter a synod of bishops from all over Italy was held to judge the pope. The bishops of northern Italy, from Liguria, Aemilia and Venetia, expressed concern that they were being summoned without papal consent and that there was no precedent for the trial of a pope by his inferiors. But the king reassured them by producing a letter from Symmachus giving his consent for the holding of a synod.[13]

The *Vita Symmachi* dismisses the trial synod in two sentences.[14]

Then the blessed Symmachus gathered together 115 bishops and a synod having been held, he was acquitted of the false accusation, and Peter of Altinum the intruder in the apostolic see and Laurentius of Nuceria were condemned because they had taken over the see while Bishop Symmachus still lived. Then the blessed Symmachus was reinstated by all the bishops and priests and deacons and the whole clergy and people with glory to sit as bishop of the holy see in the place of the blessed Peter.

But there was of course rather more to it than this.

The synod, held in the basilica of Santa Maria, was presided over by the three other Italian metropolitans, Peter of Ravenna, Laurentius of Milan and Marcellianus of Aquileia.[15] The pope duly appeared and declared that he was glad that they had gathered together to clear up the matter. But he refused to give evidence until the visitor had been removed and the administration of the Roman see restored to him. For the appointment of a visitor implied a vacancy in the see and the see could only be vacant if Symmachus was guilty, which meant that the case had been judged before the evidence had been heard. The majority of the assembled bishops thought this was fair but declared that they could not act in the matter of the visitor without the consent of the king. The king refused to withdraw the visitor until the charges had been answered, and so there was deadlock.[16]

Several bishops, terrified by the increasing mob violence, left Rome and the rest appealed to the king to withdraw the meeting of the synod to the palace in Ravenna. The king wrote to the synod on 8 August 502, saying that it was not appropriate to summon them to Ravenna and besides he was too busy with other matters.[17] They must meet again on 1 September and decide the case. If it was still not settled then, he would come to Rome himself and take a hand. He reinforced his arguments with another letter, dated 27 August, requiring the bishops to meet and end the uncertainty about the pope as soon as possible.[18] He told them also that he was sending the royal stewards to escort Symmachus across the city to attend the synod.

So, on 1 September, the synod reconvened in the *Basilica Sessoriana*. The accusers of the pope presented a *libellus* which contained at least two points deemed unacceptable by the majority of the assembly. The first was that the king already knew that Symmachus was guilty and therefore the synod should assume guilt, hear the evidence and then pass sentence. The second was to have slaves give evidence against Symmachus, something which was contrary both to canon and civil law. What was worse, as the pope set out from St Peter's, surrounded by his supporters, to cross the city, he was attacked by a Laurentian mob, many of his supporters were injured and several killed, including the priests Gordian and Dignissimus. The pope therefore retreated to St Peter's and refused to come out. The synod sent a deputation of bishops to urge him to appear but Symmachus said that he and his followers had suffered enough. He would not appear again and would leave it to God and the king to decide his case.

Symmachus's words to the synodical deputation have survived:[19]

At the beginning without any hesitation I hastened to your meeting when you came to Rome and placed my privileges at the will of the King, recognized the authority of the synod and in accordance with ecclesiastical rules demanded the return of the churches. But you did nothing for me. Then when I was coming with my clergy I suffered cruel ill-treatment. I therefore submit myself no further to your examination and it is in the power of God and my lord the King to decide what should be done with me.

Upon receipt of this reply, certain of the bishops urged the synod to return to their obedience to the pope. But they were not in a majority.[20] So the synod again petitioned the king saying that their hands were tied. They could not condemn Symmachus in his absence nor could they hold him guilty of obstinacy since he had in fact appeared. Added to which there was no precedent for bishops to try the pope. They said that they had done all they could to settle the situation. They had urged both Senate and clergy to keep the peace but their requests had been ignored. So they sought permission from the king to return home.[21] The king's reply, dated 1 October, was to insist that they must see the matter through to a conclusion.[22]

The synod dutifully assembled again, for its third session, on 23 October 502. The locale is uncertain but was perhaps the Palma, the place from which Theodoric had addressed the people in 500. The events of the two previous synods were surveyed by the bishops and they then decided that, since the pope was the successor of St Peter, they could not pass judgment on him. They agreed to leave the matter to God. The pope was freed of all charges and all who had abandoned his communion were urged to reconcile themselves to him. Furthermore, all his clerical opponents were instructed to ask forgiveness and seek from him reinstatement in their offices. It was ordered that any member of the clergy who celebrated mass in Rome without his consent in future should be punished as a schismatic. The resolutions were signed by seventy-six bishops, headed by Laurentius of Milan and Peter of Ravenna.[23]

But the opponents of Symmachus were not beaten yet. They tried every means in their power to get the synodical decisions reversed. They launched a comprehensive attack on the synod in their memorial *Contra Synodum Absolutionis Incongruae*. They claimed that the synod was unrepresentative because not all the bishops were present, that not all those present had voted for absolution and that most of them were elderly and feeble anyway. They challenged the whole basis of the synodical decision, saying that the pope had been absolved but he had not been cleared of the charges, that his accusers had not been heard and that the idea that the pope could not be judged was dangerous folly. They accused the synod of self-contradiction by asking why, if they believed they were not competent to judge the pope, they had summoned him to appear before them. Finally they accused the synod of ignoring the instructions of the king and evading their responsibility.[24]

They also petitioned the king to send Laurentius back to Rome, declaring that it was a basic rule of the church that every bishop should remain in the church where he was first consecrated, and Laurentius had been consecrated in Rome. Laurentius did return to Rome, from Ravenna, whither he had retired, according to the 'Laurentian Fragment', to avoid persecution by Symmachus,[25] but more probably to lobby on behalf of his cause. He was welcomed back eagerly by his supporters, took over many of the Roman churches and much of the papal patrimony and ruled as pope from the Lateran Palace.

But Symmachus fought back, summoning a new synod which met in his stronghold of St Peter's on 6 November 502. The synod began with a reading of the refutation of the Laurentian memorial by the deacon Ennodius, *Libellus adversus eos qui contra synodum scribere praesumpserunt*.[26] The next move, much more daring and characteristic of Symmachus, was a full-scale attack on the principle of lay interference in church affairs. The immediate object of the attack was the decree against alienation of church property promulgated by Basilius in 483. The synod expressed indignation that a layman should draw up laws for the church threatening clerics with anathema. Several leading bishops, Laurentius of Milan, Peter of Ravenna and Eulalius of Syracuse in particular, declared the edict invalid because the pope had not been present at the deliberations nor had he signed the edict and because laymen had no right to issue instructions respecting church property. The synod as a whole then pronounced the 483 edict invalid.[27]

But Symmachus's intention was only to demolish the idea of lay interference and not to abandon the principle behind the law. For a new law was now decreed declaring that no pope could dispose by sale or exchange of any estate belonging to the church and that the profits of these estates could only be used for paying the clergy, ransoming prisoners and succouring strangers. Anyone selling church property in future would suffer loss of dignity and the clergy would reclaim all illegally alienated property. This new law achieved two things. First, it demonstrated to the world that far from indulging in the alienation of church property, as his accusers alleged, Symmachus actually condemned it. Second, it demonstrated that it was up to the pope and not to the aristocracy to make dispositions regarding church property.

But just as the 498 arbitration in favour of Symmachus had failed to halt the schism, so too the 502 synodical resolution failed to halt it. Laurentius returned to Rome and for four years, according to the 'Laurentian Fragment', held the churches of Rome and ruled as pope, backed by Festus.[28] By that reckoning 506 is the year in which he finally conceded defeat, an interpretation that is confirmed by the deacon John's *libellus* of submission, which is dated 16 September 506.[29]

The years 502 to 506 were marked by activity on two fronts. In Rome the two sides simply fought each other for mastery of the city. But alongside this there was frantic diplomatic activity to get King Theodoric to step in. Violence had always been a characteristic feature of the schism. There had been fighting following the divided election. There had been violent clashes during the synods, notably the assault on Pope Symmachus's train. All parties seem to have been guilty of it. The *plebs* were obviously involved and several bishops left the trial synod because of mob violence. But the clergy and the Senate were also involved and had to be admonished by the synod to keep the peace.[30]

The *Vita Symmachi* paints a vivid picture of the conditions which obtained in Rome.[31] 'Then the ex-consul Festus the senior member of the Senate and the ex-consul Probinus began to fight within the city of Rome with other senators and especially with the ex-consul Faustus.' By this the author means that the huge senatorial households, retainers, slaves and hangers-on, will have been engaged in constant fighting.

> In their hatred they visited slaughter and murder on the clergy. Those who rightly held communion with the blessed Symmachus were openly put to the sword when found within the city. Consecrated women and virgins were expelled from their convents and houses, stripped and beaten up. Every day they waged war against the church in the midst of the city. Also many priests were killed, among them Dignissimus and Gordian, priests respectively of SS Peter *ad vincula* and SS John and Paul, whom they killed with clubs and swords; also many other christians, so that it was unsafe for any of the clergy to walk abroad in the city by day or by night.

The constant stress within this account on the fighting within the city confirms the picture of the Laurentians controlling the area within the walls with the Symmachans relegated to the suburbs. Even if only half of what is described is true, and there are cross references in other sources for some of it, this represents a frightening state of affairs.

It is small wonder that there was feverish diplomatic activity on the part of the Symmachans to end the uncertainty. Curiously enough the bulk of this activity seems to have been undertaken by two deacons who were not part of the Roman clergy at all. One of them was the Milanese deacon Ennodius. Diplomat, aristocrat and scholar, author of nine books of very turgid letters, poems, hymns and saints' lives, he was already a man of considerable accomplishment and standing, related to several important Roman noble families. He fervently espoused the cause of Symmachus and wrote the refutation of the Laurentian memorial, in which he answered their accusations point by point. He also lobbied extensively on behalf of the Symmachans at Ravenna, paying out money from the Milanese church coffers to win over important people to the cause. He had some difficulty in getting this money back from Symmachus and was in danger of having to pay it out himself, since his archbishop Laurentius of Milan was pressing for the deficit in the church coffers to be made up.[32] Nevertheless, he kept lobbying and secured the support at the royal court of the deacon Helpidius, the personal physician and confidant of the king.[33] But although the groundwork was done by Ennodius, it was another outsider, the deacon Dioscorus, who clinched Theodoric's support. An exile from the Alexandrian church, who had attached himself to Symmachus, presumably because of their similar hardline views on the East, he undertook a crucial embassy to Ravenna in 506 and it was he who persuaded Theodoric to intervene and end the destruction in Rome by confirming the synodical decision.[34]

Theodoric instructed Festus to hand over the churches in Rome to Symmachus and at this point Laurentius retired from Rome to one of Festus's estates and there fasted so rigorously that he died soon afterwards.[35] The king's intervention then, was, decisive. He issued a *praeceptum* urging unity[36] and many of the Laurentians made their submissions and came over to Symmachus. Ennodius delightedly penned a panegyric to the king.[37] But such bitterness had been generated that it is not surprising that several hard-core Laurentians, notably the deacon Paschasius, refused to be reconciled. Paschasius died still in schism from the church.[38] The 'Laurentian Fragment' claimed that Symmachus revelled openly in his victory and used it as a licence for many evil deeds, notably the open sale of office.[39] Whether or not this is true, only the death of Symmachus in 514 was to end the bitterness that had been generated by his election sixteen years before. It was his successor, Pope Hormisdas, who achieved the final reconciliation and bound up the last remaining wounds.

Chapter 6

The Symmachan Schism (ii) issues and participants

The Lay Participants

The roles of the various participants in this sordid affair repay close attention, for they throw valuable light on the part played by the laity in papal affairs, the extent of internecine strife within the clergy and the interplay between the interested parties. Of central importance is the role of King Theodoric, pledged by his own religious policy to a position of neutrality in the affairs of the Catholic church. Does he maintain this stance? He first appears in these events in 498, when the disputed election was referred to him and he found in favour of Symmachus on the grounds of majority clerical support and prior ordination. All the evidence points to a completely disinterested decision by Theodoric on the basis of the available facts. As far as he was concerned the matter was now closed.

When dissension flared up again, the position he took was once more wholly neutral. He summoned Symmachus to answer the charges before him, and only when he failed to appear did Theodoric accede to the Laurentians' request for a visitor to be appointed. In this Theodoric was following the precedent set by the emperor Honorius who had sent a visitor to Rome during the schism between Boniface I and Eulalius in 418. Theodoric ordered a synod to meet in Rome and discuss the charges against the pope, and when the north Italian bishops objected that there was no precedent for this Theodoric was able to produce letters from Symmachus agreeing to the trial. Indeed Symmachus duly presented himself at the first session. Even when his request that the visitor be withdrawn before he answered the charges was rejected by the synod, Symmachus was still prepared to attend the second session, and retreated to St Peter's only after his followers had been massacred. So there is no question of Theodoric acting in this matter without the consent of the pope.

Having once called the synod, Theodoric clearly hoped to take no further part in the matter. But the bishops acted constantly with the utmost timidity. After the first session became deadlocked, they petitioned the king to withdraw the case to Ravenna. He refused, saying that it was up to the bishops to decide. When the second session proved inconclusive they again petitioned the king, saying that their hands were tied and they could do nothing. 'The simplicity of bishops is not fit for dealing with secular cunning' they whined, and asked to be allowed to return home.[1] The king was indignant that they had once again passed the buck back to him. He replied that if he had wished to decide the controversy, he would with God's help have done so and restored the peace. He repeated that they must decide the matter. It was entirely a matter for them and their consciences. They could do whatever they wished about the pope as long as they restored the peace. The bishops, having thrice sought to avoid it, made their decision; despite the appeals of the Laurentians against its findings, Theodoric made no attempt to recall the synod or reverse its decisions. Theodoric's position then was absolutely consistent. He would not intervene. It was none of his business. He consistently stressed that his main concern was with peace and public order. It was entirely in keeping with his general policy of respecting existing Roman institutions and practices.

There is something really rather shocking about the way in which the assembled bishops of the Catholic church fell over themselves to persuade a heretic barbarian to decide who the pope should be. It makes nonsense of the idea of an articulation of a papal monarchical theory in which the church was superior to the lay authorities. Both the Symmachan and Laurentian factions appealed to the king for arbitration in 498 and both sides accepted his convocation of a synod. Symmachus, indeed, finally submitted a decision about his case to God and the king, hardly the sort of behaviour one would expect for a champion of papal supremacy. Indeed the regularity with which both sides invoked the intervention of the king strongly suggests a widely held view of his impartiality.

There are several controversial facets of his actions, however, which should be looked at more closely. First, there is the appointment of Peter of Altinum as visitor. It is on the face of it rather an odd choice. Peter was a suffragan bishop of Istria, whose metropolitan, Marcellianus of Aquileia, was the only one of the three Italian metropolitans hostile to Symmachus. But there is no reason to suppose that this hostility predated the 502 synod or that either he or Peter had a predetermined position on the case. It seems more likely that Theodoric chose him because his see was one of the furthest from Rome and he would be less likely than many others to have had direct contact with the personalities involved. Peter does seem to have favoured the Laurentians during his time as visitor, however. He was bitterly attacked by the deacon Ennodius, but Ennodius also goes out of his way to acquit Theodoric of responsibility for the visitor's actions, saying that Peter had gone outside the bounds of his task as fixed by Theodoric and joined the opposition, so that he produced discord instead of the peace desired by the king.[2] In the *Vita Symmachi* Peter was bracketed with Laurentius as an 'invader' of the Holy See.[3] It is clear from the *libellus* of the deacon John that anti-Symmachan clergy reconciled to the pope after 502 were required to anathematize Peter was well as Laurentius. Since Symmachus resented the appointment of a visitor in the first place, Peter is likely to have been a *bête noire* to the loyalists. But even if he did actively favour the Laurentians, there is no evidence that he did so on the orders of the king.

Second, there is the fact that Laurentius was allowed to return from Ravenna to Rome by Theodoric after the conclusion of the 502 synod. This is more problematic. His return prolonged the schism for a further four years. But in 499 at the synod held after the arbitration in favour of Symmachus, Laurentius had loyally attended and signed the proceedings first of all the priests. It would be logical to expect that, the synod having absolved Symmachus of the charges, Laurentius would resume his allegiance. Whatever Theodoric may have thought, there was surely no justification for retaining Laurentius in Ravenna now that the matter was officially closed.

Third, there is the question of the consular nominations. Did Theodoric show partiality to one side or another among the senatorial families supporting rival papal candidates? Again the answer seems to be in the negative. His selections for the consulship reveal impartiality. The leader of the Symmachan faction was Flavius Anicius Probus Faustus, the former *Magister Officiorum* who held the office of *quaestor sacri palatii* from 503 to 506, and his two sons, Flavius Rufus Magnus Faustus Avienus and Flavius Ennodius Messala, both became consuls during the schism, in 502 and 506 respectively. On the other hand, Flavius Rufius Petronius Nicomachus Cethegus, son of the prominent Laurentian Petronius Probinus, was consul in 504.

There have been scholars who have sought to interpret Theodoric's actions in the context of a wider *politique*. But the idea that he supported Symmachus because Symmachus opposed the Eastern empire and Theodoric had a vested interest in preventing a reconciliation between Rome and Constantinople is simply not borne out by the evidence. If Theodoric was pro-Symmachus, why did he refuse to intervene in the 502 trial synod on Symmachus's behalf, why did he send back Laurentius in 502 and why did he not intervene to settle the schism until 506? The idea that he supported Laurentius because the acceptance of the *Henotikon* by the pope was the price of his recognition as king by the emperor is also supported neither by his initial decision in favour of Symmachus nor by Symmachus's willingness to remit the case to him nor by his final settlement of the schism in Symmachus's favour. The only interpretation that fits the facts is that Theodoric was absolutely impartial. As he said himself to the bishops in his *praeceptio*: 'We do not consider it our business to decide anything concerning ecclesiastical matters'.[4] He was a man of his word.

The Emperor Anastasius, consistent with his arrangement with Festus, threw his support behind Laurentius. He wrote to Symmachus accusing him of not having been properly ordained, of being a Manichaean heretic and having conspired with the senate to excommunicate him. This provoked Symmachus to write an indignant and forthright rebuttal to the emperor, the *Apologeticus Symmachi Episcopi Romani adversus Anastasium imperatorem*.[5] In it he addressed Anastasius curtly as 'emperor' with none of the customary honorific appendages and none of the honeyed phrases of Pope Anastasius II. He denied that he was a Manichaean, revealing that he had been born a pagan but had been converted in Rome and had never deviated from the true faith since. He said that it was Acacius and not the emperor who had been excommunicated. But he went on to hector the emperor with such sentiments as: 'Because you are emperor, do you think that the judgment of God is nothing?' But Anastasius was powerless to do anything other than write letters and this accurately reflects the position of the Eastern emperor in papal politics at this time. It is, however, unquestionably the deep personal antagonism between Symmachus and Anastasius revealed by this letter that effectively prevented any progress towards the resolution of the Acacian schism as long as Symmachus lived. He dug himself into the Gelasian position, and there was virtually no contact with the imperial court for the major part of Symmachus's reign.

As to the population of Rome itself, the evidence suggests that there was an almost complete split between the senatorial aristocracy and the people during the schism. For the most part the aristocracy supported Laurentius and for the most part the people supported Symmachus. The *Vita Symmachi* says that 'only the ex-consul Faustus fought for the church' and when recording the reinstatement of the pope after his acquittal says that it was accomplished by 'all the bishops and priests and deacons and the whole clergy and people', conspicuously making no mention of the senate.[6]

On the other hand, the ex-consul Festus and the ex-consul Probinus are twice stated by the *Vita* to be the leaders of the Laurentians both in laying charges against Symmachus and in organizing the violence in Rome. The senate played an important role in getting the trial synod called. The 'Laurentian Fragment' says that the synod was called 'according to the will of the clergy and senate'[7] and this is confirmed by Theodoric's *praeceptio*.[8] They also remained hostile to Symmachus as testified by the heading of a lost document in the dossier of synodical documents from 502.[9] An opposition petition to the king headed '*Regi relatio senatu vel Marcelli(a)ni episcopi cum ceteris*' indicates that the Laurentian faction consisted of the senate, Patriarch Marcellianus of Aquileia and 'others', perhaps the dissenting bishops. Both the bishops in their letter to the king[10] and Ennodius in his defence of the trial synod speak of appealing to the senatorial families to keep the peace, by, it is implied, desisting from their opposition to Symmachus.[11]

The Symmachan camp had no doubt that it was the senate which comprised their enemies and this is reflected in the 'Symmachan apocrypha', a collection of documents concocted by supporters of the pope and circulated to gain support for his cause. In them historical and fictional episodes from the church's past are reworked to make them fit exactly the events of 502. In them the senate is always the villain, the pope the misunderstood hero and the people the supporters of the pope.[12]

The *Gesta de Xysti purgatione* recounts how two leading senators Marinianus and Bassus, who had a grudge against the pope because of his refusal to grant them church estates, accused him of debauching a nun, citing the testimony of a papal slave as evidence. The emperor Valentinian withdrew from communion with the pope on hearing this but then, bowing to popular pressure, summoned a council of clergy and senate to examine the charges. It met in the *basilica Sessoriana*, but the ex-consul Maximus declared that the pope could not be judged by his inferiors and the synod declared him innocent. Xystus promptly excommunicated Marinianus and Bassus. They tried to buy forgiveness with donations to the church but the pope remained inflexible and they died unreconciled to the church. For Xystus read Symmachus, for Valentinian read Theodoric, for Marinianus and Bassus read Festus and Probinus, for Maximus read Faustus and there you have the events of the 502 schism.

Similarly the *Gesta de Polychronii accusatione* tells of a non-existent bishop of Jerusalem, Polychronios, who was tried before a Roman synod for alienation of church property. But it was proved that Polychronios had sold church estates only to raise money to alleviate the distress of the populace during a famine, and he was acquitted and restored to his throne. This story was clearly fabricated to explain the sale of church estates which Symmachus was accused of carrying out.

The account of the trial of Pope Marcellinus at the orders of the emperor Diocletian, *Sinuessanae Synodi Gesta de Marcellino* was fabricated to prove that the pope could not be judged by his inferiors. The *Constitutum Silvestri*, the report of a Roman synod supposedly held by Pope Sylvester, decreed the same thing and also justified the Roman date for Easter, as did the *Gesta Liberii*. The latter contains an interesting and significant piece of pseudo-etymology, when it declares *omnis curia a cruore dicitur*, an untranslatable pun which roughly means 'the word senate (*curia*) is derived from blood (*cruor*)'.

It is not in fact true that only Faustus supported the pope, though he was obviously the most prominent of Symmachus's senatorial supporters. There was a group of senators in the Symmachan camp, though only a minority of the whole senate. The senate had divided into groups during the 498 election, the majority group supporting Laurentius and the minority group favouring Symmachus. The *Vita Symmachi* says 'Festus the ex-consul and senior member of the senate and Probinus the ex-consul began to fight inside the city of Rome with other senators and especially with the ex-consul Faustus.' Two of these 'other senators' supporting Symmachus are readily identifiable. One is Petrus Marcellinus Felix Liberius, patrician and former praetorian prefect, who is found intriguing on behalf of the Symmachans in the Aquileia election.[13] The other is Q. Aurelius Memmius Symmachus (no relation), ex-consul and former prefect of the city, who is addressed jointly with Faustus in a letter from Bishop Avitus of Vienne.[14] Avitus encourages them in their resistance to the trial of the pope and this, taken with the evidence of the *Gesta de Xysti Purgatione*, suggests that the lead in getting the weak-kneed bishops to acquit Symmachus may well have been taken by the handful of pro-Symmachan senators. It is possible that to this group we should add Anicius Manlius Severinus Boethius, son-in-law and close associate of Symmachus; the *vir illustris* Palatinus who gave money to Pope Symmachus for the building of the church of St Martin[15] and Caecina Decius Faustus Albinus, ex-consul, son of the praetorian prefect Caecina Decius Maximus Basilius and himself a future praetorian prefect, who built a church on his estates dedicated by Pope Symmachus to St Peter.[16]

Even though a handful of *religiosi* among the aristocracy backed Symmachus, his principal support in Rome derived from the people. One of the reasons the bishops gave for absolving Symmachus in 502 was that 'almost the whole people have bound themselves indissolubly to his communion'.[17] Ennodius claimed that support for Symmachus derived from 'the multitude of the common people devoted to God'.[18] It was mob violence on Symmachus's behalf that caused several of the bishops to leave Rome at the end of the first session of the trial synod. The 'Symmachan apocrypha' stress the support of the people for the pope. The Laurentians in their attack on the synod protested against the mob violence on behalf of Symmachus, to which Ennodius's reply was that the multitude following the pope, many of them women, came with 'lamentations not missiles'.[19]

Symmachus clearly recognized the source of his support. An early version of the *Vita Symmachi* recorded 'He loved the clergy and the poor' and the Cononian epitome records that he tripled poor relief and clerical salaries.[20] He built shelters for the poor (*habitacula pauperibus*) attached to the churches of St Peter, St Paul and St Laurentius, and in the square before St Peter's he built a public convenience (*usum necessitatis humanae*) – eloquent testimony of his concern for his followers.[21]

The Clerical Participants

While the division of support within two or three sections of the electorate – senate and people – seems fairly clear, the position of the clergy remains deeply ambivalent. Although the *Vita Symmachi* claims that Symmachus was restored by the action of 'clergy and people', it is clear from the same source that in 498 the clergy divided into two groups as the senate did, though apparently the majority voted for Symmachus. It was 'some of the clergy and senate' who laid charges before Theodoric. Again the clergy divided into factions after the charges had been laid, 'some took communion with Symmachus, others with Laurentius'.[22]

But even before the election of 498 there had been divisions within the clerical body. The attendance and subscription lists of the 487,[23] 495,[24] 499[25] and 502[26] synods testify to this. It is clear from the 495 and 499 synodical subscription lists that the parish priests of Rome signed in order of seniority. For 487 and 502 there are attendance rather than subscription lists, which are less exact but generally give approximate order of seniority. Since each of these synods had a particular character, certain deductions can be made. The 487 synod of Felix III was unconnected with the controversies which were to split the Roman church. The 495 synod was devoted to the absolution of Misenus of Cumae, which it has been argued betokened a softening of attitude towards the East. The 499 synod was the reconciliation synod after Symmachus had been awarded the papal throne by Theodoric. The 502 synod was the victory synod held by Symmachus after his absolution.

The basic figures for these synods are in themselves interesting. There were throughout this period some 28 titular or parish churches in Rome but many of them had more than one priest. There were 76 priests who attended the 487 synod and 74 the 499, though only 67 signed the latter, the missing 7 being accounted for by death or absence since the opening. However, only 58 attended the 495 synod and only 37 attended the 502 victory synod. These facts suggest a degree of opposition by a section of the priesthood to the policies or personalities of the popes. Since the 495 synod was called to rehabilitate Bishop Misenus, whose deposition had been the *cause célèbre* of the previous reign, it is reasonable to assume that the missing 18 absented themselves because they favoured the maintenance of the hard line with no concession to Eastern sentiment. The majority support for a change of attitude to Constantinople, betokened by the presence of 58 priests at the absolution of Misenus, was reflected the following year in the election of a soft-line pope, Anastasius II. The absence of some 39 priests from the 502 synod suggests that something is very wrong indeed, for Symmachus could muster only half of the available parish priests to support his cause.

But still further conclusions are possible because of our access to the seniority rankings. The information revealed by the 502 synodical attendances is significant. Of the 37 priests attending the 502 synod, 31 had attended the 499 synod and 6 were new, almost certainly replacements for the dead – Gordian and Dignissimus murdered during the rioting, Smaragdus, Maxentius, Valentine and Agapitus dying during or soon after the 499 synod. Of the 31 survivors from the 499 synod, 11 come from the group of 15 ordained since 495, most of them ordained by Anastasius II, who is known to have ordained 12. Of the remaining 20 from 499, 8 are survivors from the reign of Felix III, dating from before 487. But 7 of these are recorded at all 4 synods, 487, 495, 499, 502, suggesting that they are hard-core loyalists, who will support whichever pope is elected through thick and thin and whatever his policy. Only one, Pascasius, was absent from 495 but present at 499 and 502. The remaining 12 date from between 487 and 495 and of these only 2 (Julian and John) attended 499 but not 495, for which they would have been eligible according to seniority ranking. That gives us a possible 3 hard-liners who absented themselves from 495 but attended 499 and 502. It is certainly not sufficient for us to argue that there is evidence here of hard-line anti-Easterners among the Symmachans. For to set against these 3 are 17 who attended 495, 499 and 502, suggesting a party of loyalists prepared to abide by the 498 ruling for Symmachus, whatever their feelings about the Acacian Schism.

Far more significant than speculation about pro- or anti-Eastern feeling amongst the Symmachans are the following undoubted facts. 17 of Symmachus's 37 supporters were among the most junior of the priests, all of them ordained since 495. Put another way, only 12 of the senior 40 priests of the 499 synod supported Symmachus in 502, only 3 of the senior 20. This does conceal some unavoidable occurrences. The highest-ranking priestly supporter of Symmachus in 502 was Projectitius, ranked 15 in 499. It would have been Gordian, ranked 4 in 499, but he was murdered in 502. However, Gordian's eminence does not obscure the fact that the bulk of Symmachus's support derived from the junior clergy and that the senior priests very largely sided with the former archpriest Laurentius.

It might be argued that it would not be surprising for the senior members of the priestly establishment to rally round their chief, since his opponent Symmachus was a deacon. But let us look at the deacons. There were at this time 7 regionary deacons in Rome, most of them at the start of Symmachus's reign dating from the reign of Felix III. Gelasius had created only 2, Anastasius none. All of them attended the 499 synod: archdeacon Fulgentius and deacons Cyprian, Anastasius, Tarrensis, Citonatus, Tertullus and John. At the end, they signed in order of seniority with the curious omission of Fulgentius. But at the 502 victory synod, there was no archdeacon and only 4 deacons: Anastasius, John, Hormisdas and Agapitus. Of the old deacons 5 – Fulgentius, Cyprian, Tarrensis, Citonatus and Tertullus – were missing. Two had remained loyal, Anastasius and John, hence their ranking in seniority first and second; 2 new ones had been created and 3 were unreplaced. As with the priests, then, the most senior deacons, including the archdeacon, had defected.

It is worth lingering over Symmachus's 2 new deacons, since both of them were to become pope themselves in the future. Hormisdas was Symmachus's principal lieutenant. He read out the 483 decree at the 502 synod and he appears in the pages of Ennodius as the man with the ear of the pope.[27] Agapitus attained the papal throne in 535, thirty-three years after becoming a deacon. Interestingly he was the son of the murdered loyalist Gordian, priest of Saints John and Paul.[28] In both the cases of Agapitus and Hormisdas Symmachus was appointing ultra-loyal supporters and in both cases men who seem to have been comparatively young.

It seems that the anti-pope Laurentius created a parallel diaconate. For to add to those who had come over to him from the original staff, Laurentius created two more at least. One of them was that deacon John, who when the Laurentian movement collapsed in 506, returned to his allegiance and presented the pope with a *libellus* of submission.[29] He is unlikely to have been the John of 502 defecting at some time later since by 502 the battle lines were drawn and the 502 synod was composed of hard-core Symmachans.

The other and even more distinguished and indeed recalcitrant Laurentian deacon was Paschasius. A learned and respected scholar, the author of a tract on the Holy Ghost, a man much loved for his charity, asceticism and virtues, he remained in schism from Symmachus even after the death of Laurentius, stubbornly refusing to recognize Symmachus and dying still unreconciled at some date undetermined between 511 and 514.[30]

In addition to this, while the Symmachan cause was very well served by its literary propagandists, the ingenious and necessarily anonymous inventors of the 'Symmachan apocrypha', the Laurentian cause was almost certainly adorned by one of the most eminent men of letters in sixth-century Rome, the Scythian monk Dionysius Exiguus. Arriving in Rome during the pontificate of Anastasius II, Dionysius attached himself to the papal court and the cause of *détente*. He was responsible initially for the translation of the letter of the Alexandrian legates from Greek into Latin for the papal archives.[31]

It is the evidence of his writings which suggests his Laurentian sympathies. Rome lacked a comprehensive collection of canons and Dionysius provided it in his *Codex Canonum Ecclesiasticorum*. It was undertaken at the behest of *carissimus frater noster Laurentius*.[32] A work of such massive importance can only have been undertaken at the behest of somebody of significance and that somebody is almost certainly the *soi-disant* Pope Laurentius, for whose chancery Dionysius was providing a much-needed manual. Significantly, it was never officially promulgated by the Roman church, perhaps because of the Laurentian taint. Nevertheless, from the reign of Pope John II onwards, once the echoes of the schism had died down, it was frequently cited by the popes in their letters and Cassiodorus observed 'The Roman church honours it by constant use'.[33]

Second, there was the *Collectio Decretorum*, a collection of decrees issued by various popes from Siricius to Anastasius II.[34] Interestingly, the popes between Leo the Great and Anastasius II are represented only by a single letter of Gelasius, while the only reference to the Acacian Schism is in the conciliatory letter of Anastasius II. Given Gelasius's prodigious edict-making, this may perhaps be taken as evidence of Dionysius's partiality. The work was undertaken at the behest of the priest Julian of St Anastasia, a Gelasian ordinee, who was absent from the 495 synod but present at 499 and 502 synods, suggesting at once a pro-Symmachan and a hard-line anti-Easterner. But the fact that the collection ends with Anastasius II also suggests that it should be dated to the early years of Symmachus before the development of the schism.

Dionysius's works on the computation of Easter, notably the *Liber de Paschate*, all favour the Greek computation, a cause of contention central to the rival factions in the schism, with the Laurentians favouring the Greek date.[35] Similarly, when in 526 Dionysius was requested by Pope John I to compute the date of Easter, he settled on the Greek date.[36]

His massive corpus of literary works, including the standard codification of the canons, makes his eminence clear. It is, therefore, all the more singular that nowhere is there any record of work undertaken for, or even contact with, Pope Symmachus. Whereas Dionysius translated the letter of the Alexandrian legates for Anastasius II and later a collection of Greek canons for Hormisdas, as well as calculating the date of Easter for John I. The evidence seems clear. Dionysius served Laurentius during the schism but became reconciled along with the other dissidents, and was subsequently put to work by both of Symmachus's immediate successors.

Taken together, the statistics about the priests and deacons are decisive. It is evident that both the senior priests and the senior deacons opted for Laurentius, while the junior priests by and large favoured Symmachus. This suggests that, however it had begun, the Symmachan schism turned into a 'Young Turks' revolt against the Establishment. When you add to this the fact that the people supported Symmachus and the aristocracy Laurentius, an even more remarkable picture emerges, an alliance of youth and the lower classes against the Establishment of both the lay and ecclesiastical hierarchies. Given the added fact that Symmachus himself reigned for sixteen years at a time when the average length of papal reigns was four years and that Symmachus is unrecorded in the sources prior to his election, it is legitimate to suggest that he, like many of his supporters in the clergy, was comparatively young. Apart from a natural matter of juniors kicking over the traces and cocking a snook at the Establishment, there are two principles deducible from Symmachus's actions which might well have provided a platform attractive to his supporters in the clergy. One of the things about the Photinus affair which had angered the clergy was that Pope Anastasius admitted him to communion without consulting the clergy.[37] Symmachus conspicuously did consult the clergy, for instance in 512 when he summoned a special meeting to discuss an approach from the Eastern bishops.[38] A return to the democratic principle of consultation, then, might well have been urged by Symmachus in the heated atmosphere caused by Anastasius's actions. Similarly, the rejection of the principle of lay interference, which was the main result of the 502 victory synod, was almost certainly part of the Symmachan platform. Both these principles would seem much more attractive to the junior clergy than to a clerical Establishment, closely involved with the aristocracy.

The whole of the clergy were never reconciled to Symmachus. It was not just the deacon Paschasius who remained in bitter opposition until death. The details of Symmachus's ordinations reveal this.[39] During the course of his sixteen years' reign (498–514), he ordained for the Roman church 16 deacons. During the reigns of his three predecessors (483–98) there had been only 7 diaconal appointments and during the comparably long reign of Simplicius (468–83) only 11. There were clearly replacement deacons being ordained here in place of the defectors as well as in place of the dead. Even more striking are the priestly ordinations. Symmachus ordained 92 priests in sixteen years, 20 more than his three predecessors put together and 34 more than Pope Simplicius. Given that at least half the priesthood of 499 dates from no earlier than 492 (Gelasius and Anastasius between them ordained 44 priests) then many of the Symmachan priestly ordinations must have been to replace defecting rather than deceased priests.

The result of these personnel activities was a clean sweep of the old establishment and the creation of an entirely new and comparatively youthful papal establishment. This Symmachan 'old guard' was virtually to run the Roman church until almost the end of the Ostrogothic period. Of Symmachus's successors Hormisdas, John I, Boniface II and John II created no deacons. The only exception is Felix IV, who created 4 and they must still have been balanced by the Symmachan survivors, who would have had the edge by virtue of seniority. Of Symmachus's immediate successors Popes Hormisdas, Felix IV and Agapitus were all his diaconal creations. But, although the Symmachan personnel kept a grip on the positions of power, it is nevertheless true that the unity within the Establishment did not survive the death of Hormisdas and new issues arose to create a fundamental division within the ranks.

Within the new Symmachan establishment, it is possible to determine the pope's principal advisers, thanks to the letters of Ennodius. The Milanese deacon Ennodius, the spokesman for the Symmachan cause at Ravenna, was one of the key figures in the Symmachan camp. But what is interesting about his letters is not the large number of clerics to whom he wrote but the small number. He was far more often and more extensively in touch with the aristocracy, almost all of the most notable of whom received letters from him, some of them very frequently, men such as Liberius, Faustus, Boethius, Opilio, Venantius, Symmachus (no relation) and Pamphronius. His clerical correspondents in Rome, however, were very few. Pope Symmachus was, of course, one.[40] Besides him, there were the deacons Hormisdas and Dioscorus, who emerge as the major figures at the Symmachan court. In fact Ennodius couples the two together in one letter.[41] Hormisdas was already being spoken of by Ennodius as Symmachus's eventual successor and Ennodius specifically refers to his influence on Symmachus. Hormisdas received more letters than anyone else at the papal court. Dioscorus, on the other hand, was the refugee Alexandrian deacon who eventually persuaded Theodoric to step in and end the schism. He, too, was important enough to be considered a candidate for the papal throne and was elected to it in 530.

The only other correspondents in Rome in the papal circle were Adeodatus and Luminosus. The priest Adeodatus was an important figure in the papal camp because he was the spiritual adviser of the family of Faustus, one of the pope's leading lay supporters, and his influence was therefore crucial for the cause.[42] Luminosus *vir sublimissimus* was also an adviser of Symmachus, though of indeterminable rank.[43] Along with Hormisdas and Dioscorus, he was specifically contacted because of his influence on the pope. Ennodius having paid out Milanese church funds to further the papal cause at the royal court and being pressed by archbishop Laurentius for repayment, contacted the pope's closest confidants to get the money repaid. These confidants were Hormisdas, Dioscorus and Luminosus.

The personnel evidence fits with what we know of Symmachus's building activities. The 'Laurentian Fragment' says that Laurentius 'held the Roman church for four years' and that Symmachus asked Theodoric to hand over to him 'the churches which Laurentius held within the city'.[44] The adherence of the senior clergy would have secured for Laurentius many of the central churches, a fact which is suggested by Symmachus's choice of refuge. When he fled back from Ariminum at dead of night, he chose as his refuge not the Lateran Palace, the pope's official residence, nor any central church, but the comparatively unfashionable basilica of St Peter across the river.

Two basic facts about Symmachus's extensive building activities stand out.[45] The first is his concentration on St Peter's, which becomes his official residence for the duration of the schism. He was the first pope to single out St Peter's for special attention and his intention was obviously to make it a fitting residence for the pope. He built a sub-basilica, dedicated to St Andreas, and no less than seven oratories, three of them at the baptistery of St Peter bearing the same dedications as oratories in the Lateran (the Holy Cross, St John the Evangelist and St John the Baptist) and obviously intended to duplicate the facilities in the Lateran basilica. All these buildings were handsomely endowed with expensive silver plate and ornaments. Furthermore, he adorned the basilica of St Peter himself with marble, widened the steps leading up to the doors, decorated the fountain of St Peter with marble and mosaic, and built another fountain and a public lavatory for the use of the waiting faithful. He also extended the basilica both to the left and the right to provide a residence for himself and a headquarters for the papal staff.

Symmachus's efforts to provide proper baptismal facilities at St Peter's are duly echoed in one of the 'Symmachan apocrypha' – the *Gesta Liberii*. Pope Liberius, exiled from Rome by a heretical emperor, takes up residence outside the city walls. As Easter approaches he is distraught because he cannot perform the customary baptisms in the Lateran. But on the advice of his priests, he conducts the ceremony in the Ostian cemetery where, according to tradition, St Peter had baptized. In the meantime a baptistery is constructed at St Peter's to allow Liberius to hold the Pentecost baptisms there. It is more than likely that this accurately reflects the arrangements adopted by Symmachus.

The symbolism involved in the choice of St Peter's basilica will also not have been lost on contemporaries. Throughout the fifth century increasing stress had been laid on the role of the pope as the heir of the apostle Peter. References to Peter were by 500 a commonplace of papal propaganda, occurring for instance throughout Ennodius's *Libellus*. It was now also customary for the popes to be buried in St Peter's. The only exception during this period was Pope Felix III, who was buried at St Paul's, in order to rest beside other members of his family.

The second fact about Symmachus's building activities which is remarkable is the number of churches he built or restored in the suburbs of Rome. It suggests that this is where his strength lay and he was putting the churches under his control in order. He built a basilica to St Agatha ten miles down the *Via Aurelia* on the *Fundus Lardarius* and on the same road just outside the West Gate of the city he built a basilica to St Pancras, significantly the avenger of broken oaths. He repaired the basilica of St Felicitas outside the *Porta Salaria* and the basilica of St Agnes north of Rome.

Compared to these activities, the building work undertaken inside Rome itself, presumably after the Laurentians had been broken, is much less dramatic. He built a basilica of Saints Sylvester and Martin near the Baths of Trajan and an oratory to SS Cosmas and Damian in the basilica of St Maria. He enlarged the basilica of St Michael the Archangel, carried out renovations at St Paul's and constructed some steps inside the basilica of Saints John and Paul. The overall picture is one of Symmachus, entrenching himself in St Peter's, consciously turning it into a papal residence and at the same time renovating and building churches within his area of control, essentially the suburbs.

It is much more difficult to interpret the behaviour of the Italian bishops during the schism than it is to interpret that of the Roman clergy. The subscription lists of the synods of 499 and the trial and victory synods of 502 survive, and certain observations are possible. The numbers subscribing, 71 in 499, 76 the trial synod and 65 the victory synod suggests a certain consistency. But this consistency is delusive, for there is a marked difference in the composition of the attending bishops between the 499 reconciliation synod and the 502 trial synod. Of the 76 bishops who acquitted Symmachus in 502, 35 had not attended a Roman synod before nor had their sees been represented. They were mostly 'backwoodsmen', 10 from trans-padane northern Italy and 8 from the southernmost provinces of Sicily, Lucania and Bruttium. Only 32 of the 71 bishops at the 499 synod also attended and subscribed to the trial synod and 18 of those were inveterate synod attenders, being present at 499, and both 502 synods as well as 495. Most of the trial synod bishops stayed on to attend the victory synod, 80 of them being listed as present at the start. But by the end of the synod, the number was down to 65 because many of those with furthest to go had started for home, the north Italians, the Sicilians and the Umbrians in particular.

While 76 bishops signed the decisions of the trial synod absolving the pope, it is known that there was a group of bishops opposed to absolution. If the *Vita Symmachi*'s figure of 115 bishops attending the trial synod is correct, then 39 bishops failed to sign the proceedings absolving the pope. Some of this group must be accounted for by the unspecified number of bishops who left Rome to avoid the violence. But there was also clearly a hard-core of bishops opposed to absolving the pope. Their leader was undoubtedly the Archbishop of Aquileia, Marcellianus. The leading roles at the synod were taken by the three Italian metropolitans, Laurentius of Milan, Peter of Ravenna and Marcellianus. Although both Laurentius and Peter had at one time withdrawn from communion with Symmachus,[46] they were convinced by the arguments in favour of absolution and put themselves at the head of the growing group which believed that the synod was not competent to judge the pope, a view endorsed by Bishop Avitus of Vienne in a letter to the pro-Symmachan senators Faustus and Symmachus.[47] Marcellianus, however, refused to agree to the absolution and petitioned the king to reverse it. The opposition of so senior a churchman was a considerable embarrassment to the synod and Laurentius of Milan was sent to try to persuade Marcellianus to acquiesce in the majority decision in the interests of church unity.[48] Marcellianus refused, and when he died shortly afterwards, there was a flurry of electoral activity to secure a pro-Symmachan archbishop for Aquileia, who eventually emerged in the person of the confusingly named Marcellinus.

There are some hints as to the composition of the anti-Symmachan group amongst the bishops and interestingly these hints come from the provinces closest to Rome. Whereas 18 Campanian bishops had attended the 499 reconciliation synod only 11 signed the pope's absolution and only 6 of those 11 had attended the 499 synod. There were 13 Tuscan bishops who attended the 499 synod and 13 signed the absolution, but only 7 of those 13 were among the 499 13. It may be that the bishops who did not attend felt embarrassed at being called upon to judge the pope and wanted to stay out of it. But one of the conspicuous Campanian absentees from both the trial and victory synods of 502 who had attended the 499 synod was Bishop Misenus of Cumae, who died only in 511[49] and was therefore presumably available for the trial. The falling away of support for Symmachus among the bishops closest to Rome since 499, manifested either in absence from, or failure to sign the proceedings of, the 502 trial synod, may perhaps be attributed to disenchantment with the pope's policies, particularly the hard line on the East. The allegiance of two of the pro-Symmachan bishops is certainly determinable. The only bishops to attend the 487, 499, trial and victory synods but not the 495 absolution of Misenus were Bishops Maximus of Blera and Cresconius of Tuder. Further, Cresconius was one of the papal envoys to Constantinople in 498 who rejected the emperor's proposed compromise. Both Maximus and Cresconius spoke fervently in support of Symmachus's attack on lay interference in church affairs at the 502 victory synod. Taken together, the evidence suggests that these two bishops at least were hard-line anti-Easterners and also hard-line pro-Symmachans. But it is likely that the majority of the bishops, especially those from distant provinces who did not know the personalities of the protagonists, will have been more concerned with the abstract principle of whether or not the pope should be judged and in the last resort it was this group which carried the day in favour of absolution. But there remains a large question mark over the stance of the suburbicarian bishops from the provinces closest to Rome.

The Issues behind the Schism

Finally, we must look at the issues behind the schism. First of all, deep-rooted differences about the Anastasian policy of *détente* must have figured both in the 498 split and in the later schism of 502–6. There is no explicit mention of doctrinal differences underlying the schism either in the *Vita Symmachi* or the 'Laurentian Fragment'. But the *Vita Anastasii*, written by the victorious Symmachan faction, was obviously hostile to him, claiming unjustifiably that Anastasius II 'wished to restore Acacius'. Symmachus's policy towards Constantinople revived the Gelasian hard-line and caused the Emperor Anastasius to lament the pope's *duritia*. On the other hand, there is the testimony of the sources on the undoubted leader of the Laurentians – Festus. The *Vita Symmachi* names him as the Laurentian leader and the instigator of the troubles and Theodoric's actions recognized this when he instructed Festus to hand back the Roman churches to Symmachus. It was to one of Festus's estates that Laurentius retired to die after his bid for power had failed.

The election of 498 and the doctrinal-diplomatic situation are explicitly linked in the almost contemporary account of Theodore the Lector.[50]

A certain Festus, one of the Roman senate, was sent on political business to the emperor Anastasius and having reached the royal city, he called for the remembrance of Peter chief of the apostles and Paul to be observed with much honour and reverence. This had been done previously save that after Festus's request it was increased by so much more of the same kind of joyous festivity. Macedonius [the patriarch] wished to send communications to Anastasius bishop of Rome by the same man Festus. But he was prevented from doing so by the emperor. Festus, it is said, secretly suggested to the emperor that he prevail on the bishop of Rome to subscribe to the *Henotikon* of Zeno. But having come to Rome, he found that Bishop Anastasius had died. And so he took the trouble himself to subscribe what was required on account of the schism. And having corrupted many men with money, he called on a certain Roman whose name was Laurentius to be elected bishop contrary to custom.

This account makes it clear that Festus came to a private arrangement with the emperor to persuade the pope to accept the *Henotikon* and, faced with the fact of the pope's death, was forced to seek the election of a new pope who would do what Festus had promised the emperor. That man was the archpriest Laurentius.

It is worth noting that part of the last sentence of a life of Anastasius II prefaces the Laurentian account of the schism[51] and since the Symmachan account of Anastasius II is hostile, it is reasonable to assume that the Laurentian version is sympathetic and that the Laurentian party was committed to a similar policy of *détente*. The incomplete sentence says that the pope sent letters to the emperor via

Bishops Cresconius and Germanus which were such that anyone reading them with fear of God in his heart would be convinced that the schism between the churches was wicked and useless.

Nevertheless, Anastasius's envoys clearly had no authority to accept the *Henotikon* and that is why their part of the joint embassy failed. Pope Anastasius, although desirous of ending the schism, was not prepared to countenance a complete abandonment of Rome's position. He endorsed the dualist theory of government when he wrote to the emperor: 'just as the outstanding appellation of your piety glitters throughout all the races of the world, so too in my humble office the see of St Peter holds the *principatus* in the universal church assigned to it by God.'[52] But he was prepared to propose a simple formula to end the schism. Constantinople would condemn Acacius but Rome would recognize the validity of his sacraments. It may be that the patriarch Macedonius was prepared to accept this because the emperor pointedly refused to allow him to communicate with the pope. But acceptance of the *Henotikon* was another matter altogether. Even without the *Henotikon* question, the anti-Eastern faction in the church already believed that the papacy had gone too far along the road to *détente*, and it was driven into revolt when Anastasius received into communion a deacon of Thessalonica, a church that had been thundered against by Gelasius in his most hawkish period.[53]

At the election which followed the death of Anastasius II, Symmachus had a majority among the clergy. He was awarded the papal throne on this basis by Theodoric and also on the grounds that he had been ordained first. We known that Symmachus was chosen in the Lateran basilica and that this was therefore the proper election, conducted where papal elections were customarily conducted. The beaten faction in the election promptly retired to another church and declared their own man elected. The fact that Festus masterminded the counter-election of Laurentius, given his known policies, must mean that Laurentius was to be the mouthpiece of those policies, and that Symmachus, as his own policy towards the East demonstrates, was their opponent. What is curious is that the majority of 58 over 18 in the 495 priesthood for a soft line towards the East had been transformed by 498 into a majority for a hard-line candidate. Several things probably account for this. If, as seems likely from the figures, there was a minority group of hawks and a minority group of doves on the Acacian schism with a majority moderate centre favouring gradual progress towards reunion, many of the moderates must have been seriously alarmed at Festus's commitment to the *Henotikon*, which must have been public knowledge for Theodore the Lector to have learned about it. Many moderate clerics will have felt that acceptance of the *Henotikon* by the pope was too high a price to pay for *détente*. There must have been considerable resentment, too, at the blatant electioneering, distribution of gold and general interference by Festus, while the fact that Anastasius had admitted Photinus to communion without consulting the clergy, something Gelasius had scrupulously done when absolving Bishop Misenus, will also have alarmed more than just the minority of hard-liners.

It seems probable, therefore, that the lines of division over the Eastern question became blurred in 498 because of the immediate events. The background to the election is revealed in more detail by the election legislation promulgated by the 499 synod. It was rare in the ancient world for laws to be drawn up in the abstract. They are generally a response to existing problems and the 499 statute gives some insight into what the particular problems of 498 were.[54] The provisions of the statute were that if any priest or deacon or cleric during the lifetime of the pope and without his knowledge commits himself to support a candidate in a future election or attends a private meeting for the purpose of holding consultations and taking resolutions or promises his vote, he shall be deposed or excommunicated. The same penalty applies to anyone canvassing for the succession during the lifetime of the pope. Should the pope die suddenly and be unable to make provisions for his successor, then, if the collected clergy elect one unanimously, he shall be consecrated. If, as often happens, opinions are divided, the majority vote prevails. Every elector who, having bound himself by a promise, does not vote freely, is to be deposed. Anyone who reports any violation of this ordinance, even if he participated in the offence, shall not only remain unpunished but shall even be rewarded.

There are several indications that this statute reflects exactly what occurred in 498. The reference to the sudden death of the pope echoes the circumstances of Anastasius's death – 'struck dead by divine wrath'. The confirmation of the clergy's majority decision, pointedly omitting the senate, reflects the judgment of Theodoric which had given the papacy to Symmachus. The references to canvassing and caballing during the illness of the pope are supported by Theodore the Lector's references to Festus corrupting men with money and fixing the election for Laurentius. If these provisions have bases in fact, then the likelihood is that the rest does too.

The picture which emerges is that the hard-liners withdraw from communion with the pope over the recognition of Photinus. The pope is taken suddenly ill and there is a flurry of electoral activity. Festus, arriving back from Constantinople when the pope is either dying or already dead, whips up support for a candidate pledged to continuing the Anastasian policy of *détente*. Anastasius dies without naming a successor and at the election which follows the majority of the clergy vote for Symmachus while the majority of the senate support Laurentius.

What is interesting is that the statute implies that it was natural and customary for the pope to designate his successor. Anastasius had not been able to do this and this as much as anything else had caused problems. Also the clause prohibiting discussions about the pope's successor during his lifetime but without his knowledge implies that properly authorized discussions of the succession were permissible. These provisions throw new light on the elections of 483, 492 and 496 as well as that of 498. The acceptance of a tradition that the pope nominated his successor explains how it was that Pope Simplicius could hand over this right to the praetorian prefect Basilius in the interests of Roman solidarity. The absence of dissension either in 492 or 496 suggests that both Gelasius I and Anastasius II were nominated by their predecessors. This would make sense, given the direction of papal policy towards the East. Gelasius was the architect of Felix III's hard line and therefore the obvious successor. Anastasius played a prominent part in the rehabilitation of Misenus of Cumae and was an equally obvious successor, given the change in the climate of clerical opinion which this indicates. The line is broken by Anastasius II's failure to nominate. But it is a right which Symmachus stressed he wished to preserve and as we shall see in due course exercised. It is perhaps worth noting in this context that a 465 conciliar decree of Pope Hilarus had forbidden incumbent bishops to nominate their successors. But it is likely that this was aimed at formal designation and that the pope made an informal recommendation of the favoured cleric's candidature which, however, carried the force of an endorsement.

What occurred after Symmachus's successful installation as pope suggests that between 499 and 502 the blurred lines of division became clarified, so that by 502 there was a much more even split in the clergy between Symmachans and Laurentians. If his clerical majority in 498 indicates that the centre rallied to Symmachus, then it must during the next four years have become progressively disenchanted, so that a large section defected to join the Laurentians. One reason must have been the resumption of the Gelasian hard line towards the East, characterized by the adoption of the Roman rather than the Greek date for Easter, the act which constituted the initial charge against him and which had considerable symbolic significance. Beyond this, the fact that there was little or no contact between pope and emperor will also have alienated the moderates still committed to cautious *détente*. Apart from this, Symmachus's flight from Ariminum and his consequent failure to appear before the king to answer the charges against him put him in a very bad light and convinced many of his guilt. It has already been noted that a deep rift was developing between senior and junior clergy and this may well have stemmed not just from annoyance that the archpriest had been beaten but from dissatisfaction with Symmachus's character and style of government, an issue which also involves the lay supporters of both sides.

Despite the importance of the Eastern question, one cannot escape the implication of class conflict suggested by the straight split between the senatorial aristocracy, which supported Laurentius and the *plebs* who backed Symmachus. The uniformity of their support tends to suggest a difference of attitude to the personalities involved. Symmachus's origins and character may help to explain his position. Non-Roman and almost certainly non-noble, Symmachus was a Sardinian, born in that most benighted of Mediterranean islands, still infested with pagans as late as Gregory the Great's reign. Indeed, Symmachus himself was a pagan in early life, being converted to Catholicism in Rome and embracing it with all the crusading ardour of the true convert. He is unlikely to have been lower class; his father Fortunatus was probably a small-time landowner. But he earned the affection of the lower classes with an active policy of poor relief and donations. He was also probably quite young, as suggested by the phenomenal sixteen-year length of his reign and the suggestion that he had debauched a nun or, if the 'Laurentian Fragment' is to be believed, a crowd of women. Thus his youth and his vigour, the romantic story of his conversion from paganism, his resolute defence of orthodoxy against the scheming Greeks, his generous policies towards the poor and his opposition to aristocratic interference would all endear him to the people, just as surely as they would alienate their betters. The aristocracy would be alienated likewise by his character, fiery, precipitate, uncouth and vindictive. He must have been regarded as a stubborn upstart, who pursued policies hostile to their interests.

Aristocratic opposition is likely to have centred on Symmachus's refusal to seek a *rapprochement* with the East and his commitment to resisting aristocratic interference in papal affairs. The debate on this subject, focused on Basilius's 483 edict, that was held at the 502 victory synod[55] reveals in the bishops a similar split between the extreme hard-liners and the moderate centre to that which has been suggested for the clergy. Bishops Cresconius of Tuder, Maximus of Blera and Stephanus of Venusia all spoke against the edict, denouncing it on the grounds that it was uncanonical for laymen to interfere in internal church affairs. But the metropolitans and moderate leaders from the trial synod, Laurentius of Milan and Peter of Ravenna, joined now by Bishop Eulalius of Syracuse, preferred to attack it on the grounds that the pope had not been present and had not signed the document. Both sides concurred in the repeal of the edict but the difference in emphasis is interesting. It shows that the moderates were not prepared to rule out a role for the laity but that the extremists were. The new decree on alienation of church property forbade the laity to make any decisions respecting church property, since the care of such things was entrusted by God to the priesthood. This ordinance suggests that Symmachus may well have stood on a platform which was as much opposed to aristocratic interference as to *détente*.

However, it should be noted also that, ecclesiastical arguments aside, the schism provided the people and the aristocracy with just another excuse to fight. Its issues masked the underlying and perennial discontents of the poor, which periodically spilled over into violence against the rich. The ill-feeling between the classes survived the ending of the papal schism and flared up again in 509 in the form of circus faction riots. The correspondence of King Theodoric on the subject makes clear the class basis of these riots.[56] The Greens, who were the popular party, had so few senatorial supporters that the king was forced to designate two, the patrician brothers Albinus and Avienus, sons of Basilius the one-time patron of the faction. Their opponents are not named, but on the analogy of Constantinople were presumably the Blues, traditionally the aristocratic faction, consisting of those same noble households whose servants and hangers-on had held Rome in thrall to terror at the height of the Symmachan schism. Theodoric accused the senators of trampling on the laws with their bands of armed slaves and adjured them to keep the peace. Characteristically Theodoric was adopting an absolutely impartial position and acting in the interests of law and order. He announced that he would lend support to neither side, and would punish the guilty slaves; he also appointed two patrons for the Greens to even up the balance. Coincidentally, Albinus and Avienus were the brothers of Theodore and Importunus, prominent patrons of the Blues. This suggests a psychological masterstroke by Theodoric in offsetting factional ties against family. It is clear then that the *plebs*, as the patron-less Greens, and the senatorial households, as the Blues, continued their rivalry, even when an ecclesiastical excuse for it was gone. This suggests that the Symmachan schism provided a convenient and long-running outlet for more deep-rooted social tensions.

In sum, then, the causes of the original schism in 498 related to the immediate circumstances at the time of Anastasius II's untimely death, a heady electoral brew of personalities, principles and politics.

It seems to have been revived and prolonged in 501–2 for three more concrete reasons: the policies of Symmachus, both towards the East and the aristocracy, the power struggle within the church between the old Establishment and the 'Young Turks' and the class conflict between the upper and lower classes which was channelled at this time into the papal schism.

Chapter 7

The Rapprochement *with the East*

The death of Pope Symmachus in July 514 was a crucial test for the election regulations introduced in 499 and of the mood of the electorate after nearly sixteen controversial years of Symmachan rule. But Symmachus had done his work well. His thorough overhaul of both priesthood and diaconate meant that a Symmachan old guard was firmly in control, and after a vacancy of seven days the deacon Hormisdas was elected pope. It is likely that Hormisdas had been nominated by Symmachus, a procedure which was implicit in the electoral regulations. He had been one of Symmachus's earliest diaconal appointments and had long been regarded as heir apparent.[1] He is likely to have been more acceptable socially and personally than his predecessor both to the clergy and to the aristocracy. Ennodius describes him as 'pious, well-born and rich'[2] and unlike Symmachus, he was by nature a cautious and careful man. He was to draw up such detailed instructions for his envoys to the East, for instance, that every conceivable eventuality was covered and catered for. His constant demands for news from his envoys indeed led them to chide him for over-anxiety. He sensibly took great care to remain on good terms with King Theodoric, consulting him at every stage of his Eastern negotiations, and achieving such a high level of cordiality with the king that he received the only recorded gift of Theodoric to the Roman church, two large silver candelabra.

The first thing he did was to extinguish the last remaining embers of the Symmachan schism. His biography in the *Liber Pontificalis* recalls that 'he set the clergy in order'[3] and his epitaph listed among his achievements that 'he healed the body of the fatherland, lacerated by schism, restoring to their proper place the members wrenched therefrom'.[4] The schism had lingered on largely out of personal hatred towards Symmachus, something with which Hormisdas was apparently not tainted. Not only was he to earn the reputation of the great reconciler within the Roman church but he was also to gain similar kudos with regard to the East.

His biography is dominated by his attempts to resolve the Acacian schism. His surviving correspondence is devoted almost exclusively to this. There was bound to be some new tentative in this direction if only because there was a new man on the throne of St Peter. Relations between Symmachus and the emperor Anastasius had been virtually non-existent, due almost certainly to Anastasius's support for the anti-pope Laurentius. In 512 Symmachus had written: 'Concerning recent events in the church of Constantinople, I can only sigh and keep silent'[5] When orthodox Eastern bishops wrote to him, seeking guidance and advice about what they should do when threatened with persecution for refusing to communicate with the successor of Acacius, Symmachus replied that they should stand firm and prepare themselves for martyrdom, which one suspects is not exactly the response for which they had been hoping.[6]

Hormisdas did not announce his accession to the emperor, but early in 515 came a letter from Anastasius to Hormisdas, lamenting the 'hardness' of his predecessor which had made communication between them impossible but saying that the good reports he had received of Hormisdas had encouraged him to reopen communications.[7] Hormisdas replied, expressing his desire for the goodwill of the emperor but dutifully defending the memory of his predecessor.[8]

But there was more to this reopening of communications than merely a change of pope. Anastasius was facing a massive crisis in the East. His failure to implement a compromise policy based on the *Henotikon* had pushed Anastasius I more and more towards the Monophysites. In consequence the orthodox forces had rallied, opposition to the government had grown and in 514 this opposition burst into open revolt, under the leadership of Count Vitalian, in the Balkans, stronghold of orthodoxy. His armies defeated in battle, the emperor had retained his throne only by agreeing to call a council of the church to resolve the religious controversy.

So Hormisdas suddenly found himself in the driving seat. As a veteran of the Symmachan regime, he was of course committed to Symmachus's hard-line stand. The purge of the clergy meant that there was now majority clerical support for the policy and the old *Henotikon* party in the aristocracy had also vanished, broken by the Symmachan victory and reduced to insignificance by the deaths of its leaders, notably Festus, who by 523 had been succeeded as senior member of the senate by Symmachus, one of the pro-Symmachan senators of the papal schism. There was, then, a united hard-line front in Rome when letters arrived in 515 inviting Hormisdas to attend a council of the church to resolve the schism.[9] Having the example of the incautious Pope Anastasius II before him, Hormisdas moved with extreme care. He first consulted King Theodoric and secured his permission to negotiate and then called a synod of bishops to Rome and took their opinions.[10] Only when he had done all this did he despatch an embassy to the East. It was an embassy chosen with the utmost care, bearing in mind the unhappy precedent of Bishops Misenus and Vitalis. It bore the firm imprint of the Symmachan old guard. It was headed by his old friend and trusted colleague Ennodius, who since 513 had been bishop of Ticinum, and it included Bishop Fortunatus of Catana, the Roman priest Venantius (probably the priest of St Marcellus, ranked 65 in 499 and 29 in 502), deacon Vitalis (another Symmachan creation) and notary Hilarus. They carried with them the *Indiculus*,[11] a comprehensive set of instructions on where to stay, who to see, what to say and above all what not to do, and the *libellus*,[12] a set of conditions for reunion, which the emperor and the Eastern bishops were expected to sign as a token of their acceptance. They included an endorsement of the Chalcedonian settlement, the condemnation of Acacius and the six great heresiarchs and the reservation to Rome of the retrial of all exiled Catholic bishops, the latter demand being the latest round in the long-drawn-out battle to get Constantinople to accept Rome's jurisdictional primacy. But these proposals were completely unacceptable to the emperor and negotiations broke down. Anastasius wrote to Hormisdas to say that he had never done anything to infringe the validity of Chalcedon and that the heresiarchs Eutyches and Nestorius had already been condemned, but that any further condemnations would provoke bloodshed and that would be displeasing to God. But he left the way open to further negotiations by saying that he would write again and send his own envoys to Rome to negotiate with the pope.[13]

Anastasius's failure to meet the conditions to which he had so recently agreed led the Balkan insurgents to renew their revolt in 516. But this time they were defeated. The emperor, believing that Rome's refusal to compromise had stemmed from his political weakness, felt that now he had disposed of the threat of rebellion, he could negotiate from strength. He decided to enlist the help of the senate. Sending the promised envoys, Count Theopompus, *Comes Domesticorum*, and Count Severianus, *Comes Sacri Consistorii*, to Rome, he entrusted them not only with a letter to the pope,[14] but also a letter to the senate, which he referred to grandly as 'his senate'.[15] He called upon them to use their influence with King Theodoric and with the pope to bring about religious reunion. But his ploy failed, the senate had fallen into line with the church, and the pope wrote back to the emperor,[16] reconfirming his already stated position on reunion and telling him in so many words that there was no point in trying to stir up the senate.

But Hormisdas was prepared to despatch another embassy eastwards. In 517 Bishop Ennodius of Ticinum once again made the long journey to Constantinople, accompanied this time by Bishop Peregrinus of Messana and the subdeacon Pullio.[17] Although they were ostensibly to negotiate with Anastasius, their real mission was to rally and consolidate the ever-growing forces of orthodox opposition, thus increasing the pressure on Anastasius to capitulate. They secretly circulated letters from the pope to the main orthodox centres of opposition, while presenting the same papal terms to Anastasius. The emperor apparently resorted to the same policy of threats and bribes that had worked so effectively with Misenus and Vitalis in 484. But this time the envoys remained firm, and Anastasius broke off negotiations and despatched the envoys back to Rome, writing angrily to the pope on 11 July 517:

> From henceforth we shall suppress in silence our requests, thinking it absurd to show the courtesy of prayers to those who obstinately refuse even to be entreated. We can endure being insulted and thwarted but we cannot endure being commanded.[18]

Once again there was deadlock.

The impasse was broken by the death, on 8 July 518, of the emperor Anastasius at the age of 88. His successor was the *Comes Excubitorum*, commander of the imperial bodyguard, Justin I. By birth an Illyrian peasant, Justin was by conviction staunchly orthodox as were the two men who now became the most important influences at the imperial court: Justin's nephew and eventual successor, Count Justinian, and the former orthodox rebel leader, Count Vitalian. Chalcedonian mobs, whipped up by the extremist monks, roamed the streets of Constantinople, calling for an end to the government policy of support for Monophysitism. This was in line with the thinking of the new government whose first act was to re-establish Chalcedonian Orthodoxy as the official religion of the Empire. The way was at last clear for a reunion with Rome.

Having announced his accession and professed his orthodoxy in a letter to the pope,[19] Justin next sent an ambassador, Count Gratus, *Comes Sacri Consistorii*, to invite Hormisdas to send an embassy to the East.[20] Once again Hormisdas consulted King Theodoric[21] and it is worth noting that not only the pope but also the Eastern emperor took care to keep the king informed of the progress of negotiations.[22] Then Hormisdas held an informal meeting of senior bishops (*conventus*) to thrash out the negotiation procedure[23] and once again a detailed *Indiculus*[24] and the pope's *libellus* of reunion terms were handed to the envoys. This time the papal legates were Bishops Germanus of Capua and John (see unknown), the priest Blandus, the deacons Felix and Dioscorus, the subdeacon Pullio and the notary Peter. The unofficial leader of the group was undoubtedly Dioscorus, the brilliant Alexandrian deacon who had successfully persuaded Theodoric to end the schism in 506 and now in 519 was chosen to deploy his spell-binding oratory again in the cause of reunification. For he was the envoy chosen to expound Rome's position on the faith to the assembled aristocracy and notables of Constantinople in the presence of the emperor. His special position in the embassy is emphasized by the fact that apart from the official reports of the envoys sent back to Hormisdas and signed by them all, Dioscorus also sent his own private assessments of the situation back to the pope.

This time, however, there was no doubt about the outcome of the mission. After a triumphal progress across the Balkans, the papal envoys were met ten miles from the imperial capital by Count Justinian at the head of a high-powered reception committee of aristocrats and orthodox monkish leaders. Amidst cheering and celebration, they were escorted into the city on 25 March 519. A council was held in the presence of the emperor, Dioscorus expounded the papal view of the evils of Acacius and his followers and the entire assembly rose to its feet, crying: 'Damnation to Acacius here and in eternity'.[25] The rest was a matter of implementing the reunion. The emperor ordered that all the bishops should sign the pope's *libellus* as a token that they accepted the condemnation of Acacius, and the patriarch John of Constantinople was among the first to sign on 28 March 519. Acacius, his four successors, and the emperors Zeno and Anastasius were all condemned as heretics. The condemnation of the emperors had never been demanded by the papacy and they must have been extremely surprised to learn about it. But the new regime was happy to see the old one discredited and although the condemnation of the emperors was unique, the new dynasty, having made its point, rapidly forgot about it. There was no further mention of this particular condemnation in any of the correspondence on the subject, and imperial authority seems not to have been compromised in the slightest by it.

The reunion was an undreamed of triumph. Constantinople had accepted Rome's terms fully and had (in condemning the emperors) conceded even more than Rome had dared to demand, something not even the harshest papal critics of Zeno and Anastasius had sought. But the extent of the triumph and the restoration of unity between the churches of East and West should not blind us to the reality behind it. It was not any innate strength in Rome's position which had brought it about. The moving forces in the reunion were the emperor, his nephew and Count Vitalian. The political situation in the East had changed, the old dynasty had been replaced and Justin I, who saw himself as a new Marcian, and the other new powers at court were men who held the same views on the heresy as Rome and did not need to be convinced.

The ending of the schism did not mean that Rome gained any more power in the Eastern church than she had previously had. For all the fêting of the papal envoys, there was no acceptance of the principle of referring Eastern bishops to Rome for trial. The patriarch John of Constantinople wrote to the pope rejoicing in the reunion, but even while he was signing the *libellus*, he was adding mention of his delight that Rome and Constantinople were now one, i.e. equal in honour. In other words he was throwing in Rome's face the controversial twenty-eighth canon of Chalcedon that the papacy had never accepted.[26] Justin and Justinian simply saw themselves as reverting to the situation before the Acacian schism and that implied no enhancement of Rome's powers or position.

But then Rome had not entered the schism to enhance her powers with regard to the Eastern church or to the emperor. If she could make capital out of it in her continuing struggle to subject Constantinople to her primacy, all well and good, but the unity of the Christian world behind the Chalcedonian creed was the main objective and the routing of the Acacian heresy was part and parcel of Rome's self-appointed duty of guarding orthodoxy. Although the Acacian schism took all the headlines, there was another struggle which is rarely mentioned, which was going on alongside it – the struggle to destroy the Manichaean heresy. Gelasius's efforts in that direction have already been mentioned. But Symmachus also discovered a nest of Manichaeans in Rome and exiled them, burning their books before the doors of the Lateran basilica.[27] His successor Hormisdas discovered Manichaeans in Rome and treated them in exactly the same way.[28] The attack on Acacius and the resistance to imperial religious policy under Zeno and Anastasius was an attack on heresy and innovation and not a bid to elevate papal Rome.

The events which followed the reunion leave no room for doubt about Rome's powerlessness in the East. The papal legates stayed on for one year and three months to supervise the implementation of the reunion, finally leaving for Rome in July 520, but their stay was one of unrelieved frustration and disappointment. Hormisdas wanted Dioscorus made patriarch of Alexandria.[29] This was refused. He bombarded all the leading figures at court, including the emperor and empress, with letters seeking the immediate restoration of three exiled orthodox bishops,[30] but Justin told him that local conditions did not permit it.[31]

Hormisdas also greatly underestimated the difficulty the imperial government would have in implementing the sweeping terms of the reunion settlement. The extent of local resistance to it is symbolized in the Thessalonica incident of 519. Bishop John, one of the papal legates, was sent to Thessalonica to get the signature of Bishop Dorotheus to the *libellus*. Dorotheus, who was opposed to the terms, encouraged the people to believe that religious persecution was imminent by staging a mass baptism several days before the legate's arrival. When John did arrive, Dorotheus delayed signing and engaged in several days of negotiation as the mood of the mob grew more and more ugly. Eventually a riot broke out, the mob broke into the house where the legate was staying, murdered his host John, an orthodox *religiosus*, and two of the legate's servants, and badly injured Bishop John, who managed to flee to a nearby church for sanctuary, where he remained until extricated by the police.[32] Hormisdas, outraged by this episode, demanded Dorotheus's immediate deposition and despatch to Rome for trial.[33] The emperor refused and instead summoned Dorotheus to Constantinople, intending to deal with him himself.[34] Dorotheus set out for the capital, armed with a sum of money caustically described as 'capable of blinding not only men but angels'.[35] This sum acquired him sufficiently powerful protectors at court that he was soon back in Thessalonica, absolved and reinstated.[36] In August 520 Dorotheus cheekily wrote to the pope saying that he had in fact saved Bishop John's life at the risk of his own. He professed his own Orthodoxy and sought permission to re-enter communion with the church of Rome.[37] Making the best of a bad job, the pope sent back a chilly reply, saying he would re-admit him once he signed the *libellus*.[38]

It was incidents like this one which convinced the imperial government that there must be a softening of the reunion terms in order to make them acceptable in the East. On 9 September 520, Justin wrote to Hormisdas saying that persecution had been tried and had failed; therefore they must try conciliation based on concessions. The concessions he suggested involved dropping the demand for the condemnation of those heretics who were particularly venerated in the East. Justin tartly reminded Hormisdas that Pope Anastasius II had only sought the condemnation of Acacius.[39]

The emperor's letter was backed up by appeals from Justinian[40] and the patriarch Epiphanius of Constantinople[41] urging a policy of moderation and conciliation, Justinian declaring roundly: 'God will demand an account of the safety of all those who may at present be saved by a spirit of moderation.' The pope did not reply and Justinian was forced to write to Hormisdas again requesting his reply to the government proposal.[42] When Hormisdas finally deigned to reply on 25 March 521, he informed the emperor that the reconciliation terms could not be modified and must be enforced if need be by persecution. Any injuries inflicted on the recalcitrants would be for the good of their souls, said the pope.[43] Faced with such papal intransigence, the government simply went ahead with its policy without Hormisdas's blessing.

If Hormisdas had believed that the re-establishment of unity in 519 meant the end of difficulties with the East, he was being rapidly disabused. For not only was the imperial government backpedalling rapidly on the reunion terms, there was also yet another bid to alter the accepted tenets of the faith. The enforcement of the reunion terms by persecution gave way to a search by the government for an agreed formula that would bring the religious dissidents into the fold and banish the debilitating disunity in the Eastern Empire. The formula they alighted on was Theopaschism, the idea that the Trinity remained the Trinity even after the Incarnation. This idea, promulgated by a group of Scythian monks led by Abbot John Maxentius, was believed to be the way of bridging the gap between the Monophysite and Orthodox positions. It was enthusiastically backed by Count Vitalian, who was related to one of the Scythian monks, and, after some initial hesitation, by Justinian. The emperor referred the monks to the papal legates and asked for their opinion on Theopaschism. After several meetings with them, the legates, prompted by Dioscorus, rejected the theory as contrary to the Chalcedonian creed.[44] Denouncing the legates as Nestorian heretics, the Scythians set out for Rome to convince the pope of the validity of their formula, and Justinian sent Hormisdas an enthusiastic letter, urging him to endorse the theory.[45]

The monks arrived in Rome full of sound and fury, denouncing all opponents of Theopaschism as Nestorian heretics. Their bulldozing tactics were hardly calculated to endear them to the cautious Hormisdas. Although at a general meeting of clergy and senate, he expressed sympathy for their ideas,[46] he delayed making a definitive pronouncement until he had explored the subject thoroughly. He sought the advice of Dioscorus in Constantinople and Dioscorus wrote back fiercely denouncing the Scythians and saying that their doctrine, having previously been preached by the emperor Anastasius, was blatantly Monophysite.[47] This advice made Hormisdas even more cautious and he was further alienated by the fact that the Scythians, having failed to make the desired headway at the papal court, turned to the senate and acquired influential friends among the pro-Eastern group re-emerging after the reconciliation.

Theopaschism was endorsed both by Dionysius Exiguus and Boethius;[48] and Faustus wrote to the priest Trifolius, seeking guidance on the subject, though he received the reply that Theopaschism was clearly heretical.[49]

The return of the envoys from Constantinople in the summer of 520 set the seal on Hormisdas's hardening opposition both to the doctrine and to the monks. It is clear from the bitterness with which John Maxentius subsequently attacked him that Dioscorus's influence was decisive in clinching papal opposition. On 13 August 520 in response to an enquiry from the African bishop Possessor, Hormisdas wrote a letter in which he denounced the Scythians as 'despisers of ancient authorities; seekers after novelty'. He accused them of stirring up violence and sedition in Rome and holding unauthorized public meetings in which they posted up placards on the statues of the emperors and harangued the people, denouncing their opponents as Nestorians.[50] Possessor made the contents of the pope's letter public and this provoked a furious response from Abbot John Maxentius.

In a vitriolic *Responsio adversus epistolam Hormisdae*,[51] John first attacked the authenticity of the letter, saying that it could not possibly have come from the pope since it was both ignorant and heretical. It paid no attention to the arguments in the case and it supported the position of the legate Dioscorus, who was clearly a Nestorian. John went on to refute the charges against the Scythians point by point, denouncing the delays and frustrations they had been subjected to in Rome, saying that the pope had repeatedly promised both publicly and privately at meetings of the senate and the church to allow a public debate between them and their opponent Dioscorus. But when this promise had been ignored, they had been forced to hold a public meeting to put their case and this had been broken up by the church's bully boys, who had provoked the violence of which Hormisdas complained. Denying all charges of misconduct, John ended with a defence and definition of the Theopaschite formula.

This attack was the last straw. The Scythians left Rome and Hormisdas wrote to the emperor on 26 March 521, rejecting Theopaschism as being against the Chalcedonian settlement.[52] Hormisdas's rejection made little impression on Justinian, who continued to adhere to it, promulgated it in two successive edicts and appointed John Maxentius as bishop of Tomi. He even managed to secure the assent to his edict of popes John II and Agapitus.

So, after the high watermark of the reunion, Hormisdas's last years were effectively spent in renegotiating the terms of the reunion. Rome had gained little from it except an official end to the wounding schism between the churches of East and West. But that fact alone was to have profound repercussions both on the papacy in particular and Italy in general. Whatever the frustrations of his later years, however, the place of Hormisdas in history was secure. When he died in August 523, his epitaph, which was composed by his son Silverius, proclaimed him 'the great peacemaker', who had healed the schism within his own church and ended the long division with the East.

Hormisdas's death occasioned a vacancy of only six days before the election of Pope John I. The election passed off without difficulty but the choice of the new pope is indicative of the mood of the times, considerably changed by the reunion of the churches. It is virtually certain that the new pope was that same deacon John who had been reconciled to Pope Symmachus in 506 after initially supporting his rival. A senior deacon, a veteran and survivor of those troubled times, he was elderly and in poor health. But he was a well-known figure in the Roman church. He was regarded as an expert in liturgical matters and as such was consulted by Count Senarius, *Comes Patrimonii* to Theodoric. [53] But, more important, he was an intimate of Boethius and seems to have been the ecclesiastical father figure of the pro-Eastern group in the aristocracy. Boethius, who called him his 'saintly master and venerable father', dedicated three of his five theological tractates to him. He submitted his writings to John for correction and indicated himself fully prepared to accept such correction:

> I submit this little essay for your first judgment and
> consideration. If you pronounce it to be sound, I beg you to
> place it among the other writings of mine that you possess;
> but if there is anything to be struck out or added or changed
> in any way, I would ask you to let me have your suggestions,
> in order that I may enter them in my copies just as they leave
> your hands. [54]

This close friendship dated at least as far back as 512 when Symmachus, Boethius and John all attended a meeting of clerics and nobles called by Pope Symmachus to reply to the letter of the Eastern orthodox bishops asking for guidance about the Acacian schism. John and Boethius subsequently communicated about the discussions at that meeting and it prompted Boethius to write his tractate denouncing Eutychianism and Nestorianism. [55] As pope, John was to consult Dionysius Exiguus and accept the Greek computation of Easter, the pro-Laurentian position on a highly contentious issue. [56]

What the election of John reveals is a profound reorientation of the Roman clergy. Some historians have seen in the reunion of Rome and Constantinople an implicit alliance against King Theodoric. But there is no evidence for this. Hormisdas was careful to get Theodoric's approval at every stage of the negotiations and the Eastern emperor kept the king thoroughly informed on their progress. Theodoric remained on excellent terms with Hormisdas throughout his reign. He seems to have welcomed the reunion. There is certainly no evidence that he did not. What he had perhaps not fully realized, however, was the extent to which the existence of the Acacian schism buttressed his own position in Italy. Despite his admirable rule, his maintenance of law and order, religious toleration and the best in the Roman traditions, he was by many in the aristocracy and the church only tolerated, never accepted. The natural thing for the aristocracy and the church was to look to the East which shared their faith and their birthright. The perverse religious policies of successive Eastern emperors had strained that sympathy: the religious reunion had removed that strain. Once again it was natural and normal for senate and church to look to their fellow Romans in the East in friendly cultural, social and religious contacts. There was now no barrier to the re-emergence of a strongly pro-Eastern faction in the aristocracy, more or less dormant since the defeat of Laurentius. It did not contain the same personnel as the old faction headed by Festus, indeed it included former supporters of Pope Symmachus from the days of the papal schism. But the issues then had been complicated by other factors. Now they were clearer, but once more there was the same link – religious unity paving the way for political unity. Like the hard-line clerical faction, the pro-Symmachan senators, faced by a conflict between *Christianitas* and *Romanitas*, had put their *Christianitas* first. Now that the Acacian schism had been ended, that conflict had also been resolved. For the *religiosi*, the Arianism of the king at Ravenna came under the spotlight and appeared more offensive. Significantly, only at the end of his account of Theodoric's reign does the *Anonymus Valesianus* launch a bitter attack on the king's Arianism.[57] The alteration in circumstances meant that the pro- and anti-Eastern factions in the aristocracy, whose stances had been determined by different attitudes to the doctrinal question, were replaced by pro-Gothic and pro-Eastern factions, based on differences of approach to the political situation, the former seeking stronger links with the royal regime in Ravenna and the latter stronger links with the imperial regime in Constantinople.

It is in this climate and against this background that the election and the eventual fate of Pope John must be set. The circumstances which had given birth to the Symmachan old guard were gone. New battle lines were being drawn. But the personnel was substantially the same as under Symmachus. Only twenty-one new priests, a small proportion of the average of seventy-five to eighty deducible from the Symmachan synodical subscriptions, had been ordained since Symmachus's death. No new deacons had been ordained at all under Hormisdas. The continuity of personnel indicates that it was the issues rather than the people which were changing.

That both senate and clergy were regrouping becomes evident from the events of John I's reign. His chief recorded act was a visit to Constantinople undertaken at the behest of King Theodoric. The background to the visit is important, for it shows that events were now moving rapidly. Theodoric's foreign policy had been based on the building up for himself of the overall hegemony of Western barbarian Europe and the maintenance of good relations with the Catholic Roman world. But in the 520s this broke down. There had been a network of marriage alliances, Theodoric's daughters married to King Sigismund of Burgundy and King Eutharic of the Visigoths and his sister Amalafrida married to King Thrasamund of the Vandals, and this, combined with their adherence to Arianism, provided the bonds. Both these bonds, however, were broken. In 506 the Frankish king Clovis renounced Arianism and was converted to Catholicism, the first barbarian ruler of the West to be so. It was the thin end of the wedge. In 516 Sigismund of Burgundy became a Catholic and in 522 put to death his son, Theodoric's grandson, Segeric. In 523 Eutharic of the Visigoths, Theodoric's designated successor, died. In 523 also Thrasamund of the Vandals died and was succeeded by his cousin Hilderic, who ceased the persecution of the Catholics and inaugurated a military alliance with the Eastern Empire. He imprisoned and soon afterwards put to death Amalafrida. The ties of religion and family were crumbling and Catholic Europe was growing stronger as Arian influence shrank. When a persecution of the Arians began in the East in 523, Theodoric must have felt that it was but a short step from that to the inauguration of an attack on the Arians in the West, now principally the embattled Ostrogoths.

Theodoric took two steps. He hastily set about creating an Ostrogothic navy,[58] which had not hitherto existed and for which there had been no necessity when the Mediterranean was surrounded by friendly powers. He also despatched a top-level mission to the East early in 526. That he set great store by it is demonstrated by its membership. Pope John I was at the head, accompanied by five bishops, three of whom are known to have been Ecclesius of Ravenna, Eusebius of Fanum and Sabinus of Canusium, and a group of distinguished senators and ex-consuls, Theodore, Importunus, Agapitus and another Agapitus.[59] Its aim was to halt the persecution of the Arians and the reconsecration of the Arian churches as Catholic churches and to insist on the reconversion of the converted Arians back to Arianism. The pope was received with great honour, just as the legates of Hormisdas had been. John re-crowned Justin, celebrated Easter in Constantinople, sat on a higher throne than the patriarch of Constantinople and received many gifts.[60] The emperor also agreed that all Theodoric's requests should be met save one, namely that he could not force converted Arians to recant their Catholicism. The ambassadors returned to Ravenna, one of them, Agapitus, dying on the way, and Theodoric, not satisfied with the results, put them all under house arrest in Ravenna, where in May 526 John I, worn out by old age and illness, died.[61]

The accounts of this mission both in the *Liber Pontificalis* and the *Anonymus Valesianus* are surrounded with lurid stories in which Theodoric appears increasingly unbalanced. The *Liber Pontificalis*[62] says that Theodoric threatened to put the whole of Italy to the sword if the mission to Justin failed, and did in fact kill many priests and Christians while the pope was away. *Anonymus Valesianus* says Theodoric decreed that the Arians were to take over all the Catholic churches in Italy, but his death prevented this being put into effect.[63]

Such stories seem wildly exaggerated and completely out of character. The *Anonymus Valesianus* talks early on of Theodoric doing nothing against the Catholic religion,[64] and Cassiodorus articulated a policy of religious toleration when he wrote on Theodoric's behalf:[65] 'We cannot give orders about religious belief because no one can be forced to believe against his will.' Significantly, leading Catholics such as Cassiodorus continued to serve Theodoric loyally up to the end.

The death of John I, however, led to considerable furore. He was credited with miracles both during his lifetime[66] and after death.[67] His epitaph proclaimed: 'You have fallen a victim for Christ'.[68] He came to be venerated as a saint and martyr, and together with Boethius and Symmachus, the other victims of Theodoric, was seen as a Catholic champion against Arianism. But the religious connotation is humbug. There is no evidence of Arian–Catholic tension in Italy.[69] The real problem was political. The emergence of a strong pro-Eastern faction in clergy and senate at a time when King Theodoric was coming to see himself and his kingdom at risk compelled the king to take action in defence of the realm. Rightly or wrongly, he saw Boethius and Symmachus and to an extent Pope John as its leaders and acted accordingly. But John was neither injured nor martyred, nor is it likely that he would have been. Already old and ill when he left for the East, he was exhausted by his trip and it was Theodoric's ill-luck that, having placed the envoys under house arrest in Ravenna as a mark of his displeasure, the most eminent of them should have died on his hands, thus giving rise to the inevitable stories of martyrdom.

Chapter 8

The Gothic Reaction

The death of Pope John had been preceded, however, by an even more significant event, which revealed the split emerging in the Roman aristocracy and the growing awareness by the king of the implications for him of the resolution of the Acacian schism. This event was the trial and disgrace of Boethius.[1]

The basic facts in the case are not in dispute.[1] At a meeting of the Royal Council in Verona, the *Referendarius* Cyprian accused the ex-consul Albinus of treasonable communication with the emperor Justin. Albinus, summoned to give answer, denied the charge. Boethius, the *magister officiorum*, came to his defence and said that if Albinus was guilty, then he and the entire senate were guilty – but that the charge was false. So Cyprian extended the charge to include Boethius, produced witnesses and convinced the king. Boethius and Albinus were imprisoned in the baptistery of a church. Later Boethius was exiled to a distant country estate, the *Ager Calventianus* and there put to death. Subsequently Boethius's father-in-law Symmachus, who the king feared might be led by his son-in-law's death into plotting against the throne, was also arrested and put to death.

What is disputed about this sequence of events is the interpretation that should be put on them. What were the charges against Boethius? By whom was he tried? When was he killed? Who were his accusers? What did Boethius mean by 'if Albinus is guilty, we are all guilty'? Different sources gives different versions of the charges. Procopius says that the charge was plotting revolution.[2] The *Anonymus Valesianus*[3] says that the charge was sending letters hostile to Theodoric to the emperor Justin. Boethius himself in the *Consolatio Philosophiae*[4] says that the charges were hoping for the safety of the senate and freedom for Rome, impeding the production of documents in the Albinus case and the practising of magic. What do they amount to? The last two mentioned by Boethius are minor charges.

The magic charge probably derived from Boethius's passion for philosophy and astronomy, and impeding the production of documents was an obvious result of his intervention in the Albinus case. But the other charges, in all the sources, add up to a charge of treason, based on the evidence of letters to the East deemed conspiratorial. Boethius's cryptic answer to this is consistent with such a charge. If Albinus is guilty (i.e. of sending letters to the East), I and the whole senate are guilty (i.e. we are all sending letters to the East). But the charge is false (i.e. but the letters are not treasonable).

What is startling about the case is the eminence of the three men centrally involved. Representatives of the oldest and most distinguished families, all three had held the highest offices of state under the Ostrogoths. The most celebrated of the three is Anicius Manlius Severinus Boethius. He had had a distinguished public career. Consul in 510, he was master of the offices at the time of his arrest. Only the year before, in 522, Boethius's two young sons had been joint consuls, a mark of the particular esteem in which Theodoric held him, and Boethius had delivered to the senate an oration in praise of the king.

But there were reasons to render him suspect once he had, in effect, implicated himself in the treason of Albinus. For Boethius and his father-in-law were the leaders of a widely ramified circle whose cultural and religious interests drew them inexorably towards the East. In particular, they were deeply involved in a plan to create a scholastic tradition in the West on the Greek model.[5] To support this Boethius planned a complete translation with commentaries of the works of Plato and Aristotle. By the time of his death he had already translated and written commentaries on Aristotle's works on logic. His love of philosophy, his fluency in Greek – an increasingly rare attribute in the West – and the large numbers of his translations of Greek works must have constituted in the eyes of a beleaguered king the first point of suspicion. But added to his deep involvement in philosophy was a similarly deep interest in theology. Staunchly Catholic, as his tractate attacking Nestorius and Eutyches demonstrated, he was also an adherent of Theopaschism. Three of his five theological tractates showed support for the formula[6] and the Scythian leader John Maxentius drew on one of them when preparing a collection of documents in support of the doctrine.[7] To the king it must have demonstrated a desire for closer religious links with the East, just as the philosophical programme indicated a desire for closer cultural links. It was but one step to advocating closer political links.

Quintus Aurelius Memmius Symmachus, the senior and most distinguished member of the senate, consul in 485, former prefect of the city of Rome and author of a seven-volume history of Rome, had taken Boethius into his home after the death of his father and brought him up. Boethius had married Symmachus's daughter Rusticiana, named his younger son after him and clearly revered him.[8] Together they conceived and worked out the plan for a cultural revival, based on Greek learning. The family had close links with a cultural enclave centred on the monastery of *Castrum Lucullanum* near Naples, an important centre for the dissemination of theological works and translations from Eastern writers.[9] Abbot Eugippius of *Castrum Lucullanum*, for instance, used the library of Symmachus's daughter Proba to prepare a collection of extracts from the writings of St Augustine.[10]

There was also a close link with Dionysius Exiguus, perhaps the key figure in the translation and popularization of Eastern theological works. Dionysius, himself a Scythian, had supported the Scythian monks in their bid to gain support for Theopaschism, undertaking for John Maxentius the translation of two of the letters of Cyril of Alexandria;[11] while for one of Symmachus's daughters, probably Proba, he had translated the *Vita Sancti Pachomii*.[12] It is clear that there was a group of both laymen and clerics actively working for a theological as well as simply ecclesiastical *rapprochement* with the East. To this group we should probably add the third of the defendants, Caecina Decius Albinus Faustus, patrician, ex-consul and former praetorian prefect, who to facilitate reconciliation with the East had proposed a softening of the official papal attitude to those who had condemned Chalcedon, suggesting a different attitude to those who had merely condemned it in speech from those who had condemned it in writing.[13] When Pope John, friend and mentor of Boethius and patron of Dionysius Exiguus, is added to this group, it represents a powerful and well-defined pro-Eastern group, all of whose activities were designed to eliminate the last remaining differences between Italy and the East. That this constitutes a complete reversal of positions taken up during the Symmachan schism is demonstrated by the fact that Symmachus, Albinus and probably Boethius had been among the handful of senators supporting the pope against the anti-pope and his pro-Eastern followers, who included Dionysius and John. The ending of the Acacian schism had made possible for the senators a wholehearted alliance with the formerly Laurentian pro-Eastern group. Theodoric must have come to see the activities of this group as subversive.

If Boethius, Symmachus and Albinus represent a pro-Eastern faction in the aristocracy, do his accusers represent a pro-Gothic faction? The answer to that seems to be in the affirmative. Boethius in his *Consolatio Philosophiae*[14] lists them as Cyprian, Opilio, Basilius and Gaudentius and paints a damaging picture of them: Opilio and Gaudentius, exiled for numberless frauds, and Basilius, dismissed from the king's service and up to his ears in debt. The *Anonymus Valesianus*[15] says that Cyprian was motivated by *avaritia* in laying the charges and Procopius[16] that the accusers were motivated by envy of the devotion to justice, generosity to the poor and the practice of philosophy of Boethius and Symmachus. At least two of these charges, however, can be connected with treason – love of philosophy (pro-Easternism) and generosity to the poor (subversion of the masses).

But the 'official' view of the accusers is rather different and emerges in the letters of Cassiodorus, who succeeded Boethius as master of the offices. He praises Cyprian and Opilio as 'utterly scrupulous, just and loyal', reveals that they were brothers and grandsons of Opilio, consul in 483, and valued servants of the government.[17] Cyprian, *referendarius* in 523, was promoted *Comes Sacrarum Largitionum* in 524, no doubt as a reward for his loyalty in the Boethius case, and in 527 he became *magister officiorum*, being succeeded in his former post by his brother Opilio, who had been consul in 524 and was employed by the government to announce King Athalaric's accession to Liguria[18] and later as ambassador to Constantinople.[19] Indeed Opilio's role in the attack on Boethius seems to have been forgiven or forgotten by 534 when he received along with other interested nobles a letter on christological doctrine from Pope John II.[20] The other two accusers seem to have been less eminent. Gaudentius was probably the former governor of Flaminia and Picenum Annonarium and Basilius's position is not known, but he was a relative by marriage of Opilio.[21] In addition to all this Cyprian and his family were, significantly, able to read Gothic.[22] Given all this evidence, the attack on Boethius, Symmachus and Albinus begins to look like the attack of one aristocratic family group from the pro-Gothic faction on another aristocratic family group from the pro-Eastern faction.

Most revealing of all, perhaps, is the fact that it is Romans rather than Goths who attack Boethius, even though Boethius records that while in office he pursued a strenuous campaign against the illegalities perpetrated by leading Goths Cunigast and Triguilla.[23] But no Goths are known to have been involved in the Boethius case. It demonstrates not only that the aristocracy was breaking up into factions but that the government was also. The hierarchy which had hitherto been able to accommodate pro-Goths like Cassiodorus and Cyprian as well as pro-Easterners like Boethius and Albinus was polarizing into rival groups, just as the Roman church later did.

The sources are apparently incompatible on the question of Boethius's trial, but can in fact be reconciled upon a detailed reading. Boethius speaks bitterly of the fact that his accusers came from the ranks of the senate and that the senate not only failed to come to his aid but also passed decrees concerning him.[24] The *Anonymus Valesianus* records that the king summoned Eusebius, prefect of the city, to Ticinum and there pronounced sentence on Boethius without giving him a hearing.[25] But these were simply two different stages of the proceedings. Boethius was most probably tried by a judicial sub-committee of the senate, the *iudicium quinquevirale*, consisting of the city prefect and five senators drawn by lot.[26] He was found guilty and the prefect took the verdict to the king at Ticinum, who pronounced the sentence without hearing anything further from Boethius. What became of Albinus is not known. If he had been put to death, he would surely have been venerated as a martyr along with the others. The facts that his brothers Theodore and Importunus participated in the Eastern mission of 526 and that an Albinus was found fleeing to the East during the Gothic wars[27] suggests that somehow or other he survived, perhaps being released after a period of imprisonment

Considerable discussion, however, has centred on the question of when Boethius was killed. The *Anonymus Valesianus* makes the death of Boethius and the visit of Pope John to the East consecutive events.[28] But this is inherently unlikely. If Theodoric had wanted concessions from the East, the last thing he would have done would be to execute the most prominent pro-Easterner in Italy. The *Anonymus* also implies that death followed soon after sentence. Yet while he was in prison, Boethius had time to write his celebrated work *The Consolation of Philosophy*. From a close examination of it, C. S. Lewis[29] has concluded that it is not the work of a man under sentence of death but a man who has been ruined, who bemoans the loss of his library, his good name and his exile while not expecting death.

All this tends to support the theory that initially he was simply exiled to the *Ager Calventianus*. The most logical explanation is that his death came as a result of the failure – in Theodoric's eyes at least – of the Eastern mission. The most likely sequence of events is that Boethius was initially imprisoned in 523, had three years in which to write his book and was then put to death, together with his father-in-law, in 526. Both the *Anonymus Valesianus* and the *Liber Pontificalis*[30] say that Symmachus was executed while the envoys were in Constantinople, something which would again be extremely illogical. But one source, the *Chronicon Cuspinianeum*,[31] says that Boethius and Symmachus were executed eighteen days before the death of Theodoric.

This sort of time-scale is supported by the account of Procopius,[32] who says that Symmachus and Boethius were slandered, and Theodoric, believing the slanders, put them to death on the grounds of plotting revolution and confiscated their property. A few days later Theodoric was taken ill with a chill and retired to his chamber, haunted by morbid fancies and expressing his remorse for the deaths of Boethius and Symmachus to his physician Helpidius. The source for this seems to be Helpidius himself, who attended Theodoric during his last illness, and the whole story has the ring of truth about it.

The key to Theodoric's attitude was the international situation. It was already tense in 523 when a group of pro-Gothic senators brought charges against the two prominent pro-Easterners. The two were found guilty and imprisoned. But the international situation deteriorated further: Theodoric's sister was put to death by the Vandals, he started building a fleet and the Arians in the East were persecuted. Theodoric banked everything on a prestige mission to the East, headed by Boethius's old friend Pope John I. When it returned, having failed to obtain all his demands, Theodoric furiously placed the envoys under house arrest and the Pope died.

The sequence of events seems to hinge on the death of Pope John. It caused a tremendous popular outcry. He was at once hailed as the martyr, and his funeral cortège returning to Rome turned into a veritable triumphal procession. Miracles occurred, relics of his clothing were eagerly seized by people and senate alike, and popular sentiment depicted him as the Catholic victim of a heretic king.[33] This affected the election of a successor. There was a vacancy of fifty-eight days, clearly filled with bitter disputes almost certainly involving pro- and anti-Gothic factions in both clergy and senate. It is not unlikely that Symmachus was active during this period on the pro-Eastern side, and it is significant that thirty-two days after a pro-Gothic pope was installed, Boethius and Symmachus were put to death. Close friends of the late Pope John and undoubted leaders of the pro-Eastern faction, their fate must have been sealed by the anti-Gothic feeling manifested during the disputed election.

After their deaths both Boethius and Symmachus were depicted as Catholic martyrs, but this interpretation glosses over the real political complexion of the situation. There seems to have been little contemporary reaction to the deaths, certainly much less than to that of the pope. But in retrospect they acquired an odour of sanctity. Gregory the Great linked Pope John and Symmachus in a story in which the two of them lead the soul of Theodoric to hell,[34] and Paul the deacon, in the eighth century, talked of Theodoric being 'goaded by the fury of his iniquity to kill Symmachus and Boethius, Catholic men'.[35] By the ninth century Boethius was being celebrated as a saint.[36]

Theodoric himself saw a pro-Gothic pope installed, executed Boethius and Symmachus and died eighteen days after their death, a hundred and four days after that of John, execrated by the people he had ruled with firmness but fairness for the past thirty-three years. The *Anonymus Valesianus* observed grimly:[37]

> He who does not allow his faithful worshippers to be oppressed by unbelievers soon brought upon Theodoric the same punishment that Arius, the founder of his religion, had suffered. For the king was seized with diarrhoea and after three days lost both his throne and his life.

It seems fortuitous, to say the least, that Theodoric should have met the same fate as Arius, who had died on a lavatory in Constantinople. The truth of the matter probably is that the king, who was then 72, caught a chill, complications set in and he was carried off. He died on 30 August 526, ill-deserving the curses of the Romans, who soon had occasion to regret his passing.

The death of John I could not have happened at a worse time for Theodoric, coming as it did in the wake of the failure of the Eastern mission, the accelerating collapse of his foreign policy and the evidence of disaffection in the aristocracy manifested by the Boethius case. It is not likely that John I had had time to name his successor, and so there was now an electoral uncertainty such as had not prevailed since the death of Anastasius II. As under that pontiff, the church and the aristocracy were splitting into rival factions, not divided this time by doctrinal but by political differences and this was to have serious consequences for the papal election.

Pope John died on 18 March 526 in Ravenna and was buried in Rome at St Peter's on 27 March. Seven weeks were to elapse before the new pontiff, Felix IV, was enthroned, in direct contrast to the one week elapsing after the deaths of Symmachus and Hormisdas. The *Liber Pontificalis* is eloquently terse. It contains the single sentence 'He was ordained by order of King Theodoric'.[38] Historians have generally interpreted this to mean that Theodoric intervened in the election and imposed his own nominee. A letter from Theodoric's grandson and successor, King Athalaric,[39] seems at first sight to confirm this but a closer reading suggests something other than straight nomination.

The letter is addressed to the senate, and Athalaric expresses his pleasure that they had obediently elected the pope chosen for them by his predecessor King Theodoric. He assures them that Theodoric 'although of a different faith' had taken pains to select a pontiff who would be satisfactory to any upright man.

> Let no one any longer be involved in the old contention. There is no disgrace in being beaten when the King's power has helped the winning side. That man makes him [i.e. the winning candidate] his own who transfers to him pure affection. For what cause for regret can there be when you find in this man those very qualities which you sought in the other when you embraced his party. Even though the person you desired is taken from you, yet nothing is lost by the faithful since the longed-for priesthood is now possessed.

In other words, Athalaric is telling the senate that they have got a good pope even if it is not the one they wanted.

What the letter and the fifty-eight-day vacancy, taken together, imply is a repeat of the situation in 498: a divided election, the referral of the matter to the king and the choice by the king of one of the candidates. It is interesting that Athalaric is here addressing only the senate, implying perhaps that the senate in the main supported the beaten candidate and that a majority of the people favoured the successful candidate. The fact that Felix was ordained 'by order of Theodoric' does not necessarily mean an overruling of the electoral process, simply the king enforcing a decision he has made to resolve the electoral dispute.

On the analogy of 498, if the senate in the main supported one of the candidates, it is likely that the people swung their support behind the other. The social tensions between the classes persisted long after the suppression of the Laurentian schism. The popular base for Felix's support may perhaps be detected in his epitaph, which said:[40] 'For his humble piety he was preferred to many of the proud. By simplicity he won the lofty place. He was bountiful to the poor and comforted the wretched.' This certainly suggests a candidate pursuing the sort of policy adopted by Symmachus to endear him to the mob.

It is, however, likely that the dispute was not as clear-cut as in that of 498 when two rival candidates were elected on the same day a few days after the death of the previous pope. The reference in Felix's epitaph to his being preferred to 'many of the proud' and the seven-week vacancy before a final decision was arrived at both suggest a splintering of the clergy, with rival factions coalescing around several rival candidates, thus preventing the previous dispute criterion of majority clerical support from being invoked.

In the end the deadlock was referred to Ravenna, the king chose, and the senate, chastened perhaps by the arrest of their leader Symmachus, ratified the decision. The new pope, Felix IV, a Samnite by birth, was like Hormisdas and John before him a Symmachan deacon, almost certainly the same Felix who accompanied the 519 mission to the East to negotiate the reunion and therefore a man of some eminence at the papal court. The installation of Felix was, however, Theodoric's last success and it seems likely that for once his long-standing neutrality wavered and that, given the crisis in which he found himself, he gave his support to the pro-Gothic candidate. The circumstances were now very different for the Ostrogoths from those in which Theodoric had resolved the 498 dispute. The very survival of the kingdom was deemed by Theodoric to be in question and so for the first time in thirty-three years it is likely that political considerations took precedence over religious neutrality. But forty days after the consecration of Pope Felix, Theodoric died and was succeeded by his young grandson Athalaric, initially under the regency of his mother Amalasuntha. There can be little doubt that Felix was the pro-Gothic candidate. Royal favour towards him can be seen in the edict of Athalaric confirming the right of the papacy to judge cases concerning the clergy.[41] Only if the plaintiff was dissatisfied with the papal decision could he appeal to the secular authority. Felix's epitaph also recalls that he 'increased the wealth of the papacy'. There is no reference to this in his biography and he certainly did not receive gifts from the Eastern emperor, in contrast both to Hormisdas and John I. So perhaps he was in receipt of gifts from a grateful Gothic government.

Felix's ordinations are interesting too. In four years he ordained four deacons and fifty-five priests, contrasting with no ordinations at all under John I and only twenty-one priests and no deacons ordained by Hormisdas. The deacons will obviously have been replacements for the dead and the promoted. But the number of priests is abnormally high, even given the lack of ordinations under John; there must be a strong suspicion of a purge of dissident priests, albeit on a smaller scale than had occurred under Symmachus.

Felix's principal concern, however, was to ensure that the pro-Gothic party remained in control of the papacy after his death, and when he fell ill in 530 he sought to circumvent the sort of electoral dispute that had occurred in 526. Convoking around his sickbed a meeting of his supporters, described as 'those priests, deacons, senators and my sons the patricians whom it concerned to be present' (i.e. the pro-Gothic faction), he issued a *praeceptum*[42] addressed to the bishops, priests, deacons and the whole clergy and the senate and people. By this he nominated as his successor the archdeacon Boniface, to whom he handed over his *pallium* on condition that it should be returned to him if he recovered. He ordered the excommunication of all those who disobeyed his command and caused dissension in the church, and he announced that he had informed the king of his decision. Now although there had been a tradition of informal nomination by the popes of their successors at least since the time of Pope Simplicius, what Felix was doing and what made his actions unacceptable to many was to so formalize the process as to pre-empt completely the process of election.

Despite the presence of senators and patricians at the meeting, the senate as a whole, realizing that it had been outflanked, assumed a mask of outraged constitutionalism and issued an edict directed to the entire clergy, forbidding the discussion of the succession during the lifetime of the pope, forbidding the acceptance of the nomination by anyone and decreeing exile and confiscation of property for the infringement of the ban.[43] The senate seemed to be acting in a wholly impartial manner but this was only because the action of Pope Felix had pre-empted their own participation in the election. Furthermore, they were reverting to the practice of regulating the affairs of the church without the consent of the pope which had been one of the causes of contention under Pope Symmachus. But this time there seems to have been no outburst of clerical anger, perhaps because the majority of the clergy agreed on this occasion with the senate in censuring the action of Pope Felix.

The death of Felix followed soon after his *praeceptum* in September 530, and three days later the election was held. Once again there was a disputed election, but this time much more clear-cut than in 526. This time there were only two candidates, the archdeacon Boniface and the deacon Dioscorus. The background of the two candidates is eloquent as to their allegiance and dramatically demonstrates the deep split within the Symmachan old guard. Boniface was the nominee of the dead Pope Felix. Although born a Roman, his father was called Sigibuld, the first Germanic name to appear amongst the antecedents of the popes, and it seems likely that he was sprung from a Germanic family which had settled several generations earlier in the empire. This background would make him highly conscious of the need for close relations between the Romans and the Goths. His opponent was the deacon Dioscorus, the Alexandrian Greek who had arrived in Rome under Pope Symmachus as a refugee from Monophysite persecution and rapidly established himself as a key figure at the papal court. He was the man who had persuaded Theodoric to end the papal schism in favour of Symmachus. He had been the central figure in the successful third embassy of Hormisdas which liquidated the Acacian schism and was instrumental in persuading Hormisdas to reject Theopaschism. He was clearly regarded as patriarchal material as is indicated by Hormisdas's recommendation of him for the see of Alexandria. Nothing had come of this, perhaps because the emperor feared that under Dioscorus Alexandria might gravitate into the orbit of Rome. Nevertheless he now symbolized the strong links between Rome and the East which the pro-Eastern faction desired, and further demonstrates the importance of the resolution of the Acacian schism in removing the barrier which had divided the Symmachan supporters from Constantinople.

The election was held as usual in the Lateran basilica and Dioscorus was elected by a large majority.[44] We know from their subsequent act of submission that sixty of the Roman priests supported him, a substantial majority.[45] It is also likely that a majority of the senate supported him, given their stance in the 526 election, their decree following the *praeceptum* of Felix IV and the statement of the *Liber Pontificalis* that 'there was dissension within the clergy and senate'.[46] Faced with the majority for Dioscorus, the minority pro-Gothic faction retired to the Basilica Julia and there elected Boniface.

It is likely that Dioscorus's large majority comprised both pro-Easterners among clergy and senate and the constitutionalists outraged by Felix IV's attempted pre-emption of the election. Dioscorus was recognized as pope by the East.[47] The odds were all against Boniface. But then on 14 October, nearly a month after the election, Dioscorus died. The pro-Eastern faction was left leaderless and after a further period of uncertainty Boniface triumphed. It was over a month before the Dioscoran clergy came over but on 27 December 530, sixty of the priests who had supported Dioscorus signed a *libellus* by which they condemned the memory of Dioscorus and promised not to try anything so wicked again. This *libellus* was then deposited in the papal archives.

Once this had been done, Boniface apparently took no further action in revenge and sought to make himself acceptable to the clergy. There is no record of any priestly ordinations, by contrast with the reign of Felix IV, suggesting that there was no purge. Instead Boniface adopted a policy of reconciliation, drawing on his own family fortune to make gifts of plate to the priests, deacons, subdeacons and notaries and, when there was a danger of famine, succouring the clergy with alms.[48] Significantly neither his biography nor his epitaph talk of any gifts to the people. Boniface's prime objective seems to have been to improve his standing with the clergy. Indeed if his epitaph is to be believed he attained a measure of success:[49]

The gentle shepherd reunited his divided flock
Folding again his distressed sheep when the enemy [i.e.

Dioscorus] had fallen,
With a meek heart he abated his anger against the suppliants
And overcame all wiles by the simplicity of his spirit.

But Boniface did not forget that, like Felix before him, he was in
office to advance the cause of the Goths, and it was necessary for him
to secure the succession. So he held a synod at St Peter's at which it
was decreed that he should ordain his own successor. The decision
was ratified by oaths sworn by the clergy and a document signed by
them to this effect. Armed with this, he duly appointed as his
prospective successor the deacon Vigilius.[50] Vigilius, a comparatively young man and almost certainly one of the deacons ordained
by Felix IV, came from a family prominent in government service,
his father John being successively *Comes Sacrarum Largitionum* and
praetorian prefect and his brother Reparatus prefect of Rome. An
ambitious aristocrat, whose entire career seems to have been geared
towards the fulfilment of an ambition to occupy the papal throne, he
typifies the new era of shifting allegiances and the break-up of old
alignments.

Although Boniface had gained the sanction of a synod for his
actions, unlike Felix who had relied on a private meeting, there was
still a storm of protest. It was so widespread that Boniface felt
impelled to recall the synod, confess that his action had been contrary
to the canons, revoke his nomination and burn the *libellus*.[51] Vigilius
was despatched to Constantinople as papal *apocrisiarios*, probably to
spare him the embarrassment of being known as the discarded heir
apparent.

Boniface was therefore unable to make any provision for the
succession, and after he died in October 532 there was a vacancy of
two months and fifteen days, the longest vacancy since the end of the
Western Roman Empire and a sure sign of trouble.

Perhaps the most scandalous election campaign yet fought in the
Ostrogothic period occupied those two months as Rome plunged
into a welter of intrigue, corruption and chicanery. The details of it
are revealed in an indignant letter from King Athalaric to Pope John
II following his election.[52] There had been many irregularities,
extending as far as the sale of church plate to raise money for bribes.
To combat this, the king declared that he was confirming the election decree recently passed by the senate and extending its competence to the whole of Italy to avoid such scandals occurring elsewhere. Any promise or contract made by anyone with a view to
obtaining the see was declared null and void and anyone receiving
money as part of such a transaction and refusing to return it was
declared guilty of sacrilege. In the event of a contested election and

the decision being referred to the king, a limit of 3,000 *solidi* was placed on payment for the completion of the necessary documents, to prevent candidates bribing royal officials to support their case. No one was to give more than 500 *solidi* to the poor, to prevent the mob being bribed. Informers were encouraged to report any private transactions aimed at getting control of the papal see. The decree was ordered to be inscribed on tablets and set up for everyone to see. These detailed regulations suggest that most, if not all, of the offences subject to legislation had occurred during the election and they reveal a horrifying picture of the large-scale bribing of royal officials, the suborning of the mob and the widespread practice of summoning secret cabals. Indeed so much of the papacy's wealth was dissipated in these bribery scandals that when Pope Agapitus paid his visit to Constantinople in 536 he was compelled to pawn church plate to pay for his expenses.[53]

The precise details of the election have not survived. But Rome did eventually get a new pope, John II. Born Mercurius, a Roman, he had for many years been parish priest of St Clement on the Caelian Hill. On his consecration he changed his name to avoid disfiguring the throne of St Peter with the name of a pagan god.[54] The election of a parish priest smacks strongly of compromise. He is the only pope in the sixth century who was provably not elected from the diaconate. The choice of John II may well have been made in desperation after rival factions had been locked in combat for over two months and had been resorting to every trick in the book to secure success. Whether the king intervened is not known for certain. The ruling he makes about the bribing of palace officials suggests that he may have done. But he seems not to have plumped for an obviously pro-Gothic candidate. Although John II had dutifully attended the 531 synod of Boniface II, indicating his adherence to that controversial pontiff,[55] he has the appearance of a saintly nonentity to whom the electorate, worn out and/or disgusted by the apparently endless and endlessly scandalous intrigues, had turned as a last resort.

The reason why there was not the sort of decisive intervention that Theodoric made in the disputed elections of 498 and 526 is probably a reflection of the state of affairs in Ravenna. Athalaric was drinking himself into an early grave and his mother Amalasuntha was too pro-Eastern herself to press an anti-Eastern candidate strongly. John II therefore seems to have been acceptable to both sides, as one might expect from a compromise candidate. He received a confession of faith and handsome presents from the emperor Justinian,[56] something which neither of his immediate predecessors had. Without demur John accepted and confirmed Justinian's Theopaschite Edict, legalizing that doctrine which Hormisdas and Dioscorus had fought so bitterly against, and went so far as to excommunicate the *Akoimetae*, the papacy's staunchest allies in Constantinople, for their opposition to it.[57] The choice of the name of the so recently 'martyred' pro-Eastern pope as his new name indicates further that John II was not hostile to the East. But he was also favourably enough regarded in Ravenna for Athalaric to release at his request certain Romans held on suspicion of sedition[58] and for him to have corresponded amiably with the members of the royal council.[59] By making himself acceptable to both sides the pope could stand aloof from the factional loyalties which were riving both clergy and aristocracy.

But John, as had perhaps been intended, was only a stopgap, reigning for just two years and four months before his death in May 535. This time there was a vacancy of only six days before the new pope was consecrated, suggesting that there was no contest. John II's successor was the elderly archdeacon Agapitus. The last survivor of the Symmachan old guard, he had been ordained a deacon as long ago as 502 and was a relative, perhaps a nephew, of Pope Felix III. He had been archdeacon only since some date after 531 and this further confirms the view already expressed that he was comparatively young when ordained deacon, since it had taken him thirty years to gain seniority over the other deacons and he had survived his contemporaries among the Symmachan deacons by some ten years.

It may well be that events in the East had prompted the unopposed election of Agapitus. Justinian, who had succeeded his uncle Justin as emperor in 527, had been pursuing a policy of attempting to reconcile the Chalcedonian and Monophysite elements in the East on the basis of the Theopaschite formula. There was a virtual truce between the two sides during the early 530s but under cover of this truce and with the active support of the Empress Theodora, herself a Monophysite, the Monophysites were advancing their influence steadily. The climax of this advance came in 535 when the pro-Monophysite Anthimus of Trebizond was appointed patriarch of Constantinople. Seriously alarmed, Palestinian and Syrian monks sent a delegation to Rome to apprise the pope of what was happening. It was perhaps the resurgent Monophysite threat which prompted the election of the last of the Symmachan old guard as pope. It was not long before Agapitus was on his way to Constantinople, though not ostensibly to tackle the Monophysites.

The political situation in Italy was now extremely tense. Worn out by his excesses, King Athalaric had died in 534 and soon afterwards his mother Amalasuntha had been strangled on the orders of her cousin, the ambitious but spineless Theodahad, who had assumed the throne. But the days of the Ostrogothic kingdom were numbered. Justinian, whose grandiose schemes included not just the reunification of the Catholic faith but also the reconquest of the Western Roman Empire, had launched a successful invasion of Vandalic Africa in 533 and the rapidity with which it had crumbled led inevitably to an invasion of Italy. The murder of Amalasuntha gave the empire just the excuse it needed and Justinian declared war on Theodahad, posing as the avenger of the dead queen. Count Belisarius, the conqueror of Africa, invaded Sicily in 535.

Panic stricken, Theodahad ordered Pope Agapitus to sail for Constantinople and try to negotiate for the withdrawal of the imperial armies. Agapitus, who had begun his reign with a spectacular gesture of reconciliation by publicly burning the *libellus* of submission extracted by Boniface II from the Dioscoran clergy, was only too glad to go.[60] But when he arrived in Constantinople in the spring of 536, Agapitus immediately turned his attention to the religious problem. Justinian tried the usual imperial ploy of threatening exile unless Agapitus recognized Anthimus as patriarch. But Agapitus stood his ground and insisted on a disputation with Anthimus. The disputation was held and Agapitus demonstrated that Anthimus in fact held heretical views. Justinian accepted the pope's findings and Anthimus was removed from office and exiled. Agapitus lived just long enough to consecrate the orthodox Menas as Anthimus's successor on 13 March and then he died on 22 April. But he had made his point. After his death a synod was held in Constantinople (May–June 536),[61] attended by the ambassadors who had accompanied Agapitus: bishops Epiphanius of Aeclanum, Sabinus of Canusium, Rusticus of Faesulae and Leo of Nola, the deacons Theophanes and Pelagius and the notaries Menas and Peter. The decision was that Anthimus and the Monophysites were duly condemned and Agapitus's body was returned to Rome in a leaden coffin and buried in St Peter's on 20 September 536. The old orthodox warrior had won his last fight.

The death of Agapitus and his failure to carry out his peace mission led King Theodahad to take an extraordinary step now and one which violated the policy pursued both by Theodoric and Athalaric. Long before the body of Agapitus arrived back in Rome, Theodahad had forced through the election and consecration as pope of the subdeacon Silverius. He was ordained on 8 June 536. The new pope held the unprecedentedly low rank of subdeacon and it means that Theodahad had passed over the entire diaconate as untrustworthy. Silverius had the distinction of being the son of Pope Hormisdas, with whom Theodoric had enjoyed cordial relations, but this was not sufficient to stifle the bitter resentment caused by the wholesale flouting of the electoral procedure. The *Liber Pontificalis* gives a very precise account of what occurred:

He was appointed by the tyrant Theodahad without proper
discussion. For Theodahad had been corrupted by bribes and
he terrified the clergy so that they believed that whoever did
not support the ordination of Silverius would be punished
with death. Therefore the priests did not accept him according
to the ancient custom and confirm his appointment before
ordination; but after he had been ordained by force of fear,
then for the sake of the unity of the church and of the faith,
when the ordination was ended, the priests accepted
Silverius.[62]

It may be that Silverius was so anxious for the throne that he
bribed Theodahad, who is known to have been extremely greedy.
But it seems more likely that the main motive was to secure a
pro-Gothic pope at this time of considerable uncertainty. There still
remained a faction among the church and clergy loyal to the
Goths. The Roman priest Rusticus, for instance, was so devoted
to Theodahad that he was chosen to go to Justinian with peace
proposals in 535.[63] Bishop Aventius of Asisium was similarly entrusted by the Goths with negotiations in 547.[64] Despite the manner of his election, Silverius did command a measure of support in
the Roman church and an unspecified number of clergy refused to
accept his successor Vigilius. But the forcible installation of Silverius
effectively meant that the factional rivalry within the clergy simmer-
ing since the election of John II had burst forth again and that the
imperial invasion had brought the strife between the pro-Goths and
the pro-Easterners to crisis point.

The installation of Silverius as pope was Theodahad's last significant act. Having secured Sicily for the empire, Belisarius now
invaded Italy proper. Theodahad's son-in-law Ebrimuth, the Gothic
commander in Bruttium, surrendered without offering any resistance and Belisarius captured Naples. Theodahad did nothing to
prevent the victorious imperial advance and the Gothic army, disgusted at his cowardly inactivity, met near Terracina and raised on
their shields a new king, the warrior hero Witiges, comrade-in-arms
of the late, lamented King Theodoric. Theodahad was arrested and
put to death and Witiges withdrew his forces to the north to regroup
and prepare a counter-attack. Unopposed, Belisarius entered Rome
and Pope Silverius, so recently elevated as the Gothic nominee,
found himself in the hands of the empire.

What followed is as tangled a web of treachery and double-dealing
as can be found anywhere in papal annals. Several different versions
of the course of events following the elevation of Silverius exist. The
fullest is the *Breviarium* of archdeacon Liberatus of Carthage.[65] He

records that on the death of Agapitus the empress Theodora secretly summoned the deacon Vigilius, the papal *apocrisiarios* in Constantinople, and extracted from him a promise that in return for the papal throne, he would restore the heretic Anthimus to the patriarchate, and recognize Monophysitism. Then, giving him 700 pounds of gold and orders for Belisarius to secure his election, she despatched him to Italy.

According to Liberatus, Vigilius agreed to this 'from love of the bishopric and of gold'. But by the time he reached Rome, he found Silverius installed as pope. Whereupon he retired to Naples and there informed Belisarius of the empress's wishes, promising him part of the money if he removed Silverius and replaced him with Vigilius. So Belisarius returned to Rome, and summoned Silverius to his official residence, the Pincian Palace, and tried to persuade him to renounce Chalcedon and embrace Monophysitism. When this failed, Belisarius charged the pope with writing treasonable letters to the Goths, promising to admit them to Rome. Liberatus paints a dramatic picture of Silverius retiring to sanctuary in the basilica of St Sabina and there receiving Photius, Belisarius's son, who promised him safe conduct if he would return to the Palace for a further meeting. Silverius's advisers warned him against trusting 'the oaths of the Greeks' but he agreed to go. 'He entered the Palace alone and was never seen by his followers again.' The next day Belisarius summoned the Roman clergy and ordered them to elect a new pope and, although some of them refused, he insisted on the election of Vigilius and Vigilius was duly elected and ordained. Clerical opposition to Vigilius seems to have collapsed at once.

Silverius was sent into exile at Patara in Lycia, but the bishop of that city went to the capital and petitioned the emperor for a fair trial for the ex-pope. Justinian then ordered that Silverius should be returned to Italy, to be properly tried. If the accusations against him were true, he should be deprived of the papacy but given another see as a consolation prize, and if the accusations were false, he should be restored to the throne. Both the deacon Pelagius, who had succeeded Vigilius as *apocrisiarios* in Constantinople, and Theodora tried to stop this plan being put into effect. But Silverius was returned to Italy. However, Belisarius handed him over to Vigilius, who had him conveyed to the island of Palmaria and starved to death.

Liberatus's account is thus extremely hostile to Vigilius, depicting him as a greedy and treacherous pro-Monophysite who ousted and virtually murdered his predecessor. But the account in the *Liber Pontificalis* is hardly more favourable.[66] According to this version, Justinian, learning of Silverius's election, took counsel with Vigilius and then wrote urging Silverius to agree to the restoration of

Anthimus to the patriarchate. Silverius refused and so Theodora sent Vigilius to Belisarius with orders to depose Silverius and install Vigilius in his place. False witnesses came forward to testify that Silverius had planned to betray Rome to the Goths and although Belisarius initially did not believe them, their persistence overcame his scruples. Silverius was summoned to the Pincian Palace and there stripped of his vestments by the subdeacon John. The subdeacon Xystus then announced to the waiting clergy that Silverius had been deposed and made a monk, whereupon the clergy fled. Silverius was handed over to Vigilius, who despatched him to the island of Palmaria where he died. The *Liber Pontificalis* omits all mention of the Patara exile.

The responsibility for these events appears not to be in doubt. Both accounts make Theodora and Vigilius the principal instigators of the affair, while the actual work on the spot was done by Belisarius. Procopius mentions that Theodora and Antonina, Belisarius's wife, were responsible for disposing of Pope Silverius and promises to reveal the details in a future volume.[67] But that volume was never written. It is possible to reconstruct with reasonable accuracy the course of events when the conditions under which the two sources were written are taken into account. The *Breviarium* was written at the height of the 'Three Chapters' controversy when Vigilius was being regarded by his opponents almost as anti-Christ and Liberatus was prominent among these opponents. The *Liber Pontificalis* account seems to be a combination of two independent sources, the first part hostile to Silverius, depicting him unflatteringly as a Gothic puppet, and the second part hostile to Vigilius, depicting Silverius as a martyr to the Orthodox faith. It seems likely that the first part was contemporary with the events it described but that the second was written like the *Breviarium* during the 'Three Chapters' controversy.

Given the atmosphere in which the sources were written, certain features of the accounts can probably be discounted. The religious colouring imparted to the events is almost certainly anachronistic. The demands for Silverius and Vigilius to endorse Monophysitism and their opposing stances as the champions of Orthodoxy and heresy are almost certainly echoes of the 'Three Chapters' affair. So too are the intrigues attributed to Theodora, whose Monophysite sympathies made her an ogre to the Orthodox faction. The theory that Vigilius did his predecessor to death is also probably apocryphal, given Vigilius's own later popularity in Rome and the analogous case of the anti-Pope Laurentius who, having been deprived of the throne, starved himself to death.

But when this religious colouring is eliminated, the rest of the facts in the two accounts are substantially in agreement and probably therefore correct. They indicate that the whole episode was political in nature. At the very moment when Justinian's armies were beginning the conquest of Italy, a pro-Gothic pope was installed. It was essential for the successful accomplishment of his plans that there should be a pro-Eastern pope substituted as soon as possible. The ideal candidate was on hand in Constantinople. The deacon Vigilius's principal motivation throughout his career, as far as can be ascertained, was the desire to be pope and he was not really concerned about which faction put him there. While the Goths were in the ascendant, he was prepared to seek the throne as a pro-Gothic candidate but when Boniface II's schemes to secure the succession for him ended in his posting to Constantinople, he was quick to use his position there to make himself useful and acceptable to Justinian and Theodora. So he was duly sent back to Italy as the pro-Eastern candidate for the papal throne.

Whether or not the letters used as evidence against Silverius were forged as Liberatus alleges, Silverius's loyalty must have been in doubt. Both sources agree that he was charged with treasonable correspondence with the Goths and the official account of the wars by Procopius says the same thing.[68] It is also interesting to note that Procopius records that at the same time Belisarius banished from Rome a pro-Gothic coterie of senators, including Maximus. They were recalled when the threat to the city receded. The deposition and exile of the pope looks in this context to be part of a tightening of security on the part of the imperial commander.

So Silverius was exiled to Lycia and Vigilius ordained to succeed him on 29 March 537, thanks, as all the sources agree, to the influence of Belisarius.[69] The participation of subdeacons in the deposition and the opposition of the *apocrisiarios* Pelagius to Silverius's retrial indicate that there certainly was a group in the clergy hostile to Silverius. Both his low rank and his pro-Gothic sympathies will have told against him in certain quarters. Vigilius seems to have been generally recognized as pope, despite the initial reluctance of some of the clergy to recognize him, and an inscription of June 537 refers to him as 'the most blessed pope'.[70]

It may be that all along Justinian had intended that Silverius should be deposed after a proper trial. There is certainly no other obvious reason to explain why he was sent back from Lycia to Rome. But neither Vigilius nor Belisarius was anxious to rake over the matter again and so he was banished to the island of Palmaria off the Tuscan coast and there died on 11 November 537, removing a substantial embarrassment from Vigilius's way.

That the correct way to view the Silverius–Vigilius affair is in the light of the struggle between the pro-Gothic and the pro-Eastern factions for control of the papacy rather than the struggle between Orthodoxy and Monophysitism and that the deposition of Silverius was the culmination of that rivalry is demonstrated by the 'Laurentian Fragment'.[71] For in addition to its account of the troubles under Symmachus it lists all the popes from Symmachus to Vigilius, giving their length of reign. Whereas each reign length tallies more or less with the details given in the *Liber Pontificalis*, there is a major discrepancy for Silverius. The 'Laurentian Fragment' gives him a reign of nine months, thus reckoning him as pope only until his deposition, whereas the *Liber Pontificalis* gives him a reign of one year five months and eleven days, thus reckoning him as pope until his death. Thus the 'Laurentian Fragment' sees Vigilius in terms of the successful pro-Eastern candidate, who brings the wheel that began rolling with Laurentius full circle. It confirms a continuity of pro-Eastern feeling and a rival papal tradition surviving down until the time when the hopes of the Laurentians were finally realized and the imperial eagles were once again planted in Rome. The 'official' account, which pointedly rejects Vigilius's actual date of ordination, implicitly regarding him as a usurper until his predecessor dies, presages the stormy passage that Vigilius was to have under the empire and the rude awakening that the pro-Easterners were to have after the longed-for day of imperial restoration arrived.

Conclusions

This interpretation of papal history in the Ostrogothic period has laid great stress on factional rivalry to explain the course of events. It is important to emphasize, however, that this rivalry must not be viewed as a crude division between pro-Eastern and pro-Gothic. It is more subtle and complex, shifting and fluid than that. For one thing, the period falls into two distinct halves, the dividing line being drawn by the ending of the Acacian schism in 519. The common factor is imperial religious policy, unacceptable to many before 519 but changing dramatically with the appearance of a new dynasty. This makes it perfectly possible for someone like the deacon Dioscorus to be anti-Eastern before 519 and pro-Eastern thereafter. It also explains why anti-Eastern before 519 does not necessarily mean anti-Gothic, whereas after 519 it comes increasingly to mean just that.

The fundamental problem both for the Roman church and the Roman aristocracy was, as has previously been mentioned, the tension created by the uneasy fusion of *Christianitas* and *Romanitas* which they both embodied. There was a straight clash between the two in the latter years of the fifth century which provoked the

Acacian schism in which the papacy took its stand on *Christianitas*. But the desire of an increasingly large number of the clergy to see a restoration of harmony between the two elements led to the election of Pope Anastasius II and the inauguration of a policy of *détente* with the East. Differences of opinion about how fast and how far *détente* should go were partly responsible for the Symmachan schism, the situation being further confused by internal power struggles and personality clashes in the Roman church.

Just as a majority of the clergy at the beginning of the Acacian schism took their stand on *Christianitas*, so a majority of the senate took their stand on *Romanitas*. They were concerned to legitimize the position of Theodoric, who had after all been sent west by the emperor, and to end the religious estrangement. Emperor Anastasius saw this clearly enough when he linked the two issues in his compromise settlement. But a minority of the senate were compelled in this instance to put their *Christianitas* first.

The resolution of the Acacian schism meant both for the church and the aristocracy, the reconciliation of *Christianitas* and *Romanitas*. This now highlighted the fact which the religious estrangement had in part obscured. Italy was psychologically and even technically felt to be part of the Roman Empire and yet was in practice an independent barbarian kingdom. Although many of the Roman aristocracy served the Ostrogoths in government and there was one faction which believed that the future for Italy lay in close and continuing co-operation between Goths and Romans, there was a sizeable rival group which increasingly sought to forge closer cultural, religious and ultimately political links with the East. The Roman church, too, came to be more and more concerned with the question of what stance the papacy ought to occupy towards Ravenna and Constantinople. While its nature and its traditions drew the papacy inexorably towards the Empire, its reason and experience warned it against the danger of heresy prevalent in the East.

These rival sentiments crystallized into pro-Gothic and pro-Eastern factions both in clergy and in senate, as the international situation worsened, Theodoric's Arian regime became increasingly isolated, the king himself grew older and the succession looked insecure. The factional rivalry spilled over into the papal elections. The papal list in the 'Laurentian Fragment' suggests that there was a continuing pro-Eastern tradition in the Roman church from Laurentius down to Vigilius. Its progress was interrupted first by the doctrinal disputes with Constantinople which temporarily eclipsed the pro-Easterners and later by struggles with the pro-Goths, resulting in the ordination of successive pro-Gothic popes. The pro-Gothic faction became more and more discredited, however, as its popes tried to 'fix' elections, and finally the king flouted the election regulations completely. The problem must have seemed resolved by the restoration of imperial rule in Italy but in fact that was just the beginning of a new chapter of problems for the papacy, demonstrating that even inside the Empire the papal identity crisis went on.

Interestingly the facts reveal that although the aristocracy was deeply involved in papal elections and papal affairs generally, the roles of the highest secular authorities – the king and the emperor – were much less active. The Eastern emperors played little real part in papal affairs. Despite their support for the successive pro-Eastern candidates Laurentius and Dioscorus, they were in no position to intervene effectively. The record of gifts from the Eastern emperors to the Roman church, however, clearly indicates that they knew who their friends were. Symmachus received nothing from the East. Hormisdas, under whom the Acacian schism ended, received a great weight of gold and silver plate, robes and jewelled gospels. John I and John II similarly were in receipt of jewelled chalices, plate and gold-embroidered robes. Felix IV and Boniface II, on the other hand, received nothing. The Ostrogothic kings were a little more active but on the whole Theodoric maintained a stance of scrupulous impartiality, with the probable exception of his arbitration in favour of Felix IV. Twice he was called upon to arbitrate in disputed elections and his intervention was decisive in ending the wounding schism which disfigured the church in the early sixth century. Athalaric seems to have maintained the same sort of watchful neutrality, though the schism under Boniface II resolved itself by the death of the anti-pope and the disputed election after Boniface's death was resolved by compromise. Only Theodahad, last and weakest of the Amalung kings, breached this policy when he installed Silverius by force.

Part III

The Papacy under the Empire

Chapter 9

The 'Three Chapters' Controversy

On 13 August 554, Emperor Justinian promulgated the *Pragmatic Sanction* which officially restored Italy to the bosom of the Roman Empire. Thus we come to the second time-period of this study, in which the papacy found itself subject to the influence of two new powers which had not hitherto directly influenced its activities. Italy's 'liberation' can hardly have been the joyous event it might have seemed in anticipation, for she had been ravaged by war for twenty years and bled by tax-gatherers of both sides. For those who had not thought through the implications of imperial restoration there was to be a rude awakening. For Italy was no longer the centre of the Roman Empire. It was a mere frontier province, and the imperial government took immediate steps to reduce it to that status. The old administrative structure was dismantled and the survivors of the senatorial aristocracy, broken by the effects of the war and emasculated by the administrative changes, began to drift eastwards to seek a revival of their fortunes and their influence at the imperial court in Constantinople. Italy emerged from the Gothic wars a Byzantine province, administered by an imported Greek civil service, garrisoned by Eastern regiments and ruled from Ravenna by an imperial governor-general, soon to be known as the exarch.

Perhaps the most profound long-term implications for the papacy were the emergence of the emperor and the Italian army to fill the vacuum left by the disappearance of the Ostrogothic kings and the senatorial aristocracy. The influence of the army and its officer class, increasingly locally recruited, was not to be felt by the papacy until the seventh century. But the influence of the emperor was felt immediately and Justinian had none of Theodoric's scruples about intervening in papal affairs. After all, unlike Theodoric, Justinian was a Catholic, a Roman and above all God's chosen vessel, charged with ensuring the spiritual well-being of his people. He had confirmed Rome's primacy within the church as long ago as the reign of

John II but this did not mean that the pope was given a license to pursue a religious policy different from that of the emperor. He was expected to toe the line and if he failed to do so, then woe betide him.

The first and most obvious effect that the imperial reconquest had was on the papal elections. The *Liber Diurnus*[1] has preserved the formula letters sent out in connection with the seventh-century papal elections and the procedure in the second half of the sixth century is unlikely to have differed very greatly from the picture there revealed. On the death of the pope, the emperor and the exarch were informed and the regency immediately assumed by the archpriest, the archdeacon and the *Primicerius Notariorum*. The main function of this triumvirate was to speed the election of a new pope. It began with prayers, lasting after a decree of Boniface III for three days,[2] then the clergy, the citizens, the lay authorities and representatives of the army gathered in the Lateran basilica and elected the new pope. The election was expected to be unanimous and electoral decrees were then drawn up, signed by the electors and despatched to the emperor, the exarch, the archbishop of Ravenna and the papal *apocrisiarios* in Constantinople. The big difference between what happened under the empire and what happened under the Ostrogoths is that whereas in the earlier period the pope was generally conveyed at once to consecration following his election, in the later period consecration waited for imperial confirmation of the election. The letter sent by the papal electors to the emperor testifies conclusively to the subordinate position accepted by the church within the empire:[3]

> Therefore tearfully we your servants beg that the piety of our lords may deign to hear the appeal of their servants and conceding the desires of your petitioners, order through Your Piety's command that we may perform his ordination; so that constituted under the same pastor by the sacred sovereignty of your clemency we may perpetually pray for the life and empire of our most serene lords and the omnipotent lord and blessed prince of apostles Peter for whose church you may concede a worthy governor to be ordained.

Only after confirmation had arrived could the consecration of the pope take place. It was performed by the bishops of Portus, Albanum and Ostia on the first Sunday following the arrival of the imperial letter.

The emperor thus had a role in the creation of the pope, but it is important to remember that the emperors did not maintain a consistency of attitude towards Rome. Their attitude changed with each new occupant of the imperial throne and with each change in religious and foreign policy. It is those emperors most deeply involved in theological controversy and pursuing policies which involved Italy who were most likely to interfere with the papacy. Emperors like Tiberius Constantine and Maurice, whose interests and policies involved neither theological strife nor Italy, left the papacy to its own devices. The potential for imperial interference in papal affairs, however, remained.

Indeed, to interfere in the papacy had been one of the first things Justinian had done as soon as his armies got a foothold in Italy. Before the Ostrogoths were even vanquished the imperial commander Belisarius had deposed the pro-Gothic pope Silverius, and on the orders of the emperor had installed the pro-Eastern Vigilius in his place. But shortly before Vigilius's ordination in 537 the Goths laid siege to Rome and maintained it for a year. Vigilius's tenure of the throne of St Peter must have looked at this point as precarious as his predecessor's had. However, the death of ex-pope Silverius in November 537 removed the most obvious focus of opposition within the church, and after the raising of the siege of Rome Belisarius pursued the war against the Goths with such vigour and success that by 540 King Witiges was ready to surrender. With the war apparently all but over, Belisarius was recalled to Constantinople. But in 542 the Goths rallied, elected the warrior Totila as king and renewed the war. For ten years Totila fought a brilliant war, capturing Rome, Naples and Perusia and winning spectacular victories against the weakened, divided and increasingly demoralized imperial forces. At last, in 551, faced with the complete failure of the imperial reconquest bid, Justinian appointed a new commander-in-chief and supplied him with men, money and able subordinate generals. This new commander was the 75-year-old eunuch chamberlain Narses, who proved to be an astute strategist and a brilliant war leader with a decisive grasp of affairs. In 552 he engaged the Gothic army in a pitched battle and routed it. Totila was killed and with him died Gothic hopes of successfully resisting the imperial conquest of Italy.

But by this time Pope Vigilius was no longer in Rome. He had begun his reign conventionally enough by sending a declaration of his orthodoxy to the emperor and the patriarch Menas[4] and by beginning to repair the damage wrought during the siege of Rome.[5] The high point of these years came in 544 when the pope held a full dress assembly of the Roman church and people where he received a version of the Acts of the Apostles written in metric verse by the subdeacon Arator, once a pupil of Ennodius of Ticinum and formerly *Comes Domesticorum* of Theodoric. Arator gave public readings of his work in the church of St Peter *ad vincula* to a rapturous reception from his audience, who called repeatedly for encores.[6] It

141

was not only a dramatic and moving occasion but it was virtually the last manifestation of the cultural revival which had occurred under the Ostrogoths. Rome was to see nothing like it for centuries.

Meanwhile theological storm clouds were gathering in the East which were to precipitate another confrontation between *Romanitas* and *Christianitas*. Initially relations between the papacy and the imperial government were cordial. The papal *apocrisiarios* Pelagius, a close associate of Vigilius, had the ear of the emperor and was accorded great respect and entrusted with important missions for the government. But Justinian was still seeking a formula by which he could reconcile the Monophysites to the church. Theopaschism had not had the desired effect. So Justinian placed his faith in a new formula proposed to him by Bishop Theodore Askidas of Caesarea, who rapidly ousted Pelagius to become the emperor's principal ecclesiastical adviser. According to Theodore all that Justinian had to do was to condemn the so-called 'Three Chapters', which consisted of the writings of Theodore of Mopsuestia and Theodoret of Cyrrhus and the letter of Ibas of Edessa to Maris the Persian. It was the acceptance of the 'Three Chapters' which had tainted the Chalcedonian settlement with Nestorianism in Monophysite eyes, alleged Theodore. Their condemnation would remove a major stumbling block to the acceptance of Chalcedon by the Monophysites.

The details of the 'Three Chapters' controversy documented in the surviving contemporary sources vividly illustrate the passions aroused by it and the complex diplomatic wheeler-dealing of both pope and emperor which it provoked and which dramatically indicates the nature of their relationship. The way Justinian went about introducing his formula duplicated exactly the conditions which had produced the Acacian schism. For instead of calling a General Council of the church, he promulgated in 544 an edict, drawn up for him by Theodore Askidas, in which the 'Three Chapters' were condemned without prejudice to the authority of Chalcedon. He then proceeded to force the four Eastern patriarchs, Menas of Constantinople, Zoilus of Alexandria, Ephraim of Antioch and Peter of Jerusalem, to sign it. But Menas contrived to make their acceptance conditional upon the agreement of the pope. Despite this the emperor proceeded to bribe and browbeat the rest of the Eastern bishops into accepting it, and they also subscribed to the edict.[7]

But the Latins in the East were made of sterner stuff. For them the edict had committed the two cardinal sins. It had attacked the integrity of Chalcedon and had revived the practice of Zeno and Anastasius of legislating on doctrinal matters without reference to a church council. It was in fact the same procedure that Justinian had followed with Theopaschism, but on that occasion the papacy had

made no protest, probably because it was preoccupied with the
internal factional strife in the Roman church. The victory of the
pro-Eastern faction over the pro-Gothic, however, had removed
that preoccupation, allowing the Roman church to turn its full
attention to defending the faith.

Predictably the hostility of the Westerners was directed towards
the patriarch Menas rather than the emperor. The principal Latins
resident in the imperial capital, the new papal *apocrisiarios* Stephen,
the refugee archbishop Datius of Milan and a group of African
bishops headed by Bishop Facundus of Hermiana, broke off communion with Menas. The Africans composed a memorial to the
emperor denouncing the condemnation of the 'Three Chapters' but
avoiding any attack on the emperor and instead blaming Menas for
it. A copy of the imperial edict was sent to Rome and the pope
canvassed learned opinion about its validity. The deacons Pelagius
and Anatolius, for instance, wrote to the distinguished theologian
deacon Ferrandus of Carthage asking for his view.[8] He replied that
the 'Three Chapters' could not be condemned without compromising the entire Chalcedonian settlement.[9] Indeed as a result of his
canvassing, Vigilius found the whole of the Catholic West to be
solidly opposed to the condemnation.[10]

Faced with this unanimous expression of public opinion, Vigilius
had no alternative but to reject the edict. The *Liber Pontificalis*
account of this episode is patently anachronistic.[11] It says that
Theodora wrote to Vigilius: 'Come fulfil for us what you promised
of your own free will concerning our father Anthimus and restore
him to his office.' Vigilius wrote back:

> Far be this from me, lady Augusta, I spoke before wrongly
> and foolishly: now I do assuredly refuse to restore a man who
> is a condemned heretic. Although unworthy, I am Vicar of St
> Peter as were my predecessors the most holy Agapitus and
> Silverius who condemned him.

The *Liber Pontificalis* has got the issue wrong but the stances
probably right. The restoration of Anthimus was not the issue but
subscription to the edict was. It is likely that Vigilius had given an
undertaking or at least an impression that he would be amenable to
imperial religious policy as the price of his nomination to the papacy.
When Justinian or Theodora or both wrote to him reminding him of
this and urging him to subscribe, he refused. But Justinian was not to
be thwarted by his nominee. An imperial official, the *scribo*
Anthemius, was sent to Rome with specific orders. If Vigilius was in
St Peter's, he was to be left alone. It would be too great a scandal to
attempt anything against him in that symbolic place. But if he was in

any other place, he was to be seized and conveyed to Constantinople. Anthemius arrived in Rome on 22 November 545, to find Vigilius in the church of St Cecilia in Trastevere, celebrating the festival of its dedicatee. In the middle of the mass, a detachment of imperial troops appeared, seized the pope and marched him to the Tiber, where he was put on board a waiting ship. The crowd followed, shocked and bemused. Vigilius pronounced the final blessing of the liturgy from the deck as the ship cast off and the people on the shore cried 'Amen' before flinging stones and missiles at the ship and denouncing the imperial kidnappers in forthright terms which referred to the conditions which the imperial reconquest had brought to Rome: 'Your hunger go with you! Your pestilence go with you! You have done evil to the Romans; may you find evil where you are going!'

Some commentators believe that Vigilius connived at his own kidnapping, citing the fact that he remained in Sicily for a year after leaving Rome.[12] But the Milanese clergy[13] and Victor of Tunnuna[14] in his contemporary chronicle of the events both testify that he was removed by force, and Procopius gives the reason for the delay in Sicily when he writes: 'Vigilius now came to Byzantium from Sicily where he had been awaiting the summons'.[15] Justinian left Vigilius to cool his heels in Sicily and think over the situation.

Vigilius was conveyed from Rome to Catana and there in December 545 made dispositions for the government of Rome in his absence, another indication of the fact that he had left precipitately and without prior arrangement. He held an ordination of priests and deacons whom he sent back to Rome together with the priest Ampliatus, appointed *vicedominus*, and Bishop Valentine of Silva Candida, who were to act as regents in his absence.[16] These clerical personnel left for Rome as soon as sailing conditions permitted and with them Vigilius sent a convoy of grain ships to relieve the starving populace of Rome. But the grain ships were ambushed by the Goths, who killed their crews and captured Bishop Valentine. King Totila had the bishop's hands cut off and then sent him back to Rome.[17] Valentine survived the operation, however, and eventually rejoined Vigilius in Constantinople.

In the meantime Ampliatus took over the financial administration of the papacy together with the deacon Stephen, probably one of the Catanese emergency appointments, and from 552 to 555 they ran the financial side of affairs until Ampliatus died.[18] But Ampliatus seems not to have had the necessary authority or charisma to provide leadership in a Rome blockaded by Goths and racked by plague and famine. An unofficial regent appeared in the person of the deacon Pelagius. Pelagius had accompanied Pope Agapitus to Constantinople in 536, had replaced Vigilius as *apocrisiarios* and had remained there to serve the interests of Vigilius until recalled about 544 and replaced by the deacon Stephen, who held the post until his death in about 547.[19] Back in Rome Pelagius established himself as a trusted and senior figure at court, being charged for instance with consulting Ferrandus of Carthage on the question of the 'Three Chapters'.[20] Pelagius spent much of his personal fortune alleviating the conditions of the destitute and was chosen to go and plead with King Totila for an armistice. When Totila took Rome in 546, it was Pelagius who intervened successfully to prevent a wholesale massacre of the inhabitants. Indeed Pelagius made such an impression on the Gothic king that he was sent by him together with the orator Theodore to convey the Gothic peace terms to Justinian.[21] In this way he found himself reunited with the pope once more. Although Pelagius remained in Rome, it is clear that many of the most senior papal administrators accompanied Vigilius to Constantinople, including the archdeacon Theophanes, the deacons Sarpatus, Rusticus and Paul, the *primicerius notariorum* Surgentius and the *consiliarus* Saturninus.

While Vigilius waited in Sicily for the emperor to summon him, he was made even more aware of the deep-rooted opposition to the condemnation of the 'Three Chapters'. Archbishop Datius of Milan arrived hotfoot from the capital to brief him on developments there. An envoy came from Patriarch Zoilus of Alexandria, who claimed that he had only signed under duress, and there was a petition signed by African and Sardinian clergy urging him not to condemn the 'Three Chapters'.[22]

Having remained for a year in Sicily, Vigilius sailed for the Peloponnese, and thence travelled overland to Constantinople. All along his route bishops and other orthodox men urged him not to condemn the chapters.[23] This emboldened Vigilius to send from Thessalonica a letter to Menas denouncing the edict and threatening him with excommunication for supporting it. However, at Patras on 14 October Vigilius halted to consecrate, on the orders of the emperor, the deacon Maximian, imperial nominee to the vacant see of Ravenna.[24] Eventually Vigilius reached Constantinople on 25 January 547. He was received with great honour by the emperor, took up residence in the Placidia Palace and immediately excommunicated Menas and his followers. Menas, in retaliation, struck the pope's name from the diptychs.[25]

Vigilius had arrived in Constantinople, committed by Western opinion to rejecting the condemnation. He had received nothing but support for this position in Rome, Sicily, Greece and the Balkans. But he had not been long in the capital before he came to terms with the reality of the situation. Vigilius had not become pope by being a man of principle and he was shrewd enough to see that the emperor had set his heart on the condemnation and that out-and-out opposition to a policy on which the emperor had set his heart was simply not practicable. So on 29 June 547, thanks to the mediation of the empress Theodora, Vigilius and Menas were reconciled and withdrew their censures on each other.[26] Privately the pope gave the emperor a document in which he promised to condemn the 'Three Chapters'.[27] But before he could do this publicly he had to placate his own supporters. Many of the non-subscribing bishops from various parts of the empire, some seventy according to Facundus of Hermiana,[28] had made their way to Constantinople to await the decision of the pope. So the pope summoned a conference of his supporters to discuss the problem. Facundus said that it all turned on whether or not Chalcedon had accepted the letter of Ibas. Vigilius had to admit that he did not know the answer to this and Facundus asked for permission to present evidence that would prove his assertion. But that was the one thing Vigilius did not want; so he adjourned the conference and called for a vote. According to Facundus, the non-subscribing bishops were got at by the agents of the emperor. But the vote, carefully guided by the pope, went in favour of condemnation. Vigilius then took the names of the seventy bishops to the imperial palace and added them to the edict. On 11 April 548, he issued his *Judicatum*, addressed to Menas, giving the result of the voting and officially condemning the 'Three Chapters' without prejudice to Chalcedon. That his solution was essentially a political one Vigilius admitted three years later when he described the character and aims of the *Judicatum*,[29] saying that he had sought to avoid a hard line and had made concessions in order to quieten men's minds and 'in accordance with the need of the time we thought to settle matters medicinally'.

The papal entourage was divided over the *Judicatum*. The deacons Rusticus, Sebastian, Sarpatus and Paul and the *primicerius* Surgentius supported condemnation of the 'Three Chapters'. But others, notably the deacon Pelagius, who had arrived with the Gothic peace terms, urged a more cautious course.[30] However, outside the immediate papal circle there was a bitter and widespread rejection of the pope's actions. Many believed that he had sold out the orthodox cause. Bishop Facundus of Hermiana composed twelve books in defence of the 'Three Chapters' and presented them to the emperor.[31] When Benenatus, Metropolitan of Prima Justiniana, called a synod of Illyrican bishops in 549 to condemn the 'Three Chapters', they declared themselves in favour of the chapters, deposed Benenatus and sent a memorial to the emperor calling for the reversal of the condemnation.[32] The African bishops met in synod in 550, excommunicated the pope and sent a memorial to the emperor couched in similar terms to those of the Illyricans.[33] The Dalmatian bishops refused to accept the condemnation.[34] Zoilus of Alexandria withdrew his assent to the edict and repudiated the *Judicatum*, and Datius of Milan declared his opposition to the condemnation. The effect of this rising tide of opposition to the pope eventually rubbed off on the papal entourage itself.

The deacon Rusticus, the pope's nephew, was one of the most enthusiastic supporters of the condemnation, so much so that he illegally had copies of the document made and circulated to various churches, laymen and clerics. He constantly sang its praises and urged support for it. But then just as extremely, he swung the other way. The widespread opposition to condemnation, particularly in the Latin West, seems to have swayed him so considerably that he was soon writing to Pelagius in Italy condemning the condemnation in a letter which Pelagius prudently forwarded to the pope. Rusticus's letter was symptomatic of the increasing underground activity within the papal circle directed against the *Judicatum*. This opposition was soon out in the open. The deacon Paul accused Rusticus before the pope of fomenting opposition to the *Judicatum* in Italy and Africa and demanded his punishment. Rusticus swore on the bible that he would not depart from his obedience to the pope and the matter was dropped. But Rusticus soon joined forces with the deacon Sebastian, the ex-rector of Dalmatia, like himself initially pro-*Judicatum* but now bitterly opposed. He had journeyed to Constantinople to encourage opposition to it. The pope was particularly hurt by Sebastian's actions since Sebastian was one of his own creations. Vigilius accused him of joining the opposition to distract attention from the charge against him of consenting to simoniac ordinations while rector of Dalmatia, and there may be some substance to this accusation. However, Rusticus and Sebastian joined forces with the African monks Felix and Lampridius, already excommunicated for their opposition to the *Judicatum*, and the campaign against Vigilius's stand gathered momentum.[35] The rebels submitted a memorial to the emperor denouncing the *Judicatum* and circulated hostile reports on it as far afield as Scythia. Bishop Valentinian of Tomi wrote to the pope in March 550, reporting on the rumours and the disturbances they were causing. In reply the pope denied that the *Judicatum* infringed Chalcedon and informed him that he had excommunicated the rumour-mongers, namely Rusticus and Sebastian.[36] It is evident that after attempts to win them over had failed, Vigilius had been driven to use the ultimate ecclesiastical deterrent against his nephew.

The excommunication of Rusticus and Sebastian did little to

silence the opposition. It now gained adherents among the junior clergy. A group of subdeacons, notaries and *defensores* among the papal staff, John, Gerontius, Importunus, Severinus, John and Deusdedit, came out against the *Judicatum* and removed themselves from the papal headquarters. Bishops Julian of Cingulum and John of the Marsi were sent to reason with the rebels, but they failed to make any headway. A more high-powered delegation was sent, again including John and Julian, but also the deacon Sarpatus and prominent laymen Cethegus and Cassiodorus. Again the rebels refused to listen and the pope reluctantly excommunicated and deposed them all. Present at the sentencing with the pope were the deacons Peter and Sarpatus, *primicerius* Surgentius, the subdeacons Servusdei and Vincentius and bishops John, Julian and Zaccheus of Scyllacium. If this group constitutes the loyalist hard core of the papal entourage, then it is clear that almost all the junior clergy attending the pope in Constantinople had gone over to the opposition.[37] It is interesting to note the presence among the rebels of a John and a Gerontius. For a Gerontius, a relative of Pope Hormisdas, became *primicerius notariorum* under Pope John III and died on 24 January 565,[38] and a subdeacon John completed Pelagius I's translation of the Greek Fathers into Latin and is believed to have subsequently become Pope John III.[39] Both John III and the *primicerius* would have been junior clergy at the time of the events under discussion and their subsequent prominence suggests that they became reconciled to the pope, perhaps after he had changed his stance on the 'Three Chapters'.

Rumour and counter-rumour were rife, in the wake of these events. They reached as far as Gaul, where it was openly alleged that the pope had repudiated the four General Councils of the church, and Bishop Aurelian of Arelate wrote anxiously to Vigilius seeking reassurance on the matter. Vigilius wrote back duly reassuring him that this was not true and appointing him papal vicar in Gaul with orders to combat such false and lying rumours.[40] However, the extent of the reaction to the *Judicatum* led Vigilius to advise the emperor that a General Church Council must be held to silence the objections of the hard-liners. Vigilius was therefore given leave to withdraw the contentious *Judicatum*, and it was decided that until the decision of that Council was reached nothing further would be done for or against the 'Three Chapters'. On 14 August 550, Vigilius took another oath in writing that he would not oppose the emperor at the coming Council and would do his best to get the condemnation of the 'Three Chapters' ratified.[41] For his part the emperor swore to keep the oath secret.

Preparations for the Council got under way. The bishops of Illyricum flatly refused to attend and only seven came from Italy because of the war. But the leading African bishops turned out in force, led by Archbishop Reparatus of Carthage, the primate Firmus of Numidia and Bishops Verecundus and Primasius of Byzacena. Since the African bishops would be the hard-core opposition at the forthcoming Council, the emperor inaugurated the traditional imperial programme of threats and bribes to win them over to condemnation before the Council ever opened. Archbishop Reparatus refused to agree and was promptly deposed and banished. In his place a pliant imperial puppet, Primosus, was appointed archbishop and was installed with the help of imperial troops after he had agreed to condemn the 'Three Chapters'. However, many African bishops refused to recognize Primosus and withdrew from communion with him. Firmus of Numidia allowed himself to be bribed and was sent home, but died on the way. Primasius of Byzacena refused to condemn and was imprisoned in a monastery; but when the primacy of Byzacena fell vacant with the death of Bishop Boethius, Primasius agreed to condemn the 'Three Chapters' in return for the primacy. Verecundus refused to yield and sought the protection of the pope. Zoilus of Alexandria, continuing in his opposition, was deposed and replaced by the pro-condemnation Apollinaris as patriarch. The governor of Africa was ordered to send all those African bishops who would support condemnation to Constantinople, but to prevent all others from leaving the province.

In view of the refusal of the Illyrican bishops to attend and the likely opposition of at least some of the African bishops, Justinian tried to persuade Vigilius that they should proceed to a condemnation solely on the basis of support for it by himself and the Eastern bishops. But since this would negate the purpose of calling the Council, which was in the main to take account of Western opinion, Vigilius was forced to refuse.[42] Exasperated by the delays and opposition that he was encountering, and anxious to stress imperial dominance in church affairs, Justinian yielded to the advice of Theodore Askidas and issued a new edict against the 'Three Chapters' in July 551. It was officially read out in the imperial palace and promptly signed by Askidas and other Eastern bishops.

This action of the emperor, in breach of the agreement he had reached with Vigilius, left the pope in a terrible dilemma. He called a conference to the Placidia Palace to try and decide what to do. It was attended by both Greek and Latin bishops, including Menas of Constantinople and Theodore Askidas. Both Vigilius and Datius of Milan warned against accepting the new edict and it was decided that anyone who did so would be excommunicated. The pope said that he would urge the emperor to withdraw it.

However, Askidas and his followers left the conference, entered the church where the edict was pinned up, celebrated mass and struck the name of the anti-condemnation Zoilus of Alexandria from the church diptychs, replacing it with that of Apollinaris. This act of defiance left the pope no alternative but to excommunicate and depose Askidas and his followers. The excommunication was signed by ten Italian bishops, two African bishops and archbishop Datius of Milan, who exaggerated his competence somewhat when he declared himself to be acting as representative of the churches of Gaul, Burgundy, Spain, Liguria, Aemilia and Venetia.[43] But even now the pope was unwilling to go into open opposition to the emperor and it was agreed not to publish the condemnation immediately but to give the emperor and the condemned bishops time to change their minds. If they did not or if any violence were offered to the pope, then the edict was to be published.

The anger of the emperor at this refusal of the pope to fall into line was such that Vigilius did indeed fear for his safety and he and the western bishops fled from the Placidia Palace and took refuge in the basilica of St Peter *in Ormisda*, symbolically placing themselves under the protection of Rome's patron. There in August 551, when it was clear that there was no hope of the emperor changing his mind, the excommunication of Theodore and his followers was published.[44]

When Justinian learned of the pope's actions, he sent a detachment of armed guards to remove the western clergy from the church. The clergy resisted removal, and a fight broke out. The deacons and other clerics were dragged out by the hair and the pope clung to the altar until it fell on top of him as the troops tried to dislodge him. Meanwhile, a hostile crowd gathered outside, objecting to the maltreatment of the pope and the soldiers prudently withdrew, leaving Vigilius battered and bruised but still in sanctuary.

Faced with this, the emperor changed his tactics and sent an embassy of high-ranking officials including his nephew Justin, Count Belisarius and the ex-consuls Peter and Cethegus to offer the pope and his clergy safe conduct back to the Placidia Palace and to guarantee their safety. Only when the most solemn oaths had been given did the pope agree and he duly returned to the Placidia Palace, only for the emperor to escalate the campaign of intimidation against him to force him into accepting the new edict. The papal entourage were kept in increasingly harsh conditions and were harassed and insulted. The pope's servants were removed and an armed guard was placed on the palace. It was probably at this time that a campaign of vilification against Vigilius was begun in Italy, in order to isolate him even further. The letter of the Milanese clergy to the Frankish legates recalls that agents were sent to Italy to stir up hatred against the pope and Archbishop Datius and to persuade the people to elect new men in their place, who would support condemnation.[45] They went so far as to get one of the papal notaries to forge letters in the pope's handwriting which were taken to Italy by one Stephanus, with the Gothic legates, in order to inflame public opinion against him. The stories circulated in Rome that Vigilius had murdered his predecessor Silverius, beaten one of his own notaries to death and had had his own niece's husband beaten to death probably derive from this campaign of slander.[46]

Ultimately unable to stand the intimidation any longer, Vigilius and his followers fled once more from the Placidia Palace two days before Christmas 551 and took refuge this time in the church of St Euphemia at Chalcedon, thus again making a symbolic statement of faith. During the stay there the pope issued an encyclical letter describing his ordeal, dated 5 February 552.[47] The persecution continued. The deacons Pelagius and Tullianus were forcibly removed from the church, several of the western bishops were arrested, the African bishop Verecundus died and Vigilius himself fell seriously ill.[48] Once again the emperor changed his tactics and sent in envoys, his nephew Justin, the senior Roman senator Cethegus, the *magister officiorum* Peter and the *quaestor* Marcellinus, to persuade the pope to come out. Vigilius, who had learned his lesson after the last set of promises, would not come out but he did agree to negotiate.

After lengthy discussions, the emperor agreed that the projected General Council should be held and on 6 June 552 the pope and the emperor were officially reconciled. In August 552 Patriarch Menas of Constantinople died, and soon afterwards Datius of Milan followed him to the grave. Abbot Eutychius was appointed as the new patriarch, and sent on 6 January 553 a confession of faith to the pope, saying that he adhered to the four councils and was anxious to see the 'Three Chapters' affair settled. His letter was countersigned by Apollinaris of Alexandria, Domninus of Antioch and Elias of Thessalonica.[49] The pope replied to the letter rejoicing in the end of the separation of the churches.[50]

The emperor summoned the General Council to meet. But this was only the beginning of a new round of frustrations for the pope. He wanted to be allowed to hold a preliminary synod in Italy or Sicily so that the Western bishops could formulate an agreed policy on the 'Three Chapters'. The emperor refused to allow it, but suggested instead a smaller synod in Constantinople attended by representatives of each patriarchate. But the emperor meant by this that there should be an equal number of bishops from each patriarchate. Since there were four in the East and only one in the West this would mean a majority of Eastern bishops. The pope therefore asked if there could be equal numbers of Greek and Latin bishops. The emperor refused, and the pope declined to attend the Council.[51]

The fifth General Council of the church therefore opened without the pope on 5 May 553, attended by the patriarchs Eutychius of Constantinople, Domninus of Antioch and Apollinaris of Alexandria with legates from the patriarch of Jerusalem, and 161 bishops. The attending bishops, apart from a handful of Africans carefully vetted by the governor of Africa and committed to condemnation already, were exclusively Easterners. A deputation was sent by the Council to persuade the pope to attend, but Vigilius pleaded ill-health. The deputation came back on 8 May to renew its request. Vigilius renewed the question of equal Greek and Latin representation but was told that the Council was already in session and that this question could not be raised again. The pope asked for twenty days to consider his position, but the deputation told him he had already had long enough and left. The Council meanwhile proceeded with its work, although the result was a foregone conclusion. Presided over by Patriarch Eutychius, it began with the reading of a letter from the emperor which stressed his duty to unify the church and condemned the 'Three Chapters' giving reasons for the charge of heresy against them.[52] There was very little discussion of the matter and when the Council formulated its findings they followed the emperor's letter closely.

Meanwhile, Vigilius desperately sought a compromise, and on 14 May 553, issued a *Constitutum*,[53] which was signed by ten Italian bishops, three Asian bishops, three Illyrican bishops, one African bishop and three senior Roman clerics, Archdeacon Theophanes and the deacons Pelagius and Peter though not Sarpatus and Tullianus. It was very carefully worded and said that, having examined the proceedings of the Chalcedon Council, it condemned the works of Theodore of Mopsuestia but not those of Theodoret or Ibas. It praised the piety of the emperor but said that no one was permitted to act against the decisions embodied in the *Constitutum*. The subdeacon Servusdei was sent to the emperor with a copy of the *Constitutum*. Justinian refused to accept it and instead sent the *quaestor* Constantine to the Council with the secret document which the pope had signed promising to condemn the 'Three Chapters'. This document was accepted by the Council after Bishop Vincentius of Claudiopolis, formerly a Roman subdeacon and undoubtedly promoted to the Eastern episcopate because of his loyalty to imperial policy, testified that he had been present when the pope signed it.[54] The Council closed on 2 June 553, with the 'Three Chapters' duly condemned and with the pope declared to have agreed to this in writing. Those present, 164 in all, signed the proceedings. The emperor confirmed the decision by imperial edict and the conciliar proceedings were sent out to all provinces of the empire for non-attending bishops to subscribe.[55]

So Justinian had got what he wanted, condemnation of the 'Three Chapters' by a church Council. He now set out ruthlessly and systematically to suppress all opposition to his policy. The Roman deacon Rusticus and the African abbot Felix published an attack on the fifth Council, and they and their followers were arrested and banished to the Thebaid.[56] Bishop Victor of Tunnuna and archdeacon Liberatus of Carthage, both of whom also published attacks on the condemnation, were also banished to Egypt.[57] Bishop Facundus of Hermiana went into hiding to avoid the same fate.[58] Pope Vigilius was placed in close confinement on bread and water for six months, his principal advisers, the deacons Pelagius and Sarpatus, were locked up in monastery-prisons and the junior Roman clergy were sent to hard labour in the quarries.[59] In the absence of Pelagius and Sarpatus, who had launched bitter attacks on the *Constitutum*, the deacons Tullianus and Peter gained ascendancy over Vigilius and under their influence, the pope, his spirit broken and his health undermined by 'the stone', capitulated. On 8 December 553, in a letter to Eutychius, he declared that a misunderstanding had arisen between himself and his Eastern colleagues due to the machinations of the devil and that on further examination he had decided that his previous view had been wrong and that the 'Three Chapters' should be condemned.[60] On 23 February 554 he issued a second *Constitutum*, drawn up for him by the deacons Tullianus and Peter, in which he endorsed the findings of the fifth Council.[61] Justinian had now finished with him. He was released from prison and allowed to return to Rome. But he never reached his destination, for in Syracuse on 7 June 555 he died, nearly ten years after he had been kidnapped from the church of St Cecilia in Trastevere.

The tragic dilemma of Vigilius perfectly highlights the irreconcilable conflict of *Romanitas* and *Christianitas*. Unlike many of his predecessors, Vigilius, who owed his throne to Justinian, put his *Romanitas* before his *Christianitas*. Not only did he consistently seek to avoid offending the emperor but he twice swore in secret to endorse imperial policy despite massive opposition to it from the Western church. That he was forced into a position of defying the emperor was none of his own choosing. He was forced into it by the emperor's constant breaches of faith and autocratic over-riding of previously agreed procedures for getting the condemnation accepted. Vigilius was prepared to go to the limit to support the emperor but Justinian pushed him beyond that limit. With increasing desperation and in the face of an utterly unresponsive imperial government, Vigilius sought any face-saving device, however small, to allow him to support the emperor while at the same time appeasing to some extent Western opinion. In the end Justinian demonstrated the omnipotence of the emperor in church affairs. Having made what seemed to him the magnanimous gesture of allowing a General Church Council to meet, Justinian was just not prepared to make any further concessions. He did not need to. Once the Council had arrived at its fore-ordained decision, Justinian simply broke Vigilius to his will.

Although Justinian had been able to deal with Vigilius satisfactorily enough from his own point of view, he was still keenly aware of the prestige and influence which papal Rome enjoyed in Italy. It was in the interests of the empire that this should be diminished, and the best way of doing this was to create a counterweight to Rome in the ecclesiastical hierarchy. The obvious candidate for elevation to counterweight was the provincial capital of Ravenna, whose bishop would have the added recommendation in the emperor's eyes of being directly subject to the influence of the imperial governor. Ravenna was technically a suffragan see of Rome. But in the fifth century the pope had given the see metropolitan powers over Aemilia province, partly to please the emperor Valentinian who wanted the ecclesiastical status of his capital raised and partly to offset the power of the archbishop of Milan.

Justinian laid the cornerstone of his Ravenna policy in 546 when the death of Archbishop Victor left the see vacant. The emperor selected as the new archbishop the Istrian deacon Maximian of Pola and the compliant Pope Vigilius consecrated him in Patras while on his way to the imperial capital. This is one of the few recorded instances of imperial intervention in Western episcopal elections other than in Rome, and its timing was crucial. Vigilius was leaving Italy for what was to prove a ten-year absence at a time when Archbishop Datius of Milan was already in Constantinople. He had fled there when Milan fell to the Ostrogoths in 539 and, like Vigilius, he was destined never to return, dying in the imperial capital in 552. There was therefore no one capable of impeding the elevation, and the appointment of Maximian marks the beginning of a serious challenge to Rome's primacy, a challenge which was to grow in importance as time wore on.

The challenge was, however, almost stillborn. For when Maximian arrived in Ravenna, its citizens refused to accept him, claiming that they had been deprived of their electoral rights by the imperial nomination and urging Maximian to abdicate. Maximian was refused entry into the city and took up residence in the old Arian episcopal palace outside the city walls. But he embarked there on a clever policy of public relations, inviting civic leaders to dine, loading them with presents and gradually winning them over.[62] Soon he was able to move into the episcopal palace in Ravenna and begin the implementation of twin policies close to Justinian's heart: the elevation of Ravenna in the Italian hierarchy and the securing of Catholic predominance over Arianism, which had obviously been strong in this the former Ostrogothic royal capital.

Justinian manifested his favour towards Maximian on the two visits that the archbishop made to Constantinople after his election. He awarded to the Ravennate church a valuable piece of property in Istria, the title of which was in dispute. Maximian even asked Justinian to send the remains of St Andrew to Ravenna, so that the see could be elevated to apostolic status. Justinian baulked at this, since St Andrew was the alleged founder of the see of Constantinople, but he did load Maximian up with relics of Saints Peter, Paul, Stephen and Andrew, which would certainly enhance the prestige of Ravenna.[63]

Maximian was a man of immense industry and apparently inexhaustible energy. 'He laboured in all things more than his predecessors' wrote his biographer.[64] He compiled a great book of masses, rites and ceremonies, to bring the level of Ravenna's religious ceremonial up to that of Rome. He built many churches and in particular completed and dedicated the great new basilicas of St Vitalis and St Apollinaris *in Classis*.[65] Significantly these churches had been begun after the visit of Archbishop Ecclesius of Ravenna to Constantinople in 526. They were constructed with money and materials supplied by Justinian on land belonging to the imperial fisc and in their early stages the building was supervised by a mysterious Greek banker, Julian the *Argentarius*, who was probably working for Justinian and who died between 533 and 536, being buried by order of the archbishop in St Apollinaris.[66]

It was, however, Maximian who completed the work on St Vitalis and St Apollinaris and the lavish and splendid interior decorations and mosaic murals form a comprehensive programme of visual propaganda designed to emphasize the triumph of Orthodoxy over Arianism, the role of Justinian in the church and the importance of Ravenna *vis-à-vis* Rome. They also begin the elaboration of the legend and cult of St Apollinaris, the founder of Ravenna, in a bid to render him if not as glorious as Rome's founder then certainly as Milan's, St Ambrose.[67]

Maximian waged war on the Manichaean heretics and drove them from Ravenna, but was careful to follow the imperial line on the 'Three Chapters', as a subsequent letter of Justinian testifies:

The sacred mother church of Ravenna, truly mother and truly

orthodox, while many other churches adopted the false doctrine because of their fear and terror of princes, you preserved the true and only faith of holy Catholicism: you never altered, you withstood change, you remained unshaken by the shaking tempest.[68]

Maximian died suddenly at the age of 58 in 556. Justinian did not intervene in the election of his successor, perhaps because he had just nominated a new pope and now had his hands full elsewhere. But the work of elevating Ravenna had been spectacularly begun and the emperor was now more or less able to rely on natural momentum and ecclesiastical pride to carry it along. The new archbishop was the 70-year-old Ravennate deacon Agnellus, a former soldier, and he loyally supported the new Pope Pelagius I in the implementation of Justinian's religious policy.[69] Agnellus was neither church-builder nor apparently propagandist, but Justinian enriched his see by handing over to it all the property of the now suppressed Arian church and Agnellus initiated a programme of reconsecrating all the Arian churches as Catholic ones, thus considerably enhancing the ecclesiastical splendour of the city at a stroke.[70]

The rise of Ravenna went on. Its natural importance as the capital of the exarchate was increased by the Lombard invasions. For with Rome frequently cut off from Ravenna by barbarian incursions, the papacy was forced to concede to the archbishop supervision of those Suburbicarian bishops unable to communicate with Rome.[71] So by the end of the sixth century, the ecclesiastical province of Ravenna was coterminous with the military province and that embraced far more than just the original metropolitan area of Aemilia. Rome soon recognized the importance of Ravenna and this was manifested in several ways. In the late sixth century the papacy secured the successive election of two Romans to the see, John III (578–95) and Marinianus (595–606), in the hope of maintaining control.[72] In the early seventh century Pope Honorius I introduced the feast of St Apollinaris into the Roman liturgy and built a church in his honour in Rome.[73] It became customary to write to the archbishop of Ravenna on the election of a new pope asking him to use his influence with the exarch to secure confirmation of the election and the archbishop was addressed as *reverentissimus et sanctissimus* in contrast to the patriarch of Constantinople who was merely addressed as *dilectissimus*.[74]

However much Justinian sought to elevate Ravenna, the support of the pope was vital for the enforcement of the condemnation of the 'Three Chapters' on a uniformly hostile Italy. The death of Pope Vigilius cannot have been entirely unexpected. After all, he had been

ill for some time and his harsh treatment at the hands of the emperor
would not have done him any good. Justinian, having already successfully accomplished the deposition of Silverius and the installation of Vigilius, did not think twice about intervening again. One of
the most distinguished Romans in opposition to the condemnation
was the deacon Pelagius. He had encouraged Vigilius in his resistance to condemnation. But after the conclusion of the fifth Council,
he was removed from the pope's side and imprisoned in a monastery. After the second *Constitutum*, the emperor asked Pelagius to
justify his continuing opposition, and Pelagius in his monastery
prison wrote a *libellus* justifying his position and that of his fellow
recalcitrant Sarpatus. Written at white heat, *In Defensione Trium
Capitulorum* was a passionate defence of the 'Three Chapters' and a
bitter denunciation of everyone opposed to them, with the notable
exception of the emperor, on whom Pelagius remained tactfully
silent. He wrote angrily of Vigilius's *inconstantia* and *venalitas*, depicting him as a crafty old man dominated by even craftier cronies and
satellites, notably the deacons Tullianus and Peter.[75] Justinian, however, knew Pelagius well and had valued him highly when he was
papal *apocrisiarios*. He therefore scented an opportunity for compromise, and achieved a masterstroke.

The memory of this compromise is enshrined in a story retailed by
the *Liber Pontificalis*.[76] According to this a petition arrived from the
clergy in Rome asking for the return of the pope, and Justinian
therefore summoned the papal entourage back from their places of
exile. He addressed them in the following terms: 'Do you wish to
accept Vigilius as he was your Pope? If so, I thank you. If not, you
have here your archdeacon Pelagius and my hand will be with you.'
The clergy replied: 'May God direct your piety. Restore to us now
Vigilius and when God wills he pass from us, let Pelagius our
archdeacon be given to us according to your command.' It is unlikely
that the dialogue is verbatim but it unquestionably embodied the
substance of a deal arrived at between Justinian and the papal entourage. Justinian sent for Pelagius and offered him the papal throne in
return for his support for the condemnation. Pelagius, having
thought it over, came to the conclusion that his defence of the 'Three
Chapters' was based on biased evidence and that they should in fact
be condemned. He accepted the offer, was reconciled with Vigilius
and probably at this time appointed archdeacon in place of
Theophanes, who had presumably died. The clergy then accepted
the ailing Vigilius as pope but agreed to back Justinian's nominee
Pelagius for the succession when the time came. The anti-
condemnation historian Victor of Tunnuna gave a rather more terse
account of the events:

Pelagius the Roman archdeacon, once defender of the 'Three Chapters', returned from exile at the persuasion of Emperor Justinian and condemning those things which he had constantly defended for a long time, he was ordained as bishop of Rome by *praevaricatores*. [77]

It is clear, then, that Pelagius was known to have sold out the condemnation cause to obtain the papal throne, and this certainly contributed to the difficulties he was to experience in Rome. The first hurdle he had to get over was that of the election. Vigilius's body was transported back to Rome and buried not in St Peter's, as was the custom, but in the church of St Marcellus on the Via Salaria outside the city. [78] The reason for this is probably either that he was so unpopular because of his betrayal of the 'Three Chapters' that the usual papal resting place was denied him, or, as in the case of Pope Felix III, he chose burial in a church that had a connection with his family.

Pelagius may have been the officially designated successor, but in Rome popular feeling favoured the priest Mareas, who had been virtual unofficial ruler of Rome in recent years. His epitaph speaks of his generosity to the poor and his opposition to attempts to tamper with the faith (i.e. condemn the 'Three Chapters') and concludes 'You would have deserved the pontifical honour'. [79] But Mareas died in August 555 and there was no serious opponent to stand against Pelagius, who was duly elected pope in September 555. But even if the Roman clergy were prepared to follow the emperor's directive on the succession, Pelagius remained massively unpopular. The *Liber Pontificalis* says that 'no bishop could be found to ordain him'; it was not until 16 April 556 that Pelagius was ordained, and then by Bishop John of Perusia, Bishop Bonus of Ferentinum and the priest Andreas of Ostia, rather than by the customary bishops of Ostia, Portus and Albanum. [80] This reflects the deep opposition within the Italian episcopate to the condemnation of the 'Three Chapters'. It is an opposition that was shared by the population of Rome for the monasteries and 'a host of pious, wise and noble people' withdrew from communion with Pelagius. The *Liber Pontificalis* says it was because they believed that he had killed his predecessor. [81] This may have been one of the rumours flying around in the perfervid atmosphere but the real reason was almost certainly his support for the condemnation of the 'Three Chapters'.

But Pelagius had one ally who was to stand him in good stead, the chamberlain Narses, who had become governor of the province following the final defeats of the Goths. Narses assumed responsibility for the papacy's financial administration during the enforced interregnum and concerted with Pelagius a dramatic plan to re-establish his credibility. A solemn procession was held from the church of St Pancras, the avenger of broken oaths, on the Janiculan Hill to the basilica of St Peter's, and there before a large congregation with a bible in his hand and a cross above his head Pelagius ascended the pulpit and took an oath of innocence. According to the *Liber Pontificalis* it was innocence of doing harm to Vigilius but it was in fact innocence of impugning Chalcedon. During 557–8 he also circulated copies of a detailed declaration of orthodoxy 'to dispel suspicions about the orthodoxy of the Roman see'.[82] This seemed to satisfy the people of Rome at least and within the city opposition to him gradually subsided.

But outside Rome, in Italy and beyond, the opposition remained virulent. To silence the widespread murmuring against him in Gaul, he sent an official declaration of orthodoxy to King Childebert on 3 February 557, complaining bitterly about the calumnies circulated by heretics against him.[83] In Italy, however, the challenge to his authority was even greater and more immediate. The bishops of *Italia Annonaria* broke off communion with the papacy and, headed by the archbishop of Aquileia, remained in schism from Rome for 150 years. Initially the archbishop of Milan did the same, but when the see was moved to Genoa to escape the Lombards, the archbishop of Milan became reconciled with Rome. Even in suburbicarian Italy there were pockets of resistance to Pelagius, though they decreased as he became established in Rome. For instance, Pelagius complained bitterly about the contempt in which Bishop Secundus of Tauromenium held him.[84] There were some successes, however. Archbishop Agnellus of Ravenna remained loyal to the condemnation policy and strove to keep Aemilia in line.[85] Governor Narses and the civil authorities backed the pope, undoubtedly on the orders of the emperor. Seven bishops of Tuscia *Annonaria* withdrew from communion with Rome but were successfully either won over or dealt with.[86] It was a long haul, but by the time of his death Pelagius seems to have persuaded Suburbicarian Italy that the condemnation of the 'Three Chapters' did not invalidate Chalcedon.

His record in other fields will have helped him. For Pelagius set to work at once to repair the ravages of the Gothic wars both in the Roman church and the Suburbicarian province. His epitaph records: 'He consecrated many ministers of the divine law, staining not his immaculate hands with gold. He redeemed captives. He was quick to succour the afflicted and he never refused to share his goods with the poor.' It also adds interestingly:

As guide he revealed the venerable dogmas of the apostolic

faith which the famous fathers had decided. He cured by his eloquence those who had fallen into schismatic error so that their hearts having been pacified, they might hold to the true faith.[87]

This confirms that in *Italia Suburbicaria* at least, Pelagius's view of the 'Three Chapters' ultimately prevailed.

He undertook a comprehensive programme of restaffing the church, whose personnel had been drastically reduced as a result of the wars and the long absence of the pope. By the time Vigilius died his court circle was near to collapse. Many of its leading figures were now old men. As Pelagius wrote to his old friend Sarpatus: 'We are both old men'.[88] The archdeacon Theophanes and the *apocrisiarios* Stephen had both died in Constantinople and the *vicedominus* Ampliatus had died in Rome about 555. The *consiliarius* Saturninus died soon after his return to Italy.[89] Rusticus and Sebastian had been exiled and were heard of no more. The subdeacon Vincentius had sold out to the emperor, gained his bishopric and stayed in the East. What became of the junior clergy who had been excommunicated is not known for certain but it is possible that some of them were reconciled, given the variations in the fortunes of others at court. To halt the drift in papal affairs and restore the dilapidated state of the administration, it was necessary to act swiftly to fill important posts. Pelagius nominated his old friend the deacon Sarpatus as *apocrisiarios* in Constantinople, but in 559 yielded to his complaint that he was too old for the job and recalled him.[90] When the *consiliarius* Saturninus died early in 559 the pope replaced him with the *vir magnificus* Theodore.[91] It is likely too that the *primicerius notariorum* Surgentius died early in the reign, since the *Liber Pontificalis* mentions the fact that Pelagius appointed the godfearing Valentine as 'his notary'.[92] The appointment of a notary is nothing unusual and this should perhaps be interpreted as the appointment of a new *primicerius*. The financial administration of the papacy, in particular, seems to have been in a rundown state. After the death of the *vicedominus* Ampliatus, the imperial governor Narses had taken over the financial administration of the papacy, assisted by a trio of priests, Felix, Dulcitius and John.[93] There was clearly a lack of financial expertise in the papal administration and it may well explain the appearance at this time of a layman, the banker Anastasius, as the first known papal *arcarius*.[94] In addition, Pelagius sought to refill the papal treasury by collecting the back rents of the patrimonies and appealing for subsidies from outside Italy. For instance, he wrote to Bishop Sapaudus of Arelate asking him to urge his father the patrician Placidus, rector of the papal patrimony in Gaul, to collect and send to Rome the revenues of the church possessions, because Italy was ravaged and destitute and in need of funds, and also to send warm clothing for the poor.[95] He also wrote to the praetorian prefect Boethius of Africa urging him to send a subsidy to help provide for the flood of refugees.[96]

He made special efforts to restore the scattered church plate and this is reflected in several of his letters. He ordered Bishop Severus of Camerinum[97] to recover the plate of one of his parish churches, reportedly sold by a previous priest to a merchant. He gave permission for Bishop Hostilis (see unknown)[98] to proceed against certain of his clerics who had removed church plate. He upbraided Bishop John of Nola[99] for selling the plate of one of his parish churches on the grounds of the impoverishment of that parish and urged him instead to join it to the cathedral church and provide for it from central funds. The clergy had been reduced by their poverty to the expedient of selling church plate; the pope clearly frowned on this, ordering plate already sold to be recovered, and he forbade plate to be disposed of in future. Indeed, so concerned was Pelagius with the problem that he appointed the notary Valentine, to deal full-time with the plate problem.[100] When Pelagius died on 3 March 561 he had, during the space of only five years, made himself and the condemnation policy acceptable in suburbicarian Italy and had put a run-down, impoverished and seriously disarrayed church back on its feet. It was a considerable achievement.

Chapter 10

The Lombardic Crisis

The success of Pelagius I in gaining acceptance for imperial religious policy meant that there was no electoral controversy after his death. The see was vacant for only three months and twenty-five days, which suggests that the election followed speedily upon his death and that imperial confirmation was obtained without undue delay. The new pope, consecrated on 17 July 561, was John III. The son of a senator, he was from the same social class as Vigilius and Pelagius and, although there is no evidence of imperial interference in the election, it is unlikely that Pelagius, Narses or Justinian would have permitted the election of a successor who was hostile to the empire or the imperial religious policies. There are several indications that John was a pro-Easterner. According to Evagrius, he was born Catelinus and changed his name upon attaining high ecclesiastical office.[1] If this is so and he followed the precedent of pope John II, born Mercurius, then he chose the name of the 'martyred' pro-Eastern pope John I. It is likely that John is to be identified with the subdeacon John who completed Pelagius I's translation of the *Vitae Patrum* and compiled a collection of extracts from the Greek fathers, part of that movement seeking to make Eastern theology and culture more accessible and acceptable to the West.[2] John III's actions as pope associate him closely with the imperial authorities.

But John's reign is chiefly significant for two events over which he had no control. The first was the death of the emperor Justinian in 565 after a reign of thirty-eight years and a period of ascendancy at court of nearly fifty years. He had been a remarkable ruler. Despite personal failings of character, he had cherished a grandiose vision of a restored Roman Empire, glorious, orthodox and united and to this end had inaugurated a lavish building programme, codified the law, sought a solution to the religious problems and launched a reconquest of the lost western provinces of Italy, Africa and Spain. But the extent of his achievements should not be allowed to obscure the fact that in many ways his reign was an anomaly, a temporary damming up of the stream of history. His predecessors Zeno and Anastasius had more or less ignored the West and with major military problems confronting them in the East and in the Balkans, Justinian's successors, in particular Tiberius Constantine and Maurice, were forced to do likewise. It was essentially the logic of events which overtook and doomed the Justinianic vision of a revived Western Empire. During the seventh century, the Eastern Empire fought its own desperate battle for survival against the onslaughts of Avars, Persians and Arabs and under the impact of this, imperial foreign policy underwent a profound reorientation. From now on imperial resources and interests were concentrated primarily on the East. Italy, being geographically peripheral to the imperial heartland, inevitably took bottom place on the strategic priority list. Constantinople, despite a theoretical commitment to the old Roman ideal of a universal empire, decisively shelved Justinianic reconquest plans and satisfied itself with holding on to what remained of the Western provinces at as little cost as possible to the imperial treasury. One byproduct of this new imperial attitude which was beneficial to Rome, however, was that there was never again the sustained programme of imperial interference in papal elections that Justinian had mounted, and as time went on the empire became less and less able to carry out such a programme of imperial interference even if it had wished to do so.

The death of Justinian I, then, was in many ways the end of an era, just as the other major happening under John III were the beginning of an era. In 568 the Lombards invaded Italy and reduced a substantial part of it to subjection. The minatory presence of a new and permanently settled race of Arian barbarians put a whole new complexion on the social, political and religious situation in Italy and it was to have profound repercussions for papal Rome.

The background to the invasion was one of increasing disenchantment with imperial rule. Although in his *Pragmatic Sanction* of 554,[3] Justinian had decreed the restoration of the senate and the Roman educational and taxation systems, the restoration of misappropriated slaves, property and money and the introduction of the imperial law code, he could do little to whip up enthusiasm for the imperial reconquest in a country which was utterly impoverished and exhausted by two decades of war. Even after the Goths were finally defeated, peace still did not come, as there were two revolts by mercenary leaders seeking to establish new barbarian regimes, Widin the Gothic count defeated in 563 and Sindual, the Herulian chief, defeated in 565.

The Italians turned against Narses, who was the provincial

governor, making him the scapegoat for all their ills. Paul the deacon speaks highly of him:

> He was a pious man, a catholic in religion, generous to the poor, very zealous in restoring churches and so much devoted to vigils and prayers that he obtained victory more by the supplications he poured forth to God than by the arms of war.[4]

Not surprisingly in view of this record of exemplary piety, he enjoyed excellent relations with both Pelagius I and John III. But it was not a view shared by the Italian people who, groaning under the tax burden imposed by their liberators, found Narses's enormous personal fortune a gross affront. 'Moved by envy', therefore, the Italians sent a deputation to Constantinople in 567 to ask the new emperor Justin II to replace Narses and hinted that if this did not occur then Italy's loyalty to the empire could not be relied upon.[5] Justin II and his wife Sophia, who were in the process of reversing their predecessors' policies and replacing his appointees, used this as the opportunity to dismiss Narses and replace him as governor by Longinus. In view of his massive unpopularity in Rome, Narses retired to Naples. The fact that the year after his dismissal, the Lombards invaded gave credence to the story that he had invited them to attack.[6] But there seems to be little foundation in fact for this rumour.

Not only was there political disaffection with the empire, there was still considerable religious disaffection. The condemnation of the 'Three Chapters' may have been accepted by Suburbicarian Italy but in the north the opposition to condemnation was as deep-rooted and pervasive as it had been under Pelagius I. Both the papacy and the imperial government were despised for espousing condemnation and this fact must go some way towards explaining the almost total lack of resistance to the invaders in the north. When you add to this the paucity of Byzantine garrison troops and the enfeeblement of the population by plague and famine, the scale and speed of Lombard success are explained.

As the Lombards poured south and Governor Longinus sat in Ravenna, powerless to do anything, John III went in desperation to Naples to beg Narses to return to Rome and take charge. He agreed to do so and took up residence in the imperial palace in Rome. But unpopularity continued to dog him and was even extended to Pope John for inviting him back. It reached such a pitch that John withdrew from Rome and took up residence at the cemetery of Saints Tiburtius and Valerian on the Via Appia two miles outside the city.[7] There he carried out all his duties, including even the consecration of bishops. Despite his unpopularity Narses continued to administer Rome, dying there in about 571 at the age of 95.[8] His body and riches were returned to Constantinople. John III followed him to the grave in 574 and was buried in St Peter's on 13 July of that year.

The impetus of the Lombard invasion was checked by the murder of King Alboin in 572 and the suspension of the Lombard kingship after the murder of his successor Cleph two years later. The empire sought to take advantage of this by mounting a major military expedition under Count Baduarius in 575, but its total defeat put an end to imperial military intervention and the recognition of the Lombard presence as a permanent reality. Thereafter the imperial government pursued an Italian policy based on a combination of money and diplomacy.[9] The Italians themselves raised money, some 216,000 *solidi*, to pay for troops and sent it to Constantinople in 577 with a high-powered embassy headed by the senior member of the senate, the former praetorian prefect Pamphronius. Even then the emperor could spare them no troops and could only give them the advice to use the money to buy the services of dissident Lombard dukes or purchase help from the Franks.[10]

The emperors were not entirely inactive. Justin II sent a fleet of grain ships to combat the disastrous famine which occurred under Pope Benedict I (575–9).[11] Maurice paid King Childebert of the Franks 50,000 *solidi* to attack the Lombards.[12] But the most practical help to be given was Maurice's action in organizing the remnants of imperial Italy into a militarized province, the exarchate, centred on Ravenna. This had serious implications for Rome. For, inevitably, the better part of imperial resources and troops in Italy were deployed in the defence of the Ravenna enclave itself. This left Rome cruelly exposed; for although it was nominally the headquarters of a duke, he seems to have had few troops, little money and comparatively little real authority. It was to be the pope who was to step perforce into the vacuum.

For the papacy the Lombards constituted a two-fold problem, both of whose facets threatened her survival. They reintroduced the only recently extinguished Arian heresy into Italy to threaten the predominance of Catholicism, while they also constituted a physical threat to the existence of Rome. The threat of the destruction of the Eternal City loomed large in these years, its reality confirmed by successive sieges of Rome.

Nevertheless, though frequently reduced to a state of desperation and sometimes even exasperation with the imperial authorities, the popes remained devotedly loyal to the Roman Empire. Their *Romanitas* stood firm, emphasized if anything by the barbarian threat to that empire, which for them meant civilization and Christianity.

As an alien darkness enfolded Italy, the papacy shone forth as one of the few surviving beacons of the empire in the West. The close co-operation between Narses and both Pelagius I and John III was not an isolated episode and although few subsequent popes achieved such a *rapport* with the exarchs, and indeed sometimes found themselves at loggerheads with them, their loyalty never wavered. Indeed, though help was often pitifully inadequate and though Rome was on her beam ends, assaulted on the one hand by the swords of the Lombards and on the other by natural catastrophe in the form of famine, plague and flood, the period between the Lombard invasion and the next theological crisis (Monotheletism) was a time not of crisis of loyalty but of reaffirmation of it. *Romanitas* ruled.

The death of Justinian, the preoccupation of his successors with the East and the commitment of the papacy to the condemnation of the 'Three Chapters' took much of the imperial pressure off the papacy. Justin II, Tiberius Constantine and Maurice paid little heed to papal elections beyond granting the customary imperial confirmation. Nothing is known of the details of the elections of Benedict I or Pelagius II, though something has survived about Gregory I's election to illustrate how such matters were conducted in the latter part of the sixth century.

Little is known about either the character or reign of Benedict I, elected to succeed John III in 575, but he may not have been as insignificant as the brief notice in the *Liber Pontificalis* suggests. His reign was marked by the continuing depredations of the invading Lombards and by a serious famine, during the course of which Benedict died. But he did make some interesting appointments, taking Gregory the Great from his monastery of St Andreas and ordaining him as a deacon and appointing a Roman John III as archbishop of Ravenna, thus showing a commendable desire to strengthen his own administrative staff and ensure the maintenance of papal influence in the exarchal capital.

At the time of Pope Benedict's death in July 579, the Lombards were besieging Rome. His successor was Pelagius II, a Roman by birth but the son of a Goth, Unigild. His reign is marked by two events which might seem on the face of it to be anti-imperial. He was ordained as pope in 579 without waiting for imperial confirmation to arrive[13] and in 580 he wrote to Bishop Aunarius of Auxerre to persuade the Franks to intervene in Italy to save the church.[14] But in fact this involves no real departure from the loyalist position of the papacy at all. The ordination without permission was undertaken because the Lombards were besieging Rome and it was no time to be without a pontiff. The imperial confirmation eventually arrived and Pelagius's reign was officially dated from its receipt in

November 579. The appeal to the Franks was simply a measure of desperation induced by the absence of any material help from the empire and was entirely in line with imperial policy, having been suggested to the Italian embassy of 577 by the emperor Tiberius himself. The conditions which Rome faced, the very real fear of imminent catastrophe, are well summarized in a letter Pope Pelagius II sent in 584 to his *apocrisiarios* in Constantinople, the deacon Gregory, despatched in 579 to try to activate the emperor:[15]

> So great are the calamities and tribulations we suffer from the perfidy of the Lombards in spite of their solemn promises that noone could adequately describe them. . . . The empire is in so critical a situation that unless God prevails on the heart of our most pious prince to show to his servants the pity he feels and to grant us a commander or general, then we are lost. For the territory around Rome is completely undefended and the exarch writes that he can do nothing for us, being unable himself to defend the region around Ravenna. May God bid the emperor to come to our aid with all speed before the army of that impious nation the Lombards shall have seized the lands that still form part of the empire.

But Pelagius's loyalty remained undimmed as is testified by the inscription he added to the altar of St Peter's, which contained the prayer that 'the Roman sceptre may be guided by the divine hand so that under its rule the true faith may have freedom'.[16]

Pelagius seems to have been a vigorous and active pontiff, but his reign was cut short in February 590 when he died of the plague then ravaging Rome. What followed his death is known from the biography of his successor, Gregory the Great, and gives us the first glimpse into papal elections since the death of Pelagius I. John the deacon wrote:[17]

> The pestilence having robbed the church of its head, the clergy, senate and people combined unanimously to elect Gregory who, wishing to avoid the burden of office, claimed that he was unworthy, fearing lest worldly glory which he had rejected might possess him under the appearance of ecclesiastical administration. But when he was unable to evade the general consensus of opinion, he pretended he would accept and secretly sent letters to the emperor Maurice, to whose son he was godfather, begging him to refuse his assent to the election. But the prefect of the city, his brother, anticipated this, intercepted the letters and sent one announcing the unanimous choice by the people of Gregory and Maurice confirmed the election.

When the imperial confirmation arrived, Gregory fled from the city in disguise and hid in a cave in the woods, but was discovered, dragged back and consecrated pope in St Peter's. Whether the story of his flight is true or not, he certainly complained volubly in his letters about being forced to shoulder the burdens of the papacy, writing in such vein to the emperor's sister Princess Theoctista, the patriarch John of Constantinople, the patriarch Anastasius of Antioch, Bishop Leander of Hispalis, the *quaestor* John, Count Philip the *comes excubitorum*, Andreas *vir illustris*, the *scholasticus* Paul, the patrician Narses and Archbishop Anastasius of Corinth, to name but a few.[18]

The account of the election contains two points of interest. The first is the presence among the electors of the senate. By now it was a very much attenuated body and this is one of its last appearances before it ceased to function altogether. The second is the acceptance by all concerned of the practice of imperial confirmation. It was clearly natural and normal, despite the fact that it involved vacancies of months and sometimes even of years in the occupany of the papal throne. Gone were the short vacancies of Ostrogothic days, and with post-Justinianic Italy at the mercy of invasion and turmoil this was a very serious development. After John III's death, there was a vacancy of ten months and three days. After the death of Benedict I, it was three months and ten days, after the death of Pelagius II, three months and twenty-five days, after Gregory I's death, five months and eighteen days before imperial confirmation arrived and the new pope could properly be consecrated. The fact that the *Liber Pontificalis* remarks on Pelagius II's being consecrated before imperial confirmation was received, shows that this was unusual. There was no repetition of that upon his death, however.

All the evidence points to the election of Gregory being a case of the city turning unanimously to the best man for the job. Indeed, Gregory was destined to become the greatest of sixth-century popes and one of the most notable in the entire Middle Ages. An aristocrat and a scholar, he was more than fitted by background and experience to occupy the throne of St Peter. He had proved his administrative capability in three different spheres – the civil administration as prefect of Rome, the monastic world as founder of St Andreas *ad clivum Scauri* and the Roman church both as papal *apocrisiarios* and 'secretary of state'. His circle of contacts at the imperial court was wide and influential and this was extremely significant for a Rome urgently and constantly seeking more imperial aid. In addition his character, dedicated, austere and determined, was in keeping with the character of the times.

His activity was ceaseless, and Paul the deacon wrote of him:

He never rested but was always engaged in providing for the interests of the people or in writing down some composition worthy of the church or in searching out the secrets of heaven by the grace of contemplation.[19]

But his lifestyle remained after his election, as before it, simple and monastic. He lived the communal life in the Lateran palace in company with monks, just as he had when papal *apocrisiarios* in Constantinople.[20] He fasted rigorously and always dressed in the simplest garb.[21] Indeed John the deacon went so far as to remark: 'The Roman Church in Gregory's time resembled the church as it was under the rule of the Apostles or the church of Alexandria during the episcopate of St Mark.'[22] Yet, despite the self-effacement implicit in Gregory's adoption of the title 'servant of the servants of God' and his constantly reiterated emphasis on humility as 'the mother and guardian of virtues',[23] Gregory maintained the hierarchic pre-eminence of the church of Rome, saying for instance 'the Church of Constantinople was beyond all doubt subject to the apostolic see'[24] and successfully exercising jurisdictional primacy in a case involving Eastern monks.

For Gregory was by nature a conservative, an authoritarian and a legalist, an old-fashioned Roman of the best kind, public servant and *pater familias*. This image is stamped on everything he did: his strict insistence on justice for all, including unusually for this period, the Jews;[25] his refusal to learn Greek;[26] his use of the antique title of *praetor* to describe his tenure of the city prefecture;[27] his insistence above all on the maintenance of order and discipline. He wrote:[28]

Since it is proper to restrain men from illicit deeds and salubriously to check excesses, the punishment system must studiously be preserved. For if it is neglected, everything will fall into confusion, with one man destroying what another has built up by observing it.

His achievements as pope were considerable, his writings prodigious. He was the last of the great Western patristic authors, the popularizer of monasticism, the propagator of extensive missionary activities, the supreme administrator and organizer. Despite this Gregory's achievements were forgotten and his memory spurned in Rome for nearly three centuries after his death. The Spanish deacon Taio of Saragossa, coming to Rome in 642, found his literary works neglected. It was not until the late ninth century that a Roman life of Gregory appeared, written by John the deacon and partly prompted by the fact that both English and Lombard lives of Gregory had already appeared. The scrappy and grudging biography in the *Liber*

Pontificalis attests the contemporary neglect of his achievements.

The reason for this can probably be found in his most-daring and least documented innovation – his bid to monasticize the papacy. Gregory was the first monk to be elected pope and, although it was almost certainly his wide experience of government in many fields which prompted his election, his deep commitment to the monastic ideal led to the virtual conversion of the papal palace into a monastic establishment and the preferment of monks and ex-monks to high office both in the church administration and the episcopate. The effects of this policy were to reverberate through the papacy, dominating elections and reviving the bitter electoral disputes which had been absent from the Roman scene for nearly half a century. However, unlike the previous disputes, this is not even tinged with doctrinal issues but is purely an issue of internal church politics, with the clergy striving to wrest back control of the positions of power from the monks.

Although the clergy eventually won the battle and ousted the monks, Gregory made a great contribution to the advancement of Western monasticism. The sixth century was the period of the 'great leap forward' in the spread of monasticism in Italy. St Benedict of Nursia drew up his *Rule*, founded many monasteries and powerfully advocated the life of contemplation and withdrawal. Cassiodorus, the former praetorian prefect, his dreams of a Gotho-Roman state broken, set up a monastery at Vivarium, collected together a large library, initiated a programme of copying and translation and associated the monastic movement with the preservation of learning and the humanities. Finally, Gregory the Great carried monasticism to the papacy, popularized it and propagandized for it in his own life, his outlook and his writings, particularly his biography of St Benedict. If Gregory I can be said to have had a programme, then that programme was underlaid by the principles of St Benedict's *Rule* – absolute obedience, simplicity of life and constant occupation. 'Idleness is the enemy of the soul' was clearly a dictum Gregory not only understood but lived by.

One of the fields in which he was most active was that of missionary work. In the sixth and seventh centuries Gregory was unique for the extent of his involvement in the propagation of the faith. His greatest success came in the conversion of the English, spearheaded by a monastic mission led by the prior of St Andreas, Augustine. Fittingly, therefore, it was the English who rescued his reputation from the obscurity, to which the failure of his monasticization policy had relegated it. The earliest life of Gregory is by an anonymous monk of Whitby, and throughout the period in which he was uncelebrated in Rome Gregory was revered in England as the instigator of the island's conversion. But it was not only to England that Gregory sent missions. He was equally occupied with Africa, Sardinia and Istria. But it is important to remember that he undertook this work not because he thought it would elevate the papacy but because he believed it was his duty to see the true faith spread throughout the whole world. As Gregory himself wrote:[29]

> By the shining miracles of his preachers, God has brought to the faith even the extremities of the earth. In one faith has he linked the boundaries of the East and the West. Behold, the tongue of Britain which before could utter only barbarous sounds has lately learned to make the Alleluia of the Hebrews resound in praise of God.

There is no word of papal advancement here.

Nor did Gregory seek consciously to elevate the papacy or increase its powers in his dealings with the Lombards or the empire. The fact that he did do so was accidental. Gregory's chief desire was to maintain the *status quo*. It has been said of his writings for instance: 'Gregory has nowhere promulgated an original thought: he has rather preserved in everything the traditional doctrine.'[30] He had apparently no desire to redefine the relationship between church and state.

Gregory was, however, keenly aware that the most pressing problem facing him was the Lombards. He wrote to the *quaestor* John in Constantinople complaining: 'For my sins, I have been made bishop not of the Romans but of the Lombards, whose compacts are swords and whose favour is a punishment.'[31] Gregory was confronted both by the failure of the exarch of Ravenna to act in response to Gregory's urgent promptings and the inadequacy of the defences of Rome. He wrote to the *scholasticus* Paul in Sicily as soon as he was consecrated complaining that the city was ringed with hostile swords and threatened within by the sedition of the soldiery.[32] The source of the problem seems to have been that the exarch's strategy for the defence of the imperial territories centred on providing forces to protect the Rome–Ravenna land corridor at the expense of the garrison of Rome. But the increasing interference of the papacy in what the exarch regarded as his business led to the progressive alienation of the exarch Romanus from the pope. It had reached the state by 595 of Gregory writing of Romanus: 'I will only say that his malice towards us is worse than the swords of the Lombards.'[33]

To remedy the situation in Rome, Gregory found himself forced to act. But he did so with considerable reluctance, regarding it as a distraction from his proper duties. As he wrote in his *Homilies*:

> How can I think what my brethen need and see that the city is guarded against the swords of the enemy and take precautions lest the people be destroyed by a sudden attack, and yet at the same time deliver the word of exhortation fully and effectively for the salvation of souls. To speak of God we need a mind thoroughly at peace and free from care.[34]

Initially, however, he took only the traditional steps to help. In August 591[35] he authorized the rector Peter of Sicily to purchase extra grain to the value of 50 pounds of gold and transmit it under guard to Rome, which was afflicted by famine, drought and plague. In the same year he encouraged the bishops of Italy to take advantage of the psychological effect of the plague on the Lombards to step up efforts to convert them to Catholicism.[36]

But soon he was forced to go further than this and take effective control of the garrison of Rome and supervise the co-ordination of military operations in the duchy. In the face of imminent attack by the Lombard Duke Ariulf of Spoletium, he despatched troops from Rome to reinforce general Velox in the field and he offered the imperial commanders tactical advice on how to deal with Ariulf.[37] To plug the most serious gaps in the defensive system, he appointed in 592 Leontius, *vir clarissimus*, as commandant of Nepe and the tribune Constantius as commandant of Naples, because this vital imperial stronghold lacked a commandant and the exarch refused to appoint one.[38] Gregory threw the full weight of his authority behind the appointments, informing the population of Nepe: 'Whoever resists his lawful commands will be deemed a rebel against us and whoever obeys him will be obeying us.'[39]

Nevertheless, Ariulf attacked the duchy and captured several towns. Although ill, Gregory opened negotiations with Ariulf, who demanded heavy subsidies to conclude a treaty. When Romanus heard of Gregory's actions, he forbade them. Gregory wrote hastily to Archbishop John of Ravenna, urging him to prevail on the exarch to withdraw his objections and lamenting the fact that Romanus would neither fight nor make peace. Gregory warned that not only Rome but Naples was threatened by the exarch's inactivity and lack of adequate defensive dispositions.[40]

Despite the exarch's opposition, Gregory did conclude a treaty with Ariulf at the church's expense.[41] But Romanus, who resented Gregory's usurpation of his prerogative, immediately broke it, marched to the duchy of Rome, received the surrender of Perusia from the treacherous Lombard duke Maurisio and took Ameria,

Tuder and Luceoli.[42] He then removed so many troops from Rome to garrison his conquests that Gregory lamented that 'to hold Perusia, Rome has been abandoned.'[43]

There were even more serious repercussions for Rome when King Agilulf, concerned at the Lombard reverses, marched south to retrieve the position. He recaptured Perusia and in 593 besieged Rome. Gregory worked closely with the *magister militum* Castus and the prefect Gregory to concert defence plans. The pope had already taken on the job of paying the troops. When he came to the throne, only the Theodosiac regiment remained stationed in the city and it was mutinous for lack of pay and could hardly be persuaded to man the walls.[44] It was not until 595, after representations had been made to Constantinople, that the emperor Maurice sent their pay to Rome.[45] In the meantime in sheer desperation Gregory paid them out of the papal treasury. As he wrote to the empress Constantina: 'As at Ravenna the emperor has a paymaster for the First Army of Italy, who defrays the daily expenses as need arises, so at Rome for such purposes am I paymaster.'[46]

But the defences of the city were simply not up to withstanding a determined Lombard assault and so once again Gregory negotiated and agreed to pay Agilulf 500 pounds of gold from church funds for peace.[47] The strain of these continual payments told heavily on church resources; in 595 Gregory lamented: 'How much we have to pay them daily from the church's treasury in order to live amongst them at all is impossible to compute'.[48]

The government deeply resented Gregory's interference, however, and the emperor wrote reproaching the pope for making terms, and accusing him of being taken in by false Lombard promises. Gregory stoutly defended himself against the charges and furthermore interceded for Castus and the prefect who had fallen into imperial disfavour for supporting him in his negotiations. Nevertheless, the treaty with Agilulf was regarded as invalid.[49]

Gregory now turned his efforts to resolving the situation by persuading the Lombards and the exarch to make a general peace. He wrote to Archbishop Constantius of Milan saying that he was willing to pay out yet more church money as part of such a settlement.[50] But once again Romanus proved the stumbling block. Nevertheless, Gregory opened negotiations with Agilulf and in 595 wrote to the *scholasticus* Severus[51] in Ravenna to say that Agilulf was willing to make a *generalis pax* as long as the exarch would agree that breaches of it by either side should be submitted to independent arbitration. Agilulf was even willing to make a special peace with the pope if the exarch refused to agree to the general peace. But Gregory was unwilling to accept this because one of his reasons for wanting the general peace was to allow the empire time to regroup and rebuild and prepare for a successful assault on the Lombards. The problem of Romanus was resolved by his death in 596 and the appointment as his successor of Callinicus, who proved much more amenable to the idea of the general peace. Abbot Probus, one of the pope's closest confidants, continued the negotiations but this time with the blessing of the exarch, and then in 598, on the written instructions of Callinicus, Probus concluded the treaty.[52] It held until 601 when Callinicus took advantage of a rebellion by the dukes of Tridentum and Forumjulii to attack Parma and carry off Agilulf's daughter and her husband Gottschalk. Furious, Agilulf entered into an alliance with the Avars and attacked the exarchate, destroying Padua, devastating Istria and defeating Callinicus in battle before the walls of Ravenna. In 603 Callinicus was recalled and replaced by Smaragdus, who had served a previous term as exarch, and who now made peace, restoring Agilulf's captive daughter.[53] The peace was still in force when Gregory died.

It is quite evident from this account that Gregory considerably extended the powers of the papacy by negotiating treaties, paying the troops, appointing commanders and disposing of soldiers. But he tried throughout to work with the exarch; when the stiffnecked and resentful Romanus was replaced by the more approachable Callinicus, the exarch was perfectly willing to make use of the good offices of the church with the Lombards to advance the imperial cause.

There is no indication anywhere in Gregory's writings that the enhancement of the papacy in real terms which he had brought about in any way diminished his respect for the emperor or altered his conception of himself as a loyal subject. He wrote,

> He is guilty before Almighty God who is not sincere both in word and deed to his most serene sovereigns. In making this suggestion I, the unworthy servant of your Piety, speak not as a bishop nor as your servant by the law of the empire but as your servant in the personal sense, since, my most serene lord, you were my lord before you became the lord of all men. . . . I who thus address my sovereign, what am I but dust and a worm?[54]

Despite his frequent professions of loyalty, Gregory tenaciously defended the interests of the church if he thought them to be threatened. There were several instances where the pope found his *Romanitas* and his *Christianitas* in conflict. The way in which he sought to resolve the conflict is illuminatingly demonstrated in the first of these which arose in 593 when the emperor Maurice decreed that no one engaged in public duty should undertake any ecclesiastical office or retire into a monastery and that no soldier could become a monk until his term of service had expired. Not unnaturally Gregory protested against this law, but he concluded his letter of protest by saying:

> In obedience to your commands I have caused this law to be transmitted throughout the various countries. I have also informed my most serene sovereigns by this letter that the law is certainly not in accordance with the will of God. I have thus discharged my debts to both sides: I have obeyed the emperor and yet have not kept back what I felt ought to be said on behalf of God.[55]

In the event, after protracted negotiations between pope and emperor the law was modified to the effect that no *curialis* might be received into a monastery until released from his obligations to the state and no soldier until a careful enquiry into his previous life had been made and until he had passed a three-year novitiate, in order to ensure that he was not seeking simply to escape from his military duties but was genuinely motivated.[56]

More serious and long drawn out was the 'Oecumenical Patriarch' controversy. At a synod held in Constantinople in 588, the patriarch John IV had assumed the controversial title 'Oecumenical Patriarch' and Pope Pelagius II had promptly annulled the acts of the synod and forbidden his *apocrisiarios* to take communion with John until he repudiated the title.[57] Gregory revived the papal protest, writing to the emperor, the patriarch and other prominent figures in the East denouncing the title and predicting the destruction of church unity and indeed the downfall of the empire unless the title were abandoned.[58] John, however, refused to abandon the title and was supported by the emperor Maurice, who failed to see what all the fuss was about, writing to Gregory 'that there ought not to be ill feeling between us on account of a silly name'.[59] But Gregory became almost paranoid on the subject of the 'Oecumenical Patriarch' and wrote furiously to the Patriarchs of Alexandria and Antioch, seeking to enlist their support, and accusing anyone who presumed to assume such a title of being 'the forerunner of Antichrist'. Even when John IV died in 595 and was succeeded by Cyriacus, there was no resolution of the problem, since the new patriarch also refused to relinquish the title. So the quarrel dragged on and Gregory was still writing to Cyriacus to urge its removal the year before his death.[60] It was finally concluded in 607 when the emperor Phocas confirmed Rome's primacy by edict.[61] But it was almost certainly the resentment Gregory felt about the title which caused him to greet the murder of Maurice and the usurpation of Phocas in 602[62] with such unbecoming jubilation that his modern biographer, F. H. Dudden, wrote: 'No one who has learnt to admire the character of the hero of this biography can read these letters without deep regret.'[63]

There was also a difference of strategy between Gregory and Maurice over the Istrian schism. Having sought and failed when 'secretary of state' under Pelagius II to win the schismatics over by persuasion, Gregory as pope determined to proceed to sterner measures, and in the first year of his pontificate ordered Archbishop Severus of Grado to attend a synod in Rome to resolve the dispute.[64] But the Istrian bishops promptly petitioned the emperor, stressing their orthodoxy and their loyalty to the empire and warning that both would be endangered by Roman persecution. They further agreed to present themselves in Constantinople and plead their case once the Lombards were defeated and peace restored. Maurice, seeing the force of their arguments, wrote to Gregory ordering him not to trouble the Istrians until peace was restored.[65] Reluctantly Gregory obeyed and, while Maurice lived, he confined himself to encouraging conversion, though even in this area he was reprimanded by Exarch Callinicus for over-zealousness and he was reminded of the emperor's orders.[66] However, as soon as Maurice was dead and his successor had re-appointed as exarch Smaragdus, who during his previous term had earned papal approbation by kidnapping the archbishop of Grado and forcing him at sword-point to recant, Gregory wrote to the exarch urging the sternest measures against the schismatics and reminding him of his previous sterling work in that direction.[67]

Lastly, the Ravenna *pallium* dispute must be noted as a further step in the rise of Rome's principal rival in the Italian hierarchy. The successive appointment of two Romans to the archiepiscopal see did nothing to damp down the ambitions of the exarchal capital. Archbishop John began wearing the *pallium* in public processions and at audiences with the laity; and the Ravenna clergy started using the *mappulae,* the distinctive white linen saddle cloths hitherto exclusive to the clergy of Rome. Gregory, who seems to have regarded this as a threat to the Roman primacy somewhat akin to the 'Oecumenical Patriarch' title, was swift to react. He wrote in July 593[68] upbraiding John for his actions and saying that he had had the archives searched and had consulted various liturgical experts and could find no precedent for this indiscriminate use of the *pallium*. John replied, attaching a list of privileges granted by previous popes to Ravenna, but agreeing to suspend the wearing of the *pallium* until Gregory had made a final decision.[69] What made the matter more serious for Rome was that the civil authorities backed John, and both the exarch Romanus and the praetorian prefect George wrote in support of his stand. In October 594 Gregory sent his decision.[70] In future John was to wear the *pallium* only on the festivals of St John the Baptist, St Apollinaris and St Peter and on the anniversary of his own ordination. John not only ignored the decision and continued to wear the *pallium* indiscriminately but Gregory also learned that John was given to cracking scurrilous and insulting jokes about the pope. This provoked an angry letter from Gregory, accusing him of double-dealing, ordering him to mend his ways and thanking God that the Lombards are between them so that he cannot act as severely as he is prompted to do.[71] The death of John in January 595 temporarily halted the dispute. There was a lengthy electoral wrangle which ended with Gregory successfully installing as archbishop the Roman monk Marinianus from his own monastery of St Andreas. But this did not mean an end to the *pallium* dispute, for leading members of the exarchal administration continued to press for the approval of the position adopted by John. Gregory therefore resorted to the time-honoured device of referring the matter to a succession of official enquiries, the final outcome of which is not known to us.[72] But it is not unlikely that the increasingly independent-minded archbishops simply went ahead and used the *pallium* as they wished.

The death of Gregory I in March 604 inaugurated the battle for control of the papacy between the monkish and clerical factions that was to rage until submerged by the next great theological crisis – Monotheletism. Although this is examined in detail elsewhere, it should be noted here as a continuing theme of the first half of the seventh century. However, whichever faction in the struggle the various popes supported, their *Romanitas* remained constant and this was important at a time when the empire was facing the most serious threat to its existence for years.

The period between the death of Maurice and the beginning of the Monothelete controversy was marked by a high state of cordiality in relations between Rome and Constantinople. Phocas, probably because his predecessor had taken a contrary position, ended the 'Oecumenical Patriarch' controversy by issuing an edict confirming the Roman primacy. It was granted in 607 to Pope Boniface III, who had been Gregory's *apocrisiarios* at Phocas's court, and it was marked by the erection in Rome of a column in Phocas's honour. There was more to come. For Pope Boniface IV (608–15) sought and gained from Phocas permission to turn the Pantheon temple in Rome into a church. It was dedicated to St Maria *ad martyres* and lavishly endowed by the emperor.[73]

But during the capricious and inept reign of this same emperor the Roman Empire came suddenly and dramatically face to face with the prospect of total collapse. The Oriental provinces, long disaffected because of the religious policies of the imperial government and constantly complaining of the tax burden, fell almost without a whimper to an onslaught by the Persian king. The very survival of the empire was brought into question. A saviour appeared in the person of the emperor Heraclius, son of the exarch of Carthage, who in 610 sailed to Constantinople, overthrew the tyrant, mobilized the people in a holy war against the invader and in a succession of brilliant military campaigns won back all that had been lost. The climactic point of his reign came in 630 when he paid a state visit to Jerusalem to restore the True Cross, carried off by the Persian invaders, to its rightful resting place. This regaining of the lost Oriental provinces compelled the government to face the still unresolved problem of Monophysitism and it was the government's attempts to solve this which were to precipitate the Monothelete controversy.

In the meantime, however, the uncertainty in the East had its repercussions in Italy. The unpopularity of Greek rule, financially burdensome and militarily inadequate, manifested itself in two uprisings during the reign of Pope Deusdedit (615–18). The exarch John was murdered, together with other senior government officials in Ravenna, and in the south, John of Compsa, perhaps a local military commander, proclaimed himself emperor and seized Naples. The crisis was met by prompt action from Constantinople. A new exarch, Eleutherius, was appointed and despatched to Italy. He secured Ravenna, arresting and executing the ringleaders of the revolt there, and then he marched to Rome, where he was warmly received by the pope, and from there he proceeded to Naples which he captured, executing the usurper. Finally he paid out a donative to the Italian army to secure its loyalty to the throne.[74] Having restored imperial authority within his own territories, Eleutherius resumed the war against the Lombards, but after being soundly beaten by the Lombard general Sunduarit he concluded a treaty on the basis of an annual tribute of 500 pounds of gold.[75]

With the fate of the empire in the East still in the balance, Eleutherius decided to make a bid for the throne himself and in 619 proclaimed himself emperor in Ravenna. Archbishop John V of Ravenna, perhaps in the hope of compromising the pope, advised Eleutherius to go to Rome for his coronation. But when Eleutherius arrived at Luceoli on his way to Rome, he was seized and beheaded by the troops, who despatched his head to Constantinople and returned to their allegiance. This took place during the vacancy between the death of Deusdedit and the ordination of Pope Boniface V, but there is no evidence of any support for his rebellion in Rome.

The army were clearly still loyal to the empire and the papacy certainly was too.[76]

The death of Boniface V was followed after only a thirteen-day vacancy by the ordination of Honorius I (625–38). He was to reign for nearly thirteen years and *Liber Pontificalis* notes approvingly: 'He did many good things'.[77] The period since the death of Gregory I had been marked by a succession of short-lived, insubstantial popes, whose reigns had been filled with economic and political crisis – plague, famine, rebellion, earthquake. Honorius took the papacy by the scruff of the neck and shook it heartily, making a concerted effort to dispel the gloom and fatalism creeping over Rome.

His epitaph was to speak of him 'following in the footsteps of Gregory'[78] and there can be little doubt that Honorius was the last of the Gregorian popes committed to a programme of support for monasticism, an active pastoral administration, a continuing interest in newly converted England and the propagation of a distinctively Western clerical education, free of theological complexity and Oriental subtlety. Honorius was even from the same background as Gregory and whether his father, the consul Petronius, is interpreted as being one of the last Western consuls or a military commander in the sense 'consul' was soon to assume, there is no doubt that Honorius was a wealthy aristocrat by birth. He turned his Roman home next to the Lateran into a monastery dedicated to Saints Andreas and Bartholomew, a clear echo of Gregory here, and endowed it with money and estates; he chose as his 'secretary of state' a monk, abbot John Symponus.[79] He undertook a major programme of educating the clergy whose standard of learning had lamentably declined. He sought to revitalize the flagging English mission, by despatching Birinus to convert the West Saxons and making organizational arrangements for the see of York.[80] He may also have sent an evangelizing mission to the Croats in Dalmatia, though this is more likely to have been the work of John IV, himself a Dalmatian, who had revived the see of Spalato and sent Abbot Martin to redeem captives from the Croats.[81]

But unlike Gregory, he undertook a massive programme of church building and renovation, the first since the Gothic wars, spending lavishly to restore the pride and panoply of papal Rome. The *Liber Pontificalis* says that he built or rebuilt churches 'too numerous to mention'.[82] At least ten of these are known by name. In particular he covered the great doors of St Peter's in silver, covered the tomb of St Peter in silver and made two pairs of silver candlesticks to stand before the tomb. He gained permission from the emperor Heraclius to recover the roof of the Lateran with bronze tiles taken from the temple of Roma. His aim was clearly to do something positive and visible to stop the sight of derelict and decaying churches in Rome and its environs hastening the erosion of the faith. Some 2000 pounds of silver were utilized to restore the glamour and glitter of the sanctuaries of the faith.

But none of this was done with the idea of creating an alternative power centre. For Honorius worked closely with the imperial authorities and his aim, like that of Gregory, was to shore up the imperial structure. He gained Heraclius's permission for the use of the bronze tiles from the temple of Roma, as part of his programme of beautifying Rome. When he took decisive steps to secure papal authority in Grado by appointing the Roman subdeacon Primogenius to the archbishopric after the schismatic Fortunatus had fled to the Lombards,[83] Heraclius backed up his efforts by making good the loss of Grado's treasures.[84] Honorius acted as paymaster of the imperial troops in Rome as Gregory had done[85] and threw the church's weight behind the pro-imperial king Adaloald in the Lombard civil war.[86] He also sought to end the rivalry with Ravenna, making clear strides towards *rapprochement* by building and endowing a church in Rome dedicated to Ravenna's patron saint, St Apollinaris, and ordering a weekly litany sung in honour of Saints Apollinaris and Peter, a firm indication of alliance rather than confrontation.[87] He gave joint instructions to the notary Gaudiosus and the *magister militum* Anatolius on how to administer the city of Naples,[88] further indicating a close co-operation between papal administrators and military commandants. Like Gregory, he was not prepared to stand for the flouting of the church's rights, and when a group of excommunicated Sardinian clerics due to be shipped to Rome were spirited away to Africa by Duke Theodore of Sardinia, he sent a strong protest to the praetorian prefect George of Africa, backed up by copies of imperial laws and papal privileges.[89]

An altogether admirable ruler, whose reign marked a decisive revival of papal vigour, Honorius was described in an inscription in St Peter's as *Dux Plebis* – 'The Leader of the People'.[90] It is an interesting contrast with the view of Gregory I as 'the Consul of God'. Honorius is seen as a military leader rather than a civilian magistrate, a commander mobilizing the forces of the papacy to battle for the faith, inspiring the people by his church-building, his encouragement of spirituality as embodied by the monks and his programme of educating the clergy. He deserved a better fate than the official condemnation of his memory made at the sixth General Council of the church and subsequently incorporated into the papal coronation oath. But this condemnation and with it the final discrediting of the Gregorian programme was the direct result of the rise of Monotheletism.

Chapter 11

The Monothelete Crisis

The papacy had survived the Lombard crisis by the skin of its teeth, and by forging close links with the imperial government had achieved a measure of security. The empire itself had also undergone and survived a major crisis. But it was determined to avoid, if it could, another crisis of loyalty in the Oriental provinces. That meant finding some compromise formula that would reunite the Mono-physites to the orthodox faith, something Justinian had spent his entire reign searching for in vain. After all the effort he had put in to get the 'Three Chapters' condemned, the condemnation in the end failed to achieve the desired results and the Monophysites remained as far from reconciliation as ever. However, the patriarch Sergius of Constantinople now developed the doctrine of Monoenergism, a new formula which argued that Christ had two natures (to accommodate the Chalcedonians) but one energy (to accommodate the Monophysites). It seemed an ideal way of reconciling the two sides and was enthusiastically taken up by the emperor Heraclius, who began negotiations with the Eastern churches to get it accepted. The *Catholicus* Ezr of Armenia accepted it in 630 and this was confirmed by an Armenian church synod of 633. Cyrus, an enthusiastic suppor-ter of the doctrine, was installed as patriarch of Alexandria in 631 and the doctrine was accepted by an Egyptian church synod in 633.

As always, of course, the position of the pope was crucial. It was to Honorius I, the practical man of affairs, administrator and statesman, that Sergius wrote in 634 seeking his opinion on the new doctrine. Honorius, who was impatient of theological subtlety and pro-foundly aware of the danger to the faith that endless debates about words constituted, sought to pre-empt such a debate by making what he believed to be an authoritative statement:[1]

Truly confessing that the Lord Jesus Christ is a single operator with both human and divine natures, I would sooner that the

181

pointless, bombastic and timewasting philosophers who weigh up the two natures should croak at us like frogs than that the simple and humble people of Christ should remain in doubt.

There is no doubt that Honorius was completely orthodox in his outlook.[2] But, refreshingly ahead of his time, he failed to see the point of the endless debates on the natures and energies of Christ. Therefore he expressed himself without theological clarity and laid himself open to attack. The Monotheletes such as Patriarch Pyrrhus of Constantinople and Patriarch Macarius of Antioch were to return constantly to what they claimed was Pope Honorius's endorsement of Monotheletism. The pope's letter was to prove a major embarrassment both to the papacy and the champions of orthodoxy. Initially, however, they staunchly defended Honorius's memory. Pope John IV wrote to the Emperor Constantine III declaring that the West was scandalized by attempts to link Honorius's name with these 'novelties which are contrary to the rule of faith'.[3] Abbot Maximus, having consulted leading men at the papal court, including Abbot John Symponus, who had translated Honorius's letter from Latin into Greek, several times declared that Honorius was perfectly orthodox.[4] But it was raised yet again at the sixth General Council of the church and was argued so strongly by the Monotheletes that in the end, when Monotheletism was officially condemned, Pope Honorius was condemned along with the other heresiarchs. It was unquestionably a humiliation for the papacy and it was a permanent one. Pope Leo II assented to the condemnation, which declared that Honorius 'tried with profane treachery to subvert the immaculate faith',[5] and thereafter the oath taken by all popes at their consecration contained the condemnation of Honorius.[6]

Despite the hope of Honorius that all debate about the two natures would cease and his belief that it was all irrelevant anyway, the forces of orthodoxy took up the challenge of Monoenergism and rallied under the leadership of the octogenarian Palestinian monk and orator Sophronius, who saw Monoenergism simply as Monophysitism in disguise and as yet another bid to subvert Chalcedon. The old battle was on again. Undeterred by the mounting opposition, Sergius refined his new doctrine into Monotheletism, which claimed that Christ had two natures and two energies but only one will. The new doctrine was embodied in an imperial edict, the *Ekthesis,* promulgated in 638. It argued that however many natures or energies Christ had, he could not have two mutually contradictory wills. It would not be common sense. So it banned the teaching of one or more energies and ordered adherence to one will. But the orthodox advanced against this the same argument that it was still Mono-physitism in disguise.

Meanwhile political events were rapidly overtaking the religious crisis. The Arabs, who had risen up to fill the vacuum left by the collapse of the Persian Empire, attacked and overran the Oriental provinces of Egypt, Syria and Palestine. The empire was faced by yet another massive military and political crisis. The Byzantine army was routed at the battle of Yarmuk in 636. Jerusalem fell in 637. The Byzantine commander in Syria was captured and sewn up alive inside a putrescent camel. The emperor Heraclius, faced with the virtual collapse of his life's work, went into a rapid physical and mental decline. The Arabs swarmed on unchecked and it was as if the clock had been turned back to the dark days of 610 when Heraclius, young and confident, had taken control of the tottering empire.

Despite the Arab invasions, the work of implementing the *Ekthesis* as the basis of imperial religious policy went on. Pope Honorius I died in October 638. His death was followed by a vacancy of one year, seven months and eighteen days. The length of the vacancy was due entirely to the new religious policy. The elderly Severinus was elected to succeed Honorius and the papal *apocrisiarii* sailed for Constantinople to get imperial confirmation of the election. The patriarch Sergius had also just died, but the senior clergy of Constantinople, presumably acting on the orders of the emperor, told the envoys that they would not support the request for confirmation unless the envoys promised to get the pope to subscribe to the *Ekthesis*. The envoys, having read the document, were unwilling to agree to this but they were equally unwilling to allow the Roman see to remain vacant indefinitely. So they agreed to show the new pope the edict and ask him to sign it if he deemed it correct. This apparently satisfied the government and the imperial confirmation was granted.[7]

During the vacancy, however, the exarch Isaac in Italy decided to take advantage of the uncertainty to provide himself with funds. He sent his *chartularius* Maurice to Rome to seize the papal treasury. Maurice convinced the garrison of Rome that Pope Honorius had withheld their pay and that it was stored in the Lateran. The army stormed the Lateran, but Severinus and his followers barricaded themselves in, and the troops could not effect an entry. After three days of force, Maurice turned to guile. He and the civil officials of Rome, who were his accomplices, persuaded the pope elect to allow them to enter and seal up the treasure vaults, presumably on the grounds that this would restore peace. After this had been done, Maurice sent for Isaac, who arrived and arrested the leading Roman clerics, exiling them from Rome temporarily so that no one could resist him. Then Isaac entered the Lateran and plundered it for eight days, removing the papal treasures to Ravenna and prudently sending part of them to Heraclius to prevent imperial displeasure overtaking him.[8]

Severinus was eventually ordained on 28 May 640. But two months later he was dead. He had made no decision about the *Ekthesis* one way or another and presumably the same conditions for confirmation were offered to his successor, the archdeacon John, for he was ordained as John IV on 24 December 640, after a delay of only four months. But by now the implications of the imperial decree, which offended against the basic papal beliefs and principles in the same way that previous imperial decrees had, were obvious and Pope John's first act was to hold a synod in Rome, which discussed the *Ekthesis* and formally condemned it along with Monotheletism.[9] He wrote to inform both the new patriarch Pyrrhus of Constantinople and the emperor Heraclius of its findings. Heraclius, broken in mind and body, wrote back disowning the *Ekthesis* and blaming it on Pyrrhus.[10] Shortly afterwards he died on 11 February 641. Pope John himself died in October 642 and the election produced an interesting result.

There is little doubt that it was refugee monks and clerics from the East, particularly Palestine, fleeing from the Arab invasions, who brought word to Rome of the nature of Monotheletism and its danger to Chalcedonian Orthodoxy. It was one of these Palestinian refugees who was elected as Pope Theodore I in 642. His election suggests the presence of an influential body of Greek clergy in Rome and testifies to a desire to have a man who spoke Greek and was versed in the theological subtleties of the East on the papal throne, to avoid any future embarrassments like Pope Honorius's letter. Only one month and thirteen days elapsed between the death of John and the ordination of Theodore on 24 December 642, and, given that it would be impossible to get to Constantinople and back in that time and particularly during the winter, it is likely that the election was confirmed by the exarch. The year 641 was one of considerable confusion in Constantinople. On Heraclius's death, the throne had been vested jointly in his sons Constantine III and Heracleonas. But the sudden death of Constantine III barely three months after the death of his father aroused suspicions of poison, and popular gossip accused Constantine's unpopular stepmother, the empress Martina. Before the end of the year there had been a military coup, which ousted and banished Martina and her son Heracleonas and installed as emperor Constantine III's 11-year-old son, Constans II. The patriarch Pyrrhus, a close associate of the disgraced empress, fled to Africa, and Paul was appointed to replace him.

In an attempt to profit from the uncertainty in the East, the *chartularius* Maurice, relying on the links he had forged with the civil and military authorities in Rome, induced the Roman army to support him in a bid to unseat the exarch Isaac, claiming that Isaac was planning to declare himself emperor. But Isaac acted swiftly by sending an army under general Donus to Rome. Maurice's allies deserted him and Maurice himself fled into sanctuary at St Maria *ad Praesepe*. But he was dragged from the church, escorted to Ravenna and beheaded.[11] Soon afterwards Isaac was killed in battle with the Lombards after a distinguished eighteen-year tenure of office during which he had consolidated imperial rule and successfully kept the Lombards at bay.

Pope Theodore, who seems to have remained aloof from all this, busied himself about his religious duties, writing to the new emperor to ask why the *Ekthesis* was still in force when it had been rejected both by the late pope and the late emperor. In a characteristic piece of primatial bravado, he also declined to recognize the new patriarch Paul until two special papal envoys had conducted investigations into the circumstances surrounding the deposition of Pyrrhus.[12]

But Theodore was not in fact the leader of the orthodox forces. The successor of Sophronius, who had died during the siege of Jerusalem, was his disciple Abbot Maximus, the former secretary of Emperor Heraclius who had abandoned his public career for a monastic life and had become a brilliant theologian. Having fled from the Arab advance, he was based now in North Africa, from where he directed the orthodox resistance to Monotheletism, with the support of the exarch Gregory of Africa and other leading dignitaries. His greatest coup came in 645 when in a disputation with the ex-patriarch Pyrrhus he persuaded Pyrrhus to acknowledge his error and recant.[13] Following the debate, Maximus and Pyrrhus left Africa for Rome. There Pyrrhus issued a public recantation of his heresy in the presence of clergy and people. The pope recognized him as patriarch of Constantinople and in a solemn ceremony, he was installed on a patriarchal throne next to the altar of St Peter's and issued a donative to the people.[14] Paul, who had been urged by the papacy to abandon Monotheletism and in reply had sent a defence of the heresy to Rome, was excommunicated.[15]

In Constantinople the government was becoming seriously alarmed, for they now faced a situation which was the exact reverse of the one that had prevailed in Egypt and Syria. In those provinces the disaffection of a Monophysite population for an orthodox government had paved the way for first Persian and then Arab invasion. In Africa and Italy, orthodox opposition to a now Monothelete government might presage the same thing. In 647 the growing religious disaffection did indeed explode into political action. The exarch Gregory of Africa proclaimed himself emperor with a policy of religious orthodoxy and was supported by the population of the province and the neighbouring Moorish tribes. The Arabs chose this moment to launch their attack. They defeated and killed Gregory but then, having exacted tribute from the province, they withdrew. A surprised imperial government reasserted its authority but it remained distinctly shaky.

It was quite clear that something would have to be done to defuse a religious situation which was threatening the political stability of the western provinces. The patriarch Paul suggested a solution and this was promulgated by the emperor Constans in 648, under the name of the *Typos*. It was yet another imperial edict, which abrogated the *Ekthesis* and simply forbade discussion of the question of the two energies or the two wills under severe penalties. As always neither side was satisfied with what was in effect a bid to settle the question by the suppression of free speech. At this point the patriarch Pyrrhus, who had apparently only recanted in the hope that the exarch Gregory (now dead) and the pope might help him to regain his patriarchal throne, saw a better hope of restoration in the change in imperial policy. So he went to Ravenna and, in the expressive phraseology of the *Liber Pontificalis*, 'he returned like a dog to his vomit'.[16] He recanted his recantation and was promptly anathematized by the pope. But it got him what he wanted. For when Paul died in 655, Pyrrhus was restored to the patriarchal throne, only to die five months later.

With the *Typos* a new phase in the theological battle had been inaugurated. Hitherto there had been debate, discussion, attempts to persuade. Now there was a ban on discussion and it was a ban which the imperial government intended to enforce, insisting that the leading ecclesiastical dignitaries sign the *Typos* as a token of their agreement. The priest Anastasius, the papal *apocrisiarios* in Constantinople, refused to subscribe and was arrested and exiled to Trebizond. Other orthodox men in the capital who adopted the same attitude were punished by flogging, exile and imprisonment. The chapel in the Placidia Palace was closed down and the altar demolished.[17] But the papal authorities were careful not to blame the emperor for this. The official view in Rome was that the patriarch Paul, 'inflated by a spirit of pride', was responsible.[18]

At this critical juncture Pope Theodore died, and was buried in St Peter's on 14 May 649. Only fifty-two days later his successor was consecrated without imperial confirmation.[19] It was the deacon Martin, who had been papal *apocrisiarios* in Constantinople in the early years of Pope Theodore and had had to negotiate with the recalcitrant Paul. Martin thus knew both the personalities and the issues involved in the dispute and his position was one of uncompromising hostility to the *Typos*, a stance in which he was backed by Abbot Maximus and the ever-increasing throng of exiled monks and refugee clerics in Rome. Martin took steps to organize the anti-Monothelete opposition in Palestine by appointing the orthodox Bishop John of Philadelphia as apostolic vicar, in the absence of an orthodox patriarch. But his most important act was to summon a synod to meet at the Lateran basilica.[20] It opened on 5 October 649 and was presided over by the pope, who addressed it first, denouncing Monotheletism and recounting the sufferings of the orthodox faithful in Constantinople.[21] It was attended by 105 bishops and during its eight sessions the heresy was debated and denounced. A leading part in these debates was taken by the senior Italian prelates, Archbishops Maximus of Grado and Deusdedit of Caralis, and it is clear that the Italian hierarchy was united in opposing Monotheletism. But the principal intellectual force in the opposition was unquestionably provided by the Greek exiles and the presentation to the synod of a memorial signed by thirty-seven of them was one of the high points of the proceedings.[22] Eventually its conclusions were drawn up and signed and copies were circulated throughout East and West, one being sent to the emperor urging condemnation of the heresy. They condemned Monotheletism, the *Ekthesis* and the *Typos* and their principal champions, Sergius, Cyrus, Pyrrhus and Paul. There was no mention of the emperor.

The reaction of Constans II was characteristically swift and autocratic. Martin's actions were after all nothing less than a slap in the face. For a known opponent of the emperor's religious policy to be elected pope was bad enough but for him to be ordained without imperial consent and then to hold a council in which the government's religious policy was rejected was quite insupportable. So Constans despatched the *cubicularius* Olympius to Italy as exarch with orders to arrest the pope and get all the bishops, leading laymen and foreign priests to subscribe to the *Typos*. The inclusion of the third category indicates that the government had a good idea who was behind Roman resistance and that they hoped to neutralize it. Specifically Olympius was instructed to proceed to Rome and, if the Roman garrison could be relied upon to support him, to seize the pope. If the garrison was unreliable, then he was to withdraw to Ravenna, secure firm control of the province and as soon as a loyal body of troops could be assembled, to proceed with the arrest.[23]

What followed Olympius's arrival in Italy is known in detail and once again the age comes vividly alive, thanks to the letters of the pope from exile and a contemporary account of his sufferings known as the *Commemoratio*.[24] Olympius arrived in Rome while the city was still full of the bishops from the synod. But he found such a wide measure of support for Martin's stand that he was unable to act openly. Instead he tried to foment schism, presumably on the grounds that Martin had been improperly elected. When this failed, he tried to have the pope assassinated during mass in the church of St Maria *ad Praesepe*. When this also failed, he made his peace with the pope, revealed the emperor's orders to him and then marched south to repel an Arab attack on Sicily. There, if the witnesses who gave evidence at Martin's trial are to be believed, Olympius proclaimed himself emperor and was preparing to overthrow the legitimate authority when he succumbed to an epidemic which ravaged his army. Left leaderless, the army returned to its allegiance.[25]

Undeterred by the failure of Olympius, Constans re-appointed a former exarch Theodore Calliopas to succeed Olympius, and sent him to Italy with the *cubicularius* Theodore Pellurius, who was specifically charged with the task of arresting Martin and conveying him to Constantinople. The exarch and the *cubicularius* arrived in Rome with the Ravenna army on Saturday 15 June 653. Fearing the worst, the pope took refuge with his clergy in the Lateran basilica, sending clerical envoys to the exarch, who said that he would come next day and pay his respects to the pope. But the next day was Sunday and the pope celebrated mass in the basilica amidst such great crowds that the exarch excused himself on the grounds of fatigue and said that he would come on the following day. On Monday, then, the exarch sent Theodore Pellurius to accuse the pope of concealing arms and armed men in the Lateran Palace. The pope gave permission for the palace to be searched and nothing was found. At midday on Monday 17 June the exarch and his men entered the basilica. The pope, ill since the previous October, lay on a bed in front of the altar with a large body of clergy around him. The exarch announced that the pope had been irregularly elected, not having received imperial confirmation, and that he was unworthy of his position. Therefore he would have to be sent to Constantinople and another chosen in his place. The clergy urged the pope not to submit and there were scuffles between clerics and soldiers. To avoid bloodshed, Martin agreed to go to Constantinople, asking only that those of his clergy who wished to go with him should be permitted to do so. The exarch agreed and the pope left with him for the imperial palace on the Palatine. As they left the clergy cried: 'Anathema to him who says or thinks that Martin will change his faith.' But Calliopas diplomatically reassured them that the faith was not in question, implying that it was a matter of the lack of imperial confirmation of the election.

On Tuesday large numbers of clergy and laity began making

preparations to leave with the pope. But this did not suit the exarch at all. On Tuesday night, the city gates were closed to prevent anyone leaving and the pope, with only a handful of attendants, was hustled aboard a ship and conveyed to Portus and thence to Misenum. Martin then endured a nightmare sea voyage. Although the ship, which Martin called 'my prison', put in at various ports and islands, he was allowed ashore only once, at Naxos. There he was permitted his only bath in three months and after Naxos he was not even allowed to wash. Racked by gout, seasickness and diarrhoea, he was unable to eat and by the time he arrived in Constantinople he had lost the use of his legs. The bishops and congregations of the places where the ship stopped came to bring him gifts but were beaten up and robbed of the gifts by the guards, who said that anyone who loved Martin was an enemy of the state.

Eventually arriving in Constantinople on 17 September 653, the pope was left on deck on his back all day, exposed to public ridicule and in the evening was conveyed to prison, where he remained for three months in solitary confinement, frequently deprived of food and water and increasingly ill. Finally, he was brought to trial on 19 December 653 before a meeting of the senate, presided over by the imperial treasurer. The pope was so ill that he could not walk, and was carried to his trial on a litter. But the treasurer insisted that he stand throughout the hearing and he was hoisted from the litter and supported on either side by an attendant.

The charge against the pope was treason on two counts, conspiring with the exarch Olympius to seize the throne and sending letters and money to the Arabs. The factual basis of these charges seems to be that he enjoyed friendly relations with Olympius after the latter had stopped trying to kill him and that he had sent money and aid to Sicily to help the victims of the Arab incursions. The witnesses against him were mainly soldiers and officials of the late exarch. The principal accuser was the patrician Dorotheus, governor of Sicily, who alleged that Martin had indeed participated in the conspiracy to elevate Olympius to the throne. Despite his physical agony and the fact that the trial had to be conducted through interpreters because the pope spoke no Greek and his judges no Latin, his spirit did not desert him and with bitter irony, he complimented the prosecution on how well drilled their witnesses were, and requested that they be spared the necessity of testifying under oath because since they were all lying they would be imperilling their immortal souls. When the pope was asked to make his defence, he began by raising the question of the *Typos* but he was interrupted and told that he was not being charged on a matter of the faith, but on a political charge – treason. The pope denied the charges, saying that he had no control over what the exarch did. But realizing that the game was up, he asked them to do whatever they were going to do with him and get it over with. The pope was found guilty of treason and sentenced to death.

Martin was taken from the Judgment Hall; outside in the presence of a large crowd and watched from a balcony by the emperor, he was stripped, flogged and his head shaved. Then loaded with chains and with a drawn sword carried before him as a sign of the death penalty he was led through the streets back to prison. The pope welcomed the death sentence as an end to his sufferings but it was an end that was to be denied to him. For the patriarch Paul interceded with the emperor for the pope's life and the sentence was commuted to exile. After three more months in prison, Martin was taken on board a ship and conveyed to the Crimea. There, he suffered intensely from the cold, the shortage of food, the harsh conditions and, even more wounding, the complete neglect by Rome. He wrote sadly from his exile:[26]

> I am surprised at the indifference and hard-heartedness of my former associates. They have so completely forgotten me that they do not even want to know whether I am alive. I wonder still more at those who belong to the church of St Peter for the lack of concern they show for one of their body. If the church of St Peter has no money, it does not lack corn, oil or other provisions out of which they might send us a small supply. What fear has seized all these men that it hinders them from fulfilling the commands of God in relieving the distressed? Have I appeared such an enemy to the whole church and an adversary to them? However I pray God by the intercession of St Peter to preserve them steadfast and immovable in the orthodox faith. As to this wretched body, God will take care of it. He is at hand, why should I worry? I hope in his mercy that he will not prolong the course of my life.

He died in the Crimea on 16 September 655, and was buried there.

Soon after the condemnation of Martin, the other leader of the anti-Monothelete forces, Abbot Maximus, was arrested and conveyed to Constantinople for trial. Maximus was charged with treason (supporting the exarch Gregory's rebellion) and disrespect to the emperor (rejection of the *Typos*). Since he more than Martin was the intellectual leader of the Orthodox opposition, special efforts were made to get him to recant. Every attempt failed. He was banished to Thrace and joined there by his disciple Anastasius and Anastasius the former papal *apocrisiarios*. They were moved from place to place, subjected to increasingly harsh treatment and interrogation, and only when this failed to move Maximus, was he brought to trial in 661. He was found guilty and condemned to be flogged, banished and deprived of his tongue and his right hand, to prevent him writing or speaking against the emperor.[27] The sentence carried out, Maximus and his two companions were deported to Lazica. Anastasius the disciple died almost at once and Maximus himself died at the age of 82 on 13 August 662. Anastasius the *apocrisiarios*, who had been in exile for nearly twenty years, died on 11 October 666.[28]

The situation in Rome had been one of intense confusion. The sudden and dramatic removal of the pope and stories of his ill-treatment which filtered back from the East frightened the Roman clergy, and the exarch tried to take advantage of this to persuade them to elect a successor. But the clergy waited for the outcome of his trial and in the meantime the archdeacon, archpriest and *primicerius notariorum* functioned as regents, as was customary in a vacancy.[29] There is no evidence but that the Roman church accepted the sentence on Martin and regarded him as deposed. They must have recognized the force of the argument that he had after all been ordained without imperial confirmation, something which seriously weakened his case. Martin was venerated as a martyr[30] but he was an embarrassment to the Roman church now and they conspicuously ignored him in his Crimean exile, making no effort even to alleviate the harsh conditions in which he lived. It was nearly a hundred years since an emperor had intervened so drastically in the affairs of the papacy and the fact that he could still do so must have given the Roman clergy pause for thought. When they heard of the fate of Martin, the regents proceeded to organize the election of a successor, and Pope Eugenius I was elected, approved by the emperor and consecrated on 10 August 654. Martin had hoped that they would refuse to choose a successor but when he heard of the election, he accepted the situation.[31] There is no evidence that the authorities interfered in the election, perhaps believing that the treatment of Martin had been lesson enough for the Roman clergy. Elsewhere the imperial government proceeded to secure the adherence of the bishops to the *Typos*. The Sardinian bishop Euthalius of Sulcis, for instance, signed, though when imperial religious policy changed, he recanted and his recantation is preserved in a manuscript at Mount Athos.[32]

The choice of the new pope indicates that the Roman electors had indeed learned their lesson. For Eugenius was a complete contrast to Martin, a gentle, kindly man who spent most of his time doing good works. Indeed he was engaged in doling out alms on the very day of his death.[33] It is clear that there was a genuine desire on the part of the electors to replace confrontation with conciliation. But Eugenius proved even more conciliatory than they could have wished. He sent *apocrisiarii* to Constantinople to negotiate, and in the summer of 655 they received into communion the new Monothelete patriarch of Constantinople, Peter, on the basis of a vague formula regarding the question of the two wills of Christ.[34] Following this, Peter sent a synodical letter to Rome announcing his election to the patriarchal throne, enclosing a profession of faith in the terms agreed with the envoys and urging reconciliation between the churches. But when this letter was read out during a service in the church of St Maria *ad Praesepe*, clergy and people rioted, mobbing the pope and refusing to allow him to leave the church until he had agreed to reject the letter.[35] It is clear that the agreement reached with the envoys went far beyond what even the newly conciliatory Romans were prepared to stand. So it was popular pressure that forced Eugenius into the position occupied by his predecessor, and Constans furiously threatened direct action, writing in September 656 to Abbot Maximus: 'Know that when we get a rest from the heathen, we will treat you like the pope who is now lifted up and we will roast all of you, each in his own place, as Pope Martin has been roasted.'[36] But Eugenius avoided the fate of his predecessor by dying in June 657.

At this point it is convenient to pause and examine the religious policy of Constans II, which differs in several important respects from that of Justinian, who treated popes in almost as high-handed a manner as Constans. Both emperors pursued policies aimed at exalting the emperor in religious affairs. But the difference is that, whereas for Justinian, personally devout and deeply interested in theology, religious unity was an end in itself, for Constans the religious motive was secondary and he was not interested in theology at all. What he was interested in was maintaining the political unity of the empire in the face of the threat from the Arabs. With the Monophysite Eastern provinces lost, it was the Orthodox Western provinces whose religious beliefs were straining their loyalty to Constantinople and whose religious discontents were finding a political outlet in support for the rebellion of Olympius in Italy and Gregory in Africa. Constans's paramount aim was to bind what was left of his empire tightly together under his rule and to present a united front against Slav and Arab aggression.

Constans's own personality is important here. He was an energetic, youthful, supremely autocratic ruler, quick-tempered and with a streak of the Heraclian madness in his make-up. He simply would not brook opposition to himself or his policies. In fact he took opposition to his religious policy as being opposition to himself personally. Having made what was to him the magnanimous gesture of changing his official religious policy by promulgating the *Typos*, he assumed that that was the end of the matter. Everyone was required to accept this. He was not concerned with doctrine, as the *Typos*, which banned doctrinal discussion, demonstrates.

The reasons why Martin incurred his wrath are all too obvious. He was consecrated as pope without waiting for imperial confirmation of his election, a grievous affront to an autocrat like Constans, but also one which indicated a worrying trend towards separatism in Italy. This worry was compounded when the man sent to arrest the pope actually came to an amicable agreement with Martin, then marched south and proclaimed himself emperor. For Constans, then, there was a political charge for Martin to answer and as far as the emperor was concerned he was in fact guilty of treason. The same is true of Maximus. He had been spiritual adviser and confidant of the exarch Gregory of Africa, who had rebelled. Hence Maximus was tarred with the same brush as Martin. The first charge against him, therefore, was treason. But the second charge, unlike in Martin's case, was treasonable disrespect, and this involved his opposition to the *Typos* and his leadership of the orthodox faction. It is typical of Constans that he should regard this primarily as disrespect towards himself rather than simply as heresy.

The action taken against Martin and Maximus was, however, part of a calculated policy. There were clearly dangerous trends towards separatism in the Western provinces. After fate had knocked out their political leaders (Olympius by disease, Gregory in battle with the Arabs), Constans took it on himself to eliminate their religious leaders (Martin of Italy and Maximus of Africa). Given this policy and Constans's ferocity towards Martin and Maximus and threat of 'roasting' Eugenius, the emperor's attitude to Eugenius's successor is most intriguing. The clergy and people may have rejected the compromise worked out by Eugenius's *apocrisiarii*, but they showed no inclination to return to hard-line opposition in the election of a successor. The new pope, Vitalian, consecrated on 30 July 657, only one month and twenty-eight days after the death of Eugenius, was presumably confirmed by the exarch. But he succeeded in doing the impossible – re-establishing a *modus vivendi* with the quicksilver Constans.

The *Liber Pontificalis* insists that Vitalian 'preserved the customary ecclesiastical rule and authority in every way', implying that he made no concessions. What is different, perhaps, is a willingness to negotiate, an appearance of reasonableness. For instance Vitalian 'sent his *responsales* to the capital with his *synodica* according to the custom to the most pious emperors, announcing his ordination'.[37] These were received by Constans, who issued a confirmation of the Roman primacy and sent handsome gifts of gilded and jewelled copies of the gospels to the pope. Vitalian also wrote to the patriarch Peter urging a return to orthodoxy[38] but couching his letter in such terms that the patriarch felt able to include the name of Vitalian in the *diptychs*, the first pope so honoured since Honorius and a clear sign of cordiality between the two churches.[39]

Apart from a willingness to respond in like manner to friendly approaches from Rome, Constans's turnabout is probably to be explained by his political position. He had indicated in his letter to Maximus that he had his hands full with the 'heathen' and was unable to deal with Pope Eugenius for this reason. In 657 his hands were still full and it was necessary to keep the potentially separatist provinces sweet until he had the time to deal with them. Added to this his own position was none too secure. His popularity with his subjects had taken a nose-dive. Many of his orthodox subjects were deeply shocked at the harsh treatment of Pope Martin, Abbot Maximus and other opponents of the *Typos*, and Constans's own military reputation had suffered a severe blow only two years before when he had led the imperial fleet into a battle which had resulted in catastrophic defeat at the hands of the Arabs, from which Constans had only narrowly escaped with his life.

But Constans's position in Constantinople deteriorated even further, and in 662 he took a controversial decision. He planned and embarked on a state visit to the West, the first by a reigning emperor since the fall of the Western Empire. His decision to leave his capital was probably prompted immediately by his massive unpopularity following the execution in 660 of his brother Theodosius on a charge of treason, an act which led to his being greeted by cries of 'Cain' whenever he appeared in public. But in the context of his overall strategy a visit to the West made sense. There was no plan to transfer the seat of the empire permanently to the West, as some historians have suggested. That would have been unthinkable. Nor was Constans about to initiate a Justinianic reconquest. He had neither the men nor the money for that. His intention was to consolidate what remained of the empire and to prevent further losses. In 658 he had undertaken a successful expedition against the Slavs in the Balkans, transporting many prisoners of war to Asia Minor and compelling several tribes to acknowledge Byzantine suzerainty. In 659 he had concluded a peace treaty with the Arabs, whose empire was convulsed by civil war and in no position to continue hostilities. The opportunity was clearly at hand to deal with the troublesome Western provinces and at the same time get out of Constantinople long enough for the heat of popular anger to die down.

The trip began with a leisurely progress through Greece, calling at

Thessalonica and Athens. Then Constans sailed for Italy with an army of 20,000 in 664. Using Tarentum as a base, he launched an attack on the Lombards, taking several towns, before his progress was halted at Beneventum, the capital of the southernmost Lombard duchy which he besieged and which was saved by a relieving Lombard army. Checked there, Constans concluded a treaty, retired to Naples and did not resume the campaign. This should be seen, then, not as the first stage in an imperial reconquest but as a parallel to Constans's earlier Slavic campaign, namely a short, sharp reminder to the barbarians that the empire was still a force to be reckoned with.

From Naples he proceeded to Rome. It must have been with considerable trepidation that Pope Vitalian awaited the visit of the persecutor of Martin and Maximus. But there is no record of any popular demonstration of hostility. Vitalian and his clergy met the emperor with all due pomp at the sixth milestone outside the city and escorted him into Rome on 5 July 664. His visit lasted twelve days and Constans's initial behaviour must have been a pleasant surprise. For he went on foot to St Peter's to pray and then to St Maria *ad Praesepe*, leaving donations. On Sunday he attended mass in St Peter's and the following Saturday was entertained to an official banquet in the Lateran Palace. On the last Sunday of his visit he again visited St Peter's for mass and made his farewells to the pope. In the meantime, however, more characteristically, he had stripped the copper off the roofs of all the buildings in Rome, including the Pantheon. All this metal, together with the statuary and public ornaments which he also sequestrated, he despatched by ship to Syracuse.

The emperor's visit made a great impression on contemporaries, indeed it dominates the 'official' life of Vitalian to the exclusion of virtually everything else.[40] It indicated both a continuing interest by the imperial government in its Western possessions and a confirmation that relations between pope and emperor were restored to a level which precluded a repeat of the Martin episode. Constans returned from Rome to Naples and thence via Rhegium to Syracuse, where he set up his headquarters, sensibly choosing a point midway between the two Western provinces whose defences and loyalty he was concerned to strengthen. From Syracuse he launched attacks on the Arabs in North Africa, and organized the naval and military defences of Italy. To pay for this, he levied heavy taxes on Sicily, Africa, Sardinia and Calabria and seized church plate. But there is no evidence of any papal protest against this.

Despite the fact that a wary peace now existed between Constans and Vitalian, when an opportunity arose to put the papacy in its place and on its guard Constans did not reject it. This opportunity involved a revival of Justinian's policy of elevating Ravenna as a counterweight to Rome in the Italian hierarchy. The policy of *rapprochement* between the sees which Honorius I had sought broke down in 642 with the election as archbishop of Ravenna of the deacon Maurus, the *vicedominus* of the Ravenna church and the right-hand man of his predecessor, the elderly archbishop Bonus. He was determined to free Ravenna from subjection to Rome and he evidently had an eye to the main chance when he absented himself from the 649 Lateran synod, alleging that the people and army required his presence in Ravenna since the new exarch had not yet arrived and there was a possibility of enemy attack.[41] But it is also likely that Maurus had no wish to be compromised and saw that capital might be made out of the imperial displeasure that was bound to be directed towards Rome.

There were several quarrels between Ravenna and Rome during Maurus's episcopate (642–71). They culminated in 666 when Pope Vitalian ordered Maurus to Rome to attend a synod, the very act of his coming being seen by both sides as an act of submission. Maurus refused; both sides excommunicated each other and appealed to the emperor. Maurus carried the day. He despatched to Syracuse Abbot Reparatus with a document purporting to have been issued by the emperor Valentinian III granting Ravenna autonomy from Rome. Constans, who saw the value of balancing Rome's influence in Italy, confirmed the *Privilegium* (as it was called) on 1 March 666 and decreed that in future archbishops of Ravenna should be confirmed by the emperor and consecrated by three of their own suffragans, just as the pope was. It was a triumph for Ravenna and the highpoint of Maurus's reign. When he died in 671 his last words to the priests gathered around his deathbed were that they should not submit to Rome but should elect their own archbishop and consecrate him themselves, according to the terms of the *Privilegium*. It is not unlikely that Maurus in fact nominated his successor, for it turned out to be none other than the now elderly Abbot Reparatus of St Apollinaris, the man who had obtained the *Privilegium*'s confirmation and who was, like Maurus before him, *vicedominus* of the Ravennate church. Reparatus proudly installed in the church of St Apollinaris a picture of himself receiving the *Privilegium* from the emperor. But he reigned only five years and nine months. His death on 30 July 677 signalled the beginning of the end of the autonomy. It was doomed not by the actions of pope or emperor but by internal church politics.[42]

The trouble began with the election of Theodore to succeed Reparatus as archbishop, and the echoes of it still reverberated two centuries after his death, when Agnellus of Ravenna wrote his history of the events. 'Youthful in age, terrible in form, horrid in aspect and full of every falsehood' is Agnellus's description of the new archbishop. He altered the quadripartite division of the church revenues agreed on after a pay dispute at the time of Pope Felix IV (526–30) and took away the clerical quarter, ordering all the documents dealing with the quadripartite agreement to be burned. He extracted clerical consent for this by engrossing all the grain during a famine and refusing to let the clergy have any until they agreed to his alteration of the division of revenues. He maintained his position by playing off priests against deacons, presumably by the manipulation of pay, until he was faced with a clerical revolt. The archpriest and the archdeacon, both also called Theodore, called a mass meeting of the clergy. They went on strike, locking themselves into the church of St Apollinaris and refusing to come out or celebrate mass with the archbishop. When the archbishop sent envoys to negotiate, they threatened to go to the pope for redress of grievance and if he would not hear them, to the emperor. Seriously alarmed, the archbishop enlisted the help of the exarch. The exarch sent messages recalling the clergy to their duties, and when the clergy ignored them, he went himself, promising redress of grievance. So the clergy unlocked the church and celebrated mass with the archbishop and the next day at a meeting with the exarch the grievances were thrashed out, the quadripartite division was reinstated and the clergy were restored to their rights and their positions. But Theodore did not forget this humiliation and decided on a new ploy to strengthen his hand, enlisting the support of the pope himself. So, when an invitation arrived from Pope Agatho to attend the 680 synod, Theodore consulted with his clergy and it was agreed that since it was to discuss vital matters of the faith, he should go. But when he arrived in Rome, he entered immediate negotiations with the pope for the ending of the autonomy. It was agreed that the archbishop elect of Ravenna should in future be consecrated in Rome but that he should not remain there longer than eight days. Overjoyed at the ending of the autonomy, Agatho agreed to back Theodore in whatever he wanted to do in Ravenna. The agreement was embodied in a *Constitutum* signed by Agatho's successor, Pope Leo II, and confirmed by Emperor Constantine IV, who was well-disposed towards Rome and agreed to withdraw his father's *Privilegium*. The autonomy was over.[43]

Constans's reign came to an abrupt end on 15 July 668, when he was murdered in his bath by a conspiracy of officers, and Mezezius was raised to the purple. Loyalist forces from all parts of Italy, however, were gathered by the exarch, who marched to Sicily to suppress the rebellion.[44] Significantly, Pope Vitalian threw his support behind the legitimate successor of Constans, his son Constantine IV, who was proclaimed emperor in Constantinople and sailed for Sicily with his fleet, and Constantine never forgot the pope's loyalty.[45] It is likely that this loyalty took the practical form of persuading the army of Rome to support the rightful emperor. By the time Constantine arrived in Sicily, Mezezius was dead and the province reduced to obedience.

The religious problem still remained, however. Both Vitalian and his successor Adeodatus (672–6) refused to accept the synodical letters of successive patriarchs of Constantinople because they were unorthodox. This came to a head when patriarch Theodore asked for Vitalian's name to be removed from the diptychs and replaced by that of Honorius, who had accepted the *Ekthesis*. Constantine IV refused both because of Vitalian's loyalty during the rebellion of Mezezius and more fundamentally because, as a clear-sighted statesman, he realized that there must be change in religious policy. He had come to see that Monotheletism was now more trouble than it was worth, and his father's solution of banning discussion had not helped the situation. The doctrine had after all been formulated in order to reconcile the Eastern provinces, which had been lost to the Arabs. So its *raison d'être* was gone and it served now only to alienate the West.

It was time for a return to Chalcedonian Orthodoxy, and Constantine therefore deposed Theodore and appointed the orthodox George as patriarch in his place. Then he wrote to Pope Donus (676–8) suggesting a General Council of the church to solve the religious question, and authorizing the exarch to provide transport for and pay the expenses of the papal envoys to such a council.[46] By the time the imperial envoys arrived in Rome, Donus was dead and Agatho was pope. Agatho had no hesitation in accepting the invitation, but first authorized preparatory Western synods to formulate the official position of the Western church on Monotheletism. Synods were accordingly held at Milan under Archbishop Mansuetus of Milan and at Heathfield under Archbishop Theodore of Canterbury. But the most important gathering was the Roman synod summoned by Pope Agatho which met on 27 March 680. Inevitably the outcome was that the Western church condemned Monotheletism, affirmed its support for Chalcedonian Orthodoxy and embodied its decisions in a decree which was sent East with the papal legates. The legates included bishops John of Portus, John of Rhegium and Abundantius of Tempsa, the priests Theodore and George, the deacon John, the subdeacon Constantine, and the monks Theophanes, George, Stephen and Conon, together with the priest Theodore of Ravenna, representing the newly reconciled church of

Archbishop Theodore. Copies of the anti-Monothelete decisions of the synods of Milan and Heathfield were also sent East. It was a very high-powered delegation, including two future popes (the deacon John and subdeacon Constantine), representatives of the Eastern monks who had been at the heart of the orthodox resistance and senior Greek-speaking bishops, notably John of Portus, a key figure at the papal court.[47]

The sixth General Council of the church was held in the imperial palace in Constantinople between 7 November 680 and 16 September 681. The orthodox position was expounded by the papal legates, notably the deacon John, and won considerable support. The patriarch George of Constantinople declared himself convinced. But the patriarch Macarius of Antioch led a fierce Monothelete rearguard action, making much of Pope Honorius's endorsement of the heresy. However, the support for orthodoxy was so strong that they were beaten. Macarius of Antioch and his followers were deposed and exiled to Rome, and Abbot Theophanes, one of the Western legates, was appointed patriarch of Antioch. A total of 174 delegates signed the final decrees of the Council, with the papal legates signing first, and after the final session was concluded, the senior papal legate, bishop John of Portus, conducted mass in Latin in the presence of the emperor and the patriarchs.[48]

So once again the true faith had been restored on Rome's terms, but, as so often before, what appears to be a considerable triumph is in reality nothing of the sort. Chalcedonian Orthodoxy had triumphed at last but only because the emperor had decided that it was politically expedient to change the official government policy, which had been left behind by the course of events. Pope Agatho, when writing to the emperor to expound Rome's definition of the faith, did so in terms which indicated that Rome fully recognized the crucial role of the emperor in the maintenance of orthodoxy:[49] 'And therefore with a contrite heart and flowing tears, I beseech you, deign to stretch forth the right hand of your clemency to the apostolic doctrine, which the co-operator of your pious labours, Peter the apostle has handed down.' Pope Honorius was among the heresiarchs condemned by name by the council, almost certainly because the Monotheletes had so constantly cited him as a supporter of their cause. He had not been among those whose names the Rome synod had condemned and his was the only name added to that list at the Constantinople council. Neither the pope nor the legates made any objection and, although the doctrine of the separation of the person and the office could be invoked to prevent papal authority being diminished, it was still true that Honorius was the first pope to be condemned by a General Council of the church, that the papacy had consistently defended his actions to the end and that it must have been seen as a blow to papal prestige. The fact that Theophanes was appointed patriarch of Antioch and that John of Portus celebrated mass in Latin was pure window-dressing.[50] The see of Antioch was now purely titular since the city was in Arab hands. Constantine IV also took the opportunity of this contact with Rome to reintroduce the practice of confirmation of a new pope by the emperor in Constantinople, a right which had latterly passed into the hands of the exarch. So while with one hand Constantine was cancelling the *Privilegium* and annulling Ravennate autonomy, with the other he was reviving direct imperial confirmation of the pope and giving Rome a salutary reminder of who was really in charge.[51] All in all, the Monothelete controversy demonstrates Rome's inability to resist the will of the emperor either in the promulgation or in the enforcement of government religious policy. The sad fate of Pope Martin was a permanent reminder of that fact.

Chapter 12

The Papal Revival

The sixth General Council of the church decisively ended the Mono-thelete controversy, and papal–imperial relations returned to their wonted cordiality. Throughout the crisis, however, the popes had sought to maintain a rigorous distinction between their *Romanitas* and their *Christianitas*. Even when denouncing the *Typos*, Pope Martin had expressed his loyalty to the throne in fulsome terms and Pope Vitalian had helped to suppress the rebellion of Mezezius. The relative absence of large-scale reaction to the death of Martin, who, though regarded as a martyr, was virtually ignored after his con-demnation in Constantinople, confirms the ingrained *Romanitas* both of the institution and the men who ran it. They realized rapidly that it had been a mistake to ignore traditional electoral procedure and at the same time attack imperial policy so roundly. After the trauma of Martin's reign, there was a visible retreat from confronta-tion politics to negotiation. This was manifested in the election of successive popes who were prepared to work for a solution. Martin's immediate successor Eugenius was too conciliatory even for the Romans. But Vitalian achieved that elusive *modus vivendi* without sacrificing the points of theological principle that Rome held dear. The accession of Constantine IV had taken the heat out of the situation, and after the important fourteen-year pontificate of Vit-alian, there had been a couple of lame duck papacies, those of Adeodatus and Donus, when elderly nonentities occupied them-selves doling out alms to the poor and salary increases to the clergy. But then under Pope Agatho almost simultaneously and without any initiative from Rome the two most serious threats to the papacy – Monotheletism and Ravennate autonomy – were extinguished. Coinciding with this there was a gradual but perceptible decline of plague attacks. As a result, a new mood of optimism gripped the papacy; the last years of the seventh century and the first half of the eighth saw a desire on the part of army, clergy and people alike to build, revive and move forward. The electorate demonstrated their awareness of this new mood by electing – with one or two exceptions – a succession of able, learned and often highly influential popes who restored the glory of the city of Rome and increased the power and standing of the papacy.

As a basis for this, excellent relations were established with the emperors, and imperial favour took the form of important concessions. Pope John V obtained from Constantine IV relief from the poll tax and the compulsory state purchase of grain on the estates of the Sicilian and Calabrian patrimonies[1] and Pope Conon obtained from Justinian II the reduction of 200 different levies on the Bruttian and Lucanian patrimonies.[2] Pope Constantine paid an official visit to Constantinople, the first by any pontiff since Agapitus, and it was marked by Justinian II's renewal of confirmation of the papal primacy.[3] The net result of all this was a striking affirmation of loyalty to the crown in the reign of Benedict II, when clergy, army and people lined up with the pope to receive locks of hair from the heads of the infant sons of Constantine IV as a sign that they received the princes into their protection.[4]

In Italy, there was a reassertion of papal authority over regions that had been slipping out of her control. Under John V vigorous action was taken to stem the growing autonomy of Sardinia, whose metropolitan had taken to consecrating bishops contrary to the normal practice.[5] Under Pope Constantine the brief revival of Ravennate autonomy was snuffed out.[6] Under Pope Sergius, envoys arrived from the archbishop of Aquileia to announce the formal ending of the Istrian schism after 150 years.[7]

In Rome the popes inaugurated a programme of building and beautification unequalled since the fall of the Western Empire. There had only been two notable builders among the popes since 476, Symmachus and Honorius I, the former for propaganda reasons and the latter as a bid to revive enthusiasm in Rome. The Honorian motive lay at the back of the new spate of building, remarkable for the fact that it was sustained over successive reigns and involved not only the building of new churches and the renovation of old ones but a consistent programme of beautification, involving painting, gilding, mosaic work and the introduction of tons of new plate. Particularly notable were the reigns of John VII, for a large painting programme, and Sergius I, for a massive programme of building and church repair. The beautification was matched by the introduction of new services and ceremonial, a glittering liturgical splendour to show off the new surroundings, and to impart the new confidence in the faith and in the papacy.

But most striking of all in this period of papal revival is the fact that the emperor was no longer able to exercise his power directly over the pope, in the way Constans had been able to with Martin and Justinian I with Vigilius. This was the result of a decisive shift of power in Italy involving the army. The late seventh century saw the confirmation of the army's emergence as a major force in papal politics. The characteristic features of Byzantine government in Italy were the exarch and the army. During the massive crisis of the seventh century, in order to survive, the empire developed the *theme* system, a system of militarized provinces geared for war, whose garrisons were settled locally and were permanently on the alert. The exarchates of Ravenna and Carthage are believed to have been the prototypes for these *themes*. But one characteristic of the Eastern *themes* not inspired by Italy was increasing territorialization, local and hereditary recruitment to the provincial army. It was a natural corollary of the system, however, and in course of time it came to prevail also in Italy. This was the key to the shift in the balance of power.

Initially, of the two new elements introduced onto the Italian scene by the imperial reconquest, it was the exarch who had a direct influence on papal affairs. This influence rarely took the form of independent action, however. When the exarchs acted against the papacy, as in the arrest of Martin, they were carrying out imperial orders. The only independent interest they showed seems to have been pecuniary. The exarch Isaac seized the papal treasures after the death of Pope Honorius and one of his successors profited more subtly from a papal election.

The most important function the exarch fulfilled consistently was during that period in the seventh century when he acted on behalf of the emperor in confirming papal elections. That he took over this role at some time in the seventh century is certain. The evidence is in the reduced vacancies between the death of a pope and the consecration of his successor[8] and in the election formulae referring to the papal election in the *Liber Diurnus,* dating from the mid-seventh century. Five of them are directed to Ravenna and only one to Constantinople.[9]

It is easier to say when it ended than when it began. For it is known that after the reconciliation of the churches and the sixth General Council, Constantine IV remitted the payment customarily made by the pope elect in return for the restoration of direct imperial confirmation in Constantinople.[10] The long vacancies after the deaths of Popes Agatho and Leo II support this revival of the old practice. Then, during the reign of Benedict II, Constantine IV relented presumably because of the delays involved and the frequency with which the popes were dying, and ordered that the pope elect be consecrated at once, which meant with exarchal confirmation.[11] Thereafter there is a return to short vacancies, one to two months being the norm, a delay explained by the trip to Ravenna to get confirmation.

The evidence from the reign of Agatho onward, then, is clear. It is not so clear when the practice of exarchal confirmation, ended by Constantine IV after 680, began. Going on length of vacancies, it looks as if imperial confirmation initially lapsed after the death of Pope Deusdedit when year-long vacancies were replaced by month-long vacancies. The year was 618 and the Eastern Empire was fighting for its life against the Persians and the Avars. The same conditions obtained when the 625 election occurred and it seems reasonable to assume that as a matter of pure expediency the exarch took over the ratification of papal elections. The thirteen-day vacancy before the consecration of Honorius I seems remarkably short, but it is possible that the exarch was in or near Rome, thus reducing the necessary delay. After the death of Honorius I, however, there was a return to the practice of direct imperial confirmation. For the envoys of Pope Severinus had to haggle in Constantinople to get the confirmation. This also ties in with the known course of events. The emperor had concluded his wars and was beginning to implement a new religious policy. Naturally he wished to resume the important task of confirming papal elections. However, soon the empire was plunged into a new political crisis as the Arabs overran the Eastern provinces, and once again there was a return to short vacancies, as the exarch resumed confirmation. Pope Martin was consecrated without waiting for permission from anyone and he paid the price for it,[12] though there was no exarch at the time and Martin may have thought that the confirmation was simply a formality. If he did, he was rapidly disabused of the idea. Vitalian was also confirmed by the exarch since his biography tells us that he sent his envoys to announce his ordination to the emperor 'according to the custom'.[13] This statement indicates that it was usual by now for the exarch to confirm, for ordination to take place and then for the emperor to be informed. Apart from the brief resumption of direct confirmation under Constantine IV this continued to be the case, and the *Vita Cononis* talking of the 686 election is able to call exarchal confirmation 'customary'.[14] All the evidence points to exarchal confirmation as usual from 618 onwards with the exceptions of direct imperial resumptions for short periods by Heraclius and Constantine IV.

Actual interference by the exarchs in the electoral process appears to have been minimal, however. On the other hand an increasing role in the electoral process came to be played by the Roman army. The imperial army of Italy was divided into corps, stationed in the military duchies, Campania, Istria, Ravenna, Rome, etc. During the seventh century this army became Italianized.[15] The process by which it did so cannot be precisely traced. But the general pattern is clear. The sources of recruitment and in consequence the nature and allegiance of the Italian army underwent a major transformation. Initially the province was garrisoned by Eastern regiments. In the sixth century, for instance, the Theodosiac regiment, recruited in the Crimea, was stationed in Rome[16] and the Persoarmeniac regiment from the Eastern frontier in Grado.[17] The Sirmian regiment, from the Danube, was also in Rome.[18] But by the seventh century, native-born regiments were appearing side by side with the Eastern ones. The Ravennate regiment and the Veronese regiment, attested in seventh-century papyri, were clearly Italian in origin.[19] Furthermore, the members of Oriental regiments settled down and intermarried with the locals, and even originally Eastern regiments began recruiting from the local population, for example, the son of a *primicerius* of the Veronese regiment who is found enlisting in the Armeniac regiment.[20] By the start of the eighth century, when Justinian II sacked Ravenna and the local regiments revolted, the Eastern units once stationed in the exarchal capital are no longer recorded and the regiments are all local, from Firmum, Ravenna, Verona and Classis.[21]

The same is true of the Roman army, increasingly part of the Roman population and increasingly interested in papal elections. Their importance comes to be recognized by their inclusion as a separate and distinct element in the electorate. At the time of Gregory the Great the election was still by the traditional 'clergy, senate and people'. But by the mid-seventh century the papal election letters in the *Liber Diurnus* list the electorate as 'clergy, army and people'. Indeed, in one formula the military electorate is rhapsodically described as 'the most excellent and fortunate Roman army and its most eminent general and magnificent officers'.[22] In effect the army and its officers came to fill the vacuum left by the decline of the senate.

Gradually, as their composition and their outlook changed, the army came to identify the pope as the figurehead of Italian aspirations. It was after all the popes, such as Gregory I and Honorius I, who frequently acted as their paymasters. They were strongly committed to the orthodox faith, which the pope defended. Their officers received land grants from the papacy and settled down to become a new aristocracy.[23]

The events are perhaps brought into focus by the Monothelete controversy. In 638, when Honorius died, the Roman army stormed the Lateran Palace to get at his treasures,[24] but by 649, when the emperor Constans was planning to arrest Pope Martin, the former exarch Plato warned his successor Olympius not to attempt anything before he had won the support of the army.[25] The acquiescence of the army was eventually gained for the arrest and deportation of the pope. But it is a striking indication of the concern felt by the imperial authorities about the loyalty of the army. Pope Vitalian was able to use his influence with the army to promote the cause of Constantine IV after Constans's murder. But the solution of the Monothelete crisis averted any crucial test of the army's loyalty, for they did not as yet have to choose between pope and emperor.

The first record of a positive intervention by the Roman army comes at the end of the seventh century. In 685 the archdeacon John, one of the most eminent of Roman clerics, was elected Pope John V. He is the first seventh-century pope about whose election details have survived. The *Liber Pontificalis* says that he was elected by the *generalitas*,[26] the full assembly of electors, presumably unanimously, in the Lateran basilica and thence conveyed to the Lateran Palace to await confirmation by the exarch. But he was ill for much of his reign and died in August 686.

When the election for a new pope was held, there was a split in the electorate, the first recorded instance of a divided election since the imperial reconquest. The clergy supported the candidature of the archpriest Peter. But the army backed the priest Theodore, who ranked second after Peter in the priestly hierarchy. The difference of opinion having become clear, an army detachment seized the Lateran basilica and closed the gates, forcing the clergy to gather outside to affirm their support for Peter. In the meantime the rest of the army gathered at the basilica of St Stephen the Protomartyr, just to the west of the Lateran, and named Theodore as pope. Several days of negotiation followed with representatives of both sides seeking a peace formula. But it became clear that neither side in the dispute would accept the candidature of the other faction. Eventually the leaders of the clerical and military parties decided that a compromise candidate must be found. They settled on a classic compromise figure, the priest Conon, a man of advanced age and simple mind. The *Liber Pontificalis* lists the qualities which commended him – his old age, saintly appearance and unworldliness. But he was also the son of a soldier of the Thracesion Regiment and this probably endeared him to the army too. His candidature was clearly the result of a deal worked out by the leaders of the two sides, for the clergy entered the Lateran Palace and unanimously elected Conon. Immediately afterwards the *iudices*, the civil authorities, and army leaders arrived to pledge their support. It was several days before the rank and file of the army could be persuaded but, influenced by the unanimity between the clergy and their own leaders, they eventually declared their support also. So the electoral decree, subscribed by all the interested parties, was conveyed by representatives of army, church and people to the exarch Theodore for confirmation and Conon was duly ordained as pope on 21 October 686.[27]

Perhaps predictably, Pope Conon was a disaster, demonstrating all the weaknesses of that unworldliness which had seemed a recommendation in the perfervid atmosphere of intrigue and chicanery surrounding the disputed election. His pontificate began well enough with Justinian II writing to say that he would preserve and uphold the decrees of the sixth General Council and further displaying his friendship by reducing the taxes levied by the imperial government on the papal patrimonies of Lucania and Bruttium and releasing the peasants from estates where they were being held in pledge by the army for the payment of the taxes. But things soon started to go wrong. Conon, acting without consulting the clergy, was misled by self-interested parties into appointing the Syracusan deacon Constantine as rector of the Sicilian patrimony, a post customarily filled by a Roman cleric. Not only did Conon do this but he also conceded to him the use of the *mappulae*, a jealously guarded privilege of the Roman clergy. This caused considerable resentment not only in Rome but also in Sicily where soon after Conon's death, Constantine's extortionate regime provoked a revolt by the papal tenantry which led to Constantine's arrest by the governor of Sicily and deportation to Constantinople.[28]

However, like his predecessor, Conon was ill for much of his pontificate and unable to perform many of his regular duties. When it became apparent that he could not long survive, the archdeacon Paschal, anxious to secure the succession, wrote to the new exarch John Platyn in Ravenna, offering him a hefty bribe to secure his election. John Platyn sent orders to the new civilian officials he had appointed to govern Rome that they should ensure that Paschal was elected pope. At this point Pope Conon died and was buried in St Peter's on 21 September 687.

At the ensuing election, there was again an electoral split. One faction elected the archdeacon Paschal, but a rival faction elected the former candidate Theodore, now archpriest following the death of his old rival Peter. The two factions raced to secure the Lateran Palace. Theodore and his group arrived first and occupied the inner apartments, but Paschal's group took control of the outer parts of the palace. Since neither side would give way, the same stalemate which had existed on John V's death once again prevailed.

The *Liber Pontificalis* does not specify the composition of the rival parties and it was obviously not as clear-cut a division as that which occurred in 686. But it is possible perhaps to reconstruct the support. The *Liber Pontificalis* says that when it became clear that neither side would give way, a meeting was held at the imperial palace on the Palatine, attended by the leading civil officials and the army officers, by the majority of the clergy and particularly the priests, and a multitude of citizens. This makes it clear that minority groups within the clergy supported the rival candidates. It is hard to avoid the feeling that a hardcore of military loyalists still adhered to Theodore and that the newly appointed civil officials following the orders of the exarch adhered to Paschal. Theodore also numbered a section of the populace among his supporters. Theodore's faction on this analysis included a mixture of clergy (though few of his fellow priests), the people and military loyalists; Paschal's faction included another group of clerics and certain of the civil officials.

But the majority amongst the electorate sought a compromise candidate again and their choice fell on another priest, though this time younger and more accomplished than Conon. This was the priest Sergius, son of a Syrian from Antioch but born and brought up in Sicily. He had been in Rome for barely ten years but had already made a name for himself and won promotion within the church hierarchy. The group meeting in the palace unanimously agreed on Sergius. He was then carried by the people into the oratory of St Caesarius in the imperial palace, there hailed as pope and thence taken to the Lateran Palace. The gates of the Lateran were closed against them but Sergius's supporters stormed them and carried their chosen pontiff inside. Theodore, now twice a loser, at once capitulated and embraced the new pope. But Paschal held out and had to be forced to submit. He sent messengers to John Platyn promising him 100 pounds of gold to come to Rome and overturn the election of Sergius. John Platyn came but, finding that the support for Sergius was overwhelming, allowed the election to stand. Determined not to be deprived of his bribe, however, he refused exarchal confirmation until Sergius paid over the 100 pounds of gold. Sergius protested but John Platyn was adamant. So Sergius paid up, was confirmed and was consecrated pope on 15 December 687. Soon afterwards Paschal, still intriguing to oust Sergius, was deposed from the archidiaconate and imprisoned in a monastery on a charge of magical practices. He died five years later, impenitent and unreconciled, his soul rotted by the canker of ambition.[29]

Sergius, who reigned for nearly fourteen years, proved an able and energetic pontiff. He enthusiastically undertook a programme of church building and beautification, introducing many elaborate Byzantine ceremonies and litanies into the church calendar. He spent 1000 pounds of silver decorating St Peter's and removed the remains of Pope Leo the Great from its obscure resting place in St Peter's to a more prominent position and an ornate new tomb. He authorized repairs, extensions and decorations to the churches of Saints Cosmas and Damian, St Paul, St Euphemia, St Susanna, St Andreas and St Aurea *in Hostis*.

Fittingly in one who clearly revered the memory of Leo the Great, he stressed the primatial role of the papacy consistently. He ordained Archbishop Damian of Ravenna, the first Ravennate archbishop elected since the ending of the autonomy. He sent the *pallium* to Archbishop Bertwald of Canterbury, stressing the links with England. He ordained Willibrord, the missionary of the Frisians, as archbishop to further the work of reclaiming the heathen to the faith. He received the submission of the archbishop of Aquileia following the final extinction of the Istrian schism.[30]

The emperors had not sought to interfere in papal affairs since the arrest of Pope Martin. That event had proved that they still commanded the loyalty of the army of Italy. But when the emperor Justinian II tried to repeat the actions of his grandfather Constans he was to find that the means of carrying out his will were lacking. It was not the pope nor the emperor who had changed either in their attitudes, their motivations or their conceptions of their roles. What had changed was the loyalty of the army, which was now primarily to the pope. The crucial transfer of allegiance, not of the pope's seeking and accomplished gradually over the course of a century, had been made and the pope was now effectively beyond the reach of the emperor. It is all the more remarkable, then, that even when this fact dawned on the papacy, the popes continued to remain loyal to the empire. Significantly, it was not just the Roman army but also the Ravennate army which saw its interests in purely Italian terms and regarded the pope as a more effective representative of them than the exarch. As so often in the Byzantine world, religious discontent was the channel by which other discontents (social, political, economic) were expressed. It seems likely that the army came to regard attacks on the pope as somehow attacks on Italian interests in general.

The crisis in papal–imperial relations which revealed this shift in the balance of power was precipitated by Justinian II. In 685 the able and far-sighted Constantine IV died and was succeeded on the imperial throne by his son Justinian II, barely 16 years old. Fiery, headstrong and ambitious, Justinian inherited that streak of quick-silver madness that had coursed through the veins of his grandfather and great-great-grandfather. He seems to have set out from the first to emulate his illustrious namesake, to the extent of renaming his wife Theodora. He planned wars of conquest, extravagant building programmes and religious reform. Extremely devout, he called himself 'the servant of Christ' on his coins and was the first emperor to have a figure of Christ stamped on their reverse. Like Justinian I, he wanted a General Council of the church to preside over. But because there was no major theological matter to discuss, he hit on the idea of a council, which became known as the Quini-sext, to remedy the defects of both the fifth and sixth General Councils by bringing up to date the disciplinary regulations of the church. The Council met in the imperial palace, at some date not precisely definable in 691 or 692, presided over by Justinian himself, and it laid down 102 canons on administration and ritual. These canons were duly signed by the patriarchs of Constantinople, Jerusalem, Antioch and Alexandria. They were also signed by the papal *apocrisiarii* in Constantinople. A space was left for the signature of the pope, which Justinian believed would simply be a matter of routine.

All six copies of the conciliar decrees were accordingly forwarded to Rome for the pope's signature. Pope Sergius I refused point blank to sign them and forbade them to be read out publicly, saying that he would rather be dead than consent to such errors, for the Council had legalized various practices contrary to those of the West, rejecting the Roman fast on Saturday in Lent, allowing priests to marry and banning the depiction of Christ as a lamb. What is more it reconfirmed the contentious statute of Chalcedon which accorded the patriarch of Constantinople equal rights with Rome. This might not have been so serious had it simply been a local synod legislating for the East but it claimed to be oecumenical and legislating for the whole of Christendom. This Sergius could not brook. But he was in a difficult position in that his *apocrisiarii* had not only attended but had consented to the decrees of the council. The official papal version of the episode was that they had been tricked and that Sergius was not bound by their consent.

Negotiations between Rome and Constantinople produced no solution to the impasse, so Justinian II acted in the tradition of Constans and Justinian I. He decided to apply pressure. He sent an official, the *magisterianus* Sergius, to Rome to arrest the chief papal advisers, Bishop John of Portus and the *consiliarius* Boniface. They were conveyed to Constantinople and vanish from the pages of history. But Sergius I remained unmoved. The next step was inevitable. The *protospatharius* Zacharias was sent to secure the pope's signature to the decrees with orders to arrest him if he refused.

So far the pattern is familiar. But at this point it changes. When the armies of Ravenna and the Pentapolis heard of the arrival of the Zacharias in Rome, they marched at once to the aid of the pope. Zacharias ordered the city gates closed, but having no military support, he threw himself on the mercy of the pope, begging for protection. The troops stormed the gates, joined forces with the local citizenry and marched on the Lateran Palace, demanding to see the pope, whom rumour had it had already been smuggled out of the city and was on his way to Constantinople. The noise and violence outside was so great that the *protospatharius* hid under the pope's bed and refused to come out, gibbering with fear. The pope calmed him and then, ordering the gates of the palace opened, appeared before the soldiers and people, thanking them for their concern, calming them down and prevailing on them to spare Zacharias's life. But the soldiers and citizens would not be satisfied until Zacharias had been expelled from the city and he was driven forth amid jeering and insults to return to his master. Shortly after this episode Justinian was deposed in an uprising and having had his nose slit to render him ineligible to resume the throne, he was exiled to the Crimea. There for the moment the matter rested. But it indicated that the wheel had come the full circle and the pope need no longer fear the fate of Martin or Vigilius.[31]

Nevertheless, despite the quarrel over the Quini-sext decrees and the humiliation of Justinian II, the papacy remained firmly loyal to the empire. Sergius died in September 701 and his successor, John VI, was consecrated on 30 October 701. During his reign the exarch Theophylact, acting on the information of informers, arrested certain prominent Roman citizens and confiscated their property. He was returning from Sicily via Rome after a visit when troops from all over Italy gathered in Rome planning to revolt and murder the exarch. But the pope intervened, closed the gates of the city and sent priests among the soldiers to calm them down. The revolt was averted but the reaction of the troops to the ill-treatment of their fellow provincials is yet another symptom of the growth of a sectional Italian interest, which could only be tamed by the pope.

But there was also a sharp reminder under John VI that the Lombards were still a threat to be reckoned with. Duke Gisulf of Beneventum invaded Campania, seized the frontier towns of Sora, Hirpinum and Arcis and came within fifteen miles of Rome. He seems to have been unopposed and it looks as if the military defences in Campania were at this time minimal. But John acted quickly, sending priests with ransom money to buy off the attack, and Gisulf, satisfied with the additions he had made to his duchy, retired. Once again, however, the imperial frontier had been pushed back.[32]

In 705 John VI died and was peacefully succeeded by John VII, the first example of the son of a Byzantine functionary obtaining the throne of St Peter. John's father was Plato, *Curator Sacri Palatii*, who had settled with his family in Rome. But in that same year Justinian II was dramatically restored to the imperial throne, reigning with a golden nose to avoid the rule forbidding mutilated persons from becoming emperor. One of his first acts, not surprisingly, was to resurrect the question of the Quini-sext decrees. He despatched two metropolitan bishops to Rome with copies of the decrees, urging John VII to convene a synod and approve those canons acceptable to him while rejecting those which were not. It seems a perfectly reasonable compromise, but John VII, terrified of doing anything that might offend Justinian, returned the decrees making no emendation.[33] The decorations executed by John for the church of St Maria *Antiqua* further show him prepared to toe the official line, for they depict Christ as a human and not as a lamb – as the Quini-sext decrees ordered – and used the image of Christ on the coins of Justinian II as the model.[34] John VII also built a new papal palace at the foot of the Palatine, where he died in 708. Why he did this is not certain. It is known that Gregory III undertook major structural alterations in the Lateran Palace and it may be that it was already showing signs of decay under John. It is also interesting to note that the new palace was much closer to the Greek quarter than the old one, and that may also have influenced a pope of Greek origins who was conspicuously kowtowing to the emperor.

Justinian's change of attitude towards Rome, as embodied in his proposals about the Quini-sext, may have something to do with his hostility to Ravenna. The events involving Ravenna are extremely obscure, are mentioned only in the *Liber Pontificalis*[35] and in Agnellus of Ravenna's history[36] and they are difficult to harmonize. Apparently, some prominent Ravennates were involved in the revolt which originally overthrew Justinian and when he returned to power he determined to revenge himself on the entire city. He ordered the fleet to Ravenna, commanded by the patrician Theodore, governor of Sicily. The fleet arrested Archbishop Felix of Ravenna and other prominent citizens, burned and plundered the city and conveyed their prisoners to Constantinople, where the laymen were all executed and Felix was blinded and banished to the Crimea.

The *Liber Pontificalis* greeted this event with unseemly glee:

> By the judgment of God and the sentence of Peter, Prince of Apostles, those men who had been disobedient to the apostolic see perished by a bitter death and the archbishop, deprived of his sight, receiving a punishment worthy of his deeds was transmitted to the region of Pontus.

The attitude of the *Liber Pontificalis* is to be explained by the fact that the old rivalry between Rome and Ravenna had flared up again under Felix. Following the death of Archbishop Theodore in 691 and the election of Damian to succeed him 'a great quiet settled on the priests and people' and the old antagonisms and rivalries died down.[37] But in 708 the deacon Felix, who like Maurus and Reparatus held the post of *vicedominus* of the Ravenna church, was elected to succeed Damian. He was duly consecrated in Rome, but revived the old rivalry by refusing to sign a bond demanded by the pope, in which he promised to do nothing to disturb the unity of the church and the safety of the empire. In this defiance, he was supported by the civil authorities in Ravenna. Justinian's actions against them seemed to Rome heaven-sent. After the overthrow of Justinian in 711, Felix was recalled from exile and returned to Ravenna. But, chastened by his experiences, he made his peace with Rome.

In the meantime, however, Ravenna did not take the imperial punishment lying down. The citizens and soldiers of Ravenna rose in revolt, electing as their leader George, son of the notary Johannicius, one of the captives taken to Constantinople. The revolt was eventually put down, but how and why is not known. A new exarch, John Rizocopus, arrived in Italy, landing significantly not at Ravenna but at Naples. Either he brought reinforcements with him, perhaps from Sicily, or he gathered loyalist troops on the way. Either way, he proceeded to Rome and there executed several senior papal officials, the deacon and *vicedominus* Saiulus, the *arcarius* Peter, the *ordinator* Sergius and the abbot Sergius. The reason for this is not given in the sources but the inclusion of the papal steward and the papal treasurer among the victims suggests a bid to plunder the papal treasury, along the lines of the *chartularius* Maurice. However, he moved on to Ravenna where, it is presumed, he succeeded in putting down the revolt before himself dying of a nameless but horrible disease, to the delight of the *Liber Pontificalis* who regarded it as a judgment on him.[38]

The pope was not in the city during the visit of Rizocopus. Pope Constantine, who had been elected to the throne in 708 following the twenty-day pontificate of Sisinnius, had been summoned to Constantinople by the emperor. Attended by a prestigious retinue, he had sailed from the harbour of Rome on 5 October 710, stopping at Naples, where he exchanged greetings with the newly arrived exarch, and proceeding thence to Sicily. From Sicily, he made his way round the Italian coast to Hydruntum, where he wintered. He was joined there by the *regionarius* Theophanes with a letter from the emperor authorizing all imperial governors to accord the pope as much reverence as they would the emperor himself. Eventually, early in 711, Constantine reached the imperial capital, where he was met on behalf of the emperor by his son the 6-year-old co-emperor Tiberius, Patriarch Cyrus of Constantinople and other leading nobles and clerics. Justinian himself was at Nicaea and when he heard of the pope's arrival, he arranged to meet him at Nicomedia. There, in a dramatic meeting, Justinian kissed the pope's feet and they embraced in full view of the people and amidst considerable rejoicing. The following Sunday Constantine celebrated mass, Justinian received communion from him and all was sweetness and light.

The official version of the visit in the *Liber Pontificalis* contains no mention of the hard bargaining that took place, but it is known from the biography of Gregory II that Gregory the deacon and future pope undertook the negotiations and hammered out with the emperor an agreeable version of the Quini-sext decrees, which the pope then accepted. Justinian was well enough pleased to issue yet another imperial confirmation of papal primacy. Eventually the pope started for home and, despite recurrent bouts of illness, reached Rome on 24 October 711, amid the rejoicing of the people.[39]

Almost immediately after this, Justinian II was murdered in another uprising and the throne was seized by an Armenian Monothelete, Philippicus. He convened a council of Monothelete bishops and abbots who declared the decisions of the sixth General Council null and void. The new religious policy, a restoration of Monotheletism, was embodied in official letters to the pope. The reaction to these letters was violent. The mob rioted, refusing to allow the picture of the emperor to be put up in any church, rejected his coinage and omitted his name from the mass. The pope made no protest against this action and the omission of the emperor's name from the mass can only have been made with his consent. The exarch, however, took steps to enforce the emperor's will. Since Duke Christopher of Rome had sided with the opposition to the new policy, he despatched a new duke, Peter, to take command of the Roman army. But Peter's arrival provoked open fighting in the streets between the supporters of the government and the numerically superior followers of Christopher who called themselves the 'Christian Party'. The worst violence occurred in the *Via Sacra* beneath the imperial palace. Thirty people were killed in the fighting, which was only halted when the pope sent out a deputation of priests, carrying gospels and crosses, who prevailed on the 'Christian Party' to withdraw.

How long the pope could have prevented violence was never put to the test, for news arrived from Sicily that Philippicus had been overthrown and the orthodox Anastasius II had taken the throne. Some time later the new exarch Scholasticus arrived in Rome on his way to Ravenna and presented the pope with the new emperor's affirmation of orthodoxy. But Duke Peter was confirmed in his command, on the understanding that he would not interfere in Roman affairs.[40] It would have done exarchal prestige no good at all to have been seen to remove a properly appointed commandant as a result of popular violence. By the time Pope Constantine died in April 715, the temporary problems both with the empire and with Ravenna were resolved and the papacy had resumed its triumphal revival of prestige and influence.

Chapter 13

The Final Crisis

The last years of the life of the exarchate of Ravenna coincided with the rule of three outstanding popes, Gregory II, Gregory III and Zacharias, under whom the trends of the previous thirty years were intensified and the pope decisively emerged as the master of Rome. Papal influence increased enormously. The beautification of Rome continued. A major missionary offensive was launched in Germany with the backing of the pope, who made its leader, St Boniface, an archbishop.

But the papal revival of the early eighth century took place in an institution very different from the one that had emerged during the reign of Gregory I, and confirms that the seventh century had been a century of profound change. In part, this was a result of circumstances, but it was also in part a result of internal conflict initiated by Gregory's bid to 'monasticize' the papacy. The condemnation in 680 of Pope Honorius I, the last great exponent of the Gregorian ideal, had set the seal on the repulse of his monastic offensive.

Gregory would hardly have recognized the papacy if he had returned in 715. The familial, monastic 'kitchen cabinet' style of government and the 'apostolic' simplicity of court life, with monks in positions of power and lay chamberlains banned from the palace, had given way to a vast, complex and ramified bureaucracy, staffed by the clergy, and servicing a glittering and splendid court, where the lay chamberlains were back in favour. The monks, far from forming an alternative power centre, were being harnessed to the clergy by being put to work performing services in the great basilicas. Gregory's bid to keep singing in its place and prevent it usurping too much of the time of senior clerics, his championship of the Latin rite, his opposition to foreign innovation and his propagation of a simple Latin western pastoral tradition in church scholarship had all been eclipsed. Instead the church had been flooded with Greek ceremonies, hymns and practices, singing flourished and was a passport to high office, and the Greek theological tradition in scholarship prevailed.

Gregory's reluctance to be involved in secular affairs and his strict delimitation of the secular and ecclesiastical spheres had (by force of circumstance) been replaced by a situation in which the popes were willing to undertake diplomacy and statecraft almost full time. There was indeed a growing acceptance of this as a regular part of their functions by kings and dukes, by army and people and even by the exarch, who was ultimately reduced to calling on it to save the exarchate. The influence that the popes were able to exercise over the Lombards by virtue of their money and their championship of orthodoxy could not be equalled anywhere in Italian society and was therefore a vital component of imperial policy in the province.

But a change was coming sooner than anyone perhaps realized and the seeds of that change were sown on 25 March 717, when Leo III was crowned Emperor in Constantinople, inaugurating the Syrian Dynasty and decisively concluding the twenty years of terror and confusion that had followed the first deposition of Justinian II. He faced formidable problems. In the first place there were the Arabs who besieged his capital for a year soon after his accession. This was significantly to be the last time that the Arabs besieged Constantinople and in a very real sense the turning of the tide that had been threatening to engulf the Eastern Empire for nearly a hundred years. The capital held out, Leo inaugurated a military alliance with the Khazars and fought back against the Arabs with considerable and lasting success. After securing his frontiers, Leo's next problem was to restore the internal order, stability and financial viability of his empire. He harnessed the turbulent circus factions, whose violent excesses constituted an ever present threat to law and order in the capital. He improved the discipline and efficiency of the army. He reorganized the provincial government. He published a new legal manual to streamline and update the administration of justice. But he was also forced to take unpopular fiscal measures to refill the empty treasury and these were to bring him his first problems with Italy.

There had already been some trouble. During the siege of Constantinople, Duke Sergius of Sicily had raised a puppet emperor Basil whom he renamed Tiberius. But the despatch of a single ship under the *chartularius* Paul was sufficient to recall the Sicilian army to its obedience. Letters from the emperor were read out, Sergius fled to the Lombards and Basil-Tiberius, left behind, was beheaded. His followers were flogged, mutilated, fined or banished according to their degrees of complicity.[1]

But the next problem was to be more serious since it concerned finance. Leo III doubled the taxes to raise much-needed revenue and this involved him in conflict with the pope. On the death of Constantine, his principal adviser, the deacon Gregory, a wealthy Roman and the obvious successor, was elevated to the throne. He was consecrated on 19 May 715 and was to reign for fifteen years, eight months and twenty-four days.

The emperor's taxation demands were resisted by the pope, not because they involved hardship to the Italians but because they threatened to bankrupt the church. But Gregory's resistance made him the reluctant symbol of opposition to the fiscal burdens of the Byzantine government in general. The dating of the quarrel is not precisely determinable, but it certainly occurred in the early part of Gregory's pontificate, between 717 and 726. The general opposition to the taxes which accompanied papal resistance led to an assassination plot aimed at the pope. A group of leading imperial officials in Rome, duke Basil, the *chartularius* Jordanes and their cohort the subdeacon John Lurion, a disaffected cleric, decided to murder the pope. Presumably Basil and Jordanes were involved in the tax-collecting operation and therefore on the receiving end of papal opposition. The plotters got the backing of the Duke of Rome, Marinus. But their plans were temporarily scotched when Marinus was taken ill and had to leave Rome. However, the arrival of a new exarch, Paul, gave them courage and they proceeded with the plan, which was apparently to stir the populace up against the pope. They should have known better. For when they learned of the plan, the people turned on the conspirators. Lurion and Jordanes were murdered and Basil only escaped by entering a monastery and taking holy orders. Nothing more effectively demonstrates the continuing hold of the papacy on the affections of the Roman people.[2]

According to the *Liber Pontificalis*, the exarch Paul also had orders to kill the pope and replace him with a more amenable figure. This may mean no more than that Paul wanted to implement imperial financial policy. He sent a new duke to Rome to carry out his orders, whatever they were, but the resistance of the people prevented their being carried out. So Paul resorted to force and despatched an army detachment under the count of Ravenna to Rome. However, the Roman army and the Lombards from nearby Spoletium rallied to the defence of the pope. All entrances to Rome were blocked and the Ravennate forces returned to Ravenna with their mission unfulfilled. There was clearly a congruence of interest here with both Gregory and the Romans opposed to additional taxation and the Lombards using internal dissension inside imperial territories to embarrass the exarch. But it also shows the army now virtually ignoring its nominal commander, the duke, when his orders conflict with their interests.[3]

But there was worse to come. For in Constantinople Leo III embarked on a new religious policy, the introduction of Iconoclasm. On the religious level, it was a puritanical movement which attacked the worship of religious images and sought to purge the faith of superstition and worldliness. But it had a political dimension, too, in that it was an attack by a centralizing government on the local, unofficial centres of power – the monasteries, the ikons and the holy men; it was an affirmation also of the importance of the regular church hierarchy, the capital and the paramount role of the emperor. Leo III was devoted to Iconoclasm both as a personal faith and a political policy and in 726 he began negotiations to get it accepted as the true faith of the empire. He wrote to the pope informing him that images were heretical and should be banned from all churches. If the pope agreed to this, he would be restored to the emperor's good grace and his resistance to the taxes forgotten. If he opposed this new policy, he would be deposed. Gregory II replied in a letter, whose authenticity in whole or in part has been challenged, denouncing Iconoclasm in forthright terms as a heresy and warning the emperor not to abandon the traditional methods of determining doctrine:

> Dogma is not the business of Emperors but of priests . . . just as a priest does not have the right to look into the affairs of the palace and to propose the distribution of imperial dignities, so also the emperor does not have the right to supervise the church and judge the clergy, nor to consecrate or distribute the blessed sacraments. . . . We invite you to be a true emperor and priest.

Leo had referred to himself in his letter conventionally as 'emperor and priest' and in the manner of Felix III and Gelasius, Gregory was reminding him what those functions involved according to tradition. In a realistic acknowledgment of the changed situation in Italy, he warned the emperor not to try to get at him because he only had to move a few miles to be beyond the reach of imperial arms.[4]

Once again as in all previous theological controversies the protagonists had taken up their familiar positions. Gregory II, despite his harsh words to the emperor, was careful to distinguish his *Romanitas* from his *Christianitas*. Whatever the tone of his letters, Gregory's actions drown them out. He was instrumental in securing the return to the empire of the key fortresses of Cumae and Sutrium. In 717, when the Lombards seized Cumae and ignored both the pope's letters of protest and offers of money, he took the necessary action. Duke John of Campania had made no move towards recapturing the fortress. So Gregory wrote to him, offering him 70 pounds of gold if he would retake the fortress. With the papal rector of Campania, the subdeacon Theodimus, at his side and inspired by the thought of the 70 pounds, John mounted a night attack on Cumae; he recovered it, killing 300 Lombards and capturing a further 500.[5] In 727, when the Lombards took Sutrium and held it for 140 days, Gregory bombarded them with letters and wiped out his personal fortune in money payments until they agreed to return it, 'out of respect for St Peter and St Paul'.[6]

However, events on the Iconoclast front began to move fast. The new religious policy of the government provoked a revolt in Greece, which was easily suppressed but which indicated that feelings were running high. Negotiations both with the pope in Rome and the aged patriarch Germanus in Constantinople failed to produce any agreement, and finally Leo acted to promulgate in 730 an edict banning religious images. On 17 January 730, the patriarch Germanus was deposed and replaced by a compliant successor, Anastasius, who accepted Iconoclasm. Leading dignitaries of church and state in Constantinople subscribed to the edict and the emperor initiated a persecution of its opponents. Receiving the synodical letters of the new patriarch, the pope wrote warning Anastasius to reject the heresy on pain of losing office and urged the emperor to desist from the heresy.

When the Iconoclast edict actually arrived in Italy, it was spontaneously rejected by the Italian populace, who saw it as a signal to revolt. The armies of Ravenna and the Pentapolis, genuinely attached to orthodoxy no doubt, but smarting also under the recent financial exactions, mutinied, denounced both the exarch and the emperor and overthrew those officers who remained loyal to the regime, electing their own generals to lead them. The exarch Paul rallied the loyalist forces, attempted to restore order but was killed. The armies discussed the possible election of an emperor to lead them against Constantinople in support of the faith. The one fixed point of loyalty in this rapidly changing situation was the pope. When Gregory was consulted about the plan, he rejected it and dissuaded them from implementing it; he refused to countenance revolution against the legitimate ruler and placed his faith in the hope of converting Leo from his error. The only beneficiaries of this internecine strife were the ever-watchful Lombards, who while this was going on captured the important fortress of Auximum in Pentapolis and five Aemilian fortresses.

But the whole of Italy was caught up in the rebellion which, while primarily directed against Iconoclasm, must also be seen as a potent expression of generalized Italian discontents with the imperial government. Exhilaratus, duke of Campania, and his son Adrian, who had a grudge against the papacy because a Roman synod had condemned him for marrying a deaconess, raised troops and marched on

Rome to enforce the emperor's will. They were engaged in battle, defeated and killed by the Roman army; after this Duke Peter of Rome was accused of writing anti-papal letters to the emperor and was blinded by his troops.

The patrician Eutychius, a former exarch, was now sent back to Italy to restore imperial authority. He landed at Naples, still a loyal imperial stronghold, and despatched a messenger to Rome urging those still loyal to the emperor to murder the pope and the principal citizens supporting him. The messenger was taken and would have been murdered by the people had not the pope intervened to save his life. But the Romans held a mass meeting, at which they condemned the exarch and pledged themselves to allow no harm to come to the pope and to die in his defence. Eutychius now wrote to the Lombard king Liutprand and the Lombard dukes promising them lavish gifts if they would refrain from supporting the pope. They rejected his approaches and pledged their support for the pope. Gregory was in an extraordinarily difficult position. Spending his time fasting and praying and holding daily litanies, he distributed lavish alms for the poor and addressed the people thanking them for their support and urging them to remain steadfast in the faith; but he warned them 'not to desist from their love or faith in the Roman Empire'. Gregory was determined to preserve imperial rule despite all the pressures on him to reject it from the Romans, the Lombards and the hostile imperial government itself. Only his personal charisma buttressed the imperial authority in Rome, but it was for the moment sufficient to halt the stampede towards separatism.

Almost at once Gregory's position became vulnerable, for Eutychius and Liutprand came to an arrangement. Liutprand was increasingly worried about the growing strength of the duchies of Spoletium and Beneventum and Eutychius agreed to aid him in subjecting them in return for a guarantee of freedom of action in Rome. Liutprand's fear was that the forging of a close alliance between Rome and the duchies would lead to the creation of a rival Lombard power base that might eclipse his own kingdom. So he marched on Spoletium, took hostages and pledges of loyalty from both dukes and advanced on Rome, pitching camp in the *Campus Neronis* and preparing to join forces with Eutychius.

Gregory decided to repeat the famous act of Pope Leo the Great and he went out of the city at the head of his clergy to meet Liutprand. Of their discussions there is no record but it is likely that Gregory reminded him of the common faith that they shared and the danger to it represented by Iconoclasm. It is likely too that, potent as these religious appeals were, Liutprand was as much persuaded by the subjugation of the dukes without imperial help; as long as the pope was willing not to encourage them, there was no need for an unholy alliance of king and exarch. Recalled to his support for the faith, Liutprand fell on his knees and promised that no harm would come to the pope. In token of his pledge, he laid his arms and armour, together with a golden crown and a silver cross, on the tomb of St Peter. But he also stayed long enough to effect a reconciliation between Gregory and Eutychius, which would also reduce the likelihood of the pope seeking closer relations with the duchies.

Eutychius took up residence in the imperial palace in Rome and relations between him and the pope were patched up. Almost immediately news arrived that one Tiberius Petasius, probably an army officer, had proclaimed himself emperor in Tuscia and had received oaths of allegiance from the garrison towns of Luna, Blera and Manturia. The exarch, who seems to have had few troops, was seriously alarmed, but Gregory, true as always to the empire, ordered the Roman army out to help him. Thus reinforced, Eutychius marched out and suppressed the rebellion, putting Petasius to death. Both the fact of his co-operation in suppressing the revolt and the fact that he could now virtually dispose of the Roman army indicate both the potential power and the unshakable loyalty of the pope. After all he had endured at the hands of imperial officials, Gregory was not prepared to countenance any alteration in Rome's status as a subject of the empire.

Although his reign was dominated by the Iconoclast issue and the whole question of papal–imperial relations, it was also marked by a continuation of beautification and rebuilding in Rome. Gregory ordered the city walls to be repaired and helped to repair the ravages of a flood which inundated large parts of Rome for seven days when the Tiber burst its banks early in his pontificate. He also rebuilt ruined churches, 'too many to list', and rebuilt and repopulated deserted and decaying monasteries. He made extensive decorative additions to St Peter's and turned his family home into a monastery dedicated to St Agatha, which he endowed with 930 pounds of gold and silver ornaments and plate.

There is one other important event in Gregory's reign which needs to be noted here, though in detail it belongs more properly to the story of the christianization of Western Europe. In 718 the English missionary monk Boniface arrived in Rome seeking papal approval and backing for his evangelizing mission among the pagan Germans. Gregory willingly gave him the papacy's blessing and letters of commendation, and they had detailed discussions on the evangelization programme. Thereafter Boniface enjoyed a special relationship with the papacy. He made three visits to Rome and maintained an extensive correspondence with Gregory II and his successors. Boniface, who had been born Winfrith in the Devon town of Crediton, shared with Willibrord, the apostle of the Frisians, who also adopted a Roman name (Clement), that peculiar English veneration for St Peter and Rome that was the palpable legacy of Augustine's mission. They were imbued with the desire to propagate among the heathen of the continent that brand of Roman Christianity which had brought their own countrymen to the light. But the initiative in both these missionary enterprises came not from the papacy but from the missionaries themselves. Rome blessed their enterprises, made both Boniface and Willibrord archbishops, gave advice and support; though for immediate practical on-the-spot help and protection they turned to the Frankish kings. The papacy's influence was inspirational rather than practical, its prime motive almost certainly, as with the Gregorian missionary enterprise, the winning of souls for Christ.[7] But as to the missionaries being agents of papal monarchical expansionism, as one historian has wisely put it: 'of this abstract claim . . . the missionaries assuredly had no knowledge'.

Gregory II died in February 731, having demonstrated perfectly that it was possible to 'render unto God that which was God's and unto Caesar that which was Caesar's'. This, however, was not how his actions were seen in the East. His prominence in the resistance both to the taxes and the Iconoclast policy caused his staunch defence of the imperial frontiers and unswerving opposition to rebellion to be overlooked. The chronicler Theophanes reflected this Eastern view when he wrote of him:

> In the elder Rome also Gregory, that holy and apostolic man and worthy successor of Peter, chief of the apostles, was refulgent in word and deed: who caused both Rome and Italy and all the western regions to revolt from their civil and ecclesiastical obedience to Leo and the Empire under his rule.[8]

It is a view that is both untrue and unjust but it does indicate that Constantinople at least was aware of who now held the balance of power in Italy.

There was no problem about the successor to Gregory. During the pope's funeral procession, the people rose up and seized the priest Gregory, carried him off to the Lateran basilica and unanimously elected him as Pope Gregory III. Five weeks later, after exarchal permission had been obtained, the new pope was consecrated.

The first act of the new pope was to write to the emperor denouncing Iconoclasm. But the priest George, entrusted with the delivery of the letter, was so frightened that he did not dare to deliver it and returned with it to Rome. Furious, the pope planned to degrade him from office, but on the intercession of the bishops assembled for the annual St Peter's day synod, he was given a second chance. Again he failed but this time because he was arrested by imperial officials in Sicily *en route* for Constantinople and detained there for a year.

The synod called by Gregory and held at St Peter's on 1 November 731 passed decrees condemning Iconoclasm. It was attended by ninety-three Italian bishops plus the archbishops of Grado and Ravenna. The *defensor* Constantine was entrusted with the decrees and despatched to the imperial court. But he too was arrested, imprisoned for a year and then sent back. Messengers from all parts of Italy sent to remonstrate with the emperor on behalf of the ikons were all arrested and detained by Sergius, governor of Sicily. At last the *defensor* Peter succeeded in reaching Constantinople and handing over letters denouncing Iconoclasm to the emperor.[9]

When he read the letters, Leo decided to act in the time-honoured method of Justinian and Constans. He sent a fleet under admiral Manes to deal with the pope. But it was wrecked in the Adriatic and the expedition abandoned. So Leo instead instituted economic and religious sanctions. He confiscated the papal patrimonies in Sicily and Calabria, the only areas in which imperial authority effectively still held sway.[10] This was a serious blow and hit the papacy hard, since these patrimonies were worth 250,000 *solidi* a year in revenue to Rome. Leo also transferred the ecclesiastical provinces of Illyricum and Sicily from the jurisdiction of the papacy to that of the patriarchate of Constantinople.[11]

Even these blows did not diminish the active loyalty of the papacy. When Duke Transamund of Spoletium seized the fortress of Castrum Gallensium, Gregory paid out a heavy ransom for its recovery, ordering it to be restored to the empire and garrisoned by the Roman army. He strengthened the fortifications of Centumcellae and rebuilt the walls of Rome, paying out of his own pocket the wages of the workmen and the cost of the lime. Although the evidence is somewhat confused, it seems that around 737 Ravenna was actually captured by Hildebrand, the nephew of Liutprand, and Duke Peredeo of Vincentia.[12] The exarch Eutychius fled to the Venetian islands, where a local autonomy had grown up but allegiance to the empire was still acknowledged. He besought their aid, and the Venetian fleet sailed with him back to Ravenna and assisted in the recapture of the exarchal capital. However, during this supreme crisis for the exarchate, the pope wrote urgently to the Venetian duke Ursus[13] and to Archbishop Antoninus of Grado, exhorting them to give aid to the exarch.[14] To Antoninus, he wrote:

Your brotherly holiness ought to cleave unto him and in our

stead strive alongside him in order that the city of Ravenna may be restored to its former status in the sacred empire and to the imperial service of our lords and sons the great Emperors Leo and Constantine so that with the zeal and love of our holy faith we may by the Lord's help be enabled firmly to remain in the confines of the empire and in the imperial service.

It may have been the extreme precariousness of imperial rule at this point which prompted Gregory III most unwisely to succumb to the politics of desperation. Since the most immediate threat to Rome seemed to be posed by Duke Transamund, Gregory entered into a defensive alliance with the dukes of Spoletium and Beneventum. But this immediately brought down on his head the wrath of King Liutprand, who was dedicated to a policy of preventing this sort of conjunction. Liutprand descended on Spoletium with his army and Transamund fled to Rome. The pope, backed by the military commander Duke Stephen, refused to hand over Transamund to Liutprand and the king therefore descended on the duchy of Rome with fire and sword, capturing the towns of Ameria, Horta, Blera and Polymartium.[15] Gregory III hastily despatched the priest Anastasius and the subdeacon Adeodatus to ask Liutprand to return the towns, and wrote urging the bishops of Tuscia Langobardorum to assist his envoys, reminding them of the oath they had taken at their ordination to further the cause of peace between the empire and the Lombards. But the pleas fell on deaf ears.[16]

So Transamund and the Romans took council, and the Romans decided to help Transamund to regain his throne, probably reasoning that this was the best way of bringing Liutprand to heel. In return Transamund promised to restore the four lost towns to the duchy. So the Roman army marched into the duchy of Spoletium, carrying all before them and triumphantly installing the duke back in his capital. But as soon as he had regained his throne, Transamund repudiated the agreement he had made with the Romans. Liutprand moved south with his army, intending to deal both with the duchy of Spoletium and the duchy of Rome. At this crucial point, Gregory III died.

Although it was in line with the 'divide-and-rule' policy so long a favourite of Byzantine diplomacy, Gregory III's policy of alliance with the Lombard dukes had been fundamentally misguided, since it was bound to provoke the wrath of the ultimately more powerful Lombard king. As the *Liber Pontificalis* ruefully admits, 'There was much disturbance of spirits between the Romans and the Lombards because the Beneventans and the Spoletans held with the Romans.'[17]

Gregory felt the lack of a secular protector so much that he wrote in desperation to the Frankish ruler Charles Martel in 740.[18] He said that the church of Rome was deserted, its Ravenna patrimony wasted by fire and sword and its estates around Rome plundered and destroyed by the Lombard kings Liutprand and Hildebrand. He said that the dukes of Spoletium and Beneventum were persecuted by the king because of their refusal to attack the Roman church. He ended by saying:

> Before God and the coming judgment we exhort you, most Christian son, to come to the aid of the church of St Peter and its particular people and with all speed beat back those kings and order them to return to their own homes.

This letter in no way suggests, as some have claimed, that Gregory III contemplated transferring the papacy to Frankish territory or even Frankish control. It was a parallel of Pelagius II's appeal to the Franks in similar straitened circumstances 150 years before. The appeal was ignored and Gregory died in December 741.

Apart from his diplomatic and doctrinal activities, Gregory III continued and intensified the beautification programme. During his pontificate the splendour of the churches surpassed anything that had been seen before. The basilicas of Rome became a veritable riot of silk veils, jewelled crucifixes, gold plate, embroidered altar cloths, inlaid pavements, silvered roof beams, gem-studded gospels, precious ikons. The introduction of the many holy images of course served a dual purpose – beautifying the churches but also defying Iconoclasm. An image of the Virgin with gold and jewelled diadem was installed in the oratory of the Saviour, the Virgin and all the Saints and Martyrs in St Peter's. Images of the Saviour, the Apostles and the Virgin were engraved on the silver-covered roof beams added to St Peter's. A golden image of the Virgin and Child was placed in a new oratory built by Gregory in St Maria *ad Praesepe*. He undertook repairs on the cemeteries around Rome and an extensive programme of re-roofing churches, many of them stripped of their tiles by Constans. He also began a move back to the Lateran. It seems that not only the Lateran Palace but the area around it had become very run-down. The building of a new papal palace near the Palatine by John VII reflects a desire to get away from the Lateran. But Gregory III prepared the way for a rehabilitation of the Lateran, rebuilding the ruined monastery next to the palace and building a new church dedicated to Saints Marcellinus and Peter near the Lateran.[19]

Eight days after the death of Gregory III, his successor Zacharias was consecrated pope. The last and in many ways the most notable of the thirteen Greek Popes, he seems to have been ordained without either exarchal or imperial confirmation. Nevertheless, despite the continuing Iconoclast controversy, he sent envoys to Constantinople with letters announcing his consecration and stating his commitment to orthodoxy.[20] The emperor Leo III had died on 18 June 741, but his son and successor, Constantine V, was equally committed to Iconoclasm and determined to implement it. But when the envoys arrived early in 742, they found that during the absence of Constantine, who had left his capital to fight the Arabs, his brother-in-law Artavasdes had seized the throne and proclaimed a policy of religious orthodoxy, in order to draw support from those sections of the populace opposed to Iconoclasm. It was necessary for Zacharias to move carefully. In April 743 the pope was still dating his letters by the regnal years of Constantine.[21] But by September 743 when it seemed as if the change of ruler had been successfully accomplished, papal documents bore the regnal years of Artavasdes.[22] But the emperor Constantine had simply been taking time to gather together his strength and in 743 he launched a bid to regain his throne, which culminated in his triumphal entry into Constantinople in November 743. Once again Zacharias was careful and for more than a year after the entry into Constantinople the papacy still dated its documents by the years of Artavasdes. Finally, Constantine's regnal years were reinstated, at the latest by October 745.[23]

The recognition of Artavasdes by the papacy seems not to have upset the restored Constantine V, for when he sent the papal envoys back to Rome, it was with a grant to the papacy of two large and rich estates, Nimphas and Normiae, situated to the north of Rome and still in the possession of the emperor.[24] This magnanimous gesture, which must have gone part of the way towards offsetting the loss of the Sicilian and Calabrian patrimonies, bespeaks a dramatic change of attitude from that of Leo. Considering Constantine's fervent Iconoclasm, this is a little difficult to fathom. But however fanatical he was, Constantine was also a political realist and if, as Theophanes's *Chronography* implies, Constantinople recognized the pivotal role of the pope in determining the course of Italian affairs, the emperor will have wanted to keep Rome sweet while he attended to more pressing commitments elsewhere. He probably had neither the resources nor at this time the inclination to deal with the pope in the manner of his father. Interestingly there is no mention of Iconoclasm in Zacharias's biography and, although it is known that he took up the same orthodox position as his predecessors,[25] it may be that he established with Constantine the same sort of *modus vivendi* as Vitalian had with Constans. This would have meant both sides

holding to their existing positions but not trying anything outrage-
ous to force each other towards a solution. After all, with Constantine concentrating his energies on the Arabs and the Bulgars and
Zacharias tackling the problem of the Lombards, it made no sense to
weaken the empire further by a revival of theological strife. Other
popes may not have weighed the political consequences perhaps but
Zacharias was above all a statesman and he was to need all his
qualities of statesmanship to deal with the threat hanging over the
papacy.

The advance of King Liutprand on Spoletium brought the quarrel-
ling Romans and Spoletans together again. They joined forces to face
Liutprand and inflicted a severe defeat on his forces in the valley of
the Metaurus. Zacharias saw his opportunity to negotiate from
strength and arranged a meeting with Liutprand. The pope saw quite
clearly that his predecessor's policy had been mistaken and he abandoned it, coming to an agreement with the king by which Liutprand
agreed to return the four captured towns and Zacharias promised
him the help of the Roman army to put down Transamund. So the
tables were turned. Taking their orders from the pope, the army
joined forces with Liutprand, and in the face of this opposition
Transamund surrendered. He went into a monastery, giving up his
throne to Duke Agiprand of Clusium, Liutprand's nephew.

But like Transamund, Liutprand showed no sign of carrying out
his bargain and held on to the towns. So in 742 Zacharias determined
on another personal interview and set out with a large body of clergy
to meet the king at Interamna. From Narnia, the pope was escorted
by a welcoming delegation of Lombard courtiers and he met the
king at the church of St Valentine in Interamna. They greeted each
other cordially, prayed together and then retired to the tents outside
the city where the talks were to take place. The result was a personal
triumph for the pope. Liutprand agreed not only to restore the four
Tuscian towns but also the towns of Narnia, Auximum, Ancona,
Humana and the Magna Valley near Sutrium and the Papal patrimony in Sabina, which had been in Lombard hands for thirty years.
All this was done 'out of respect for Peter, the Prince of Apostles' but
it is likely to have involved an agreement on the pope's part not to
revive the Gregorian policy of allying with the dukes. A twenty-year
treaty was concluded with the duchy of Rome and all captives in
Lombard hands were freed. On the Sunday following the meeting,
the pope ordained a bishop for Caesena, an Aemilian town in Lombard hands; after mass, the king entertained the pope to dinner, an
occasion at which the pope was so witty and charming that the king
later said he had never enjoyed a dinner so much. Then on Monday
Zacharias took his leave, returned via the four towns, which were

officially handed over to him, and entered Rome in triumph, celebrating with a procession of people singing the litany from the Pantheon to St Peter's.

Despite the fact that a political agreement underlay the treaty, Liutprand's generosity in the restoration of territory needs more explanation. That explanation can only rest in Liutprand's genuine attachment to Catholicism and its ecclesiastical head, Rome, and on the impact of Zacharias's charismatic personality and skill in diplomacy. Liutprand certainly saw the treaty as being with the pope alone. He still regarded the exarch as fair game and in 743 launched a fresh attack on the now attenuated exarchate. The exarch, Archbishop John VI of Ravenna and the leading citizens petitioned the pope to intercede on their behalf. The pope sent Bishop Benedict of Nomentum, his *vicedominus*, and the *primicerius notariorum* Ambrose to the king with presents and letters urging him to withdraw and restore captured Caesena to Ravenna. The embassy returned empty-handed. So Zacharias determined on a third face-to-face confrontation. He left Rome in the charge of Duke Stephen, indicating that he was now its unquestioned master, and set out for Ravenna. He was met by the exarch and the Ravennate people at the church of St Christopher at Aquila. The people cried: 'Welcome to our shepherd who has left his own sheep and has come to rescue us who were ready to perish.' The sight of the exarch begging the pope to save him from the Lombards testifies more powerfully than anything else to the utter enfeeblement of the exarchate and the effective transfer of authority in Catholic Byzantine Italy from the imperial governor to the pope. From Ravenna Zacharias again sent the *primicerius* Ambrose, this time with the priest Stephen, to see Liutprand. Once in Lombard territory, they took fright and sent letters to the king instead of going in person. Zacharias finally decided to go himself, crossed the frontier and headed for Ticinum. He halted outside the city walls at the church of St Peter *ad Coelum Aureum* to celebrate mass and the following day, 29 June on the feast of Saints Peter and Paul, undoubtedly chosen for its symbolism, the pope entered Ticinum and met Liutprand in the royal palace. For some time the king resisted, but was finally persuaded to restore the country districts around Ravenna which he had taken, together with two-thirds of the Caesena territory. The remaining third of the territory together with Caesena itself was to remain in his hands as a pledge of the exarch's good behaviour until 1 June next, to await the outcome of a mission by the Lombards to the emperor in Constantinople. The content of the final agreement makes it clear that the pope was here negotiating on behalf of the empire and had been empowered so to do by the exarch. The mission to Constantinople suggests that Liutprand was now thinking in terms of a treaty of long duration, based on restitution of conquered territory. If this was the way his mind was working, it makes sense of the generous restorations made to the Duchy of Rome in the Interamna agreement. Liutprand accompanied the pope personally as far as the banks of the Po and sent officers with him to superintend the hand-over of agreed territory to the pope.

The papal magic had worked for the third and last time on Liutprand. For he died in January 744 after reigning for thirty-one years, his death being greeted with jubilation by the *Liber Pontificalis* which described him as 'that ambusher and persecutor'. His immediate successor, Hildebrand, was soon deposed and succeeded by Duke Ratchis of Forumjulii. Ratchis kept the peace as agreed by Liutprand, until pressure from his bellicose nobles forced him to break it. There was a growing feeling in the aristocracy that the exarchate was there for the taking and it was nonsense to wait. In 749 Ratchis embarked on a bid to capture Perusia, the key to the Rome-Ravenna land corridor. Once again the pope (armed with lavish gifts) hastened from Rome to avert catastrophe and once again the combination of personal charisma and hard cash worked on a Lombard sovereign. Ratchis raised the siege of the city and soon afterwards abdicated and entered the monastery of Monte Cassino. But his fierce brother Aistulf took the throne and it was he who in 751 put an end to the lingering death of the exarchate by taking and holding Ravenna.[26] So what had threatened for so long had finally occurred. The exarchate was extinguished. The emperor did nothing about it apart from sending an envoy to ask for it back. From now on Byzantine rule was confined to Sicily and southern Italy, Greek-speaking and Greek-cultured. The imperial government, committed to a religious policy alien to Rome and deeply embroiled with wars in the Balkans and the East, accepted the loss of the exarchate with a mixture of relief and resignation. Constantinople had lost interest in the exarchate. It was more trouble than it was worth.

But the end of the exarchate and of the imperial presence in Latin Catholic Italy was much more significant for the papacy. The papacy had never sought the overthrow of imperial authority, had resolutely defended it even at the moments of most acute crisis, and at the end the papacy alone had stood between the exarchate and destruction. But with the fall of Ravenna, the papacy was compelled to look elsewhere for a secular protector. Isolated in the midst of a race which it had never trusted, the papacy looked outside Italy. In 752 the first steps were taken which were to lead eventually to a special relationship with the Franks. Pippin, mayor of the palace and effective ruler of Frankish Gaul, wrote to the pope asking if it was right that one man should rule and another be king. Zacharias replied that it was not, and effectively sanctioned the transfer of power in France from the decadent Merovingians to the vigorous and ambitious Carolingians.[27] It was the beginning of a new era for France and it was to signal a new era too for the papacy; but that is another story.

So the reign of Zacharias saw the culmination of the developments in papal history since 680. The pope now ran the Roman army and civil administration, negotiated with the Lombards, even protected the exarchate. But his pontificate also saw other significant developments. In order to resettle abandoned land and provide additional sources of revenue to replace those lost in the confiscation of the Sicilian and Calabrian patrimonies, Zacharias developed the *domusculta*. These were estates held in perpetuity by the Roman church and worked directly by and for the Roman church. Basilicas were built on them to serve as foci for re-settlement. The introduction of *domuscultae* seems to have begun with the bequest to the church by the aristocrat Theodore, son of Megistus, of his paternal estates five miles from Rome. The pope bought up the surrounding land, renovated and decorated the oratory of St Cecilia already there, built an oratory to St Cyrus and launched the first *domusculta*. Others followed on the same pattern: a *domusculta* on the papacy's Tuscian patrimony fourteen miles from Rome, at Lauretum, where two great estates were joined together, and on properties at Antium and Formiae, bequeathed to the church by Anna, widow of the *primicerius* Agatho, a Greek military officer.[28] The practical result of this activity was soon seen when the episcopate of Tres Tabernae was revived. It had been derelict since 592, but in 761 as a result of the re-settlement programme, its first bishop since the days of Gregory the Great attended a Roman council.[29]

Zacharias also completed the rebuilding and beautification programme in Rome, moving back to the Lateran Palace after a major rebuilding programme undertaken by the *primicerius* Ambrose. A new papal dining-room was built, constructed out of marble and decorated with mosaics and murals. The oratory of St Silvester and the colonnade were redecorated with sacred images. A tower and colonnade were built in front of the *scrinium* with bronze doors, engraved with an image of the Virgin. Above the tower and reached by a flight of stairs another dining-room was built, decorated with verses and a map of the world.[30]

By the time Pope Zacharias died in March 752, the papacy had finally taken over as master of Rome and as guardian and inheritor of the Roman tradition in the West. It had come about gradually, almost imperceptibly, in response to trends and events – the respect accorded to the papacy by the Lombards, the resistance by the papacy of a succession of Eastern heresies, the transfer of allegiance of the army from the emperor to the pope, the increasing divergence of interest between East and West. But none of it had been planned by the popes, who had throughout – despite extreme provocation at times – seen themselves as the loyal subjects of the empire. The basic policies of the papacy were not really any different in 752 from what they had been in 476. They were in religion, the defence of papal primacy and the orthodox faith and in politics, the defence and preservation of the interests of the Christian Roman Empire. Any alternative policy would have been unthinkable because the papacy believed that the union of *Romanitas* and *Christianitas* had been ordained by God, who had also sanctioned the definition of the faith at Chalcedon. The abandonment of these fundamental principles would have meant chaos. There had been no innovative papal governmental theory, no advance on the definition of roles of church and emperor made in the Constantinian settlement, on the part of Rome. If anything it was the emperors who had tried to alter the situation, by legislating independently on doctrine and supporting heresy. But when that occurred, the popes simply sought to guide them back to the true path. It was in the last resort, then, the course of events which placed the papacy in the position where it was forced by harsh reality to consider an alternative to the system it had lived by and defended for so long.

Part IV

The Popes

Chapter 14

Class Origins

During the period covered by this book, there were forty-four popes. Having looked at the history of the institution they governed, it is necessary to turn to an examination of the men themselves. Who were they? Where did they come from? What were their qualifications for office? What was their standard of learning? The answers to these questions throw important light on the social structure of early medieval Italy and on the criteria sought by the papal electors.

In an examination of the class origins of the popes, there are two dates of immediate significance, which in retrospect assume the role of watersheds – 483 and 604. 483 was the year of the *admonitio* of Pope Simplicius, which involved the senatorial order, in the person of its leader Basilius, in the process of electing his successor. The outcome of this, as has been seen, was the election of Felix III, the first demonstrably aristocratic pope. His election indicates both the importance of the senate in papal elections after the fall of the Western Empire and the extent to which the senatorial order had been permeated by Christianity. Men of aristocratic origin were now increasingly making their careers in the Roman Church rather than in secular government.

But Felix's election is significant for more than just his own social background, for his family was to provide two further popes within the century after his death – Agapitus (535–6) and Gregory I (590–604). It is a veritable papal dynasty and its ramifications throw important light on the involvement of the aristocracy in the church.

It has long been known that Gregory I was descended from one of his predecessors. On two occasions he recounted the story of how Pope Felix appeared to his saintly aunts Tarsilla and Aemiliana to warn them of their impending deaths.[1] Gregory does not say which Pope Felix this was but describes him as *meus atavus* — 'my great-great-grandfather' or more loosely 'my ancestor'. It was not until the mid-nineteenth century that this *atavus* was identified by J. B. De

235

Rossi as Felix III.[2] De Rossi based his case on the discovery of a collective tombstone in the pavement of the Roman basilica of St Paul. This tombstone recorded the reburial of the members of the deacon Felix's family, taken from their individual resting places and collectively reburied at some time between 489 and 492 in a common family tomb. These were Petronia, 'wife of the deacon' who had died in 472, Paula *clarissima femina*, her daughter who had died in 484, Gordianus *dulcissimus puer*, her son who had died in 446 and Aemiliana *sacra virgo* (relationship unspecified) who had died in 489. They were clearly members of the same family and, what is more, two of the names (Gordianus and Aemiliana) were also borne by members of Gregory's immediate family, his father and his aunt. Given the conservative attitude of old Roman families in the choice of names, this establishes an indisputable link.

The *Liber Pontificalis* provides the evidence that identifies Petronia's husband, the deacon Felix, with Pope Felix III.[3] For Felix, alone of the popes in this era, was buried in St Paul's; the rest were interred in St Peter's. The presence of the tombstone indicates a touching desire to be buried with the rest of his family. But why should the family be buried in St Paul's in the first place? The answer to this lies in another family link. The *Liber Pontificalis* names Felix's father as Felix, *presbyter tituli Fasciolae*, one of the parish priests of Rome. De Rossi identifies him as the priest Felix, who together with the deacon Adeodatus had been ordered by Pope Leo the Great to repair the church of St Paul. The priest Felix died in 471 and was buried in St Paul's, where his tombstone testified to his part in the rebuilding.[4] The deacon Adeodatus, who died in 474, and his wife Maria who died in 451 are also buried in St Paul's.[5] Taken together, all the evidence points to Petronia's husband being the man who became Pope Felix III.

The next stage is to link Felix with Gregory. The son of Felix, Gordianus, died young and his daughter Paula was presumably unmarried, since she was buried with her own family rather than her putative husband's. There is, however, both on the collective tombstone and on the individual tombstone of Petronia, discovered in 1959, reference to the mother being mourned by *natae* — 'daughters'.[6] It must have been one of these daughters who married and gave birth to Gregory's great-grandfather. The same church of St Paul provides a possible husband for this unnamed daughter. Next to the collective tombstone of Petronia and her family is that of Felix, described as *Primus Apostolice tenuit qui scrinia sedis*, in other words *primicerius notariorum*.[7] The tombstone reveals that he was married and had children, whose education he entrusted to his wife when he took orders. Furthermore it talks of him 'following the model and pattern of his outstanding father'. It used to be argued that this 'outstanding father' was Felix III and that Felix the *primicerius* was the pope's son and Gregory's great-grandfather.[8] But the reference to daughters alone mourning Petronia makes it clear that Felix III had no surviving son at the time he became pope. It is possible that Felix the *primicerius* was Felix's son-in-law, which argues a looser but still permissible reading of 'father' and still permits him to be Gregory's great-grandfather. Aemiliana *sacra virgo* is likely to have been Felix III's sister. An elderly, unmarried nun, dying three years before the pope, she would most naturally have been buried with her brother's family.

The second pope provided by this family is Agapitus. Once again there is a link with Gregory. Gregory's father, Agapitus's father and Felix's son all share the same name – Gordianus. Agapitus's father Gordianus was priest of Saints John and Paul on the *Clivum Scauri*. Agapitus began his career as a *clericus* in the same church[9] and Agapitus's family owned a house opposite the church which he turned into a library as part of a plan he had concerted with Cassiodorus for a Christian University of Rome.[10] The university failed to materialize, but the library passed into the hands of Gregory the Great, whose family also owned property on the *Clivum Scauri*.[11] This property was turned into the monastery of St Andreas by Gregory and the library of Agapitus was incorporated into it. The passing of the property on the *Clivum Scauri* from one Gordianus, the father of Agapitus, to another Gordianus, the father of Gregory, establishes the family tie.

It is perhaps possible to define this relationship even more precisely. Gordianus, the priest of Saints John and Paul, was one of the most senior clerics in the Roman hierarchy, ranked fourth at the 499 synod.[12] He supported Pope Symmachus, and after Gordianus's murder during the rioting which convulsed Rome at that time,[13] his son Agapitus was appointed a deacon by Symmachus in 502.[14] He was the most junior of the new batch of deacons and, given that although ordained a deacon in 502 he did not become archdeacon until after 531, he is unlikely to have been much older than 25 – the minimum age for the diaconate. We can assume that from his senior rank, his father was at least in his sixties. The necessity for a close relationship with Gregory's father and therefore with the family of Pope Felix III so that the property on the *Clivum Scauri* could pass from one Gordianus to the other, coupled with the coincidence of the names, makes it probable though not finally provable that the priest Gordianus was Felix III's younger brother and that Pope Agapitus was therefore Felix's nephew. In this context it is perhaps worth noting that the only basilica built by Felix was dedicated to St

Agapitus,[15] perhaps a favourite saint of the family in the same way that St Hormisdas was a favourite of the family of Justus of Frisino, father of the future Pope Hormisdas.

Gregory the Great himself was the son of Gordianus and Silvia, who both displayed the exceptional piety that seems to have been a hallmark of this family.[16] Silvia went into religious seclusion at Cella Nova near the basilica of St Paul on the death of her husband. Gordianus, who was almost certainly dead by the time Gregory embraced the monastic life in the 570s, was, according to John the deacon, a *regionarius*. John describes an ancient painting in which Gordianus is depicted holding the hand of St Peter, confirming that he did indeed hold an administrative post in the church.[17] What John means by *regionarius*, however, is not entirely clear. But it seems likely that he has retrospectively applied to Gordianus the title his office would have carried with it in John's own time (the ninth century) and that what is meant here is *defensor*. It was Gregory himself who created the regionary *defensor* though the office of *defensor* had long existed previously. Such an office, involving minor orders, is feasible for Gordianus, given that there are several examples from Gregory's own pontificate of wealthy married land-owners like Gordianus holding this office.

Other members of Gregory's family are known. Gregory's three paternal aunts, Tarsilla, Aemiliana and Gordiana, lived in their own house as nuns under strict religious discipline. The first two, renowned for their saintliness, died in the odour of sanctity after seeing a vision of their ancestor Pope Felix. The youngest, Gordiana, who had always chafed at the religious life, immediately threw it up and married the steward of her estates.[18] Another aunt was Pateria, who in 591 was living in straitened circumstances in Campania, and to whom Gregory authorized a subvention.[19] He calls her *mea thia*, which can mean either maternal or paternal aunt. But since Gregory in the story of the other three aunts expressly states 'my father had three sisters', she is probably to be identified as a sister of Silvia.

Finally, there is the long-vexed question of Gregory's brother. In May 591 Gregory writes to the Rector Peter of Sicily asking him to send his brother's money to Rome as he had asked[20] and in June 599 he asks the Rector Sergius of Calabria to return a runaway slave to his brother.[21] Most authorities have admitted defeat in the matter of Gregory's brother's name.[22] But it is recoverable from the sources. When Gregory was elected pope, he wrote to the emperor Maurice asking him not to consent to the election. The Prefect of Rome intervened, however, stopped the letter and sent instead a decree of Gregory's unanimous election, thus causing the emperor to confirm it. Gregory of Tours, the earliest authority to write about this episode, says *sed praefectus urbis romanae germanus eius anticipavit nuntium*.[23] Most authorities read this as 'but the prefect of Rome Germanus anticipated his messenger'. But it could equally well be translated as 'but the prefect of Rome his brother anticipated the messenger'. No prefect Germanus is attested anywhere in the sources for the period and Gregory's brother could very well have held the position Gregory himself had before entering the church.

But there is more evidence. In 598 Gregory suggests that the peace treaty with the Lombard King Agilulf be signed on his behalf by the archdeacon, a bishop or *gloriosum fratrem nostrum*.[24] By this time the brother would have ceased to be city prefect, since someone called John is attested holding that office in the period 597–9.[25] The brother would thus have been free to act as a representative of the Roman church, without compromising a government position. There is a further reference which gives us the elusive name. This is the reference to *gloriosus frater meus palatinus patricius* in a letter to the ex-consul Leontius, dated 600.[26] It makes it clear that Gregory's brother with the title of *gloriosus* and rank of *patricius* is called Palatinus. Against this, it has been argued that Palatinus is an office and not a name and that *frater* means a spiritual and not a blood relationship.[27] Both these objections are invalid. There was an official called a *palatinus* but the office would not be held by anyone with the exalted rank of *gloriosus*. Palatinus is certainly a name, as the existence of the *vir illustris* Palatinus in the early years of the sixth century confirms.[28] *Frater* in the spiritual sense is reserved for fellow churchmen and Gregory invariably refers to laymen as *filii*. So if a man who is obviously a layman, the patrician Palatinus, is Gregory's *frater*, then he must be his brother by blood.

The context of the letter lends further weight to the suggestion that Gregory's brother was city prefect. For there had arisen some question about the *cautio* of the Sicilian praetor Libertinus during the inspection tour of the ex-consul Leontius. The matter had been referred to Gregory, who consulted with his legal adviser Theodore *consiliarius* and with Palatinus *vir gloriosus*. If Palatinus is the former city prefect, he is just the man to consult about the terms on which other imperial officials served. The evidence of the letters then strongly suggests that Palatinus was the name of Gregory's brother and it seems highly likely that he was the former city prefect.

Further supporting evidence might be found in the letter of Gregory concerning his aunt Pateria. In the same letter, he also authorizes subventions to two other ladies, *domina* Palatina, widow of Urbicus, and *domina* Viviana, widow of Felix.[29] In the letter Gregory remarks: 'If we have compassion towards the needs of our relations, we will find compassion from God towards our needs', suggesting that like

Pateria, Palatina and Viviana are relatives. In this group of names, there are two (Palatina and Felix), already argued as names in the Gregorian family circle. They are not aunts because Gregory distinguishes Pateria alone as *thia*. But they are probably relatives at a more distant remove, cousins perhaps, or great-aunts.

There are several conclusions which can be drawn from this picture. The first is that a single Roman family provided three popes in the period of a little over a century. This family was wealthy, propertied and aristocratic. Gregory I owned enough land in Sicily to endow six monasteries and turned his palatial family home on the *Clivum Scauri* into the monastery of St Andreas. Gregory of Tours describes Gregory the Great as *de senatoribus primis* – 'from among the leading senators'.[30] This is confirmed by the fact that first Gregory and then probably his brother Palatinus held the office of prefect of Rome, and that Palatinus attained the loftiest rank of all as *vir gloriosus* and *patricius*. Palatina, arguably a relative, was a *femina illustris*. All this indicates a rise in the social scale of comparatively recent date. Felix III was from the lower reaches of the aristocracy, his daughter Paula being only a *clarissima*. John the deacon also describes Gregory's father as *vir clarissimus*. The family boasts none of the familiar names of the greatest Roman aristocratic clans, the Decii or the Anicii. The likelihood is that Gregory's family rose in importance as other, more eminent families died out or moved East in the wake of the mid-century troubles.

Nevertheless, it is a wealthy aristocratic family and demonstrates the fact that whole establishment families and not just individuals were now prepared to seek careers in the church and, if not careers, to devote themselves to the religious life. For if the relationships postulated above are correct, this one family produced Pope Felix III, who is the son of the priest Felix, the brother of the priest Gordianus and the nun Aemiliana, the uncle of Pope Agapitus and the father-in-law of the *primicerius* Felix. A generation or so later, Felix's great-great-grandson became Pope Gregory I, the son of the *regionarius* Gordianus and Silvia, who became a nun on her husband's death, and the nephew of three nuns, two of them saints and the third a backslider.

It begins to look as if there was after all something in the often-derided suggestion of the emperor Constans that the clergy should become, like the army, a closed and hereditary caste.[31] With the evidence of the family of popes Felix III, Agapitus and Gregory in mind, then, we need to look for evidence of, on the one hand, members of the aristocracy becoming pope and, on the other, of families of *religiosi* attaining the throne of St Peter.

In the mid-sixth century a succession of aristocrats of the highest rank attained the papacy. The first and most distinguished was Vigilius. Marked out as early as the reign of Boniface II as a potential pope, he eventually succeeded to the throne as the imperial nominee on the deposition of Pope Silverius. He was the son of the consul John, who had held successively the posts of *comes sacrarum largitionum*, vicar of Rome and praetorian prefect under the Ostrogothic kings.[32] While Vigilius chose a career in the church and rose rapidly and controversially, his brother Reparatus became successively prefect of Rome and praetorian prefect. Reparatus was one of the eminent men who fell victim to the Gothic wars. After escaping one massacre of senators at Ravenna under Witiges, he finally met his death when the Goths took Milan.[33] Responsibility for Reparatus's children devolved on Vigilius; he discharged this responsibility assiduously, marrying his niece Vigilia to the consul Asterius[34] and ordaining his nephew Rusticus, who had followed him into the church, as a deacon, specifically giving as the reason for the promotion their family tie.[35]

Vigilius's successor, Pelagius I, was almost equally distinguished. His father, also called John, had been *arcarius*, *referendarius*, vicar of Rome and a member of the Gothic privy council.[36] Besides being nobly born, Pelagius was also very rich, earning great popularity by using his fortune to alleviate the sufferings of the citizenry during the siege of Rome.[37] Pelagius's successor, John III, was the son of the *vir illustris* Anastasius, a man of senatorial rank who has been identified as the governor of the provinces of Flaminia and Picenum Annonarium in the period 523–6.[38] According to the Eastern historian Evagrius, John's real name was Catelinus and he changed it on his accession.[39] Bearing in mind that the previous Pope John II had also changed his name, from Mercurius, this is at least plausible, though it is not mentioned in any Western source.

The chronology of this trio of aristocratic popes is interesting. It is more than coincidental that the three most eminent aristocratic popes occur immediately after the imperial reconquest. At least the first two and possibly the third were nominees of the emperor Justinian. They were men from a social group which favoured reconquest on the whole and who spoke the same language as the emperor. All three supported imperial policies, often in the face of extreme opposition from their flock.

There is no information on the class background of John III's two successors, Benedict I, a Roman and the son of Boniface, and Pelagius II, a Roman and the son of Unigild. Pelagius's father, however, bears the first Gothic name to appear among the papal progenitors. He had a family home in Rome which he turned into an old people's home; it seems likely that he came from a fairly well-to-do Christianized Gothic family, settled in Rome. But the sixth century ends with a return to senatorial eminence in the person of Gregory I.

By comparison, there is much less evidence of senatorial eminence amongst the popes of the Ostrogothic period. Felix III certainly came from the upper classes, though not from the upper reaches of the upper classes. He was a middle or lower rank aristocrat, with strongly religious connections. There were other aristocrats under the Ostrogoths, Felix III's nephew Agapitus and Boniface II. Boniface the son of Sigibuld was certainly rich – he distributed his family plate among the clergy to win their favour after his hotly disputed election.[40] The Germanic name of his father suggests a relationship with that Sigibuld who had been consul in 437; it indicates perhaps membership of a Romanized barbarian family settled in Rome and incorporated into the aristocracy for over a century. But there were none of the front-rank blue-bloods of the post-conquest papacy.

There is evidence of provincial nobles gaining the throne, however, and one of them provides another family group. Pope Hormisdas, described by his friend Ennodius as 'pious, wellborn and rich',[41] was born in the Campanian town of Frisino, the son of one Justus.[42] Since both Hormisdas and his son Silverius are described as Campanians by birth, they were clearly members of the provincial rather than the Roman aristocracy. Hormisdas's son, Silverius, a subdeacon in the Roman church, became pope in 536 after the intervention of the Gothic King Theodahad. Another relative was Gerontius, described as 'linked by blood to Pope Hormisdas',[43] who entered the notariate, and by the time of his death in 565 has risen to be *primicerius notariorum*. Hormisdas's curious Persian name probably derives from the popularity in the West of St Hormisdas, an exiled Persian noble celebrated in the Roman martyrology (8 August) but not so honoured in the East. Certainly the names of Hormisdas's father and son suggest a straightforward Italian pedigree.

The evidence on Pope Felix IV suggests an origin not dissimilar to that of Hormisdas. A Samnite, the son of Castorius, Felix IV was obviously not a Roman aristocrat.[44] But under Gregory the Great a Castorius, son of Felix a *nobilis* of Nursia, and a subdeacon in the Roman church, became bishop of Ariminum.[45] The coincidence of names and the proximity of geographical origins suggests a family tie and the distinct possibility that Felix IV was also from the provincial aristocracy. It is worth noting that of these three popes claimed as provincial aristocrats, Felix and Silverius were Gothic nominees and Hormisdas enjoyed supremely cordial relations with Theodoric. This fits in with the known tendency of Theodoric to favour the utilization of provincial aristocrats in his central administration, men like Cassiodorus.

There is not a drop of blue blood, however, in the antecedents of the other popes in the Ostrogothic period. Gelasius I, son of Valerius, was an African. John I, who did have close contacts with the aristocracy but only on the basis of his intellectual attainments and pro-Eastern sympathies, was a Tuscan, the son of Constantius. Anastasius II, a Roman, was the son of the priest Peter. John II, a Roman, was born Mercurius, the son of Projectus. Symmachus was perhaps the rankest outsider of them all. A Sardinian, born a pagan, the son of one Fortunatus, he was the ultimate provincial nobody. Admittedly we have only the evidence of names and geographical origins to go on with this group but, given the extremely conservative behaviour of the Roman aristocracy in the choice of names, it is fair to say that few of the names in this group of popes or the names of their fathers or in many cases their places of origin have the ring of the nobility about them.

Between 483 and 604, therefore, of seventeen occupants of the throne of St Peter, seven are certainly or probably from Roman aristocratic families (Felix III, Agapitus, Gregory I, Vigilius, Pelagius I, John III, Boniface II) and three certainly or probably from provincial aristocratic families (Hormisdas, Silverius, Felix IV). The rest are almost certainly non-aristocratic in origin (Gelasius, Anastasius II, John I, John II, Symmachus, Benedict I, Pelagius II). In other words, well over half of the sixth-century popes are aristocratic or upper class. Moreover, a single family provides three of these aristocratic popes and another family two. Eight popes had relatives who were also in the church in one capacity or another. (Felix III, Anastasius II, Agapitus, Silverius and Gregory I had fathers in the church, Hormisdas had a son, Vigilius a nephew, Felix IV a relative.)

Certain conclusions are possible from this data. First, when Eastern emperors interfered in papal elections, they chose members of the Roman aristocracy as pope; when the Gothic kings interfered they chose scions of the provincial aristocracy. The reasons for this are both political and social. The Eastern emperors derived support from some sections of the Roman aristocracy, the Gothic kings from some sections of the provincial aristocracy. Either way they were all from the upper class and therefore *au fait* with aristocratic thinking.

Second, it seems that it was only in the later Ostrogothic period (i.e. after the death of Theodoric) that members of top-flight Roman aristocratic families sought careers and power in the church. The barbarian regime, which many Roman aristocrats were prepared to serve in its heyday, was by the 530s increasingly isolated and unpopular. Many felt that there was no longer any point in continuing to seek to prop it up. The religious reunion with the East had removed the major barrier between Rome and Constantinople. The Ravenna government was no place for the ambitious and far-sighted. It is perhaps symptomatic of the move towards the church that at least two leading figures from Theodoric's government abandoned the secular life and took holy orders. Cassiodorus, *magister officiorum* under Theodoric and praetorian prefect under Athalaric, became a monk. Arator *vir illustris, comes domesticorum* and *comes privatarum* under Theodoric became a subdeacon in the Roman church. It was in this period, too, that young aristocrats Vigilius, Pelagius and John began their ecclesiastical careers which culminated in the papal throne.

Third, there does seem to be a tradition of family involvement in the church. Two notable ecclesiastical families have already been mentioned, but in all eight popes had relatives, often more than one, in the church. It is thus distinctly an age of pious and churchly families.

A very different picture, however, emerges in the seventh century. For one thing the geographical origin is different. Of the seventeen popes between 483 and 604 eleven were Romans. But of the twenty-seven popes between 604 and 752 only eight were Romans, affording much less access to the throne for Roman aristocratic candidates, if any. But in addition, eleven of these twenty-seven were not even Italians but mainly Greeks from Greece, Syria or Palestine. Of the non–Roman Italians, few can have been aristocratic. Indeed, the origins of two of them (Pope Martin, a Tuscan, and Pope Agatho, a Sicilian), are so obscure that even the names of their fathers are not recorded. Few of the others suggest origins of distinction. Pope Sabinian, a Tuscan of Blera, the son of Bonus; Boniface V a Campanian from Naples, the son of John; Vitalian, a Campanian from Signia, the son of Anastasius; Leo II, a Sicilian, the son of Paul; none of these details smack of the aristocracy. Equally, few of the Romans indicate noble birth: Eugenius I, the son of Rufinianus; Adeodatus, the son of Jovianus; Donus, the son of Maurice; Benedict II, the son of John; Gregory II, the son of Marcellus and Honesta.

The Greek popes were obviously not members of the Roman aristocracy. But only one of them, John VII, son of Plato *curator sacri palatii* and Blatta *femina illustris*, boasts a distinguished origin. The details of the rest are virtually devoid of information about social origins. John V, a Syrian from Antioch, was the son of Cyriacus; Sergius, born and brought up in Panormus in Sicily, was the son of an Antiochene expatriate Tiberius; John VI's father was unknown; Sisinnius, a Syrian, was the son of John; Constantine, a Syrian, was the son of John; Gregory III, a Syrian, was the son of John; Zacharias, a Greek, was the son of Polychronios. Only Pope Conon, the son of a soldier of the Thracesion regiment, adds to our knowledge of the social origins of the popes in this period.

What can be gleaned about the popes in the period before the Greek influx, however, suggests that where identifiable, their origins are in the professional middle classes. Boniface IV was the son of a doctor from Valeria[46] and had a relative Stephen who was a priest;[47] John IV, a Dalmatian, was the son of a lawyer;[48] Deusdedit, a Roman, was the son of the subdeacon Stephen;[49] Pope Theodore was the son of a Palestinian bishop.[50] Boniface III, though Roman-born, was the son of John Catadiochus,[51] who sounds like a Greek immigrant, perhaps a soldier or civil servant.

But of the twenty-seven popes between 604 and 752 only two give any hint of Roman aristocratic origin. Pope Honorius I, a Campanian by birth, was the son of the consul Petronius; yet he had a family home in Rome which he turned into a monastery and he made enormous donations to the church.[52] He was clearly rich and aristocratic. His father, who does have one of the old aristocratic names, was perhaps one of the last Western consuls. It is worth noting that Honorius's epitaph speaks of his imitating Gregory the Great.[53] It is known that he turned his home into the monastery of Saints Andreas and Bartholomew, in emulation of Gregory; if the parallel is to be carried through completely, Honorius will have been a wealthy aristocrat, perhaps even a government functionary, who renounced the world, made his property over to the church and then entered the clergy.

Honorius's successor was Severinus, a Roman and the son of Avienus.[54] Alone among the names of the seventh-century popes and their fathers these two shine out with the aristocratic lustre of the previous century. Avienus and Severinus were names borne by several members of the wealthy and important Basilii and Anicii families, who had dominated the social and political life of pre-conquest Rome. But beyond the actual names, the evidence fails. It could be coincidence, for Severinus had become a common name with the popularity of the cult of St Severinus of Noricum. Even if noble birth is somewhat dubiously ascribed to Severinus, at most only two seventh-century popes can be even conjecturally linked with the Roman aristocracy.

This absence of upper-class popes during the seventh century is confirmed by the evidence of donations. Gregory I presented 100 pounds of gold to the Roman church; Pope Honorius gave 2,000 pounds of silver. But from then until the reign of Sisinnius donations totalled a meagre 42 pounds of gold and 310 pounds of silver.[55] During the eighth century things improved considerably as a succession of popes with private fortunes took the throne, but they were non-aristocratic rich men.

Despite the paucity of the evidence, the contrast between the sixth and seventh centuries is striking. After the death of Gregory I, only one pope is provably of aristocratic origin. All the other evidence of names, origins, professions and donations, is negative. Most popes, given the basic need to be literate, would have been middle class, some richer than others, some non-Roman and non-Italian. But the involvement of the aristocracy had dramatically declined. Interestingly there is also an apparent decline in the incidence of clerical dynasties; only two popes (Deusdedit and Theodore) had fathers in the church. This bears importantly on the composition of the Roman clergy. But, on the question of class origins, how does the virtual absence of aristocratic popes after 604 accord with what is known of the senatorial aristocracy in post-Ostrogothic Italy?

After the restoration of imperial rule in Italy, there are only four references to the Roman senate. Justinian's *Pragmatic Sanction* mentions the senate but gives it only control of weights and measures, suggesting the reduction of this once-proud body to the status of a municipal council.[56] On the other hand, committing the appointment of provincial governors to the bishops and leading inhabitants of the provinces attests a clear shift in the patterns of power. Thereafter the senate only appears in the sources on three occasions. The Debtors' Law of 556 is addressed to Narses, the praetorian prefect Pamphronius and the senate.[57] In 579 a deputation from Italy, including members of the senate, visited Constantinople to plead for aid from the government.[58] Finally, in 603, there is reference in the Gregorian Register to the acclamation of the statues of the emperor Phocas and empress Leontia 'by the whole clergy and the senate', after which the pope ordered the statues to be placed in the chapel of the imperial palace on the Palatine.[59] The senate appeared merely as a group of laymen attached to the clergy and not under the leadership of the city prefect or the senate leader, and the pope, rather than the senate, ordered the removal of the statues. Such evidence confirms the impression that the senate had ceased to be a significant constitutional or administrative body.

In these circumstances, it is not possible to dismiss the statements of Gregory the Great and Agnellus of Ravenna on the senate as mere rhetoric. In 593 Gregory wrote 'Where is the senate? Where are the people? The senate is vanished, the people have perished.'[60] Agnellus, dating the disappearance of the senate to the end of the sixth century, says: 'Then little by little the Roman senate disappeared.'[61]

The silence of Gregory's letters on the subject of the senate is in itself eloquent. There is not a single mention of the senate in the

Register, apart from the ceremony of the images already mentioned, even when the pope is concluding treaties with the Lombards. The Register also reveals how thin on the ground high-born aristocrats were. Only eight *gloriosi* appear in the pages of the Register, a handful of the distinguished names of the Ostrogothic period (Cethegus, Faustus, Venantius, Clementina), most of them living by then in Sicily or Campania, a pale remnant of the once-flourishing senatorial order. There are only six *illustres* in the Register. All this compares unfavourably with the 354 senators listed in Sundwall's prosopographical study,[62] most of them dating from before the reconquest. It has been estimated that in the reign of Odoacer alone the senate had sixty to eighty members.[63]

The evidence points inexorably to the imperial reconquest as the great watershed, during which the old senatorial families were destroyed or dispersed. Two overriding causes for this disappearance can be discerned. First, there was the succession of massacres of Roman senators and, more importantly, their children. In 536, when Witiges was made king, he took most of the Roman senators as hostages to Ravenna. In 537 he ordered them to be wiped out and many were.[64] At least two, Vergentinus and Reparatus, escaped to Milan, only to get caught up in the siege of that city in 539. Reparatus was killed when the city fell, but Vergentinus escaped yet again, and this time ensured his safety by leaving Italy for the East.[65] In 552, in the despair of defeat, the Goths sought out and executed all the aristocrats they could find and more seriously put to death 300 noble children held hostage north of the Po.[66]

To avoid death, many aristocrats fled to the East, following the example of the prudent Vergentinus. Some, like Cethegus, Basilius and Albinus, left everything they had behind and turned up in Constantinople destitute.[67] Others who went East recouped their position by taking service in the imperial administration. For instance Liberius, a former prefect of Gaul under the Ostrogoths, became Justinian's prefect of Egypt. The nobles who both stayed behind and avoided the massacres found their privileged position eroded by the war. Procopius talks of senators reduced to poverty and forced to beg in the streets.[68]

Second, once imperial rule was re-established, there was no incentive for the survivors to stay in Italy or for the exiles to return. The fall of the Ostrogothic kingdom meant the end of the old administrative system, headed by the Roman aristocracy. Its place was taken by a new provincial organization, staffed by Greeks. The centre of power, the obvious magnet for the rich and well-born, was now Constantinople rather than Ravenna. The patriciate ceased to be awarded in Italy and the consulship ceased to be awarded at all. For imperial titles and honours, for favour and influence, the aristocracy had to go East.

The ecclesiastical evidence confirms the theory that the aristocracy withered away in Italy, broken by massacre, impoverishment and the loss of influence. Throughout the Ostrogothic period, the senate had been deeply involved in papal elections, playing a vital role in the elections of Felix III, Symmachus, Felix IV, Boniface II and John II; after the reconquest there is no further evidence of senatorial involvement in elections. The seventh-century *Liber Diurnus* names the papal electors as the clergy, the people and the army, making no mention of the senate, which would have been inconceivable unless it had ceased to exist. In 684 an imperial ordinance about the ratification of the papal election was addressed by Emperor Constantine IV to clergy, people and garrison of Rome, with no mention of the senate. The army had emerged to fill the vacuum left by the aristocracy, a vacuum further evidenced by the virtual absence of aristocratic popes after the death of Gregory I.

A study of the class origins of the popes thus confirms, first, the increasing incidence of aristocrats in the ranks of the Roman church during the sixth century and second, their subsequent disappearance in the wake of the decline of the senate, which as a social and political force had lost all significance by the early seventh century.

Chapter 15

Age and Experience

Of all the possible qualifications for the office of pope the one which emerges most often is old age. Old age went hand in hand with wisdom in the thinking of the ancient world. Given the strength of the hierarchical principle, there was a built-in prejudice in favour of senior clerics and that inevitably meant old popes. But old age was valued for itself, quite apart from seniority, as is evidenced by the choice of Pope Conon, whose 'white hairs' were regarded by the electors as a prime recommendation.

Between 483 and 752, forty-four popes occupied the throne of St Peter. During the same period there were only twenty-two emperors in Constantinople. The average papal reign was four to five years. It is clear from this fact alone that very old men were often elected and the indications are that long reigns, such as Vigilius's seventeen years, Symmachus's sixteen, Gregory's fourteen and Sergius I's fourteen probably betoken comparatively young men. Gregory, for instance, is known to have to have been born about 545 and was therefore only in his forties when he became pope. Sergius had entered the Roman clergy only fifteen years before becoming pope.

There are of course concealed variables. Pope Pelagius II, for instance, died of plague in 590 and there is no indication of how old he was. But it is not necessary to deduce old age simply from length of reign. There is abundant evidence in the sources pointing firmly to the fact that the bulk of the popes were old men. Boniface II, who reigned for two years twenty-six days, is described in his epitaph as *senex*.[1] John I, who reigned for two years nine months and seventeen days, was 'elderly and infirm' when he set out on his visit to Constantinople.[2] The epitaph of Pope Deusdedit, who reigned for three years and twenty-three days, talks of his 'old age'.[3] Pope Severinus, who reigned for two months and four days, was described by Abbot Maximus as 'aged'.[4]

In general, it is true to say that if an archdeacon was elected pope, he was an old man and his reign was short. The great exception to this is Vigilius, though his appointment as archdeacon was perhaps a political one rather than on strict seniority. Pelagius I, who had been archdeacon, ruled only four years ten months and eighteen days and admitted in a letter to the deacon Sarpatus 'We are both old men'.[5] The other known archdeacons to be elected, Boniface II, Agapitus, John IV and John V all reigned for two years or less.

Ill health, the concomitant of old age, was also a recurring characteristic of the early medieval popes. The most extreme example is perhaps Pope Sisinnius. Consecrated on 15 January 708, he was so badly crippled with gout that he could not even feed himself. He died twenty days after his consecration.[6] John I was ill when he left for Constantinople on his official visit and died upon his return.[7] Both Popes Vigilius[8] and Constantine[9] suffered seriously from illness while they were in Constantinople. John V suffered from an illness so severe that he could not even perform routine ordinations.[10] Conon suffered in the same way with the same effect on the administration.[11] Benedict II is described as being ill from the beginning of his ten-month reign to the end.[12] Pope Agatho, who took on the job of *arcarius* because he could not find anyone suitable to do it, was forced to relinquish it because of ill health.[13] Pope Martin had been ill for eight months at the time of his arrest and by the time he reached Constantinople was unable to walk.[14] Even a comparatively young man like Gregory the Great suffered. But in his case it was partly his own fault. He had ruined his digestive system by protracted fasting and had so undermined his constitution that he was a prey to fever. For two whole years (598–600) he was so ill that he was unable to leave his bed.[15] In view of this interminable parade of infirmity and incapacity it is a wonder that the papacy achieved anything at all.

Old age in the popes generally also betokened experience. But what sort of experience? Since the personnel of the church divide essentially into two branches, the administrative (deacons, sub-deacons, *defensores*) and the spiritual (priests, clerics, acolytes), a preference for one or other of these branches should reveal something about the criteria of choice operating during elections.

As with the question of class origins, there seems to have been a definite split between the sixth and seventh centuries, with the reign of Gregory I once again assuming a crucial significance. Our starting point must be the statement made at the end of the sixth century by the patriarch Eulogius of Alexandria that the papacy was limited to the diaconate and that priests were not eligible.[16] This was not true, but it must reflect the practice in sixth-century Rome as observed from outside.

The evidence for the period 483–615 strikingly bears out Eulogius's contention. Of the twenty popes between 483 and 615 only two are provably not deacons – and both of these were elected under special circumstances. Pope Silverius, who had the unprecedentedly low grade of subdeacon, was elected by force on the intervention of King Theodahad.[17] Pope John II was elected as Mercurius, priest of St Clement on the Caelian.[18] A fragmentary inscription in the church of St Clement indicates that he had been a priest there at least since the reign of Pope Hormisdas.[19] He is not recorded at any of the Symmachan synods and so was presumably ordained as a priest at some time after 502. But he is ranked second of the forty-one priests attending the 531 synod of Boniface II and was therefore a priest of some seniority.[20] He was almost certainly a compromise candidate chosen after a bitterly divisive election. This is suggested by his epitaph, composed by his successor, Pope Agapitus:[21]

Living with a pious mind, brought up in the palace of Christ
And rejoicing in excellent simplicity alone;
Charming in obedience and full of pure love,
Rightly living a peaceful, quiet life;
You, pleasing to the people and worthy of the high honour,
Assumed the papal honour from your merits
And preserved in piety the whole flock committed to you.

It indicates a saintly, non-political figure called upon to restore the unity of the Roman church and succeeding during his short reign (two years four months six days).

Apart from Silverius and John II, all the other popes in this period were probably or provably deacons. Felix III, elected in 483, was a deacon and had been for at least eleven years. By birth an aristocrat, he had married and fathered several children before taking holy orders.[22] Both his background and his experience commended him as a man fitted to deal with the major problems confronting the Roman church – relations with the East and with the barbarian regime in Italy.

His successor in a sense virtually chose himself in 492. Gelasius, African-born but a long-time cleric in the Roman church, had increasingly come to take charge of the vexed question of relations with the East.[23] He wrote many of Felix's letters on the subject of the Acacian schism to the East and briefed the papal envoys on how to handle the slippery Greeks. As effective 'secretary of state', he was almost certainly a deacon and perhaps even archdeacon. The attendance list of the 487 synod which includes virtually all the Roman priests of the time contains no priest called Gelasius.

The changing attitude in Rome to the East towards the end of Gelasius's reign manifested itself in the selection of his successor in 496. Like Gelasius, Anastasius II was a career cleric and probably a deacon. His epitaph tells us: 'The son of a priest, born among the duties, I chose the principles of the life and service of God. Having been a servant to the orders of the Popes with a pious heart, I obtained the great apostolic name'.[24] This reveals both that Anastasius's father Peter had been a priest and that he himself was probably a senior cleric, given that he had served several popes. This in itself suggests the diaconate, as does a curious reference in the *Liber Pontificalis*.[25] The *Liber Pontificalis* account adds after the usual details of birthplace and father (*Anastasius natione Romanus ex patre Petro*) the phrase *de regione V caput Tauri*. The mention of one of the regionary districts further suggests Anastasius's position as one of the seven regionary deacons of Rome.

He was certainly not one of the parish priests of Rome. The only known parish priest called Anastasius, the priest of St Anastasia, attended the 495 synod, ranked forty-one, the 499 synod, ranked thirty-six and the 502 synod, ranked twenty-three.[26] There was, however, a deacon Anastasius. He played a prominent role in the proceedings of the 487 and 495 synods, the only named deacon to do so, and was therefore an important figure at the papal court.[27] To complicate matters, a deacon Anastasius attended the 499 and 502 synods as an adherent of Pope Symmachus.[28] But in view of the other evidence, the only reasonable conclusion is that there were two deacons called Anastasius, one of whom became pope in 496 and the other of whom was a Symmachan loyalist. On balance, then, Anastasius II was probably a deacon and also probably an important and trusted senior adviser at the courts of both Felix III and Gelasius.

The divided election on Anastasius's death produced two candidates, whose ranks are certainly known. Laurentius was archpriest and Symmachus a deacon. This does not mean a clash between the two orders but resulted from a conflict of policy and personality. Laurentius was the most senior of the Roman priests, having attended both the 487 and 495 synods, being ranked nine and two respectively, and having succeeded Castinus as archpriest some time between 495 and 498.[29] Symmachus, on the other hand, was unknown to history before the election, unlike his three predecessors, all of whose pre-papal careers have some documentary evidence. His strong support amongst the junior clergy and his exceptionally long reign (fifteen years) suggests a comparatively young man, certainly a younger man than any of his predecessors.

The capitulation of the Laurentian faction and the subsequent clerical purges ensured that Symmachus and his followers maintained a tight hold on the clerical establishment, and it was his principal lieutenant, the deacon Hormisdas, who eventually succeeded him in 514. He had been regarded as heir-apparent since as long ago as 506, at least by Ennodius who was in a good position to know.[30] He had been one of the earliest Symmachan diaconal appointments, appointed in the dark days of 502, and had played a prominent part at the Symmachan victory synod. His election confirmed the hold that the Symmachan old guard had secured over the Roman church.

But this hold was shaken by external events. The reconciliation with the East and the ending of the Acacian schism brought about a realignment within the establishment not on the religious grounds, which had underlain the Symmachan schism, but on more strictly political grounds. This is reflected in the 523 election when, on the death of Hormisdas, the elderly deacon John was elected.[31] He was a veteran of the Laurentian pro-Eastern faction, who had made his peace with Symmachus in 506.

The new tensions within the church and the electorate provoked three successive electoral disputes, in which all but one of the major participants were from the diaconate. In 526 after the death of John I, the pro-Gothic candidate, the deacon Felix, was installed as pope. Not one of the Symmachan old guard, he first appears in 519 when he was sent by Pope Hormisdas as one of the envoys to negotiate the end of the Acacian schism. His inclusion in that vital embassy demonstrates that he was an important and trusted figure at the papal court.[32]

Felix, however, endeavoured to fix the succession by nominating during his own lifetime the pro-Gothic Boniface, who was then archdeacon. In recommending him, the pope declared that 'from his earliest years he has served in our church', a fact confirmed by Boniface's epitaph.[33] It may be that the diaconate and archidiaconate date only from the reign of Felix and that Boniface is the former *primicerius notariorum*, who under John I was engaged in determining the date for Easter in 526,[34] and who as a simple notary, appears in 517 producing documents from the papal archives for Pope Hormisdas to send to Spain.[35] If we can conflate the two Bonifaces, the lifetime career mentioned in the papal recommendation is explained. With Felix IV planning the succession during his lifetime, the promotion of his candidate to be deacon and archdeacon at a time of diaconal 'monopoly' would be calculated to ensure wider acceptance for him. In the event Boniface only got the throne because his more popular opponent died. For he was opposed by the deacon Dioscorus, a key figure both in negotiating the end of the Symmachan schism in 506 and the Acacian schism in 519. A refugee Alexandrian, he had arrived in Rome at the height of the Symmachan schism, attached himself to Symmachus's party and become an influential figure at the papal court both under Symmachus and under Hormisdas. By the time of his election to the papal throne in 530, he had been a deacon for at least twenty-four years and is likely to have been quite old.

Like Felix, Boniface II tried to nominate his successor, choosing the deacon Vigilius, but popular opposition forced him to withdraw his backing and on his death there was a ferocious and stale-mated election which led to the compromise choice of the priest Mercurius as John II. John's successor in 535 was the archdeacon Agapitus, the last of the Symmachan old guard. Son of the priest Gordian and perhaps a nephew of Pope Felix III, he had begun his career as a *clericus* in his father's church of Saints John and Paul on the *Clivum Scauri*. Promoted to the diaconate as a hard-line loyalist after the death of his father in 502, he had thus been a deacon for thirty-three years by the time he became pope. But the fact that he had only attained the archidiaconate after 531, when Tribunus is recorded as holding the post, indicates that he had probably been extremely young when first appointed.[36]

His immediate successor was the ill-fated subdeacon Silverius, but Silverius's successor was a man long marked out as a future pope, Vigilius. Vigilius had been nominated by Boniface II as his successor in 531 in an act subsequently revoked. Vigilius was at that time a deacon, almost certainly a creation of Felix IV, the first pope since Symmachus to create any deacons, and probably quite young. When he eventually became pope, he reigned for seventeen years and six months, the longest pontificate of any pope in the period covered by this book.

There is some confusion about his actual rank at the time of his election. Soon after his abortive bid for the papal throne, he departed for Constantinople as *apocrisiarios*. In Liberatus's account of his rise, he is described as a deacon.[37] But in the *Liber Pontificalis* account, he is described first as deacon and legate and later as archdeacon and legate.[38] This is probably due to the fact that the *Liber Pontificalis* represents a conflation of two different accounts of the pontificate of Silverius, but it probably also represents a true picture of Vigilius's career.

When Pope Agapitus arrived in Constantinople, Vigilius was still there as deacon and *apocrisiarios*. But Agapitus appointed the deacon Pelagius as the new *apocrisiarios*. It must be at this point that Vigilius was promoted to the archidiaconate, a position vacated by Agapitus himself when he became pope. The *Liber Pontificalis* account says that Vigilius was described as archdeacon in the letters sent by Theodora to Belisarius and promotion by Agapitus would be the only possible explanation. It gives Vigilius so short a spell in the job that it also explains why subsequent writers, such as Liberatus, ignored his tenure of it. The appointment may have been a political one, with Agapitus succumbing to imperial pressure to name Vigilius as virtual heir-apparent. But it is possible that Vigilius was senior deacon, for with Felix IV and Agapitus creating four deacons each, few of them can have been appointed before 526.

Vigilius's successor, Pelagius I, was also archdeacon and is so described by Victor of Tunnuna, Procopius and the *Liber Pontificalis*.[39] But a similar question mark hangs over his career. For much of his documented career he was a deacon. He first appears in 536 accompanying Pope Agapitus on the visit to Constantinople.[40] Agapitus appointed him *apocrisiarios* in succession to Vigilius, presumably when Vigilius was raised to the archidiaconate.[41] He stayed on in Constantinople[42] after Agapitus's death, attended the church council and was confirmed in his office by Pope Vigilius, whose interests he defended by opposing the plan to return ex-Pope Silverius to Italy for trial.[43] Pelagius returned to Italy about 543 and became one of the most important figures at the papal court, unofficially taking charge of Rome after the departure of Vigilius for Constantinople.[44] Subsequently he followed Vigilius east and signed his *Constitutum* in 553.[45]

But the *Constitutum* was also signed by the archdeacon Theophanes, which indicates that Pelagius remained a deacon as late as 553. If we examine the references to Pelagius as archdeacon, we find that both Victor of Tunnuna and the *Liber Pontificalis* refer to his archidiaconate in connection with events immediately leading up to his elevation to the papal throne. The other archidiaconal reference, in Procopius, refers to events occurring during his apocrisiariate and is therefore patently anachronistic. It can probably be explained by Procopius's retrospectively applying to him his highest pre-papal rank, even though it was attained many years later.

Pelagius broke with Vigilius after the pope accepted the condemnation of the 'Three Chapters' and he was imprisoned. While in prison and writing his tract in defence of the 'Three Chapters' in 554, Pelagius was still describing himself as a deacon.[46] But soon after this, with Vigilius mortally ill, Pelagius sold out to the emperor in return for a promise of the papal succession; the most likely explanation of his archidiaconate is that Vigilius and Pelagius were reconciled just before the former's death and Pelagius was promoted to ensure his acceptance in Rome.[47]

255

Between Pelagius I and Gregory I the secure evidence fails, but Eulogius's statement on pre-papal ranks suggests that John III, Benedict I and Pelagius II were all deacons. This is confirmed in John's case if he is, as has been suggested, the subdeacon John who made a collection of extracts from the Greek fathers and completed the translation into Latin of the *Vitae Patrum* begun by Pelagius I.

The next pope whose pre-papal career is documented in detail is Gregory I. Born about 545 a wealthy aristocrat, he had become Prefect of Rome by the 570s. On the death of his father, he turned the family home on the *Clivum Scauri* into a monastery, which he entered as a monk. But his wide experience of public life and of dealing with the powerful led Pope Benedict I to withdraw him from his monastery and appoint him a deacon.[48] Pelagius II sent him to Constantinople as *apocrisiarios*[49] and on his return in 586, he acted as secretary of state, writing on the pope's behalf to the Istrian schismatics.[50] But Gregory never became archdeacon.

During his lengthy reign, Gregory I built up a staff of experienced administrators, several of whom succeeded to the papal throne. The careers of his three immediate successors can be traced in the Gregorian Register. Sabinian had been deacon and papal *apocrisiarios* in Constantinople from 593 to 597.[51] Boniface III had been deacon and Papal *apocrisiarios* in Constantinople from 603 to 604.[52] Boniface IV had been deacon and *dispensator* at the papal court from at least as early as 591.[53] It is worth noting that of the nine popes between the imperial restoration and 615, five were former *apocrisiarii* and this perhaps indicates the electors' concern to choose someone who had the ear of the emperor and could represent their interests in that quarter.

Even more significant than the prominence of *apocrisiarii* amongst the popes, however, is the fact that Gregory's pontificate represents a watershed in personnel policy. Gregory was the first monk to become pope. It is unlikely that he became pope because he was a monk but rather because he was the 'secretary of state' and former *apocrisiarios* of his predecessor Pelagius II. Even if his monastic background was not the reason for his elevation, however, it determined his style of government and unleashed a dispute the repercussions of which were felt for nearly a century. One of Gregory's most significant innovations was a thoroughgoing bid to monasticize the papacy. It was an attempt which caused so much resentment that, despite his celebrity in Britain as the instigator of Augustine's missionary offensive and in the East because of his writings, he was consigned to obscurity in Rome itself for 250 years.[54]

As pope, Gregory continued to live a communal monastic life in the Lateran Palace and, according to John the deacon, removed from his counsels all laymen and chose only the most prudent clerics as his familiars.[55] It is instructive in this context to examine the Gregorian inner circle of advisers. According to John, there were eight confidants, four clerics (the deacon Peter, the notaries Aemilianus and Paterius, the *defensor* John) and four monks (Abbot Maximian of St Andreas, Abbot Probus of Saints Andreas and Lucia, Abbot Claudius of Classis and the monk Marinianus of St Andreas). But this must be qualified, since by 595, three of the monks (Maximian, Marinianus and Claudius) were gone from Rome for good and the *defensor* John would have been away a great deal by the nature of his duties.

The Gregorian Register allows us to complement this list and arrive at a truer picture of the inner circle, and reveals that at its heart was a team of trusted administrators which Gregory built up and in whom he demonstrated his confidence by promotion. It is a group that shared his outlook and sympathies and may reasonably be called Gregorian.

In September 591 Gregory deposed the archdeacon Laurentius for *superbia*.[56] Laurentius had just been passed over for the succession in favour of the more junior Gregory and had also seen his power curtailed by the creation of a permanent *vicedominus*, so it might not be placing too great a strain on the evidence to see in the alleged *superbia* a manifestation of disgruntlement at the turn of events. Laurentius was replaced as archdeacon by the deacon Honoratus, *apocrisiarios* in Constantinople[57] and prior to that associated with Gregory during the latter's own apocrisiariate.[58] The deposition of the archdeacon, coupled with the elevation of the *vicedominus*, must have been seen in some quarters as an assault on the clerical hierarchy. To fill the newly created posts of *vicedominus* and *primicerius defensorum* Gregory chose the deacon Anatolius and the *defensor* Boniface respectively, subsequently manifesting his confidence in them further by appointing them successively to the post of *apocrisiarios*.[59] The pope's effective executive lieutenant, however, was the deacon Boniface (later Pope Boniface IV), who held the office of *dispensator* (probably treasurer) and also seems to have functioned as 'secretary of state'.[60]

Gregory made four promotions to the diaconate: his disciple and favourite the subdeacon Peter, the Isaurian monk Epiphanius, the *primicerius defensorum* Boniface and the subdeacon Florentius, previously Gregorian candidate for the bishopric of Naples.[61] Of these Peter was unquestionably the most important. Gregory describes him as a close friend from the earliest days of his youth and a companion in the study of the scriptures. This strongly suggests that Peter had begun his career as a young monk at St Andreas in the period 574–8 when Gregory himself was there. He seems to have left the monastery at the same time as his mentor to embark on a clerical career, holding successively the ranks of *defensor* and subdeacon. After Gregory's election, he was appointed both rector and vicar of Sicily and, after his return, acted as interlocutor in the *Dialogi*. He remained thereafter a close confidant and seems to have been Gregory's ideal cleric, combining like the pope himself a devotion to the simple, spiritual life of contemplation and prayer and at the same time a practical grasp of affairs based on personal experience of administration.[62] Gregory's confidence was also enjoyed by three notaries: Aemilianus, to whom he dictated his *Homilies on the Gospels*, Exhilaratus and Paterius, who made a volume of collected extracts from the pope's works. The two latter successively held the post of *secundicerius notariorum* and all three seem to have functioned as favoured private secretaries.[63]

Two characteristics of this group may be noted, lending force to the suggested direction of Gregorian personnel policy. There was an absence of laymen, confirming John the deacon's statement on the subject. Apart from his brother Palatinus, the only layman known to have exerted any influence on Gregory's circle is the *consiliarius* Theodore. He was a lawyer but seems to have been neither rich nor powerful, in contrast to Vigilius's *consiliarius*, for instance. For in January 593 Gregory sent him a Sicilian slaveboy to reward his loyal service because he had no servants.[64]

On the other hand, there is a marked preference for men of monkish background and sympathies. The residents of the Lateran Palace, we know, lived a communal monastic life, and John the deacon has indicated that half of Gregory's inner circle were by his reckoning monks. As far as can be ascertained, the deacons Peter and Epiphanius and the *secundicerius* Exhilaratus all began their careers as monks, while the deacon and *dispensator* Boniface showed strong monastic sympathies, for instance turning his family home into a monastery. It is also clear that Gregory drew heavily on his own foundation, St Andreas, as a continuing source of recruits for important bishoprics and abbacies. From St Andreas, Gregory appointed Maximian bishop of Syracuse, Marinianus archbishop of Ravenna, Augustine archbishop of Canterbury, Sabinus bishop of Callipolis, Claudius abbot of Saints John and Stephen in Classis and Caesarius abbot of St Peter *ad Baias* in Sicily. The regime was thus formed in Gregory's own image, that particular blend of a contemplative life and administrative experience that he himself embodied, and its monastic bias was to provoke a fierce clerical backlash as the regular clergy found themselves ousted from the positions of power.

The Roman clergy was fiercely jealous of its power and prerogatives and also intensely conservative and hierarchical. This underlies several episodes in papal history in the sixth century: the support of the senior clergy for the archpriest Laurentius in the Symmachan schism; the hostile reaction to the forced election of the subdeacon Silverius, partly explicable in terms of his low rank; the archdeacon Laurentius's bitterness at being passed over for the papacy in favour of Gregory I; the dispute under Gregory with the Ravenna church over their attempt to adopt some of the exclusive trappings of the Roman clergy. The Roman clergy not unnaturally reacted fiercely to Gregory's bid. In retrospect the seventh century can be seen as the period in which they fought for, ensured and tightened their control on the church.

There was, however, a Gregorian party and it fought back, winning the throne for Boniface III, Boniface IV and Honorius I who sought to implement the Gregorian programme. This programme involved the advancement of monasticism and the creation of a familial administration on the monastic model; a commitment to converting the heathen and in particular support for the English mission; a policy of close co-operation with the imperial authorities and involvement in the preservation of the province from the Lombards; and commitment to a new form of learning epitomized by the *Dialogi*, *Homilies* and *Regula Pastoralis* of Gregory. The new learning was simple, straightforward and accessible to ordinary people, a pastoral, allegorical, inspirational form of culture which laid great stress on the character, spirituality and endurance of the 'holy man'. It constituted a clean break with the old high culture of the sixth century centred on an intellectual elite, deeply immersed in the theological complexity and philosophical traditions of the East, exemplified by men like Boethius, Eugippius and Dionysius Exiguus. The new culture, strongly influenced by the monastic ideal, emphasized simple truths – suffering, spirituality and goodness – rather than the mastery of abstruse points of theological dogma. It promoted a religion of example and intercession and although its importance was realized in the East, imitated by John Moschus in his *Pratum Spirituale* and promoted by Pope Zacharias's Greek translation of the *Dialogi*, it was eclipsed in the West with the influx of émigré Greek monks and clerics, raised in the Eastern tradition and epitomized by Abbot Maximus, aristocrat, intellectual and prodigious writer on matters theological, liturgical and exegetical.

The Gregorian popes can be seen to have been committed to all or most of these facets of the Gregorian programme. Boniface IV and Honorius I interested themselves in the affairs of Britain.[65] Boniface

IV held a synod to regulate monastic affairs.[66] All of them favoured the monastic establishment over the clerical. All worked closely with the imperial authorities. Honorius I carried the dislike of theological philosophers to its greatest height in his celebrated denunciation of them as 'croaking frogs'. But it was his discrediting and eventual condemnation by the General Council of 680 that set the seal on the defeat of the Gregorian movement.

Events overtook the programme. The rise of Monotheletism meant a new wave of theological speculation and, although monks were prominent in this, they were Eastern monks and played an intellectual and inspirational role rather than administrative one. There was no lessening of the papacy's commitment to England or to the Empire. But the monastic bid for power in the administration was decisively defeated. By the eighth century the monasteries, far from providing an alternative power centre, had been absorbed into the orbit of the clerical administration. Monks were servicing the great basilicas and dispensing charity under the aegis of a clerically dominated papal administration.[67]

The fight for power began on the death of Gregory the Great in 604. Battle lines were drawn and the anti-Gregorian party candidates took great pains to stress their qualifications for office and to advance the clerical faction with rewards and promotions. This became a vital consideration for the electorate in the first half of the seventh century.

Gregory's successor on the papal throne was the deacon Sabinian, unquestionably elected as the candidate of the clerical party. His epitaph stated his credentials: 'He did not receive the papal crown as a result of instant fame, but this holy man earned it by working his way up the clerical ladder'.[68] There is an implied rebuke here perhaps against Gregory, swept straight from his monastery into the diaconate and thence to the papal throne. Sabinian, by contrast, had worked his way steadily to the top through all the regular grades of the clergy. He probably predated Gregory, in fact, in the service of the Roman church. This was the sort of pope the clerical faction wanted and not an intruded non-clerical outsider.

It is recorded of Sabinian that 'he filled the church with clergy'.[69] This does not mean the creation of extra priests; Sabinian created none at all. It enshrines the reversal of Gregory's policy of filling the papal court with monks. The recall of the clergy was only part of a more general anti-Gregorian reaction. For it is known that after his death Gregory's memory was execrated by the people of Rome. He was blamed for the famine which gripped the city and there was a bid by the mob to destroy his writings which was only averted by the intervention of Gregory's disciple, the deacon Peter.[70]

But Sabinian was soon to learn the fickleness of the mob for himself. He was consecrated on 13 September 604 and his short reign was marked by disaster. There was a renewal of war with the Lombards after a lengthy truce; there was famine in the wake of an intense frost, which killed the vines; and a plague of mice and a corn blight.[71] Sabinian was accused of profiteering in grain when he sold rather than gave away the contents of the papal granaries.[72] The people turned back to Gregory, and the legend that Sabinian died because the ghost of Gregory kicked him in the head for profiteering in grain at a time of famine encapsulated the extent of popular feeling against Sabinian.[73] At the height of his unpopularity, Sabinian died in February 606 and his funeral procession had to detour outside the city walls to avoid hostile demonstrations.[74]

The advantage was once again with the Gregorians, the populace having been alienated from the anti-Gregorians by the actions of Sabinian. There was a vacancy of eleven months and twenty-six days before the new pope was consecrated, and while this may simply be due to an unavoidable delay in getting imperial confirmation, it is possible that there was a disputed election. There had only been a five-month delay after Gregory I's death. In addition, the principal recorded act of the new pope, Boniface III, during his eight-month reign (February–November 607) was a synod, attended by seventy-two bishops and thirty-three priests and all the deacons and clergy, to make regulations about the papal electoral procedure, a fact which suggests – on the analogy of previous reigns – a disputed election.[75]

This synod forbade simony in connection with the papal election and forbade any discussion on the succession during the lifetime of, or for three days after the burial of, the pope. It seems likely that just those things had been happening during the final illness of Pope Sabinian. There is no need to look any further than the Gregorian and anti-Gregorian parties for the rival factions in this power struggle.

The synodical attendance attests the full support of the diaconate for the new pope. But this was still the Gregorian diaconate, Sabinian having created no deacons. The priestly attendance of thirty-three was less than half the numbers attending the Symmachan synods. This implies a less than full-hearted attitude by the priesthood towards the new pope, who was very much one of Gregory's handpicked team. The former *primicerius defensorum*, Boniface had been promoted deacon and *apocrisiarios* by Gregory. His stay in Constantinople and his acquaintance with the emperor Phocas stood him in good stead, for Phocas ended the 'Oecumenical Patriarch' controversy by confirming once again papal primacy.

Boniface III died in November 607 and was succeeded by an

unquestionable Gregorian, Boniface IV, consecrated on 25 August 608. The former deacon and *dispensator*, he had worked closely with Gregory, and his epitaph speaks of him imitating the 'merits and examples of his master Gregory'.[76] His actions eloquently bespeak the same monkish bias that Gregory had displayed. He turned his house into a monastery and endowed it. He held a synod in Rome to draw up orders for the life and peace of the monks.

Boniface's ordinations are interesting too. He ordained no priests during his reign; indeed, no new priests were ordained between the death of Gregory in 604 and the election of Deusdedit in 615. But Boniface did ordain no less than eight new deacons, suggesting that the Gregorian diaconate was dying out and that the pope was seeking to replace it by men of the same persuasion. These facts, coupled with the attendance figures at the 607 synod, suggest something of a split between the diaconate and the priesthood, with the former largely supporting the Gregorian programme and the latter in part opposing it. The balance in the elections may well have been held, therefore, by the people. So far as can be judged, their decisions were dictated by external events. It was famine which led to Gregory's posthumous disgrace and contributed to the election of the anti-Gregorian Sabinian. It was the continuance of the famine and the revival of war that led to the disgrace of the pro-clerical faction and the election of two successive Gregorians, Boniface III and Boniface IV. But Boniface IV's reign was a period of almost continuous disaster in the form of famine, plague and flood and the inevitable consequence was electoral disaster.[77]

Boniface IV died in May 615, having reigned for six years eight months and thirteen days, and on 19 October 615, his successor, Pope Deusdedit, was consecrated. The five-month vacancy implies a normal election and customary imperial ratification. The remarkable fact about Deusdedit is that he was a priest and had been for forty years. He is the first priest known to have been elected to the papal throne since John II in 533. This breach with the tradition of diaconal monopoly on the papal throne, which had grown up in the sixth century, is not so surprising if we accept, as has been argued, that the diaconate was in 615 largely Gregorian in outlook. It was, after all, the exclusive creation of Gregory I and Boniface IV; no intervening pope had created any deacons. If the anti-monastic party was looking for a candidate, it would therefore have to turn to the priesthood. The candidate it chose fulfilled the same criteria that Sabinian had. Deusdedit's epitaph talks of his old age, and stresses the fact that he had been raised in the church since childhood and had served in the priesthood for forty years.[78] Of Deusdedit's pro-clerical sympathies there can be no doubt. The *Liber Pontificalis* records of him 'He greatly loved the clergy and recalled the priests and the clergy to their former positions'.[79] This confirms the fact implicit in the sympathies of his predecessor but nowhere explicitly stated that Boniface IV had in fact restored the familial, monastic administration of Gregory and had truly, as his epitaph stressed, imitated the 'examples of his master Gregory'. Deusdedit was reversing this action. He also ordained fourteen priests during his reign, the first to have been ordained since Gregory's death.

There are two continuing sources of evidence which should be noted at this point, for they provide valuable pointers to the sympathies of the pontiffs in the seventh century. The first is that the clerically composed *Liber Pontificalis* begins to give little character sketches of the popes, revealing both for what they say and what they do not say. The second is the tradition, beginning with Deusdedit, of making funerary bequests to the clergy, again revealing because not all popes did so.[80] If we go back to the beginning of the seventh century, the *Liber Pontificalis* gives no character to Sabinian and his epitaph talks mainly of the disastrous conditions of his reign – famine, plague and war. The two Gregorians, Boniface III and Boniface IV, as might be expected, are given no characters and make no bequests. Boniface III's epitaph describes him as 'custodian of justice, upright and patient, benign, cultivated in speech and pleasing in piety', a model Gregorian indeed, but speaks of no generosity.[81] Boniface IV's epitaph speaks only of his imitating Gregory I. Deusdedit's epitaph calls him 'wise, shrewd and simple'. But he was not so simple that he did not know where his support came from and he made on his deathbed the first recorded funerary bequest, *unam integram rogam*, which probably means that he decreed the payment to each cleric an equivalent amount to their full salary.

In August 618 there was a major earthquake followed by an outbreak of a scab disease, during the course of which, in November 618, Deusdedit died. But its effects had apparently not percolated through to the electorate in time to affect the choice of a successor. There was a vacancy of one year one month and sixteen days before the new pope was consecrated, but Boniface V, whose pre-election rank is unfortunately unknown, was pro-clerical. The *Liber Pontificalis* says 'he loved the clergy' and like Deusdedit, he bequeathed to the clergy *integra roga*.[82] His legislative decrees show his keenness to preserve clerical prerogatives. He ordered that only priests, not acolytes, might translate the relics of martyrs. Nor should acolytes take the place of deacons at baptisms. This suggests that the junior clergy had been kicking over the traces, perhaps during the long vacancy, and had been usurping the functions of their seniors, a situation Boniface took steps to remedy. But it was clearly necessary for him, in view of the catastrophes which had preceded his election, to base his appeal on more than just the pro-clerical faction. The people were crucial, and the evidence points to outstanding generosity to the people being a feature of Boniface V's reign. The *Liber Pontificalis* calls him 'most holy and kindly disposed above all men and compassionate'. His epitaph calls him 'generous, wise, chaste, sincere and just' and records that he distributed his own personal fortune in alms and talks of the 'phalanxes of orphans and troops of blind men' he had helped.[83]

Despite this, after Boniface V's death in October 625, the pendulum swung back again towards the Gregorian party. The reigns of Deusdedit and Boniface had been a period of both natural and man-made disorder, for in addition to the scab disease, there had been a rebellion by the exarch Eleutherius and a revival of war with the Lombards. It was time for an able, energetic administrator in the Gregorian mould and that man was elected and consecrated only thirteen days after the death of Boniface V. He was Honorius I, who was to rule for twelve years eleven months and seven days.

Although Honorius's pre-papal rank is unknown, he was an aristocrat, builder and administrator, whose epitaph talks of him following in the footsteps of Gregory.[84] He turned his Roman home next to the Lateran into a monastery dedicated to Saints Andreas and Bartholomew – a clear echo of Gregory – and endowed it with money and estates.[85] He chose as his 'secretary of state' a monk, abbot John Symponus.[86] He made the first recorded grant of monastic exemption from episcopal control when he decreed that Bobbio should be directly dependent on Rome.[87] He sought out and delighted in the company of Abbot Bertulf of Bobbio during his stay in Rome.[88]

There can be little doubt then that Honorius revived the promonastic policy of Gregory I and Boniface IV. Coupled with the evidence of his actions is the fact that, although the *Liber Pontificalis* admits 'he did many good things', it gives him no character and says nothing about generosity, or love of the clergy.[89] His epitaph similarly concentrates on his concrete achievements. Although he spent 2000 pounds of silver beautifying the churches, Honorius, unlike his two predecessors, made no funerary bequest to the clergy.

The reign of Honorius I was the last fling of the Gregorians. After he died in October 638, the clerical faction reasserted its control. Pope Severinus, whose rank is not known, was pro-clerical. Characterized as 'holy, good above all men, a lover of paupers, generous and most kind', he is also said to have 'loved the clergy'. He manifested this love by increasing all clerical salaries and granting the *integra roga* on his death.[90]

John IV (640–2), although uncharacterized by the *Liber Pontificalis*, also granted the *integra roga*.[91] He was the archdeacon at the time of his election, the first known holder of that office to be elected pope for nearly a hundred years and a sure sign of the reassertion of clerical control.[92] By now the papacy was in the midst of the Monothelete controversy and it seems likely that this submerged the internal power struggle temporarily. By the time the controversy was resolved, Pope Honorius (and the Gregorian cause) had been disgraced and the Greek émigrés had taken charge of the papacy.

Their orthodoxy and their handling of the emperor seem to have been the principal credentials of the three main popes at the height of the controversy: Theodore I (642–9), Martin I (649–55) and Vitalian (657–72). None of them made funerary bequests. Only one of them is characterized; Theodore is described in the *Liber Pontificalis* as 'a lover of paupers, generous, good above all men and compassionate'.[93] Only Martin's pre-papal career, deacon and *apocrisiarios*, is known. The reigns of all three seem to have been dominated by the political and theological issues.

The single exception during this period is Eugenius (654–7), characterized as 'good, kind, gentle, affable to all and outstanding in sanctity'. He was a lifetime cleric (*clericus a cunabulis*) and the attachment of a region to his name (*Regio I Aventinense*) suggests a regionary deacon. He certainly decreed *integra roga* to clergy and people on the day of his death.[94]

As the heat was taken out of the Monothelete crisis, the electors turned from the strong-willed statesmen they had chosen at the height of the troubles, elevating a succession of short-lived, elderly, saintly figures, chiefly distinguished for their generosity to the people in general and the clergy in particular. The control of the papal court and administration by the clergy was ensured.

The papal election formulae in the *Liber Diurnus*, dating from the mid-seventh century, take it for granted that the pope had served since his early years in the clergy, a reflection perhaps of the state of affairs as it had emerged since the death of Honorius. Pope Donus (676–8), whose pre-papal rank is unknown and who is uncharacterized in the *Liber Pontificalis*, promoted everyone during his short reign.[95] Pope Agatho (678–81), who was 'so good and gentle that he was happily approved of by all', and whose takeover of the post of *arcarius* suggests a pre-papal training in the finance departments of the papal bureaucracy, also promoted everybody and gave out *integra roga* upon his death.[96] Pope Leo II (682–3), 'a lover of the poor who worked hard to alleviate their condition', seems not to have been as fond of the clergy, to whom he made no bequest.[97] But this was rectified by the election of Benedict II (684–5). A priest, ranked eleventh in 679, Benedict had entered the clergy in childhood and served in every order of the clergy during his career.[98] Characterized as 'lover of the poor, humble, gentle, and having compassion for all and a most generous hand', he promoted everybody and left 30 pounds of gold for distribution amongst the clergy and the diaconal monasteries.[99]

The only apparent exception during this period of short pro-clerical reigns is that of Adeodatus (672–6). He was a monk, the first to be elected since Gregory I, but he was a very different sort of pontiff from Gregory. The *Liber Pontificalis* says of him: 'He was of such greatness, most kind and good that he freely received all men from the great to the small. He showed compassion to foreigners and granted to anyone whatever he demanded without hesitation.'[100] Far from pursuing an anti-clerical policy, Adeodatus increased all salaries, and this careful display of generosity can only mean that the clergy now felt secure enough in their control of the administrative machine to permit the election of a monk.

By 685 clerical control was so secure that the senior clerics were coming to regard election to the papal throne once again almost as a prescriptive right, on the age-old principle of Buggins's turn. Benedict II's successor, John V (685–6), was archdeacon and extremely distinguished.[101] As a deacon, he had been sent to Constantinople as one of the papal delegation to the General Church Council of 680 and there had played a leading role in the discussions leading to the suppression of Monotheletism. He left 1900 *solidi* to the clergy and the diaconal monasteries in his will.[102]

On John's death in 686 there was a struggle for power based not on differences of policy or principle but simply on conflicting ambition. The electors split between the archpriest Peter and the priest Theodore, second in seniority to Peter. The result was a compromise choice, the priest Conon, specifically chosen for his 'angelic aspect, white hairs, true speech, advanced age, simple mind, quiet life' and his pursuit of a purely religious existence in which he never got involved in secular affairs.[103] The search for spirituality was an inevitable reaction to the worldliness of a hard-fought election campaign. But Conon continued the pro-clerical policy of the past half-century by leaving 30 pounds of gold to the clergy and diaconal monasteries when he died in 687.[104] Once again, there was a revival of electoral dispute with the election split between the archdeacon Paschal and the archpriest Theodore, the candidate in the previous election now promoted following the death of his erstwhile rival.

This time the compromise choice, another priest, Sergius, was young and vigorous. The *Liber Pontificalis* tells us something of his career.[105] He had arrived in Rome from Sicily as recently as the reign of Adeodatus and had been enrolled by him in the clergy. He had distinguished himself by his fine singing and had been attached to the *Schola Cantorum*. He rose steadily through the ranks of the clergy and attracted the attention of Leo II, himself a fine singer and much interested in church music. Leo made Sergius priest of St Susanna on the Quirinal, a position he still held at the time of his election to the papal throne. He reigned for thirteen years eight months and twenty-three days. With Sergius's reign, the tradition of lavish bequests to the clergy starts to tail off; this suggests that clerical control of the papacy was now established beyond a peradventure, enhanced if anything by the condemnation by the Council of Constantinople of the last great Gregorian, Honorius I. Sergius is given no character in the *Liber Pontificalis* and he made no bequest to the clergy. The same is true of his successor John VI (701–5), of whose pre-papal career nothing is known.

John VII (705–7) was an administrator. From the epitaph he put up to his mother Blatta, it is known that he was rector of the Appian patrimony in 687, which implies subdiaconal rank and suggests that he was probably a deacon by the time of his election.[106] His epitaph records his acts of charity and generosity with his personal fortune.[107] But there is no record of a bequest to the clergy. Nothing is known of Sisinnius, who reigned for twenty days in 708. But his successor, Constantine (708–15), is probably the same as the subdeacon Constantine who accompanied the ecclesiastical embassy to the Council of Constantinople in 680[108] and was subsequently entrusted by the emperor with delivery of a letter to Pope Leo II.[109] His inclusion in such an important embassy indicates that he was already highly thought of, a promise confirmed by his election twenty-eight years later, probably from the diaconal grade. The *Liber Pontificalis* calls him 'the gentlest of men' but he made no bequests to the clergy.[110]

Constantine's successor was Gregory II (715–31). He had been brought up since childhood in the church, entering the administrative grade of the clergy and rising to become subdeacon and *sacellarius* under Pope Sergius I. Later he had been put in charge of the papal library as *bibliothecarius,* and finally he had been appointed deacon and had accompanied Pope Constantine on his visit to Constantinople, where he had taken a leading role in the negotiations with Emperor Justinian II and the resolution of the problems arising from the Quini-sext council. He had clearly been an important figure at the papal court for some years and his elevation to the throne then was the natural culmination of a regular clerical career.[111] He bequeathed 2160 *solidi* to the clergy and the diaconal monasteries, reviving the recently unfashionable practice of funerary bequests.[112]

Gregory II's successor was Gregory III (731–41). He was a priest and had been for at least ten years, when he was elected by popular acclaim immediately after the funeral of his predecessor.[113] The *Liber Pontificalis* calls him 'a most gentle and wise man' and rhapsodizes about his learning,[114] culture, generosity, charity, defence of Orthodoxy and encouragement of good works. He made no bequest to the clergy, however. Finally, there is Zacharias (741–52), a deacon for at least nine years, described as

> a most soft and suave man, adorned with every goodness, a lover of the clergy and people of Rome, slow to anger and swift to pardon, returning evil for evil to no man, nor distributing punishment according to deserts. But pious and generous from the time of his ordination, he returned good for the evil of those who persecuted him, promoting them to honours and enriching them.

As part of this general goodness and generosity, he doubled all salaries.[115]

During the sixth century, then, the papacy was a virtual diaconal monopoly; electors consistently chose men of proven administrative ability and seniority. After the imperial reconquest particular favour was shown towards former *apocrisiarii*, who would have that all-important access to the ear of the emperor. But, with Gregory I's bid to monasticize the papacy, there began a battle between pro- and anti-Gregorian factions for control of the papal administration. It ended in the late seventh century with the decisive assertion of clerical control. This initially involved a breach with the diaconal monopoly, because in the early part of the seventh century the diaconate was dominated by the Gregorians. The situation was complicated in the seventh and eighth centuries by the fact that there were ten popes whose pre-papal ranks are unknown, but in most cases their pro- or anti-monastic sentiments are clear. The distinction between the priesthood and the diaconate *per se* seems to have been much less crucial after 615 than the attitude of the candidate, whether priest, monk or deacon, to the clerical establishment.

Chapter 16

Geographical Origins and Cultural Attainments

It was a basic rule of episcopal elections that the electors should look to the clergy of their own church first to fill a vacant see. This was unquestionably followed by the Roman electors, but an examination of the actual birthplaces of the popes throws valuable light on the composition of the Roman clergy in our period.[1]

Of the seventeen popes between 483 and 604, eleven were natives of Rome and four came from provinces close to Rome and inside the Suburbicarian Province. There are only two exceptions, Gelasius, an African, and Symmachus, a Sardinian. But both had entered the service of the Roman church, Symmachus after being converted from paganism. So they are clearly special cases. In general, as one might expect, the popes were Romans or at least Italians. It is interesting to note the general absence of Germanic and Gothic names in the background of the popes. The only exceptions to this are Boniface II, son of Sigibuld, and Pelagius II, son of Unigild. Both men were born in Rome and counted as Romans, and it has been suggested above that Boniface's family had probably been settled in the empire for a century. This indicates both that there was nothing to stop Goths or Germans entering the clergy and rising to high office but also that not many did, certainly not enough to alter the composition of the clergy substantially.

In the first three-quarters of the seventh century there is a slight change of emphasis. Between 604 and 678, there were fourteen popes, of whom six were Romans and six from provinces near Rome and within the limits of Suburbicarian Italy. Again there were two exceptions, both explicable: John IV, a Dalmatian, probably a refugee from Slavic inroads and Theodore, a Palestinian Greek, almost certainly a refugee from the Arab invasions. The increase in the proportion of non-Roman Italians can probably be explained by the Lombard invasions, which caused widespread dislocation and made Rome a centre for refugees, some of whom were absorbed into

269

the Roman clergy. However, it is interesting to observe that on no occasion either in the sixth or seventh century was someone from northern Italy elected to the papal throne.

A dramatic change came over the papacy in the last quarter of the seventh century and the first half of the eighth. For between 687 and 752, of the thirteen popes elected, only two were Romans (Gregory II and Benedict II). All the rest were Greek-speaking: two Sicilians, four Syrians and five Greeks. If intervention by the emperor or the exarch is ruled out – as it must be in the absence of any evidence for it – this can only mean that the composition of the clergy had drastically changed during the course of the seventh century.

There are some hints on the origins of these Greek popes. Some were children of imperial functionaries stationed in Italy. Conon, who is described as 'Greek by birth, brought up in Sicily' was the son of a soldier of the Thracesion regiment, then stationed in Italy;[2] John VII was the son of Plato, who held the office of *curator sacri palatii* and was a civil servant stationed in Rome.[3] The important fact about both these families, however, is that they settled in Italy, their children were brought up there and in the cases of Conon and John entered the Roman clergy and eventually attained the throne. So one source of Greeks in the Roman clergy was the imperial administration, both civil and military.

But another, and perhaps more significant, source was refugees. It has already been suggested that flight from the Arabs explains the appearance in Rome of Pope Theodore, son of a Palestinian bishop.[4] But there is hard evidence in the case of Pope Sergius I, born in Panormus in Sicily but the son of a Syrian, Tiberius of Antioch, who had migrated from there, undoubtedly as a result of the Arab invasions.[5] Sergius himself came to Rome in the pontificate of Pope Adeodatus (672–6), became a distinguished musician and was ordained a priest in 682–3.

Sicily itself had become the subject of Arab attacks in the mid-seventh century and this perhaps accounts for the influx of Sicilians into the Roman clergy, their presence being attested by the elections of Popes Agatho, Leo II, Sergius I and Conon.

The Greek popes for the most part seem to have belonged to a single wave of clerics, which included both refugees and the children of refugees. John V, for instance, was born, like Pope Sergius's father, in Antioch and was perhaps part of the same exodus. Many of the Greek popes were elderly and short-lived, the extreme example being Sisinnius, who reigned for twenty days. By the mid-eighth century this wave had spent itself and Romans were once again elected to the papal throne.

The extraordinary consistency of Greek elections between 678 and

752 strongly suggests that the Roman clergy had been swamped by Easterners, and indeed all the evidence points to the inescapable fact that during the seventh century, and particularly the latter part of the seventh century, Rome, its cultural ambiance, language and outlook became saturated by Eastern influences in the form of a large, vocal, articulate and influential Greek presence. It is only necessary to compare Rome at the end of the sixth century with Rome at the end of the seventh century to appreciate the changes that have been wrought.

It must be stressed that there is nothing sinister or untoward in this Hellenization. It used to be argued that there was a deliberate policy of Hellenization of Italy carried out by the exarch, that this was undertaken, in the case of the church, to reduce its power and subject it to the imperial will and, in the case of the state, to bind the Italian province closer to the Eastern Empire.[6] There is no evidence to support this theory. Ecclesiastical historians who have fostered the idea of a 'Byzantine captivity' of the Roman church have done so from the *a priori* assumption that there was something degrading in the adoption of Eastern liturgical practices and in the pursuit of a policy of co-operation with the imperial government. But this is a value-judgment unsupported by contemporary evidence. There are no seventh-century laments about 'the Byzantine captivity' of the church and it is high time that we got away from the idea that there was something sinister, degrading or corrupt about Greek influence on the West.

It has recently been pointed out that an artificial and over-rigid distinction is often made between East and West, whereas there was a much more real division between North and South. East and West were after all part of a Mediterranean world and culture, which shared traditions and outlooks in common, particularly the Roman imperial idea.[7] There had been a long tradition of interchange with the East. In the clerical sphere, refugee Eastern clergy were welcomed in Rome and were sometimes incorporated into the Italian church. The refugee Patriarch John Talaia of Alexandria became bishop of Nola. The Alexandrian deacon Dioscorus became a key figure at the courts of Popes Symmachus and Hormisdas and only narrowly missed becoming pope in 530. The Isaurian monk Epiphanius became a Roman deacon under Gregory I. Eastern scholars and intellectuals were welcomed, and enriched the cultural life of Italy. Gregory of Agrigentum, Eastern monk and theologian, took up residence in a Roman monastery and ultimately became bishop of Agrigentum. John Moschus, author of the *Pratum Spirituale*, similarly resided in a Roman monastery for a time. The Scythian monk Dionysius Exiguus became the most celebrated canonist in sixth-century Rome. What happened in the seventh century as far as the church was concerned was an intensification of this process as a flood of refugees from the Arabs, the Persians, the Avars, the Slavs and from Monothelete persecution headed for Rome.

There was bound to be a substantial lay presence. After all, Italy was a Byzantine province, governed by a predominantly Greek staff of army officers, senior civil servants and Exarchal administrators. Some of them brought their families and settled, their presence reinforcing the Greek element in Italian society. Plato the *curator* father of Pope John VII, was one of these. The land grants made in the eighth century by the papacy to Eastern army officers often included the stipulation that the grant was for the lifetime of themselves, their children and grandchildren – further evidence of settlement.

But this should not be overstressed. The surviving documents and inscriptions are in Latin, indicating that it remained the official language. The composition of the rank-and-file of the regiments of the army changed from Greek to Latin as local recruitment took over. The garrison army, in line with trends elsewhere in the empire, was transformed during the course of the seventh century into a local militia, on permanent standby. There had also always been Greek merchants in Rome; they had been the targets of satirists like Martial and Juvenal in the first century. Indeed, they had become so powerful by the early fifth century that they were expelled after a nativist outburst among the Latin populace and Greek merchantships were banned from Western ports. But the ban was soon lifted, and the emperor Valentian III recalled the merchants to Rome. They soon resumed their former eminence, their position being unassailable after the imperial reconquest. There was a Greek quarter in Rome at the foot of the Aventine and this became the heart of the city, a fact recognized by the siting of the new papal palace of John VII near by.[8]

So it is not so much that there was a quantitative change in the population of Rome or indeed of Italy; but there was a qualitative change. The ruling elites were drawn from Greek-speaking, Eastern-oriented groups. The social, cultural and religious tone of society was set by these groups. It is, therefore, the transformation in the nature and composition of the Roman clergy with its consequent effects on both the papacy and the outlook and ambiance of Rome that is crucial, and here, uniquely, there does seem to have been a quantitative change too.

The process of Hellenization which this change involved can be traced in every branch of the church's activities and structure. The election of a succession of Greek popes has already been noted. This was accompanied, however, by the increasing dominance of the

Greeks in court circles. Their rise to the positions of power can be tantalizingly charted from the scraps of evidence that survive. On the death of Pope Severinus in 640, the three senior clerics who assumed the regency were the archpriest Hilarus, the archdeacon John and the *primicerius notariorum* John.[9] Of them, Hilarus, from his name, must be Latin and the archdeacon John, the future John IV, is known to have been a Dalmatian.

So by 640 the Greek influence had not yet reached the top levels, but it was already making an impact. Abbot John Symponus, 'secretary of state' to Honorius I and John IV, was a Greek and dealt with the all-important papal correspondence with the East.[10] The deacon Sericus, Honorius's *apocrisiarios* in Constantinople, was from his name probably also a Greek and his influence increased after the election of the refugee Palestinian Theodore as pope in 642.[11] The elevation of Theodore, who must have been Greek-speaking, may well have provided an additional impetus to the Greek influx. Under Theodore, Sericus became archdeacon and was despatched again to Constantinople together with the new papal *apocrisiarios*, the Tudertine deacon Martin, to examine the canonical status of the patriarch Paul, successor of the deposed Pyrrhus.[12] It was Martin, already deeply involved in anti-Monotheletism and committed to a strongly orthodox position, who was elected Theodore's successor in a wave of anti-Monothelete feeling. But the Lateran Synod of 649, held to formulate the official papal position on the question, was dominated by thirty-seven Greek refugee monks and clerics, who presented a crucial petition. The proceedings themselves, which included the reading out of various documents, letters and statements, highlighted the prominence of Greeks in the notariate. For the participants were the *primicerius notariorum* Theophylact and the senior notaries Paschal, Exuperius, Theodore, Anastasius and Paschasius, who bore Greek names, and were able to translate fluently from Latin into Greek.[13]

But there was not yet a Greek monopoly of office. Senior clergy who had begun their careers before the Greek influx survived and rose up the scale. Eugenius's archdeacon, the friend of St Wilfrid of Hexham, was the Latin Boniface and Vitalian's *primicerius notariorum* had the distinctively Latin name of Gaudentius.[14] Vitalian selected as archbishop of Canterbury the distinguished Greek monk, Theodore of Tarsus, but he sent to England with him the African abbot Adrian of Nisida, to ensure that there was not a widespread introduction of alien Greek customs to swamp already established Latin tradition.[15] This perhaps indicates a papacy on its guard against Greek innovation, in part possibly because of fear of the Monotheletes. But with the Monothelete crisis, the pressure of the Greeks on the positions of power was irresistible. In view of the increasing Greek dominance in the second half of the seventh century, especially in the senior clerical echelons, it is perhaps surprising that it was not until 685 that the first true Oriental, Syrian-born archdeacon John, became pope as John V. This opened the floodgates but there was nothing sinister about this. It meant that an Oriental had reached the top of the clerical hierarchy by a normal career course and from that eminence had attained the throne. But it does look as if there was an avoidance of Greek popes, despite the evident hierarchical seniority of the Greeks, until the Monothelete crisis was safely resolved.

There was a takeover, if not of the entire hierarchy, certainly of the positions of influence at court. The envoys sent by Pope Agatho to the sixth General Council of 680 demonstrated this.[16] On this crucial mission were the priests Theodore and George, the deacon John, the subdeacon Constantine, Bishops Abundantius of Tempsa, John of Rhegium and John of Portus, and a monastic delegation consisting of Abbot Theophanes of St Caesarius *ad Baias* in Sicily, George priest and monk of Saints Andreas and Lucia, Conon and Stephen, priests and monks of the *Domus Arsicia*. The flavour was overwhelmingly Greek. The envoys participated in the Council speaking in Greek and they signed in Greek. The deacon John is the future John V, a known Syrian, and the subdeacon Constantine, another Syrian. The monks were all Greek. Bishops Abundantius and John of Rhegium were from the increasingly Hellenized southern provinces of Italy. Added to this the priests Theodore and George sound distinctly Oriental and are probably identical with the priests of the same name who signed four and five at the 679 council and were thus senior members of the priesthood.

Bishop John of Portus seems to have been a major figure at the papal court during these years. Senior envoy to the Constantinople Council, deputed with Bishop Andreas of Ostia to look into the appeal of St Wilfrid of Hexham,[17] he was later during the reign of Sergius I arrested by order of the emperor in order to put pressure on the papacy in the Quini-sext dispute.[18]

After the death of Pope John V in 686 the bitter struggle for the succession involved the most senior dignitaries of the clergy, who have predominantly Greek-sounding names. In 686 the archpriest Peter and the priest Theodore, his immediate junior in the priestly hierarchy, contested the election, but the throne went to a compromise choice, the priest Conon. In 687 Theodore, now archpriest following Peter's death, and the archdeacon Paschal, contested the throne but it went to a compromise choice, the priest Sergius. Of the protagonists in these elections Conon and Sergius are known to have been Greeks and most of the others are likely so to have been. It is possible that the senior echelons were temporarily discredited by this unholy scramble for power, for interestingly the imperial authorities discerned as the chief advisers of Sergius I not the archpriest or archdeacon but a bishop, John of Portus, and a layman, the *consiliarius* Boniface.

Perhaps the fullest glimpse we ever get of the papal hierarchy at this time comes when Pope Constantine makes his official visit to the East in 710.[19] His entourage included Bishops Nicetas of Silva Candida and George of Portus, the priests Michael, Paul and George, the deacon Gregory, the *secundicerius notariorum* George, the *primicerius defensorum* John, the *sacellarius* Cosmas, the *nomenclator* Sisinnius, the *scriniarius* Sergius, the subdeacons Dorotheus and Julian. Although of this group the deacon Gregory is known to have been Roman and the future Pope Gregory II, the rest sound overwhelmingly Greek and not just Greek but Byzantine, bearing names like Nicetas, Michael, Sisinnius and Cosmas, which were wholly alien to the West. The archdeacon, archpriest and *primicerius notariorum* were clearly left behind as regents. They escaped the visit of the exarch John Rizocopus unscathed, but other senior papal officials were less fortunate and a group including the deacon and *vicedominus* Salius, the *arcarius* Peter, the abbot Sergius and the *ordinator* Sergius, another distinctively Greek-sounding group, were executed.

The prominence of Gregory the deacon at Constantine's court, evidenced by the leading role he played in hammering out a settlement of the Quini-sext dispute with Justinian II, was reflected in his election to the papal throne in 715, the first non-Greek pope for thirty years. Both his successors, Zacharias and Gregory III, were Greeks and the evidence of the diaconal subscriptions to the 721, 731 and 743 councils is of a continuing and strong Greek presence.[20] The successive archdeacons were called Peter (721), Moschus (731) and Theophylact (743) and evince a predominant Eastern flavour. But the Roman influence was about to revive and the inclusion among the deacons of 743 of the Roman Stephen, the future Pope Stephen II, was a pointer to things to come. So too was the eminence at court of the *primicerius notariorum* Ambrose, entrusted by Zacharias with the restoration of the Lateran Palace and chosen envoy to the Lombard king,[21] and of Bishop Benedict of Nomentum, papal *vicedominus* and, together with Ambrose, envoy to Liutprand.[22] Both were clearly Latins and their prominence means that the Latin influence, entering the lower ranks, had now in the natural course of things percolated to the highest. The old generation of Greek immigrants and immigrant families was about to be overtaken.

It was clearly not just the senior clergy but also the rank-and-file who changed as a result of the Greek influx. At the end of the sixth century Gregory I complained about the lack of Greek interpreters in

Rome who could translate important documents from the East into Latin.[23] By the 649 Lateran synod, the senior papal notaries were freely and fluently translating from Greek into Latin.[24] A similar change is reflected in the priestly subscription lists for the synods of the sixth and seventh centuries. Without taking any individual cases, the overwhelming flavour of the lists by the end of the seventh century is Greek. The sixth-century lists were dominated by Latin names. But the seventh- and eighth-century lists boast hosts of men called Sisinnius, Theodore and George. Since popes with distinctively Eastern names, Sisinnius, Sergius and Conon for instance, are provably Greek, it seems reasonable to assume that many of the other Roman priests with similarly Oriental names are of the same provenance. The overwhelming Greek dominance in the subscription lists also coincides exactly with the succession of Greek and Greek-speaking popes.

There is the evidence also of the monasteries.[25] Those founded in the sixth century or before in Rome were, as far as can be ascertained, exclusively Latin, but by the seventh century there were at least six Greek monasteries in the city, some new, some taken over. The monastery of St Anastasius *ad Aquas Salvias*, founded according to tradition in the sixth century by Governor Narses, was by 649 occupied by a community of Cilician monks. The Boetiana monastery, whose name indicates a connection with the family of the philosopher senator Boethius and similarly suggests sixth-century foundation, was discovered in 676–8 to be full of Syrian Nestorian monks. The otherwise unknown *Domus Arsicia* monastery sent two Greek-named and almost certainly Greek-speaking monks to the 680 General Council in Constantinople, indicating a Greek community. The monastery of St Erasmus on the Caelian Hill, from which the Roman-born Pope Adeodatus was elected in 672, became a Greek foundation soon afterwards, judging from the evidence of Greek inscriptions found there. The monastery of Saints Andreas and Lucia, a Latin foundation in the reign of Gregory the Great when Probus, nephew of the Bishop of Reate, was appointed abbot, was by 649 described as 'the monastery of the Armenians' and had undergone a change of dedication. Now the abbey of Saints Maria and Andreas, it sent its abbot with the distinctively Oriental name of Thalassius to the 649 Lateran synod and a priest called George to the 680 General Council. The monastery of St Saba, from the evidence of its buildings and frescoes, was a Greek foundation of the early seventh century.

These monasteries, and perhaps others still unidentified, were the intellectual power-houses of the Greek émigrés, in the struggle against Monotheletism. Their appearance in the seventh century and the prominence of some of their representatives confirms the impression of a stream of clerical refugees making their way to Rome to escape Arab invasion and Monothelete persecution. The evidence of the six monasteries already cited indicates the presence of communities from Cilicia, Armenia and Syria in Rome. Their importance is attested by the admittance to the 649 Council of four Greek abbots, described as 'for a long time resident in the city of Rome': John abbot of St Saba in Rome, Theodore abbot of St Saba in Africa, Thalassius abbot of Saints Maria and Andreas in Rome and George abbot of Aquae Salviae. They presented to the council a petition signed by thirty-seven exiled monks, priests and deacons from Africa, Palestine, Armenia and points East denouncing Monotheletism and outlining the true faith.[26]

The extent of the Greek presence both in Rome and in the positions of influence as early as 649 is evidenced by the fact that Abbot Maximus, the spiritual leader of the anti-Monothelete forces and himself a refugee from the Arab invasions, arrived in Rome from Africa about 646 and survived there for several years without knowing any Latin.[27] From these refugee ranks sprang several important and respected figures. Abbot John Symponus, 'secretary of state' to Popes Honorius I and John IV, responsible for translating their letters from Latin into Greek, was still alive and flourishing at the time of the debate of Pyrrhus and Maximus and was a friend of both Abbot Maximus and his disciple Anastasius.[28] Abbot Theodore, appointed by Pope Martin as envoy to Palestine,[29] and abbot Theophanes of St Caesarius *ad Baias* in Sicily, George, priest and monk of Saints Maria and Andreas, and the monks, Conon and Stephen, of the *Domus Arsicia*, appointed envoys to the sixth General Council, were also important in these Greek monastic circles.[30]

The Greek influence even extended beyond Rome to the Italian episcopate. Eddius Stephanus, the biographer of St Wilfrid of Hexham, noted rather disapprovingly that when his hero presented himself to a synod in Rome in 704 to argue his case against deprivation of his see, the bishops present chatted and joked amongst themselves in Greek.[31] Several important bishops seem to have been Greek. Bishop John of Portus, senior papal envoy to the 680 council, spoke fluently in Greek during the proceedings and signed in Greek, as did his fellow episcopal envoys, Abundantius of Tempsa and John of Rhegium, both southern and probably natively Greek-speaking bishops.[32] Bishop Leontius of Naples, who introduced the Byzantine festival of the Exaltation of the True Cross to his city some fifty years before it reached Rome, sounds to have been a Greek exile.[33] Bishop Nicetas of Silva Candida, companion of Pope Constantine on his visit to the East, is another prelate with a striking Byzantine name.[34]

There are several other late seventh-century bishops from the areas around Rome with Eastern-sounding names. But the ones listed above are those most likely to have been Greeks.[35]

The influence of the Greek personnel filling the various branches of the Roman church was inevitably felt in the area of ceremonial and ecclesiastical decoration. There was a large-scale introduction of the cults of Greek saints, Greek rites and rituals and even Greek church institutions into Rome. The seventh century, for instance, saw the development in Rome of Greek-style *diaconia*, charitable monasteries attached to churches and chapels of decidedly Greek provenance – St Maria *in Cosmedin*, St George *in Velabro*, Saints Cosmas and Damian, Saints Sergius and Bacchus, St Theodore, St Hadrian. Most of these churches date from the time of the Greek influx, many of them dedicated to warrior saints particularly associated with the army.[36]

The changes in ritual are even more striking. At the end of the sixth century Gregory I, in a letter to Bishop John of Syracuse, indignantly denied that the Roman church copied any of the liturgical practices of the Eastern church, saying that the current practices were all ancient customs of the Roman church.[37] This pride in Rome and Roman ways harmonizes with Gregory's mistrust of the heresy-prone Greeks and in particular his failure to learn Greek. But the situation was certainly different by the early eighth century. By the reign of Leo II the festival of the *Theophania* had been introduced, and Leo built a church to the Eastern warrior saint George,[38] whose head Pope Zacharias produced from the Lateran and installed in a place of honour.[39] Sergius I introduced the quintessentially Eastern festivals of the Exaltation of the True Cross, the Annunciation, Dormition and Nativity of the Virgin Mary and the cult of the martyr St Symeon. Several Greek hymns were introduced into the church services, and in particular Sergius I introduced the Syrian hymn, *Agnus Dei*.[40]

It is possible that in the seventh century there was still a residual feeling that Hellenization constituted a potential danger to the purity of the Roman tradition. Italian-born Pope Vitalian sent the African Abbot Adrian of Nisida to England with the newly appointed Greek archbishop of Canterbury, Theodore of Tarsus, to ensure that the latter did not introduce alien Greek customs and throw the English, converted and brought up in the Latin tradition, off balance.[41] But this may have been a special case and it is certain that fear of Hellenization had disappeared from Rome to such an extent by the mid-eighth century that Roman-born Pope Paul I could found a Greek monastery for the singing of Greek chant.[42] Greek customs, rituals and practices were clearly, therefore, accepted as a normal part of church life in Rome. This acceptance may have been helped by the stance of one of the most notable Hellenizers, Sergius I. Not only did he transfer the body of Pope Leo the Great to a new, splendid and prominent tomb, thus emphasizing his links with the Roman tradition, but he also keenly resisted attempts by the emperor Justinian II to legislate against the traditional practices of the Roman church. This demonstrated beyond a peradventure that the Greek innovations were not a bid to subvert the Latin tradition.

Associated with this development was a major artistic movement, spurred on by the arrival of refugee Alexandrian artists. It centred on church decoration and in particular the painting of frescoes and images and the designing of ikons in the Byzantine fashion. At its height during the reign of John VII, it was to become in part an element in the assertion of orthodoxy against Iconoclasm but it was also a supreme reflection of the Hellenization of the church and city of Rome. The basilicas of the city, handsomely endowed and lavishly decorated by the Greek popes, became in their Oriental opulence veritable Byzantine temples, shimmering with silk gauze draperies, glittering with jewelled chalices, embroidered altar cloths, hanging crucifixes, inlaid silver roof-beams, gold and silver ikons, and ornamental arches, iridescent with multi-coloured frescoes and mosaic floors.

They became in fact the perfect setting for the dramatic alterations in the liturgy, for during the seventh and early eighth centuries there emerged in direct reflection of Byzantine ecclesiastical and court ceremonial a new papal rite alongside the old Roman rite. It has been described as

> a rigid etiquette admitting neither change nor improvisation on the part of the assistants, an awe-inspiring solemnity of ceremonies and a unique grandiose *organum* chant [which] become symbols of Papal sovereignty in the West, turning the congregation into spectators and listeners.[43]

The distinguishing feature of the Roman rite, which was symbolic of the Roman community and was here displaced, was the participation in the ritual by the congregation as well as the clergy. The new papal rite excluded the congregation and was built around the glorification of the pope. But it should not be taken to mean a change in papal ideology. It implies nothing more than that the Greeks were bringing in the sort of liturgical arrangements they were used to and familiar with. In context, it is the ceremonial counterpart of the introduction of Greek-style diaconal monasteries, the cult of the warrior saints and Alexandrian-style frescoes.

The development of the papal chant used to be ascribed to Gregory I. But it is much more likely that its elaboration and expansion took place under Gregory II, the cultivation of a trend which had begun under Pope Vitalian and reflected the increasingly Oriental nature of the clergy. The importance of the chant is testified to in the heights reached by some of its most expert practitioners, and contrasts starkly with the situation that obtained under Gregory I.

Gregory enacted at the 595 synod a decree with regard to cantors.[44] It stated that the reprehensible custom had crept into the Roman church of ordaining cantors as deacons because of their beautiful voices rather than their good works; furthermore after ordination they still spent their time singing rather than in preaching or caring for the poor. It was, therefore, ordered that deacons could only sing the gospel during mass and that they should take no other part in singing the other lections or psalms, which would be assigned to subdeacons and minor orders. Gregory had, however, introduced extra masses during his reign, to console the people during the troubles. To provide sufficient cantors to carry out singing duties, without needing to call on the deacons further, Gregory set up a *Schola Cantorum*, with two branches, one at St Peter's and the other at the Lateran basilica, to train singers in the urban rite. However, the introduction of the new Eastern forms led under Pope Vitalian to the setting up of a new *Schola Cantorum*, specifically to train singers in the Byzantine-style papal rite. Its members were known as *Vitaliani* after their founder. One of its most distinguished graduates was Pope Sergius I, who enrolled there under Vitalian's successor Adeodatus.[45] Far from giving up their singing to concentrate on their other duties, several future popes attracted attention precisely because of their singing, something which bears out the importance of the new papal rite and of singing in general under the Greek popes. Popes Leo II, Benedict II and Sergius I were all noted for their singing.[46] John, archcantor of the Roman church, was entrusted by Pope Agatho with an important mission, ostensibly to teach singing in England but in fact to report to Rome on the state of the English church.[47] The prominence of the new Eastern-influenced ceremonial was confirmed by the issue of new mass books probably by Gregory II, which were to form the basis of the earliest surviving version of the papal rite, the eighth-century *Ordo Romanus I*.[48]

The succession of Greek popes also had a significant effect on learning and culture. For one thing there seems to have been a positive desire on the part of the electors for a learned and accomplished pope. There is no evidence during the sixth or for most of the seventh centuries that learning was among the attributes sought by the electorate in a pope. The learned popes were the exception rather than the rule. Gelasius I with his works on heresy, his hymns and sermons; Pelagius I with his translations from the Greek fathers and his tract in defence of the 'Three Chapters'; and of course Gregory the Great, the author of the *Regula Pastoralis*, the *Dialogi*, the *Homilies* and the many works of Biblical exegesis, all stand virtually alone. Furthermore, at least four popes, Vigilius,[49] Gregory I,[50] Honorius I[51] and Martin I[52] were unable to speak Greek, all the more remarkable in view of the fact that three of them had been Papal *apocrisiarii* in Constantinople and all had reigned after the imperial reconquest of Italy.

By contrast, the Greek popes showed fluency in both Latin and Greek and wide-ranging knowledge. Pope Agatho quoted learnedly and profusely from Greek works when writing to the emperor Constantine IV,[53] Pope Leo II translated the proceedings of the sixth General Council from Greek into Latin, and the *Liber Pontificalis* said of him that he was

> a most eloquent man, adequately instructed in the holy scriptures, erudite in the Greek and Latin tongue, outstanding in chant and psalmody and polished in those senses by the most subtle exercise of them; also learned in language and polished in speaking by greater reading, the encourager of all good works and he brought knowledge to the people splendidly.[54]

It later gave the same character to Pope Gregory III.[55] Of Benedict II it said: 'He so applied himself to the divine scriptures and to the chant in boyhood and the priestly dignity that he showed himself worthy of his name',[56] of John V 'a most strenuous man and endowed with learning',[57] of John VII 'a most erudite man and eloquent',[58] of Gregory II 'chaste, learned in scripture, eloquent and firm'.[59] To them may be added Zacharias, who translated Gregory's *Dialogi* into Greek.[60] This trend towards the election of learned men stemmed perhaps from several impulses. First, there would have been the desire after the disgrace of Pope Honorius to ensure that sufficiently qualified theologians occupied the papal throne and could combat the intellectual threat posed by Monotheletism and Iconoclasm. Second, there would have been the need for Greek popes to establish their intellectual credentials both with a predominantly Greek clergy and with a Latin citizenry. Last, the trend reflects the general revival of the papacy and of Rome in the late seventh and early eighth centuries, the desire to re-establish the standing, culture and self-respect of the Roman church after a period of confusion and uncertainty.

The election of learned popes can be seen as part of a general cultural revival, resulting from the influx of émigré Greek clerics and finding expression in the creation of libraries, the undertaking of translations, the reforms in church services and chant, the co-ordinated programmes of painting and beautification. It was a revival that was, however, essentially Eastern-based and Greek-inspired and it marked the repulse of the new Western-based pastoral culture pioneered by Gregory I.

As in so many fields of life and endeavour, the imperial reconquest had provided a watershed in the area of culture and learning. The Ostrogothic period had seen a considerable flowering of culture in Italy. Schools flourished in Ravenna, Rome and Milan and the old academic life, based on the teaching of grammar, rhetoric and philosophy, continued until the mid-sixth century. Theodoric actively encouraged learning by maintaining state professorships. Monastic centres like Vivarium and Castrum Lucullanum gathered together precious manuscripts and undertook translation work and copying. A pro-Eastern group, including the consuls Symmachus and Boethius, abbot Eugippius, Dionysius Exiguus and others, produced works of history, theology and philosophy in a conscious bid to introduce in particular the practices of the Nisibis school and in general Eastern modes of thought and argument into the West. At the same time the Goth Jordanes, perhaps a bishop, and the Roman Cassiodorus, the former praetorian prefect, both writing in the East, were composing their histories and seeking to propagate closer links between the Romans and the Goths. Although Cassiodorus and Pope Agapitus planned to found a Christian University of Rome and although many distinguished scholars of the period were churchmen, such as Bishop Victor of Capua and Bishop Maximian of Ravenna, who prepared new editions of the gospels, and Bishop Ennodius of Ticinum, whose prodigious output included hymns, letters, saints' lives and poems, the Roman church did not play a major role in the propagation of learning. Much of it was done under the aegis of aristocratic patronage or in clerical establishments not directly dependent on Rome.[61]

The destruction of the senatorial order and the ravages of wars and invasions in the mid-sixth century had a profound effect on learning, and indeed education. Although Justinian officially re-established the schools, there is no evidence that they reopened. Libraries had been broken up and dispersed. By the time of Gregory the Great there were no copies of the *Acts of the Martyrs*, the writings of Irenaeus or the decrees of the second General Council in Rome.[62] Greek interpreters were lacking and that meant restricted access to the major Greek works. The effect of this was seen in the decline in the standard of education among the clergy. Honorius I inaugurated a programme of clerical education.[63] But Pope Agatho was still forced to apologize to the emperor Constantine IV for the quality of men he sent as envoys to the sixth General Council, saying: 'Among men situated in the midst of the enemy and forced to seek their daily sustenance by manual labour, how can one expect to find knowledge of the scriptures'.[64]

But just as the army replaced the senate in politics, so too did the Roman church replace the senate in the field of culture. Gregory I inaugurated the move to create a new simplified, accessible Western culture. He rejected classical learning, denouncing Bishop Desiderius of Vienne for his interest in secular learning, his lectures on grammar and public readings from the poets: 'Consider how offensive, how abominable a thing it is, for a bishop to recite verses which are unfit even to be recited by a religious layman.'[65] He praised St Benedict, on the other hand, for rejecting secular learning, calling him 'skilfully ignorant and wisely unlearned'.[66] He also rejected the old aristocratic high culture of men like Boethius and Symmachus, preferring a hortatory, pastoral, homiletic learning, accessible to the many and underpinned by simple truths. Among his followers this rejection of the theological subtlety of the East was carried to its fullest extent by Honorius I.

However, the need to refute the arguments of the Monotheletes, coupled with the arrival of the refugee clergy from the East, doomed the Gregorian attempt to oust the old-style culture. The papacy remained a vital force in the field of learning, but it was henceforth committed to the traditional forms. The successful repulse of the Monothelete heresy confirmed their validity, and the upward turn in the papacy's fortunes found the clergy valuing the erudite as well as the doctrinally sound amongst their choices for the papal throne. It was in part perhaps a reaction to the level of education attained by the clergy before the arrival of the Greeks but it also indicates the extent to which the Greek clergy and their values had come to dominate the Roman church.

Conclusions

It is very rare for the sources to give the reasons for the election of a specific pope. It is, therefore, of great interest to find in the *Liber Pontificalis* account of the election of Pope Conon, the statement that he was selected for his 'angelic aspect, white hair, true speech, advanced age, simple mind and quiet life' and a specifically religious life in which he never mixed in secular matters.[67] It indicates a concern with 'image' and appearance that would not discredit contemporary media politicians. But it would be unwise to generalize from this, because Conon was a compromise choice, his election a reaction to the disgraceful politicking of a disputed election, his reign a disaster and the result a different sort of ruler chosen to succeed him. It is, however, valuable as a glimpse at the electors at a particular point in papal history and teaches several lessons.

The first and most obvious is that each election was determined by the circumstances surrounding it. But it is also clear that there were certain recurring characteristics either throughout the period or for parts of it which weighed with electors. Old age, in particular, was a continuing recommendation and the overwhelming number of popes were old men.

The electorate was not monolithic, and different attributes some-times appealed to different groups. Indeed the electorate changed, from clergy, senate and people in the fifth and sixth centuries to clergy, army and people in the seventh and eighth. The importance of the senate in the first half of our period, however, is reflected in the election of men of senatorial rank to the papal throne. It is not that men were elected because of their class origins. The occupancy of the papal throne in the Ostrogothic era was determined almost exclu-sively by the political and theological positions of the candidates with regard to the East and to the Goths. For instance, the senate supported Laurentius and Dioscorus because of their pro-Eastern sympathies. But class origin was a consideration and did influence style of government. There seems to have been the feeling that upper-class clerics could move amongst and talk the language of the governing classes. It cannot have been pure coincidence that all three popes under Justinian (Vigilius, Pelagius I and John III) were aristo-crats, and at least the first two were handpicked by the emperor. While social origin was of limited importance overall in determin-ing the choice of pope, it is of significance in demonstrating the extent to which the aristocracy were willing to participate in the Roman church, which until the fifth century had been essentially a non-aristocratic institution.

Turning to pre-papal rank, it is clear that in the sixth century the diaconate had a virtual monopoly of the papal throne, suggesting that there was a general feeling that administrative experience was important in a pope. This monopoly was broken by the Gregorian programme of monasticization, which saw the clergy as a whole close ranks against the monks in a bitter struggle for control of the positions of power. The clergy won but the diaconate never regained its monopoly. Of the last ten popes in the period, only five are known to have been deacons, indicating that clerical origin from whatever branch was what counted rather than simply diaconal training.

Finally, there is geographical origin. Romans or Italians were almost exclusively elected until the latter part of the seventh century, when the influx of Greek refugee clergy meant a succession of Greek popes, who undertook a thoroughgoing Hellenization of the church and among whom learning was particularly prized.

Looked at *in toto*, it is clear that particular issues dominated particular parts of the period and determined the criteria of papal elections. The hour frequently produced the man, such as Gelasius I to combat Monophysitism and Martin I to combat Monotheletism. Ongoing issues such as relations with the Goths, the Gregorian programme of monasticization, the influx of Greek refugee clergy dominated the decision-making of the electorate. When there was not a burning issue in the forefront of affairs, it seems that age and character carried the day and this perhaps explains the appearance in the doldrum days of the seventh century of a number of elderly men of saintly character and extreme generosity who gave lavish handouts to all and sundry and promptly dropped dead.

Part V

The Papal Administration

Chapter 17

The Central Administration

Structure

The emergence of the pope as a central figure in the secular as well as the spiritual life of Italy meant more work and increased importance for the papal administration. The personnel of the church can be divided essentially into two branches: the priestly branch concerned with teaching, preaching, hearing confession and celebrating mass, and the administrative branch, deacons, subdeacons, notaries and *defensores*, who were in charge of the mechanics of poor relief, the proliferating papal correspondence and the administration of the papal estates. Collectively they formed the Roman clergy, an elitist cadre with jealously guarded privileges and distinctive dress, the body from amongst whose members the most powerful churchman in the West was elected. The strength of this elitist feeling was demonstrated fully when Gregory I tried to introduce a new element, the monks, into the centres of power.

It was possible to enter the Roman clergy from many different directions and at virtually any age. Popes Felix III and Hormisdas were married men with children when they first entered the church. Pope Gregory I and the subdeacon Arator forsook public careers of distinction to enter the church. But increasingly it was the tendency for devout parents to offer their children to the church at an early age. Popes Boniface II, Eugenius I, Benedict II and Gregory II had been in the Roman church since childhood. With the effective loss of the civil service as a career and the decline of the educational system in the wake of the Gothic wars, the church came to be seen as one of the few remaining respectable careers and sources of education.

The promotion ladder was strictly fixed; advancement was by seniority and only came about when there was a vacancy. There was a strict age limit – a subdeacon had to be at least 20, a deacon at least 25, a priest at least 30. The principle of seniority was a cornerstone of the structure. Pope Gelasius I, for instance, wrote to Bishop Bellator of Ostia saying that promotion must be by seniority, as decreed in the ancient canons and reconfirmed in the 494 Roman synod.[1] So he vetoed the promotion of the deacon Maro to the Ostian archidiaconate and insisted that the deacon Laurentius be given the post by virtue of his seniority. But he added that if Maro was as industrious and worthy as Bellator seemed to think, he could certainly be entrusted with the management of ecclesiastical affairs. Thus the pope overruled an appointment by merit in favour of an appointment by seniority but was also hinting that the spirit of the law could be ignored even if the letter could not; in other words, Maro could undertake the duties but Laurentius must hold the title. It was an ingenious compromise and in a way typical of the sort of balance that often needed to be struck if the church was to be effectively run. Gregory I maintained the Gelasian principle when he wrote to archbishop Januarius of Caralis in August 591, ordering that the deacon Liberatus, who had aspired to the archidiaconate without the proper seniority, should be ranked last among the deacons as a punishment for his 'reprehensible spirit of ambition'.[2]

The immediate effect of this principle on the papacy was to make it a gerontocracy. The heads of the two senior colleges, the archpriest and the archdeacon, were invariably the oldest clerics, and the pope was generally chosen from among the senior members of these two colleges. The papal administration was collegiate: the priests formed a college, headed by the archpriest; but this was much less important than the diaconal college, headed by the archdeacon. One only has to compare the number of archpriests (none) who are known to have become pope with the number of archdeacons (at least 7) who did so. There was also a college of notaries, headed by a *primicerius*. These original three colleges were later joined by colleges of *defensores*, also headed by a *primicerius*, and subdeacons.

The busiest grade was perhaps the notaries, the staff of the papal chancery, career bureaucrats in minor orders, generally entering the service of the papacy in adolescence. From the earliest times the papacy kept an archive (the *scrinium*), but while the church was a subversive organization, it was difficult for it to develop. Only when the church acquired legal status under the Emperor Constantine I was it possible for the archive to be properly run and maintained. At the time of Pope Damasus (366–84) the archives were kept in the basilica of St Laurentius *in Prasina* but at some date after that, probably in the fifth century, they were transferred to the Lateran Palace. There were kept the registers of papal correspondence, the account books of the papal estates, conciliar decrees, the records of papal decisions, which formed a core of precedent, and a collection of books. The *scrinium* can be seen in operation in the record of the proceedings of the 649 Lateran synod, when books and documents were constantly being requisitioned during the course of the discussions, brought in from the archives, quoted from by notaries under the direction of the *primicerius* Theophylact and then returned. The library side of the archive's activities expanded so much by the seventh century that a *bibliothecarius* was appointed specifically to head the papal library. The first known holder of the post was the future Pope Gregory II, then a subdeacon, appointed *bibliothecarius* by Pope Sergius I and combining that job with that of *sacellarius*.[3] By 829 the post was important enough to be held by a bishop.

Not all documents were kept in the archive. Particularly important documents, such as the confession of faith signed by incoming popes, were kept at the tomb of St Peter. The *Liber Pontificalis* relates that the *cautio* of Archbishop Felix of Ravenna was deposited there by Pope Constantine, but after he reneged on his agreement with Rome, it was discovered miraculously burned.[4]

Besides servicing the archive, the notaries formed the staff of the papal secretariat, based in the Lateran Palace and closely modelled on its imperial counterpart. The papal writing office was a hive of activity, its staff beavering away constantly at the ever-growing mounds of papal correspondence. So much of this business was routine that a collection of formula letters was drawn up in the seventh century and embodied in the *Liber Diurnus* for the use of notaries.[5] It gives us an important insight into the range of business conducted by the chancery: petitions to exchange and lease papal land, petitions for permission to build or repair or consecrate oratories, baptisteries, altars, churches; requests for holy relics; notifications of episcopal vacancies, elections, the amalgamation of sees; deeds of grant, sale and exchange of papal slaves; invitations for bishops to visit Rome for synods; arrangements for the provision of transport and hospitality for papal couriers; instructions for papal rectors; letters granting the use of the *pallium* to new bishops. These were only the routine matters. Beyond this there were a host of other matters requiring the dictation of personal letters by the pope which could involve the notaries concerned becoming confidants and advisers. The number of notaries is unknown, but their head, the *primicerius notariorum*, was sufficiently important to be one of the regents during a vacancy in Rome.[6]

Most of the surviving references to the *primicerius* are in connection with the archive and it is clear that he was very much the keeper of the papal past, the guardian of tradition, the expert on precedent. For instance Boniface, *primicerius notariorum* of John I, appears when the pope ordered him to search the archives for the correct date of Easter.[7] Surgentius, *primicerius notariorum* under Vigilius, was ordered to deposit the poem *De Actibus Apostolorum* by the sub-deacon Arator in the archives.[8] Gaudiosus, *primicerius notariorum* of Gregory I, was consulted about the use of the *pallium* in Ravenna.[9] Essentially bureaucrats, none of them is known to have gained the papal throne during this period. The job of the notaries was to provide for the efficient functioning of the machine rather than to control the decision-making.

The *defensores* came to be incorporated into a college much later than the notaries. As their name implies, they were charged with defending the rights of the Roman church and protecting the oppressed. The formula of appointment was vague enough to allow them to undertake virtually any duty on behalf of the church.[10] It reads:

> Having regard for the good of the church, we have decided that if you are not ineligible by virtue of your condition or status and you have not been a cleric in another city and there is no canonical impediment against you, you should accept the office of *defensor ecclesiae* and in whatever shall be enjoined on you for the good of the poor, you shall strive honestly and diligently to make use of the privilege that we have bestowed on you with due deliberation. In carrying out all things which shall be enjoined on you by us, you should show yourself faithful in your work so that you justify our decisions under God by your actions.

This shows that they were very much the executive agents of the papal will. There was a corps of *defensores* in Rome and staffs of *defensores* on all the important patrimonies. The Gregorian Register indicates that at least eight *defensores* were operating in Sicily between 590 and 604.[11] They functioned under the control of the rector. But their detailed involvement in the day-to-day running of the patrimonies made them obvious candidates for the rectorship and of the eight Sicilian *defensores* mentioned in the Gregorian Register, two (Fantinus and Romanus) gained promotion to Sicilian rectorships. Pelagius II's Sicilian Rector was the *defensor* Antoninus.[12] In all at least ten *defensores* are known to have become patrimonial rectors under Gregory I.[13]

The potential power and importance of the job is attested by the fact that many men usurped the title of *defensor* and committed illegal acts cloaked in the protection afforded by the name of the Roman church. In August 591 Gregory I warned against the Sicilian *pseudo-defensores* who were extorting money from bishops,[14] and in October 598 he ordered the rector Romanus to hold an investigation into the usurpation of the job and send details of the false *defensores* to Rome so that they could be dealt with.[15] It was also Gregory who recognized the importance of the *defensores* by organizing them into a college along the same lines as the deacons and notaries with a *primicerius* at their head.[16]

The most important college was undoubtedly that of the deacons. The diaconal college initially consisted of the seven regionary deacons of Rome who, with a staff of subdeacons and acolytes, were concerned with poor relief and the management of property. As the administrative burdens of the papacy increased, so too did the power and responsibility of the diaconate. Its number rapidly rose from the original seven. For when deacons were detached from Rome and sent abroad on other duties, new deacons were promoted *in loco absentium*. Pope Vigilius specifically made this point when upbraiding the deacon Sebastian, who was so promoted, for his subsequent ingratitude towards his benefactor.[17] These supernumerary appointments resulted in a diaconal college of no fewer than nineteen at the accession of Gregory I.[18]

Some deacons were detached for rectorial duties, including Pelagius II's Sicilian rector the deacon Servusdei,[19] Gregory I's Sicilian rector the deacon Cyprian[20] and Honorius I's Sicilian rector, the deacon Cyriacus.[21] Some were sent on diplomatic missions, for instance the deacons Felix, Vitalis and Dioscorus who accompanied Pope Hormisdas's peace missions to the East.[22] But unquestionably the most prestigious diaconal secondment was as *apocrisiarios,* the pope's permanent representative in Constantinople, a post created with the re-establishment of friendly relations following the liquidation of the Acacian schism. It was a position which demanded consummate diplomatic skill and considerable theological accomplishment if the holder was to be able to pick his way through the labyrinthine subtleties of Christological debate and the filigree intricacies of Byzantine court procedure and emerge unscathed. It carried with it not only great responsibility but great influence: an official residence at the Placidia Palace, the presidency of General Councils in the absence of the pope and the ear of the emperor.

Several of the papal *apocrisiarii* not surprisingly eventually became popes themselves. For it was both a rigorous and a searching training in the finer points of high diplomacy and an invaluable opportunity to make friends in high places. Vigilius, *apocrisiarios* of John II and Agapitus, wormed his way into the confidence of Justinian and Theodora so successfully that he received their backing in his bid to unseat pope Silverius and gain the throne.[23] Pelagius, appointed by pope Agapitus to succeed Vigilius as *apocrisiarios* and maintained in that office by Pope Vigilius, similarly obtained a position of considerable influence with the emperor and was active in religious affairs in the East. He was instrumental in securing the election to the vacant see of Alexandria of the Chalcedonian monk Paul in 538; he was duly ordained in the presence of Pelagius and the patriarchal nuncios of Antioch and Jerusalem. But Paul had no sooner arrived in Alexandria than he was implicated in the murder of the deacon Psoius, *oeconomos* of the Alexandrian church, and formally deposed – again by Pelagius, acting this time with the patriarchs of Antioch and Jerusalem and the bishop of Ephesus. Zoilus was ordained in Paul's place. Pelagius later interceded with the emperor on behalf of his close friend the Roman aristocrat Liberius, dismissed as Prefect of Egypt. On his way back from Egypt, Pelagius uncovered a nest of Origenists in Palestine and reported on them to the emperor, who instituted their persecution.[24] Soon after this, about 543, Pelagius returned to Rome. But the emperor's remembrance of their cordial relations in these days helped in securing for him the papal throne on the death of Vigilius. Gregory I, while *apocrisiarios*, became godfather to the emperor Maurice's eldest son[25] and established a wide circle of influential friends which included members of the imperial family, the government and aristocratic circles whom he was able to lobby on matters concerning the Roman church after his election to the throne.

Of the twelve known *apocrisiarii*, six became pope – Vigilius, Pelagius I, Gregory I, Sabinian, Boniface III and Martin. But it was a position not without its dangers. Gregory I wrote to the emperor Phocas that he had been unable to find anyone at his court willing to take the job while the emperor Maurice was alive because it was believed to be too dangerous.[26] The arrest and exile of the *apocrisiarios* Anastasius by the emperor Constans II for opposing his religious policy indicates that a very real danger could exist for the occupants of the Byzantine hot seat. Indeed Anastasius was never recalled from exile and spent twenty years being shunted from place to place, finally dying in the Crimea in 666.[27] It was a recurrence of theological dispute between Rome and Constantinople and the undoubted fears for the safety of papal personnel there that led to the discontinuation of permanent papal representation at the imperial court some time during the reign of the Iconoclast emperor Leo III.

Of the known *apocrisiarii*, only one was not a deacon – the priest Anastasius, the victim of Constans II. All the rest were deacons: Vigilius *apocrisiarios* about 533–6, Pelagius I 536–c. 543, Stephen 544–7 (died in office),[28] Sarpatus 556–9,[29] Gregory 579–86,[30] Honoratus 586–93,[31] Sabinian 593–7,[32] Anatolius 597–601,[33] Boniface 603–4,[34] Sericus under Honorius I[35] and Martin under Pope Theodore.[36] There are known to have been papal *apocrisiarii* in Constantinople under John IV[37] and Severinus,[38] Eugenius[39] and Vitalian[40] but their names and ranks are not known.

Despite this division into colleges, with notaries handling the papal correspondence, *defensores* estate management and the deacons central administration and poor relief, all Roman clerics were at the disposal of the pope and could be detached from their duties and despatched on special missions whenever the pope deemed it necessary. This was most frequently the case with regard to notaries and *defensores*. Under Gregory I, for instance, the *defensor* Optatus was sent to Nursia to correct indiscipline among the clergy there,[41] the *defensor* Redemptus was sent to Sardinia to examine charges against the archbishop Januarius of Caralis[42] and the *defensor* John was charged in 603 with the highly delicate mission of investigating the appeals against deposition of the Spanish bishops Januarius of Malaca and Stephen (see unknown).[43] Of the notaries, Pantaleo seems to have acted as a sort of papal troubleshooter, sent off on a bewildering variety of jobs, all of which he seems to have handled with great expertise and success. In 593 he was in Sipontum investigating the alleged seduction of a deacon's daughter by the bishop's grandson.[44] In 598 he was in Sicily to collect church plate taken there by refugee clerics and allegedly being sold to alleviate their poverty.[45] In 600 he was supervising the election of the new archbishop of Milan and attending to the affairs of the Roman church in the Cottian Alps.[46] In 603 he was back in Sicily investigating financial abuses in the Syracusan patrimony.[47] Other popes deployed their personnel in much the same way. Pope Symmachus sent the *defensor* Julian to Valeria to escort Abbot Equitius to Rome to answer charges of illegal preaching.[48] Pope Pelagius I sent the *defensores* Oclatinus and Basilius to Umbria to assist in the arrest of Bishop Paulinus of Forumsempronii who had been ordered to Rome for trial.[49] But such missions were not exclusively the province of *defensor* and notary. Pelagius I sent the deacon Menantius to Capua to bring a ravished nun to Rome[50] and Pope Hormisdas sent the subdeacon Pullio to Ephesus to collect the signatures of the local bishops to his *libellus* of orthodoxy.[51] More importantly clerics of every grade, even the priesthood, were despatched from Rome to serve as patrimonial rectors.

There is no question but that the sixth and seventh centuries saw an unparalleled expansion of the central papal administration. This has to be reconstructed from the merest fragments of evidence and has perhaps not yet been given the recognition its importance merits. But it demonstrates the dramatic expansion in the powers and responsibilities of the Roman clergy, responsibilities which were yearly increasing due to the pressure of events rather than the dictates of ideology.

The growing strength and importance of the *defensores* was recognized by Gregory I when he organized them into a *schola*, giving them corporate status for the first time in 598.[52] A *primicerius* was appointed to head the *schola* and the seven senior *defensores* were given the style of *regionarius*. The first *primicerius defensorum* in fact subsequently became Pope Boniface III. In the seventh century the subdeacons were also organized into a *schola*, but details of that operation are lacking.

The expansion in all fields of papal activity is marked by the appearance, particularly in the seventh century, of a whole succession of new offices. Several important new financial officials appeared and it is clear that the financial side of papal business was becoming clear-cut, defined and differentiated from the rest. Revenue came in the main from two sources. There were bequests and donations from the faithful, sometimes earmarked for specific functions. The *Liber Pontificalis* described the papal treasures sequestrated by the exarch Isaac in these terms, defining the purpose of such bequests as 'for the redemption of their souls so that they could be paid out in relief to the poor for all time and for the ransoming of prisoners'.[53] The Register of Gregory I contains details of some specific donations. Princess Theoctista, sister of the emperor Maurice, sent 30 pounds of gold to Rome for use in ransoming prisoners from the Lombards and subsidizing needy nuns.[54] Maurice himself sent 30 pounds of gold for distribution among the priests and persons in need.[55] The patrician Rusticiana, a Roman émigré aristocrat, sent 10 pounds of gold for the ransoming of prisoners.[56] The ransoming of captives had always been a traditional duty of the papacy, and Pope Symmachus, for instance, is known to have used papal money to ransom captives in Liguria.[57] But the onset of the Lombards made this duty a regular and heavy burden on the papal treasury, with Gregory I, for example, ransoming the inhabitants of Crotona[58] and John VI those of Campania.[59] Pope John IV, himself a Dalmatian, went further afield by sending Abbot Martin to Dalmatia to ransom captives of the Slavs.[60] In addition, the maintenance of swarms of refugees became another continuing charge after the Lombard invasion. Pope Symmachus had sent money to maintain exiled African Catholic bishops in their places of banishment.[61] But these isolated acts of charity became permanent and systematic by the end of the sixth century.

The other source of income was the revenue of the papal estates, the details of which will be considered when we look at the structure of the patrimonial administration. According to tradition, the revenues of the Roman church were divided into four parts, an arrangement known as the *quadripartitum*.[62] They were earmarked respectively for paying the Pope, for clerical salaries, for the maintenance of church buildings and for charity. Under the latter heading fell the rapidly burgeoning field of social services – poor relief, hospitality, the maintenance of hostels, redemption of captives, etc. How much money came into the papal coffers annually during this period is unknown. But there are figures for Ravenna, one of the richest and most powerful sees in Italy after Rome. Pope Felix IV arbitrated at some date between 526 and 530 in a dispute about the division of Ravennate revenue and in the course of this it emerged that one quarter of the revenue, the clerical fourth, amounted to 3,000 *solidi*, suggesting an overall annual revenue of 12,000. But there were in addition payments in kind, estimated at 888 hens, 266 chickens, 8,800 eggs, 3,760 pounds of pork, 3,450 pounds of honey, plus geese and milk.[63] Rome's revenue will have been a great deal more.

The most important of the new financial officials was the *arcarius*, the papal treasurer, who first appeared in the reign of Pelagius I. The first known papal *arcarius* was not a cleric but a banker, Anastasius, found receiving the receipts of the papal patrimonies in 560.[64] But at some time late in the sixth century the office was being filled by a cleric. It was important enough indeed to be filled by a deacon, Dometius, known from a funerary inscription to have held the position of *arcarius* at some date not precisely determinable in the sixth century.[65] By 680 the job was so important that Pope Agatho himself unprecedentedly took it on until forced by ill health to relinquish it.[66] The office of *dispensator*, literally papal paymaster, held by the deacon Boniface and only encountered in connection with him was probably *arcarius* by another name.[67]

By the end of the seventh century it had become necessary to differentiate, as in secular states, between the treasurer of the institution – the *arcarius* — and the keeper of the privy purse – the *sacellarius*, who dealt with the pope's day-to-day expenses. Initially *sacellarius* was a position of lesser importance than that of *arcarius*, held when first encountered under Sergius I by a subdeacon, the future Gregory II.[68] But by 745 it was held by one of the seven senior notaries, Theophanes.[69] It was this differentiation of duties which led to the *sacellarius* Cosmas accompanying Pope Constantine on his official visit to Constantinople while Peter the *arcarius* remained behind in Rome (fatally, as it transpired, since he was executed along with several other high-ranking papal officials by the exarch John Rizocopus).[70]

The other area of significant expansion is that of court ceremonial and court business. A *nomenclator* appears, first in the reign of Agatho when he is found assisting the pope to run the papal treasury.[71] But his main function was as master of ceremonies, presenting petitions and visitors to the pope, issuing the pope's replies and arranging orders of precedence at feasts and receptions. In time, he came to deal with the actual petitions as well as the petitioners, sifting them, putting them in order of importance and doing preliminary background work on them. Not surprisingly this increasingly powerful official accompanied the papal delegation to the East in 710.[72] The first indication of the rank of the *nomenclator* comes in 745 when the position was held by the regionary notary Gregory, who had the job of presenting Archbishop Boniface to the Roman synod.[73] The *nomenclator* was probably assisted in his work by the *ordinator*, who first appears in the reign of Pope Constantine when the *ordinator* Sergius was one of the victims of the exarch John Rizocopus.[74] With the *nomenclator* Sisinnius accompanying the pope to Constantinople, it would have been natural for his deputy to remain behind to deal with ongoing business. Another new official, the *bibliothecarius*, the papal librarian, also appeared in the late seventh century and has already been noted in connection with the work of the archives.

Perhaps the most important of the new offices outside the financial branch was that of *vicedominus*, steward of the papal palace. This position first appeared in 545 when Pope Vigilius, on leaving for Constantinople, appointed the priest Ampliatus as *vicedominus* to run the Lateran in his absence.[75] But it seems to have been an ad hoc job, made permanent by Gregory I in 590 when he appointed the deacon Anatolius as *vicedominus*.[76] The *vicedominus* takes precedence over the previously existing *maior domus*, the distinction apparently being that the *maior domus* was a domestic steward of the household whereas the *vicedominus* was much more involved in central administration. Pelagius II's *maior domus* Peter, for instance, was a ferocious figure who mistreated the papal slaves and died about 586.[77] Gregory I certainly appreciated the distinction between the *vicedominus* and the *maior domus* since he advised Bishop Paschasius of Naples to appoint one of each to assist him.[78] In the hands of the diaconate, however, the *vicedominate* became one of the senior administrative posts in the papal bureaucracy. The deacon Saiulus, *vicedominus* of Pope Constantine, was one of the officials left behind to run the city in his absence.[79] Later still the position was important enough to be filled by bishops, Benedict of Nomentum under Pope Zacharias and Theodore under Stephen III.[80]

One important consequence of the creation of the new specialist offices was the weakening of the position of the archdeacon. His administrative pre-eminence in the past had come to be regarded frequently as a passport to the papal throne, as is evidenced by the careers of popes Boniface II, Agapitus, Vigilius and Pelagius I. But thereafter between 561 and 827 only two archdeacons are known to have been elected to the throne – John IV[81] and John V.[82] It is not unlikely that the creation of a permanent *vicedominus* by Gregory was designed in part specifically to weaken the archdeacon's position. For it cannot be coincidental that the appointment of a *vicedominus* by Gregory was swiftly followed by the deposition of the archdeacon Laurentius for *superbia*.[83]

Two conclusions can perhaps be drawn from this creation of new posts. First, the obvious specialization and increasing differentiation of functions of the papal administrators indicates a massive increase in pressure of work and, since senior notaries were holding the posts both of *nomenclator* and *sacellarius* by 745, it seems reasonable to assume that these particular offices and the branches of government they concerned themselves with had grown out of the previously undifferentiated mass of duties undertaken by the notarial college. Second, the appearance of officials, the *nomenclator* and the *ordinator*, concerned with ceremonial, presentation and orders of precedence, indicates both the triumph of the clerical faction over the monastic, the victory of the hierarchical set-up over the familial, and confirms the influence of imperial Byzantine court procedure on the papal court, already noted as part of the general papal revival of the late seventh and early eighth centuries, precisely the period when these officials first appear.

Naturally all the positions mentioned were filled by clerical personnel. But there was one non-clerical papal job, that of *consiliarius*, legal adviser. It was a post generally held by a prominent layman. The first known *consiliarius* was Saturninus, who was a *vir illustris* and legal adviser to Pope Vigilius.[84] Some idea of his duties can be gained from the Register of Gregory the Great. His *consiliarius* was Theodore *vir magnificus* and Gregory appointed him in 598 together with the deacon Peter to handle the mass of complaints against Archbishop Januarius of Caralis that were being received in Rome.[85] In 600 he was called in to read with Gregory and his brother Palatinus the documents sent by the imperial inspector-general, Leontius, in which Leontius set out to prove the guilt of Praetor Libertinus of Sicily.[86] They were both the sorts of jobs for which legal knowledge would be helpful.

But the *consiliarius* could also be involved in less strictly legal matters, such as when the *consiliarius* John was called in to help the papal regents draft a letter to the Irish bishops in 640 about the date of Easter and the evils of Pelagianism.[87] A later *consiliarius*, Boniface, was sent by Pope Benedict II to try to dissuade from his heresy the deposed Monothelete patriarch of Antioch, Macarius, then imprisoned in a Roman monastery.[88] Regarded as one of the leading papal advisers, Boniface was subsequently arrested by the emperor Justinian II in an attempt to put pressure on Pope Sergius I and was removed to Constantinople.[89]

The process by which the church took over from the state the effective running of Rome can clearly be seen in the area of supply. When imperial rule in Italy was restored, Justinian I ordered in his *Pragmatic Sanction* of 554 that the *Annona* – the free grain dole to the people – which Theodoric had made should be continued.[90] Initially, then, the imperial government continued its responsibility for this particular service. Rome depended on it and the Register of Gregory I shows his concern for it, as he writes to the Praetor of Sicily in 590 urging that the grain be delivered to Rome.[91]

But at some point after the reign of Gregory I the *annona* ceases. There is no known *praefectus annonae*, the official in charge of the grain dole, after the sixth century, and it seems likely that the *annona* in Rome ceased at the same time as the free grain dole in Constantinople was cancelled by the emperor Heraclius at the height of the Persian crisis. Into the vacuum created by this cancellation stepped the church, though not initially the papacy itself.

The papacy had its own granaries in Rome (*horrea nostrae ecclesiae*) which were in fact inundated and their contents ruined by the great floods of 590.[92] They were close to the quayside and were kept supplied from the papal estates. They were used to feed the papal court and to supply the regular charitable distributions by the papacy which initially co-existed with the imperial *Annona*. In emergencies the papacy would supply the entire city from its own grain stores, as Popes Gelasius I, Vigilius and Gregory I did on specific occasions to relieve famine.[93] It was a source of great resentment, then, when Pope Sabinian sold rather than gave away grain from the church store during the famine of 604.[94] There was, at least from the time of Gregory I on, a systematized distribution of food to the needy and there was a regular hand-out of money for the purchase of food. The *Liber Pontificalis* recounts of Pope Zacharias that he ordered

> that on frequent days the cash dole for food purchase which up to this time is called the *elymosina* should be carried out of the Palace and distributed to paupers and visitors to St Peter and he ordered the same distribution to be made to all the needy and sick in the regions of Rome.[95]

But when the regular grain dole by the state ceased, a new ecclesiastical institution appeared in Rome to take its place – the *diaconia*. There were already *diaconia* in Naples, Ravenna and Pisaurum in Gregory the Great's reign but apparently none as yet in

Rome.[96] The *diaconia* were charitable institutions which originated in the East, being known in Palestine and Egypt long before their appearance in Italy. Though some of them functioned as hospitals and hostels, their main function was the distribution of food to the poor. They were staffed by monks, who had a chapel attached to their diaconal building. Indeed they resembled in many ways a socially active monastery. They were founded by wealthy benefactors, who could be either lay or ecclesiastical. For instance, Pope Gregory II endowed the *diaconia* of St Eustathius with three estates and fifty-four farms,[97] and the benefactions of Duke Eustathius to St Maria *in Cosmedin* and of Duke Theodotos to St Angelus *in Pescheria* are recorded in inscriptions.[98] They were maintained by such donations of land and although they performed regular services in their chapels, their principal *raison d'être* was supply. This is confirmed by the fact that many of the Roman *diaconia* were built on the sites of the old imperial grain distribution centres, thus for instance the *diaconia* of St Maria *in Cosmedin*, St George *in Velabro* and St Theodore. Also at least eight of the eighteen known Roman *diaconia* were built near to the Tiber quayside so that the grain ships could be unloaded directly into their granaries. The predominance of Greek and Eastern saints among the titulars of the *diaconia* further confirms their Eastern origin and suggests their foundation by Greek popes, clerics and laymen at some time in the seventh century after the popularization of these saints in Rome.

The first mention of the *diaconia* in Rome comes in the *Liber Pontificalis* Life of Benedict II, who on his death in 685 bequeathed money to the diaconal monasteries, an example followed by his successors John V and Conon.[99] It indicates a clear papal involvement at an early stage, at least, in their financing.

By the time of Pope Hadrian I there were eighteen such *diaconia*. They were headed by a *dispensator* or *pater*, an honorary position accorded as a measure of respect which could be held either by a layman or a cleric; thus, for instance, the subdeacon Theodimus, Gregory II's rector in Campania, was *dispensator* of the *diaconia* of St Adrian *ad Nidum* at Naples and Theodotos, *primicerius defensorum* of Pope Zacharias, was *dispensator* of St Maria Antiqua in Rome, while under Stephen II Duke Eustathius was *dispensator* of St Maria *in Cosmedin*. Their foundation and development alike derived from acts of charity, as in the case of ordinary monasteries. Their appearance in Rome was almost certainly a byproduct of the influx of Eastern clerical refugees and part of the gradual transformation of the city, in its externals at least, from a Latin city into a Greek one.

What happened in the eighth century, however, was that the popes first interested themselves in the development of the *diaconia* and eventually took them over – part of a continuing process of absorption of all religious institutions into the papal maw. This can be traced in the pages of the *Liber Pontificalis*. Benedict II, Conon, John V and Gregory II made handsome funerary bequests to the *diaconia*; Gregory II endowed the *diaconia* of St Eustathius; Gregory III expanded and extended the buildings of the *diaconia* of Saints Sergius and Bacchus, an indication of what was to occur in the reigns of his successors. Some of the monasteries were converted into churches, shed their charitable activities and became part of the regular structure of the Roman parishes, and others still were taken over by the papacy. However, although the evidence is fragmentary, the overall picture is quite clear. Imperial control of supply in Rome ended around the early seventh century; and its place was jointly taken by the papal charitable operations and the foundation of new charitable monasteries. Eventually, the latter were taken over by the papacy and the whole field of food distribution became a papal domain.

Personnel

It is clear that the sixth and seventh centuries were crucial for the expansion and development of the administrative machinery of the papacy far beyond the imaginings of the early church fathers. Modelling itself closely on the imperial administrative systems and methods, the church administration increased its personnel and its ceremonial and increasingly specialized and differentiated between areas of activity. More and more it was actively equipping itself to take over those tasks which the imperial government proved increasingly unwilling or unable to undertake in Rome.

It is unfortunately not possible to tie many of the new developments to particular reigns, but there are several popes who stand out in the field of administrative development and personnel policy, in particular Gelasius I, Pelagius I and Gregory I.

Gelasius I, who made important developments in patrimonial administration, also took steps to strengthen the Roman clergy, presumably to meet the growing responsibilities of the papacy. The brief biography of Gelasius in the *Liber Pontificalis* twice records that he increased the number of clergy, suggesting that this was a significant feature of his reign.[100] It does not mean that he increased the number of parish priests, which stood at about seventy-six in 487 and about seventy-five in 499. His large number of priestly ordinations (thirty-two in five years as opposed to Felix's twenty-eight in nine years and Simplicius's fifty-eight in fifteen years) simply means that he inherited an elderly priesthood in which there had been comparatively few changes, and increased mortality meant an increased replacement rate. It means rather that he increased the number of junior clergy, both in the administrative and priestly grades. He was keenly interested also in the quality as well as the quantity of clerics. He concerned himself with the training of candidates for the priesthood, seeking to imbue them with the characteristics he himself embodied.[101] The complete strength of the Roman clergy at this time is not known for certain, though it was much the greatest in the Italian church. In the mid-third century, the total clergy of all grades had numbered some 154.[102] By the early sixth century the Ravenna church, one of the biggest in Italy, could still only muster 60.[103] There are isolated examples of numerical strength. The subscriptions to the late-fifth-century Roman synods suggest a priesthood of seventy-five to eighty, double the number in the mid-third century. There are known to have been nineteen deacons at the time of Gregory I's election to the throne. The Neapolitan clergy under Gregory numbered 226. So while complete figures are lacking, the Roman clergy was certainly numerous.

Gelasius I, like Gregory I, also took on the responsibility for emergency supply and like Gregory, was prompted to it by sheer desperate necessity, in his case as a result of three years of civil war. The *Liber Pontificalis* records that he 'delivered the city of Rome from the danger of famine'.[104] This danger seems to have been in part due to stormy winter seas which prevented the arrival of grain ships.[105] He presumably supplied the city from nearby papal estates. But he also became deeply involved with feeding refugees and with poor relief. He sent the *defensor* Peter to King Theodoric to get help in feeding the paupers.[106] He urged a leading layman, Januarius, to protect those concerned with poor relief.[107] He thanked Firmina *illustris femina* for helping to get sequestrated papal estates restored because their produce was needed to help feed refugees.[108] He even used his own private fortune in the work of poor relief.[109]

There was a major personnel crisis in the Roman church as a result of the Gothic wars and this was tackled with vigour and authority by Pope Pelagius I. The *Liber Pontificalis* says of his reign: 'There was no one in the church who was capable of being promoted'. So the pope issued a unique statement saying:[110]

I beg of you to grant my request that whoever deserves promotion in the holy church and is worthy of it, from a doorkeeper to a bishop, should accept advancement, though not for gold or any promises: you all know that that is simony. But whoever is learned in the works of God, and leads a good life, we bid him not by bribes but by honest *conversatio* to rise to the first rank.

During his nearly five-year reign he accordingly ordained twenty-six priests, eight deacons and forty-nine bishops, a substantial increase on his predecessor Vigilius who in seventeen years had ordained only forty-six priests, sixteen deacons and eighty-one bishops. Pelagius ordained on average twice as many bishops a year as had Vigilius and three times as many priests, indicating the filling up of vacancies. He also took firm action to ensure that all the silver and gold plate and holy vestments of the churches which had been scattered during the troubles be collected up and restored to their proper places.[111]

Pelagius's letters indicate his detailed concern in the choice of new priests and in the maintenance of standards in restaffing. He wrote in March 559 to Bishop Marcellus of Sabiona giving him specific instructions which probably reflected his guiding principles in personnel policy.[112] He urged him to make a record of the places of origin of the refugee clergy in his diocese so that they could be returned whence they came. He gave permission for the bishop to draw on the monasteries for candidates for the priesthood, so long as the monasteries did not become denuded of inmates. But there was a desperate shortage of clerics. In March 559 Pelagius wrote to Bishop Florentinus of Clusium,[113] giving permission for the promotion to the diaconate of a cleric, who after the death of his wife cohabited with his housekeeper and fathered several sons, on condition that the housekeeper went into a nunnery. Pelagius reckoned that the cleric would now be too old for suspicion of incontinency to attach to him in future and if the housekeeper was safely behind nunnery walls, all temptation would be removed. Similarly in March 559 he authorized the promotion of the cleric Valentine of Sabiona because his wife had previously been engaged rather than married and although canon law forbids a cleric to marry a widow, this does not apply to someone who was only engaged elsewhere before her marriage.[114] He agreed to the ordination of three laymen to be priest, deacon and subdeacon for Centumcellae.[115] But he does draw the line at accepting the recommendation of the ladies Antonina and Decia that a monk be made a *defensor*, on the grounds that the two lifestyles are incompatible: the monk having a life of quiet, prayer and manual labour and the *defensor* being involved in lawcases, legal agreements and whatever business the church's good requires.[116] This selection from Pelagius's correspondence gives a clear insight into the kind of pressure the pope was under in the personnel field.

The next known major administrative advance occurred in the reign of Gregory I. Typically, Gregory applied to the central administration a comprehensive system of discipline and rationalization. This was done centrally, of course, so comparatively little of it has percolated into the Gregorian Register. But there are hints enough to show us Gregory's line of attack.

He organized the *defensores* as a *schola* with a *primicerius* at its head. He made permanent the office of *vicedominus*, thus creating a counterweight to the archdeacon. Indeed, he insisted on a division of duty and authority and the creation of a system of checks and balances to prevent any one official from becoming too powerful.[117] He reduced the singing duties of the deacons to give them more time for administration; lastly, and perhaps most characteristically, he excluded the lay attendants from the papal household and surrounded himself entirely with monks and clerics.[118] Indeed, his biographer John the deacon goes so far as to say that laymen were left only with armsbearing and farming and that all other duties were now confined to clerics. This contains the kernel of a policy inaugurated by Gregory that was to reverberate throughout the seventh century. Sadly none of the later developments are precisely datable, but the later seventh century was to see the most extensive expansion of the central administration for centuries, an expansion which coincided with the victory of the clerical faction in their struggle to repulse the monasticization policy inaugurated by Gregory.

A word of warning should perhaps be added in conclusion. It was not necessarily in the burgeoning administrative structure that the actual power centres were to be found. As with most human agencies, so too with the papacy, there was an unofficial element – the 'kitchen cabinet', the inner circle, the papal confidants. These were the men who helped to shape the pope's thinking and determine his stance on issues.

Stress has been laid on these coteries elsewhere. But it is worth summarizing briefly what we know of them here. The profound crisis which overtook the papacy early in the reign of Symmachus led to a dramatic purge of the clergy and the emergence of what I have called the Symmachan old guard, a tightly knit group whose members more or less controlled the papacy until the end of the Ostrogothic period. Prominent in this group were the deacon and later Pope Hormisdas, the deacon Dioscorus and Bishop Ennodius of Ticinum, who played decisive roles in determining the course of papal history in the first quarter of the sixth century.

The final extinction of the old guard was accompanied by the reconquest of Italy by the Empire, whose nominee on the papal throne, Vigilius, created a new establishment. He raised his nephew Rusticus to the diaconate in an open and admitted act of family patronage.[119] The matter-of-fact way in which the pope subsequently referred to this indicates that such family patronage was not unusual or unexpected and did not carry with it the opprobrium attached to sale of office. Other examples have been quoted of members of papal families playing important parts and filling important posts at court.

But this new Vigilian establishment was torn apart by the 'Three Chapters' controversy. Many of the senior papal administrators spent much of the reign in the East, leaving Rome to be run by a scratch team of emergency appointments. The constantly changing position of the pope on the subject of the 'Three Chapters' meant the constant rise and fall in influence of divergent groups among his entourage. It is abundantly clear that for part of his stay Vigilius was much under the influence of the deacon Pelagius and that later this influence was supplanted by that of the deacon Tullianus.

The election to the throne of Gregory I provoked perhaps the most long-lasting conflict between power groups, as monastic and clerical groups fought for mastery of the positions of authority. This provided the human element of personal conflict and political controversy which ran alongside administrative growth and is perhaps too often overlooked.

Chapter 18

The Patrimonial Administration

Introduction

As with the central administration, so also the patrimonial administration made great strides in organization and expansion in the
period 476–752. The landed estates of the papacy, collectively
known as the patrimony of St Peter, provided one of the principal
sources of revenue of the Roman church. These estates had been
acquired over the years by endowment and bequest, ever since the
legalization of bequests to the church in 321.[1] One of the earliest and
most lavish benefactors was the imperial family. But its last great
donation was probably the lands of the Arian church in Italy, confiscated after the extinction of the Ostrogothic kingdom and handed
over in 554 to the Catholic church. Rome did not of course get it all
but is likely to gained a substantial proportion. There were, however, subsequent smaller donations, such as the granting of the
estates of Normiae and Nymphas by Constantine V as a token of
goodwill.

How much revenue these estates actually brought in is very difficult to estimate, though there are some hints. According to the
chronicler Theophanes, the value of the Sicilian and Calabrian patrimonies confiscated in 729 by Emperor Leo III was 250,000 *solidi*.[2]
These were unquestionably the largest, richest and most profitable
of the papacy's landed holdings and their loss must have been a
considerable blow financially. The annual revenues of the Ravennate
patrimony in Sicily in the mid-seventh century are known to have
been 31,000 *solidi*, 50,000 *modii* of wheat and sundry other goods.[3]
Rome's will have been much more.

The papacy must have been used to fluctuations in the fortunes of
its landed estates. Mainland Italy was subjected to war and disturbance for much of this period and the effect told heavily on the papal
patrimony. For instance, the Picene estates, estimated under Gelasius
at an annual value of 30 pounds of gold (2,160 *solidi*),[4] had by the

reign of Pelagius I dropped in value to a mere 500 *solidi* per annum.[5] Indeed the thirty years of warfare had a very serious effect on the mainland estates in general as Pelagius I testified in 560–1 when he wrote:[6]

> After the continuous devastations of war which have been inflicted on the regions of Italy for 25 years and more and have scarcely yet ceased, it is only from the islands and places overseas that the Roman church receives some little revenue, however insufficient, for the clergy and the poor.

On a smaller scale there had been similar disruption during the war between Theodoric and Odoacer. During the fighting, papal estates had been seized and ravaged by both sides and Gelasius took active steps to recover them, enlisting the aid of sympathetic aristocrats like Firmina *femina illustris* to intercede on behalf of the Roman church.[7]

While both the civil war and the Gothic wars eventually ended, providing breathing spaces during which the Roman church could regroup and retrench, the invasion of the Lombards initiated an entirely different state of affairs – nearly 200 years of intermittent warfare and progressive conquest, which was bound to affect the papal estates severely. The Picene patrimony was certainly swallowed up. Parts of the Samnite, Sabine and Apulian patrimonies which fell within areas of Lombard occupation were lost. There was also considerable loss of population on some of the estates which remained, Gregory I referring to the 'few peasants' still left on the Callipolis estates.[8] It was a continuing process. Gregory III wrote sadly to Charles Martel that Lombard armies attacking Ravenna had destroyed 'all St Peter's farms and carried off what livestock remained'.[9] As if the devastations of the Lombards were not enough, the conflict between Rome and Constantinople over Iconoclasm led to the confiscation of the estates in Sicily and south Italy, a grievous blow because of the extent, productivity and value of these lands. Not only this but the overseas estates were all eventually lost due to changing political events. There is no reference to the Gallic patrimony after 613.[10] The African patrimony will have been lost with the fall of that province to the Arabs, and the Dalmatian patrimony was attacked and eventually overwhelmed by Slavic invaders.

But all was not gloom. There was some restoration of lost property as relations between Rome and the Lombards became more cordial. The papal estates in the Cottian Alps, which were admittedly small, were twice captured by the Lombards and twice restored to the papacy as a gesture of goodwill, once by Aripert to John VII and once by Liutprand to Gregory II.[11] The Sabine patrimony overrun about 712 was restored to the papacy thirty years later after the meeting of Liutprand and Zacharias at Interamna.[12] Also, to compensate for the heavy loss of Sicily and Calabria, Pope Zacharias inaugurated a new policy, enthusiastically followed by his successors, aimed at ensuring a regular supply of revenue and resources for the papacy and encouraging the resettlement of the abandoned and ravaged areas of Latium and Campania. This was the system of *domusculta*, which combined the creation of farms with the building of churches, a stimulus for economic and demographic growth.[13]

The Structure

The patrimony of St Peter consisted of several individual regional patrimonies; by the time of Gregory the Great some fifteen. Each of these was subdivided into estates, leased out by the Roman church to tenants (*conductores*), who paid rent and farmed the land. The manager of the patrimony was the rector, appointed by the pope and holding office at his will. Designated in Rome, he would take an oath on the tomb of St Peter to defend the interests of the church and protect the poor. He received letters of appointment, the estate account book and a detailed set of instructions from the pope pertaining to his area.[14] Letters would also be sent to the *coloni* and *conductores* of the patrimony enjoining their obedience to the new rector and letters of commendation sent to local bishops and imperial officials.[15]

Obviously one of their major duties was the actual management of the patrimonial estates. They collected rents and forwarded them to Rome.[16] They supplied the papal court with produce such as grain, horses and timber.[17] They granted out leases on the estates.[18] But there were other important areas of involvement for them. They were charged with the protection of the oppressed, relief of the poor and the upkeep of the church hostels (*xenodochia*). They dealt with much minor litigation. In the field of ecclesiastical discipline, the rectors were the maintainers of order and propriety. They oversaw episcopal elections. They kept up the welfare of churches and monasteries. They rectified abuses in churches, monasteries and hospitals. They acted against heretics. They enforced discipline and punished offences.[19]

Over the activities of the rectors and patrimonial officials the pope needed to keep a watchful and informed eye. There were many opportunities for misconduct. The position of the Roman church as a landlord was extremely powerful and its name carried considerable weight and was sometimes used as a licence to plunder. Gregory I, for instance, frequently had to deal with complaints against the representatives of the patrimonial administrators involving such matters as the illegal seizure of land, ships, slaves and countless financial extortions and swindles.[20]

The pope had to be constantly on his toes when it came to overseeing estate administration. He needed to choose his rectors carefully. If they were trusted, the rectors were often given a bewilderingly varied range of duties. A single letter written in July 592 by Gregory I to his Sicilian rector Peter gives a good insight both into the spheres of competence of the rector and the detailed nature of papal oversight.[21] The pope instructed Peter on property disputes, law suits, the sale of unprofitable herds, the reduction of estate duty paid by converted Jews to encourage conversion, hostel management, the selection of personnel for patrimonial administration, the building of a monastery, the payment of poor relief and subsidies to individuals, the using of his influence with the Bishop of Syracuse in the case of two individuals, the payment of gifts to imperial officials to ensure their goodwill towards the church, the execution of various provisions in the will of a deceased churchman, and the provision of horses for the pope.

The most complete list of patrimonies available can be drawn from the Register of Gregory I and checked against fragmentary references from elsewhere. During the sixth century there were four areas of papal estates outside Italy proper, none of them apparently extensive. There was a Gallic patrimony, small and situated apparently in the area around and between Arelate and Massilia. Gregory describes it as a *patrimoniolum*.[22] The 400 *solidi* in rental revenue which Gregory received from Gaul in 593 might seem at first sight large for a so-called *patrimoniolum* but it almost certainly includes rent arrears, for there were periods in which a backlog of money built up.[23] There was a problem with the revenue from these estates in that rents seem to have been paid in a locally struck coinage of a different weight and type from the official imperial coinage and to prevent depreciation, the popes encouraged the spending of the money locally.[24] Pelagius I urged the rector Placidus of Gaul to spend part of the revenues buying warm clothing and to send it to Rome for the use of refugees.[25] Gregory I himself suggested the spending of the revenues on buying warm clothing for the poor and also teenage English slave boys for service in the Roman monasteries.[26]

The last reference to these estates was in 613 under Boniface IV when there was still a resident papal rector.[27] The beginning of this silence coincides with the failure of the locally minted coinage, the last example of which dates from the reign of the emperor Heraclius (610–41). It is probable that at some time in the first half of the seventh century the papal estates were quietly absorbed by local bishops or magnates.

The Roman church possessed estates in North Africa, probably given or at least restored to her after the Byzantine reconquest and equally probably held until the Islamic conquest. They seem to have been located principally around Germanicia in Numidia.[28] There were also estates in Illyricum, described by Gregory as a *patrimoniolum*, like the Gallic estates.[29] Some of the papal possessions were around Salona and others in Praevalitana,[30] though both generally came under the control of a single papal rector. They are attested also in the reigns of Gelasius I and Vigilius.[31]

There were papal patrimonies also in Sardinia and Corsica, which islands, although they came within the patriarchal jurisdiction of the pope, were not part of the exarchate of Ravenna. They were in fact subject to the exarch of Africa, probably because before the reconquest they had formed part of the Vandal Kingdom. The islands were administered by a *dux*, who was a subordinate of the African exarch and who was resident in Caralis, the Sardinian capital and also the metropolitan see of the island. During the whole of Gregory I's reign the archbishop of Caralis was the aged, petulant and hopelessly incompetent Januarius and for much of the reign the *dux* was the grasping and tyrannical Theodore. Between the two of them the Sardinian people seem to have had a hard time of it.

The importance of all the extra-Italian patrimonies for the papacy seems to have been primarily political rather than fiscal. In the Sardinian and Corsican correspondence, for instance, there is comparatively little mention of estate business. The papal rectors there were employed in checking the excesses of the bishops, supplying Rome with information on the running of the Sardinian church and keeping a watchful eye on the lay authorities. This seems to have been the pattern of business in all the non-Italian patrimonies. They were useful papal footholds outside Italy proper but Rome did not depend on them overly for revenue.

The principal revenue-producing estates were in Italy itself. The smallest papal patrimony was probably in the Cottian Alps, where Gregory describes the estates as *possessiuncula*.[32] There has been some confusion over this patrimony. The properties were situated in the area known classically as Liguria, i.e. the coastal enclave around Genoa. But references in John the deacon's biography of Gregory to the Cottian Alps led scholars to believe that there were also papal estates in the classical Cottian Alps.[33] But this confusion was resolved by Paul Fabre, who demonstrated that some time between 533 and 553 the organization of the provinces in Northern Italy was changed and the classical Liguria and Cottian Alps both disappeared to be replaced by new provinces with the same names but different boundaries.[34] The new Cottian Alps province embraced the coastal area of classical Liguria and the papal *possessiuncula*, meaning in effect that the papal estates in Liguria and the Cottian Alps were one and the same.

The richest and most extensive of the papal patrimonies was in Sicily, where by the time of Gregory I these were sufficient farms to support some four hundred *conductores*. By Gregory's reign, in fact, the patrimony had become so large that the pope divided it into two rectorships, centred on Panormus and Syracuse respectively. The Syracusan rector was always the senior of the two and some idea of the extent of the papal patrimony in Sicily can be gauged from the fact that his bailiwick included properties in Catana, Messana and Agrigentum as well as Syracuse itself.[35] The papal patrimony had existed at least as early as the reign of Pelagius I[36] and almost certainly for a lot longer than that. The churches of Ravenna and Milan also owned patrimonies on the island.[37]

Another rich and important papal patrimony was that of Campania, centred on Naples, the headquarters of the papal rector, and also existing at least since Pelagius I and almost certainly earlier.[38] It seems to have been extensive enough to absorb Lombard depredations. But several other once important patrimonies were less fortunate. The patrimony of Lucania and Bruttium, controlled by a single rector resident in Rhegium, was an important source of timber for the repair of the Roman churches.[39] It had existed at least since the time of Pelagius I[40] but its area would have been curtailed by the ravaging of Lucania and the loss of imperial control over much of that unhappy province. There were similarly estates in Apulia and Calabria, which had also existed at the time of Pelagius I,[41] but the Apulian estates were much reduced by the loss of most of the province to the Lombards. A papal rector remained in residence in the imperial enclave of Sipontum, administering what was left of the Apulian patrimony, but his isolation made it difficult for him to exercise such close control over the Calabrian estates, in particular those at Callipolis.[42] In Samnium, only Hortona and the area around it remained in imperial hands, but since there was a papal rector in the city,[43] papal properties in the enclave must have remained, a rump of the Samnite patrimony. The Sabine patrimony was certainly reduced in size. It seems to have been substantial at one time, consisting of estates around Carseoli, Praeneste and Tibur.[44] The patrimony probably came in the main to the Roman church after the imperial reconquest and comprised the estates of King Totila's father, Hildibad.[45] A pre-Gregorian rector of the patrimony is described at the time of Gregory as 'Rector of the patrimony of Sabina and Carseoli'.[46] But in the same letter the same patrimony is described as 'Tiburtine', the name by which it is referred to in the registers of

Gregory II and Zacharias.[47] This seems to indicate and acknowledge a reduction in size of the original patrimony. Since Carseoli is known to have been right on the frontier of imperial territory, it seems likely that the headquarters of the rector was moved to Tibur for safety. One patrimony completely lost by the time of Gregory was the Picene patrimony, attested both in the reign of Gelasius I and that of Pelagius I.

Close to Rome itself were the Appian patrimony, a cluster of estates around the Appian Way yielding oil for the lamps of the Roman churches,[48] and the Tuscian patrimony, which included estates around Blera and was safely within the boundaries of the Duchy of Rome, as indicated by its survival and attestation under Zacharias.[49] Finally, there were papal estates in Ravenna and Istria, administered from Ravenna by a rector who also acted as papal *apocrisiarios* at the exarchal court.[50] The position was a vital one, since it involved dealing with and keeping an eye on the exarch, the archbishop of Ravenna, the Lombards and the Istrian schismatics, all of whom could prove difficult and frequently did, sometimes all at once.

During the sixth century, there seems to have been some eleven Italian patrimonies in the possession of the Roman church, many of them curtailed by the Lombard invasion. By the first half of the eighth century, for which parts of the land registers of Gregory II and Zacharias survive, a somewhat different picture emerges. Judging by these admittedly incomplete registers, there does seem to have been a shift in the structure of the patrimony of St Peter. The overseas patrimonies have gone and so too have the Sicilian and Calabrian estates. But the activities of the papacy seem to have been little affected by this and there is no sign of a slowing up in its charitable activities or its building programme.

The answer is in part suggested by the registers. It looks as if the amount of land in papal hands in Latium, Campania and Tuscia, the provinces closest to Rome, had dramatically increased since the sixth century. The most obvious reason for this is bequests. The combined effects of plague, celibacy and war will have caused the extinction of many propertied families and in a world in which the papacy was coming to tower above any other institution in Italy, it will have been the obvious recipient of the properties. It is known from the *Liber Pontificalis*, for instance, that Gregory I, Gregory II, Honorius I, Pelagius II and Boniface IV at least were the last representatives of their families, because they turned their Rome family homes into monasteries or charitable institutions. There must have been many similar cases. The accretions and acquisitions became so extensive as to warrant the division of several patrimonies, something which had only previously happened in Sicily so far as is known. The eighth-century land registers, however, reveal a division of estates in Campania, with one block centred on Naples and another on Gaieta.[51] The extent of the Campanian patrimony is also indicated by the fact that Rome owned property at Misenum and Surrentum as well as the entire island of Capri, leased by Gregory II to the consul Theodore for twenty-nine years at an annual rent of 109 *solidi* and 100 *megarici* of wine.[52]

Some 143 separate farms are leased in the surviving registers and they help us to see the structure of the patrimonies, which seem to be grouped around the roads radiating outwards from Rome. There was one entirely new patrimony, the *Labicana*, which was grouped apparently around the Via Labicana, which drove south-eastwards from Rome.[53] It extended east as far as the Via Praenestina, including property at Gabii and Praeneste, and reached at least as far as Anagnia forty miles from Rome. The Via Praenestina seems to have been the boundary of the Tiburtine patrimony, grouped around the Via Tiburtina and including property on the Via Praenestina as well as inside the town of Tibur itself.[54] The Appian patrimony reached at least twenty miles down the Via Appia and stretched westwards to include territory on the Via Ardeatina.[55] The Tuscian patrimony, stretching north from Rome, centred on the Via Aurelia and the Via Clodia at least as far as Forum Clodii twenty-five miles north of Rome.[56] Both the Tuscian and Appian patrimonies had lands described as set in the suburban patrimonies and there seems to have been a ten-mile cut-off point beyond which was the patrimony proper.[57]

It is clear from what evidence survives that a considerable area around Rome in all directions belonged to the papacy. A policy of extending it even further and bringing back into cultivation and settlement abandoned areas was inaugurated by Pope Zacharias in his *domusculta* programme; and this must have gone some way towards compensating for the confiscation of the Sicilian and Calabrian estates by the imperial authorities. There was therefore a shift of emphasis in the geographical structure of the patrimony, with outlying estates vanishing and the central core being considerably strengthened and extended.

The Patrimonial Rectors

It seems to have been Gelasius I who took the first steps towards organizing the papal patrimony into a coherent administrative unit. For it is from his reign that the *Polyptycum*, the great account book of the patrimony, dates.[58] This probably resulted from a full-scale investigation of the papal estates, prompted by the need to check on war damage. A letter of 17 January 494 records part of the process when Pope Gelasius ordered the deacon Corvinus to make a *descriptio* of the merits and revenues of the papal estates lying in Picenum.[59] It will have been surveys of this kind which helped to build up an over-all picture of the estates and their income, as enshrined in the *Polyptycum*. The *Polyptycum* was still in use in the ninth century.

There is, however, some evidence to suggest that there was as yet no regular rectorial system in operation under Gelasius. For Corvinus seems to have been ordered to Picenum specifically to make a *descriptio*. A letter to one Agilulf, clearly a layman, asking him to defend the Dalmatian patrimony and to carry out whatever archbishop Honorius of Salona and the individual *conductores* of the estate think best for its welfare, suggests that these estates were unsupervised except in an advisory capacity by the Dalmatian metropolitan.[60]

By the time of Pelagius I, however, there was a fully operational rectorial system, but it was not as yet entirely staffed by clerics of the Roman church. In Gaul the papal rector was the patrician Placidus, father of Bishop Sapaudus of Arelate.[61] Bishop Maurus of Praeneste administered the Tiburtine patrimony between 552 and 558 and Bishop Julian of Cingulum administered the Picene estates.[62] Other patrimonies did have Roman clerical administrators: *defensor* John in Sicily, *defensor* Constantine in Campania, subdeacon Melleus in Lucania-Bruttium and *defensor* Dulcitius in Calabria-Apulia.[63] But they do not seem to have been entirely satisfactory. Melleus was reprimanded by the pope for withholding revenue from the patrimony, none of which he had paid over since he was appointed, and Dulcitius was upbraided for trying to embezzle money by falsifying the patrimonial accounts.

At some point between the reigns of Pelagius I and Gregory I it became customary for Roman clerics to administer the Italian patrimonies. Although their chief duty was the supervision of the estates and the collection of rent, by the time of Gregory the papal rectors had become the instruments of the papal personnel policy, the eyes and ears of the papacy in the regions, the regulators of clerical, even episcopal, behaviour. This had been a gradual and inevitable development of the introduction of permanent papal representatives in the localities. There is no evidence of their involvement in elections under Pelagius I but there is of other aspects of non-estate management activity. For example, the *defensor* John, the Sicilian rector, was ordered by Pelagius to deprive Bishop Secundus of Tauromenium of his *pallium* and send him to Rome to be disciplined because he was spending his time in private lawsuits to the detriment of his official duties.[64]

315

Unfortunately, it is not possible to trace the steps by which the rectors acquired these additional powers and responsibilities but the process was clearly gradual and cumulative during the sixth century. The Gregorian Register presents the first real opportunity to assess the nature and structure of the fully formed rectorial system.

Gregory instituted certain important reforms in the system. First and foremost of these was Gregory's determination to bring all the patrimonies, not just the Italian ones, under the control of Roman clerics. As John the deacon noted, Gregory 'appointed industrious men of his own church as *rectores patrimonii*' in order to safeguard church affairs and look after the poor.[65] This was of particular significance in the extra-Italian patrimonies, where in some cases it was happening for the first time. For there is no doubt that Gregory saw these rectors not primarily as agents of estate management but as the unofficial envoys of the papal see resident abroad.

The Gallic patrimony had always been administered by local dignitaries, lay or ecclesiastical. Under Pelagius I, the rector had been the governor of Provence, the patrician Placidus;[66] under Pelagius II it was Placidus's son, Bishop Sapaudus of Arelate.[67] On Sapaudus's death in 586 the local governor, the patrician Dynamius, had once again assumed the job. Dynamius was a complex character. He is depicted by Gregory of Tours as interfering in episcopal elections and plotting against King Childebert, but the poems of Venantius Fortunatus praise him for his benevolence, piety and love of letters.[68] In the autumn of 595, however, Dynamius retired from public life and entered a monastery.[69] This gave Gregory the opportunity he wanted. He did not appoint as papal rector Dynamius's successor as governor, the patrician Arigius. He simply allowed Arigius to administer the patrimony until a new rector could arrive from Rome. But to be on the safe side, he was not to be allowed to collect rents. The *conductores* were to nominate one of their number to collect and hold the rents until the new rector arrived.[70]

The new rector was the Roman priest, Candidus, who duly arrived in Gaul to take over the administration of the patrimony.[71] Someone whom the pope could trust was certainly needed. Rents collected by the bishop of Arelate ten years before, when he had been rector, had still not been paid in 596.[72] But this was not the only or indeed arguably the main reason why Gregory wanted a Roman cleric as rector of Gaul. The point of choosing a priest, a member of the spiritual arm, rather than a representative of one of the administrative orders, emphasizes this. The job was to be predominantly a missionary one. He was to try to expedite Gregory's long-cherished and ultimately unsuccessful project to instigate a great synod in Gaul to reform the Gallic church, in which abuses were rife. In September

597 for instance, Gregory wrote deploring the widespread prevalence of paganism and tree worship, the indiscriminate promotion of laymen to bishoprics and the universality of simony.[73] Even allowing for emphatic exaggeration, the situation sounds bad. In 599 and 601 Gregory mounted an all-out bid to promote a reform synod, writing to leading bishops and members of the royal family. Both times he failed. Candidus clearly played an important part in all this, acting as a permanent one-man pressure group to advance papal policy in Gaul. He stayed on in Gaul after Gregory's death and was last heard of in 613 still acting as papal rector.[74]

Gregory's African rector was the notary Hilarus who had held the same office under Pelagius II and was confirmed in it by Gregory.[75] The few references in the Register to his activities indicate that his role was similar to that of Candidus in Gaul, representing the Roman presence and papal authority, seeing as far as possible that episcopal discipline and clerical good behaviour were maintained; this meant in effect keeping the Donatists down and staying on good terms with the civil authorities.[76]

The incumbent rector of Dalmatia on Gregory's accession was Bishop Malchus, a local prelate of unknown see.[77] Accused of the sale of church property and other illicit acts, he was summoned to Rome for trial and, after a lengthy and circuitous journey via Ravenna and Sicily, necessitated by the closing of the Rome–Ravenna land corridor by war, he eventually reached Rome, was tried and found guilty late in 593 or early in 594. However, that same night, having been taken home to dinner by the notary Boniface, Malchus died. This unhappy event gave rise to a rumour which circulated freely in Constantinople that the bishop had been done to death by the pope, a story that Gregory was at pains to correct in a letter to his *apocrisiarios* Sabinian.[78]

By the removal of Malchus from office, however, Gregory did gain the opportunity to install one of his own clergy, the Roman subdeacon Antoninus, appointed Dalmatian rector in March 592.[79] Again given the paucity of the papal estates in the province, his role was very much that of a papal representative, looking into the irregular deposition of Bishop Florentius of Epidaurus, for instance, and more importantly overseeing the arrangements for the election of a new archbishop of Salona. There was in this election a papal candidate, the archdeacon Honoratus, and a non-papal candidate, Maximus. In the event, papal plans went awry when Maximus was installed as archbishop of Salona by imperial troops and in the ensuing violence and confusion, subdeacon Antoninus was forced to flee for his life.

Thereafter during the prolonged dispute between Gregory and Maximus, there was no resident papal representative in Salona, as is evidenced by the fact that during this period Gregory always had to write direct to the Dalmatian bishops to make his views known. However, after the reconciliation between Rome and Salona was effected in August 599, it was safe, and indeed desirable, to send a papal rector to keep an eye on the now officially recognized archbishop Maximus. This rector was another Roman cleric, the notary John.[80] It is interesting to note that in the three countries, Gaul, Africa and Dalmatia, the only incumbent rector to keep his job under Gregory was the sole Roman cleric; the other non-Roman rectors were replaced by Roman clerics.

What the arrangements in Sardinia and Corsica had been before Gregory is not known. But certainly under Gregory, Roman clerics were sent as papal rectors, and their jobs corresponded very much with those of the other overseas rectors. This seems to have been recognized by the inhabitants of the islands, both lay and clerical. For instance, in 599 archbishop Januarius of Caralis's clergy, deserting their duties and refusing to obey him, resorted to the protection and patronage of the papal rector Vitalis. Gregory ordered this to stop but did permit Vitalis to act as an intercessor on their behalf in disputes with the archbishop when he thought that the clergy should be pardoned rather than punished.[81]

The first known Sardinian rector was the *defensor* Sabinus, ordered in May 593 to see that Archbishop Januarius came to Rome to answer criminal charges.[82] There was extensive correspondence with his successor as rector, the *defensor* Vitalis, who first appears in September 598, ordered to ensure that the excommunication order against the 'perverse counsellors' of Januarius was carried out.[83] The content of the Sardinian letters makes it clear that the rectors were chiefly preoccupied with the affairs of the Sardinian church.

Two rectors of Corsica are known from the Register. The first, *defensor* Symmachus, was ordered in June 591 to choose a suitable defensive position for a new monastery, to enforce celibacy amongst the Corsican priesthood and to correct irregularities among the monks of Gorgona.[84] His successor, the *defensor* Boniface, had similar duties enjoined on him. In February 599, he was urged to exhort bishops not to cohabit with women and in August 601 was ordered to encourage the inhabitants of Adjacium and Aleria to elect bishops to fill the vacant sees and to see that clerics were not held in custody by laymen but tried by their bishop.[85] Again, there is no mention of patrimonial business and the whole tenor of the correspondence suggests that the Corsican rectors were concerned chiefly with ecclesiastical discipline and organization.

Within Italy Gregory maintained the tradition of appointing Roman clerics as rectors. But he made some innovations in practice in the interests of improved honesty and efficiency. He rarely permitted one rector to stay at his post throughout the reign, changing them after a few years to prevent complacency or the entrenchment of interest. Gregory's immediate predecessor, Pelagius II, seems to have been guilty of appointing some unsatisfactory rectors. He used local bishops, such as Malchus for Dalmatia and Sapaudus of Arelate for Gaul, and they proved less than satisfactory. He also employed wealthy propertied men in minor orders with locally based families who seem to have been guilty of irregularities. The *defensor* Antoninus in Sicily and the *defensor* Constantius in Campania fall into this category.[86] A process of fluidity and transfer prevented the consolidation of power in the hands of one man, as did the important development of the division in Sicily.

The known transfers of power occur in Lucania-Bruttium, where the notary Peter was replaced by the subdeacon Sabinus,[87] in Apulia where the *defensor* Sergius was replaced by the notary Romanus,[88] in Ravenna where the notary Castorius was replaced by the subdeacon John[89] and in Tuscia where the *defensor* Candidus was replaced by the notary Eugenius.[90] In addition to these apparently routine changeovers, there are two cases of transfer known to have been for reasons of unsatisfactory conduct. In Samnium, the rector was the *defensor* Scholasticus, son of Bishop Blandus of Hortona. After his father's death he refused to hand over the episcopal palace to the new bishop Calumniosus and held on to vestments and other property properly belonging to the bishop. He also detained in the name of the Roman church land rightfully belonging to the Hortona church. He was ordered by the pope in July 599 to hand over the illegally retained property. It is not unlikely that this behaviour led to his replacement by the *defensor* Benenatus.[91]

There was also a change connected with unsatisfactory performance in Campania. The first Gregorian rector there was the subdeacon Anthemius, who first appears in the job in February 591.[92] He had frequently to be reminded of his duty towards the poor which he apparently neglected and there is evidence that monastic discipline in his area was very lax and that monasteries were riddled with abuse.[93] It is probably this poor record which led to Anthemius's recall, for between 591 and 594 he is lost to view. In his place the subdeacon Peter was appointed rector of Campania, first mentioned in September 592 and last in July 593.[94] It has often been assumed that this was the same subdeacon Peter who was rector of Sicily. But that identification is impossible, for Peter of Sicily was recalled and promoted deacon in time to act as Gregory's interlocutor in the *Dialogi*, written in 593 when the other Peter was still in Campania. It is more likely that the Campanian Peter was the subdeacon appointed by Gregory to be bishop of Triocala in 594, which would explain his disappearance from Campania at about that time. Anthemius, who had by now apparently proved himself in other duties, was reappointed to Campania by July 594 and seems to have remained there.[95] There is only one patrimony where no change of rector is known and that is Appia, for which only one rector, the subdeacon Felix, is attested, but the evidence is so scanty on this patrimony that it would be unwise to draw any firm conclusions from this. In general, apart from known cases of removal because of unsatisfactory performance, Gregory seems to have pursued a calculated policy of periodic replacement of patrimonial rectors, changes being deemed useful in keeping the administrators up to scratch.

Apart from the implementation of this general principle, Gregory's reign also saw various internal adjustments in structure and staffing. The Cottian Alps patrimony was initially administered by an exiled Milanese priest Magnus,[96] but he died at some point before 600 when the notary Pantaleo was sent to Genoa to attend to church business and supervise the election of a new archbishop of Milan.[97] Soon after this Gregory brought the Cottian Alps patrimony back under direct Roman control by appointing the *defensor* Hieronymus as Rector.[98]

An adjustment was necessary in the Apulia-Calabria patrimony because of the political situation. The rector remained resident in Sipontum, cut off from the Calabrian estates. In 599 Gregory became concerned about the danger to the Calabrian estates around Callipolis, threatened by enemy attack, the diminution of the tenant population and the oppression of the local military commandant. So he detached the estates from the control of the Apulian rector and placed them under Bishop Sabinus of Callipolis, who happened to be an ex-monk of Gregory's monastery and was therefore trustworthy. Gregory ordered him to investigate the rent roll and see that the *coloni* paid only what they could afford in relation to their possessions. It is a clear indication that the pope was prepared to sanction a reduction in rent to keep his diminishing tenant force. Admittedly he broke his own rule about not employing bishops as rectors but since the bishop in question was one of his own patronage appointments, the breach was more one of letter than spirit.[99]

In Sicily there was an even more spectacular structural change, the division of the patrimony into two. Gregory's reign opened with the appointment of his friend and disciple Peter the subdeacon as rector of the Sicilian patrimony and also vicar of the Sicilian church. His tasks were to overhaul the patrimonial administration at all levels and begin the Gregorianization of the episcopate. He held office from September 590 to July 592.[100] On his recall the patrimony was divided into two, one half centred on Syracuse and the other on Panormus, the former maintaining a supervisory capacity over the latter. To the senior post, the deacon Cyprian was appointed.[101] The appointment of a deacon as a patrimonial administrator, though rare, was not unprecedented. Interestingly, such cases appear most frequently in connection with Sicily, a measure of its importance. The last Sicilian rector under Pelagius II had been the deacon Servusdei.[102] Honorius's rector of Sicily was the deacon Cyriacus.[103]

To the junior Sicilian post in Panormus the notary Benenatus was appointed.[104] But by July 594 he had been replaced by one of his subordinates, the *defensor* Fantinus, previously one of several *defensores* operating in the patrimony.[105] Cyprian is last attested in Sicily in November 597 and was probably recalled some time in 598.[106] There was a hiatus before the appointment of a new rector, and in the interim Bishop John of Syracuse was given charge of the papal patrimony, an arrangment which seems to have been resisted by some of the *defensores* who refused to obey his orders and had to be threatened with punishment by the pope.[107] Like Sabinus at Callipolis, John was an appointee of the pope and could therefore be trusted with the temporary administration of the patrimony.

Eventually, the *defensor* Romanus was appointed as the new Syracusan rector. As manager of a *xenodochium*, he had been reprimanded by the pope for devoting too much time to making money and not enough to spreading it among the poor.[108] But in practical terms his efficiency commended itself so much that, after being entrusted with a mission to Constantinople in 597,[109] he was appointed Syracusan rector in 598.[110] He held the position until August 601, but eventually overreached himself. In February 601 Gregory wrote reprimanding him for taking cognizance of cases involving clerics not just in Syracuse but elsewhere. He had released on his own initiative certain clerics put to penance by Bishop John of Syracuse, thus overriding episcopal rights. Gregory ordered that the clerics be returned to penance and commanded Romanus to cease interfering in clerical cases.[111]

It was a basic principle for Gregory that the ecclesiastical hierarchy must be preserved and episcopal rights maintained. He explained firmly to Romanus: 'If the jurisdiction of each and every bishop is not preserved, what else will happen but that the ecclesiastical order will be thrown into confusion by us by whom it ought to be preserved?' Soon after this *contretemps*, Romanus was recalled and replaced by the notary Adrian, first encountered in the Register in January 603.[112] He had been acting rector of Panormus during the absence of the rector Fantinus, probably in Rome in connection with the trial of Bishop Exhilaratus 601–3. Adrian was promoted to the senior rectorship on the return of Fantinus to Panormus, eloquent testimony to his good stewardship.[113] The surviving details of the rectorial arrangements for Sicily indeed give us a valuable insight into the workings of the papal administrative system and some of the ideas behind it.

Gregory's reign, then, saw positive advances in the rectorial system. Men from all grades of the administrative service were used as rectors and they were changed fairly frequently to prevent abuses. Gregory kept a close eye on their activities, used them to implement his personnel policies but did not allow them to step outside their limits and infringe the rights of the episcopate. His innovations lay in bringing outlying and extra-Italian patrimonies directly under the control of Rome by the appointment of Roman clerics to administer them and by making various internal adjustments in the interests of greater efficiency. His watchwords throughout were prestige, efficiency and discipline.

It is clear that Gregory's reign was very important in the development of the rectorial service and although after his death the outlying patrimonies were gradually lost, the principles he established seem to have been maintained, so far as can be ascertained from the highly fragmentary evidence. Certainly the principle of using Roman clergy exclusively as rectors was so well-established by 687 that when Pope Conon appointed a Syracusan deacon, Constantine, as Sicilian rector he caused a storm of protest, and eventually Constantine's extortionate regime led to his arrest and imprisonment.[114]

Chapter 19

The Papacy and the Episcopate

Just as circumstances and the course of events saw an increase in the powers of the papacy and the scope of its activities, so too did the episcopate in general come to be thrust more and more into the mainstream of life; it was expected on a day-to-day basis to involve itself in matters previously outside its ken. The imperial reconquest and the subsequent Lombard invasion was the great watershed. With the aristocracy broken and dispersed and with imperial military forces, at least initially, badly organized, badly officered and badly paid, it fell more and more onto the shoulders of the bishops to undertake such responsibilities as the handling of refugees, the negotiation of treaties, the provisioning of cities, the making of defence dispositions. The people came to look to the bishops – as they did to the pope – to protect them from the wrath of the barbarians, and as the Lombards gradually became civilized and Christianized, it was the bishops and the pope to whom they listened. It was therefore increasingly important that the bishops be versed in statecraft and the techniques of man management.

This extension of episcopal involvement in secular matters was reflected in the Law Code of Justinian. He gave the bishops effective oversight in the whole field of local government when he demanded that they report infringements of the law by imperial officials and that they bring the complaints of the people before the emperor. They were expected to oversee the treatment of prisoners, orphans, foundlings and lunatics, civic expenditure, public works, aqueduct maintenance, public order and the supply of foodstuffs to the troops.[1] In the *Pragmatic Sanction*, drawn up to regulate the newly created province of Italy, the bishops were even given the task of helping to choose provincial governors.[2] All in all, it constituted an awesome responsibility. Practical examples of episcopal involvement can be found in the fragmentary sources of the seventh century. In the first half of the century, the young Bishop Gaudiosus of

Salernum negotiated a truce between the Roman inhabitants of Salernum and the Lombards of Beneventum;[3] Bishop Agapetus of Surrentum was involved in negotiating the withdrawal of and payment of ransom to Duke Radoald of Beneventum after a Lombard attack on the city.[4]

Both as patriarch of the Western church and metropolitan of Suburbicarian Italy, it was the pope's duty to maintain a supervisory interest in the activities of the bishops. The enhancement and extension of episcopal duties made this supervision more imperative than ever. It meant that for some popes at least the higher needs of an overall papal personnel policy might have to take precedence over the local desires of the inhabitants in the matter of election to the episcopate – in short the operation by the pope of a system of selective patronage. By patronage, I mean the intervention of the pope in episcopal elections either directly or through his agents to secure the appointment of a man known to be fitted for the enhanced responsibilities of the office. To say that the popes indulged in patronage is not to allege anything sordid or simoniac in their conduct. Sixth- and seventh-century popes had a consistent record in denouncing simony.

Personnel management was not pursued consistently from reign to reign. Its operation depended entirely on contemporary circumstances and on the experience and personality of the man on the throne. It is unlikely that the unworldly figures who occupied the papal throne during parts of the seventh and eighth centuries were either interested or active in personnel management – and even if they were, the shortness of the reigns would have precluded systematic interest.

The operation of a comprehensive patronage policy is demonstrable only for Gregory I, though that may be because only from his reign have a substantial number of papal letters survived. There is, however, one clue to the operation of patronage in general terms. While we can never be sure that the election of a local man has not involved patronage, the election of a Roman cleric to a bishopric generally does imply papal involvement. The episcopal lists for the period are extremely fragmentary but such runs of evidence as exist suggest that few Romans were elected to provincial bishoprics and that in general elections did remain local affairs. For the episcopal succession in Ravenna during this period, there are details in Agnellus's *Liber Pontificalis Ecclesiae Ravennatis*. Though the origins of every archbishop are not mentioned, unusual origins are. The only known non-Ravennates elected to the see were Maximian, the Istrian deacon appointed by Justinian I,[5] and the Romans John III and his nephew Marinianus. John, who by his own testimony had been brought up in the Roman church and was perhaps originally a notary,[6] was appointed in 578 by Pope Benedict I, and Marinianus in 595 by Gregory I.[7] Again, all the seventh-century archbishops of Grado were Istrians apart from Primogenius, a Roman subdeacon, and Maximus, a Dalmatian and probably a refugee.[8] It is not very much to go on, admittedly, but these are premier sees where one might legitimately expect papal intervention.

There are known to have been 'one-off' patronage appointments by the pope but these were generally under special circumstances. Pope Honorius I appointed the Roman subdeacon Primogenius as archbishop of Grado after archbishop Fortunatus went schismatic and fled to the Lombards, and the clergy had petitioned Honorius for a replacement.[9] The priest Wighard, archbishop elect of Canterbury, died of plague in Rome before he could be consecrated, and Pope Vitalian therefore appointed the Greek monk Theodore of Tarsus as archbishop.[10]

In 484, following the death of Bishop Felix of Nola,[11] Pope Felix III nominated as his successor the exiled patriarch of Alexandria, John Talaia. Although Liberatus says that John remained there 'many years',[12] he must have died soon afterwards, for his successor as bishop of Nola, Theodosius, died there on 7 December 490,[13] indicating a comparatively short reign for John and one which would harmonize with his failure to reappear in the pages of history after his appointment to Nola.

There was also a tradition that the failed candidate in a disputed papal election should receive a bishopric, partly as a consolation prize but also partly to get him out of Rome and remove a focus for discontent. In 366, after the death of Pope Liberius, the succession was disputed by Damasus and Ursinus. A council of priests was called to break the deadlock and decided in favour of Damasus, whereupon Ursinus was awarded the bishopric of Naples. In 419, following the death of Pope Zosimus, there was a disputed election between the archdeacon Eulalius and the priest Boniface. It was settled by the intervention of the emperor Honorius, who called a synod which awarded the papacy to Boniface. Eulalius received the bishopric of Nepe. In 499 after the resolution of the election dispute in favour of Symmachus, the archpriest Laurentius was awarded the bishopric of Nuceria. It was also a tradition invoked by the emperor Justinian when he sent ex-pope Silverius back to Rome, suggesting a consolation bishopric for him.

We might *a priori* expect to find evidence of papal patronage in operation during the embittered in-fighting which accompanied the Symmachan schism. The 'Laurentian Fragment' 's claim that after his acquittal, Symmachus sold off ecclesiastical offices in droves, if it is anything more than simply losers' sour grapes, could contain a distant echo of a policy of installing Symmachan loyalists in local sees.

The epitaph of Bishop Andreas of Formiae records that he lived for seventy years, was a priest in Rome for seven years and bishop for twenty-eight years ten months and twenty-two days.[14] He died on 19 October 529 and was therefore consecrated on 9 December 501. This is slightly at odds with the known facts concerning Andreas and Formiae but the problem can be resolved with a little ingenuity. The see of Formiae was represented at four of the five synods during the period. Bishop Martinian of Formiae attended the 487 and 495 synods and Bishop Adeodatus of Formiae the 499 and 502 trial synods. Formiae was not represented at the 502 victory synod, held in November of that year. By postulating a scribal error (twenty-eight for twenty-seven), we can put Andreas's ordination in December 502 after the close of the victory synod, which, if Adeodatus died before its convening, would account for the absence of a bishop of Formiae from its deliberations. It is interesting and significant that a Roman priest should have been ordained bishop of Formiae at the comparatively early age of 42 at this crucial period of papal history.

Another Symmachan appointment was the *defensor* Julian, who, according to the *Dialogi* of Gregory the Great, became bishop of Sabina.[15] Julian was sent by the pope to bring the holy man Equitius to Rome for preaching without a licence. This must have occurred early in the reign, for Equitius became the abbot and father of many Valerian monasteries and later in the reign was involved with the magician Basilius. It is worth noting that Dulcitius, bishop of Sabina, was present at the 495 and 499 synods, voted for the pope's absolution in 502 and was present at the beginning but not the end of the 502 victory synod. If he died during the course of the synod, the opportunity for the pope to appoint a faithful Roman *defensor* to the vacant see would have arisen.

The eighteenth-century chronicler, Pirri, working from earlier records which have not survived, records that the successor of Eulalius as bishop of Syracuse was the otherwise unknown Stephanus, whom he records was 'a Roman by birth, whom the Syracusans did not recognize.'[16] Unfortunately he does not quote the source of his information, but the unique appearance of a Roman in the premier Sicilian see to succeed a man who had played a prominent role at the 502 victory synod would fit in with a Symmachan patronage policy, aimed at keeping sees which fell vacant in sympathetic hands.

The proceedings of the 502 trial synod include the signature of

Aprilis, *episcopus ecclesiae Laterianae*.[17] This is probably a scribal error because at the 502 victory synod he signed himself as bishop of Nuceria, the see so recently awarded to the anti-pope Laurentius.[18] Either Laurentius never took it up or Symmachus deposed him, but it is interesting to note that the new bishop voted for the pope's absolution at the trial and turned up at the victory synod thereafter. It may be that we should see Symmachus's hand in this too.

However, the greatest patronage coup came in Aquileia. The trial synod was presided over by the three Italian metropolitans, Laurentius of Milan, Peter of Ravenna and Marcellianus of Aquileia.[19] When the synod pronounced for Symmachus's absolution, the first two duly recognized him. But Marcellianus did not. Dissatisfied with the verdict, he went over to the Laurentians. He did not sign the synodical proceedings nor did he attend the 502 victory synod. Instead he submitted a petition to the king on the subject, together with the senate and 'certain others'.[20] Marcellianus's opposition to the absolution was very serious and boded ill for the unity of the Italian church. A private mission was sent to win him over but failed.[21] Shortly afterwards, however, Marcellianus died and the deacon Ennodius wrote exultantly to the pope of his enemy's death.[22]

There now had to be an election and the letters of Ennodius suggest, when you cut through the incredible turgidity and circumlocution, that there was a deliberate bid by aristocratic supporters of the papal cause to fix the election. Ennodius wrote to his relative, the *vir magnificus* Avitus, suggesting that he ensure the election of a pro-papal candidate.[23] Later, he wrote to the patrician Liberius, applauding his intervention in the election, praising his circumspection in achieving this end without opposition and praising his candidate, the new archbishop Marcellinus.[24] Ennodius described the new prelate as *ignotus*. He may have been unknown to Ennodius, but the chronicle of Andrea Dandolo supplies information which provides a suggestive link.[25] He describes Marcellinus uniquely among the Aquileian archbishops as a Roman. The date of his election is not certainly known, but computed from length of reigns was probably 503–4. Even if Dandolo's information is discounted, it looks as if action was taken to secure the installation of a Symmachan loyalist in Aquileia. Despite the rather scrappy nature of the evidence, it does look as if there was patronage activity by Symmachus to ensure the loyalty of the episcopate after his confirmation as pope.

On the other hand, there is evidence from the reign of Pelagius I to suggest that he did not intervene in episcopal elections to secure his shaky throne. The key role played by the imperial governor Narses in securing his acceptance as pope prefigures the role that the laity were to play in Pelagian personnel management. Entrusting visitation of Catana to Bishop Eucarpus of Messana in the autumn of 558, the pope lamented the fact that there was no one else in the Syracusan half of Sicily to whom he could entrust ecclesiastical duties, indicating the widespread degree of vacancy Pelagius had to tackle.[26] Indeed Pelagius issued a general appeal, urging all those who were qualified to accept promotion when it was offered.[27] We know that during his reign he ordained forty-nine bishops, twice the annual average of ordinations of bishops per year per reign, computed from the figures given for other popes. His epitaph, too, confirms that he ordained 'many ministers for the divine law' without sullying his hands with simony.[28]

But the shortage of bishops was so acute that even unsatisfactory ones had to be tolerated. In March 559 Pelagius wrote to Bishop Priscus of Capua, saying that although many things were alleged against him, Pelagius had taken action on none of them but something had now arisen which it was impossible to ignore.[29] A nun Juliana, carried off by one Severus, had escaped, claimed sanctuary from the church and had been handed back to her abductor by the bishop. Pelagius therefore sent the deacon Menantius from Rome to see that the nun was returned to her nunnery or sent to Rome. Priscus was threatened with excommunication or suspension unless he carried out this order. In the autumn of 558 Bishop John of Narnia, who had confessed himself unequal to his duties or the maintenance of discipline, requested permission to appoint the priest Constitutus as effective regent of the see.[30] The pope was forced to agree, adjuring the Narnian clergy to retain their reverence for John while obeying Constitutus in day-to-day affairs.

The details of the handful of elections which the Pelagian Register preserves are instructive. In February 559 Pelagius wrote to the patrician Cethegus saying that because he knew that Cethegus wanted it thus he had consecrated the bishop of Catana immediately upon his arrival in Rome.[31] But although Cethegus wanted the same for the bishop of Syracuse, Pelagius was unable to oblige, partly because of the bishop's character and partly because he had a wife and sons, to whom he feared that church property would be alienated. He had delayed for a year, hoping that the Syracusans would choose again but they said that they could find no one else and the praetor Leo of Sicily wrote to say that they would choose no one else. So Pelagius gave way. He held a council, extracted from the bishop elect the written promise that he would allow no church property to pass to his family and then consecrated him.

This, in the light of Gregory's activities, is amazing. If a man was not suited to the episcopate by reason of character and marriage,

Gregory would certainly have disallowed him and nominated someone in Rome, especially since the see involved was Syracuse, the premier city in Sicily. There is no mention of the papal rector in the letter, someone with whom Gregory would have been in constant touch during the election. Pelagius also accepts the dictation of laymen, the patrician Cethegus and the praetor Leo, whose detailed involvement suggests that they backed the bishop elect. Pelagius simply seems to have left things for a year, hoping that the people would change their mind, and when they had not, he had accepted their choice as a *fait accompli*. There seems to have been no bid to change their opinion, no exercise of the veto and no involving of the rector to swing popular feeling on the spot. Suitable candidates may have been scarce but Gregory would not have allowed the chance to nominate the senior Sicilian bishop to pass.

It is probable that the Syracusan bishop thus elected was Eleutherius, who received three of the surviving ninety-six Pelagian letters but whose see is not explicitly named.[32] He appears to have been a local notable of propertied family (his mother built and endowed an oratory on an estate in Sicily).[33] His name is Greek and would fit a native Sicilian. His backing by Cethegus and Leo suggests someone of their social class. The long vacancy intervening before his consecration can also be invoked to explain why as early as March 559 he was complaining that he could not, as he had promised on his consecration, carry out daily vigils because his clergy, puffed up with insolent pride, refused to attend the services and moreover neglected their duties; busying themselves with their own affairs.[34] One of them in particular, the priest Petronius, was refusing to obey a judgment of the episcopal court. The long vacancy seems to have encouraged the priesthood to become fractious and discipline was proving difficult to restore. Eleutherius was later urged to pursue a policy of mediation, kind words and mutual reconciliation when lawsuits arose and this, taken in conjunction with the case of Petronius, suggests that an element of partisanship existed in the bishop's judgments.[35] Whatever interpretation is placed on the letters, it is evident that Eleutherius did not enjoy a smooth passage in his episcopate.

There was trouble too in the Catana election. Bishop Eucarpus of Messana was appointed visitor in the autumn of 558 to oversee the election.[36] But the election was divided. The majority of the electors supported the deacon Elpidius, but a section of the clergy under the deacon Paul and certain powerful laymen backed Anastasius, the son of the late bishop. It was alleged that he had promised them immunity for their illegal acts in return for their support. The praetor Leo, coming to Rome, assured the pope that Elpidius was the majority choice, and the patrician Cethegus urged his immediate ordination. So Pelagius ordered Elpidius and the electoral documents to Rome and there ordained Elpidius, commanding him not to promise or give anything to anyone or promise favourable judgments in court cases. These obviously were the sorts of practices spawned by disputed elections, in which rival candidates bid for support.

Anastasius was put on trial for his actions – presumably interfering with due electoral process.[37] But he rejected the judges appointed by the pope as biased. Pelagius therefore committed the case to the praetor Leo, in whose good faith and integrity he had the utmost confidence. Pelagius urged Elpidius to become reconciled with the deacon Paul and the clergy who had opposed his election so that they could all work together for the good of the church. Once again, then, there is an election in which the pope fails to make a decisive intervention. As with Syracuse, he accepted the candidate backed by prominent laymen Leo and Cethegus. Indeed, he made a point of writing to Cethegus to say that he had consecrated Elpidius according to his wishes.[38] In the light of this prominent lay involvement in Sicilian church affairs, it is worth noting that in February 559 Pelagius wrote to another lay notable, *vir illustris* Cresconius, asking him to see that the bishop of Syracuse did not exact from his priests more than the customary 2 *solidi* as *cathedraticum* and that he also saw to it that bishops did not demand excessive entertainments and feasts when travelling round for confirmations because too much money was being spent on entertainments and not enough on poor relief.[39]

For Lucania, we have the details of the Consilinum election. In March 559 Pelagius wrote to Bishop Tullianus of Grumentum saying that he had received Tullianus's letters announcing the election of his deacon Latinus as bishop of the neighbouring city of Consilinum (also known as Marcelliana).[40] This fact had been confirmed by the visitor and other inhabitants of the city. So, if he had been unanimously elected and was of good character and had his bishop's permission to leave Grumentum, Latinus could come to Rome for consecration. This looks like an entirely local affair, uninfluenced by the pope, who evidently did not know the bishop elect.

But in Apulia the Luceria election indicates a similar situation to the one prevailing in Sicily. In February 559 Pelagius wrote to the *defensor* Dulcius of Apulia ordering him to inform the *magister militum* Aemilianus, the *iudex* Constantine and the *vir magnificus* Ampelius that the deacon Anastasius had been ordained bishop of Luceria as they had desired.[41] It looks as if here the three leading local laymen had put their heads together and picked a local deacon, whom the pope had obediently consecrated.

The evidence is clear and consistent. Where we might have

expected, given the Gregorian experience, to find Pelagius I operating a full-scale patronage system, particularly in key sees, the
evidence to the contrary indicates that he rarely intervened, never
proposed candidates and in fact left elections and indeed episcopal
oversight very much in the hands of powerful local laymen and
government officials. This may have been part of Pelagius's general
strategy. A nominee of the emperor Justinian, he worked closely
with Governor Narses and would therefore expect to be able to call
on the imperial government and its functionaries for help. It may
also be that Pelagius did not concern himself overly with the
mechanics of elections because he was vitally concerned with the
other side of personnel management, the maintenance of discipline.
The disciplinary problems he faced, and which have been referred to
elsewhere, were immense. Since they were in part the result of his
own insecure position, he may have felt that open interference in
episcopal elections would merely serve to exacerbate that insecurity.
The differing responses of Symmachus and Pelagius to a not dissimilar situation underlines the lack of consistency in personnel policy.

Such evidence as we have, then, suggests that systematic interference in the electoral process did not begin until the late sixth century,
coinciding with the extension of episcopal responsibilities after the
reconquest. Gregory I practised it but he may not have been the first
to do so. Pelagius I explicitly did not, probably due to the circumstances of his own election, and Gelasius I seems not to have done,
although the evidence is based on a partial selection of his letters. It
seems likely, however, that in the period up to the Gothic war popes
intervened in episcopal elections only on special occasions. After the
Lombard invasions it became more necessary to practise a consistent
personnel policy, both to provide suitable men in the key sees and to
utilize displaced personnel. Gregory I's policies of employing exiled
bishops to govern vacant sees as well as uniting depopulated sees
became so standard that formula letters authorizing these expedients
appeared in the *Liber Diurnus*.[42] Regrettably the papal registers of the
seventh- and early eighth-century popes are lost, and it is not possible to assess the extent to which Gregory's successors pursued
similar policies.

The other side of personnel management of course involves the
maintenance of discipline and standards. Here the powers of the
pope were well defined both by canon and secular law. If a bishop
was accused of a crime, then he was investigated and if the charge had
any foundation he was tried, often in Rome but sometimes by a panel
of provincial bishops under papal licence. If the bishop was proved
guilty, he could be disciplined – by suspension, excommunication or
deposition, depending on the seriousness of the charge. A bishop

could be accused of usury, simony, dereliction of duty, but the admittedly incomplete evidence suggests that while, as one might expect, bishops came under punishment for heresy and immorality, the most frequent charge was that of the malversation of church property. This is not perhaps so surprising when two factors are taken into consideration. First, some sees were very poor. The bishopric of Ferentis, for instance, possessed only one small vineyard.[43] Second, the malversation often seemed to involve the bishop's family, and this reflects the number of family men who attained episcopal thrones. The emperor Constans I had envisaged a hereditary clerical caste, and there were some eminent episcopal families. There exists a remarkable tombstone from the late fifth century celebrating Bishop Pancratius of Narnia, son of Bishop Pancratius and brother of Bishop Herculius.[44] But the emperor Justinian I had discerned a problem here when he legislated against the alienation of church property to the families of bishops.[45] It was a problem the pope needed to watch carefully, and when Bishop Importunus of Atella bequeathed two-thirds of his property to his daughter-in-law, Gregory I ordered the will checked to see that he was not leaving what was not his own.[46]

There were in Gelasius I's reign two scandalous *causes célèbres* of ecclesiastical discipline, which give a valuable insight into the working of the system under that pope. The first was the Scyllacium case.[47] The Bishop of Scyllacium (unnamed) was murdered during a riot by a church trustee (*creditarius*). The murderer was himself cut down and in the aftermath there was plundering of church property. Archdeacon Asellus, instead of investigating the bishop's death and protecting church property from attack, promptly compelled the clergy to elect him as bishop without informing the pope and without going through the full and proper electoral procedure. Gelasius acted swiftly and firmly. He appointed Bishops John of Vibona and Majoricus of Tempsa as visitors and ordered Asellus to be deprived of office until Gelasius decided what to do with him. The pope subsequently informed the visitors that, since the bishop had been at the centre of all the strife in Scyllacium he would remove the cause by permitting no election for the time being. In other words, there was to be 'a cooling-off period'. John and Majoricus were to remain visitors and were ordered to stamp out the Manichaeanism which had reportedly emerged in the see, further evidence of a disturbed situation there. Subsequently the priest Celestine was convicted of complicity in the bishop's murder and excommunicated for a year. Whether Asellus eventually got his episcopal throne is not known.

The other case involved Bishop Eucharistus of Volaterra, charged by the *defensor* Faustus with the illegal sale and misuse of church property for his own benefit.[48] The pope summoned both Faustus and Eucharistus to the papal court for judgment. But Eucharistus came alone, Faustus being detained by illness. Eucharistus presumably hoped to get his case heard in the absence of his accuser but when this proved impossible, he left again. When his accuser arrived, the pope sent the *defensor* Anastasius to urge Eucharistus to present himself for trial. He refused and was deposed.

But this was only the beginning. The Gothic Count Teias took up the case and wrote to the pope that Faustus had previously been a friend of Eucharistus and had praised him in the past. He also threw doubt on Faustus's credibility by saying that various of Faustus's relatives had been found guilty of a crime. On these grounds, he suggested that Faustus's evidence be disregarded. But the pope replied that someone who knew Eucharistus as well as Faustus had would be well acquainted with his conduct; whatever his relations had done, Faustus was bringing the charge and not them. Teias's suggestion that the pope should remit the case back to the bishops of the province for judgment was therefore rejected by the pope, who upheld the original sentence.

Eucharistus himself now appealed, countering Faustus's charges with the amazing defence that Faustus could not be trusted because Eucharistus had paid him a bribe of 63 *solidi* in order to get the bishopric, despite the fact that his life and conduct made him unworthy of it. Faustus's answer was that the money had been given to him to pay off Eucharistus's election campaign expenses, including bribes to various people. The pope had the accounts checked and the evidence of expert witnesses taken and once again it supported Faustus's version of the events. Eucharistus's appeal was therefore rejected. The archdeacon Justus and the *defensor* Faustus were instructed to recover the property and estates sold or granted away by Eucharistus and to render a full account to the new bishop. The pope subsequently asked the new bishop Elpidius to associate a third colleague with them, so that there should be no suspicion of dishonesty. The whole story reveals a tangled web of corruption and intrigue, through which Gelasius picked his way with wisdom and firmness.

The key to the selection of satisfactory bishops obviously lay in the election. The procedure following the death of a bishop in the suburbicarian see is clearly outlined in papal letters. Notice of an episcopal vacancy was sent to Rome, the metropolitan see. The pope then appointed a visitor, usually a neighbouring bishop, to administer the see, preserve its rights and revenues and provide for a speedy election. The letters of Gregory I are very precise in the standard instructions to visitors.[49] The pope ordered the visitor to arrange an

333

election so that the clergy and people might get together with one consent, choose a bishop who would be worthy of the office and against whom there was no canonical impediment. The bishop elect was then to be despatched to Rome together with the electoral decree testifying to his literacy, countersigned by the visitor, to be ordained by the pope. Elections were supposed to take place within three months of the death of the incumbent bishop.

The actual electorate consisted of clergy, nobles (*ordo*) and people and their vote had to be unanimous. Pope Leo I wrote 'He that is to preside over all must be chosen by all'.[50] But it does not take too much imagination to suspect that the chief clergy and the local nobles fixed things between them in general. The Council of Laodicea indeed went so far as to ordain that 'the mob should not be allowed to make the choice of those to be appointed bishops'.[51] But technically the people still participated in the election.

Officially, then, the election was decided in the local church. But the pope as ordainer of the bishop had considerable legal powers which he could use to influence the choice. He was legally entitled to veto an election on canonical grounds. If a man had a criminal record, if he was illiterate, if he held a government position, if he was a layman, if he had been married twice or if he had married a divorcee, if he was under thirty, then he could not become a bishop. There was a ban on the translation of a bishop from one see to another.

In the event of a deadlock dragging the election beyond three months, the pope was empowered by the canons to choose and ordain a candidate himself. However, what the pope invariably did – and this indicates his full awareness of local sensitivity in the matter – was to summon representatives of the clergy and citizens to Rome and there, in discussion with them, to choose a mutually acceptable candidate. Though more often than not it would be a case of the pope suggesting and the electors agreeing.

What usually happened in cases like this is described in the *Vita S. Zosimi*.[52] When Bishop Peter of Syracuse died about 648, there was a divided election. The *plebs* chose Abbot Zosimus of St Lucia in Syracuse, a man renowned for his good works and love of the poor; the clergy chose the priest Venerius, a 'vain and ambitious man'. The case was referred to Rome and Pope Theodore pronounced in favour of Abbot Zosimus, who was duly ordained.

Another saint's life, *Vita S. Gregorii Agrigentini*, indicates how the pope could use such a split election to interpose a candidate of his own.[53] Bishop Theodore of Agrigentum died probably some time in 589 and there was a disputed election. Rival factions among the clergy supported rival candidates, the priest Sabinus and the deacon Crescentinus. In the circumstances Archdeacon Euplus and the majority of the people suggested referring the matter to the pope. So a delegation of 'selected men of the church and other leading figures' from the diocese sailed to Rome to lay the matter before the pope. Admitted to the papal presence, the delegation was adjured to settle its differences and give a unanimous vote to one of the candidates. However, rioting broke out and the pope ordered the delegates to be removed from his presence. Three days later the pope, 'divinely inspired', sent for the distinguished Eastern churchman and theologian, Gregory, who was currently residing in one of the monasteries in Rome, and appointed him bishop. This sort of papal patronage was probably resorted to quite often under similar circumstances.

So much for the pope's legal powers. What, however, if a man was elected without dispute against whom there was no canonical objection but whom the pope for reasons of state did not want to see in office? There was no legal way of preventing his taking office, and this raised a problem that the pope must seek to obviate at the roots by interference in the electoral process itself.

There were certain important limitations, however, to the making of patronage appointments. The first was the strength of local resentment to outside interference. There are several examples of bishops who came up against this. Archbishop Maximian of Ravenna, an Istrian by birth and a patronage nominee of the emperor Justinian, was locked out of the city and only gained admittance by some judicious greasing of palms with imperial gold.[54] This ingrained hostility to outsiders also underlies the story of St Laurence the Illuminator, a Syrian who, elected bishop of Spoletium by the clergy against the will of the people, only gained admittance to his city by the performance of an opportune miracle, which convinced the sceptical populace of his fitness for office. This is, in fact, a fictional story, a hagiographical account written in the early sixth century, but it undoubtedly reflects the author's knowledge of the potential danger for an outsider elected to an Italian bishopric.[55] Pope Pelagius II was equally aware of the dangers when he appointed Gregory bishop of Agrigentum, which was why he sent another bishop with him to his see to help smooth his passage. Local feeling, then, was a major factor to be reckoned with and required skilled and sensitive handling.

Much more basic, however, was the desperate shortage throughout the period of suitable candidates for all grades of the clergy, from the episcopate down. The three-and-a-half years of war accompanying the Ostrogothic takeover of Italy seriously disrupted the ecclesiastical hierarchy, causing Pope Gelasius I to issue a major *Constitutum*, the details of which have survived in a version sent to the bishops of Lucania, Bruttium and Sicily on 11 March 494.[56] The reason for the promulgation of the *Constitutum* was clearly stated by the pope. It is 'for the restoration of the clergy, which in various parts of Italy has been so consumed by the onset of war and famine that in many churches everywhere there is a lack of clergy'. The source of Gelasius's information on this was archbishop John of Ravenna, whose area of jurisdiction was precisely that most affected by the war. But clearly its consequences, both direct and indirect, had caused serious problems not just in the northern provinces but also in the southern, where the illegal ordination of slaves as clerics testifies to a shortage of suitable candidates.[57]

Although Gelasius said that to meet the crisis there had to be a temporary relaxation of the rules relating to clerical ordination, the *Constitutum* also testifies strongly to Gelasius's overriding desire to stress the maintenance of tradition and to quell all unwelcome innovation. The extent of the personnel crisis is revealed by precept 2 of the *Constitutum*, in which the pope gave permission in the event of a dearth of suitable candidates for both monks and laymen to be ordained. They were to be investigated and, if unmarried, literate, and free of a criminal record, they were to be made lector, *defensor* or notary at once; after three months, acolyte; after six months, subdeacon; after nine months, deacon; and after a year, priest. But this was not intended in any way to relax the high standards expected of candidates for the priesthood. There was an absolute prohibition on the promotion of illiterates (precept 16), women (precept 26), proven criminals (precept 18) and the physically deformed (precept 17). Furthermore, no one was to receive a fugitive from another church and promote him in his own church (precept 23), so that the local nature of clerical recruitment might be preserved. This latter precept was something about which the pope felt very strongly and also stressed in his letters.[58] Certainly stringent safeguards were being proposed, but the fact remains that the church had been overtaken by a serious shortage of suitable candidates for ordination.

The Gothic wars, followed by the lengthy absence of the pope and leading Italian bishops in Constantinople during the 'Three Chapters' controversy, told heavily on clerical personnel too. The Milanese clergy wrote frantically to the Frankish legates in Constantinople at the height of the controversy begging them to persuade Archbishop Datius of Milan to return and ordain new bishops for the province. For during his fifteen-year absence almost all the bishops he had ordained had died and ordinary people were dying unbaptized in droves.[59] The suburbicarian province faced a similar crisis of personnel. Pope Pelagius I, returning from the East to tackle it, lamented 'the defects of our time in which we lack not only meritorious candidates but any candidates at all'.[60] He inaugurated a major restaffing programme but the coming of the Lombards plunged the ecclesiastical hierarchy once more into confusion. Gregory I's own personnel policy was seriously hampered by the lack of suitable promotion material. He wrote sadly to the patrician Venantius of Panormus: 'Your excellency knows that it is difficult for us to send you a priest because the necessity of ordaining priests for other destitute places is in no way diminishing.'[61]

The standard of education of the clergy appears to have been low, as indicated in the seventh century in the *Liber Pontificalis*, which included among the great deeds of Pope Honorius I the fact that 'he educated the clergy.'[62] In spite of Honorius's activity, Pope Agatho still had to write to the emperor Constantine IV in 680 apologizing for the quality of men he was sending as papal envoys to the General Council of the church.[63]

The reasons for the continuing shortage of suitable candidates for the episcopate and even for the priesthood, are linked to the continuous wars, first Gothic and then Lombard, and to the onset of the plague, which took such a heavy toll of the Italian populace. But it should also be noted that reluctance to stand for election, which according to papal directives had to be respected, might also be an important reason for the manpower shortage. Such reluctance is not hard to understand. The life of a bishop in the Dark Ages was not at all a bed of roses. There are many gruesome examples of the sticky ends met by the episcopate of Italy. For instance, Bishop Herculanus of Perusia was beheaded and flayed by the Gothic king Totila.[64] Bishop Valentine of Silva Candida had his hands cut off by the same man.[65] Bishop Cethegus of Amiternum was executed by the Lombards for treason, after ladders were discovered leaning against the city walls near the episcopal palace during an attack by imperial troops.[66] Bishop John of Spoletium was murdered by drunken Gothic soldiers.[67] Bishops Alexander of Faesulae and Gerontius of Ficuclae were murdered by highwaymen.[68] The Gelasian bishop of Squillace was murdered by members of his own clergy during a riot.[69] Bishop Callistus of Tuder was murdered by members of his own congregation whose immoral lives he had denounced in a sermon.[70] The bishop of Tibur during the Gothic wars was slaughtered in a manner too horrible for even Procopius to repeat.[71] The elderly bishop Sabinus of Canusium narrowly avoided being poisoned by his archdeacon who was tired of waiting for him to die and wanted to expedite his own succession to the see.[72] So the difficult task of selecting suitable men for bishoprics was rendered doubly difficult by the reluctance of candidates to stand.

It is undoubtedly this situation which led to a relaxation in the rules about the ordination of monks and laymen as bishops. Initially neither were eligible for the episcopate. Successive popes and church councils had banned the election of laymen. Gregory I repeated the ban. Yet driven by necessity, popes can be found approving lay candidates on several occasions. Archbishop Sergius of Ravenna in the early eighth century was a layman and a married man.[73] Bishop Redux of Naples, ordained by Pope Pelagius II, was a layman.[74] Even Gregory I himself was prepared to countenance the election of the layman Oportunus as Bishop of Aprutium.[75]

Lay candidates, however, remained comparatively rare. Not so monkish candidates. In the late fourth century Pope Siricius had relaxed the ban on them by permitting their ordination to the priesthood if they had reached the age of thirty but not permitting them to be elected directly to the episcopate.[76] But by the end of the fifth century Pope Gelasius was forced to allow it in the event of shortage of any other suitable candidates.[77] Gregory I's election to the papacy effectively killed the ban, and his personnel policy provided a powerful fillip to monkish elections. There had already been monkish bishops before Gregory. Eulalius of Syracuse,[78] Herculanus of Perusia,[79] Gregory of Agrigentum[80] and an unnamed bishop of Ancona are known sixth century examples.[81] But Gregory actively promoted them as a principle. Despite this, the election of clerical candidates to the episcopate remained the norm, as evidenced by the *Liber Diurnus*, which accepts a deacon as the usual grade of candidate.[82]

It is worth noting finally that there was practically no imperial interference in episcopal elections. The only known example is the appointment of Archbishop Maximian of Ravenna by the emperor Justinian in 546.[83] There may have been an imperial hand in the election of Bishop Laurentius of Sipontum, allegedly chosen by the Emperor Zeno,[84] and the appearance of a Byzantine hymnographer George as Bishop of Syracuse during the sojourn there of Emperor Constans II[85] suggests imperial intervention, but the evidence in both cases is fragile and cannot be pushed very far.

Chapter 20

Gregory the Great and the Episcopate

The Principles of the Gregorian Personnel Policy

The most coherent policy of patronage and personnel management emerges from the Register of Gregory the Great, the most complete set of papal letters surviving from the period. Gregory's policy assumed a distinct pattern and possessed the sort of coherence one might expect from someone with his background in both secular and ecclesiastical administration. It is important to stress that the policy stemmed not from an ideological desire to dominate the episcopate but from a pressing practical need to ensure good government, for which, as a good Roman of the old school, he saw a need to organize. It was not for nothing that his epitaph called him the 'Consul of God', a title that he would have been the first to appreciate.

Gregory constantly stressed in his correspondence, particularly on elections, the need to secure good men in bishoprics. But what constituted for Gregory an ideal bishop? On this the evidence is conflicting both in principle and practice, a conflict which perhaps reflects the battle within Gregory between monastic withdrawal and administrative involvement.

His standard visitation letters contain the interesting order 'that no one from another church shall be allowed to be elected unless no one can be found among the clergy of the church under visitation, which we do not believe likely'.[1] This affirms a desire to maintain the local character of the episcopate and one which conflicts directly with the idea of nominating known Roman clerics to key bishoprics. This principle is important to bear in mind when looking at the detailed working of the Gregorian programme.

Gregory has in fact left a whole book on his ideal bishop – the *Liber Regulae Pastoralis* – in which he paints a characteristic picture of the sort of bishop he envisaged. It was highly influential during the Middle Ages, particularly in Gaul and Britain. But while it might express an ideal, it is not a realistic guide to the practice. The paragon Gregory sought can be deduced from a typical extract:

> He ought by all means to be drawn to become an example of right living, he who, dead to all fleshly passions, already lives spiritually; who disregards worldly prosperity; who fears no adversity; who desires only spiritual things; whose intention thus well known the body does not oppose by weakness nor the spirit by disdain; who is not led to covet the goods of others but gives freely of his own; one who through the bowels of compassion is moved to grant pardon but is never plucked from the citadel of righteousness by pardoning more than is fitting; who perpetrates no illicit deeds but deplores those perpetrated by others as if they were his own; who out of heartfelt feeling sympathizes with another's infirmity, and rejoices in another's good fortune as if it were his own; who so suggests himself to others as an example in all that he does, that he has nothing to blush for in his own past deeds; who studies so to live that he may be able to water even the dried-up hearts with streams of the faith; who has already learned by the use and practice of prayer that he can obtain what he has requested from the Lord.[2]

He goes on to say that someone of great gifts should not allow selfish love of quiet to hinder exercising them in the public interest, that a ruler must be pure in thought, totally unbiased and ruled by reason, that he should at all times preserve humility and that he should show himself to his people 'as a mother in piety and as a father in discipline'.[3]

It clearly emerges from Gregory's meditation on his own office, so reluctantly assumed, that the care of souls, teaching and preaching both actively and by example of life are the keynotes of the bishop's life and it was this he stressed in his letters of encouragement to other newly ordained bishops, such as Constantius of Milan.[4]

It is evident that Gregory's thinking on episcopal character was much in line with his thinking on personnel policy in the central administration. The spirituality, humility and pastorality of the ideal bishop, devoted to teaching, preaching and meditation, reflects the sort of life he himself led with his monastic establishment in the Lateran. But it was at odds with the needs of the day in terms of practical administrative experience. In fact, a much shorter and pithier phrase from one of his letters sums up the attitude of *realpolitik* which determined his dealings with, for instance, elections in the major provincial capitals. He wrote:

You know that at this time such a one ought to be constituted in the citadel of government who knows not only how to be solicitous for the safety of souls but also for the external advantage and security of his subjects.[5]

It is on the basis of this maxim that Gregory rejected as a possible bishop of Syracuse Trajan, a man who amply fulfilled the ideal of the *Regula Pastoralis* but lacked the requisite administrative experience for a senior see in the dark days of the late sixth century. His policy in practice, therefore, is seen sometimes to stray from the glowing idealism of the book into the realistic demands of practical government.

Gregory's personnel operations took three forms, all of them eminently practical under the circumstances: the union of sees, the utilization of existing personnel and above all, interference in elections. The union of sees was an obvious expedient, to husband resources and preserve valuable manpower. It was frequently done, expecially on the frontier where town populations decreased dramatically in the face of continual Lombard attack.[6] In those provinces particularly ravaged by the Lombards, Gregory was compelled to create semi-vicarial posts, grouping several sees under a single bishop, for instance the Lucanian coast under the bishop of Acropolis and imperial Apulia under the bishop of Sipontum.[7] He was also quick to utilize the talents of refugee bishops, who would otherwise have been unemployed, appointing the Dacian bishop John of Lissus to the see of Scyllacium in Bruttium and Agnellus of Fundi to neighbouring Terracina.[8]

But perhaps the most interesting aspect of his policy is his electoral activity. Unfortunately, lack of space prevents my discussing in detail his patronage operations on the mainland. I shall, however, examine them in detail in my forthcoming biography of Pope Gregory the Great. For the moment, I must be content to summarize in brief and let Sicily stand as a detailed case study.

We are fortunate in possessing, thanks to John the deacon, what is in effect a disguised patronage list.[9] John writes: 'He took care to ordain as bishops the best men wherever he could find them' and adds that from the Roman priesthood, he ordained Boniface as bishop of Rhegium, Donus as bishop of Messana and Habentius as bishop of Perusia; from the Roman subdeacons, he ordained Gloriosus as bishop of Ostia, Festus as bishop of Capua, Peter as bishop of Triocala and Castorius as bishop of Ariminum; and from the monks of his own monastery, he ordained Marinianus as bishop of Ravenna, Maximian as bishop of Syracuse and Sabinus as bishop of Callipolis. What is interesting about this list is not just that it is a unique record of papal patronage, indicating the three sources on which Gregory drew for bishops, but that, with the exceptions of Messana and Triocala, Sicilian sees for which special circumstances will be argued, the other sees are all important cities and, in several cases, provincial capitals. The consistency certainly seems to imply the implementation of a carefully thought-out plan and the details of some of the patronage operations are recoverable from the Gregorian Register. But the effects of the nominations were far from what he must have hoped. The bishops of Capua and Rhegium became embroiled in bitter arguments with their clergies and the bishop of Ariminum was driven insane by the hostility of his flock and forced to resign.[10] Gregory wrote angrily to the Ariminates to denounce the *inquietudo* and *tribulatio* which had brought Castorius to this sad end.[11]

Gregory's greatest patronage coup, however, was on the whole successful and that was the installation of a handpicked nominee in the see of Ravenna, Rome's greatest rival in the Italian hierarchy. The incumbent archbishop at the time of Gregory's elevation was John III, himself a Roman and probably the result of some earlier papal patronage operation. Initially he was on excellent terms with Gregory but relations between them soured as a result of the *pallium* dispute, discussed earlier, and when John died early in 595, Gregory acted decisively to fill the vacancy. The papal nuncio in Ravenna chose a delegation of Ravennate electors, the pope vetoed the candidate favoured by the exarch and produced from his monastery of St Andreas the monk Marinianus, whom he had known for years and who had the added advantage of being the nephew of the late archbishop John. There was initial opposition to the appointment, but this gradually subsided and Marinianus was eventually accepted as archbishop of Ravenna.[12]

Gregory the Great and the Sicilian Episcopate

For a perfect case study in detail of Gregory's policy of episcopal personnel management we have only to turn to Sicily. Sicily presents several features of interest. Throughout his reign, Gregory showed particular interest in Sicily, as more than 200 of the surviving letters attest. The reasons for this are fairly obvious. Rich in fruit, grain and manpower, Sicily was the site of the wealthiest and probably the largest block of papal estates. It was the furthest of the Suburbicarian provinces from Rome and was governed, as a separate province, by a governor, called a *praetor* in the sixth century and in the seventh century a *strategus*. Resident in Syracuse, he was directly responsible to the emperor in Constantinople and not to the exarch in Ravenna.

It was the largest single unit free of Lombard control and as such ripe for papal intervention.

Gregory was consecrated as pope on 3 September 590 and it is significant that his first recorded letter, dated that same month, was to the bishops of Sicily.[13] First, it announced that the Roman sub-deacon Peter had been appointed rector of the Sicilian patrimony. It was not unusual for a new pope to replace his predecessor's rectors. Second, it announced that Peter had been appointed vicar. This is most important, for it is the only occasion in the entire Register when a man of such low rank receives this exalted honour. It was conferred on the bishops of Prima Justiniana, Arelate and Syracuse.[14] But here the honour went to a mere subdeacon. But this was not just any subdeacon. For Peter was one of Gregory's closest friends and advisers, the man he represented as his interlocutor in the *Dialogi*, whom he subsequently raised to the diaconate and who, after Gregory's death, during the wave of anti-Gregorian feeling which swept Rome, defended Gregory's memory in the face of a hostile, book-burning mob. Third, Gregory released the Sicilian bishops from the obligation of journeying annually to Rome, the metropolitan see, by authorizing their own annual provincial synod, presided over by his personal representative, the Vicar. This was partly a mark of Gregory's confidence in Peter, but also partly a reflection of the delicate political situation. Later letters reveal that the Sicilian praetor had been attempting to prevent the bishops leaving Sicily for the Roman synod and Gregory's actions were clearly in part dictated by the desire to avoid a head-on clash with the secular authorities. But Gregory was fully aware that the vicarial appointment was unusual and likely to cause resentment among senior bishops, unaccustomed to being presided over by a mere subdeacon. There was therefore a stern injunction: 'From this council let hatreds, the nourishment of crimes, be absent and let internal jealousies and discord of spirits, which is most dreadful, melt away.'

So Gregory's first step was to appoint an utterly loyal and trust-worthy friend as both rector and vicar of Sicily, thus giving him direct power not only over the papal estates but also over the persons of the bishops and clergy themselves. With regard to the latter power, Gregory gave Peter an explicit directive about his task in January 591,[15] informing him that if any Sicilian cities were without pastoral care because their bishops had been deposed for misconduct, he should seek their successors from amongst the clergy and the monasteries and send them to Rome for ordination. He adds:

But if you should find any vacant places and there is no one from that church fitted for such an honour, inform us after careful enquiry so that God may provide someone whom he has judged worthy of such ordinations.

In other words, Gregory was declaring his willingness to intervene in episcopal elections, when it was necessary to replace lapsed bishops.

There were thirteen attested sees in existence in Sicily at Gregory's accession: Syracuse, Catana, Panormus, Messana, Agrigentum, Tyndaris, Lipara, Lilybaeum, Melita, Tauromenium, Triocala, Leontini and Carina. Probably vacant in 591 were Syracuse, Tauromenium, Carina and perhaps Lipara; certainly not vacant were Panormus, Catana, Agrigentum, Melita, Messana and probably not Triocala. There is no evidence on Leontini, Tyndaris or Lilybaeum. Of these sees unquestionably the most important was Syracuse, the seat of the governor and the rector, the administrative capital of the island and the oldest episcopal foundation. It was therefore vital as a first step in any episcopal personnel policy that a reliable bishop of Syracuse be secured.

The first mention of a bishop of Syracuse occurs in a letter dated October 591 and addressed to bishop Maximian of Syracuse.[16] It conferred on him the apostolic vicariate, with two major limitations – the reservation to the pope of all major cases and the granting of the office to Maximian personally and not to his see in perpetuity. The job was conferred on Maximian because Gregory knew and trusted him, but would not necessarily know and/or trust his successor. If this is the case, why had not Maximian been made vicar in 590? The answer must be that he was not in office then and this is borne out by the facts of Maximian's career.

Maximian had been a monk serving with Gregory in Gregory's own foundation, St Andreas *ad clivum Scauri* in Rome.[17] When Gregory was withdrawn from his monastic quiet and sent to Constantinople as a deacon and papal *apocrisiarios*, Maximian went with him. He was recalled in October 584 by Pelagius II to become abbot of St Andreas.[18] He was still abbot when Gregory was elected pope, and is listed by John the deacon among Gregory's closest friends and advisers and among his episcopal nominees.[19] He was someone who perfectly balanced the contrary needs underlying the personnel policy – the personal qualities of dedication and spirituality from his monkish vocation and the necessary administrative know-how from his abbatial experience.

It is not unlikely that the grant of the vicariate followed soon after his election, which probably took place some time in mid-591. With the appearance on the scene of a reliable bishop of Syracuse, Peter's job was done. First, he unloaded the vicariate – in October 591 –

clearly conferred on him initially as an emergency measure, and second, in July 592 he was recalled to Rome, and his rectorship ended.[20] What had happened is that one close and trusted friend, Peter, had been replaced by another, Maximian, who by becoming bishop of the senior Sicilian see, would be able to manage the Sicilian episcopate for Gregory, much more unobtrusively and uncontroversially than the papal rector could.

All the evidence points to the first successful Gregorian intervention in an election. The absence of any mention of a Syracusan bishop before the appearance of Maximian in the Gregorian Register, in October 591, suggests the possibility of a long vacancy and perhaps a disputed election. There had been a vacancy of seven months between the death of Pelagius II and Gregory's consecration, during which time there was no one to ordain a new bishop for Syracuse. There would be ample time for feelings to run high in the Sicilian capital. It is probable, then, that the deadlock over the choice of a new bishop led to the matter being referred to Rome and the choice by Gregory 'in consultation with representatives of the Syracusan electorate' of a suitable candidate. In fact, Gregory must have certainly hand-picked the abbot of his old monastery and his long-time companion and friend to be the cornerstone of his episcopal policy in Sicily.

After Syracuse, the three most important sees were Panormus, Catana and Agrigentum. All three had incumbent bishops at the time of Gregory's accession: Victor in Panormus, Leo in Catana and Gregory in Agrigentum. In August 591 Gregory informed the rector Peter that, since their suit with the praetor Justin prevented them from leaving the island, the bishops were not to be compelled to come to Rome for the annual St Peter's Day synod.[21] However, three bishops were specifically excluded from this exemption – Gregory, Victor and Leo. They were ordered to Rome before the winter. The reason soon emerged. Two of them were wanted for trial.

Of the charges against Leo we learn nothing except that they were disproved.[22] The case of Gregory of Agrigentum was more prolonged. The pope wrote to Maximian of Syracuse in November 592, ordering him to send to Rome at once the accusers, documents and petitions in the case, and complaining that he had written already, asking for them, without result.[23] The reason for Victor's summons comes in a letter dated April 593.[24] It would seem from this letter that reports of widespread misbehaviour by the inhabitants of Panormus had reached Rome, bespeaking dereliction of his pastoral duties by bishop Victor and that Gregory had ordered him to undertake a city-wide clean-up campaign. The evidence suggests that the campaign began on the return of Victor from Rome where he had been summoned for a stiff lecture on his duties and the advice that he should take steps to suppress the evil-doing in his city.

It cannot be pure coincidence that the three leading Sicilian bishops after Syracuse were summoned to Rome within a year of the accession of the new pope, two for trial and the third, as I have suggested, for a pep talk. It is not unlikely that the occasion for the charges against Leo and Gregory was the very fact of a change in the occupant of the throne of St Peter, a change which detractors of the two bishops sought to utilize to obtain revenge on them for some wrong, real or imagined. The attempts failed. Leo was acquitted swiftly, Gregory's acquittal took longer but came eventually. But the importance as far as the pope was concerned was that these two trials and the disorder in Panormus gave him just the excuse he needed to get these three prelates to Rome and examine them at close quarters over a long period, to ginger them up with advice and instruction and form estimates of their characters and capabilities, which he would need when planning any personnel arrangements for the island.

While Leo and Gregory were acquitted, two other Sicilian bishops were not so fortunate. The bishops of Triocala and Lipara were deposed. In July 593 the pope wrote to Maximian of Syracuse, ordering him to see that the church of Lipara provide 50 *solidi* for the sustenance of Agatho, 'their former bishop', who had been deposed for his crimes.[25] Since he had received the prescribed canon punishment, the pope thought it only common humanity for him to be given enough to live on. That Agatho had been deposed for these unspecified crimes within Gregory's pontificate is indicated by earlier correspondence on the subject of the Liparitan see.

In March 591 Gregory ordered the rector Peter to collect together the monks of bishop Paulinus of Tauriana, who were wandering about Sicily as refugees since the sack of Tauriana by the Lombards in the previous year.[26] He was then to install them in the monastery of St Theodore at Messana. This establishment being conveniently in need of an abbot, the same Bishop Paulinus was to be appointed as its abbot.

Then, in February 592, Gregory announced to Paulinus his appointment as bishop of Lipara, ordering him to reside in that see but visit Tauriana whenever he deemed it necessary.[27] At the same time Gregory ordered Maximian of Syracuse to see Paulinus installed in Lipara without delay and to see that the clergy of Lipara were obedient to him.[28] The previous bishop must have been that same Agatho who by July 593 was in financial difficulties, and it seems likely, therefore, that the deposition occurred some time between March 591 and February 592. The deposition of a bishop was a very serious matter and the pope probably considered that the choice of a successor was too important to be left to the electors. Clearly someone of proven ability and beyond personal reproach was needed to correct the impression left by the ex-bishop. In the event the man Gregory chose appears to be admirably qualified for the task on hand. He had administrative experience as bishop of Tauriana in Bruttium and abbot of St Theodore in Messana. Reference to his monks and the very fact of his appointment as abbot suggest a monkish origin and the likelihood that, as bishop, he continued to live in community with his monks, as Gregory himself did. This background would be the strongest possible recommendation as far as Gregory was concerned. The simple, austere communal life, the devotion to prayer and meditation which this background implies would make him the ideal person to restore the tarnished image of the episcopate, while his administrative experience would enable him to carry out his duties efficiently.

It should be pointed out that Paulinus's appointment to Lipara, while still bishop of Tauriana, did not contravene the canonical prohibition of the translation of bishops. For technically, Tauriana and Lipara were being temporarily united in Paulinus's person and he retained all his rights over Tauriana while being resident in Lipara. Tauriana was almost certainly derelict following the Lombard attack but Lipara was separated from it only by a short sea voyage and so it could be visited when necessary.

The uniting of the sees was effected by Gregory himself through the exercise of the papal prerogative (*ex nostra auctoritate*), thus obviating the need for an election. The apostolic vicar was brought into play to secure his peaceful acceptance and Gregory's own rule about local men being elected once more went by the board. Agatho's deposition, probably occurring late in 591, makes it likely that he was the first victim of the episcopal overhaul begun by Peter and now in the hands of Maximian.

Agatho was not the only bishop to fall by the wayside. In July 593 Gregory wrote to bishop Theodore of Lilybaeum, who, it is clear, was undertaking the visitation of some unnamed see.[29] He praised him for his efforts to date and urged him to press on with his investigations, reporting all his findings to Maximian. The ex-bishop Paul was to remain in the monastery to which he had been consigned for penance.

Bishop Paul was another victim of the Gregorian purge. His crimes appear to have been embezzlement of church property and dereliction of his duties. But what was his see? Of the thirteen attested sees in 593, ten are accounted for, having incumbent bishops, and Carina is derelict. That leaves two. Leontini and

Triocala. Bearing in mind that visitation normally went to a neighbouring see, Leontini is ruled out, being on the opposite side of the island from Lilybaeum. The see must therefore have been Triocala, which was quite close to Lilybaeum.

In November 594 Gregory wrote to a bishop Peter of Triocala to inform him that he was to be paid for acting as visitor of Agrigentum.[30] Peter was another Gregorian nominee. John the deacon includes him in his patronage list as a Roman subdeacon who became bishop of Triocala.[31] Since, as has been argued, Triocala was under visitation in July 593, following the deposition of bishop Paul, it must have been some time between then and November 594 that Peter was elected to succeed him.

His very origins betray the circumstances of his appointment. The ex-bishop had demeaned his office and neglected his duty, and so the same conditions as in Lipara apply. Peter, as a subdeacon and probably the ex-rector of Campania, would be familiar with administration and his character would be known to the pope. Whether a stage-managed election in Triocala or direct suggestion by the pope in Rome was involved, there can be no doubt that Peter was Gregory's man.

His appointment as visitor of Agrigentum shows that Gregory of Agrigentum was still absent and that his absence had now been so prolonged that a substitute was needed. Who better than the Gregorian loyalist peacefully ensconced in nearby Triocala? How long the visitation lasted is not known. But that Gregory was ultimately cleared and did return to Agrigentum is apparent from the next explicit reference to him in January 603 when, as a matter of routine, the new Syracusan rector was commended to him.[32] We can safely assume that the deposition of Paul of Triocala occurred early in 593, making him the second known victim of the Gregorian purge in Sicily and creating the second opening for a papal nominee.

The fourth Gregorian patronage appointment occurred in Messana. The incumbent bishop of Messana on Gregory's accession was Felix, who appears from the evidence to be a bad lot, at the very least an opportunist and probably worse. In 591 he wrote asking the pope for permission to reduce his clergy's salary, backing up his request with a costly gift of robes.[33] Gregory forbade it and, regarding the gift as a bribe, returned its value in cash. It was a typical attempt to put something over on a new pope.

Felix died in 595 and in September of that year Gregory conceded the *pallium* to his successor Donus.[34] John the deacon lists him as another of the Gregorian nominees, drawn this time from among the priests of Rome.[35] John's statement is confirmed by the synodical decrees of 5 July 595, among the signatories to which is listed Donus, priest of the church of St Eusebius.[36] Gregory's dissatisfaction with Felix and the state of affairs in Messana had prompted another intervention, perhaps after a disputed election.

The bishop of Tauromenium during the reign was Secundinus. He first appears in August 591 when Gregory ordered Peter the rector to restore to him the house, lands and goods, seized by officers of the Roman patrimony but rightfully belonging to the church of Tauromenium.[37] He also ordered him to meet with Secundinus and discuss how certain monies lost during the time of his predecessor, bishop Victorinus, could be recovered in the best interests of the church.

This letter strongly suggests a recent vacancy in Tauromenium, exploited by overzealous officers of the patrimony. This impression is reinforced by the subscription list of the 595 Roman synod.[38] Every indication points to the fact that the bishops signed in order of seniority; Secundinus signed after Candidus of Vulsinum, who became bishop sometime between December 590 and October 591 and before Homobonus who was ordained as bishop of Albanum in 592.

The evidence also points to the probability that Secundinus was a friend of Gregory. For Secundinus was the only Sicilian bishop present at the 595 synod. It was to Secundinus that Gregory sent two books of his *Homilies* for correction and comment,[39] while, throughout the reign, Gregory entrusted him with important investigations and arbitrations, an indication of the faith he placed in his judgment.[40]

But beyond this point we cannot go. John the deacon does not mention him among the list of Gregorian friends and nominees. The Register is silent on the circumstances of his election. He seems to have been elected in 591 and to have been a friend of Gregory. There the evidence stops but arguing by analogy, there must be a suspicion here of a Gregorian intervention, which must remain unproven.

The remaining bishops of Sicily appear to have been satisfactory for the moment. They were Theodore of Lilybaeum, praised for his energy and vigilance as visitor of Triocala;[41] Eutychius of Tyndaris, encouraged in his efforts to convert the pagans and heretics in his diocese;[42] Zeno of Leontini;[43] and Lucillus of Melita, who was ordered to see that those of his clerics who held possessions of the African church paid their rent, which they had been refusing to do.[44]

But the entire carefully built-up structure was threatened when its pivotal agent, Maximian of Syracuse, died suddenly in November 594.[45] It was a bitter blow to Gregory, both personally and politically. For he had been an old friend and he had implemented the Gregorian episcopal policy with great efficiency. We know that he was charged with installing Paulinus of Lipara[46] and it must also have fallen to him to smooth the passage of the other outsiders in their early days. Though it is never stated, he probably presided – in his capacity as vicar – over the trials of Agatho and Paul. We know that Gregory made Theodore the visitor of Triocala, responsible to Maximian.[47] He undertook investigations and arbitrations and was directly responsible for the maintenance of discipline among the bishops. He must have taken much of the burden from Gregory's shoulders in the matter of Sicilian ecclesiastical affairs, which was of course the reason for his appointment. At the time of his death he was engaged in a campaign against clerics who were castrating themselves in imitation of Origen.[48]

Unless Gregory's hold over the ecclesiastical organization of the island was to be lost, it was vital that he secure an acceptable bishop of Syracuse. We are fortunate in possessing an extremely revealing series of letters on the subject of this election. It may well have been letters on this pattern, now lost, that furnished John the deacon with his episcopal patronage list.

The first was to Cyprian the rector and is dated February 595.[49] After expressing his regret over Maximian's death, he got down to the important business of the election. He urged him to see that a worthy successor to the late, lamented bishop was elected:

> And indeed I believe that the majority would choose the priest Trajan, who, as is said, is of a good disposition but, as I suspect, not fit to rule in that place. Yet if a better cannot be found and if there is no charge against him, compelled by extreme necessity it can be yielded to him. But if my will in this election is sought, I indicate secretly to you what I wish: it seems to me that there is no one in that church so worthy to follow the lord Maximian as John, archdeacon of Catana. If his election can be brought about, I believe that he will be found an extremely suitable person.

So, despite his good disposition and his popularity with the majority of the electors, Gregory did not propose to allow Trajan to become bishop. He lacked the requisite qualities for governing a great see. The pope did not say what these were but they surely included being known to and trusted by the pope. Cyprian was asked by Gregory to arrange with Bishop Leo of Catana for John to stand in the election, and to carry out Gregory's wishes regarding him.

The moral of this letter is quite clear and it underlies the whole field of patronage operations. Whatever the will of the majority may be, the interests of the church as discerned by Gregory must be served first. There can be very little doubt about his active concern with and involvement in elections after this.

Unfortunately this election did not go smoothly. The next letter on the matter, dated July 595, reveals this.[50] Gregory wrote to the nobles of Syracuse, praising their decision to opt out of the election process and leave the choice of bishop to Gregory. The letter also reveals that the clergy and people of Syracuse had nominated for bishop a certain Agatho and certain others, another nominee unnamed. Gregory ordered that both candidates be sent to Rome so that he might decide between them.

Reading between the lines, the story unfolds as follows. On Maximian's death, there was a large measure of support for the priest Trajan. This was undermined, probably as a result of the activities of the rector Cyprian in privately communicating the pope's wishes to certain influential people. The nobles agreed to support whomever Gregory should choose. The clergy and people, two-thirds of the voting body, now transferred their support to Agatho, almost certainly another local cleric. They had perhaps accepted the disqualification of Trajan but, still preferring a Syracusan to a Catanian, had settled on another local man Agatho, who they hoped would be more acceptable to the pope.

The pope, however, wants Archdeacon John of Catana and he is almost certainly the unnamed candidate, supported by the minority of the electorate, a group mobilized undoubtedly by the papal rector. There seems to have been a straight split between the nobles, who understood and supported the papal need to choose the right man for this key position, and the majority of the clergy and people whose natural sentiment was to favour a local man.

However, once the case was withdrawn to Rome for arbitration, the result was a foregone conclusion, and by October 595 John was installed as bishop of Syracuse.[51] It seems likely that Gregory knew him personally, for to put someone he did not know into this key position would have been asking for trouble.[52] The most obvious opportunity for a meeting would be if John accompanied Bishop Leo to Rome for his trial in 591 and in Rome favourably impressed the pope. The important fact is that Gregory wanted him and he got him, despite majority local support for two successive non-Gregorian candidates. In this context it is worth mentioning that it was about this time that the priest Donus was sent down from Rome as bishop of Messana. It might be that, given the amount of support for rival candidates to John in Syracuse, Gregory had seen fit to strengthen his hand on the Sicilian episcopal bench and with it the committed support and backing for John by the introduction of another loyalist.

The election of John to Syracuse more or less brings to a close the first phase of Gregory's personnel policy in Sicily. The final seal is set on this by the letter, dated May 597, in which Gregory conceded that the Sicilian bishops needed to come to Rome in future not every three but every five years on the anniversary of St Peter.[53] This concession could not have been made had Gregory not felt strong enough and confident enough to leave the day-to-day running of affairs in Sicily to his handpicked bishop of Syracuse, who had now had two years to establish himself.

A glance at the Gregorian achievement during the period 591–5 reveals clearly enough why he should feel this confidence. When he came to the throne, the Sicilian episcopate was to him an entirely unknown quantity. He had no personal representatives on the episcopal bench and few, if any, friends. In this situation, there was nothing for it but an emergency measure. He despatched to the island as rector and vicar one of his closest friends and advisers, the subdeacon Peter. Gregory's greatest coup was the appointment of two successive bishops of Syracuse, first Maximian and then John, who were able to replace the rector as the operator of papal personnel policy on the high level. The arrival of the new bishop, together with his vicariate, meant that episcopal policy could now be left to him.

From the existing episcopal bench, three bishops, Leo of Catana, Gregory of Agrigentum and Victor of Panormus, were summoned to Rome and kept there for some time in 591, the first two for trial, the third for a lecture on his duties. Two more, Agatho of Lipara and Paul of Triocala, were deposed and two more still, Felix of Messana and Lucillus of Melita, were threatened with canon punishment unless they kept up to scratch. Of those left Tyndaris and Leontini were of minor importance and rarely mentioned and Lilybaeum was apparently satisfactory.

By 595, then, the Sicilian bench had been completely Gregorianized. Gregorian nominees ruled in Syracuse, Messana, Lipara, Triocala (with lengthy visitation in Agrigentum) and just possibly in Tauromenium. Catana and Panormus had been vetted at close quarters, Melita was under observation and the rest stood. This is a major achievement and one which had been managed with subtlety, skill and a great measure of success.

Phase two of Gregorian policy was rather less active than phase one. The hierarchy had been successfully remoulded and the policy from 595 on was one of maintaining the new system and upholding discipline, with changes in the episcopal structure dealt with individually as they arose.

The key man in the operation of this policy was, of course, John of Syracuse. There is no specific mention in the Register of the grant of the vicariate to John but it is likely that he received it, in view of the extended interval between visits of the Sicilian bishops to Rome and the extensive judicial activity in which John was involved.

In the management of the episcopal bench, John had less to do than his predecessor. The absence of any mention of further bishops of Triocala and Messana suggests that the two Gregorian nominees, Peter and Donus, outlived their patron. Paulinus of Lipara did not survive. His death in 602 brought to an end the temporary unification of Tauriana and Lipara.[54] There is no mention of a successor in the surviving papal correspondence.

Of the three old stagers, Leo, Gregory and Victor, the first two probably outlived the pope. Leo of Catana had a rather chequered career. He seems to have been something less than satisfactory and the Register is regularly punctuated with letters reprimanding his remissness.[55] There was indeed a second investigation of his conduct, undertaken by the papal rector Romanus in 598, as a result of charges laid by the imperial inspector-general, ex-consul Leontius.[56] But Leo survived this just as he had survived his trial in Rome.[57] The picture of him that emerges is of an easy-going, rather too good-natured prelate, who needed periodic promptings to keep him up to the mark. There can, however, be little doubt that if there had been anything seriously wrong with his government, he would have been deposed as other miscreants had been.

While Leo and Gregory survived the pope, Victor of Panormus did not. He died some time in 602, for in the November of that year Bishop Barbarus of Carina was appointed visitor and ordered to arrange for an immediate election.[58]

What followed is revealed in a letter from Gregory to the patrician Venantius, dated November 602.[59] Gregory began by saying that he was delighted by the news that Venantius had nominated for bishop, Urbicus, abbot of St Hermes in Panormus. But he added:

> Because someone else is proposed by the rest, we cannot disturb his quiet so that while he advances externally, he shall decline internally, lest when we promote him to higher things, we compel him to a life of turbulence.

This has been quoted as an example of Gregory's solicitude for people – an unwillingness to withdraw Urbicus from his monastic quiet and plunge him into the cares of office.[60] But there is perhaps more to it than that.

Urbicus was a Gregorian *par excellence*. He was the abbot of one of the monasteries founded by Gregory on his Sicilian family estates and had been entrusted with several important jobs in the past by the pope.[61] He certainly fulfilled the requirements of administrative experience and being known to and trusted by Gregory. In addition, he seems to have been a native Sicilian.[62]

Venantius seems to be acting as the head of the pro-papal faction in the electorate, probably drawn from the *nobiles* – on the analogy of Syracuse. He emerges as a devout layman and trusted friend of the papacy.[63] It may well be that Venantius, who knew Urbicus well and had served on commissions of enquiry with him, believed him to be the best man for the job. But the involvement of Gregory in such detail suggests that he may have been acting for the pope in the matter. Who better than this respected local notable to arrange the election of a Gregorian?

Finally, the reference to Urbicus being disturbed by *fluctus* if he were elected should be looked at in the context of the unhappy outcome of other Gregorian patronage appointments. Three notable cases, Castorius of Ariminum, Festus of Capua and Boniface of Rhegium, stand out. All three had experienced the utmost difficulty in gaining acceptance from their own clergy and in the case of Castorius, the experiment ended in dismal failure. It was precisely this that Gregory sought to avoid and which prompted his suggestion that the candidacy of Urbicus be dropped.

The other candidate, clearly a majority choice, was the deacon Crescens. He was almost certainly a local man and, with the aristocracy favouring Urbicus, the clergy and people were the likely electors. Since he did not know the man, Gregory asked Venantius to investigate the character and qualifications of Crescens, in particular the running of the *xenodochium* of which he had charge. If the investigation proved that he was satisfactory, then Venantius was to see to it that the election became unanimous, i.e. that he swung his own, pro-Urbicus party behind Crescens. If, however, he proved unsatisfactory, then Venantius was to get the electorate to nominate an alternative to be sent with Crescens to Rome to enable the pope to choose between them. If, on the other hand, there was no viable alternative in Panormus – and for once the pope did not say that he thought this unlikely – then he was to see to the nomination of the alternative from another church. If all else failed and no fit person was to be found in Panormus or elsewhere, then the electors were to choose representatives, empowered to decide in their name, and send them to Rome to see if they could find some suitable candidate there.

The pope seemed genuinely reluctant to involve himself here, for reasons already suggested. He seemed to be laying down a purely disinterested procedure. But this disinterest is belied by the choice of Venantius as investigator of the character of the prospective bishop. In nearly all the other recorded cases, the visiting bishop did this. But of Barbarus the visitor there is no mention in these proceedings.

Instead of the presumably impartial visiting bishop, Gregory entrusted the evaluation of the rival candidate to the leader of one of the factions in the election.

The pope's involvement in the election is further expressed in the instruction to Venantius that he ask of the messengers who took his letter to Rome what they had discussed with the pope in detail. From the juxtaposition of sentences in this part of the letter it is possible for us to reconstruct the discussions that took place in Rome. The mesengers apparently presented to the pope the situation as it was. A majority of the electorate favoured the deacon Crescens, a minority favoured Abbot Urbicus. Venantius seems to have asked the pope either to summon the candidates to Rome and declare in favour of Urbicus or, failing that, to send down from Rome another hand-picked candidate from the Roman clergy. Gregory replied that he did not want to promote Urbicus against the will of the majority if it would cause trouble with his flock. He also did not have sufficient people for ordination to the vacant sees already existing and could not spare one for Panormus. There were sufficient Gregorians on the Sicilian bench to prevent Panormus being a vital see and there was no pressing situation such as a deposition which demanded intervention. Therefore, Gregory proposed that if Crescens was found suitable – by a layman Gregory knew and trusted – he should be elected. Failing that, another candidate should be chosen from inside or outside Panormus – again by Gregory's agent on the spot. So the Panormus election represents an interesting halfway stage in papal electoral intervention.

The next we hear is in a letter dated July 603 conferring the *pallium* on the new bishop of Panormus, John.[64] Crescens had clearly been overruled and another candidate introduced but who, how and from where? One possibility is that he was another local cleric, selected as suitable by Venantius. But in the light of the previous letter, it seems more likely that the choice was the result of consultations carried out in Rome by the pope and the representatives of the Panormitan electorate.

In this context, the wording of the *pallium* letter is interesting. We possess other Gregorian *pallium* letters: to John of Syracuse and Donus of Messana.[65] They are completely formulary and consist of an injunction to live up to their high office and a confirmation of the customary privileges of the church. The standard chancery formula to Sicilian bishops is very similar in wording to these.[66]

But the letter to John of Panormus contains instructions not usually part of the formula and inserted into the middle of the letter. He is ordered to ensure that no one questions the authority of the pope. The absence of this injunction from the other *pallium* letters can only mean that in Panormus there was some reason why the authority of the pope might be questioned and the over-ruling of a favourite son in favour of an outsider would constitute such a reason.

There is another letter which might also be adduced in support of this hypothesis. Dated July 603, it is a letter to John giving papal confirmation to what is in effect a Bill of Rights demanded by the clergy and already confirmed by John.[67] It includes an annual publication of the accounts, drawn up with the participation of the clergy; the distribution of clerical salaries on merit; the right to the clergy to buy wine from the ecclesiastical estates, something hitherto denied them; the right for charges against clerics to be fully investigated before the bishop passes sentence.

The presentation of this bill by the clergy again suggests that John is an outsider, imposed on them by Rome. They were seeking to ensure that he made no restrictive innovations and indeed in some cases to secure a better deal than they enjoyed under Victor. Acceptance of the bill by John and Gregory was the price they paid for the peaceful acceptance of the new bishop by the clergy and the avoidance of attacks on papal authority. The evidence is admittedly circumstantial but it does point to a Gregorian intervention and the admittance of an outsider to Panormus. As to who John was, there is no hard evidence.

Of the other important sees, Tauromenium probably remained under Secundinus throughout the reign. But there were changes in Lilybaeum and Melita. By February 595, Theodore of Lilybaeum was dead and his will was being investigated by the rector Cyprian to ensure that the church suffered no loss from its bequests.[68] But the election did not go smoothly. There was deadlock, and the canonical three months was well exceeded. In September 595 Gregory informed Cyprian that a deputation of the Lilybaetan clergy had come to Rome to look for a suitable bishop and Gregory had given them permission to search for one.[69] They had come up with Decius *presbyter forensis*. But whether he was *forensis* just to Rome or to Suburbicarian Italy in general is not clear. He was most likely a refugee from the Lombards or the Istrian schism. They requested his ordination and with some reluctance the pope agreed. This reluctance may be explained by his order to Cyprian to lose no opportunity to help Decius because the regime of bishop Theodore had left much to be desired and many things which he ought to have amended he left untouched. Theodore had been praised for his energetic and effective visitation of Triocala but since his death his mismanagement at home had become known in Rome. In these circumstances Gregory was reluctant to appoint someone he did not know to the see.

However, he did ordain him and there is no evidence that he tried to force anyone else on them. It is worth remembering that at just this time he was involved in settling the Syracusan election, which was of far greater moment than Lilybaeum. So Lilybaeum got their bishop, Decius, and he apparently proved satisfactory.

The case of Lilybaeum, like that of Panormus, is an interesting example of an election in which the pope was concerned and rather unhappy about the outcome, but in which he was not prepared to push the issue. He had probably hoped that their search for a bishop in Rome would lead them to choose a Roman cleric who was known to him. But it did not and he therefore made the best of it.

Even after the Gregorian purge of the episcopal bench, however, there was still misconduct among the bishops and the case of the bishop of Melita is a good reminder that discipline could never be relaxed, even when a bench had been as successfully reconstituted as the Sicilian one had. In September 598, Gregory wrote to John of Syracuse to say that since his trial had proved the guilt of bishop Lucillus of Melita, he was to be deposed.[70] In view of the accusations against certain of his priests and deacons, alleged to be his accomplices, there was to be a full investigation of the clergy and all those found guilty were to be stripped of their ranks and relegated to monasteries. The worst offenders were to be excommunicated. The clergy and people of Melita were to be admonished to elect a new bishop.

But Lucillus remained contumacious, and in the autumn of 599 Gregory ordered the rector Romanus to see that Lucillus and his son Peter restored to the new bishop Trajan the property they had removed from the church.[71] It seems that they had not only removed church property but had also pocketed the sums earmarked for church repair, leaving the buildings to decay. The pope ruled that unless they returned what they had taken, they should answer for their behaviour to John of Syracuse.

Perhaps even more interesting is the rest of the letter, which fills in the background of the new bishop of Melita. He requested that four or five monks from the monastery in Syracuse, of which he had been abbot, should be sent to him for company, as he was a stranger in Melita and knew no one. He further asked that certain private property which he had in the monastery should be sent to him, including certain books and a slave boy purchased with his own money. Gregory agreed to the first request but not to the second since monks were not allowed to own private property.

So Trajan was abbot of a monastery in Syracuse. But he was not a Sicilian. Born in Valeria, apparently of wealthy parents, he had become a monk in a monastery founded by his father. But he had fled from Valeria when the Lombards came and had taken refuge in Sicily where he had become abbot of the Syracusan monastery founded by Capitulina.

It is not unlikely that he was the same Trajan who stood for election to the see of Syracuse in 595. Trajan is an unusual name. Its only bearers in the entire Register are the would-be bishop of Syracuse and the Syracusan who became bishop of Melita. The fact that the Syracusan candidate is described as 'priest' presents no real difficulty. For in many monasteries, monks were ordained as priests in order to be able to say mass for the brethren. Presumably he became abbot after his disappointment in the 595 election.

What is significant is that although Gregory found him incapable of governing Syracuse, he made no objection to his governing Melita. It may, of course, be that by 598 he had made such a good job of governing the monastery of Capitulina that his ability was at last recognized. The situation in Melita in 598 was one which, on the analogy of Triocala and Lipara, called for intervention. Bishop Lucillus and his son and a ring of ecclesiastical embezzlers had been systematically mulcting the church of its property and income. To restore the prestige of the see, to maintain discipline and to win back the faithful a reliable and trusted man is needed. Trajan seems to fit the bill. He had had the administrative experience as abbot. His monkish calling was a good guarantee of his leading a life fitted to serve as an example to his new parishioners. His intention to live in community with his monks indicated an emulation of Gregory's own practice which would not have harmed his standing in the pope's eyes. Gregory himself had commented on his 'good disposition' at the time of the Syracusan election.

Given the fact that John of Syracuse had been charged with conducting the investigation of the clergy and arranging for the Melitan election and that in 599 Trajan was lonely and friendless in Melita, given also that Trajan came from John's own see of Syracuse and indeed was prominent enough to have been considered for the episcopate of that city, the odds are here on another intervention, not by Gregory but by John. It is a good indication of how far John, as Gregory's representative in Sicily and knowing Gregory's requirements in personnel policy, had taken over the running of the ecclesiastical set-up in the island. It was, then, probably John who selected and installed Trajan. Trajan apparently settled down well enough. For he is last heard of alive and well in January 603, and presumably outlived the pope.[72]

The two least important sees in Sicily were probably Leontini and Tyndaris. Both changed their bishops during the course of the reign but the changeovers appear to have been routine, to have been left in the hands of the local electors and to have involved local clerics.

Bishop Zeno of Leontini was succeeded some time between 595 and 599 by Bishop Lucidus.[73] Bishop Eutychius of Tyndaris was succeeded some time between 593 and 599 by Bishop Benenatus.[74]

There remain, however, two controversial cases to be considered: those of Bishop Barbarus of Carina and Bishop Exhilaratus (see unknown). In the first case the problem lies in the the two letters of Gregory specifically devoted to Carina. The first, dated September 595, is a letter to Bishop Boniface of Rhegium.[75] Although Carina was destitute of a bishop, the desertion of the place and the diminution of its population made an election for a new bishop impracticable. Therefore Gregory united the see to Rhegium, giving Boniface the usual episcopal powers over Carina. The second, dated November 602, appointed Bishop Barbarus of Carina visitor of Panormus, with orders to see to the arrangement of the election of a new bishop.[76]

Commentators have never been able to reconcile the uniting of the see of Carina, which must from the second letter be close to Panormus, with a see many miles away in Bruttium. However, what has long been inexplicable in geographical terms becomes explicable in terms of patronage. First, Boniface of Rhegium was a Gregorian patronage appointment, a Roman parish priest appointed to that see in the early years of the reign and the only such appointee in Lucania and Bruttium. Second, there is the timing. Carina and Rhegium were united in September 595, the very time that John was being installed after a hard-fought election in Syracuse. It might have been anticipated that his early passage would be rough, and another trusted ally on the Sicilian bench to back him up would be welcome. That Boniface counted as a Sicilian bishop in his capacity as Bishop of Carina is evidenced by a letter of May 597, ordering the Sicilian bishops plus the bishops of Lipara and Rhegium to Rome.[77] This does not mean that Lipara and Rhegium were two non-Sicilian bishops being added to the group for that occasion; it refers to the fact that both were double sees. The bishop of Tauriana was also bishop of Lipara but resident in the latter; the bishop of Rhegium was also bishop of Carina but resident in the former. This explains the titulature. Gregory mentioned them so that the rector Cyprian would be sure that he meant all Sicilian bishops, including those who had other duties as bishops in Bruttium.

There can be no doubt, then, that Boniface counted as bishop of Carina until some time between 597 and 602. By the latter date, the situation had changed, either because John's standing in Sicily had improved or because the size of the population of Carina had increased, perhaps both. An independent election in Carina was permitted and Bishop Barbarus chosen.

Then there is the case of Bishop Exhilaratus, who, we learn from a letter to the Panormitan rector Fantinus, dated September 603, had been on trial in Rome.[78] The story which emerges seems to run as follows. Exhilaratus had been charged with excessive severity towards his clergy, or some of them, in punishments imposed after some case. They had complained to the pope who had summoned Exhilaratus to Rome for trial and kept him there for a long time. However, Bishop Leo of Catana had come to his aid, by declaring that he too was a judge in the case, and therefore by implication, Exhilaratus was not pursuing some private grudge or indulging in personal excesses. So Gregory acquitted him. But considerable ill-feeling remained in the clergy and the rector Fantinus was charged with patching up good relations between bishop and clergy on the basis of mutual charity.

Where is the see? There are certain clues that we can follow up. The involvement of Fantinus, rector of Panormus, clearly puts the see somewhere in his bailiwick and therefore rules out the Syracusan patrimony which we know to have included Syracuse, Catana, Agrigentum, Messana, Tauromenium, Leontini and Melita, all of which were occupied anyway in January 603. By a process of elimination that leaves Lipara, Tyndaris, Panormus, Lilybaeum, Triocala and Carina. Panormus is accounted for and Carina was occupied as recently as November 602. Of the remaining four, Benenatus of Tyndaris is last attested in July 599, Decius of Lilybaeum in August 599, Peter of Triocala in winter 598 and we know Lipara to have been vacant in January 603. No vacancies are known for the other sees but the absence of any mention after the dates listed makes vacancy a possibility.

There is another factor to be considered, the participation of Leo of Catana as judge with Exhilaratus. This suggests the probability that Exhilaratus's see was somewhere between Panormus and Catana, but within the Panormitan sphere of influence. Only two sees fit the bill – Lipara and Tyndaris. The circumstances of the case suggest a build-up of ill-feeling in the see, which can only have taken place over a fairly long period, and on top of this Exhilaratus is known to have been detained in Rome for a long time. This would rule out Lipara.

Tyndaris is all we are left with. If Bishop Benenatus died soon after we last hear of him in mid-599, his successor would have had three years in which to stir up the storm against him and spend at least a year in Rome undergoing investigation. In the circumstances Tyndaris seems a reasonable hypothesis.

Finally, there is one more example of patronage to consider, one which, this time, did not come off, but which is admirable evidence of Gregory's administration of patronage on the island. There is a letter, dated June 595, to Bishop Sebastian of Rhisinum, a Dalmatian prelate, who had gone to Constantinople to escape the barbarian inroads and who was an old friend of Gregory.[79] Hearing that he had been offered and had refused a see in the patriarchate of Antioch, Gregory wrote to say that if ever he wanted another see, there were sees vacant in Sicily, any of which he would be welcome to take and rule. The offer was apparently not taken up but it indicates the extent to which Gregory was willing to treat the Sicilian sees as a useful patronage reserve – in this case, for employing the talents of exiled bishops.

Phase two of Gregory's reign ended with his death on 12 March 604. In retrospect it can be seen to have been much quieter and less active than phase one. Bishop John of Syracuse remained in firm control and gradually more and more responsibility was delegated to him. There were fewer direct personal interventions in personnel changes than in phase one. The Panormus election and the Exhilaratus trial prompted papal intervention. But the trial of one bishop of Melita and the election of another were left to John. There is no evidence of papal interference in the episcopal changes in Lilybaeum, Leontini, Tyndaris, Carina and Lipara, beyond a mild reluctance to ordain Decius for Lilybaeum. The policy had become one of maintaining the *status quo* as it existed by the time of the election of John of Syracuse.

What conclusions can be drawn from the operation of papal personnel policy under Gregory? First, there was active involvement in elections – whether at grassroots level or by arbitration in Rome. Of the fourteen elections known to have occurred in Sicily under Gregory, six, including Boniface of Rhegium's appointment to Carina, were certainly Gregorian patronage appointments; two were probably so (Trajan of Melita and John of Panormus) and one was possibly (Secundinus of Tauromenium). There were also six trials of bishops, some of them held in Rome but at least one (Lucillus of Melita) in Syracuse. Of these six trials, three bishops were acquitted (Leo, Gregory and Exhilaratus) and three were deposed (Lucillus, Paul and Agatho). The pattern of involvement is that there was considerable activity in the early years of the reign when the episcopate was unknown and under review but that this activity declined when key episcopal positions were filled to papal satisfaction.

It is clear that Gregory was above all vitally concerned to secure a suitable appointment to the premier see in the province, and in two successive elections for Syracuse his nominees carried the day. He also became deeply involved in the aftermath of a deposition, which will have damaged the prestige of the church – hence his appointments to Lipara, Triocala and Melita. Also when there was evidence of episcopal delinquency which fell short of deposition – as in Messana and Lilybaeum – there was an actively expressed papal concern.

Besides involvement in elections and in trials, there are two other salient factors of papal personnel policy to note. One is his unification of sees, usually for demographic reasons. The other is the re-deployment of experienced ecclesiastical personnel who had lost their posts through enemy action (Paulinus of Tauriana to Lipara, the offer of a see to Sebastian of Rhisinum). The criteria for a good appointment were both administrative experience and being known to and trusted by the pope, as was clearly the case in the appointment of Abbot Maximian to Syracuse and Archdeacon John to Syracuse, subdeacon Peter to Triocala, the priest Donus to Messana and Bishops Boniface and Paulinus to Lipara and Carina. It was the fact that he did not know and/or trust Decius or Trajan or Crescens that worried Gregory about their candidature for Lilybaeum and Syracuse and Panormus. There is also the characteristic Gregorian prejudice for men of monastic background (Maximian, Paulinus, Trajan), especially when reinforced by administrative experience. It is the existence of so much detailed information on Gregory's personnel policy which makes the absence of comparable material for his successors so vexing. Yet even if only for Gregory, this information does focus attention clearly on a papal preoccupation largely neglected by historians.

Afterword

It has been asserted that the study of papal history is meaningless if it is not about the transmission of ideas. That may be so, but it is also meaningless if it is only about the transmission of ideas – and even more so if those ideas are wrong. For years now the study of the medieval papacy has been dominated by the theme of the development of the idea of papal monarchy. Its proponents have turned this idea into an all-dominating, all-pervading 'Grand Theme' into which every event and every significant personality has to be fitted. Its dominance means the judging of individual popes and indeed entire eras in terms of their contribution to the theme. But this inevitably involves *a priori* judgments, the distorting of facts, the ignoring of contradictory evidence, the misinterpretation of concepts and events, the wrenching of important texts out of their literary, ecclesiastical and intellectual context, the attribution of motivations unproved and unprovable.

What I have tried modestly to do in this study of the early medieval papacy is to suggest that we need to restore the context of papal history and counterbalance the emphasis on papal ideology by stressing social and economic conditions, political developments, intellectual constraints and personality differences. The restoration of context, for instance, shows the similarities in outlook between Gregory I and Gelasius I, always claimed as the most important popes of the period. Their differences – the philosophy of humility propounded by Gregory, the narrow-minded, high-handed attitude informing the pronouncements of Gelasius – emerge as differences not of ideology but of style, personality and circumstance. In the wider sense, what emerges is the picture of an era important for aspects of papal development which were not ideologically new or startling but in the main 'gut' responses to the changing situation – the expansion of responsibility and influence, the building up of the bureaucracy, the maintenance of loyalty to the empire. The restora-

363

tion of the context, then, demonstrates that the principal characteristic of the period was not adherence to or deviation from the idea of papal monarchy but the irreconcilable paradox of *Christianitas* and *Romanitas*, a paradox resolved not by the papacy but by the Lombards, who in conquering the exarchate of Ravenna removed the imperial presence from the papacy's purview.

Appendix 1 The Popes

Name	Reign	Birthplace	Father
Simplicius	468–83	Tibur	Castinus
Felix III	483–92	Rome	Felix
Gelasius I	492–6	Africa	Valerius
Anastasius II	496–8	Rome	Peter
Symmachus	498–514	Sardinia	Fortunatus
Hormisdas	514–23	Frisino	Justus
John I	523–6	Tuscia	Constantius
Felix IV	526–30	Samnium	Castorius
Boniface II	530–2	Rome	Sigibuld
John II	533–5	Rome	Projectus
Agapitus	535–6	Rome	Gordianus
Silverius	536–7	Campania	Hormisdas
Vigilius	537–55	Rome	John
Pelagius I	556–61	Rome	John
John III	561–74	Rome	Anastasius
Benedict I	575–9	Rome	Boniface
Pelagius II	579–90	Rome	Unigild
Gregory I	590–604	Rome	Gordianus
Sabinian	604–6	Blera	Bonus
Boniface III	607	Rome	John Catadiochus
Boniface IV	608–15	Valeria	John
Deusdedit	615–18	Rome	Stephanus
Boniface V	619–25	Naples	John
Honorius I	625–38	Campania	Petronius
Severinus	640	Rome	Avienus
John IV	640–2	Dalmatia	Venantius
Theodore	642–9	Palestine	Theodore
Martin I	649–53	Tuder	Unknown
Eugenius	654–7	Rome	Rufinianus

Name	Reign	Birthplace	Father
Vitalian	657–72	Signia	Anastasius
Adeodatus	672–6	Rome	Jovianus
Donus	676–8	Rome	Maurice
Agatho	678–81	Sicily	Unknown
Leo II	682–3	Sicily	Paul
Benedict II	684–5	Rome	John
John V	685–6	Antioch	Cyriacus
Conon	686–7	'Raised in Sicily', the son of a soldier	Unknown
Sergius I	687–701	Born in Sicily of Syrian parentage	Tiberius
John VI	701–5	'Greek'	Unknown
John VII	705–7	'Greek'	Plato
Sisinnius	708	Syria	John
Constantine	708–15	Syria	John
Gregory II	715–31	Rome	Marcellus
Gregory III	731–41	Syria	John
Zacharias	741–52	'Greek'	Polychromios

NB 'Greek' does not necessarily mean from Greece but probably from the Eastern Empire generally.

Appendix 2 Papal Vacancies

After Simplicius	6 days
After Felix III	5 days
After Gelasius I	7 days
After Anastasius II	4 days
After Symmachus	7 days
After Hormisdas	6 days
After John I	58 days
After Felix IV	3 days
After Boniface II	2 months 15 days
After John II	6 days
After Agapitus	1 month 28 days
After Silverius	No time lapse given
After Vigilius	3 months 5 days
After Pelagius I	3 months 25 days
After John III	10 months 3 days
After Benedict I	3 months 10 days
After Pelagius II	6 months 25 days
After Gregory I	5 months 18 days
After Sabinian	11 months 26 days
After Boniface III	10 months 6 days
After Boniface IV	6 months 25 days
After Deusdedit	1 month 16 days
After Boniface V	13 days
After Honorius I	1 year 7 months 17 days
After Severinus	4 months 24 days
After John IV	1 month 13 days
After Theodore	52 days
After Martin	No time lapse given
After Eugenius	1 month 28 days
After Vitalian	2 months 13 days
After Adeodatus	4 months 15 days

After Donus	2 months 15 days
After Agatho	1 year 7 months 5 days
After Leo II	11 months 22 days
After Benedict II	2 months 15 days
After John V	2 months 18 days
After Conon	2 months 23 days
After Sergius I	1 month 20 days
After John VI	1 month 18 days
After John VII	3 months
After Sisinnius	1 month 18 days
After Constantine	40 days
After Gregory II	35 days
After Gregory III	8 days
After Zacharias	12 days

Appendix 3
Papal Ordinations

Simplicius (468–83)   58 priests, 11 deacons, 88 bishops
Felix III (483–92)   28 priests, 5 deacons, 31 bishops
Gelasius I (492–6)   32 priests, 2 deacons, 67 bishops
Anastasius II (496–8)   12 priests, 16 bishops
Symmachus (498–514)   92 priests, 16 deacons, 117 bishops
Hormisdas (514–23)   21 priests, 55 bishops
John I (523–6)   15 bishops
Felix IV (526–30)   55 priests, 4 deacons, 29 bishops
Boniface II (530–2)   No ordinations
John II (533–5)   15 priests, 21 bishops
Agapitus (535–6)   4 deacons, 11 bishops
Silverius (536–7)   14 priests, 18 bishops
Vigilius (537–55)   46 priests, 16 deacons, 81 bishops
Pelagius I (556–61)   26 priests, 9 deacons, 49 bishops
John III (561–74)   38 priests, 13 deacons, 61 bishops
Benedict I (575–9)   15 priests, 3 deacons, 21 bishops
Pelagius II (579–90)   28 priests, 8 deacons, 48 bishops
Gregory I (590–604)   39 priests, 5 deacons, 62 bishops
Sabinian (604–6)   26 bishops
Boniface III (607)   21 bishops
Boniface IV (608–15)   8 deacons, 36 bishops
Deusdedit (615–18)   14 priests, 5 deacons, 29 bishops
Boniface V (619–25)   26 priests, 4 deacons, 29 bishops
Honorius I (625–38)   13 priests, 11 deacons, 81 bishops
Severinus (640)   4 bishops
John IV (640–2)   18 priests, 5 deacons, 18 bishops
Theodore (642–9)   21 priests, 4 deacons, 46 bishops
Martin I (649–53)   11 priests, 5 deacons, 33 bishops
Eugenius (654–7)   21 bishops
Vitalian (657–72)   22 priests, 1 deacon, 97 bishops
Adeodatus (672–6)   14 priests, 2 deacons, 46 bishops

Donus (676–8)	10 priests, 5 deacons, 6 bishops
Agatho (678–81)	10 priests, 3 deacons, 18 bishops
Leo II (682–3)	9 priests, 3 deacons, 23 bishops
Benedict II (684–5)	12 bishops
John V (685–6)	13 bishops
Conon (686–7)	16 bishops
Sergius I (687–701)	18 priests, 4 deacons, 97 bishops
John VI (701–5)	9 priests, 2 deacons, 15 bishops
John VII (705–7)	19 bishops
Sisinnius (708)	1 bishop
Constantine (708–15)	10 priests, 2 deacons, 64 bishops
Gregory II (715–31)	35 priests, 4 deacons, 150 bishops
Gregory III (731–41)	24 priests, 3 deacons, 80 bishops
Zacharias (741–52)	30 priests, 5 deacons, 85 bishops

Abbreviations

≈⋙⊙⋘≈

Acta SS.	*Acta Sanctorum*
ACO	*Acta Conciliorum Oecumenicorum*
ASR	*Archivio della Reale Deputazione Romana di Storia Patria*
BHL	*Bibliotheca Hagiographica Latina*
BZ	*Byzantinische Zeitschrift*
Chron. Pat. Grad.	*Chronica Patriarcharum Gradensium*
CIL	*Corpus Inscriptionum Latinorum*
CJ	*Codex Justinianus*
CSEL	*Corpus Scriptorum Ecclesiasticorum Latinorum*
CTh.	*Codex Theodosianus*
ep.	*Epistulae*
HL	Paulus Diaconus, *Historia Langobardorum*
ILCV	*Inscriptiones Latinae Christianae Veteres*
Jaffe	P. Jaffe, *Regesta Pontificum Romanum*
JEH	*Journal of Ecclesiastical History*
JRS	*Journal of Roman Studies*
JTS	*Journal of Theological Studies*
LD	*Liber Diurnus*
Lib. Pont. Rav.	Agnellus Andreas, *Liber Pontificalis Ecclesiae Ravennatis*
Loewenfeld	S. Loewenfeld, *Epistulae Pontificum Romanum Ineditae*
LP	*Liber Pontificalis*
MAH	*Mélanges d'archéologie et d'histoire de l'Ecole française de Rome*
Mansi	J. D. Mansi, *Sacrorum Conciliorum Nova et Amplissima Collectio*
MGH	*Monumenta Germaniae Historica*
MGH aa	*Auctores Antiquissimi*
ep. Lang.	*Epistolae Langobardicae*

ep. Wisigoticae	*Epistolae Wisigoticae*
ep. Merov.	*Epistolae Aevi Merovingici*
Poet. Lat.	*Poetae Latinae*
Scr. Merov.	*Scriptores Rerum Merovingicarum*
Scr. Rer. Lang.	*Scriptores Rerum Langobardicarum et Italicarum*
NA	*Neues Archiv der Gesellschaft für ältere Deutsche Geschichtskunde*
PG	J. P. Migne, *Patrologia Graeca*
PL	J. P. Migne, *Patrologia Latina*
PLS	*Patrologia Latina Supplementum*
RAC	*Rivista di Archeologia Cristiana*
Rer. It. Script.	L. A. Muratori, *Rerum Italicarum Scriptores*
Settimane	*Settimane di Studio del Centro Italiano di Studi sull' Alto Medioevo*

Notes

Chapter 1 The Ideological Context

1 Mansi, 3, p. 559.
2 Mansi, 7, p. 370.
3 Gelasius I, *Tractate*, 4, p. 558.
4 Gelasius I, *ep*. 26, p. 405.
5 *Collectio Avellana*, 159.
6 Justinian I, *Novel*, 131, ch. 2.
7 *Collectio Avellana*, 159.
8 Notably *CJ*, I, i, 7, 8.
9 *Collectio Avellana*, 139.
10 *Collectio Avellana*, 117, 119.
11 Mansi 11, pp. 196, 201.
12 *LP, Vita Bonifacii III*, p. 316.
13 *LP, Vita Vitaliani*, p. 343; *LP, Vita Constantini*, p. 391; Mansi, 11, pp. 684–5.
14 Mansi, 10, p. 914.
15 Mansi, 10, p. 893.
16 For the full story of the Roman Primacy see F. Dvornik, *Byzantium and the Roman Primacy* (New York, 1966).
17 Gelasius I, *ep*. 4.
18 Rev. J. J. Taylor, 'Eastern Appeals to Rome in the Early Church: a little known witness', *Downside Review*, 89 (1971), pp. 142–6. Cf. also P. Bernadakis, 'Les Appels au pape dans l'église grecque jusqu'à Photius', *Echos d'Orient*, 6 (1903), pp. 30–42, 118–25, 249–57; J. P. Whitney, 'The Growth of Papal Jurisdiction before Nicholas I', *Reformation Essays* (London, 1939).
19 Felix III, *ep*. 17, p. 275.
20 Gelasius I, *ep*. 10; Gregory I, *ep*. v, 27.
21 *Collectio Avellana*, appendix 4.
22 *CJ*, I, i, 7.
23 Margaret Deanesly, 'The Anglo-Saxon Church and the Papacy', *The English Church and the Papacy in the Middle Ages*, ed. C. H. Lawrence (London, 1965), pp. 31–62.
24 Optatus of Milevis, *De Schismate Donatistarum*, appendix 7, p. 212.
25 Justinian I, *Novel*, 6, *Praefatio*.
26 Mansi, 4, p. 1291.
27 *PL*, 54, p. 735.
28 *PL*, 69, p. 22.
29 For a full discussion of the theories see F. Dvornik, *Early Christian and Byzantine Political Philosophy* (Dumbarton Oaks, 1966), 2 vols.
30 Gelasius I, *ep*. 12.
31 Gregory I, *Regula Pastoralis*, iii, 4.
32 Symmachus I, *ep*. 10, p. 704.
33 Martin I, *ep*. 3, p. 139.
34 Jaffe, 2180.
35 Gregory I, *ep*. xiii, I.
36 *LP, Vita Constantini*, p. 392.

37 For full details of the development of Monophysitism see W. H. C. Frend, *The Rise of the Monophysite Movement* (Cambridge, 1972).

38 Hugo Koch, 'Gelasius im kirchenpolitischen Dienst seiner Vorgänger Simplicius und Felix III', *Sitzungsberichte der Bayerischen Akademie, philhist. abt. 1933*, vol. 6; Nelly Ertl, 'Diktatoren frühmittelalter Papstbriefe', *Archiv für Urkundenforschung und Quellenkunde des Mittelalters*, 15 (1937), pp. 61–6.

39 Felix III, *ep.* 1, p. 222.

40 Felix III, *ep.* 15, p. 270.

41 Felix III, *ep.* 8, p. 250.

42 Gelasius I, *ep.* 12.

43 Gelasius I, *Tractate* 6.

44 *LP, Vita Gelasii*, p. 255.

45 Gelasius I, *ep.* 6.

46 Gelasius I, *ep.* 4, 5.

47 Gelasius I, *Tractate* 5.

48 *LP, Vita Gelasii*, p. 255.

49 Gelasius I, *Tractate* 1.

50 Gelasius I, *Tractate* 3.

51 Gelasius I, *Tractate* 4.

52 Gelasius I, *ep.* 12.

53 E. Caspar, *Geschichte des Papsttums* (Tubingen, 1933), ii, pp. 65–71, 753–5.

54 W. Ullmann, *The Growth of Papal Government in the Middle Ages* (London, 1955), pp. 14–28.

55 F. Dvornik, *Early Christian and Byzantine Political Philosophy*, ii, pp. 805–6.

56 A. K. Ziegler, 'Pope Gelasius and his teaching on the relation of Church and State', *Catholic Historical Review*, xxvii (1941–2), pp. 412–37.

57 Anastasius II, *ep.* 1, 620.

58 Gelasius I, *Tractate* 4, pp. 567–8.

59 Gelasius I, *ep.* 14.

60 Loewenfeld, *ep.* 33.

61 Gelasius I, *frag.* 7.

62 Gelasius I, *frag.* 25.

63 Gelasius I, *frag.* 17.

64 Loewenfeld, *ep.* 9.

65 *MGH, aa*, xii, p. 423.

66 W. Ullmann, *A Short History of the Papacy in the Middle Ages* (London, 1972), p. 40.

67 *ibid.*, p. 52.

68 *ibid.*, p. 54.

69 W. Ullmann, *Growth of Papal Government in the Middle Ages* (London, 1965), p. 38.

70 P. D. King, *Law and Society in the Visigothic Kingdom* (Cambridge, 1972), p. 123.

Chapter 2 The Political and Religious Context

1 The 527–8 edict (*CJ*, I, i, 5) and the 533 edict (*CJ*, I, i, 6).

2 *Collectio Avellana*, 84.

3 *Ibid.*

4 *Collectio Avellana*, 91.

5 A. H. M. Jones, 'The Constitutional Position of Odoacer and Theodoric', *JRS*, 52 (1962), pp. 126–30.

6 Jordanes, *Getica*, 59.

7 W. G. Sinnigen, 'Administrative Shifts of Competence under Theodoric', *Traditio*, 21 (1965), pp. 456–67.

8 *Anonymus Valesianus*, 59–60.

9 Procopius, *De Bello Gothico*, v, 1.

10 Cassiodorus, *Variae*, ii, 27; *Anonymus Valesianus*, 81, 82.

11 Cassiodorus, *Variae*, ii, 27.

12 On the Arian Church see Jacques Zeiller, 'Étude sur l'Arianisme en Italie à l'époque Ostrogothique et à l'époque Lombarde', *MAH*, 25 (1905), pp. 127–46; C. Cecchelli, 'L'Arianesimo e le chiese Ariane

d'Italia', *Settimane*, 7, ii (1960), pp. 743–74.

13 Cassiodorus, *Variae*, i, 9; Gelasius I, *frag.* 11, 12, 13.

14 Felix III, *ep.* 1, p. 225.

15 The Lombard invasion is described in detail in Paul the deacon's *Historia Langobardorum* (*MGH, Scr. Rer. Lang.*, pp. 45–187); on settlement evidence, see G. Luzzatto, *An Economic History of Italy* (London, 1961), p. 20.

16 *HL*, ii, 25.

17 *HL*, ii, 12.

18 *HL*, iii, 31.

19 See F. Lanzoni, *Le Diocesi d'Italia* (Faenza, 1927) and F. Savio, *Gli Antichi Vescovi d'Italia* (Milan, 1899) on the survival of North Italian sees.

20 *HL*, iii, 26.

21 Gregory I, *ep.* iv, 2.

22 Gregory I, *ep.* iii, 30.

23 Gregory I, *ep.* iii, 30.

24 Gregory I, *ep.* iv, 37.

25 *HL*, iii, 20, 26.

26 Gregory I, *ep.* v, 56; xii, 13.

27 *HL*, iv, 33; *Chron. Pat. Grad.* 3.

28 *MGH, ep. Lang.*, I.

29 *Chron. Pat. Grad.*, 6.

30 *MGH, ep. Lang.*, 3.

31 *Chron. Pat. Grad.*, 7.

32 Gregory I, *ep.* i, 17.

33 *HL*, iv, 6.

34 Gregory I, *ep.* ix, 49, 166; xii, 39; ix, 59, 107.

35 *HL*, iv, 8.

36 Gregory I, *ep.* iv, 2, 37.

37 *HL*, iv, 42; Gregory I, *Dialogi*, iii, 29.

38 Columban, *ep.* 5.

39 *MGH, ep. Wisigoticae*, 5.

40 *HL*, iv, 41.

41 *MGH, ep. Lang.*, 2; Fredegar *Chronicon*, iv, 49.

42 *MGH, ep. Lang.*, 2.

43 *MGH, ep. Lang.*, 4.

44 Jonas, *Vita S. Bertulfi*; *MGH, Scr. Merov.*, iv, pp. 143–8.

45 *HL*, iv, 46.

46 Mansi, 10, pp. 1162–70.

47 Gregory I, *Dialogi*, iii, 11.

48 L. Schiaparelli, *Codice Diplomatico Longobardo* (Rome, 1929), p. 17.

49 *MGH, Poet. Lat.*, iv, 2, p. 728.

50 *HL*, iv, 42.

51 Gian Pietro Bognetti, Gino Chierici and Alberto de Capitani d'Arzago, *Santa Maria di Castelseprio* (Milan, 1948), pp. 237–62; Enrico Cattaneo, 'Missionari Orientali a Milano nell'età Longobardo', *Archivio Storico Lombardo*, series 9, vol. 3 (1963), pp. 215–47; P. M. Conti, 'Missioni Aquileiesi, Orientali e Romane nel regno Longobardo', *Studi Romani*, 17 (1969), pp. 18–26.

52 *HL*, vi, 4; the letter itself survives, *PL*, 87, pp. 1261–8.

53 J. B. De Rossi, *Inscriptiones Christianae Urbis Romae* (Rome, 1888), vol. 2, i, p. 170; *Acta SS.*, April, ii, pp. 91, 92.

54 *Carmen de Synodo Ticinensi*, p. 730.

55 *LP, Vita Constantini*, pp. 391, 392.

56 *HL*, v, 33.

57 *HL*, v, 38.

58 Carlo Troya, *Codice Diplomatico Longobardo* (Naples, 1852), p. 338.

59 Mansi, 11, pp. 767–76.

60 *LD*, 76.

61 U. Pasqui, *Documenti servire per la storia della città di Arezzo nel medio evo* (Florence, 1899), vol. I, nos. 5, 6, 7, 11.

62 *Vita S. Barbati* (*MGH, Sc. Rer. Lang.*, pp. 557–63).

63 *LP, Vita Sergii*, p. 376.

64 *MG, Legum*, iv, p. 124.

65 *MGH, ep. Lang.*, 8, 9.

66 *MGH, ep. Lang.*, 16.

Chapter 3 The Social and Economic Context

1 Gregory I, *Homiliae in Evangelia*, ii, 6, 22.

2 Cassiodorus, *Variae*, iv, 5; xii, 28; ix, 5; x, 27; xi, 5; xii, 25; xii, 26.

3 Procopius, *De Bello Gothico*, v, ·10.

4 *ibid.*, vi, 21.

5 *ibid.*, vii, 10.

6 *ibid.*, vi, 20.

7 *ibid.*, vi, 20; *LP, Vita Silverii*, p. 291.

8 Procopius, *De Bello Gothico*, vii, 9.

9 Gregory I, *Dialogi*, i, 4; iii, 28; iii, 27; iv, 21, 22, 23.

10 Gregory I, *ep.* i, 39; v, 9; i, 42; iv, 42; ix, 209; ii, 38; x, 1.

11 Gregory I, *ep.* i, 48.

12 Gregory I, *ep.* i, 8; i, 77; ii, 44; ii, 48; iii, 13; iii, 20; ix, 60.

13 *HL*, v, 29.

14 The sees were: Myria, Velia, Consilinum, Grumentum, Lippiae, Egnathia, Venafrum, Cales, Nuceria, Aecanum, Larinum, Carmeia, Salapia, Herdonia, Caudium, Acheruntia, Venusia, Volturnum, Compulteria, Casinum, Aquinum, Antium, Suessa, Subaugusta, Trebiae, Aquaviva, Tarquinii, Forumclodii, Hispellum, Tadinum, Plestia, Histonium, Bovianum, Aufidena, Sulmo, Truentum, Pausulae, Ocriculum, Matelica, Urbs Salvia, Potentia and Tolentinum.

15 Evagrius, *Historia Ecclesiastica*, iv, 29.

16 *ibid.*

17 *Auctarium Marcellini, MGH, aa,* xi, p. 107.

18 J. B. Bury, *History of the Later Roman Empire* (London, 1923), ii, p. 62.

19 Gregory I, *ep.* ix, 232.

20 *HL*, ii, 4.

21 *HL*, ii, 26.

22 *Auctarium Marcellini*, p. 107.

23 *HL*, ii, 4; iv, 4.

24 Gregory I, *Dialogi*, iv, 26.

25 Marius of Aventicum, *Chronicon*, p. 238.

26 *LP, Vita Benedicti*, I, p. 308.

27 *HL*, iii, 23.

28 Gregory of Tours, *Historia Francorum*, x, 1; *HL*, iii, 24; *LP, Vita Pelagii II*, p. 309.

29 Gregory I, *Dialogi*, iv, 18, 26, 36; *HL*, iii, 24; *LP, Vita Pelagii II*, p. 309.

30 Gregory I, *ep.* ii, 4.

31 *HL*, iv, 4.

32 *HL*, iv, 2.

33 *HL*, iv, 14.

34 Gregory I, *ep.* ix, 232.

35 *HL*, iv, 29.

36 *LP, Vita Bonifacii IV*, p. 317.

37 *LP, Vita Deusdedit*, p. 319.

38 *LP, Vita Adeodati*, pp. 346–7; *HL*, v, 15.

39 *LP, Vita Doni*, p. 348; *HL*, v, 31.

40 *HL*, vi, 5.

41 *LP, Vita Benedicti II*, p. 364; *HL*, vi, 9.

42 Theophanes, *Chronographia*, a.m. 6238.

43 *MGH, Sc. Rer. Lang.*, p. 425.

44 *LP, Vita Gelasii I*, p. 255.

45 Procopius, *De Bello Gothico*, vii, 15.

46 Pelagius I, *ep.* 4, 9.

47 Pelagius I, *ep.* 85.

48 Joannes Diaconus, *Vita Gregorii*, ii, 24–30.

49 *LP, Vita Sabiniani*, p. 315.

50 Gregory I, *ep.* i, 39; ii, 38; ix, 136; iii, 55; iv, 43; iv, 28; iv, 31.
51 Joannes Diaconus, *Vita Gregorii*, ii, 27.
52 *LP, Vita Symmachi*, p. 263.
53 *Continuatio Prosperi Havniensis*, 22.
54 *LP, Vita Gregorii II*, pp. 400, 407.
55 *LP, Vita Gregorii III*, p. 420.
56 Gregory I, *ep.* ii, 45; iii, 40, 16; vi, 32; v, 46; vii, 13, 35, 23, 25; viii, 22.

Chapter 4 The Acacian Schism

1 Pope Simplicius's illness was lengthy, as Pope Felix III reported to the Emperor Zeno (Felix III, *ep.* 1, p. 223).
2 *MGH, aa*, xii, p. 445.
3 His daughter Paula was *clarissima femina*. See Part 4, chapter 14.
4 W. Ullman, *A Short History of the Papacy in the Middle Ages*, p. 30.
5 *LP, Vita Felicis III*, p. 252.
6 Felix III, *ep.* 2, p. 237.
7 Gelasius I, *ep.* 26, p. 409.
8 Felix III, *ep.* 1, p. 223.
9 Felix III, *ep.* 1, 2.
10 Evagrius, *Historia Ecclesiastica*, iii, 21.
11 Felix III, *ep.* 6, 7, 10.
12 Felix III, *ep.* 8.
13 Felix III, *ep.* 11, 12.
14 *LP, Vita Felicis III*, p. 252.
15 Felix III, *ep.* 1, p. 223.
16 Felix III, *ep.* 14.
17 Felix III, *ep.* 15.
18 Felix III, *ep.* 16.
19 Felix III, *ep.* 17, 18.
20 The letter has not survived but is mentioned in Gelasius I, *ep.* 10, p. 342.
21 This is also mentioned in Gelasius I, *ep.* 10, p. 346.

22 Gelasius I, *ep.* 12, p. 350.
23 *PL*, 59, p. III.
24 *PL*, 67, p. 231.
25 Gelasius I, *ep.* 10, p. 341.
26 *MGH, aa*, xii, p. 445; Marini, *Papyri*, no. 83.
27 *Anonymus Valesianus*, 49.
28 *Anonymus Valesianus*, 53.
29 Gelasius I, *ep.* 10.
30 Gelasius I, *ep.* 12.
31 *Anonymus Valesianus*, 57.
32 *ibid.*, 64.
33 Gelasius I, *ep.* 12.
34 *LP, Vita Gelasii*, p. 255; Gelasius I, *ep.* 30.
35 Anastasius II, *ep.* 1.
36 *Collectio Avellana*, 102.
37 Theodore the Lector, *Historia Ecclesiastica*, ii, 17.
38 *LP, Vita Anastasii II*, p. 258.

Chapter 5 The Symmachan Schism
(i) the events

1 *LP, Vita Symmachi*, p. 260.
2 *MGM, aa*, xii, p. 402 – *popularem tumultum*.
3 *LP, Vita Symmachi*, p. 260.
4 'Laurentian Fragment', p. 44.
5 *LP, Vita Symmachi*, p. 260.
6 'Laurentian Fragment', p. 44.
7 Ennodius, *ep.* iii, 10; vi, 16, 33.
8 Theodore the Lector, *Historia Ecclesiastica*, ii, 17.
9 *Acta Synodi ad 499, MGH, aa*, xii, pp. 399–415.
10 *Anonymus Valesianus*, 65–7.
11 *LP, Vita Symmachi*, p. 260. 'Laurentian Fragment', p. 44.
12 *LP, Vita Symmachi*, p. 260.
13 *MGH, aa*, xii, p. 427.
14 *LP, Vita Symmachi*, p. 260. The trial synod has traditionally been dated 501 but a date of 502 had been conclusively established by G. B. Picotti in his article 'I Sinodi Romani nello Scisma Laurenziano',

Studi Storici in onore di
Gioacchino Volpe, ii (Firenze,
1958), pp. 743–86.

15 Acta Synodi ad 501 (502 on
revised dating), MGH, aa, xii,
pp. 416–37.

16 MGH, aa, xii, p. 428.

17 Praeceptio Regis, III, MGH, aa,
xii, pp. 419–20.

18 Praeceptio Regis IV, MGH, aa,
xii, pp. 420–1.

19 MGH, aa, xii, pp. 428–9.

20 'Laurentian Fragment', p. 45.

21 MGH, aa, xii, p. 423.

22 Praeceptio Regis, MGH, aa, xii,
p. 424.

23 The proceedings of this session
are preserved in MGH, aa, xii,
pp. 426–37. The text of the
proceedings does not mention
where the session met. But it is
headed Synodus Palmaris,
suggesting the Palma.

24 This work has not survived but
its contents are known from
the summary given in
Ennodius, Libellus adversus eos
qui contra synodum scribere
praesumpserunt, MGH, aa, vii,
pp. 48–67.

25 'Laurentian Fragment', p. 45.

26 MGH, aa, vii, pp. 48–67.

27 Acta Synodi ad 502, MGM, aa,
xii, pp. 438–55.

28 'Laurentian Fragment', p. 45.

29 Symmachus, ep. 8.

30 MGH, aa, xii, p. 423.

31 LP, Vita Symmachi, pp. 260–
261.

32 Ennodius, ep. iii, 10.

33 ibid., ep. vii, 7.

34 'Laurentian Fragment', p. 46.

35 ibid.

36 MGH, aa, xii, p. 392.

37 Ennodius, Panegyricus, MGH,
aa, vii, pp. 203–14.

38 Gregory I, Dialogi, iv, 40.

39 'Laurentian Fragment', p. 46.

Chapter 6 The Symmachan Schism
(ii) issues and participants

1 MGH, aa, xii, p. 423.

2 MGH, aa, vii, p. 61.

3 LP, Vita Symmachi, p. 260.

4 MGH, aa, xii, p. 424.

5 Symmachus, ep. 10.

6 LP, Vita Symmachi, pp. 260–1.

7 'Laurentian Fragment', p. 44.

8 MGH, aa, xii, p. 420.

9 ibid.

10 ibid., p. 423.

11 MGH, aa, vii, p. 64.

12 The 'Symmachan Apocrypha'
consists of: Gesta de Xysti
Purgatione (Pierre Coustant,
Pontificum Romanum Epistolae
Genuinae, i (Gottingen, 1796),
pp. 117–120), Gesta Liberii
(Coustant, pp. 89–94),
Sinuessanae Synodi Gesta de
Marcellino (Coustant, pp.
29–36), Gesta de Polychronii
Accusatione (Coustant, pp.
120–4), Constitutum Silvestri
(PL, 6, pp. 11–20).

13 Ennodius, ep. v, 1.

14 Avitus, ep. 34.

15 'Laurentian Fragment', p. 46.

16 LP, Vita Symmachi, p. 263.

17 MGH, aa, xii, p. 431.

18 MGH, aa, vii, p. 61.

19 ibid., p. 57.

20 LP, Vita Symmachi, p. 263,
n. 2.

21 ibid., p. 262.

22 ibid., p. 260.

23 Felix III, ep. 13, pp. 259–60.

24 Gelasius I, ep. 30, p. 437.

25 MGH, aa, xii, pp. 399–402,
405–15.

26 ibid., pp. 438–43.

27 Ennodius, ep. v, 13; vi, 33.

28 LP, Vita Agapiti, p. 287.

29 Symmachus, ep. 8.

30 Gregory I, Dialogi, iv, 40.

31 Collectio Avellana, 102.

32 F. Maassen, *Geschichte der
   Quellen und der Literatur des
   canonischen Rechts* (Gratz, 1870),
   pp. 960–2.
33 *PL*, 70, p. 1137.
34 *PL*, 67, pp. 231–316.
35 *PL*, 67, pp. 483–511.
36 *ibid.*, pp. 513–20.
37 *LP, Vita Anastasii II*, p. 258.
38 Boethius, *Tractate* 5, pp. 72, 74.
39 *LP, Vita Symmachi*, p. 263.
40 Ennodius, *ep.* iv, 1, 29, 8, 22,
   31.
41 Ennodius, *ep.* vi, 33. To
   Hormisdas alone Ennodius sent
   ep. iv, 34; v, 13; vii, 12; viii, 33,
   39; ix, 5; to Dioscorus, vi, 28.
42 Ennodius, *ep.* iii, 7; vi, 36; vii,
   28; viii, 30; ix, 32.
43 Ennodius, *ep.* iii, 10; iv, 11; vi,
   16.
44 'Laurentian Fragment', pp.
   45–6.
45 The building activities are
   detailed in *LP, Vita Symmachi*,
   pp. 261–3.
46 *MGH, aa*, vii, p. 59.
47 Avitus, *ep.* 34.
48 Ennodius, *ep.* iv, 1.
49 *CIL*, X, 3299.
50 Theodore the Lector, *Historia
   Ecclesiastica*, ii, 17.
51 'Laurentian Fragment', p. 44.
52 Anastasius II, *ep.* 1.
53 Gelasius I, *ep.* 18.
54 *MGH, aa*, xii, pp. 402–5.
55 *ibid.*, pp. 445–51.
56 Cassiodorus, *Variae*, i, 20, 27,
   30, 31, 32, 33.

Chapter 7 The *Rapprochement*
   with the East
 1 Ennodius, *ep.* viii, 39.
 2 Ennodius, *ep.* viii, 33.
 3 *LP, Vita Hormisdae*, p. 269.
 4 J. B. De Rossi, *Inscriptiones
   Christianae*, p. 108.
 5 *Collectio Avellana*, 104.

 6 Symmachus, *ep.* 12.
 7 *Collectio Avellana*, 107.
 8 *ibid.*, 108.
 9 *ibid.*, 109
10 *LP, Vita Hormisdae*, p. 269.
11 *Collectio Avellana*, 116.
12 *ibid.*, 116a.
13 *ibid.*, 125.
14 *ibid.*, 111.
15 *ibid.*, 113.
16 *ibid.*, 112.
17 *LP, Vita Hormisdae*, p. 269.
18 *Collectio Avellana*, 138.
19 *ibid.*, 141.
20 *ibid.*, 143.
21 *LP, Vita Hormisdae*, p. 270.
22 *Collectio Avellana*, 114, 147, 199.
23 A. A. Vassiliev, *Justin the First*
   (Harvard, 1950), pp. 166–7.
24 *Collectio Avellana*, 158.
25 *ibid.*, 167; *LP, Vita Hormisdae*,
   p. 270.
26 *Collectio Avellana*, 159.
27 *LP, Vita Symmachi*, p. 261.
28 *LP, Vita Hormisdae*, pp. 270–1.
29 *Collectio Avellana*, 175.
30 *ibid.*, 202, 203, 207, 210, 221.
31 *ibid.*, 193.
32 *ibid.*, 225, 226.
33 *ibid.*, 227.
34 *ibid.*, 185.
35 *ibid.*, 186.
36 *ibid.*, 185.
37 *ibid.*, 208.
38 *ibid.*, 209.
39 *ibid.*, 232.
40 *ibid.*, 235.
41 *ibid.*, 233.
42 *ibid.*, 243.
43 *ibid.*, 236, 237.
44 *ibid.*, 216, 217.
45 *ibid.*, 191.
46 *ACO*, 4, ii, 3.
47 *Collectio Avellana*, 216, 224.
48 Viktor Schurr, *Die Trinitätslehre
   des Boethius im Lichte der
   Skythischen Kontroversen*
   (Paderborn, 1935).

49 *PL*, 63, pp. 534–6.
50 *Collectio Avellana*, 231.
51 *ACO*, 4, ii, pp. 46–62.
52 *Collectio Avellana*, 236.
53 *PL*, 59, pp. 388–408.
54 Boethius, *Tractate* 5, p. 72.
55 *ibid*.
56 *PL*, 67, pp. 513–20.
57 *Anonymus Valesianus*, 88, 94, 95.
58 Cassiodorus, *Variae*, v, 16–20.
59 *Anonymus Valesianus*, 90; *LP, Vita Johannis I*, p. 275.
60 Marcellinus, *Chronicon* ad 525, p. 102.
61 *LP, Vita Johannis I*, p. 275.
62 *LP, ibid*.
63 *Anonymus Valesianus*, 94.
64 *ibid*., 60.
65 Cassiodorus, *Variae*, ii, 27.
66 Gregory I, *Dialogi*, iii, 2.
67 *Anonymus Valesianus*, 93.
68 J. B. De Rossi, *Inscriptiones Christianae*, ii, 57.
69 G. B. Picotti, 'La Politica Religiosa di Teodorico', *Settimane*, iii (1956), pp. 173–226.

Chapter 8 the Gothic Reaction

1 *Anonymus Valesianus*, 85–7, 92.
2 Procopius, *De Bello Gothico*, v, 1.
3 *Anonymus Valesianus*, 85.
4 Boethius, *Consolatio Philosophiae*, i, 4.
5 There is a full discussion of Boethius's cultural role in Pierre Courcelle, *Late Latin Writers and their Greek Sources* (Cambridge, Massachusetts, 1969), pp. 273–330.
6 Viktor Schurr, *Die Trinitätslehre des Boethius im Lichte der 'Skythischen Kontroversen'* (Paderborn, 1935).

7 John Maxentius, *Collectio Palatina* (*ACO*, i, 5, pp. 3–215).
8 Boethius calls him 'one of the most precious ornaments of the human race' (*Consolatio Philosophiae*, ii, 4).
9 For a detailed discussion of this circle see J. A. Moorhead, 'The Catholic Episcopate in Ostrogothic Italy' (Liverpool Univ. Ph.D. thesis, unpublished), pp. 136–76.
10 *CSEL*, ix, p. 1.
11 *PLS*, iv, 20–1.
12 Dionysius Exiguus, *Vita Sancti Pachomii* (ed. H. Van Craneburgh, Brussels, 1969).
13 *Collectio Avellana*, 173.
14 Boethius, *Consolatio Philosophiae*, i, 4.
15 *Anonymus Valesianus*, 85.
16 Procopius, *De Bello Gothico*, v, 1.
17 Cassiodorus, *Variae*, v, 40, 41.
18 *ibid*., viii, 16.
19 Procopius, *De Bello Gothico*, v, 4.
20 *PL*, 66, p. 20.
21 Cassiodorus, *Variae*, viii, 17.
22 *ibid*., viii, 21.
23 Boethius, *Consolatio Philosophiae*, i, 4.
24 *ibid*.
25 *Anonymus Valesianus*, 87.
26 L. H. Coster, *The Iudicium Quinquevirale* (Cambridge, Massachusetts, 1935), pp. 40–63.
27 *LP, Vita Vigilii*, p. 298.
28 *Anonymus Valesianus*, 87–8.
29 C. S. Lewis, *The Discarded Image* (Cambridge, 1964), p. 77.
30 *Anonymus Valesianus*, 92; *LP, Vita Johannis I*, p. 276.
31 *LP, Vita Johannis I*, p. 277, n. 7.
32 Procopius, *De Bello Gothico*, v, 1.
33 *Anonymus Valesianus*, 93.

34 Gregory I, *Dialogi*, iv, 30.
35 *PL*, 95, p. 978.
36 On this question see W. Bark, 'The Legend of Boethius' Martyrdom', *Speculum*, 21 (1946), pp. 312–17. Cf. H. R. Patch, 'The Beginnings of the Legend of Boethius', *Speculum*, 22 (1947), pp. 443–5.
37 *Anonymus Valesianus*, 95.
38 *LP, Vita Felicis IV*, p. 280, n. 5.
39 Cassiodorus, *Variae*, viii, 15.
40 J. B. De Rossi, *Inscriptiones Christianae*, ii, p. 126.
41 Cassiodorus, *Variae*, viii, 24.
42 *LP, Vita Bonifacii II*, p. 282, n. 4.
43 *ibid.*
44 *LP, Vita Bonifacii II*, p. 281.
45 *ibid.*, p. 282, n. 8.
46 *ibid.*, p. 281.
47 Mansi, ix, p. 263.
48 *LP, Vita Bonifacii II*, p. 281.
49 De Rossi, *Inscriptiones Christianae*, i, no. 1029.
50 *LP, Vita Bonifacii II*, p. 281.
51 *ibid.*
52 Cassiodorus, *Variae*, ix, 15.
53 *ibid.*, xii, 20.
54 *LP, Vita Johannis II*, p. 285.
55 Mansi, viii, p. 740.
56 *LP, Vita Johannis II*, p. 285; Liberatus, *Breviarium*, 20.
57 *Collectio Avellana*, 84.
58 Cassiodorus, *Variae*, ix, 17.
59 *PL*, 66, p. 20.
60 *LP, Vita Agapiti*, p. 287.
61 Mansi, 9, pp. 873–1162.
62 *LP, Vita Silverii*, p. 290.
63 Procopius, *De Bello Gothico*, v, 6.
64 Auctarium Marcellini, ad 547, p. 108.
65 Liberatus, *Breviarium*, 22.
66 *LP, Vita Silverii*, pp. 292–3.
67 Procopius, *Anecdota*, i, 14.
68 Procopius, *De Bello Gothico*, v. 25.

69 *ibid.*; Liberatus, *Breviarium*, 22; Marcellinus, *Chronicon, Continuatio* ad 537.
70 J. B. De Rossi, *Inscriptiones Christianae*, i, p. 482.
71 'Laurentian Fragment', p. 46.

Chapter 9 The 'Three Chapters' Controversy
1 *LD*, 58–63.
2 *LP, Vita Bonifacii III*, p. 316.
3 *LD*, 58.
4 *PL*, 69, pp. 21–5.
5 Louis Duchesne, 'Vigile et Pelage', *Revue des questions historiques*, 36 (1884), p. 378.
6 Arator, *De Actibus Apostolorum; CSEL*, 72, p. xxviii.
7 Facundus of Hermiana, *Pro Defensione Trium Capitulorum*, iv, 3, 4; Facundus of Hermiana, *Liber Contra Mocianum*, pp. 863–5.
8 *PL*, 67, pp. 921–8.
9 Ferrandus, *ep.* 6.
10 Facundus, *Pro Defensione*, iv, 3.
11 *LP, Vita Vigilii*, pp. 296–7.
12 Louis Duchesne, 'Vigile et Pelage', p. 385.
13 Mansi, 9, p. 152.
14 Victor of Tunnuna, *Chronicon* ad 544.
15 Procopius, *De Bello Gothico*, vii, 16.
16 *LP, Vita Vigilii*, p. 297. The *Vita Vigilii* calls Valentine bishop of Saints Rufina and Secunda. But he was in fact bishop of Silva Candida as his signature to the 1st *Constitutum* of Vigilius (*Collectio Avellana*, 83) attests. As he lacked hands, the actual signing was done on Valentine's behalf by Bishop Zaccheus of Scyllacium.

17 Procopius, *De Bello Gothico*, vii, 15.
18 Pelagius I, *ep.* 14.
19 Facundus of Hermiana, *Pro Defensione Trium Capitulorum*, iv, 3–4.
20 *PL*, 67, pp. 921–8.
21 Procopius, *De Bello Gothico*, vii, 16, 20, 21.
22 Facundus, *Pro Defensione*, iv, 3–4.
23 *ibid.*, iv, 3.
24 Agnellus, *Lib. Pont. Rav.*, 70.
25 Facundus, *Liber Contra Mocianum*, p. 862.
26 Theophanes, *Chronographia*, a.m. 6039.
27 Facundus, *Liber Contra Mocianum*, p. 861.
28 *ibid.*
29 *PL*, 69, p. 60.
30 *PL*, 69, p. 44.
31 Facundus of Hermiana, *Pro Defensione Trium Capitulorum Concilii Chalcedonensis*, *PL*, 67, pp. 527–854.
32 Victor of Tunnuna, *Chronicon* ad 549.
33 *ibid.* ad 550.
34 Mansi, 9, p. 154.
35 *PL*, 69, pp. 43–51.
36 Mansi, 9, p. 359.
37 *PL*, 69, pp. 43–51.
38 *ILCV*, 1312.
39 *PL*, 73, p. 49.
40 Jaffe, 925.
41 Mansi, 9, p. 349.
42 *ibid.*, 9, p. 154.
43 *ibid.*
44 *PL*, 69, pp. 59–62.
45 Mansi, 9, p. 155.
46 *LP, Vita Vigilii*, p. 297.
47 *PL*, 69, pp. 53–9.
48 Mansi, 9, pp. 56–7.
49 *Collectio Avellana*, 83, pp. 231–2.
50 Jaffe, 932.

51 *Collectio Avellana*, 83, pp. 234–6.
52 Mansi, 9, pp. 178–86.
53 *Collectio Avellana*, 83.
54 Mansi, 9, p. 349.
55 *ibid.*, 9, pp. 202–346.
56 Victor of Tunnuna, *Chronicon* ad 553.
57 *ibid.* ad 555.
58 Facundus, *Liber Contra Mocianum*, pp. 853, 855.
59 *LP, Vita Vigilii*, p. 298; Pelagius I, *ep.* 80.
60 Jaffe, 936.
61 Mansi, 9, p. 457.
62 Agnellus, *Lib. Pont. Rav.*, 70–1.
63 *ibid.*, 74, 76.
64 *ibid.*, 77.
65 *ibid.*, 72–81.
66 *ibid.*, 72–81.
67 For a detailed discussion see Otto von Simson, *Sacred Fortress* (Chicago, 1948).
68 Agnellus, *Lib. Pont. Rav.*, 85.
69 Agnellus, *Lib. Pont. Rav.*, 84; Pelagius I, *ep.* 37, 50, 74.
70 Agnellus, *Lib. Pont. Rav.*, 85; Marini, *Papiri*, 87.
71 Gregory I, *ep.* ii, 28.
72 *ibid.*, *ep.* iii, 57; vi, 2.
73 *LP, Vita Honorii*, p. 323.
74 *LD*, 1, *superscriptiones*, 7, 9.
75 Pelagius I, *ep.* 80: Pelagius Diaconus, *In Defensione Trium Capitulorum*, ed. Robert Devreesse, *Studi e Testi*, 57 (1932), see especially pp. 31, 41, 55, 56, 65.
76 *LP, Vita Vigilii*, p. 299.
77 Victor of Tunnuna, *Chronicon* ad 558.
78 *LP, Vita Vigilii*, p. 299.
79 J. B. De Rossi, *Inscriptiones Christianae*, ii, pp. 83, 117.
80 *LP, Vita Pelagii I*, p. 303.
81 *ibid.*
82 Pelagius I, *ep.* 11.

83 *ibid., ep.* 7.

84 *ibid., ep.* 41.

85 *ibid., ep.* 37, 50, 74.

86 *ibid., ep.* 10.

87 J. B. De Rossi, *Inscriptiones Christianae*, ii, p. 208.

88 Pelagius I, *ep.* 77.

89 *ibid., ep.* 42.

90 *ibid., ep.* 77.

91 *ibid., ep.* 42.

92 *LP, Vita Pelagii I*, p. 303.

93 Pelagius I, *ep.* 14.

94 *ibid., ep.* 83.

95 *ibid., ep.* 9.

96 *ibid., ep.* 85.

97 *ibid., ep.* 82.

98 *ibid., ep.* 51.

99 *ibid., ep.* 17.

100 *LP, Vita Pelagii I*, p. 303.

Chapter 10 The Lombardic Crisis

1 Evagrius, *Historia Ecclesiastica*, v, 16.

2 Sigebert, *Liber de Scriptoribus Ecclesiasticis*, 116; *PL*, 73, p. 49. See Pierre Courcelle, *Late Latin Writers and their Greek Sources*, p. 359, n. 35, though he mistakes John's rank, calling him a deacon when at the time he did his compilation he was only a subdeacon.

3 Justinian, *Novellae*, Appendix 6–7.

4 *HL*, ii, 3.

5 *LP, Vita Johannis III*, p. 305.

6 *HL*, ii, 5; *LP, Vita Johannis III*, p. 305.

7 *LP, Vita Johannis III*, pp. 305–6.

8 Agnellus, *Lib. Pont. Rav.*, 95.

9 W. Goffart, 'Byzantine Policy in the West under Tiberius II and Maurice', *Traditio*, 13 (1957), pp. 73–118.

10 Menander, *Fragmenta*, 62. Cf. P. Goubert, *Byzance Avant L'Islam* (Paris, 1965), 2, ii, p. 17.

11 *LP, Vita Benedicti I*, p. 308. The emperor is erroneously referred to here as Justinian. But Justin II must be meant, since Justinian was dead.

12 *HL*, iii, 22.

13 *LP, Vita Pelagii II*, p. 309.

14 *MGH, ep. Merov*, 9.

15 Gregory I, *ep.* appendix 2.

16 J. B. De Rossi, *Inscriptiones Christianae*, ii, p. 145.

17 Joannes Diaconus, *Vita Gregorii*, i, 39.

18 Gregory I, *ep.* i, 5, 3, 4, 7, 6, 29, 41, 30, 31, 26.

19 Paulus Diaconus, *Vita Gregorii*, 15.

20 Joannes Diaconus, *Vita Gregorii*, i, 26; ii, 11, 12.

21 *ibid.*, iv, 80.

22 *ibid.*, ii, 12.

23 Gregory I, *ep.* ii, 38.

24 *ibid., ep.* xii, 5.

25 *ibid., ep.* i, 39a; viii, 25.

26 *ibid., ep.* vii, 29; iii, 63; xi, 55.

27 *ibid., ep.* iv, 2.

28 *ibid., ep.* ix, 107.

29 Gregory I, *Magna Moralia*, xxvii, 21.

30 Adolf von Harnack, *Lehrbuch der Dogmengeschichte*, iii (Leipzig, 1890), p. 233.

31 Gregory I, *ep.* i, 30.

32 *ibid., ep.* i, 3.

33 *ibid., ep.* v, 40.

34 Gregory I, *Homiliae in Ezechiel*, i, 2, 26.

35 Gregory I, *ep.* i, 70.

36 *ibid., ep.* i, 17; ii, 4.

37 *ibid., ep.* ii, 7, 32, 33.

38 *ibid., ep.* ii, 14, 34, 45.

39 *ibid., ep.* ii, 14.

40 *ibid., ep.* ii, 45.

41 *ibid., ep.* v, 36.

42 *HL*, iv, 8.

43 Gregory I, *ep.* v, 36.

44 *ibid., ep.* ii, 45.

45 *ibid., ep.* v, 30.

46 *ibid., ep.* v, 39.
47 *Continuatio Prosperi Havniensis,* 17.
48 Gregory I, *ep.* 39.
49 *ibid., ep.* 36.
50 *ibid., ep.* iv, 2.
51 *ibid., ep.* v, 34.
52 *ibid., ep.* ix, 11.
53 *HL,* iv, 20, 23–5, 28.
54 Gregory I, *ep.* iii, 61.
55 *ibid.*
56 *ibid., ep.* viii, 10.
57 *ibid., ep.* v, 39, 41, 44.
58 *ibid.*
59 *ibid., ep.* vii, 30.
60 *ibid., ep.* vii, 28; xiii, 43; cf. *ep.* vii, 31.
61 *LP, Vita Bonifacii III,* p. 316.
62 Gregory I, *ep.* xiii, 34.
63 F. Homes Dudden, *Gregory the Great* (London, 1905), ii, p. 263.
64 Gregory I, *ep.* i, 16.
65 *ibid., ep.* i, 16b.
66 *ibid., ep.* ix, 154.
67 *ibid., ep.* xiii, 36.
68 *ibid., ep.* iii, 54.
69 *ibid., ep.* iii, 66.
70 *ibid., ep.* v, 11.
71 *ibid., ep.* v, 15.
72 *ibid., ep.* ix, 167.
73 *LP, Vita Bonifacii IV,* p. 317; *HL,* iv, 36.
74 *LP, Vita Deusdedit,* p. 319.
75 *Continuatio Prosperi Havniensis,* 21–2.
76 *LP, Vita Bonifacii V,* p. 321; *Continuatio Prosperi Havniensis,* 23.
77 *LP, Vita Honorii,* p. 323.
78 J. B. De Rossi, *Inscriptiones Christianae,* ii, p. 127.
79 *PG 91,* pp. 244–5; *LP, Vita Honorii,* p. 324, cf. also *Vita S. Bertulfi,* 6.
80 Bede, *Historia Ecclesiastica,* ii, 17, 18, 19; iii, 7.
81 Constantine Porphyrogenitus, *De Administrando Imperii,* 31;

LP, Vita Joannis IV, p. 330; cf. also D. Mandic, 'Dalmatia in the Exarchate of Ravenna', *Byzantion,* 34 (1964), pp. 371–2.
82 *LP, Vita Honorii,* pp. 323–4.
83 *MGH, ep. Lang.,* 3.
84 *Chron. Pat. Grad.,* 7.
85 *LP, Vita Severini,* p. 328.
86 *MGH, ep. Lang.,* 2.
87 *LP, Vita Honorii,* p. 323.
88 Jaffe, 2034.
89 *ibid.,* 2015.
90 *LP, Vita Honorii,* p. 325, n. 2.

Chapter 11 The Monothelete Crisis

1 *PL,* 80, pp. 470–4.
2 V. Grumel, 'Recherches sur l'histoire de Monothélisme', *Echos d'Orient,* 28 (1929), pp. 272–82.
3 *PL,* 80, p. 603.
4 *PG,* 91, pp. 244–5; *PL,* 129, 572.
5 Mansi, 11, p. 732.
6 *LD,* 84.
7 Mansi, 10, pp. 677–8.
8 *LP, Vita Severini,* pp. 328–9.
9 Mansi, 10, p. 607.
10 Mansi, 11, p. 9.
11 *LP, Vita Theodori,* pp. 331–2.
12 *PL,* 87, pp. 78–9.
13 Maximus, *Disputatio cum Pyrrho, PG,* 91, pp. 287–354.
14 *LP, Vita Theodori,* p. 332; Theophanes, *Chronographia,* a.m. 6121.
15 *LP, Vita Theodori,* p. 333.
16 *ibid.,* p. 332.
17 Mansi, 10, p. 879; *PG,* 90, pp. 171–96.
18 *LP, Vita Martini,* p. 336.
19 *PL,* 87, p. 201.
20 Mansi, 10, pp. 863–1188.
21 *ibid.,* p. 879.
22 *ibid.,* p. 903.
23 *LP, Vita Martini,* p. 337.

24 Martin I, *ep*. 14, 15; *Commemoratio, PL*, 87, pp. 119–98.
25 *LP, Vita Martini*, pp. 337–8.
26 Martin I, *ep*. 17.
27 Anastasius, *Relatio motionis factae inter domnum Maximum et socios eius et principes in secretario, PG*, 90, pp. 109–30.
28 Anastasius, *Epistola ad Theodosium presbyterum Gangrensem, PG*, 90, pp. 171–94.
29 Martin I, *ep*. 15.
30 *LP, Vita Martini*, p. 338.
31 Martin I, *ep*. 15, 17.
32 A. Guillou, 'L'Italia Bizantina', *Bolletino dell'Istituto Storico per il Medio Evo*, 78 (1967). pp. 1–20.
33 *LP, Vita Eugenii*, p. 341.
34 *PL*, 129, p. 613; *PG*, 90, p. 122.
35 *LP, Vita Eugenii*, p. 341.
36 *PL*, 129, p. 653.
37 *LP, Vita Vitaliani*, p. 343.
38 Mansi, 11, p. 572.
39 *ibid.*, p. 200.
40 *LP, Vita Vitaliani*, pp. 343–4; *HL*, v, 11.
41 *PL*, 87, pp. 103–6.
42 Agnellus, *Lib. Pont. Rav.*, 112, 115.
43 *ibid.*, 117–24.
44 *LP, Vita Adeodati*, p. 346.
45 Mansi, 11, p. 200.
46 *ibid.*, pp. 195–201.
47 *LP, Vita Agathonis*, p. 350.
48 Proceedings of the Constantinople Council, Mansi, 11, pp. 189–922, incorporating the decrees of the Roman synod of 680, pp. 767–76.
49 *PL*, 87, p. 1168.
50 *LP, Vita Agathonis*, p. 354.
51 *ibid.*, pp. 354–5.

Chapter 12 The Papal Revival
1 *LP, Vita Joannis V*, p. 366.
2 *LP, Vita Cononis*, p. 369.

3 *LP, Vita Constantini*, p. 391.
4 *LP, Vita Benedicti II*, p. 363.
5 *LP, Vita Joannis V*, p. 366.
6 *LP, Vita Constantini*, p. 389.
7 *LP, Vita Sergii*, p. 376.
8 Appendix 2.
9 *LD*, 58–63.
10 *LP, Vita Agathonis*, pp. 354–5.
11 *LP, Vita Benedicti II*, p. 363.
12 Martin I, *ep*. 15.
13 *LP, Vita Vitaliani*, p. 343.
14 *LP, Vita Cononis*, p. 368.
15 On the Italian army see A. Guillou, *Régionalisme et indépendance dans l'empire Bizantin au VII siècle: L'exemple de l'exarchat et la pentapole d'Italie* (Rome, 1969), pp. 147–63; E. Patlagean, 'Les armes et la cité à Rome', MAH 86 (1974), pp. 25–62.
16 Gregory I, *ep*. ii, 45.
17 *CIL*, X, 1591.
18 Marini, *Papiri*, 141.
19 Marini, *Papiri*, 109, 95.
20 Marini, *Papiri*, 95.
21 Agnellus, *Lib. Pont. Rav.*, 140.
22 *LD*, 60.
23 Jaffe, 2199, 2208, 2214, 2216, 2217, 2225.
24 *LP, Vita Severini*, p. 328.
25 *LP, Vita Martini*, p. 337.
26 *LP, Vita Joannis V*, p. 366.
27 *LP, Vita Cononis*, p. 368.
28 *ibid.*, p. 369.
29 *LP, Vita Sergii*, pp. 371–2.
30 *ibid.*, pp. 374–6.
31 *ibid.*, pp. 372–4.
32 *LP, Vita Joannis VI*, p. 383.
33 *LP, Vita Joannis VII*, pp. 385–6.
34 J. Breckinridge, 'Evidence for the Nature of Relations between Pope John VII and the Byzantine Emperor Justinian II', *Byzantische Zeitschrift*, 65 (1972), pp. 364–74.
35 *LP, Vita Constantini*, p. 389.

36 Agnellus, *Lib. Pont Rav.*,
136–45.
37 *ibid.*, 125.
38 *LP, Vita Constantini*, p. 390.
39 *ibid.*, pp. 389–91.
40 *ibid.*, p. 392.

Chapter 13 The Final Crisis
1 Theophanes, *Chronographia*,
a.m. 6210.
2 *LP, Vita Gregorii II*, p. 403.
3 *ibid.*, pp. 403–4.
4 The authenticity of the letters
of Gregory II to Leo III has still
not been satisfactorily
established. The older
commentators almost
uniformly dismissed them as
forgeries, thus for instance L.
Duchesne, *Le Liber Pontificalis*,
i, pp. 413–14, n. 45; Thomas
Hodgkin, *Italy and her Invaders*,
vi (Oxford, 1896), pp. 501–5;
L. Guérand, 'Les lettres de
Grégoire II à Léon l'Isaurien',
MAH, 10 (1890), pp. 44–60.
More recently their authenticity
has been accepted, for instance,
by E. Casper, 'Papst Gregor II
und der Bilderstreit', *Zeitschrift
für Kirchengeschichte*, 52 (1933),
pp. 72–89. But the most
convincing work on the letters
is by G. Ostrogorsky, 'Les
débuts de la querelle des
images', *Mélanges Charles Diehl*,
ii (Paris, 1930), pp. 232–55. He
argues that the letters have
survived in much later copies
and although the basic text is
probably authentic, the letters
have suffered from
interpolation, faulty translation
and copyists' errors. It is
therefore still very dangerous
to base any arguments on them.
5 *LP, Vita Gregorii II*, p. 400.
6 *ibid.*, p. 407.

7 R. E. Sullivan, 'The Papacy and
Missionary Activity in the
Early Middle Ages', *Medieval
Studies*, 17 (1955), pp. 46–106.
8 Theophanes, *Chronographia* a.m.
6221.
9 *LP, Vita Gregorii III*, pp.
415–17.
10 Theophanes, *Chronographia*,
a.m. 6224.
11 M. V. Anastos, 'The transfer of
Illyricum, Calabria and Sicily
to the jurisdiction of the
Patriarch of Constantinople in
732–3', *Studi Bizantini e
neoellenici in onore di S. G.
Mercati* (Rome, 1957), pp.
14–31. Against this V. Grumel,
'L'annexion de l'illyricum
oriental, de la Sicile et de la
Calabre au patriarchat de
Constantinople', *Recherches de
science religieuse*, 40 (1952), pp.
191–200, has argued that this
action was taken not by Leo III
but by his son Constantine V
after the fall of the exarchate.
12 *HL*, vi, 54.
13 *MGH, ep. Lang.*, 11.
14 *MGH, ep. Lang.*, 12.
15 *HL*, vi, 55; *LP, Vita Zachariae*,
p. 426.
16 *MGH, ep. Lang.*, 16.
17 *LP, Vita Zachariae*, p. 426.
18 *Codex Carolinus* 2; Fredegar,
Chronicle Continuation, 22.
19 *LP, Vita Gregorii III*, pp.
417–20.
20 *LP, Vita Zachariae*, p. 432.
21 St Boniface, *ep.* 52, 53.
22 *ibid.*, *ep.* 57, 58.
23 *ibid.*, *ep.* 59.
24 *LP, Vita Zachariae*, p. 433.
25 *PL*, 91, p. 1222.
26 All this is recounted in *LP,
Vita Zachariae*, pp. 426–31, 433.
27 *MGH, scriptores*, i, pp. 136,
138.

28 LP, Vita Zachariae, pp. 434–5.

29 O. Bertolini, 'La Ricomparsa della sede episcopale di Tres Tabernae nella seconda metà del secolo VIII e l'istituzione delle domuscultae', ASR, 75 (1952).

30 LP, Vita Zachariae, p. 432.

Chapter 14 Class Origins

1 Gregory I, Dialogi, iv, 16; Gregory I, Homiliae in Evangeliis, 38.

2 J. B. De Rossi, Inscriptiones Christianae, i, pp. 371–3.

3 LP, Vita Felicis III, p. 252.

4 J. B. De Rossi, Inscriptiones Christianae, i, p. 366.

5 ibid., i, pp. 351–2.

6 Antonio Ferrua, 'Nuove Iscrizioni della Via Ostiense', Epigraphica, 21 (1959), pp. 97–116.

7 J. B. De Rossi, Inscriptiones Christianae, ii, p. 69.

8 Ildefonso Schuster, 'Les ancêtres de St. Grégoire et leur sépulture de famille à St. Paul de Rome', Revue Bénédictine, 21 (1904), pp. 112–23.

9 LP, Vita Agapiti, p. 287.

10 Cassiodorus, De institutione divinarum litterarum, Praefatio, PL, 70, p. 1105.

11 H. I. Marrou, 'Autour de la Bibliothèque de Pape Agapit', MAH, 48 (1931), pp. 124–69.

12 MGH, aa, xii, p. 411.

13 LP, Vita Symmachi, p. 261.

14 MGH, aa, xii, p. 443.

15 LP, Vita Felicis III, p. 252.

16 Joannes Diaconus, Vita Gregorii, i, 9.

17 ibid., iv, 83.

18 Gregory I, Dialogi, iv, 16; Homiliae in Evangeliis, 38.

19 Gregory I, ep. i, 37.

20 ibid., ep. i, 42.

21 ibid., ep. ix, 200.

22 For instance: F. Homes Dudden, Gregory the Great, i, 8; Walter Stuhlfath, Gregor der Grosse (Heidelberg, 1913), Appendix 3, pp. 95–7; P. Fedele, 'Il fratello di Gregorio Magno', ASR, 42 (1919), pp. 607–13; P. Ewald and L. M. Hartmann, MGH, Registrum Epistolarum Gregorii I Papae (Berlin, 1887), i, 66, n. 5.

23 Gregory of Tours, Historia Francorum, x, 1.

24 Gregory I, ep. ix, 44.

25 ibid., ep. vii, 34; ix, 116.

26 ibid., ep. xi, 4.

27 P. Fedele, 'Il fratello di Gregorio Magno'.

28 'Laurentian Fragment', p. 46.

29 Gregory I, ep. i, 37. A subsequent letter (ep. i, 57) gives Palatina's rank more precisely as illustris.

30 Gregory of Tours, Historia Francorum, x, 1.

31 CTh., 16, ii, 9, 349.

32 LP, Vita Vigilii, p. 296.

33 Procopius, De Bello Gothico, v, 26; vi, 21.

34 LP, Vita Vigilii, p. 297.

35 Mansi, 9, p. 351.

36 LP, Vita Pelagii I, p. 303.

37 Procopius, De Bello Gothico, vii, 16.

38 LP, Vita Johannis III, p. 305.

39 Evagrius, Historia Ecclesiastica, v, 16.

40 LP, Vita Bonifacii II, p. 281.

41 Ennodius, ep. viii, 33.

42 LP, Vita Hormisdae, p. 269.

43 ILCV, 1312.

44 LP, Vita Felicis IV, p. 279.

45 Gregory I, Dialogi, i, 4.

46 LP, Vita Bonifacii IV, p. 317.

47 Gregory I, Dialogi, iii, 20.

48 LP, Vita Joannis IV, p. 330.

49 *LP, Vita Deusdedit*, p. 319.
50 *LP, Vita Theodori*, p. 331.
51 *LP, Vita Bonifacii III*, p. 316.
52 *LP, Vita Honorii*, p. 323.
53 J. B. De Rossi, *Inscriptiones Christianae*, ii, p. 127.
54 *LP, Vita Severini*, p. 328.
55 P. Llewellyn, *Rome in the Dark Ages* (London, 1971), p. 139.
56 Justinian I, *Novellae*, appendix 8.
57 *ibid.*, appendix 9.
58 Menander, *fragmenta*, 62.
59 Gregory I, *ep.* xiii, I.
60 Gregory I, *Homiliae in Ezechiel*, ii, 6, 22.
61 Agnellus, *Lib. Pont. Rav.*, 95.
62 J. Sundwall, *Abhandlungen zur Geschichte des ausgehenden Römertums* (Helsinki, 1919).
63 A. Chastagnol, 'Le Sénat Romain sous la règne d'Odoacre', *Antiquitas*, series 3, fasc. 3 (1966).
64 Procopius, *De Bello Gothico*, v, 11, 26.
65 *ibid.*, vi, 21.
66 *ibid.*, viii, 28–33.
67 *LP, Vita Vigilii*, p. 298.
68 Procopius, *De Bello Gothico*, vii, 20.

Chapter 15 Age and Experience

1 J. B. De Rossi, *Inscriptiones Christianae*, i, 1029.
2 *LP, Vita Johannis I*, p. 275.
3 J. B. De Rossi, *Inscriptiones Christianae*, ii, p. 127.
4 *PG*, 91, p. 143.
5 Pelagius I, *ep.* 77.
6 *LP, Vita Sisinnii*, p. 388.
7 *LP, Vita Johannis I*, pp. 275–6.
8 *PL*, 69, pp. 53–9.
9 *LP, Vita Constantini*, p. 391.
10 *LP, Vita Johannis V*, p. 367.
11 *LP, Vita Cononis*, p. 369.
12 *LP, Vita Benedicti II*, p. 363.

13 *LP, Vita Agathonis*, p. 350.
14 Martin I, *ep.* 15.
15 Paulus Diaconus, *Vita Gregorii*, 5; Gregory I, *Dialogi*, iii, 33; Gregory I, *Homiliae in Evangeliis*, ii, 34, 1; Gregory I, *ep.* ii, 45; x, 14.
16 *PG*, 103, p. 533.
17 *LP, Vita Silverii*, p. 290.
18 *LP, Vita Johannis II*, p. 285.
19 *ibid.*, p. 285, n. 1.
20 Mansi, 8, p. 740.
21 J. B. De Rossi, *Inscriptiones Christianae*, ii, p. 126.
22 See Part 3, chapter 9 for details.
23 Gelasius I, *ep.* 12.
24 J. B. De Rossi, *Inscriptiones Christianae*, ii, p. 126.
25 *LP, Vita Anastasii*, p. 258.
26 Gelasius I, *ep.* 30; *MGH, aa*, xii, pp. 413, 443.
27 Felix III, *ep.* 13; Gelasius I, *ep.* 30.
28 *MGH, aa*, xii, pp. 415, 443.
29 Felix III, *ep.* 13; Gelasius I, *ep.* 30; *MGH, aa*, xii, p. 410.
30 Ennodius, *ep.* viii, 33, 39.
31 See Part 2, chapter 7 for details.
32 *LP, Vita Hormisdae*, p. 270; *Collectio Avellana*, 149, 159, 170, 185, 192, 213, 217, 218, 219, etc.
33 J. B. De Rossi, *Inscriptiones Christianae*, i, 1029.
34 *PL*, 62, p. 513.
35 Hormisdas, *ep.* 26.
36 Mansi, 8, p. 741.
37 Liberatus, *Breviarium*, 22, 24.
38 *LP, Vita Silverii*, p. 292.
39 Victor of Tunnuna, *Chronicon ad 558*; Procopius, *Anecdota*, 27, 17; *LP, Vita Vigilii*, p. 299.
40 Liberatus, *Breviarium*, 22.
41 *ibid*
42 Mansi, 8, pp. 970, 1143.
43 Liberatus, *Breviarium*, 22.

44 Procopius, *De Bello Gothico*, vii, 16, 20, 21.

45 *Collectio Avellana*, 83, p. 320.

46 Pelagius Diaconus, *In Defensione Trium Capitulorum*, ed. Robert Devreesse, *Studi e Testi*, 57 (1932).

47 *LP, Vita Vigilii*, p. 299.

48 Joannes Diaconus, *Vita Gregorii*, i, 25.

49 Paulus Diaconus, *Vita Gregorii*, 7; Joannes Diaconus, *Vita Gregorii*, i, 26.

50 *HL*, iii, 20.

51 Gregory I, *ep.* v, 6, 15, 37, 44; vi, 58; vii, 33; etc.

52 Gregory I, *ep.* xiii, 41, 43; xiv, 2, 8.

53 Gregory I, *ep.* i, 50; iv, 11; vi, 31; xiv, 8.

54 P. Llewellyn, 'The Roman Church in the 7th Century: the legacy of Gregory the Great', *JEH*, 25 (1974), pp. 363–80.

55 Joannes Diaconus, *Vita Gregorii*, ii, 11.

56 Gregory I, *ep.* ii, 1.

57 Gregory I, *ep.* v, 44.

58 *MGH, Registrum Epistolarum Gregorii I*, ii, appendix 2; *MGH, ep. Merov.*, 32.

59 Gregory I, *ep.* i, 11; vii, 27, 28; xi, 29; xii, 6; i, 25, 26; viii, 16; xiii, 41.

60 Gregory I, *Dialogi*, iii, 20; *ep.* ix, 72; i, 50; iv, 11; vi, 31.

61 Joannes Diaconus, *Vita Gregorii*, iii, 7; Gregory I, *ep.* v, 35; xiii, 45; xiv, 3 (on Epiphanius); Gregory I, *Dialogi*, ii, 8; *ep.* ix, 8 (on Florentius).

62 Gregory I, *Dialogi, Praefatio*; *ep.* vi, 24; iii, 54; ii, 38; ix, 11, 219.

63 Joannes Diaconus, *Vita Gregorii*, ii, II; Gregory I, *ep.*

xi, 15 (on Aemilianus); Gregory I, *ep.* v, 26; vi, 12; ix, 97; xi, 15; Joannes Diaconus, *Vita Gregorii*, ii, 11 (on Paterius); Gregory I, *ep.* v, 6; vii, 29; *Dialogi*, ii, 18 (on Exhilaratus).

64 Gregory I, *ep.* iii, 18.

65 Bede, *Historia Ecclesiastica*, ii, 4, 17, 18, 19. Pope Honorius encouraged his correspondents to read the works of Gregory.

66 Bede, *Historia Ecclesiastica*, ii, 4.

67 *LP, Vita Gregorii II*, pp. 397–8; *LP, Vita Gregorii III*, p. 419.

68 J. B. De Rossi, *Inscriptiones Christianae*, ii, p. 127.

69 *LP, Vita Sabiniani*, p. 315.

70 Joannes Diaconus, *Vita Gregorii*, iv, 69.

71 *HL*, iv, 24.

72 *LP, Vita Sabiniani*, p. 315.

73 Paulus Diaconus, *Vita Gregorii*, 29.

74 *LP, Vita Sabiniani*, p. 315.

75 *LP, Vita Bonifacii III*, p. 316.

76 J. B. De Rossi, *Inscriptiones Christianae* ii, 128, 208.

77 *LP, Vita Bonifacii IV*, p. 317.

78 J. B. De Rossi, *Inscriptiones Christianae*, ii, p. 127.

79 *LP, Vita Deusdedit*, p. 319.

80 *ibid.*

81 J. B. De Rossi, *Inscriptiones Christianae*, ii, 126, 141.

82 *LP, Vita Bonifacii V*, p. 321.

83 J. B. De Rossi, *Inscriptiones Christianae*, ii, p. 128.

84 J. B. De Rossi, *Inscriptiones Christianae*, ii, p. 127.

85 *LP, Vita Honorii*, p. 324.

86 *PG*, 91, pp. 244–5.

87 *PL*, 80, pp. 483–4.

88 Jonas, *Vita S. Bertulfi*, 6.

89 *LP, Vita Honorii*, p. 323.

90 *LP, Vita Severini*, p. 329.

91 *LP, Vita Johannis IV*, p. 330.
92 Bede, *Historia Ecclesiastica*, ii, 19.
93 *LP, Vita Theodori*, p. 331.
94 *LP, Vita Eugenii*, p. 341.
95 *LP, Vita Doni*, p. 348.
96 *LP, Vita Agathonis*, pp. 350, 355.
97 *LP, Leonis II*, p. 359.
98 Mansi, 11, pp. 1085, 179.
99 *LP, Vita Benedicti II*, pp. 363–4.
100 *LP, Vita Adeodati*, p. 346.
101 J. B. De Rossi, *Inscriptiones Christianae*, ii, p. 129.
102 *LP, Vita Johannis V*, p. 367.
103 *LP, Vita Cononis*, p. 368.
104 *ibid.*, p. 369.
105 *LP, Vita Sergii*, p. 371.
106 *LP, Vita Johannis VII*, p. 386, n. 1.
107 C. Vogel, *Le Liber Pontificalis*, iii (Paris, 1957), p. 99.
108 *LP, Vita Agathonis*, p. 356.
109 Jaffe, 2118.
110 *LP, Vita Constantini*, p. 389.
111 *LP, Vita Gregorii II*, p. 396.
112 *ibid.*, p. 410.
113 *LP, Vita Gregorii III*, p. 415; Mansi, 12, pp. 264–6.
114 *LP, Vita Gregorii III*, p. 415.
115 *LP, Vita Zachariae*, p. 435.

Chapter 16 Geographical Origins and Cultural Attainments

1 See appendix I for details of papal birthplaces.
2 *LP, Vita Cononis*, p. 368.
3 *LP, Vita Johannis VII*, pp. 385–6.
4 *LP, Vita Theodori*, p. 331.
5 *LP, Vita Sergii*, p. 371.
6 C. Diehl, *Etudes sur l'administration dans l'Exarchat de Ravenne* (Paris, 1888), pp. 241–7.

7 P. Brown, 'Eastern and Western Christendom in Late Antiquity: A Parting of the Ways' in *Studies in Church History 13*, ed. Derek Baker (Oxford, 1976), pp. 1–24.
8 *LP, Vita Johannis VII*, p. 385.
9 Bede, *Historia Ecclesiastica*, ii, 19.
10 *PG*, 91, pp. 244–5; *PL*, 129, p. 572.
11 Honorius I, *ep.* 5.
12 *PL*, 87, pp. 78–9.
13 Mansi, 10, pp. 863–1188.
14 Jaffe, 2093; Eddius Stephanus, *Life of Bishop Wilfrid, c.* 5.
15 Bede, *Historia Ecclesiastica*, iv, 1.
16 *LP, Vita Agathonis*, p. 350.
17 Eddius Stephanus, *Vita S. Wilfridi*, 29.
18 *LP, Vita Sergii*, p. 373.
19 *LP, Vita Constantini*, p. 389.
20 Mansi, 12, pp. 264–6; *LP, Vita Gregorii III*, pp. 422–3; Mansi, 12, pp. 381–4.
21 *LP, Vita Zachariae*, pp. 429, 430, 432.
22 *LP, Vita Zachariae*, pp. 429; Boniface, *ep.* 90.
23 Gregory I, *ep.* i, 28; vii, 27; x, 14, 21.
24 Mansi, 10, pp. 863–1188.
25 G. Ferrari, *Early Roman Monasteries* (Rome, 1957).
26 Mansi, 10, pp. 903–10.
27 *PG*, 90, p. 155. At his trial, Maximus declared: 'I love the Romans because we share the same faith, the Greeks because we share the same language.'
28 *PG*, 91, pp. 327–30.
29 *PL*, 87, p. 162.
30 *LP, Vita Agathonis*, pp. 350, 354; Mansi, 11, p. 211.
31 Eddius Stephanus, *Life of Bishop Wilfrid*, 53.
32 Mansi, 11, pp. 667, 670.

33 *Gesta Episcoporum Neapolitanorum*, 32.
34 *LP, Vita Constantini*, p. 389.
35 For example, George of Ostia, Maurice of Tibur, Nicetas of Gabii, Sergius of Praeneste. For full episcopal lists see P. B. Gams, *Series Episcoporum Ecclesiae Catholicae* (Ratisbon, 1873).
36 On the development of the *diaconia* see Part 4, chapter 14.
37 Gregory I, *ep.* ix, 26.
38 *LP, Vita Leonis II*, p. 360.
39 *LP, Vita Zachariae*, p. 434.
40 *LP, Vita Sergii*, p. 376.
41 Bede, *Historia Ecclesiastica*, iv, 1.
42 *LP, Vita Pauli I*, p. 465.
43 S. P. Van Dijk, 'Gregory the Great – Founder of the Urban *Schola Cantorum*', *Ephemerides Liturgicae*, 77 (1963), p. 336.
44 Gregory I, *ep.* v, 57a.
45 S. P. Van Dijk, 'Gregory the Great', pp. 345–56.
46 *LP, Vita Leonis II*, p. 359; *Vita Benedicti II*, p. 363; *Vita Sergii*, p. 371.
47 Bede, *Historia Ecclesiastica*, iv, 18.
48 *Ordo Romanus Primus*, edited and translated by E. G. C. F. Atchley (London, 1905).
49 Mansi, 9, p. 98.
50 Gregory I, *ep.* vii, 32; xi, 74.
51 *PG*, 91, pp. 244–5.
52 *PL*, 87, p. 114. Martin's testimony at his trial had to be delivered through an interpreter.
53 *PL*, 87, p. 1185.
54 *LP, Vita Leonis II*, p. 359.
55 *LP, Vita Gregorii III*, p. 415.
56 *LP, Vita Benedicti II*, p. 363.
57 *LP, Vita Johannis V*, p. 366.
58 *LP, Vita Johannis VII*, p. 385.
59 *LP, Vita Gregorii II*, p. 396.
60 *LP, Vita Zachariae*, p. 435.

61 On the cultural history of the period see especially P. Riché, *Education et culture dans l'Occident barbare* (Paris, 1962); P. Courcelle, *Late Latin Writers and their Greek Sources* (Cambridge, Massachusetts, 1969); A. Momigliano, 'Cassiodorus and the Italian culture of his time', *Proceedings of the British Academy*, 41 (1955), pp. 207–45; M. L. W. Laistner, *Thought and Letters in Western Europe 500–900* (London, 1957, 2nd ed); H. I. Marrou, *A History of Education in Antiquity* (London, 1957).
62 Gregory I, *ep.* viii, 28; xi, 40; vii, 31.
63 *LP, Vita Honorii I*, p. 323.
64 Agatho, *ep.* 1.
65 Gregory I, *ep.* xi, 34.
66 Gregory I, *Dialogi,* ii, *Prolegomena.*
67 *LP, Vita Cononis*, p. 368.

Chapter 17 The Central Administration

1 Loewenfeld, *ep.* 14.
2 Gregory I, *ep.* i, 81.
3 *LP, Vita Gregorii II*, p. 396; P. Courcelle, p. 394.
4 *LP, Vita Constantini*, p. 389.
5 Th. Sickel, ed., *Liber Diurnus Romanorum Pontificum* (Vienna, 1889).
6 *LD*, 59, 61–3.
7 *PL*, 62, p. 513.
8 *PL*, 68, p. 55.
9 Gregory I, *ep.* iii, 54.
10 Gregory I, *ep.* v, 26.
11 Scholasticus (ix, 43); Candidus (iv, 28; ix, 40); Vitus (ix, 97; ix, 118); Peter (ix, 128); Cyriacus (iv, 38); Fantinus (i, 42); Romanus (ii, 38); Gaudiosus (ix, 109).
12 Gregory I, *ep.* i, 39.

13 Urbicus in Sabina (iii, 21),
Scholasticus in Hortona (ix,
194), Sergius in Apulia (viii, 8,
9; ix, 88, 110, 112, 169, 200,
206), Vitalis in Sardinia (ix, 2,
123, 203, 204; xi, 13; xiv, 2)
Symmachus in Corsica (i, 50),
Sabinus in Sardinia (iii, 36),
Boniface in Corsica (ix, 110),
Fantinus in Sicily (iv, 43),
Romanus in Sicily (ii, 38; ix,
29; xi, 59) and perhaps
Boninus (ix, 191).

14 Gregory I, *ep*. i, 68.

15 Gregory I, *ep*. ix, 22.

16 Gregory I, *ep*. viii, 16.

17 *PL*, 69, p. 46.

18 Joannes Diaconus, *Vita
Gregorii*, iii, 7.

19 Gregory I, *ep*. iv, 34; xiii, 22;
i, 42.

20 Gregory I, *ep*. iii, 35; v, 28;
viii, 7.

21 Honorius I, *ep*. 14.

22 *LP, Vita Hormisdae*, pp.
269–70.

23 *LP, Vita Silverii*, pp. 292–3.

24 Liberatus, *Breviarium*, 23;
Procopius, *Anecdota*, xxvii, 17,
19.

25 Joannes Diaconus, *Vita
Gregorii*, i, 40; Gregory of
Tours, *Historia Francorum*, x,
1.

26 Gregory I, *ep*. xiii, 41.

27 Mansi, 10, p. 853; *PG*, 90, pp.
174–94.

28 Facundus of Hermiana, *Pro
Defensione Trium Capitulorum*,
iv, 3–4.

29 Pelagius I, *ep*. 77.

30 Joannes Diaconus, *Vita
Gregorii*, i, 26; Paulus
Diaconus, *Vita Gregorii*, 7.

31 Gregory I, *ep*. i, 6; ii, 36; v, 44.

32 *ibid*., iii, 51, 52, 66; vii, 23, 25,
29, 31.

33 *ibid*., vii, 27, 28; xi, 29.

34 *ibid*., xiii, 41.

35 Honorius I, *ep*. 5.

36 *LP, Vita Martini*, p. 337.

37 Mansi, x, 667, 678.

38 *ibid*.

39 *PG*, 90, p. 122.

40 *LP, Vita Vitaliani*, p. 343.

41 Gregory I, *ep*. xiii, 38, 39.

42 *ibid*., viii, 35.

43 *ibid*., xiii, 47, 48, 49, 50.

44 *ibid*., iii, 40, 41.

45 *ibid*., viii, 26; ix, 19.

46 *ibid*., xi, 6, 14.

47 *ibid*., xiii, 37.

48 *ibid*., Dialogi*, i, 4.

49 Pelagius, I, *ep*. 70, 71.

50 *ibid*., ep*. 49

51 Hormisdas, *ep*. 19, 20.

52 Gregory I, *ep*. viii, 16.

53 *LP, Vita Severini*, p. 328.

54 Gregory I, *ep*. vii, 23.

55 *ibid*., v, 30.

56 *ibid*., viii, 22.

57 *LP, Vita Symmachi*, p. 263.

58 Gregory I, *ep*. vii, 23.

59 *LP, Vita Joannis VI*, p. 383.

60 *LP, Vita Joannis IV*, p. 330.

61 *LP, Vita Symmachi*, p. 263.

62 Simplicius, *ep*. 1; Gelasius I,
ep. 16, 17; Gregory I, *ep*. xi,
56.

63 Agnellus, *Lib. Pont. Rav.*, 60.

64 Pelagius I, *ep*. 83.

65 J. B. De Rossi, *Roma
Sotterranea*, ii, 3, p. 521.

66 *LP, Vita Agathonis*, p. 350.

67 Gregory I, *Dialogi*, iii, 20.

68 *LP, Vita Gregorii II*, p. 396.

69 Mansi, 12, p. 384.

70 *LP, Vita Constantini*, pp.
389–90.

71 *LP, Vita Agathonis*, p. 350.

72 *LP, Vita Constantini*, p. 389.

73 Mansi, 12, p. 384l.

74 *LP, Vita Constantini*, p. 390.

75 *LP, Vita Vigilii*, p. 297.

76 Gregory I, *ep*. i, 11.

77 *ibid*., Dialogi*, iv, 36.

78 *ibid., ep.* xi, 53.
79 *LP, Vita Constantini*, p. 390.
80 *LP, Vita Zachariae*, p. 429; *LP, Vita Stephani III*, p. 470.
81 Bede, *Historia Ecclesiastica*, ii, 19.
82 J. B. De Rossi, *Inscriptiones Christianae*, ii, p. 129.
83 Gregory I, *ep.* ii, 1.
84 *PL*, 69, p. 47.
85 Gregory I, *ep.* ix, 11.
86 *ibid.*, xi, 4.
87 Bede, *Historia Ecclesiastica*, ii, 19.
88 Mansi, 12, p. 1035.
89 *LP, Vita Sergii*, p. 373.
90 Justinian, *Pragmatic Sanction*, 22.
91 Gregory I, *ep.* i, 2.
92 Gregory of Tours, *Historia Francorum*, x, 1.
93 Gelasius I, *Tractate*, 6, p. 603; Procopius, *De Bello Gothico*, vii, 15; Gregory I, *ep.* i, 70.
94 *LP, Vita Sabiniani*, p. 315.
95 *LP, Vita Zachariae*, p. 435.
96 Gregory I, *ep.* xi, 17; x, 8; v, 25.
97 Jaffe, 2220, 2213.
98 J. Lestocquoy, 'L' Administration de Rome et Diaconies du VII au IX siècle', *Rivista di archeologia cristiana*, 7 (1930), pp. 277–82.
99 *LP, Vita Benedicti II*, p. 364.
100 *LP, Vita Gelasii*, p. 255.
101 *PL*, 67, p. 231.
102 Eusebius, *Historia Ecclesiastica*, vi, 43.
103 Agnellus, *Lib. Pont. Rav*, 60.
104 *LP, Vita Gelasii*, p. 255.
105 Gelasius, *Tractate*, 6, p. 603.
106 Gelasius, *frag.* 36.
107 *ibid., frag.* 34.
108 *ibid., frag.* 35.
109 *PL*, 67, p. 231.
110 *LP, Vita Pelagii I*, p. 303.
111 Pelagius I, *ep.* 16, 17, 51, 82.

112 *ibid.*, 57.
113 *ibid.*, 47.
114 *ibid.*, 57.
115 *ibid.*, 43.
116 *ibid.*, 27.
117 Joannes Diaconus, *Vita Gregorii*, ii, 54.
118 *ibid.*, ii, 15.
119 Mansi, 9, p. 351.

Chapter 18 The Patrimonial Administration

1 *CTh.*, xvi, 2, 4.
2 Theophanes, *Chronographia*, a.m. 6224.
3 Agnellus, *Lib. Pont. Rav.*, III.
4 Jaffe, 633.
5 Pelagius I, *ep.* 83.
6 *ibid.*, 85.
7 Gelasius I, *frag.* 35.
8 Gregory I, *ep.* ix, 205.
9 *Codex Carolinus*, 2.
10 *MGH, ep. Merov.*, 12.
11 *HL*, vi, 28; *LP, Vita Johannis VII*, p. 385; *LP, Vita Gregorii II*, p. 398.
12 *LP, Vita Zachariae*, p. 428.
13 See Part 3, chapter 13.
14 Gregory I, *ep.* xiii, 37; *LD*, 52.
15 *ibid.*, ix, 20; v, 21; ix, 33; v, 56; i, 2; ix, 31.
16 *ibid.*, i, 37; ii, 38; ix, 84; ix, 236.
17 *ibid.*, i, 42, 70; ii, 38; ix, 124–7.
18 *ibid.*, ii, 10.
19 *ibid.*, i, 18; iii, 22, 35, 39; v, 9; ix, 142; i, 67; v, 23; viii, 23; ix, 170; i, 39, 40, 50, 60; v, 33; ix, 120; xiv, 2; ii, 46; viii, 23; i, 82; ii, 22, iii, 1; iv, 6; x, 4.
20 *ibid.*, i, 71; ix, 40; ix, 192; v, 33; i, 42.
21 *ibid.*, ii, 38.
22 *ibid.*, vi, 6, 51.
23 *ibid.*, iii, 33.
24 P. Grierson, 'The *Patrimonium Petri in Illis Partibus* and the Pseudo-Imperial Coinage in

Frankish Gaul', *Revue Belge de Numismatique*, 105 (1959), pp. 95–111.

25 Pelagius I, *ep.* 4, 9.
26 Gregory I, *ep.* vi, 10.
27 *MGH, ep. Merov.*, 12.
28 Joannes Diaconus, *Vita Gregorii*, ii, 53.
29 Gregory I, *ep.* ii, 23.
30 *PL*, 69, pp. 43–51.
31 Gelasius I, *frag.* 2; *PL*, 69, pp. 43–51.
32 Gregory I, *ep.* xi, 6.
33 Joannes Diaconus, *Vita Gregorii*, ii, 53.
34 Paul Fabre, 'Le patrimoine de l'église Romaine dans les Alpes Cottiennes', *MAH* 4 (1884), pp. 283–420.
35 Gregory I, *ep.* ix, 29.
36 Pelagius I, *ep.* 41, 44.
37 Pelagius I, *ep.* xi, 8; Cassiodorus, *Variae*, ii, 29; Agnellus, *Lib. Pont, Rav.*, III.
38 Pelagius I, *ep.* 22, 54.
39 Gregory I, *ep.* ix, 124–7.
40 Pelagius I, *ep.* 64, 88.
41 *ibid.*, 12, 29, 64.
42 Gregory I, *ep.* ix, 205.
43 *ibid., ep.* ix, 194.
44 *ibid.*, iii, 21; Pelagius I, *ep.* 14.
45 Pelagius I, *ep.* 14.
46 Gregory I, *ep.* iii, 21.
47 Jaffe, 2201, 2220, 2226, 2302.
48 Gregory I, *ep.* xiv, 14.
49 *ibid.*, ix, 96.
50 Joannes Diaconus, *Vita Gregorii*, ii, 53; Gregory I, *ep.* iii, 54; ix, 234.
51 Jaffe, 2217, 2218, 2214.
52 *ibid.*, 2222, 2205, 2216.
53 *ibid.*, 2210, 2225, 2298, 2190.
54 *ibid.*, 2201, 2220, 2302.
55 *ibid.*, 2221, 2209, 2211.
56 *ibid.*, 2191, 2219.
57 *ibid.*, 2219, 2196, 2198, 2211.

58 Joannes Diaconus, *Vita Gregorii*, ii, 24; Gregory I, *ep.* ix, 199; ii, 38.
59 Jaffe, 633.
60 Gelasius I, *frag.* 2.
61 Pelagius I, *ep.* 4, 9.
62 *ibid.*, 14, 83, 84.
63 *ibid.*, 4154; 28, 64, 88; 12, 29.
64 *ibid.*, 41.
65 Joannes Diaconus, *Vita Gregorii*, ii, 53.
66 Pelagius I, *ep.* 4, 9.
67 Gregory I, *ep.* vi, 51.
68 Gregory of Tours, *Historia Francorum*, ix, 12; Venantius Fortunatus, *Carmina*, 9, 10.
69 Gregory I, *ep.* vi, 6; vii, 12, 33.
70 *ibid.*, v, 31.
71 *ibid.* The new rector was almost certainly the priest of St Clement in Rome, who attended the 595 Synod (*ep.* v. 57a).
72 *ibid.*, vi, 51, 53.
73 *ibid.*, viii, 4.
74 *MGH, ep. Merov.*, 12.
75 Gregory I, *ep.* 73, 74, 75.
76 *ibid.*, i, 82; ii, 46; xii, 8, 9.
77 *ibid.*, i, 36.
78 *ibid.*, ii, 22, 45; iii, 22; v, 6.
79 *ibid.*, ii, 23.
80 Joannes Diaconus, *Vita Gregorii*, ii, 53.
81 Gregory I, *ep.* ix, 203, 204.
82 *ibid.*, iii, 36.
83 *ibid.*, ix, 2.
84 *ibid.*, i, 50.
85 *ibid.*, ix, 110; xi, 58.
86 *ibid.*, i, 42, 63; ix, 92.
87 *ibid.*, ii, 3; v, 9; ix, 88; xiv, 9.
88 *ibid.*, viii, 8, 9; ix, 112; Joannes Diaconus, *Vita Gregorii*, ii, 53.
89 *ibid.*, iii, 54; ix, 234; xi, 16; xii, 13.
90 Joannes Diaconus, *Vita Gregorii*, ii, 53; Gregory I, *ep.* ix, 96; ix, 110.

91 Gregory I, *ep.* ix, 194;
Joannes Diaconus, *Vita
Gregorii*, ii, 53.
92 Gregory I, *ep.* i, 23.
93 *ibid.*, i, 37, 53, 57.
94 *ibid.*, iii, 1, 39.
95 *ibid.*, iv, 31.
96 *ibid.*, iii, 26, 29.
97 *ibid.*, xi, 6, 14.
98 Joannes Diaconus, *Vita
Gregorii*, ii, 53.
99 Gregory I, *ep.* ix, 205, 206.
100 *ibid.*, i, 1; ii, 38.
101 *ibid.*, iii, 35.
102 *ibid.*, iv, 34; xiii, 22; ix, 8.
103 Honorius I, *ep.* 14.
104 Gregory I, *ep.* iii, 27.
105 *ibid.*, iv, 43; cf. i, 42.
106 *ibid.*, viii, 7.
107 *ibid.*, ix, 22.
108 *ibid.*, ii, 38.
109 *ibid.*, vii, 27.
110 *ibid.*, ix, 29.
111 *ibid.*, xi, 24.
112 *ibid.*, xiii, 22.
113 *ibid.*, xiv, 4, 5.
114 *LP, Vita Cononis*, p. 369.

Chapter 19 The Papacy and the Episcopate

1 *CJ*, I, iv; Justinian, *Novellae*, 86,
134.
2 Justinian I, *Pragmatic Sanction*,
12.
3 *Acta SS.*, October, xi, pp.
906–9.
4 *Homilia in laudem SS. Renati et
Valerii*, F. Ughelli, *Italia Sacra*,
vi, pp. 600–1.
5 Agnellus, *Lib. Pont. Rav.*,
69–70.
6 Gregory I, *ep.* iii, 57; Agnellus,
Lib. Pont. Rav., 98.
7 Gregory I, *ep.* v, 51.
8 Andrea Dandolo, *Chronica*, pp.
89, 91, 100, 101.
9 *MGH, ep. Lang.*, 3; *Chron. Pat.
Grad.*, 6.

10 Bede, *Historia Ecclesiastica*, iii,
29.
11 *CIL*, 10, 484.
12 Liberatus, *Breviarium*, 18.
13 *CIL*, 10, 1345.
14 *CIL*, 10, 1, 6218.
15 Gregory I, *Dialogi*, i, 4.
16 R. Pirri, *Sicilia Sacra*, i, p. 605.
17 *MGH, aa*, xii, p. 436.
18 *ibid.*, p. 453.
19 *ibid.*, p. 419.
20 *ibid.*, p. 420.
21 Ennodius, *ep.* iv, 1.
22 *ibid.*, iv, 29.
23 *ibid.*, iv, 31.
24 *ibid.*, v, 1.
25 Andrea Dandolo, *Chronica*, p.
64.
26 Pelagius I, *ep.* 18.
27 *LP, Vita Pelagii I*, p. 303.
28 J. B. De Rossi, *Inscriptiones
Christianae*, ii, p. 208.
29 Pelagius I, *ep.* 49.
30 *ibid.*, 15, 16.
31 *ibid.*, 33.
32 *ibid.*, 44, 86, 96.
33 *ibid.*, 44.
34 *ibid.*
35 *ibid.*, 96.
36 *ibid.*, 18, 23.
37 *ibid.*, 72.
38 *ibid.*, 33.
39 *ibid.*, 25.
40 *ibid.*, 56.
41 *ibid.*, 29.
42 *LD*, 9.
43 Gregory I, *Dialogi*, i, 9.
44 *ILCV*, 1030.
45 *CJ*, I, ii, 24; Justinian, *Novellae*,
131, 13, 7, *Praefatio*; *CJ*, I, iii,
41, 44.
46 Gregory I, *ep.* ix, 142.
47 Gelasius I, *ep.* 36, 37, 38.
48 Gelasius I, *frag.* 23; Loewenfeld,
ep. 9, 22.
49 Gregory I, *ep.* ii, 39; vi, 21; vii,
16; xiii, 16.
50 *PL*, 67, p. 288.

51 Mansi, 2, p. 578.
52 *Acta SS.*, March, iii, pp. 835–9.
53 *PG*, 98, pp. 550–715.
54 Agnellus, *Lib. Pont. Rav.*, 26.
55 A. Dufourq, *Études sur les Gesta Martyrum Romains* (Paris, 1907), iii, pp. 62–5.
56 *LP, Vita Gelasii*, p. 255; Gelasius I, *ep.* 14.
57 Gelasius I, *ep.* 20, 21, 22, 23, 24.
58 *ibid.*, 16, 12; Loewenfeld, *ep.* 19.
59 *PL*, 69, pp. 113–19.
60 Pelagius I, *ep.* 47.
61 Gregory I, *ep.* xiii, 14.
62 *LP, Vita Honorii I*, p. 323.
63 Agatho, *ep.* I.
64 Gregory I, *Dialogi*, iii, 13.
65 Procopius, *De Bello Gothico*, vii, 15.
66 *Acta SS.*, June, ii, pp. 688–93.
67 *Acta SS.*, September, vi, pp. 30–1.
68 *Acta SS.*, June, iv, pp. 749–51 and May, ii, p. 461.
69 Gelasius I, *ep.* 36, 37, 38.
70 *Acta SS.*, August, iii, p. 168.
71 Procopius, *De Bello Gothico*, vii, 10.
72 Gregory I, *Dialogi*, iii, 5.
73 Agnellus, *Lib. Pont. Rav.*, 154.
74 C. Troya, *Codice Diplomatico Longobardo*, i, pp. 30–3.
75 Gregory I, *ep.* xii, 4.
76 *PL*, 67, p. 237.
77 Gelasius I, *ep.* 14.
78 Fulgentius Ferrandus, *Vita S. Fulgentii Ruspensis*, 12.
79 Gregory I, *Dialogi*, iii, 13.
80 Leontius, *Vita S. Gregorii Agrigentini, PG*, 98, pp. 550–715.
81 Gregory I, *Dialogi*, i, 5.
82 *LD*, 3.
83 Agnellus, *Lib. Pont. Rav.*, 70–1.
84 *Vita S. Laurentii Episcopi Sipontini*, p. 544.

85 D. G. Lancia di Brolo, *Storia della Chiesa in Sicilia nei Dieci Primi Secoli del Cristianesimo* (Palermo, 1880–4), ii, pp. 34–7.

Chapter 20 Gregory the Great and the Episcopate

1 E.g. Gregory I, *ep.* vii, 16.
2 Gregory I, *Regula Pastoralis*, i, 10.
3 *ibid.*, i, 15; ii, 2, 6.
4 Gregory I, *ep.* iv, 1.
5 *ibid.*, x, 19.
6 E.g. Formiae and Minturnae (Gregory I, *ep.* i, 8), Narnia and Interamna (*ep.* ix, 60), Misenum and Cumae (*ep.* ii, 44), Nomentum and St Anthimus in Cures (*ep.* iii, 30), Velitrae and Tres Tabernae (*ep.* ii, 46).
7 Gregory I, *ep.* ii, 42; i, 51; iii, 41.
8 *ibid.*, ii, 37, 39, 40; iii, 13, 14.
9 Joannes Diaconus, *Vita Gregorii*, iii, 7.
10 Gregory I, *ep.* iii, 34; ix, 129, 134; i, 55, 56; ii, 28; iii, 24.
11 *ibid.*, iii, 25.
12 *ibid.*, v, 21, 24, 51; vi, 2, 28, 63; vii, 39, 40; ix, 139, 149, 155, 177, 178, 234; xi, 21.
13 *ibid.*, i, 1.
14 *ibid.*, v, 10, 16, 58; ii, 8.
15 *ibid., ep.* i, 18
16 *ibid.*, ii, 8.
17 Joannes Diaconus, *Vita Gregorii*, i, 6.
18 *MGH, Registrum Epistolarum Gregorii I*, ii, appendix 2; Gregory I, *Dialogi*, iii, 36.
19 Joannes Diaconus, *Vita Gregorii*, iii, 7, cf. Gregory I, *Dialogi, i,* 8; iii, 36; iv, 32.
20 Gregory I, *ep.* ii, 38.
21 *ibid.*, i, 70.
22 *ibid.*, ii, 30.

23 *ibid.*, iii, 12.
24 *ibid.*, iii, 27.
25 *ibid.*, iii, 53.
26 *ibid.*, i, 39.
27 *ibid.*, ii, 19.
28 *ibid.*, ii, 51.
29 *ibid.*, iii, 49.
30 *ibid.*, v, 12.
31 Joannes Diaconus, *Vita Gregorii*, iii, 7.
32 Gregory I, *ep*. xiii, 22.
33 *ibid.*, i, 64.
34 *ibid.*, vi, 8.
35 Joannes Diaconus, *Vita Gregorii,* iii, 7.
36 Gregory I, *ep*. v, 57a.
37 *ibid.*, i, 71.
38 *ibid.*, v, 57a.
39 *ibid.*, iv, 17a.
40 *ibid.*, ix, 75; viii, 3, 30; v, 57, 62.
41 *ibid.*, iii, 49.
42 *ibid.*, iii, 59.
43 In September 595 Gregory ordered the Syracusan Rector Cyprian to give 1,000 *modii* of wheat to Bishop Zeno (see unspecified) because his people were in dire need (Gregory I, *ep*. vi, 4). There is only one Sicilian see unaccounted for at this time and that is Leontini.
44 Gregory I, *ep*. ii, 43.
45 *ibid.*, v, 20.
46 *ibid.*, ii, 51.
47 *ibid.*, iii, 49.
48 *ibid.*, v, 32.
49 *ibid.*, v, 20.
50 *ibid.*, v, 54.
51 *ibid.*, vi, 18.
52 *ibid.*, vi, 40.
53 *ibid.*, vii, 18.
54 *ibid.*, xiii, 21.
55 *ibid.*, iv, 34; vi, 30; viii, 7.
56 *ibid.*, ix, 32.
57 *ibid.*, ix, 238.
58 *ibid.*, xiii, 16.
59 *ibid.*, xiii, 14.
60 Dudden, *Gregory the Great*, i, p. 387.
61 Gregory I, *ep*. ii, 38; v, 4; vi, 39; vi, 47; ix, 20, 21, 38; xi, 30.
62 *ibid.*, ii, 38.
63 *ibid.*, ix, 38; xi, 19; ix, 119.
64 *ibid.*, xiii, 40.
65 *ibid.*, vi, 8, 18.
66 *LD*, 48.
67 Gregory I, *ep*. xiii, 46.
68 *ibid.*, v, 23.
69 *ibid.*, vi, 13.
70 *ibid.*, ix, 25.
71 *ibid.*, x, 1.
72 *ibid.*, xiii, 22.
73 *ibid.*, xii, 15; xiii, 22.
74 *ibid.*, ix, 180.
75 *ibid.*, vi, 9.
76 *ibid.*, xiii, 16.
77 *ibid.*, vii, 19.
78 *ibid.*, xiv, 4.
79 *ibid.*, v, 40.

Bibliography

Primary Sources

Collections
Acta Sanctorum, collecta a. socii s, Bollandianus (Antwerp, 1643).
Acta Conciliorum Oecumenicorum, ed. E. Schwartz (Berlin and Leipzig, 1922).
Corpus Inscriptionum Latinarum.
Codex Justinianus, ed. P. Krueger (Berlin, 1877).
Codex Theodosianus, ed. T. Mommsen (Berlin, 1905).
Inscriptiones Latinae Christianae Veteres, ed. E. Diehl (Berlin, 1925–31).
P. Jaffe (ed.), *Regesta Pontificum Romanum* (2nd ed. by W. Wattenbach, S. Loewenfeld, F. Kaltenbrunner and P. Ewald, Leipzig, 1885), S. Loewenfeld, *Epistulae Pontificum Romanum Ineditae* (Leipzig, 1885).
J. D. Mansi, *Sacrorum Conciliorum nova et amplissima collectio* (Venice, 1759–98).
J. P. Migne, *Patrologia Graeca* (Paris, 1857–66), 161 vols.
J. P. Migne, *Patrologia Latina* (Paris, 1841–64), 217 vols.
Monumenta Germaniae Historica, ed. G. H. Pertz *et al.* (Berlin/Hanover, 1826–   ).
L. A. Muratori (ed.), *Rerum Italicarum Scriptores* (Milan, 1723–51), 25 vols.
U. Pasqui, *Documenti servire per la storia della città di Arezzo nel Medio Evo* (Florence, 1899).
De Rossi, J. B., *Inscriptiones Christianae Urbis Romae* (Rome, 1861–88).
De Rossi, J. B., *Roma Sotteranea* (Rome, 1864–77).
L. Schiaparelli, *Codice Diplomatico Longobardo* (Rome, 1929).
A. Thiel (ed.), *Epistulae Romanorum Pontificum Genuinae* (Brunsberg, 1868).
C. Troya (ed.), *Codice Diplomatico Longobardo* (Naples, 1852).

Individual Works
Pope Agatho, *Epistulae*, PL, 87, pp. 1161–1259.
Agnellus Andreas, *Liber Pontificalis Ecclesiae Ravennatis*, MGH, Scr. Rer. Lang., pp. 265–391.
Pope Anastasius II, *Epistulae*, Thiel, pp. 615–27.

Anastasius, *Apocrisiarios, Epistulae, PG*, 90, pp. 171–94.

Anastasius the Monk, *Relatio Motionis Maximi, PG*, 90, pp. 109–30.

Anonymus Valesianus, *MGH, aa*, ix, pp. 306–28.

Arator, *De Actibus Apostolorum, CSEL*, 72.

Bede, *Historia Ecclesiastica*, ed. B. Colgrave and R. A. B. Mynors (Oxford, 1969).

Avitus of Vienne, *Epistulae, MGH, aa*, vi, pp. 35–103.

Boethius, *Consolatio Philosophiae, CSEL*, 87.

Boethius, *Tractates*, ed. H. F. Stewart and E. K. Rand (Harvard, 1918).

St Boniface, *Epistulae, MGH, ep*. iii, pp. 215–433.

Cassiodorus, *Variae, MGH, aa*, xii, pp. 3–385.

Catalogus Episcoporum Mediolanensium, Rer. It. Script., i, 2, pp. 96–103.

Chronica Patriarcharum Gradensium, MGH, Sc. Rer. Lang., pp. 329–97.

Codex Carolinus, MGH, ep. iii, 2, pp. 469–657.

Collectio Avellana, CSEL, 35.

Columban, *Epistulae, MGH, ep*. iii, pp. 154–90.

Commemoratio eorum quae saeviter . . . , PL, 87, pp. 119–98.

Coustant, P., *Pontificum Romanum Epistolae Genuinae* (Gottingen, 1791).

Andrea Dandolo, *Chronica, Rer. It. Script.*, xii, pp. 9–327.

Dionysius Exiguus, *Opera, PL*, 67, *PLS*, 4.

Dionysius Exiguus, *Vita S. Pachomii*, ed. H. Van Craneburgh (Brussels, 1969).

Eddius Stephanus, *Vita S. Wilfridi*, ed. B. Colgrave (Cambridge, 1927).

Ennodius, *Opera, MGH, aa*, vii.

Epistula Legatis Francorum, *PL*, 69, pp. 113–19.

Eulogius, *Contra Novatum, PG*, 103, p. 533.

Eusebius, *Historia Ecclesiastica*, ed. K. Lake and J. E. L. Oulton (London, 1926–32).

Evagrius, *Historia Ecclesiastica, PG*, 86, pp. 2415–886.

Facundus of Hermiana, *Liber Contra Mocianum, PL*, 67, pp. 854–68.

Facundus of Hermiana, *Pro Defensione Trium Capitulorum, PL*, 67, pp. 527–854.

Pope Felix III, *Epistulae*, Thiel, pp. 222–78.

Pope Felix IV, *Epistulae, PL*, 65, pp. 9–23.

Fredegar, *Chronicon IV cum continuationibus*, ed. J. M. Wallace-Hadrill (London, 1960).

Fulgentius Ferrandus, *Epistulae, PL*, 69, pp. 878–950.

Fulgentius Ferrandus, *Vita S. Fulgentii Ruspensis, Acta SS.*, Jan., I, pp. 32–45.

Gelasius I, *Epistulae*, Thiel, pp. 287–483.

Gelasius I, *Fragments*, Thiel, pp. 483–510.

Gelasius I, *Tractates*, Thiel, pp. 510–607.

Gesta Episcoporum Neapolitanorum, MGH, Sc. Rer. Lang., pp. 398–424.

Gesta Liberii, Coustant, i, 89–94.

Gesta de Marcellino Sinuessanae Synodi, Coustant, pp. 25–36.

Gesta de Polychronii Accusatione, Coustant, pp. 120–4.

Gesta de Xysti Purgatione, Coustant, pp. 117–20.

Goscelin, *Vita S. Augustini, PL*, 80, pp. 43–95.

Gregory I, *Dialogi*, ed. U. Moricca (Istituto Storico Italiano, Rome, 1924).

Gregory I, *Epistulae, MGH, ep.* i, ii.

Gregory I, *Homiliae in Evangeliis, PL,* 76, pp. 1075–1313.

Gregory I, *Homiliae in Ezecheliem, PL,* 76, pp. 785–1072.

Gregory I, *Magna Moralia, PL,* 75, p. 515–*PL,* 76, p. 782.

Gregory I, *Liber Regulae Pastoralis, PL,* 77, pp. 13–128.

Gregory of Tours, *Historia Francorum, MGH, Sc. Rer. Merov.,* i.

Pope Hilarus, *Epistulae,* Thiel, pp. 127–70.

Pope Honorius I, *Epistulae, PL,* 80, pp. 469–94.

Pope Hormisdas, *Epistulae,* Thiel, pp. 741–990.

Joannes Diaconus, *Vita Gregorii Magni, PL,* 75, pp. 59–242.

Pope John II, *Epistulae, PL,* 66, pp. 9–26.

John Malalas, *Chronographia, PG,* 97, pp. 65–717.

John Maxentius, *Collectio Palatina, ACO,* i, 5, pp. 3–215.

Jonas, *Vita S. Bertulfi, MGH, Sc. Rer. Merov.,* iv, pp. 143–8.

Jordanes, *Getica, MGH, aa,* v.

Justinian, *Novellae,* ed. R. Schoell and W. Kroll (Berlin, 1963).

'Laurentian Fragment', ed. L. Duchesne, *LP,* I, pp. 44–6.

Leontius, *Vita S. Gregorii Agrigentini, PG,* 98, pp. 550–715.

Liber Diurnus Romanorum Pontificum, ed. Th. Sickel (Vienna, 1889).

Liber Pontificalis, ed. L. Duchesne (Paris, 1955–7), 3 vols.

Liberatus, *Breviarium causae Nestorianorum et Eutychianorum, PL,* 68, pp. 968–1054.

Marcellinus Comes, *Chronicon, MGH, aa,* xi, pp. 37–105.

G. Marini, *I Papiri Diplomatici* (Rome, 1805).

Marius of Aventicum, *Chronicon, MGH, aa,* xi, 2, pp. 232–9.

Martin I, *Epistulae, PL,* 87, pp. 119–204.

St Maximus Confessor, *Opera, PG,* 90.

Menander Protector, *Fragments, Fragmenta Historicorum Graecorum,* ed. C. Muller (Paris 1851), vol. 4, pp. 201–69.

Die Nichtliterarischen Lateinischen Papyri Italiens aus der Zeit 445–700, ed. T. O. Tjader (Lund, 1955).

Ordo Romanus Primus, ed. E. G. C. F. Atchley (London, 1905).

Optatus of Milevis, *De Schismate Donatistarum, CSEL,* 26.

Paulus Diaconus, *Historia Langobardorum, MGH, Sc. Rer. Lang.,* pp. 45–187.

Paulus Diaconus, *Vita Gregorii Magni, PL,* 75, pp. 42–60.

Pelagius I, *Epistulae quae supersunt,* ed. P. M. Gasso and C. M. Batlle (Monserrat, 1956).

Pelagius Diaconus, *In Defensione Trium Capitulorum,* ed. R. Devreesse, *Studi e Testi,* 57 (1932).

Pelagius II, *Epistulae, PL,* 72, pp. 703–50.

Procopius, *Wars* and *Anecdota,* ed. H. B. Dewing (London, 1914–40), 7 vols.

Prosper Havniensis, *Continuatio, MGH, aa,* 9, pp. 337–9.

Sigebert, *Liber de Scriptoribus Ecclesiasticis, PL,* 160, pp. 547–88.

Pope Simplicius, *Epistulae,* Thiel, pp. 174–214.

400

Stephanus, *Carmen de Synodo Ticinense*, *MGH, Poet. Lat.*, iv, 2, pp. 728–31.

V. Strazzulla, 'Museum Epigraphicum,' *Documenti per servire alla storia di Sicilia* (Palermo, 1897), series 3, vol. 3.

Pope Symmachus, *Epistulae*, Thiel, pp. 642–734.

Pope Theodore I, *Epistulae*, *PL*, 87, pp. 75–102.

Theodore Lector, *Historia Ecclesiastica*, *PG*, 86, pp. 165–226.

Theophanes, *Chronographia*, *PG*, 108, pp. 63–1164.

Venantius Fortunatus, *Carmina*, *MGH*, *aa*, iv, pp. 1–292.

Victor of Tunnuna, *Chronicon*, *MGH*, *aa*, xi, pp. 184–206.

Pope Vigilius, *Epistulae*, *PL*, 69, pp. 9–328.

Vita et translatio S. Sabini episcopi Canusini, *MGH, Sc. Rer. Lang*, pp. 586–9.

Vita S. Alexandri episcopi Faesulani, *Acta SS.*, June, iv, pp. 749–51.

Vita S. Barbati episcopi Beneventani, *MGH, Sc. Rer. Lang*, pp. 556–63.

Vita S. Callisti episcopi Tudertini, *Acta SS.*, Aug., iii, p. 168.

Vita S. Cerbonii Populoniensis, Ughelli, *Italia Sacra*, iii, pp. 703–9.

Vita S. Gerontii Ficuclensis, *Acta SS.*, May, ii, p. 461.

Vita S. Joanni Spoletani, *Acta SS.*, September, vi, pp. 30–1.

Vita S. Laurentii episcopi Sipontini, *MGH, Sc. Rer. Lang.*, pp. 543–5.

Vita S. Terentii Lunensis, *Acta SS.*, July, iv, p. 96.

Vita S. Zosimi episcopi Syracusani, *Acta SS.*, March, iii, pp. 835–9.

Pope Vitalian, *Epistulae*, *PL*, 87, pp. 999–1010.

Secondary Sources

Alessandrini, A., 'Teoderico e Papa Simmaco durante lo scisma Laurenziano', *ASR*, 67 (1944), pp. 153–207.

Anastos, M. V., 'Justinian's Despotic Control over the Church', *Mélanges Ostrogorsky*, 2 (Belgrade, 1964), pp. 1–11.

Anastos, M. V., 'The transfer of Illyricum, Calabria and Sicily to the jurisdiction of the Patriarch of Constantinople in 732–3', *Studi Bizantini e Neoellenici in Onore di S. G. Mercati* (Rome, 1957), pp. 14–31.

Andrieu, M., 'La Carrière Ecclésiastique des Papes et les documents liturgiques du Moyen Age', *Revue des sciences religieuses*, 21 (1947), pp. 90–120.

Antonelli, F., 'I Primi Monasteri di Monaci Orientali', *RAC*, 5 (1928), pp. 105–21.

Baker, D. (ed.), *The Orthodox Churches and the West* (Oxford, 1976).

Bardenhewer, O., *Geschichte der Altkirchlichen Literatur* (Freiburg, 1932).

Bark, W., 'The Legend of Boethius's Martyrdom', *Speculum*, 21 (1946), pp. 312–17.

Bark, W., 'Theodoric v. Boethius: Vindication and Apology', *American Historical Review*, 49 (1944), pp. 410–26.

Barrett, H. M., *Boethius: Some Aspects of his Time and Work* (Cambridge, 1940).

Batiffol, P., 'Librairies Bizantines à Rome', *MAH* (1888), pp. 297–308.

Batiffol, P., 'L'Empereur Justinien et la siège apostolique', *Recherches des sciences religieuses*, 16 (1926), pp. 193–264.

Bernadakis, P., 'Les appels au Pape dans l'Eglise Grecque jusqu'à Photius' *Echos d'Orient*, VI (1903), pp. 30–42, 118–25, 249–57.

Bertolini, O., 'L'Aristocrazia e il Senato di Roma come forza politica sotto i regni di Odoacre e di Teodorico', *Atti del 1 Congresso Nazionale di Studi Romani* (Rome, 1929), pp. 462–75.

Bertolini, O., 'Le Chiese Longobarde dopo la conversione al Catolicesimo ed i loro rapporti con il Papato', *Settimane*, vii, I (Spoleto, 1960), pp. 455–92.

Bertolini, O., 'La Fine del Pontificato di Papa Silverio in uno studio recente', *ASR*, 47 (1927), pp. 325–43.

Bertolini, O., 'I Papi e le Relazioni Politiche di Roma con i Ducati Longobardi di Spoleto e di Benevento', *Rivista di Storia della Chiesa in Italia*, 6 (1952), pp. 1–46; 8 (1954), pp. 1–22.

Bertolini, O., 'Per la storia delle diaconie Romane nell'alto medio evo alla fine del secolo VIII', *ASR*, 70 (1947), pp. 1–145.

Bertolini, O., 'I Rapporti di Zaccaria con Constantino V e con Artavasdo nel racconto del biografo e nella probabile realtà storica', *ASR*, 78 (1955), pp. 1–21.

Bertolini, O., 'La ricomparsa della sede episcopale di *Tres Tabernae* nella seconda metà del secolo VIII e l'istituzione della *domusculta*', *ASR*, 75 (1952), pp. 103–9.

Biraben, J. N. and LeGoff, J., 'La Peste dans le Haut Moyen Age', *Annales*, 24 (1969), pp. 1484–1510.

Bognetti, G. P., 'La continuità delle sedi episcopali e l'azione di Roma nel regno Longobardo', *Settimane*, vii, I (Spoleto, 1960), pp. 415–54.

Bognetti, G. P., Chierici, G., and de Capitani d'Arzago, A., *Santa Maria di Castelseprio* (Milan, 1948).

Borsari, S., *Il Monachesimo Bizantino nella Sicilia e nell'Italia Meridionale PreNormanne* (Naples, 1963).

Breckinridge, J. D., 'Evidence for the Nature of Relations between Pope John VII and the Byzantine Emperor Justinian II', *BZ*, 65 (1972), pp. 364–74.

Brehier, L., 'Les colonies d'Orientaux en Occident au commencement du Moyen Age', *BZ*, 12 (1903), pp. 1–40.

Bresslau, H., *Handbuch der Urkundenlehre* (Leipzig, 1889).

Brown, P., 'A Dark Age Crisis: aspects of the Iconoclastic Controversy', *EHR*, 88 (1973), pp. 1–34.

Browning, R., *Justinian and Theodora* (London, 1971).

Bury, J. B., *History of the Later Roman Empire* (London, 1923), 2 vols.

Cappelletti, G., *Le Chiese d'Italia* (Venice, 1844–70), 21 vols.

Caron, P. G., 'Les élections épiscopales dans la doctrine et la pratique de l'église', *Cahiers de Civilisation Médiévale*, xi, 4 (1968), pp. 573–585.

Casper, E., *Geschichte des Papsttums* (Tubingen, 1933), 2 vols.

Casper, E., 'Papst Gregor II und der Bilderstreit', *Zeitschrift für Kirchengeschichte*, 52 (1933), pp. 72–89.

Casper, E., 'Die Lateran synode von 649', *Zeitschrift für Kirchengeschichte*, 51 (1932), pp. 25–73.

Cattaneo, E., 'Missionari Orientali a Milano nell'età Longobardo', *Archivio Storico Lombardo*, series 9, vol. 3 (1963), pp. 215–47.

Cecchelli, C., 'L'Arianesimo e le chiese Ariane d'Italia', *Settimane*, 7, ii (1960), pp. 743–74.

Cessi, R., 'Dallo Scisma Laurenziano alla Pacificazione Religiosa con L'Oriente', *ASR*, 42 (1920), pp. 209–321.

Cessi, R., 'Lo Scisma Laurenziano e le origini della dottrina politica della Chiesa di Rome', *ASR*, 42 (1919), pp. 5–229.

Chamard, F., 'Les Papes du VIᵉ siècle et la seconde concile de Constantinople', *Revue des Questions Historiques*, 37 (1885), pp. 540–73.

Chapman, J. B., *The Condemnation of Pope Honorius* (London, 1907).

Chapman, J. B., *St. Benedict and the Sixth Century* (London, 1929).

Charanis, P., *Church and State in the Later Roman Empire: The Religious Policy of Anastasius I* (Madison, Wisconsin, 1939).

Charanis, P., 'On the question of the Hellenization of Sicily and Southern Italy in the Middle Ages', *American Historical Review*, 52 (1946), pp. 74–87.

Chastagnol, A., *Le Sénat Romain sous la règne d'Odoacre* (Bonn, 1966).

Constantelos, D. J., 'Justinian and the Three Chapters controversy', *Greek Orthodox Theological Review*, 8 (1962–3), pp. 71–94.

Conti, P. M., 'Missioni Aquileiesi, Orientali e Romane nel regno Longobardo', *Studi Romani*, 17 (1969), pp. 18–26.

Coster, C. H., *Late Roman Studies* (Cambridge, Massachusetts, 1968).

Courcelle, P., *Late Latin Writers and their Greek Sources* (Cambridge, Massachusetts, 1969).

Crivelluci, A., 'Le Chiese Cattoliche e i Longobardi Ariani', *Studi Storici*, 4 (1895), pp. 385–423; 5 (1896), pp. 154–77; 6 (1897), pp. 93–115, 345–69.

Deanesly, M., *Augustine of Canterbury* (London, 1964).

Deanesly, M., 'The Anglo-Saxon Church and the Papacy', *The English Church and the Papacy in the Middle Ages*, ed. C. H. Lawrence (London, 1965), pp. 31–62.

Devreesse, R., 'Lo scisma dei Tre Capitoli', *Atti del 4 Congresso di Studi Romani* (Rome, 1938), I, pp. 341–50.

Devreesse, R., 'La Vie de St. Maxime le Confesseur et ses recensions', *Analecta Bollandiana*, 46 (1928), pp. 5–49.

Diehl, C., *Études sur l'administration Byzantine dans l'exarchat de Ravenne* (Paris, 1888).

Duchesne, L., *L'Eglise au Sixième Siècle* (Paris, 1925).

Duchesne, L., 'L'Empereur Anastase et sa politique religieuse', *MAH,* 32 (1912), pp. 305–36.

Duchesne, L., 'Les Évêches de Calabre', *Mélanges Paul Fabre* (Paris, 1902), pp. 1–16.

Duchesne, L., 'Les Évêchés d'Italie et l'invasion Lombarde', *MAH,* 23 (1903), pp. 83–116; 25 (1905), pp. 365–99.

Duchesne, L., 'Les Schismes Romains au VI siècle', *MAH*, 35 (1915), pp. 222–56.

Duchesne, L., 'Le Sedi Episcopali nell'Antico Ducato di Roma', *ASR*, 15 (1892), pp. 478–503.

Duchesne, L., 'Vigile et Pelage: étude sur l'histoire de l'église Romain au milieu du VI siècle', *Revue des Questions Historiques*, 36 (1884), pp. 369–440.

Dudden, F. H., *Gregory the Great: His Place in History and Thought* (London, 1905), 2 vols.

Dufourq, F., *Études sur les Gesta Martyrum* (Paris, 1907).

Dvornik, F., *Byzantium and the Roman Primacy* (New York, 1966).

Dvornik, F., *Early Christian and Byzantine Political Philosophy* (Dumbarton Oaks, 1966), 2 vols.

Dvornik, F., *The Idea of Apostolicity in Byzantium* (Cambridge, Massachusetts, 1958).

Dvornik, F., 'Pope Gelasius and the Emperor Anastasius', *BZ*, 44 (1951), pp. 111–18.

Dvornik, F., 'The See of Constantinople in the first Latin Collections of Canon Law', *Mélanges Ostrogorsky* (Belgrade, 1963), i, pp. 97–101.

Eidenschink, J. A., *The Election of Bishops in the Letters of Gregory the Great* (Catholic University of America, Canon Law Studies 215, Washington, 1945).

Ensslin, W., 'Papst Agapet I und Kaiser Justinian I', *Historische Jahrbuch*, 77 (1958), pp. 459–66.

Ensslin, W., 'Papst Johannes I als Gesandter Theoderichs des Grossen bei Kaiser Justinos I', *BZ*, 44 (1951), pp. 127–34.

Ensslin, W., *Theoderich der Grosse* (Munich, 1974).

Ertl, N., 'Diktatoren frühmittelalter Papstbriefe', *Archiv für Urkundenforschung und Quellenkunde des Mittelalters*, 15 (1937), pp. 61–6.

Ewald, P., 'Die Papstbriefe der Brittischen Sammlung', *NA*, 5 (1880), pp. 277–414.

Ewald, P., 'Studien zur Ausgabe des Registers Gregors I', *NA*, 3 (1878), pp. 433–625.

Fabre, P., 'Le Patrimoine de l'Eglise Romaine dans les Alpes Cottiennes', *MAH*, 4 (1884), pp. 283–420.

Fedele, P., 'Il Fratello di Gregorio Magno', *ASR*, 42 (1919), pp. 607–13.

Ferrari, G., *Early Roman Monasteries* (Rome, 1957).

Ferrari, L. A., 'A proposito dei Patrimonii delle chiese di Ravenna e di Milano in Sicilia', *Studi Storici*, 4 (1895), pp. 551–6.

Ferrua, A., 'Gli Antenati di San Gregorio Magno', *La Civiltà Cattolica*, 115, vol. 4 (1964), pp. 238–46.

Ferrua, A., 'Nuove Iscrizioni della Via Ostiense', *Epigraphica*, 21 (1959), pp. 97–116.

Finley, M. I., *Ancient Sicily* (London, 1968).

Fischer, Balthasar, 'Die Entwicklung den Instituts der Defensoren in der Römischen Kirche', *Ephemerides Liturgicae*, 48 (1934), pp. 443–54.

Fliche, A. and Martin, V. (eds), *Histoire de l'Eglise* (Paris, 1934–64), vols 4, 5, 6.

Frend, W. H. C., *The Rise of the Monophysite Movement* (Cambridge, 1972).

Galtier, P., 'La Première Lettre du Pape Honorius', *Gregorianum*, 29 (1948), pp. 42–61.

Gams, P. B., *Series Episcoporum Ecclesiae Catholicae* (Ratisbon, 1873).

Gay, J., 'Quelques Remarques sur les Papes Grecs et Syriens avant la querelle des iconoclastes', *Mélanges offerts à Gustave Schlumberger*, i (Paris, 1924), pp. 46–54.

Goffart, W., 'Byzantine Policy in the West under Tiberius II and Maurice', *Traditio*, 13 (1957), pp. 73–118.

Goubert, P., 'Autour du voyage à Byzance du Pape Jean I', *Orientalia Christiana Periodica*, 24 (1958), pp. 339–52.

Goubert, P., *Byzance Avant l'Islam* (Paris, 1965), 2 vols.

Gouillard, J., 'Les lettres de Grégoire II à Léon III devant la critique du XIVe siècle', *Mélanges Ostrogorsky*, i (Belgrade, 1963), pp. 103–10.

Greenslade, S. L., '*Sede Vacante* Procedure in the Early Church', *JTS*, 12 (1961), n.s., pp. 210–26.

Gregorovius, F., *Rome in the Middle Ages* (London, 1894).

Grierson, P., 'The *Patrimonium Petri in Illis Partibus* and the Pseudo-Imperial Coinage in Frankish Gaul', *Revue Belge de Numismatique*, 105 (1959), pp. 95–111.

Grisar, H., *History of Rome and the Popes in the Middle Ages* (London, 1912).

Grumel, V., 'L'annexion de L'Illyricum Oriental, de la Sicile et de la Calabre au patriarchat de Constantinople', *Recherches de science religieuse*, 40 (1952), pp. 191–200.

Grumel, V., 'Recherches sur l'histoire du Monothélisme', *Echos d'Orient*, 29 (1930), pp. 16–28; 27 (1928), pp. 6–16; 28 (1929), pp. 19–34, 272–82.

Guérand, L., 'Les lettres de Grégoire II à Léon L'Isaurien', *MAH*, II (1890), pp. 44–60.

Guillou, A., 'L'Italia Bizantina', *Bolletino dell'Istituto Storico per il Medio Evo*, 78 (1967), p. 120.

Guillou, A., *Régionalisme et indépendance dans l'Empire Byzantin* (Rome, 1969).

Haller, J., *Das Papsttum: Idee und Wirklichkeit* (Hamburg, 1965).

Hallinger, K., 'Papst Gregor der Grosse und der Hl. Benedikt', *Studia Anselmiana*, 42 (1957), pp. 231–319.

Halphen, L., *Études sur l'administration de Rome au moyen âge* (Paris, 1907).

Harnack, A. von, 'Der erste deutsche Papst (Bonifatius I) und die beiden letzen Dekrete des Romischen Senats', *Sitzungsberichte der Preussischen Akademie der Wissenschaft* (1924), pp. 24–42.

Harnack, A. von, *Lehrbuch der Dogmengeschichte* (Leipzig, 1890).

Hartmann, L. M., *Geschichte Italiens im Mittelalter* (Stuttgart, 1923), 2 vols.

Hartmann, L. M., *Untersuchungen zur Geschichte der Byzantinischen Verwaltung in Italien 540–750* (Leipzig, 1889).

Head, C., *Justinian II of Byzantium* (Madison, Wisconsin, 1972).

Hefele, C. J., *History of the Councils of the Church* (translated W. R. Clarke, Edinburgh, 1895).

Hildebrand, P., 'Die Absetzung des Papstes Silverius', *Historisches Jahrbuch*, 42 (1922), pp. 213–49.

Hodgkin, T., *Italy and her Invaders* (Oxford 1896), vols 3, 4, 5, 6.

Howorth, H. H., *Gregory the Great* (London, 1912).

Hughes, P., *The Church in Crisis* (London, 1960).

Hurten, H., 'Gregor de Grosse und der Mittelalterlich Episkopat', *Zeitschrift für Kirchengeschichte*, 73 (1962), pp. 16–41.

Jalland, T. G., *The Church and the Papacy* (London, 1944).

Jones, A. H. M., 'Church Finance in the 5th and 6th Centuries', *JTS*, n.s., II (1960), pp. 84–94.

Jones, A. H. M., 'The Constitutional Position of Odoacer and Theodoric', *JRS*, 52 (1962), pp. 126–30.

Jones, A. H. M., *The Later Roman Empire* (Oxford, 1964), 3 vols.

King, A., *The Liturgy of the Roman Church* (London, 1957).

King, P. D., *Law and Society in the Visigothic Kingdom* (Cambridge, 1972).

Koch, H., 'Gelasius im kirchenpolitischen Dienst seiner Vorgänger Simplicius und Felix III', *Sitzungsberichte der Bayerischen Akademie* (1933), vol. 6.

Laistner, M. L. W., *Thought and Letters in Western Europe 500–900* (London, 1957, 2nd edn).

Lancia di Brolo, D. G., *Storia della Chiesa in Sicilia nei Dieci Primi Secoli del Cristianesimo* (Palermo, 1880–4), 2 vols.

Lanzoni, F., *Le Diocesi d'Italia* (Faenza, 1927).

Lecrivain, C., *Le Sénat Romain depuis Dioclétien* (Paris, 1888).

Lestocquoy, J., 'L'Administration de Rome et Diaconies du VIIe au IXe siècle', *RAC*, 7 (1930), pp. 261–98.

Lewis, C. S., *The Discarded Image* (Cambridge, 1964).

Llewellyn, P., 'The Roman Church in the 7th Century: the Legacy of Gregory the Great', *JEH*, 25 (1974), pp. 363–80.

Llewellyn, P., *Rome in the Dark Ages* (London, 1971).

Lowe, H., 'Theoderich der Grosse und Papst Johann I', *Historische Jahrbuch*, 72 (1953), pp. 83–100.

Luzzatto, G., *Geschichte der Quellen und der Literatur des canonischen Rechts* (Gratz, 1870).

Mandic, D., 'Dalmatia in the Exarchate of Ravenna', *Byzantion*, 34 (1964), pp. 347–74.

Mann, H. K., *Lives of the Popes in the Middle Ages* (London, 1906–32), vols 1, 2.

Markus, R. A., 'Reflections on Religious Dissent in North Africa in the Byzantine Period', *Studies in Church History*, iii (London, 1966), pp. 140–50.

Marrou, H.-I., 'Autour de la bibliothèque du Pape Agapit', *MAH*, 48 (1931), pp. 124–69.

Marrou, H.-I., *A History of Education in Antiquity* (London and New York, 1957).

Marrou, H.-I., 'L'Origine orientale des diaconies romaines', *MAH*, 57 (1940), pp. 95–142.

Martroye, F., 'Les *Defensores Ecclesiarum*', *Bulletin de la société des antiquaires de France* (1920–1), pp. 241–9.

Martroye, F., 'Les *Defensores Ecclesiae* aux Ve et VIe siècles', *Revue historique de droit français et étranger*, series 4 (1923).

Martroye, F., *L'Occident à l'époque Byzantine* (Paris, 1904).

Milik, J. T., 'La Famiglia di Felice III', *Epigraphica*, 28 (1966), pp. 140–2.

Miller, D. H., 'The Roman Revolution in the 8th Century', *Medieval Studies*, 36 (1974), pp. 79–133.

Minasi, G., *Le Chiese di Calabria del quinto al duodecimo secolo* (Naples, 1896).

Mochi Onory, S., *Vescovi e città* (Bologna, 1933).

Momigliano, A., 'Cassiodorus and the Italian Culture of his Time', *Proceedings of the British Academy*, 41 (1955), pp. 207–45.

Moorhead, J. A., 'The Catholic Episcopate in Ostrogothic Italy', (Liverpool Univ. Ph.D. thesis, unpublished).

Moresco, M., *Il Patrimonio di San Pietro* (Turin, 1916).

Morosi, G., *Studi del Dialetti Greci della terra d'Otranto* (Lecce, 1870).

Morrison, K. F., *Tradition and Authority in the Western Church 300–1140* (Princeton, 1969).

Musset, Lucien, *The Germanic Invasions* (London, 1975).

Nelson, J. L., 'Gelasius I's Doctrine of Responsibility: A Note', *JTS*, n.s., 18 (1967), pp. 154–62.

Norberg, D., *In Registrum Gregorii Magni Studia Critica* (Uppsala, 1939).

Ostrogorsky, G., 'Les débuts de la querelle des images', *Mélanges Charles Diehl*, 2 (Paris, 1930), pp. 232–55.

Ostrogorsky, G., *History of the Byzantine State* (Oxford, 1968).

Partner, P., *The Lands of St. Peter* (London, 1972).

Patch, H. R., 'The Beginnings of the Legend of Boethius', *Speculum*, 22 (1947), pp. 443–5.

Peeters, P., 'Une Vie grecque du pape S. Martin I', *Analecta Bollandiana*, 51 (1933), pp. 225–62.

Picard, J. C., 'Etude sur l'emplacement des tombes des Papes du IIIe au Xe siècle', *MAH*, 81 (1969), pp. 725–82.

Picotti, G. B., 'La Politica Religiosa di Teodorico', *Settimane*, 3 (Spoleto, 1956), pp. 173–226.

Picotti, G. B., 'Il Senato Romano e il Processo di Boezio', *Archivio Storico Italiano*, series 3, vol. 7 (1931), pp. 205–28.

Picotti, G. B., 'I sinodi Romani nello Scisma Laurenziano', *Studi Storici in Onore di Gioacchino Volpe*, ed. G. C. Sansoni (Florence, 1958), pp. 743–86.

Picotti, G. B., 'Sulle Relazioni fra Re Odoacre e il Senato e la Chiesa di Roma', *Rivista Storico Italiano*, series 5, vol. 4 (1939), pp. 363–86.

Pietri, C., 'Le Sénat, le peuple chrétien et les partis du cirque à Rome sous le pape Symmaque', *MAH*, 78 (1966), pp. 123–39.

Pirri, R., *Sicilia Sacra* (Palermo, 1733).

Poole, R. L., *The Papal Chancery* (Cambridge, 1915).

Riché, P., *Education et culture dans L'occident barbare* (Paris, 1962).

Rohlfs, G., *Scavi Linguistici nella Magna Graecia* (Rome, 1933).

Romano, G. and Solmi, A., *Le Dominazioni Barbariche* (Milan, 1940).

Rubin, B., 'Theoderich und Justinian', *Jahrbücher für Geschichte Osteuropas*, I (1953).

Salaville, S., 'L'Affaire de l'Hénotique', *Echos d'Orient*, 19 (1920), pp. 49–68, 415–33.

Santifaller, L., 'Saggio di un Elenco dei Funzionari Impiegati e Scrittori della Cancellaria Pontificia dall'inizio all'anno 1099', *Bolletino dell'istituto storico Italiano per il medio evo*, 56 (1940), pp. 1–841.

Savio, F., *Gli Antichi Vescovi d'Italia dalle origini al 1300* (Milan, 1899).

Schurr, V., *Die Trinitätslehre des Boethius im Lichte der 'Skythischen Kontroversen'* (Paderborn, 1935).

Schuster, I., 'Les ancêtres de St. Grégoire et leur sépulture de famille à St. Paul de Rome', *Revue Bénédictine*, 21 (1904), pp. 112–23.

Schuster, I., *St Benedict and his Times* (London, 1953).

Schwartz, E., 'Zur Kirchenpolitik Justinians', *SB Bayerische Akad. wiss. Phi.-hist. Abt.* (1940), pp. 32–81.

Sherwood, P., 'An annotated date-list of the works of Maximus the Confessor', *Studia Anselmiana*, 30 (1952), pp. 1–64.

Simson, O. von, *Sacred Fortress* (Chicago, 1948).

Sinnigen, W. G., 'Administrative Shifts of Competence under Theodoric', *Traditio*, 21 (1965), pp. 456–67.

Sola, G., 'Santi Bizantini a Roma', *Atti del 3 Congresso di Studi Romani* (Bologna, 1935), vol. 2–3, pp. 139–41.

Spearing, E., *The Patrimony of the Roman Church in the time of Gregory the Great* (Cambridge, 1918).

Stein, E., 'La disparition du sénat de Rome à la fin du VI siècle', *Bulletin de la classe des lettres de l'Académie Royale de Belgique*, series 5, vol. 25 (1939), pp. 308–22.

Stein, E., *Histoire du bas empire*, 2 (Paris, 1968).

Stein, E., 'La période byzantine de la papauté', *Catholic Historical Review*, 21 (1935–6), pp. 129–63.

Stuhlfath, W., *Gregor der Grosse* (Heidelberg, 1913).

Sullivan, R. E., 'The Papacy and Missionary Activity in the Early Middle Ages', *Medieval Studies*, 17 (1955), pp. 46–106.

Sundwall, J., *Abhandlungen zur Geschichte des ausgehenden Römertums* (Helsinki, 1919).

Taylor, J. J., 'The Early Papacy at work: Gelasius I', *Journal of Religious History*, 8 (1974–5), pp. 317–32.

Taylor, J. J., 'Eastern Appeals to Rome in the early Church', *Downside Review*, 89 (1971), pp. 142–6.

Testa, O. M., 'La Chiesa di Napoli nei suoi rapporti con Papa Gregorio I', *Rivista Storica Italiana*, 7 (1890), pp. 457–88.

Townsend, W. T., 'Ennodius and Pope Symmachus', *Studies in honour of E. K. Rand* (New York, 1938), ed. L. W. Jones, pp. 277–83.

Townsend, W. T., 'The Henotikon Schism and the Roman Church', *Journal of Religion*, 16 (1936), pp. 78–86.

Townsend, W. T., 'The so-called Symmachan forgeries', *Journal of Religion*, 13 (1933), pp. 165–74.

Treccani Degli Alfieri, G. (ed.), *Storia di Milano* (Milan, 1953).

Ughelli, F., *Italia Sacra* (2nd edn, revised by N. Coletti) (Venice, 1717–33), 12 vols.

Ullmann, W., *The Growth of Papal Government in the Middle Ages* (London, 1965).

Ullmann, W., 'Leo I and the Theme of Papal Primacy', *JTS*, n.s., II (1960), pp. 25–51.

Ullmann, W., *A Short History of the Papacy in the Middle Ages* (London, 1972).

Vaccari, P., 'Roma e l'Oriente nei Rapporti Ecclesiastici del Secolo VI', *Atti del 4 Congresso di Studi Romani*, I (Rome, 1938), pp. 416–19.

Van Dijk, S. P., 'Gregory the Great – Founder of the Urban *Schola Cantorum*', *Ephemerides Liturgicae*, 77 (1963), pp. 345–56.

Van Dijk, S. P., 'Urban and Papal Rites in 7th and 8th Century Rome', *Sacris Eruditi*, 12 (1961), pp. 411–87.

Vassiliev, A. A., *Justin the First* (Harvard, 1950).

White Jr, L., 'The Byzantinization of Sicily', *American Historical Review*, 42 (1936), pp. 1–21.

Zeiller, J., 'Étude sur l'arianisme en Italie à l'époque ostrogothique et à l'époque lombarde', *MAH*, 25 (1905), pp. 127–46.

Ziegler, A. K., 'Pope Gelasius I and his Teachings on the Relations of Church and State', *Catholic Historical Review*, 27 (1941–2), pp. 412–37.

Index

Note: all clergy listed are from the Roman church unless otherwise stated

410